Organising and Managing Work

By the same author

The Personnel Managers (1977)

Sociology, Work and Industry (1980, 1987, 1995)

Management, Organisation and Employment Strategy (1986)

In Search of Management (1994, 2001)

The Emergent Manager, with P. Harris (1999)

Strategic Human Resourcing, edited with J. Leopold and L. Harris (1999)

Organising and Managing Work

Organisational, managerial and strategic behaviour
in theory and practice

Tony J. Watson

FT Prentice Hall
FINANCIAL TIMES

An imprint of **Pearson Education**
Harlow, England • London • New York • Boston • San Francisco • Toronto • Sydney • Singapore • Hong Kong
Tokyo • Seoul • Taipei • New Delhi • Cape Town • Madrid • Mexico City • Amsterdam • Munich • Paris • Milan

Pearson Education Limited
Edinburgh Gate
Harlow
Essex CM20 2JE
England

and Associated Companies throughout the world

Visit us on the World Wide Web at:
www.pearsoned.co.uk

First published 2002

ISBN 0273 63005 9

British Library Cataloguing-in-Publication Data
A catalogue record for this book is available from the British Library

Library of Congress Cataloging-in-Publication Data
Watson, Tony J.
    Organising and managing work: organisational, managerial, and strategic behaviour in
theory and practice / Tony Watson.
        p. cm.
    Includes bibliographical references and index.
    ISBN 0-273-63005-9
    I. Organization. 2. Management. I. Title.

HD31 . W3547 2001
658--dc21   2001050141

10 9 8 7 6 5 4 3
07 06 05 04 03

Typeset in 9.5/12.5 pt Stone Serif by 30

Printed by Ashford Colour Press Ltd, Gosport

Brief Contents

Chapter 1   Organising and managing work: study and practice   1

Chapter 2   Organisations and management: the *systems-control* orthodoxy   33

Chapter 3   Organising and managing: a *process-relational* perspective   57

Chapter 4   People, identity and culture   93

Chapter 5   Experience and work: orientation, emotion and managing
to manage   125

Chapter 6   Organising and strategy-making   169

Chapter 7   Structure, culture and the struggle for management control   221

Chapter 8   Choice and constraint in the shaping of structure and culture   251

Chapter 9   Shaping tasks and winning cooperation   275

Chapter 10   Power, decision-making and organisational mischief   321

Chapter 11   Organising, managing and human resourcing   367

Chapter 12   Managing in a changing world: capability, learning, trust
and morality   415

Contents

List of Cases and Conversations   xiii
List of Activities   xv
List of Figures   xvii
List of Tables   xviii
Introduction   xix
Acknowledgements   xxiv
Endorsements for *Organising and Managing Work*   xxv

Chapter 1   Organising and managing work: study and practice   1

- Objectives   1
- Managing work   2
- Building on the Organisational Behaviour tradition   11
- Work Organisation and Management Studies   16
- Common sense and social science   20
- The critical study of organising and managing   21
- Knowledge and the informing of practice   26
- Summary   31
- Reading   32

Chapter 2   Organisations and management: the *systems-control* orthodoxy   33

- Objectives   33
- Talking and thinking about organising and managing: assumptions and perspectives   34
- Modernism, management and the search for control   36
- Modernism and the management of systems   38
- Organisations and management: the systems-control orthodoxy   43
- Systems-control thinking and the problem of organisational goals   45

- From mainstream modernism to pragmatic modernism   50
- Managerialism and managism: twin pathologies of mainstream modernism and systems-control thinking   52
- Summary   54
- Reading   56

Chapter 3   Organising and managing: a *process-relational* perspective   57

- Objectives   57
- Going beyond the orthodoxy   58
- Organisations and organising: a process-relational perspective   58
  - In what sense do organisations actually exist?   61
- Management and managing: a process-relational perspective   64
  - Three dimensions of management: management, managing and managers   65
  - Task and social-status aspects of management   70
- Official blueprints and negotiated orders   74
- Coming to terms with uncertainty and ambiguity   81
- Making sense of what managers do   84
- Summary   91
- Reading   92

Chapter 4   People, identity and culture   93

- Objectives   93
- Individuals and organisations: beyond 'either or' thinking   94
- The systems-control view of people – dualisms in action   97
  - Linearity and dualism in analysing human behaviour   98
  - Language and action   102
- A process-relational view of people, work and organisations   105
- Individuals, societies and the role of culture in the managing of human existence   110
- Narratives and stories in culture and identity-management   115
- Discourse, language and human practices   118
- Summary   123
- Reading   124

Chapter 5   Experience and work: orientation, emotion and managing to manage   125

- Objectives   125
- Strategic exchange, work orientations and implicit contracts   126

- Feelings, emotions and the experience of stress   138
  - Emotional labour   145
  - Stress, strain and distress   148
- Managing and not managing   154
- Manager talk and controlling the uncontrollable   160
  - The challenge of managerial work   166
- Summary   167
- Reading   168

Chapter 6   Organising and strategy-making   169

- Objectives   169
- Strategy-making and managing in an uncertain world   170
- Strategy-making and the work of all managers   173
- The systems-control view of strategy-making   177
- The process-relational view of strategy-making   185
- Directed evolution: a general trend in strategic thinking and practice?   189
- Strategy-making, organisational effectiveness and survival into the long term   198
- Strategic exchange and the managing of resource dependencies   202
- The influence of strategy-makers themselves on strategy (and vice versa)   213
- Summary   218
- Reading   220

Chapter 7   Structure, culture and the struggle for management control   221

- Objectives   221
- Structure, culture and the struggle for control   221
  - Organisational and societal structures and cultures   225
  - Official and unofficial aspects of structure and culture   228
  - The closeness and overlap of structure and culture   230
- The logic of managerial attempts to shape organisational structures and cultures   234
- The ubiquity and inevitability of bureaucracy   239
- The failings and contradictions of bureaucracy   242
- Summary   249
- Reading   250

Chapter 8   Choice and constraint in the shaping of structure and culture   251

- Objectives   251

■ Direct and indirect options in the pursuit of managerial control 251
■ Enactment, contingency and argument in structural and cultural shaping 255
■ Cultural analysis and manipulation 266
■ Summary 274
■ Reading 274

Chapter 9 Shaping tasks and winning cooperation 275

■ Objectives 275
■ Beyond motivation, leadership and job design 276
■ From 'worker motivation' to work orientations and strategic exchange 279
■ From 'motivating people' to the manipulation of implicit contracts 281
■ Breaking the bounds of motivation and leadership theories 291
■ Equity, balance and expectancies in work orientations 298
■ Direct and indirect control principles of work design 302
■ Modernity, industrialism and the hesitant embracing of direct control work design 305
■ Dilemmas and choices in shaping work tasks and gaining co-operation 311
■ Summary 319
■ Reading 320

Chapter 10 Power, decision-making and organisational mischief 321

■ Objectives 321
■ Power and exchange at interpersonal, organisational and societal levels 322
■ The inevitability of organisational politics or 'micropolitics' 325
■ Organised anarchy and decision-making in the garbage can 338
■ Workplace mischief and the organisational underlife 346
■ Sexuality, humour and the struggle for control 358
■ Summary 365
■ Reading 366

Chapter 11 Organising, managing and human resourcing 367

■ Objectives 367
■ Human resourcing and the employment relationship 368
■ 'HRM': an ambiguous and confusing term? 369
■ Human resource management: a process-relational view 375
■ The essentially strategic nature of human resourcing 378
■■ The centrality of human resourcing issues to processes of organisational strategy-making 378
■■ Human resourcing and the handling of tensions and contradictions

underlying the employment relationship 382

  ■   The necessarily corporate and long-term focus of HRM 384

■   HR specialists and other managers: tensions and ambiguities 388

■   Choices and constraints in human resource strategy-making 390

  ■   Flexibility and dual human resourcing strategies 396

  ■   HR strategy-making in practice 398

■   Selection, choice and discrimination in human resourcing 404

■   Summary 412

■   Reading 414

Chapter 12   Managing in a changing world: capability, learning, trust and morality 415

■   Objectives 415

■   Continuity, change and managerial choice in the managing of work 416

■   Global trends, technological possibilities and organisational options 419

  ■   Globalisation? 425

  ■   Virtual organisations? 426

  ■   Portfolio careers? 427

■   Achieving organisational effectiveness 429

  ■   The pursuit of flexibility 429

  ■   Reciprocity and high trust relations 430

  ■   Stakeholding or trading? 435

■   Achieving manager effectiveness 437

■   Managing right and wrong 447

  ■   Ethical ambiguity and the inevitability of moral dilemmas 455

  ■   Morality and managerial practices 458

■   Summary 463

■   Reading 464

Concept guide 465

Reading guides 477

Reading Guide 1   The nature and study of organisations 477

Reading Guide 2   The nature and study of management 480

Reading Guide 3   Human identity, culture and language 482

Reading Guide 4   Narrative, ethnography and pragmatism 483

Reading Guide 5   Managerial behaviour and practices 485

Reading Guide 6   Ambiguity, uncertainty and managerial decision-making 487

Reading Guide 7   Power and politics in organising and managing 488

Reading Guide 8   Emotion and stress in work and organisations 489

Contents

Reading Guide 9   Manager insecurity and changing careers   490
Reading Guide 10   Manager competence and leadership   491
Reading Guide 11   Management learning and development   492
Reading Guide 12   Fads, fashions and gurus in management thinking   494
Reading Guide 13   Critical management and organisation studies   494
Reading Guide 14   Strategy and strategy-making   495
Reading Guide 15   Learning organisations and knowledge management   497
Reading Guide 16   Bureaucracy, organisational structures and re-engineering   498
Reading Guide 17   Work design, empowerment and teams   500
Reading Guide 18   Changing organisational, technological, global and 'postmodern' patterns   502
Reading Guide 19   Cultural aspects of organisations   504
Reading Guide 20   Cross-cultural and comparative patterns   506
Reading Guide 21   Human resource management and employment relations   507
Reading Guide 22   Work orientations, careers, contracts and motivations   512
Reading Guide 23   Gender in organisations and management   514
Reading Guide 24   Mischief, humour and joking in organisations   516
Reading Guide 25   Ethics, trust and morality in organising and managing   518

Reading guide index   521

Index   529

List of Cases and Conversations

1.1	Managing people and herding cats	3
1.2	The madness of Hands-off Harry	7
1.3	Managing Ward 17	9
1.4	Rose takes over The Canalazzo	18
1.5	Rose and The Canalazzo under threat	25
2.1	Billy Daviot's bread, pies and lemonade	41
3.1	Don Belivat addresses the management of Tradespark Gears	66
3.2	One step forward and one step back at Meikle Printers	71
3.3	The board within the board at Eagle Buses	78
3.4	Peter Brodie reviews his day	88
4.1	Grant Park gets thirsty, or does he?	99
4.2	Colin's ups and downs	108
4.3	Jane Cawdor, heroine and engineer	117
4.4	Mike Kilrock promotes himself	120
5.1	Ravi Barr gets oriented	132
5.2	Sacha and the seven dwarves	135
5.3	Ken Steary laughs, cries and falls over	140
5.4	Cindy sets the limits	146
5.5	A tale of two deputies	150
5.6	Kurt crawls back from the edge	161
6.1	Mats and the reluctant strategist	174
6.2	Tigermill goes strategic	180
6.3	Ali and Dina come into their own	192
6.4	Crunch time at Strath Guitars	208
7.1	Jan and Mohammed come to Mountains	226
7.2	Walt and Roger go into the country	232
7.3	Charles Cawdor at war and peace	235
7.4	Ronnie falls into the Seaforth Arms	246
8.1	Getting on track at Motoline	260

9.1	Dal Cross and the recalcitrant yardies	283
9.2	Dal and the yardies' 'triumph of change management'	287
9.3	Cam Toon confronts the magic triangle	294
9.4	Re-engineering the Doocot	315
10.1	The rise and rise of Derek Duffus	331
10.2	God, Todd, Plod, Wad, Bods and Oddjob in the garbage can	342
10.3	Hazel and Jenny probe the underworld	353
10.4	Messages from the underworld	360
11.1	Sue Ridgebridge gets cross about HRM	371
11.2	Malcolm Lossie plays it canny	379
11.3	Jack fights his corner	385
11.4	'Viewfields, how can I help you?'	399
11.5	Francesca dismantles the sausage machine	406
12.1	Carlo contemplates the future	420
12.2	Faith, trust and the future of Firthside	432
12.3	My company right or wrong?	449

List of Activities

1.1   Mark Merryton's notion of management   2

1.2   The doubtful realism and moral unacceptability of 'people management'   5

1.3   Harry Carse's notion of management   7

1.4   Sadie Rait's notion of management   9

1.5   Management and the curriculum   12

1.6   Applying the social sciences to the Rose Markey story   18

1.7   Applying critical analysis to the Rose Markey story   24

1.8   Pragmatist criteria of 'truth' and three ways of 'framing' management   29

2.1   The value and weakness of the living system metaphor   39

2.2   Analysing organisations as open systems   41

2.3   Playing The Inquisitive Martian game   46

3.1   Don Belivat's three uses of the word 'management'   65

3.2   Three dimensions of management in Meikle Printers   70

3.3   Making changes at Meikle Printers   73

3.4   The negotiated order in Eagle Buses   78

3.5   Analysing Peter Brodie's day   88

4.1   Grant Park's coffee, needs and motivation   99

4.2   Grant Park and the influence of imaginary others   103

4.3   Colin Darnaway's identity and fragility   108

4.4   Instincts and culture   112

4.5   Careers and the stories we are told   116

4.6   Using discursive resources to get a job   120

5.1   Ravi Barr's orientations to work   131

5.2   Analysing one's career and work orientations   135

5.3   Patterns of variety and change of work orientation in one department   137

5.4   Emotional troubles at the hotel   140

5.5   Sex work, acting and emotional labour   146

5.6   Personal resources and coping with stress   150

5.7   What popular books, articles and advertisements say about management   155

5.8   Managerial talk and managing to manage   161

5.9   The managerial styles of Kurt Delnies and Peter Brodie   166

6.1   Strategy-making and the work of all managers   174

6.2	Takeover and strategic change at Tigermill	180
6.3	Starting again at Tigermill	186
6.4	Brodie, Clunas and logical incrementalism	190
6.5	Directed evolution at Tigermill	191
6.6	Criteria of organisational effectiveness	198
6.7	Identifying an organisation's key constituencies	205
6.8	Strategic patterns in Strath Guitars	208
6.9	The personal orientations and practices of strategy-makers	216
7.1	Culture inside and outside the organisation	226
7.2	The relationship between official and unofficial organisational practices	230
7.3	Relating structural and cultural aspects of organisations	231
7.4	The limited possibilities of managerial control	235
7.5	Means blocking ends – in the Seaforth pub and in one's own experience	245
8.1	Analysing Mick and Joy's change management at Motoline	260
8.2	Cultural analysis in Motoline	272
9.1	Work orientations revisited	279
9.2	Implicit contracts and the yard gang	283
9.3	Job redesign, teamwork and a change in implicit contract	287
9.4	Making sense of the Maslow needs hierarchy	294
9.5	Equity, fairness and motivation	299
9.6	Walt, Roger and socio-technical thinking in practice	310
9.7	Choice, contingency and job design	312
9.8	Contingencies, contradictions and BPR at Dovecote Components	315
10.1	Three dimensions of power in Dovecote Components	324
10.2	The micropolitical moves of Derek Duffus	331
10.3	Micropolitics observed	338
10.4	Analysing the Leisure Centre garbage can	341
10.5	Making sense of organisational mischief with Hazel and Jenny	353
10.6	Sex, work and anxiety	358
10.7	Reading messages from the underworld	360
11.1	The problematic concept of 'HRM'	371
11.2	Relating HR and corporate strategies	379
11.3	The necessity or otherwise of a corporate HR department	385
11.4	High commitment HRM and trade unions in Motoline	396
11.5	Changing the HR strategy at the call centre	399
11.6	Two ways of thinking about people and doing HRM	406
12.1	Making sense of the future with Carlo Relugas	420
12.2	High commitment employment policies, the pub and the call centre	428
12.3	Effectiveness and stakeholder thinking at Firthside	432
12.4	The strengths and weaknesses of stakeholder thinking	436
12.5	Managers, management and managing revisited	438
12.6	'Good' and 'bad' managers observed	440
12.7	The competencies of successful general managers	444
12.8	Moral thinking and managerial practice	449
12.9	Ethical responses to race and gender discrimination	454
12.10	The managerial skills of women and men	454

List of Figures

1.1 Three ways of talking about organising and managing 11
1.2 Work Organisation and Management Studies (WOMS) and other 'subjects' 14
1.3 A critical Work Organisation and Management Studies 23
2.1 Systems-control and process-relational frames of reference and a strategic exchange focus 35
2.2 A living open system 39
2.3 The organisation as a big open-system machine 41
2.4 The Inquisitive Martian 46
4.1 Descartes and the 'thinking self' as the ghost in the machine 96
4.2 The human individual as a system 97
4.3 Linear and processual relationships between cognition and action 101
4.4 Organisations and managers in their societal and human-existential context 114
5.1 The strategic exchange and implicit contract between the individual and the organisation 127
5.2 The individual's perceived implicit contract at the centre of their work orientation 130
6.1 Two uses of the term 'emergent strategy' 188
6.2 Organisational strategic exchange constituencies – one possible pattern 204
6.3 Strath Guitars' pattern of strategic exchange constituencies 210
6.4 The strategic exchange between managers/strategy-makers and the organisation 215
7.1 Linear and processual relationships between strategy, structure and culture 223
7.2 The logic of managerial attempts to shape organisational structure and culture 234
8.1 Direct and indirect approaches to the pursuit of managerial control 252
8.2 Contingency thinking and the black box 257
8.3 Choice and contingency in organisational shaping 258
8.4 Three levels of 'visibility' of cultural elements 268
9.1 Direct and indirect control principles of work design 304
10.1 Organisation hierarchies are both control structures and – narrowing – career ladders 328
10.2 The variety of factors at play in the decision-making garbage can 340
10.3 Glimpsing into the abyss 364
11.1 Systems-control and process-relational views of the relationship between corporate and HR strategy-making 381
11.2 Contingency and choice in human resourcing strategy 392

List of Tables

1.1 Focal and supporting social science disciplines for Work Organisation and Management Studies   17

1.2 Two types of common sense in practice   21

1.3 Three ways of deciding the 'truth' of knowledge   27

2.1 Systems-control views of organisations and management   44

2.2 Ten textbook definitions of organisations   45

2.3 A dozen management students' answers to the question, 'What is this "management" that you do?'   47

2.4 Mainstream and pragmatic modernism   51

3.1 Three dimensions of management   67

4.1 Systems-control and process-relational views of the human individual   105

5.1 Books to help you manage: excerpts from a book club brochure   156

5.2 Organisational expressions heard being used by managers   164

7.1 Organisational structure and culture   223

7.2 The organisational paradox of consequences and its relationship to a fundamental organisational contradiction   245

8.1 Elements of organisational culture to be considered in cultural analysis   270

9.1 Two ways in which we talk about 'motivation' in the work context   279

9.2 An input–reward representation of how employees perceive their implicit contract with the employing organisation   282

11.1 A summary of how much academic writing on HRM tends to contrast an aspired to 'HRM' with the 'personnel management' which it rejects   370

11.2 Three dimensions of human resource management   377

11.3 General organisational and managerial options and aspirations related to the basic high commitment/low commitment HRM choice   394

12.1 Broad characteristics of more able and less able managers   441

Introduction

Organising and Managing Work takes a distinctive and innovative approach to what is often called the 'behavioural' aspects of work organisations. It both uses and contributes to the continually developing social-science thinking that is such a valuable resource for understanding modern work activities and how they are managed. This is done in a critical manner, challenging ways of thinking about organisations and management that are taken for granted. It is believed that adopting a critical attitude to knowledge puts us in a much better position to make effective decisions about our work and managerial activities than if we simply follow conventional ways of thinking and acting.

Organisational and managerial activity is deeply and inevitably implicated in the way modern societies themselves are organised and a political and ethical awareness of this has just as much relevance to those working as managers – indeed to their very 'effectiveness' as managers – as it does to people who prefer to keep a critical distance from managerial work itself. But, whatever one's interest in the management of work, it is necessary to adopt some clear criteria for judging the relative value of the various approaches that are available for the study of organisational and managerial practices. Currently available texts rarely do this. Such a concern is central to *Organising and Managing Work*. The book's *pragmatist* approach argues in favour of our evaluating knowledge about organisational and managerial activities according to how effectively these ideas and frameworks inform the fulfilment of human projects in the working part of our lives, whatever those projects might be. This recognises that a 'good' theory of managerial control, for example, would be as helpful to us when we find ourselves subject to – and perhaps wanting to resist – such controls in our working lives as it would if we were attempting to exert such controls as managers.

There are many books that usefully set out the variety of 'schools of thought' or academic 'perspectives' that are on offer for understanding work organisations. These tend to leave it to the reader to decide how valuable or relevant each might be. *Organising and Managing Work* avoids this by suggesting that theories and perspectives can be judged in terms of relevance to practice, as we have suggested. But it goes further. It takes these organisational and managerial practices as its main focus. Its starting point is the everyday practices and understandings of people actively involved in managing work activities. It then turns to theoretical and research-based materials as a means of helping us achieve a better – a critical and potentially 'more useful' – understanding of these practices and 'taken-for-granted' ideas.

It is in this spirit of judging knowledge in terms of its relevance to human practices that *Organising and Managing Work* questions and goes beyond what it calls the systems-control orthodoxy about organisations and management. A degree of systems thinking is invaluable in understanding organised human activities. But over reliance on systems-control assumptions tends to encourage a rather mechanistic view of managerial work. It encourages a view of managerial work as primarily concerned with designing and controlling work organisations as if they were big machine-like systems rationally devised to meet unambiguous 'organisational goals'. The alternative *process-relational* way of thinking presented here recognises that in managing their lives and their working activities people continually strive to make sense of what they are doing in a highly ambiguous world. This is a world in which there are numerous crosscutting and conflicting goals and purposes. It is a world in which managers and non-managers alike constantly have to make and remake bargains, exert power, resist power, cope with conflicts of interest and negotiate understandings with others in order to make sure that the hospital's patients get treated, the factory's goods get produced, the shop's goods get sold or the university's students get educated. Like it or not, these are the 'realities' that confront everyone involved in working and managerial relationships.

As well as being innovative in combining academic and critical rigour with a focus on practice, *Organising and Managing Work* challenges the academic convention of artificially dividing up the 'behavioural' component of work organisations into separate 'subjects' like organisational behaviour, corporate strategy and human resource management. As soon as one moves outside the classroom to look at how work organisations operate in practice, the futility of treating human behaviour *within* the organisation as if it were unconnected to the organisation's strategic relationship with the world *outside* soon becomes apparent. And the pointlessness also becomes apparent of studying the manipulation of *human resources* of effort, skill and capability as if this were not part of a managerial effort to shape both internal organisational behaviours and the overall strategic performance of the corporation. Accordingly, *Organising and Managing Work* rejects the artificial and increasingly unhelpful academic division of labour between 'OB', strategy and 'HRM'. It treats all three 'areas' as closely interrelated components of the overall phenomenon of work organisation and management.

A further innovative intent behind *Organising and Managing Work* is that of providing a textbook which combines a teaching and learning role with the theoretical integrity of a research-based analysis of work organisation and management. The device that links these two aspects of the book is the set of Cases and Conversations that runs through it. These stories and dialogues, and the pictures that go with them, are not included as simple adornments to the text, or as illustrations of the text's argument. They are an integral part of the argu-

ment. Because they derive from the author's research within organisations and managerial work, they reveal important aspects of the 'grounding' in which the overall analysis is rooted. But the cases and conversations have an equally important purpose of imaginatively involving and *engaging* the reader in the text. It is hoped that the cases and conversations will enable the reader regularly to relate what they are reading to their own experiences and to dilemmas arising in their own lives. The use of narrative forms, conversations and pictures parallels Lewis Carroll's approach in *Alice's Adventures in Wonderland* (first published in 1865). At the beginning of that story, Alice peeps into the book her sister is reading and, seeing that it lacks such features, asks herself, 'what is the use of a book . . . without pictures or conversation?' (Carroll, 1962, p. 3, Reading Guide 4).

The cases and conversations have all been derived from interview and field notes collected by the author over several decades of research in work organisations. A significant proportion of this research has involved participant observation within managerial roles. Some of the conversations are direct transcriptions of recorded interviews, while others have been constructed by bringing together elements from more than one interview. Some of the stories stay very close to the events encountered in the research, others have been constructed by bringing together elements from several research projects. Here, fiction-writing techniques have been used to create a coherent and structured account that links to the issues being discussed in the text. Such a use of 'creative writing' techniques in social-science research is especially helpful in handling problems of research confidentiality (Watson, 1995, Reading Guide 4) and in respecting the commercial sensitivity of information gathered in strategy research. The technique has been helpful in this respect with much of the material used in the present book. However, the technique of *ethnographic fiction science* which is used has the further advantage of enabling closer matching of theoretical concerns and fieldwork observations than would be possible if the account was limited to 'what actually happened' in the circumstances of a single case study (Watson, 2000, Reading Guide 4). Although a piece of ethnographic fiction science cannot be strictly 'true' in the *correspondence* sense of truth ('this is exactly what happened'), it is written to be true in the *pragmatist* terms that are explained later in Chapter 1 (pp. 27–9). All the Cases and Conversations that are presented in *Organising and Managing Work* – the fictionalised and the less 'crafted' ones alike – are intended to give sharp insights into the actualities of organisational and managerial life and to foster a practical as well as a theoretically sound understanding of the issues being covered.

The observations and experiences of organisational and managerial work that have informed the writing of *Organising and Managing Work* have occurred in several countries. Events have been observed and discussions held with managers in cultural settings varying from the Far East and southern Africa to Central and Eastern Europe and the UK. These have all been drawn upon in the Cases and Conversations, without national settings being explicitly indicated in most cases. While emphasising that there are significant cultural variations from one organisational setting to another, the book concentrates on the underlying *processes* of organising and managing work that are common to organisations across industrial and capitalist societies generally. Within these general processes, there will be cultural variations from country to country, from region to region and from organisation to organisation. The way in which choices and contextual variations come together in any specific organisational situation is fully recognised in the book's theorising and in its case studies. This, together with the recognition that certain basic principles underlie all of these variations, gives *Organising and Managing Work* relevance across national borders.

The writing of *Organising and Managing Work* has been influenced by an enormous amount of literature, as well as by first-hand research work. This has covered all the main aspects of work organisation, management, strategy, human resource management and organisation theory as well as the social sciences generally and a certain amount of philosophy and history. If direct reference to even a fraction of this were made in the body of the book, the text would become overloaded with citations. For this reason, direct citations in the text have been kept to a minimum and readers directed at various points (including at the end of each chapter) to relevant and helpful books and articles in the 25 Reading Guides that come at the end of the book. These bring together the various functions of a further reading guide, reference source and bibliography and spare the reader from having to navigate too large and unwieldy a bibliographic apparatus at the end of the book.

Although the book has been written to follow a single and coherent narrative from its beginning to its end, it is recognised that people might want to consider the areas it covers in a different order from that built into the chapter structure. Some readers might want to enter the book through its consideration of strategy, for example, and others might start with an interest in the human resourcing aspect of management or with organisational mischief. To make it possible for readers to choose their own order for reading *Organising and Managing Work*, without losing sight of material from other parts of the book that supports the section they are reading, a system of *link boxes* are built into the text. Sometimes these point forward in the text and sometimes they point back. This device should help readers to navigate the book in the way that is most relevant to their own interests and priorities. It should also help academic tutors fit the book into their own teaching programmes. Tutors can obtain a free *Tutor's Guide* from the publisher for further support on this and on other aspects of using the text in their programmes.

Organising and Managing Work is written to be interesting, useful and stimulating to as wide a range of readers as possible. A great deal of effort has gone into making a lot of complex ideas meaningful and accessible, and care has been taken to respect the range of views and values that different users of the book will bring to their reading of it. It will not have been possible to please everyone but the writing of the book will have been justified if most readers have got some intellectual stimulation from its arguments, have got a reasonable amount of pleasure from its stories and characters and, above all, have found the book helpful and relevant to their own experiences with the organising and managing of work.

Acknowledgements

My gratitude goes to all of those from whom I have learned about managing and organising – workplace colleagues, research contacts, students and many other 'helpful friends'. Discussions and exchanges with academic colleagues have enriched and been enriched by this. My special thanks go to Emily Watson for using her creative imagination and drawing skills to give life and extra personality to the cast of characters who appear throughout this book.

Endorsements

Tony Watson's thinking is state-of-the-art. He is at the forefront, both as a scholar and as a researcher. But he is also a brilliant teacher, and this book will entice its readers into learning. The book is clear, interesting, highly original, brilliantly structured, totally sound theoretically, well grounded in organisational life, and full of good stories. No one gives you more new thoughts per page.

(David Sims, Professor of Organisational Behaviour and Head, School of Business and Management, Brunel University)

Yet again Tony Watson has written a 'must buy' book. His new text, Organising and Managing Work, *provides an insightful, sophisticated and critical dialogue between systems-control and process-relational perspectives on organisation/organising, that confronts head-on the tensions between structure and agency in the workplace. The text examines working life from a holistic and ethically sensitive standpoint, vividly brought to life with pointed 'cases and conversations' that clearly illustrate the old dictum that there is nothing so practical as good theory. Beautifully written and highly integrated, this is the text for the theoretically-inclined practitioner, the new breed of MBA student that academics aspire to.*

(Karen Legge, Professor of Organisational Behaviour, Warwick Business School)

This is quite simply the most exhilarating, instructive and witty aid to the study of management and organisations that I have come across for a long time. It will change irrevocably for the better teaching and learning in these areas. Buy it and enjoy it!

(Yiannis Gabriel, Professor of Organisational Theory, Imperial College Management School)

CHAPTER 1

Organising and managing work: study and practice

Objectives

Having read this chapter and completed its associated activites, readers should be able to:

- Appreciate the value of a focus on the management of work as a starting point for thinking about work organisations and their management.

- Recognise the advantage of a *management of work* focus over both a 'people management' or a 'structures and procedures' way of talking and thinking about management and work organisation.

- See how the style of *Work Organisation and Management Studies* adopted in the present book builds upon and goes beyond the traditional business school subject of *Organisational Behaviour*.

- Note the contribution which various social science disciplines make to Work Organisation and Management Studies.

- Recognise a continuity between social-science thinking and a critical form of common sense.

- Understand the importance and value of developing Work Organisation and Management Studies as a critical study.

- Discriminate between perspectives, theories and research findings in terms of how useful (or 'true') they are when it comes to relating theory and practice.

Managing work

To create the goods, services and quality of life people look for in the modern world some rather complex patterns of cooperative human behaviour have to be orchestrated or 'managed'. The academic study of the organising and managing of work involves taking a step back from our day-to-day involvement in these patterns of behaviour and trying systematically to understand how they come about. Such a study also has the potential to help us achieve a better quality of productive cooperation than we typically manage in contemporary work organisations.

We study work organisation and its management because we are interested in the various individual human motivations, interests, values and meanings which play a part in bringing about the patterns of behaviour we see in workplaces ranging from shops, offices and factories to schools, hospitals and universities. But the study also has to concern itself with the ways in which these patterns of human activity and meaning themselves come to be an influence on what occurs in the world. Once human beings create groups, societies, cultures, classes, governing institutions and organisations, what they do in their lives becomes significantly shaped by them. One of the things which makes the study of the organising and managing of work so challenging is that it has to understand how individual choices and initiatives, on the one hand, and already existing and *emerging* structures and patterns on the other hand, both play their parts in social life. And these two influences – of human initiative and structural context – do not work separately. They are inextricably intertwined.

To understand these complexities is not simply an exciting intellectual challenge. It is not just something one might do as an alternative to getting practically involved in work organisation and management. The complexities are ones with which we have to come to terms if we are to be more than direction-less and muddled practitioners in the world of work organisation. In this first chapter of *Organising and Managing Work* we will be looking carefully at ways in which we can take up these challenges. A further key aim of the chapter, however, is to establish, from the start, a critical frame of mind and to challenge some of the over simplifications which we tend to make in our ordinary or 'everyday' thinking about work and its management. Let us consider one of these tendencies now – and look at how we can usefully challenge such apparently reasonable ways of looking at work management.

Activity 1.1

Look carefully at what Mark Merryton has to say about the most difficult aspects of his job, in Cases and Conversations 1.1. Ask yourself what you think his notion of being a manager is – beyond the obvious role of applying the market research skills that he has 'at his fingertips' and being 'creative' about customers.

Managing people and herding cats

What would you say is the most difficult aspect of your job as marketing director for the company, then?

Oh, without doubt it's the people side, if you know what I mean.

Trying to work out what the customers are going to want next – that sort of thing?

Good heavens, no. That's the straightforward side. I think I know what I'm doing on that one. I've got the market research techniques at my fingertips and I'm sharp enough to keep on top of things customer-wise and product-wise. But since my last promotion I find that managing the department has almost wholly become a matter of managing the people in it.

So the problem is . . . ?

It's the people management thing. It's handling the people who work for me. They are a constant headache. I've tried to read the books and I've been on people management courses. I didn't miss one of the OB classes on my MBA course. But I still despair at the difficulty I have with managing the people in my function: sorting out who is going to do what, getting them to do the things I want, getting them to finish things on time, even getting them to be where I want them. And that's before I get into all the recruiting, training, appraising and all that stuff.

Why is this do you think?

Perhaps it's because they are marketing people. We often say that managing marketing people is like herding cats. Can you imagine trying to herd cats? It's a powerful image, isn't it?

Indeed it is. And I've heard it numerous times. Only the other day I heard it applied to university lecturers by a faculty dean. And I've heard it applied to engineers, shop workers, hospital staff, secretaries . . .

Yes, I'm sure. And just look at my secretary. I'm meant to be her boss. She can be quite good but I often feel that she is managing me more than I am managing her.

So it's not just marketing people then?

No, I suppose it's not.

And what about your fellow managers, how do you get on with them?

Some good and some bad. But there are some really difficult people in the business I have to deal with. And this includes several people that I don't myself manage – you know, people in other functions. They can make life difficult. I think it's down to their not being properly managed. The managing director himself is not very good at managing his top team. And my finance director friend is utterly hopeless at managing the people who work for him.

This conversation will surprise no one who has been involved in managerial work. As you read this you may be puzzled at why your attention is being drawn to language that is utterly normal in many workplaces – to wording that you hear every day and take for granted. But, as has already been implied, a key purpose of this book is to encourage you to stop short from time to time and think about just what is going on beneath the 'taken-for-granted' surface of everyday organisational life. To pause and reflect critically from time to time on what one is saying, how one is framing reality, and what is happening as a consequence of this, is a valuable habit for any organisational practitioner. Mark Merryton appears to subscribe to a popular notion of what 'management' is about. Let us examine his arguments carefully.

One of the key themes to be developed and applied throughout the book is the idea that the way we talk and think about the world is closely implicated in how we act in the world. We will be considering the idea that the language and concepts we apply to the world around us can be seen as a *framing of reality* that, to a certain extent, brings about that reality. This is similar to an insight which people often draw upon when explaining how a particular 'mindset' shaped the way someone behaved in a certain situation. Without going into a detailed explanation of this idea at this stage, we can helpfully apply the 'framing' idea to the above conversation. Mark Merryton is in effect telling the interviewer about how difficult people are to relate to or 'deal with' at work. This is a fairly straightforward point to make. We all know that our fellow human beings are quirky, unpredictable and not readily amenable to doing what anyone else tells them to do. But Mark is more specific in the way he frames this general argument. He adopts as a key framing idea the notion of *managing people.* He sees part of his job as one of 'managing the people in my department' and he mentions the courses on 'people management' that he has attended. He tells us that he believes he should be 'managing' his secretary and that the managing director should be 'managing' the directors in his 'top team'. Not only does he refer to the finance director as being bad at 'managing the people' in the finance function, he speaks of the people in that department *working for* the finance director as opposed to working for the organisation which is their actual employer.

The idea of people management and the concept of employees working for a particular 'boss', as opposed to working for the employing organisation is probably a widely accepted notion in modern culture. One of the leading British management magazines, for example, is called *People Management*. But is this title one that can easily be accepted as a realistic and helpful way of thinking about or 'framing' managerial work? Let us think hard about this often taken-for-granted notion.

Activity 1.2

-It is common to hear talk about managers *managing people* or to come across books and courses on *people management*. Given that the word 'manage' generally implies controlling and directing (and, in Mark Merryton's case at least, 'herding'), consider the extent to which this way of talking and thinking about managerial activity is:

■ Morally acceptable – is it at all ethical to ask some people to 'manage' other people?

■ Realistic – is it at all feasible or practicable for some human beings to be given the job of 'managing' other human beings?

Each reader will have answered the first question according to his or her own personal feelings about work and authority. It is not the place of an academic text to lay down or prescribe one particular moral position rather than another. However, it is one of the key arguments of this book that moral issues and choices run through every aspect of organisational and managerial work. It is therefore important to note that Mark Merryton was taking a particular ethical position about work and employment generally and his managerial role specifically when he spoke in the way he did. He may or may not have fully thought out his personal ethical view of the relationship between managers and the people working in the area for which they have responsibility. But such a position is implicit in the words he uses. To help us reflect on what this might be, let us set out a contrary view to the one Mark expresses.

It can be argued that a manager does not have the moral right to direct, manage or 'boss' any individual in their area of responsibility *as a whole person* or in *the totality of their workplace behaviour*. Instead, they have a limited authority to give instructions to employees in tightly prescribed and limited areas of activity. The moral basis of that authority lies in its purpose – to fulfil those work tasks in which the employees have contractually agreed to participate. Employees in modern democratic societies do not sign a contract of employment on the assumption that managers appointed by their employer will have the right to manage them as a person. The manager is appointed to manage the work tasks – and as part of this has limited rights to instruct people. But these rights only exist as means to specific organisational ends and not because of any 'right to command' over the person as a whole. It is thus morally improper to encourage a view of managerial and organisational work based on a principle of 'managing people'.

Is this ethical view simply an alternative to the one implicit in Mark Merryton's words, one that we can adopt or reject solely in terms of our personal ethical position? It is not. It is much more than this. While accepting that it has been expressed in words that might not be fully acceptable to everyone, this ethical position is one implicit in the cultures of modern democratic societies. Moving out of an ethical mode of discussion, then, back into a social-science analytical mode, one can argue that there is a conflict between the 'managing people' view of managerial authority that some managers take and the values or the morality of the wider society of which they are a part. And this suggests that to adopt a focus on people management when one is looking at the 'human aspects' of work organisation is unrealistic – as well as morally dubious.

To recognise a clash between a 'people management' ethic and the ethical assumptions of the wider society, then, is already to accept one significant way in which such a framing of managerial activity is unrealistic. And further grounds readily suggest themselves if we go on to think generally about the people who are allegedly to 'be managed'. While there may be people in the labour markets of modern societies who are happy to subjugate themselves to the wills of 'bosses' at work, such individuals are surely very rare. We will be looking more closely at the complex issue of just what a human being is in Chapter 4. For present purposes, however, it is sufficient to note that one of the key ways that members of the human species differ from other animals is that they are active agents in the shaping of their lives. However meek or submissive particular individuals might be, each human being is nevertheless always the owner and shaper of their own identity, to some degree. As far as the historical record can tell us, no human group in the history of the human species has yet found another group over which it could exert complete control. And this applies even in the extreme conditions of slave societies or extermination camps, where human beings have still demonstrated what looks like an inherent tendency of the species – to resist being managed. We might say that it is not just that cats are inherently 'un-herdable' but that human beings are inherently 'unmanageable'. Which, of course, is not to say that work tasks, involving human beings, cannot be managed.

What is to be concluded from all this reflection? It is to suggest that the widespread tendency to frame – to think about and understand – managerial and organisational work in terms of the management of people is unwise and misleading. It is unrealistic and impracticable, therefore, to focus on the 'management of people' when studying organisational and managerial behaviour. The focus, instead, needs to be on the management of work. The starting point for any consideration of organisational and managerial behaviour is more usefully taken to be the work tasks that are to be carried out. It is these which are organised and 'managed', not the people who carry out the tasks. To understand the behaviours that arise when work tasks are to be done, it is necessary to recognise that work tasks are always *to an extent managed by everyone involved in those tasks*. Work management is not simply what people formally designated as 'managers' do. The nature of the work done by people holding managerial posts will be a concern of Chapter 3. However, there is another common and over simplified idea about management that we need to address at this stage of our thinking – one that perhaps needs even more critical attention than the 'people management' conception that we have looked at.

Activity 1.3

The manager we are about to meet in Cases and Conversations 1.2, 'The madness of Hands-off Harry', has a conception of his job which seems to have little of the 'people management' con- cerns which were expressed by Mark Merryton. Compare Harry's way of 'framing' managerial work with that of Mark. How would you characterise his view of how work should be managed?

The madness of Hands-off Harry

You've heard what the team leaders call me, haven't you?

What is that, Harry?

Come on, I'm sure they've told you that they call me Hands-off Harry.

Well yes, now that you mention it. Do you mind?

Not at all. Well, I did at first because I thought they weren't taking me seriously. I thought they might be laughing at the way I talk about running the department in a 'hands-off' manner. I think they understand my philosophy though, really.

And that philosophy is?

That the manager's job is to lay down all the procedures, the schedules, the targets and the monitoring systems and to keep an eye on all the reports that come up from the shopfloor and all that. You ensure that everyone's been trained in the training school in exactly how to do the job and that they value the job they've got in such a modern facility. They know they will get the pay they want if they meet the targets. Nothing should go wrong if I, as the manager, have got all these systems running properly.

And have you?

More or less – I recognise that things have to be tweaked as you go along. But the team leaders can do that. You just don't need the manager to go out there and, well, sort of get in the way.

But surely people don't simply go along with all the rules and procedures coming from an invisible figure in this office at the end of this long corridor.

Oh, so you've heard the 'invisible man' quip from Joe, have you? He's never been happy with the team leader role but, as I have said to him, modern factories should not need overseer types watching over them. But I do respect what you are saying. And you are right, that all my brilliant paperwork procedures are not enough. There is also the set of values that everyone has absorbed – they've all been through the total quality scheme. All those cultural things are in place. Maybe it doesn't all work like clockwork. But it does work, as long as I do my bit here with my charts and things – and do all the business at the management meetings – I can be Hands-off Harry in the department.

What it appeared that Harry Carse did not know was that the machine operators in his department treated their invisible manager with contempt. They would joke that he stayed in his office (which was indeed at the end of a long corridor off the shopfloor) because he was a madman. They did, however, more or less meet all the targets that Harry set – albeit working in a generally sullen manner. So perhaps it did not 'matter' that Harry remained remote. The three team leaders in the department argued, however, that if Harry 'managed in a more hands-on manner' and 'got to know' the machinists, that there was a strong possibility that much higher output and quality targets could be set.

It is impossible for us to know whether these team leaders are right about whether the department might increase its output if Harry managed it in a different way. However, his case is useful because he talks about managing in a way which helpfully contrasts with Mark Merryton's. He frames managerial work very much as a matter of setting up formal arrangements, procedures, structures and so on. These are not entirely mechanistic notions. His concept of formal arrangements includes cultural matters like 'values' and the idea of people being influenced by principles such as those of total quality management. This means that we cannot argue that he necessarily rejects the idea of 'managing people' – he might argue that he does this but does it remotely – as his nickname of Hands-off Harry implies. However, in the terms preferred here, we can say that his conception of managing work is one that prioritises the structural arrangements side of things rather than the human initiatives side of things.

As we implied earlier we must not go too far in separating out the two aspects of work organisation and management – the direct human initiative aspect, and the structural arrangements aspect. The two are intertwined. Harry Carse may appear simply to run his department through systems, rules and values rather than through direct 'human' interventions. But those procedures and principles were devised by human initiatives taken by Harry and by other managers. Rules, structures and procedures – as much as they sometimes seem to take on a life of their own – do not exist separately from either the human initiatives that are behind them or from the human interpretations of those whose actions at first sight are shaped by them. And it is important to remember that part of the justification for focusing on the 'management of work' in a broad sense was to recognise that the formal managerial work done by 'the manager' – whether it takes the form of setting up procedures or directly attempting to influence people – is only one part of the overall way in which the organisation and management of work is achieved. This is something which appears to be recognised in what Sadie Rait has to say about the case of hospital Ward 17.

Activity 1.4

Read what Sadie Rait has to say in Cases and Conversations 1.3 about her job as a hospital ward manager. Ask yourself:

- What is Sadie's idea of being a manager?
- How does her concept of managerial work differ from that of Mark Merryton or Harry

Managing Ward 17
Cases and Conversations 1.3

Although I am called the Ward Manager, the job is not very different from when my predecessor did it. She was called the Ward Sister though.

Does the new title mean you are a 'manager' in any sense that she was not, would you say?

No, I wouldn't – except strangely that she was much more a manager type than I am. Strange perhaps, but she managed things much more than I do. It was much more, 'You do this, you do that'. She was the one you might want to call a manager rather than me.

In what sense are you less a manager than she was, then?

Thinking about it, I wouldn't actually. We are both managers, but I see management in a different way. You would see Mary Ann obviously 'managing', if you know what I mean. But I work differently. The way I see it is that there is a great deal on the ward that has to be managed – and that I cannot take all of that on. So every nurse, porter, ancillary and clerk is managing the place.

And the doctors?

Whoops, sorry. I suppose them too. Well what I was going to say – and perhaps it's why I forgot the doctors – but perhaps not [laughing], was that the nurses as a team manage this ward. I don't manage the nurses. I wouldn't even try. What I say to them is that I am just the first among equals. I say we manage it together and that I just have watch how it all adds up – and, of course, be accountable to Hospital Trust management.

So you don't find yourself giving people instructions or even disciplining nurses who fall short?

Oh yes I do. I draw up work rosters for example and I've had to do formal disciplines on several occasions. I frequently have to chase people up. But, you see, that is all within the whole set of rules that the Trust sets. The hospital is managed by people but also through rules, systems, procedures, protocols, professional knowledge we all bring with us – all that.

By The Trust, you mean . . .?

Well, the management board have done a lot to change how the hospital's work is managed – through the mission and key values statements they've developed and the new culture that everybody has had a say in.

From this account of her approach to hospital ward management we can identify something of Sadie Rait's style of relating to the people who work on the ward. But what is most interesting to us at this stage is not so much how she manages relationships in her job. It is that she appears to 'frame' the managerial task in the hospital as one that many people contribute to, in addition to the not insignificant directing role undertaken by herself as the official 'manager' – including 'chasing people up'. And without taking on a Hands-off Harry type of faith in the power of structures and procedures, she clearly frames the management of work as something going well beyond managerial *behaviours* as such. Work is managed through structures, procedures and meanings (the hospital is 'managed through rules, systems, procedures, protocols, professional knowledge . . . mission and key value statements . . . the new culture') as well as by specific actions of human actors – managerial and non-managerial. The work of Ward 17 is managed by the day-to-day actions and initiatives of Sadie and her staff but it is also in part managed by the structures and procedures of the hospital. Not only this but the factors which might impede or undermine the effective managing of the ward include both these types of factor. Members of staff choosing for personal reasons not to work cooperatively with others would be an example of the human choice and initiative type of factor. And a set of financial circumstances which meant that the ward was always short of the necessary number of nurses would be an example of the more structural type of factor.

We have then identified three ways of talking about management or 'framing' it, as we see in Figure 1.1. The preference here is clearly for Sadie Rait's notion of what management is – her way of 'framing' her managerial role. It is preferred because it is a much more realistic way of talking about the activity, not least in its recognition that the management of work is only partly done by 'managers'. It also implies that what occurs in workplaces is not just an outcome – or sum – of direct human actions. It also involves structures or arrangements which stand in some sense outside specific actions as such. This

Managing people   Managing structures and procedures   Managing work through relationships and procedures

FIGURE 1.1   **Three ways of talking about organising and managing**

latter facet of work organisation is given primacy of attention by Harry Carse while, it would seem, Mark Merryton lays emphasis on the direct action side of things. The relationship between these two facets of work management and organisations – the direct action and the structural – is an important matter for understanding the organising and managing of work. However, the importance of looking at how relatively direct and individualistic actions like 'leading' or 'motivating' are related to more structural phenomena like bureaucratic structures or cultural patterns is rarely acknowledged in the 'subject' of Organisational Behaviour (OB) as it is taught in business and management courses. It is in giving a fuller consideration to such matters that we go beyond orthodox organisational behaviour thinking.

Building on the Organisational Behaviour tradition

The latter part of the twentieth century has seen enormous growth in institutions engaged in educating people for careers in business and management. Increasingly these activities have been concentrated in the departments of management or the 'business schools' of universities and colleges. A fairly standard type of curriculum has developed in the business schools of the USA and other English speaking countries that have followed the American lead in this style of education. This has involved dividing up the knowledge and teaching relevant to the directing of complex work enterprises into different 'subjects'. Some of that packaging follows an immediately obvious logic. Knowledge related to dealing with customers, for example, has been gathered into the subject area of *marketing* while issues of finance and accounting control form another subject and techniques of planning and coordinating production and service activities a further one of *operations management*. Other parts of the curriculum deal with areas which similarly reflect the way businesses tend to be functionally divided – purchasing, personnel or human resource management for example. But how much attention is given to the issue of how the enterprise as a whole is to be managed?

Activity 1.5

Look at the basic curriculum of a business school you know about or a general management programme within the school and ask yourself (or even a tutor!):

■   Is there a section of the programme or a 'subject' called 'management' available for study?

■   If there is not, where in the curriculum are all the specialist or functional elements brought together into an overview of how the enterprise or *the organisation as whole* is managed or directed?

Quite often there is no such subject as 'management', even within those university or college departments which name themselves 'school of management' or where there are individuals with the title, 'Professor of Management'. This might seem strange. This does not mean, however, that there is no attempt to provide an integrative subject. And the area where one will typically be told the curriculum provides the kind of integrative study we have in mind is in a subject called 'Strategy' or, sometimes, 'Strategic Management'. This gets students to study the way organisations – and predominately commercial business organisations – behave or 'perform' as entities in their economic and societal environment. It is here one might therefore expect to see the social sciences used to analyse how such complex patterns of human activity and structural dynamics come about and are *managed*. But generally, and with the exception of the use of a limited amount of material from economics, there is only a marginal use of theoretical or research insights in strategy teaching into how human behaviours and meanings are shaped into the complex patterns of activity which enable them to relate to their customers, clients, markets or environments. A large part of the time spent studying 'strategy' involves students reading, talking and writing about descriptive case studies of relationships between corporations and their efforts to compete with other corporations. Strangely perhaps, issues of human patterning of behaviour and cooperation and the task of demonstrating the potential of social science analysis are handed over to another subject: organisational behaviour or 'OB' as generations of business students have come to know it.

One might expect a subject with the title of 'Organisational Behaviour' to study the managing and organising of cooperative activities in the context of how the organisation relates to all those external bodies upon which its future is dependent. OB only does part of this job however. It intends to look 'inward', leaving much of the 'outward' focus of the study of organisational performance to the subject of strategy. Its emphasis tends to be on the 'means' through which organising is brought about, with little reference to the 'ends' that it serves. And in doing this, it seriously risks its analytical integrity since these 'ends' – in practice if not in the classroom – fundamentally influence the organisational 'means'. Issues of profitability, market share or government policy, for example, lie in the realm of the strategists while the OB people look at the individual human behaviours, the group formations, the job designs and the organisation structures *in their own terms*, isolating them from their vital strategic context. But even attention to these internal processes is limited in the typical OB curriculum – restricted in large part to the more formal or official aspects of management. It gives only limited attention to the ambiguities, confusions and conflicts which are as much a part of work management activities as all the motivational and leadership efforts, the job and organisation designing, the culture and organisational change initiatives which form the bulk of the curriculum. Even at the level of formal managerial processes, a proportion of these is left to another area of the curriculum. Where are the processes of selecting, recruiting and dispensing with organisational members or the relationships with organised labour dealt with? By and large, these are left to the subject of 'human resource management'.

Organisational Behaviour is a thriving area of teaching and study activity and, indeed, of book publishing. It is developing in sophistication. There are attempts to develop the curriculum in places by bringing into the story the politics of managerial relationships or devoting chapters to conflict more generally. And some attention is given to contextual influences on certain aspects of organisational choice in the guise of 'contingencies' (covered below in Chapter 8). But the tendency for books and courses to run through unlinked accounts of matters of individual behaviour in one section, group behaviours in another and structural and change issues in others is dominant. At a theoretical level, this means that a fault line runs beneath the whole OB landscape. There is a deep hole beneath the surface created by the neglect of what is perhaps the most fundamental challenge which social science has grappled with over the years. This is the issue, referred to earlier, of understanding how the aspects of human choice and initiative in social life, on the one hand, relate to structural and cultural aspects on the other. Leadership, for example, has to be seen as related to wider cultural patterns and not just to the characteristics and actions of particular individuals. What happens at the level of group behaviour must be seen in the context of the overall structural pattern of the organisation, if not of the whole society, in which the group is located. We need to have some understanding of these matters if, for example, we are going to recognise where as human actors in organisational contexts we have choices and where we are structurally constrained. It has to be understood if we want to recognise where we can influence matters by direct actions and where we have to influence them by devising structures and procedures and encouraging shared understandings. These are surely vital things for us to understand if we are interested in how work is managed or might be managed differently. To do this we have both to build upon and 'go beyond' OB.

One of the first things that has to be done to go beyond OB is to abandon the popular device used in many texts or presenting a whole series of different theoretical approaches (the classical approach, the human relations approach, the systems approach and so on) and, after some limited indication of the strengths and weaknesses of each of these, leaving the reader to make up his or her own mind. This might sound fair-minded and liberal, but it is an opting out of the social science writer's responsibility to provide the reader or student with some general criteria by which they might judge what is a useful or a misleading model, a good theory or a bad theory. The failure to develop an integrative theoretical framework makes it very difficult for any connections to be drawn between, say, the 'motivations' of individual organisational members and the prevailing culture of the organisation or, say, between the principles of job design adopted in an organisation and the values and beliefs of the senior managers. OB books fail badly in this respect by, for example, discussing individual 'motivation' in one section of the book and 'organisational culture' in another, without seriously examining how these relate to each other.

Organising and Managing Work, while trying to overcome this problem, is not turning its back on the organisational behaviour tradition. While dealing with many of the issues traditionally tackled in OB and looking at much of the work normally covered in the subject, it attempts both to overcome some of the existing weaknesses and to build upon the firmer base thus laid down. It will do this by:

- organising and integrating the various areas and levels of analysis within a single unifying theoretical perspective – one which has at its heart a recognition of the constant interplay between individual initiatives and structural circumstances;

- explaining and then applying a commitment to a particular style of critical management studies;

- providing the reader with a criterion for judging how some perspectives and theories are 'better' than others;

- connecting the concerns normally associated with the 'subject' of Organisational Behaviour with some of those generally tackled in the separate subjects of Strategic Management and Human Resource Management, as represented in Figure 1.2.

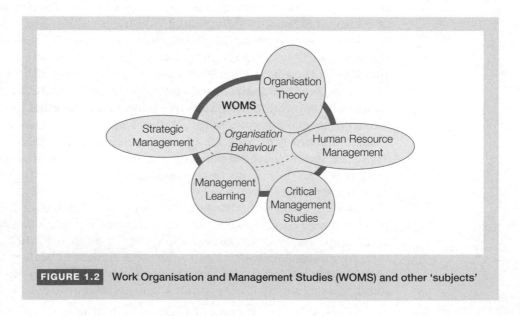

FIGURE 1.2 Work Organisation and Management Studies (WOMS) and other 'subjects'

Figure 1.2 includes three further 'subjects' alongside the fairly standard business school subjects of Strategic Management and HRM. These are Organisation Theory/Organisation Studies, Management Learning, and Critical Management Studies. The first of these looks at many of the same issues as OB but does it with a primarily academic focus – concerning itself first and foremost with scholarly understanding rather than with the implications of such understandings for practice. The materials to be found in journals such as *Organisation Studies* or many of the books listed in Reading Guide 1 are nevertheless invaluable for the more practice-oriented *Work Organisation and Management Studies*. This is especially so because the subject has been much more attentive to the question of relating individual level activities to bigger 'structural' patterns. It has also been more concerned with taking a critical stance than OB, something which has also informed the emergence of Critical Management Studies (Reading Guide 13) – in effect an application of the more critical ideas of Organisation Theory directly to issues of managerial activity. Management Learning is another emergent field of specialist study with its own academic journal, *Management Learning*, and a concern to bring together theoretical developments in the understanding of human learning processes with issues of both educating and 'developing' managerial practitioners (see Reading Guide 11). *Organising and Managing Work* is informed by this development in its recognition of the central importance of issues of learning to all aspects of the organisation and management of work.

All of these developments in the study of the organisation and management of work in modern societies can be understood, perhaps ironically, as aspects of work organisation themselves. This is to say that these different 'subjects' have not 'come about' straightforwardly to reflect different aspects of human activity which exist 'out there' in the world of work and its management. There is no chunk of work activity going on in the world which is 'strategic management' and which can be separated from another chunk of reality which is 'management learning'. In part, the academic subjects reflect a division of labour among managerial practitioners. Some managers, for instance, are paid to operate more 'strategically' than others are. However, the pattern of academic subjects we tend to see in business schools are probably more an outcome of the ways in which teachers, researchers, writers and publishers have chosen to carve up their territories than a straightforward reflection of the 'realities' of organisational practice. This carving up involves all the career building interests, interpersonal conflicts, market pressures, confusions and ambiguities which characterise all work organisations and the people who work in them. We cannot expect those working in academic organisations to be immune to any of this.

These comments inevitably apply to the writing of *Organising and Managing Work* itself, of course. We will shortly consider the justification that can be offered for such a departure and what it involves. First, however, it is time to clarify formally where we have got to with our notion of Work Organisation and Management Studies.

Work Organisation and Management Studies

Work Organisation and Management Studies, as a subject which both incorporates and goes beyond existing ways of looking at work organisation and management, can be formally defined.

Work Organisation and Management Studies	Concept
The analysis of the human aspects of work organisation and its management which draws on the social sciences to develop insights, theories and research findings with a view to informing the choices, decisions and actions of people who have a practical involvement with organisations.	

We need to note several things about this concept of Work Organisation and Management Studies.

- What is studied is the 'human aspects of work organisation and its management'. This language is not meant to imply that attention is only paid to 'human aspects' at the level of the human individual. The focus is on work *organisation* and management, which means that patterns of human activity and thinking going beyond the level of the individual are as important as thinking about the human individual. As has already been explained, the concern is with the interplay of factors at the level of human initiative and choice and factors at the level of social, political and economic context, or structure.

- The subject *informs* the choices, decisions and actions of people involved in practices in organisations. There is no question of developing an academic subject which can tell people what they should do in the complex area of work management. The area is far too complex for there to be any basic rules or even sets of guidelines about 'how to do management'. Not only this but, given the moral factors which must come into every human situation where power and authority are involved, it would be quite wrong for a textbook to attempt to provide guidance in this way. What it can do, however, is to provide insights into the range of factors and issues which are relevant to any particular choice (of, say, job design or planning an organisational change programme). The actual choice or decision that is made is a matter for those involved in the particular organisational situation – with all the political, moral and specific local considerations coming into play alongside the insights which can be derived from academic study of the managing and organisation of work.

- Reference is made to 'organisational practitioners' rather than 'managers' as the potential 'users' of the subject. This is done in recognition of the fact that people other than those formally designated as managers are closely involved in the way work tasks are managed. If there are ideas in Work Organisation and Management Studies which would be helpful to a manager in an organisational situation wishing to have his or her understanding enhanced by academic thinking then surely those ideas are going to be equally relevant to anyone else concerned with that situation. This would be the case regardless of the person's formal authority in the organisation or, for that matter, their degree of commitment to official organisational policies.

● The social sciences are 'drawn on' by Work Organisation and Management Studies. The subject is not seen as a social science in its own right. A variety of social science disciplines can be turned to provide research findings, theoretical resources or insights that might be helpful in understanding organisational issues. This does not mean, however, that we simply turn in a random or *promiscuous* manner to the vast bank of social science materials every time they wish to analyse a particular situation. Each individual is likely to build up their set of preferred social science concepts as their learning proceeds. They then turn to the books and journals for further insight, as the need arises, and incorporate the new learning into their ever-developing personal framework of understanding.

Organisational behaviour has tended to draw primarily on the social science disciplines of sociology, psychology and social psychology. Work Organisation and Management Studies, as conceived of here, follows this and similarly supports the contributions of the main disciplines with insights from economics, political science and anthropology. The key concerns of each of these are outlined in Table 1.1.

All of these disciplines can be seen as providing resources which can be drawn upon when wishing to understand the organising and managing of work in general or any particular organisational situation or problem in particular. Many of the human issues that can arise in the organisational context do not fall into any one obvious disciplinary territory and many of them might use ideas from more than one discipline. Bearing this in mind, see how you get on with Activity 1.6.

TABLE 1.1 Focal and supporting social science disciplines for Work Organisation and Management Studies	
Focal social science disciplines	**Supporting social science disciplines**
Psychology focuses on individual characteristics and behaviour and on such matters as learning, motivation and individual ('personality') differences	**Economics** supports the sociological concern with the economic context and, also, the psychological concern with decision-making (through its attention to 'rational' decisions made by economic actors)
Social psychology focuses on group characteristics and behaviour, on roles, attitudes, values, communication, decision-making and so on	**Political science** supports the sociological concern with power and conflict and the social–psychological concern with decision-making (through its concern with the state and other institutions handling matters of power and difference of interest)
Sociology focuses on structures, arrangements or patterns and how these both influence and are influenced by individual and group behaviour. It is concerned with the structure of the social and economic system as well as with the organisational structure and issues of technology, conflict, power and culture	**Anthropology** supports the social-psychological concern with norms, values and attitudes and the sociological concern with cultures (both organisational and societal) with insights taken from the study of non-industrial or 'less advanced' societies about such things as rites, rituals, customs and symbols

Activity 1.6

Read the story about Rose Markey taking over as the manager of The Canalazzo restaurant (Cases and Conversations 1.4), thinking about the issues which Rose is going to have to deal with to satisfy her employers. Following the characterisations of the six social sciences set out in Table 1.1, note the factors or issues that you think might be identified as, respectively, psychological, social–psychological, sociological, economic, political and anthropological.

Rose takes over The Canalazzo
Cases and Conversations 1.4

Rose Markey had been working for a national chain of restaurants for only a couple of years when they asked her to take over a restaurant which they had recently acquired. They had bought The Canalazzo restaurant from the Italian family which had established the business some twenty or so years previously. The family had decided to return to Italy and to warmer summers. The company had originally put in one of their older managers to run the newly acquired restaurant. However, they were very disappointed with what was being achieved. Their director of finance argued that the turnover of the business simply did not justify the investment that had been made in the purchase of the business and in the redecoration of the premises. When they challenged the first manager they had put in, he talked of his resentment at being asked to move to a new part of the country at the age of 55. He persuaded the company to give him an early retirement settlement so that he could return to the part of the country he had lived in for most of his life. They were pleased to do this because it was clear, the human resources manager told Rose, that this man's poor motivation and attitude to customers was increasingly being reflected in the way the staff of the restaurant went about their work.

When Rose arrived at the restaurant she soon learned that her predecessor had clashed on several occasions with local police officers about serving late drinks. This was likely to get back to the magistrates and the

restaurant would be in danger of failing to have its drinks licence renewed when it was next due for review. The manager's defence was that he was simply following local customs in the town whereby customers would have a night out that would bring them into the restaurant only after spending most of the evening in a public house. It was not his fault, he said, that the police officers and the magistrates all lived outside of the town and didn't know about this.

When it came to the problems with the staff, Rose found that her predecessor had set up a strongly hierarchical set of relationships among them. This seemed to be accepted, albeit grudgingly, by the people who worked in the kitchen. But it was resented by the waiting staff who were largely part-time workers studying at the local university. Not only this, but the group of waiters – who all knew each other from the university – and the kitchen workers, all of whom had left school at 16, tended only to speak to members of their own group. The chef, who was a middle-aged Italian, regularly fell out with the headwaiter – a woman a dozen years younger than him. Their respective ideas about how young female staff should be treated were poles apart and these differences led to frequent arguments. Overall there was very little coordination between the kitchen and the restaurant. All of this, Rose decided, seriously affected the quality of service the customers received.

Perhaps psychological factors are the first to suggest themselves here, ranging from issues of differences of personality and temperament among different employees of the restaurant to ones of motivation and personal commitment. The varying sets of attitude in the restaurant are clearly a matter of social–psychological interest as are the problematic patterns of communication and the way the two groups of kitchen and restaurant staff have developed to create a division among the junior staff as a whole. All of this feeds into the sociological factors and issues. There is a power structure within the restaurant and this has elements which relate to sociological variables such as age, gender and ethnicity – all of which relate to the way society as a whole is organised. But there are also sociological factors about the way the restaurant fits into the local economy and community, both as a provider of services and a source of labour. Here there is a clear overlap with economic issues of market organisation and this, in turn, relates to the most obvious economic issues of financial performance, turnover (and, by implication, profitability) and investment. Issues of a formal political nature (i.e. relating to issues of the role of the state) are present with regard to the police and magistrates, and there are obvious informal 'political' issues running right through the whole set of relationships in the restaurant. This is in addition to whatever the 'informal' politics of the relationship between local police officers and restaurant managers might be. Anthropological issues of informal customs might also be involved but, more obviously, the anthropological notions of custom and ritual are highly relevant to the patterns of restaurant use which influence the pattern of work which has to be managed by Rose Markey and the rest of the staff of The Canalazzo.

Common sense and social science

One of the first thoughts occurring to anyone trying to make sense of the problems of The Canalazzo restaurant might be that 'common sense' is likely to be just as helpful as ideas from psychology, sociology or anthropology. It has, nevertheless, been a tradition of social science teachers to contrast social science thinking with common-sense thinking and, not surprisingly, to argue that social science analysis is to be preferred to common sense. But an alternative response might be to say, 'It all depends on what you mean by common sense'. This is necessary, in fact, because there are two quite different usages of the term 'common sense' that often get muddled up. It is useful to distinguish between *everyday common sense* and *critical common sense*.

Everyday common sense	*Concept*
Analysis based on unthought-out, taken-for-granted, immediately 'obvious', everyday assumptions about the world and human activity within it.	

Everyday common sense is necessary for 'getting by' in our daily lives. We all make quick assumptions about what is going on around us, drawing on all kinds of stereotypes, half-remembered experiences and simplistic cause–effect connections. This is necessary to cope with our daily lives. We would not cope with life if we stopped, sat back and deeply pondered on every eventuality that faced us between getting up in the morning and going to bed at night. But perhaps we can see why social scientists claim that their more analytical style of thinking has advantages over this. In the work context, for example, individuals frequently offer woefully simplistic generalisations such as 'People only go to work for the money' – typically adding, 'It stands to reason' or, 'It's obvious' or, 'It's common sense isn't it?' This is a good example of everyday common sense, based as it is on easy, unthought-out, taken-for-granted assumptions. Assumptions like these make life simpler – at first sight, anyway. But such assumptions are often dangerous guides to action on matters of any importance or complexity such as designing a pay system or 'reward structure', for example.

We therefore turn to critical common sense as a style of thinking which involves being essentially logical or rational about things in the way which is common to all human beings when they are alertly and critically putting their mind to whatever matter is in hand.

Critical common sense	*Concept*
Analysis based on the basic logic, rationality, hard-headedness to be found in human beings whenever they step back from the immediate situation and critically put their minds to an issue or problem.	

This is the kind of common sense that we can more reliably use as a guide to action when more complex matters of work organisation and management arise. It is an activity of the same order as that in which the scientist engages. Science,

TABLE 1.2 Two types of common sense in practice	
Everyday common sense and pay	**Critical common sense and pay**
If you pay employees in proportion to their output they will produce more than if they get the same wage whatever they turn out	Pay for output might work. But employees might prefer the comfort of a steady work rate and the security of a steady wage. They might resent the pressures of a bonus system on group relations
They will clearly work better under a performance-related pay system	It would be wise to find out what the particular employees' requirements are before deciding for or against a performance-related pay system

in this view, is essentially a formalised version of critical common sense. Scientific thinking – in principle if not always in practice – is the more formal, systematic and painstakingly analytical application of critical common sense.

Critical common sense analysis tends to start from a consideration of the most obvious or likely explanation of what is going on; the everyday common sense explanation in fact. But it then goes on to ask whether things are really as they seem at first. Alternative explanations are considered and attention is paid to available evidence in judging the various rival explanations. We can see the two types of common sense compared in Table 1.2 and the managerial implications of applying each of them, in this case in deciding for or against a performance-related pay system.

The considerations about performance related pay connected in Table 1.2 to a critical common sense way of thinking about work behaviour are indeed similar to ones which have emerged from social science research and theorising about the relationship between pay and behaviour.

 Link   See, in particular, the 'expectancy' theory of work motivation explained in Chapter 9, p. 300. Similar arguments to these critical common sense ones were developed in the light of one of the famous Hawthorne experiments – The Bank Wiring Observation Room experiment – by Roethlisberger and Dickson (1939, Reading Guide 1).

The critical study of organising and managing

A critical common sense frame of mind is obviously relevant to any kind of practical human endeavour. But it has particular relevance to academic work – and especially to studies that claim to be scientific. Scientific analysis, as has already been suggested, can be understood as an especially rigorous or systematic application of critical common sense. And this would suggest that we could not do social science at all without being critical in the sense of constantly questioning taken-for-granted ideas and practices. However, there has been a growing trend of questioning the extent to which social-science study of work behaviour and managerial practice has been sufficiently critical.

The crux of the problem that all writers and researchers interested in managerial issues have to face up to is the fact that managerial activities are always and inevitably implicated in issues of power and relative advantage and disadvantage between human groups and human individuals. Everyone engaged in management research and management education is therefore faced with a dilemma. How do they reconcile providing knowledge that might help improve the effectiveness of work activities with the fact that in doing so might help some people ('managers' and the employers of managers, say) more than others ('the managed', for example)? Helping make work organisations more efficient or more effective is not a politically neutral matter.

In a world where valued resources tend to be scarce and there is continuous competition for the goods, services and rewards provided by work organisations, any intervention can involve one in taking sides between the relatively advantaged and the relatively disadvantaged. The social scientist is in danger of becoming a 'servant of power', as an early polemic on such matters put it (Baritz, 1960, p. 39, Reading Guide 13). One way of handling this dilemma is suggested by some members of the emergent 'critical management studies' movement. Their strategy amounts, in effect, to 'going on the attack' against managerial ideologies and activities that are felt by the critical scholar to be 'wrong' or 'harmful'. Critical research and writing would, for example, offer its students 'an appreciation of the pressures that lead managerial work to become so deeply implicated in the unremitting exploitation of nature and human beings, national and international extremes of wealth and poverty, the creation of global pollution, the promotion of "needs" for consumer products etc.' (Alvesson and Willmott, 1996, p. 39, Reading Guide 13). Such a critical management study is committed to exposing the political implications of managerial work with an ambition of helping achieve 'emancipatory transformation' – the transformation of both people and society. And, in the workplace itself, a 'critical' version of the concept of empowerment is called for, 'empowering employees to make more choices and to act more effectively to transform workplace relations' (Thompson and McHugh, 1995, p. 22, Reading Guide 13).

These advocates of critical management studies, critical management education and critical organisation studies want their work to help change the balance of power in the worlds of work and employment. But they are not just critical of the existing patterns of power prevailing in organisations and society at large. They also aim their critical fire at the type of writing and teaching which constitutes the orthodoxy in contemporary business and management schools. And the main thrust of this critique is against the assumption behind much of this orthodoxy that success in managerial and organisational work comes from acquiring, developing and applying *skills* and *techniques* – skills and techniques which are neutral and 'innocent' in a political sense. Issues of power, inequality, conflict (at interpersonal, group and class levels), gender and ethnicity are either ignored or treated as peripheral matters which, from time to time, get in the way of smooth organisational functioning. Sympathy with this latter criticism has been an important inspiration for the writing of the present text and it informs the critique of what is called the *systems-control* orthodoxy and its displacement

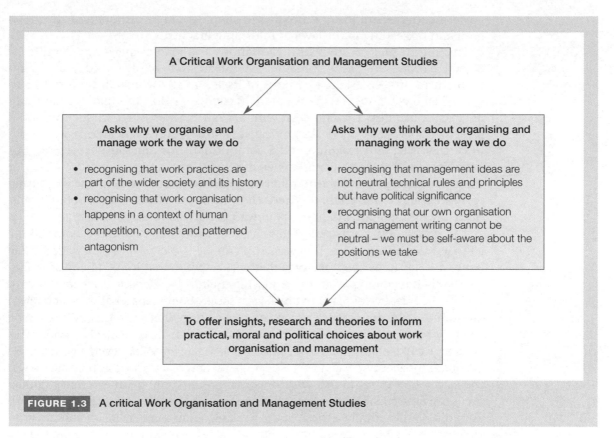

A Critical Work Organisation and Management Studies

Asks why we organise and manage work the way we do

- recognising that work practices are part of the wider society and its history
- recognising that work organisation happens in a context of human competition, contest and patterned antagonism

Asks why we think about organising and managing work the way we do

- recognising that management ideas are not neutral technical rules and principles but have political significance
- recognising that our own organisation and management writing cannot be neutral – we must be self-aware about the positions we take

To offer insights, research and theories to inform practical, moral and political choices about work organisation and management

FIGURE 1.3 A critical Work Organisation and Management Studies

by a more realistic and politically sensitive *process-relational* perspective. But the whole text is underpinned by a particular notion of a critical organisation and management study, which is summarised in Figure 1.3. It is a notion that shares much ground with the work being produced under the flag of 'critical management studies' but its overlap is only partial, as the earlier Figure 1.2 suggested.

The conception of a critical organisation and management study adopted in *Organising and Managing Work* differs from that taken by some of the critical thinkers whose ideas were looked at above. This is primarily with regard to the issue of arguing for 'transformation', at both the personal and the social levels. It is felt that the choices that these transformations would entail are a matter for political and moral debate in society generally and for contestation within organisations themselves. They are not transformations which social science can or should push people towards. What the social sciences can do is to illuminate or inform those debates with information and insights derived from both research investigations and theoretical reflections. And if these insights, research contributions and theories are going to have any real potential to *make a difference* to practices in the world outside the classroom and library, there has to be an openness about the fact that all social science analysis is itself value-laden. To contribute to either societal or organisational debates about how work tasks are to be organised and managed as if this were simply a matter of deciding which power-neutral technique or procedure to adopt would be dishonest at the moral level and misleading at the level of informing practice.

This means that no study of organisations and management can claim to be objective or in some sense 'value-free'. A critical study of organisation and management must keep asking questions of itself – as the words on the right-hand side of Figure 1.3 suggest. This entails recognising that the management and organisational ideas that are dealt with are not matters of technique or neutral principles, devoid of political significance. It also requires a degree of self-aware-ness in writing and teaching and a commitment to judiciously revealing our own biases and moral inclinations where this is necessary to help the reader or student take one's inevitable partiality into account. This principle was followed early in the present chapter where the notion of 'people management' was *engaged with* as a matter of morality as well as pragmatic realism.

The writing of the early part of this chapter was also relevant to the words on the left-hand side of Figure 1.3. The essence of critique is *questioning* and a critical study has to ask questions about the organisational activities that it is studying as well as constantly questioning what it is producing itself in its 'literature'. We looked criti-cally at the way several practising managers speak about managerial work and raised questions about the practice of speaking of management in terms of 'managing people' or 'managing structures and procedures' rather than 'managing work'. This argument will be built upon as *Organising and Managing Work* develops. And as we ask questions about how and why work organisation practices are as they are we will constantly bear in mind that work organisations are only in an extremely limited way a separate phenomenon from the economy and society of which they are part. They did not historically 'evolve' in the working out of some divine or abstract prin-ciple of increasing organisational efficiency. The hierarchy of jobs in today's organisations, for example, is both an outcome of and a contributor to the hierarchy of class and status which has developed in society as individuals and groups have competed with each other for advantage over the years. By the same token, markets do not exist 'out there' as part of the 'economic context' of business organisations. They are *made* by organisational initiatives as much as they are served by organisa-tions. A critical perspective also requires us constantly to observe that differences of interest – and the frequent alignment and re-alignment of interests – are inherent in organisations. They permeate the managerial strata of organisations as well as under-lying the basic tensions between employees and employers.

Activity 1.7

Quickly re-read Cases and Conversations 1.4 and how Rose Markey 'took over' at The Canalazzo restaurant. Then read the sequel to that story (Cases and Conversations 1.5), 'Rose and The Canalazzo under threat'. Make a note of all the ways in which an understanding of both parts of The Canalazzo story would require attention to factors to which, it is argued above, a critical study of organisation and management draws attention. The wording on the left-hand side of Figure 1.3 is a starting point for your analysis.

After six months' managing The Canalazzo restaurant, Rose Markey prepared for her annual performance appraisal at the headquarters of the company which owned the restaurant. She was still finding her job quite a struggle. She had begun to adjust to living in the north of the country, having only ever lived in the south previously. She had established good relationships with the local police and the worry about losing the drinks licence had disappeared. However, she was having difficulties with the chef, who resented a woman being in charge of the restaurant. The problems with the chef were exacerbated by the fact that the kitchen staff seemed pleased to see her discomforted whenever she got into an argument with him. And the kitchen staff's uncooperative attitude towards the waiters had got worse. They knew that Rose was a university graduate and frequently mocked her southern middle-class accent in the same way they regularly mimicked what they called the 'posh' accents of the largely-student waiting staff. They saw Rose and the waiters as people who were only in their present jobs as a means towards something better later on.

In spite of these difficulties, Rose felt sure she could succeed in improving the restaurant's popularity. She believed she could win over the chef in the long run, by encouraging him to develop some more adventurous menus and attracting a new clientele. This, she thought, would encourage him to discipline his kitchen staff more effectively – especially with regard to their relationships with the waiters.

Rose was excited about explaining all of this to the manager who was to do her appraisal. However, before she could even begin to talk about what she was doing, he told her that the company was considering closing the restaurant. A rival had ousted the chief executive of the company. The new managing director wanted, she said, to take the whole business 'up-market'. A restaurant in a northern town with a declining local economy did not 'fit into the new scheme of things'. Rose was to be offered redundancy – the terms of which she was invited to go and discuss with the Human Resources manager.

When Rose found the HR manager, he immediately invited her to go to a nearby wine bar for a drink. He explained that as an old friend of the former managing director he had felt it wise to seek a job with another business. He had been successful in this and therefore felt able, he said, to let Rose know that he believed she had been badly treated. He said that the possibility of closing the restaurant had arisen before Rose had been moved there. Rose had been chosen to take the Canalazzo job because one or two of the headquarter's managers felt that her 'face did not fit'. She was not only the one graduate trainee manager they employed. She was the only one with a black face.

The story of Rose and The Canalazzo involves many of the normal problems that someone is likely to face when trying to manage work – in a struggling restaurant or anywhere else. Alongside the obvious problems about the nature of the market for the particular services offered, and the need to achieve better coordination of the restaurant's division of labour, are a whole series of interpersonal and intergroup relationship problems. But most of these relate in some way to the patterns of conflict, inequality and discrimination existing in the wider culture and society. A critical organisation and management study would take all of this into account in an analysis of what was occurring. This would take it well beyond attention to orthodox issues of motivation, leadership and group relations. But it would also recognise the wider pattern of economic ownership which was relevant to issues in The Canalazzo and observe the way in which boardroom politics can affect what happens at a local workplace level in an organisation. There are politics at every level – workplace, organisation and society. A critical Work Organisation and Management Studies would see these as centrally important matters, not merely as ones providing the 'context' in which the basic day-to-day application of managerial techniques and motivational skills have to be applied.

By now, after two visits to The Canalazzo restaurant, two things should be apparent about analysing all the complexities of organisational and managerial behaviour as it occurs in 'real life' (as opposed to how it appears in the idealised world of standard management texts). First, as we saw in Activity 1.7, we have to look critically at facets of social, cultural, political and economic life that go way beyond a simple search for efficient management techniques. A whole series of moral issues arise in the Canalazzo story. Second, as we saw in Activity 1.6, we have to turn to a range of social-science sources for help in analysing these matters. But each of these social sciences itself has a range of perspectives, models, concepts, theories and research studies on which we might draw when analysing whatever organisational or managerial issues interest or concern us. How do we choose between these?

Knowledge and the informing of practice

One of the ways in which we said that we needed to 'go beyond' Organisational Behaviour was to avoid the very popular OB textbook device of organising material according to a variety of different 'schools' or theoretical approaches or perspectives (the 'classical', 'human relations' or 'systems', for example). Although some texts point out the merits and demerits of each of these, readers are more or less left to decide for themselves which way of looking at organisations they prefer. However fair and reasonable this may seem at first, it avoids the issue of advising students of work organisation and management about what broad criteria they might apply to any piece of research or theorising they come across when trying to understand organisational or managerial practices. And this militates against taking a critical stance with regard to the study of work organisation and management itself. How do we make judgements about the relative value of one piece of analysis or knowledge compared with another?

To deal with this question we have to get involved with issues of *epistemology*. This is the branch of philosophy that deals with the relationship between the way the world is and the knowledge we have of that world. And it has a specific concern with the sort of truth claims that can be made for particular propositions or pieces of knowledge. This might seem a rather complex issue for us to get involved in here, something we can leave to philosophers while we get on with looking directly at organisations and their management. However, we really cannot duck the matter. It is vital to any understanding of how we relate 'theory and practice'.

Whether we like it or not, we all make epistemological judgements every day of our lives. We may have to decide, for example, 'how much truth there is' in the story we just read in our newspaper about an imminent business takeover. We might be concerned with 'how much truth there is' in the picture of society painted by the politician whose speech we have just listened to. Or we might be anxious about 'how much truth there is' in stories we have heard about a local school 'failing' and being closed down. Broadly speaking there are three approaches or 'theories' we can apply to such matters – approaches we can also take to the sort of accounts and analyses we come across when studying organisations and management. These are shown in Table 1.3.

TABLE 1.3 Three ways of deciding the 'truth' of knowledge	
Three ways of deciding the 'truth' of an item of knowledge	**For example . . .**
Correspondence theories of truth judge an item of knowledge in terms of how accurately it paints a picture or gives a report of what actually happened or 'is the case'	A jury is asked to apply this principle (qualified by the notion of 'beyond reasonable doubt') when deciding between the accounts given by the prosecution and the defence. A judgement has to be made as to whether 'x' actually did or did not kill 'y'
Coherence/plausibility theories of truth judge an item of knowledge in terms of how well it 'fits in with' everything else we have learned about this matter previously	We might apply this principle when deciding whether a piece of gossip about somebody we know is true or false. We ask whether or not it fits with everything else we have seen of them and heard about them
Pragmatist theories of truth judge knowledge in terms of how effectively one would fulfil whatever projects one was pursuing in the area of activity covered by the knowledge, if we based our actions on the understanding of those activities which it offers	We might apply this principle when comparing what a promotional tourist brochure says about a foreign city we are going to visit and what is said in a book by an independent author drawing on their first-hand experiences. We have to decide which account of that city we are going to heed when deciding what to wear, how to address local people, how to find food that we like, or avoid being robbed

In everyday life we apply all three ways of deciding the validity of a piece of knowledge. We do this in organisational contexts as much as we do in the other areas of life used in the examples in Table 1.3. But the pragmatist approach to making judgements is obviously the most relevant to deciding what practices we are going to follow in any situation, in the light of the knowledge about that situation which is available to us. In the case of deciding which of the two tourist guides to trust, we would clearly be wise to apply the pragmatist 'theory of truth'. We would similarly be wise to apply this principle if we were considering taking a job with a particular organisation and had available to us, say, both the organisation's recruitment brochure and an article written by a researcher who had carried out participant observation research in that organisation. Which of these two 'pieces of knowledge' is the 'truer' one, we would tend to ask. And we would ask ourselves this question because we would be concerned to decide the most appropriate way to behave when entering the organisation. We would, in this respect, be applying a pragmatist theory of truth claims in the same way that we do when we compare the account of a product given in the manufacturer's advertisement and a report on the product published by an independent consumer association.

In the light of these examples, it is clear that a pragmatist approach to judging the sorts of material one comes across in studying organisations and management is invaluable. The wisdom of such an approach derives from its pragmatically realistic acceptance to two things:

● It is impossible when looking at organisational issues to have enough information – free of interpretation, free of biased reporting, free of the tricks of human memory and free of ambiguity – to apply the correspondence theory of truth. This applies to social life in general as well as to organisations specifically. Because everything we are told about the world is mediated by language and interpretation, we can never receive an account which accurately reports or 'mirrors' that world.

● There are no absolute truths or 'final laws' which social scientific analysis can offer with regard to organisations or any other aspect of social life. One proposition, theory or research study can be judged to be truer than another, however. But this is only to the extent that it will tend to be a *more trustworthy*, *broad guide to practice* in the aspect of life it covers than the other. It cannot be wholly correct, totally true, or completely objective. One piece of knowledge is simply more useful than the other as an account of 'how things work' which we can use to inform our practices.

This pragmatist approach to judging the validity of the sorts of material we are going to study derives from a particular school of philosophy, the pragmatist philosophy of Charles Pierce, William James and James Dewey as well as, in part, the neo-pragmatist thinking of Richard Rorty (see Reading Guide 4). But it also fully accords with the relatively straightforward notion of *critical common sense* looked at earlier. It leads us to the eminently sensible critical common sense practice of reading management and social science books (or considering any other kind of knowledge for that matter) and asking ourselves, 'To what extent should I take into account this knowledge when deciding what to do in practice?'. If one theory, one research study, or even one piece of fictional writing, is thought to be more helpful in informing our practical projects than another, then it is a *better* theory, article or book. It is 'truer' in the pragmatist sense of 'true'.

To emphasise the relevance of pragmatist criteria for evaluating pieces of organisational and management knowledge is not to argue for completely turning our backs on the other criteria for judging truth. The concept of justice applied in many societies requires us to work with the correspondence theory of truth, for example, in courts of law or other types of judicial or bureaucratic enquiry. Yet, even here, as we noted earlier, the ultimate impossibility of this is recognised in the acceptance that a judgement can only achieve a reliability which is 'beyond *reasonable* doubt'. We are therefore much safer, for most purposes, applying the more modest pragmatist criterion for judging truth claims. And we are certainly much safer applying this approach than making too much use of coherence or plausibility theories of truth. We apply these all the time – when, for example, we ask how one statement on some issue 'stacks up against' everything else we have heard on that matter. At the level of ordinary or everyday common sense we have to do this. But it is not good enough when we are engaged in the more rigorous and critical common sense type of thinking which we frequently have to do in the complex area of organising and managing work. Too many poor theories in the organisational and management sphere have an immediate plausibility, one that soon disappears when rigorous and critical common sense is applied to them.

 Link   The endlessly taught and cited 'hierarchy of needs' theory of work motivation is subjected to this kind of analysis in Chapter 9, pp. 291–7, and shown to fall down badly in pragmatist terms.

The reader of *Organising and Managing Work* is invited to apply the pragmatist criterion of validity to everything that is offered in the forthcoming chapters. It is the criterion that has been applied to the arguments developed throughout the book. It informs the recommendation of a *process-relational* perspective for looking at organising and managing work, instead of the orthodox *systems-control* perspective which is critically examined in Chapter 2, for example. Also, it can be applied to the different ways of talking about managerial work that we have considered in the present chapter. Activity 1.8 can help demonstrate this.

Activity 1.8

Apply the 'pragmatist theory of truth' to the view of managerial work expressed in Cases and Conversations 1.1, 1.2 and 1.3, respectively, by Mark Merryton, Harry Carse and Sadie Rait (summarised in Figure 1.1). You can do this by assuming that you are planning to take up a managerial career and are wondering which of these informal 'theories of management' is likely to be most useful to you when deciding how you will act once in a managerial post.

This activity should help you see why Sadie Rait's account of 'what management is all about' was identified earlier as a 'more realistic way' of talking about that activity than the way Mark and Harry 'framed' managerial work. Pragmatist thinking suggests that anyone doing managerial work is likely to be more effective at whatever they are trying to do in that job if they recognise that:

● 'management' is done by non-managers as well as managers;

● that managerial work involves *both* dealing directly with 'people' and setting up structures and procedures.

Mark and Harry's 'theories of management' were much more simplistic than this and would tend to be less helpful when it came to informing practice. They are less 'true' than Sadie's account in the sense that they would be less useful as indicators of 'how things work' in managerial activities and would thus be less useful when it comes to informing practice.

One way in which this broad principle of utility applies to all scientific thinking is in science's use of concepts.

Concepts
Concept

Concepts are the working definitions that are chosen or devised to make possible a particular piece of scientific analysis. They are the way scientists define their terms for the purpose of a specific investigation. They therefore differ from dictionary definitions which tend to have a much more general applicability.

In our everyday lives, we are used to looking for *correct definitions* of phenomena, ones that will be generally helpful to us when communicating within a broad public language. If we wish to analyse phenomena with the greater degree of rigour and focus that distinguishes scientific analysis, however, we find ourselves having more carefully to *conceptualise* phenomena. This means devising working definitions which are helpful to us in trying to analyse and understand some aspect of the world. Thus an economist will conceptualise money more rigorously than the person in the street will 'define' it. Psychologists will do similarly with regard to 'intelligence' – working with different concepts of intelligence at different times. What this means is that in engaging in an enterprise like writing *Organising and Managing Work*, one develops concepts that are useful to one's purposes. One does not turn to a dictionary for the universally 'correct' definition. Thus, every time there is a 'defining of terms' in this book (usually using the device of a 'concept box'), it is done to be *helpful* to the purposes of the book – and *useful* to the readers who are interested in improving their understanding of how work is organised and managed. The whole enterprise of the book is based on the notion that some ways of conceptualising, 'management' or 'organisation', say, are more useful than others. The intent is not to find a 'correct' definition of what 'management' or 'organisation' is but to use concepts that help us critically engage with the world.

The pragmatist style of thinking is also relevant, in a very basic way, to the arguments set out earlier for the *critical analysis* of *Work Organisation and Management Studies*. Doing this, it was argued, involved appreciating that work organisation happens in a context of contest, inequality and conflict and that management ideas are more than neutral rules, principles or guides to action; they always have political significance. Knowledge of organisations and management which gives full recognition to these matters, according to the pragmatist principles, would be better – as a set of resources for informing practice – than knowledge which ignored them. This is because an organisational practitioner, managerial or non-managerial, would be better placed to succeed in whatever their purposes might be if they were informed in this way. We might go as far as to say that an individual who tried to undertake any kind of organisational task without a strong awareness of the political dimension of organisational life would be a fool! It follows from this that critical thinking is equally relevant to a manager, a non-managerial worker or someone wishing to challenge and undermine the whole enterprise. To put this another way, there cannot be 'managerially biased' knowledge – other than inadequate or misleading knowledge. If there is work organisation knowledge which helpfully informs the practices, projects and purposes of managers, then it is likely to be equally helpful to anyone else operating in that context – including someone wishing to oppose 'managerial' initiatives. The same principle applies to other spheres of human activity: knowledge which helps a government rule can also help an opposition to bring it down; knowledge which helps a police force fight crime can equally help criminals carry out crimes more successfully, for example.

As far as *Organising and Managing Work* is concerned, everything in the book is intended to inform people involved in the management of work – whatever the nature of that involvement might be. The book should be helpful to those designated as 'managers'. But it should be equally relevant to someone whose 'project' is to have a quiet life at work, make an investment or customer decision about a work organisation or set out in some way to oppose the managers of an organisation. In this spirit, we now move forward in Chapters 2 and 3 to look at some of the major ways in which our understanding of organisations and managerial work is changing – and changing in a direction which can make it more effective than previously as a resource for informing our practices in the management of work.

Summary

In this chapter, the following key points have been made:

- The most helpful way to think about issues of work organisation and management is to focus on all those activities which contribute to the management of work tasks, only then considering how such activities are divided up between people who have the title of 'manager' and those which do not.

- There are both moral and practical problems with the notion of 'managing people'.

- Approaches to managerial work that focus on the 'management of structures and procedures' are equally inadequate.

- There are both 'people' elements and 'structure-procedure' aspects to managerial work, and both have to be taken into account both in thinking about management and engaging in it. Managerial work needs to be recognised as something which entails both directly relating to people and establishing working structures or procedures. The interplay between these two aspects of management – and between the choices that are possible and the factors which influence those choices – is complex and will be a theme of much of what is to follow in later chapters.

● Although the academic subject of Organisational Behaviour has been the main vehicle for bringing social science thinking into the study of management and organisation, it has a number of inadequacies. The present book attempts to overcome many of these.

● Work Organisation and Management Studies, as a subject attempting to build upon and go beyond Organisational Behaviour, is linked with several other established and developing academic subjects, including management learning, critical management studies, strategic management and human resource management.

● Work Organisation and Management Studies is the study of the human aspects of work organisation and its management which draws on the social sciences to develop insights, theories and research findings with a view to informing the choices, decisions and actions of organisational practitioners.

● The social science disciplines drawn upon by *Organising and Managing Work*, and their analytical styles, are not essentially different from 'common sense' thinking. In fact, they have a close continuity with what can be called 'critical common sense'.

● In the spirit of 'critical common sense', the style of *Work Organisation and Management Studies* adopted here can be identified with certain aspects of the emergent tradition of 'critical management studies'. This entails continually asking, first, why work is organised and managed in the way it is and, second, why we think about and study work and its management in the ways we do. It also involves continuous recognition of the extent to which work organisation happens in a context of human competition, context and patterned antagonism as well as recognising that management ideas are not neutral technical rules and principles but always have political significance.

● To be able to relate what we study to issues of practice in the organisational and managerial world we need some criteria for judging the relative merits of the theories, research studies and other materials that are available to us. The most useful criterion we can apply to judging theories, and the rest, is one derived from pragmatist philosophy. There is no way of judging absolute truth or validity. But some accounts can be seen as 'truer' than others. It is suggested that one piece of material may be judged to be 'truer' than another to the extent to which it better informs human practices or 'projects' in the aspect of human activity with which it deals.

Reading

Reading Guides 1, 2, 4 and 13 contain material that supports and takes further much of what is covered in Chapter 1.

Organisations and management: the *systems-control* orthodoxy

<table>
<tr>
<td></td>
<td>

Having read this chapter and completed its associated activites, readers should be able to:

- Locate the origins and underlying assumptions of orthodox ways of thinking about work organisation and management in the distinctively *modernist* way of looking at the world – one which is concerned with asserting human control over the world as a means to bringing about general progress in the human condition.

- Understand the centrality of the notion of *systems* to the orthodox way of thinking about work organisations and their management.

- Recognise the focus on organisational goals and objectives which also characterises the current orthodoxy.

- Identify the weaknesses of the *systems-control* way of looking at organising and managing, and, in particular, its dependence on systems thinking and on the notion of organisational goals.

- See how a shift from mainstream modernist thinking to a more realistic *pragmatic modernism* can change the way we think about work organisation and management – in a direction which is more realistic and, in effect, more helpful.

- Become aware of two dangers which mainstream modernism and *systems-control* thinking present both to democratic principles at the societal level and the effective fulfilling of work tasks at the organisational level – *managerialism* and *managism* – and appreciating how these dangers reinforce arguments for developing an alternative way of thinking about and carrying out the organising and managing of work.

</td>
</tr>
</table>

Talking and thinking about organising and managing: assumptions and perspectives

Before we can properly study processes of organising and managing work we need to give careful attention to the way we talk about and think about 'organisations', whatever they are, and 'management', whatever that is. Some progress has already been made on these matters in the first chapter where we concentrated on the different ways in which managers themselves can be seen to be thinking about the nature of managerial work. What we should have established by now is that the way we 'frame' any given activity has important implications for how we practically involve ourselves in that activity. We saw, for example, the different ways in which three managers, Mark Merryton, Harry Carse and Sadie Rait, frame *management* in Cases and Conversations 1.1, 1.2 and 1.3. Mark frames his work in terms of 'managing people', Harry uses a 'managing through structures and procedures' framework while Sadie's frame of reference is one which incorporates elements of both of these. Sadie's understanding of managerial work – an understanding which provided her with guiding principles for her practice – was one which recognised the need both to relate directly to the people in her ward and, at the same time, to develop structures and procedures for getting things done. It was argued that this third way of framing management is a better one than the other two.

The grounds upon which we are able to judge some ideas, theories or frames of reference to be better than others was also established earlier (pp. 26–9). The pragmatist way of judging truth claims suggests we can treat one account or theory as truer or 'better' than another if the former has the potential to inform our practical projects better than the latter. Thus, Sadie's way of framing managerial work is to be preferred because, all things being equal, it is likely to be a more realistic guide to successful practice than the other two ways.

In Chapter 3 we will develop a more formal and explicit framework which enables us to recognise that it is not a matter simply of there being two aspects of managerial work that every manager needs to deal with – a 'relating to people' and a 'structures and procedures' aspect. The two are closely interrelated. The broad frame of reference for studying work organisation and management which is to be developed in the next chapter, a *process-relational* one, gives full recognition to this. But that perspective is difficult to appreciate without setting it in the context of the standard or orthodox framework (or 'frame of reference') that the perspective seeks to supersede. This *systems-control* perspective is closely examined in the present chapter, though not simply in order to contextualise what will follow in Chapter 3. The ideas that it incorporates are so powerful and so widely accepted that any *critical* study of organising and managing work must examine it closely and subject it to careful critique. It contains many of the assumptions which influence the way we both study organisations and the practices which occur within them. It is thus vital to consider how valid those assumptions are – with a view, in the subsequent chapter, to suggesting alternative assumptions which might be more helpful both to organisational analysis and managerial practice.

At first sight, in discussing two rival frameworks for studying organising and managing across these two chapters, we might appear to be retreating back to the conventional 'organisation behaviour' practice of dividing up material into various 'schools', 'approaches' or 'perspectives' which was criticised earlier (pp. 13–14). But no, the intention is still to avoid treating the subject as a sequence of separate scholarly 'inputs' or as a series of debates between different academic stances. We must not allow the lenses that are available to us for looking at the world to become more the objects of study than the human activities that they are meant to focus on. We must avoid the examination of the *means* of study becoming an *end* in itself, which means not spending too much time gazing at the tools we have to hand at the expense of actually getting on with the job that the tools are intended to help us with. Nevertheless, we do have to make sure that we have the most useful conceptual tools lined up to help us with our studies, which means that certain academic debates about the strengths and weaknesses of different ways of looking at the world have to be taken into account. The purpose of these two chapters, therefore, is to develop the most useful general 'analytical tool kit' that can be put together in the light of ongoing academic debates. This will be done in two stages:

- in the present chapter, critically examining the orthodox *systems-control* framework, noting both its strengths and weaknesses, and establishing some basic principles for developing an alternative perspective (without abandoning all its insights);

- in Chapter 3, identifying the emerging and alternative *process-relational* framework which organisational researchers and writers are increasingly adopting, one which goes beyond the current orthodoxy but which does not abandon some of the valuable insights which that orthodoxy incorporates. And in Chapter 5 the concept of *strategic exchange* will be introduced, a

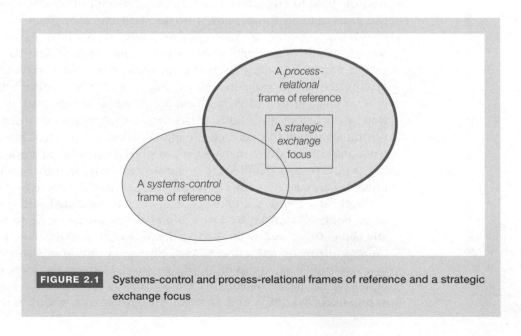

FIGURE 2.1 Systems-control and process-relational frames of reference and a strategic exchange focus

theoretical device that crystallises much of the thinking which distinguishes the *process-relational* frame of reference.

Figure 2.1 represents pictorially the relationship between the two general frames of reference and the more specific *strategic exchange* focus.

Modernism, management and the search for control

History is not just 'the past'. What we are and what we do in the present must always be understood in the light of where we have come from historically. If we don't do this we will fail to see that the way things are for us in the world is not the only way it can be. The ways in which we organise and manage work, for example, are the relatively haphazard outcomes of a whole series of particular decisions, accidents, conflicts, alliances, achievements, mistakes and failures made by human beings as they have struggled with the world and with each other to solve the challenges of scarcity and desire which the human species has always faced. It was partly in recognition of this that a historical awareness was put at the centre of the critical conception of *Organising and Managing Work* explained in the previous chapter (pp. 21–6). Only when we have recognised that there is no fixed and pre-given way of ordering human affairs will we engage our critical faculties and ask ourselves whether we might be able to do things 'better' (better, that is, in the light of whatever it is we value in life).

The basic ways in which we organise our work activities in the early part of twenty-first century – as well as the ways we think about or 'frame' them – can only be understood in the light of major changes which have taken place over the last several hundred years, originally in Europe and increasingly across what we now tend to talk about as a 'globalised' world. Most obviously we have seen the growth of an industrialised world, with much of the work that people do involving complex technologies and advanced divisions of labour within bureaucratically structured work organisations, with these organisations paying people wages and salaries in return for their efforts and commitment. In spite of attempts in certain societies to organise all of this within socialist principles whereby the means of production are publicly owned and 'managed' by the state on behalf of its citizens, it has been a capitalist set of social and economic principles which has become the globally dominant one. This means that the work activities and the managerial aspect of those work activities for an increasing proportion of people across the world occurs within a context of market pressures and the dynamics of competitive corporate activity.

All of these changes, and the thinking that is associated with them, can be seen as elements of *modernity* and *modernism* ('modernity' referring to the historical era and 'modernism' to the ideas and principles central to it). If we locate this era of human history on the whole scale of human evolution it is still very new, and it takes up only a tiny proportion of that scale. Many of the basic modernist principles which have shaped this era of human existence were originally given expression by French and Scottish Enlightenment philosophers in the mid-eighteenth century. The Enlightenment thinkers were building on and systematising ideas which had been unfolding for some time – especially the questioning of religious faiths and traditions and the growing scientific way of thinking about the physical world. Taking up the principle established by Descartes in the seventeenth century of applying rational thought to a world from which human beings can separate themselves, the French 'philosophes' Voltaire and Montesquieu were greatly influenced by the English philosopher John Locke and the English scientist Isaac Newton. Their ideas were built upon first by Hume in Scotland and Rousseau and Diderot in France and, later, by the Scots Adam Smith and Adam Ferguson, the French Marquis de Condorcet and the German Immanuel Kant.

It might be asked at this stage what all of this can have to do with management and work organisation. The answer is, a great deal. Alongside all of these ideas, and by no means unrelated to them, was the growing interest in commercial and technological innovation that came to be known as the industrial revolution. This had two particular implications of interest to us here:

- it involved a growth in the size of work enterprises that required the specialised involvement of some people in the managerial aspects of organising work;
- it encouraged a search for principles of organising work and administration that would be more effective and efficient than traditional methods had been.

But related to both of these developments – the origins of the occupation of 'the manager' and the application of bureaucratic principles of work structuring (a key concern of Chapter 8) – was the key principle of Enlightenment or 'modernist' thought, one which sought control through the application of reason.

Modernism *Concept*

The key principle of modernism is the application of rational or scientific analysis to social, political and economic affairs – work organisation included – to achieve greater human control over the world and to bring about general progress in the condition of humankind.

Out of the application of this principle has come the growth of managerial jobs within ever-larger and consciously structured work organisations. But it has also provided the basis for the very idea of social science and such business school subjects as 'organisational behaviour'. More significantly, however, it has shaped what has become the orthodox formal thinking about the work of managers over the last century or so.

Management, the modernist conception of managerial work *Concept*

This sees managers as specialised 'experts' within work organisations who rationally analyse the tasks for which the organisation was set up and the resources required to complete them and, in the light of these analyses, design work systems which achieve sufficient control over work activities to ensure successful task completion.

It is to achieve the level of expertise implicit in modernist aspirations that so much time, money and effort has gone into the development of business schools, the writing of management books and the creation of such academic subjects as 'management science' and 'organisational analysis'. Indeed, the opportunity to write *Organising and Managing Work* arose within the context of this principle – even though the book subjects the principle to critical review. But before we can come fully to terms with the problems inherent in this way of dealing with the question of what management is, we need to look closely at the way the modernist orthodoxy has made central use of the notion of *system*.

Modernism and the management of systems

The concept of *system* is one of the most powerful that has been developed for thinking about work organisations. Its origins lie in the attempts which thinkers have made over many centuries to deal with the problem of making sense of those aspects of the social world which appear to exist outside and beyond the experiences and activities of the individuals. This was often done by saying that the society, the tribe or the church was like a human body. Christians, for example, often speak of their church as 'the body of Christ' and the practice was developed long ago of referring to the person in charge of any social grouping as its 'head'. The word 'corporation', typically used to refer to what we are here calling organisations, derives from 'corpus', the Latin word for body, and the very word 'organisation' makes clear reference to the biological notion of 'organism'. All of this had great potential for managerial ideologists who wanted to justify the trend for work organisations to differentiate between managers and non-managers. The division between manager and worker, it could be claimed, was as natural and necessary as that in a living body between hand and brain (and, indeed, it was quite normal at one time to refer to workers as 'farm hands' or 'factory hands').

The system idea, when applied to organisations, effectively *gives a life of its own* to the organisation. This makes it very convenient to both managers and people studying organisations. The buzzing confusion of a mass of people going about a multitude of activities that we actually see when we get near an organisation can be reduced to something seemingly much more *manageable* if we conceive of these organisational elements as the body parts or movements of a big animal. The attraction of thinking in this way is increased further once we notice an interesting parallel between an organisation and a living creature: they both take resources 'into themselves' and they both produce outputs – with these two activities necessarily being related to each other. They can thus both be seen as open systems.

Open systems thinking   *Concept*

A way of analysing any complex entity in terms of system inputs, system outputs and an internal conversion process – with communication links or 'control actions' monitoring the outputs to enable any necessary process adjustments to be made.

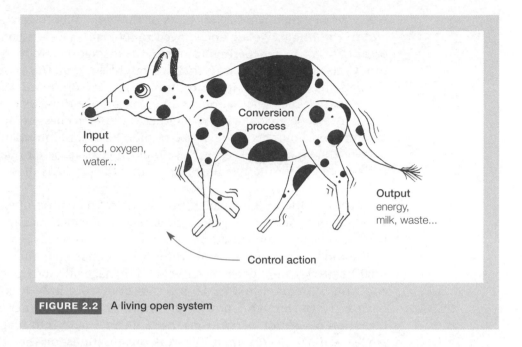

Input
food, oxygen,
water...

Conversion process

Output
energy,
milk, waste...

Control action

FIGURE 2.2   A living open system

Figure 2.2 portrays an imaginary living creature in open-systems terms. Inputs to this living system include food, water and oxygen and the internal functions of the creature convert these into energy, fat, muscle, waste and so on. The creature will also have evolved with a set of internal control mechanisms which, for example, monitor these outputs in case adjustment has to be made to the inputs. If the animal's body temperature begins to fall, for example, its instinctive control mechanism will lead it to seek shelter or sunlight. Similarly, if its energy levels fall in a threatening way, it will seek food.

Activity 2.1

Look closely at Figure 2.2 and consider:

■ What value, or insight, is there in thinking of a work organisation as if it were a living creature, like the one in the picture?

■ Where does the metaphor break down or become unhelpful? Where do the parallels between a living creature coping with its environment and an organisation functioning in the social and economic world fail to be helpful?

Some useful insights can follow from looking at the organisation as if it were a living creature. We are made aware, for example, that the various work activities going on in the organisation need to be mutually supportive to some degree and contribute to a certain extent to the functioning of some broader scheme of things. To put it another way, the metaphor encourages us to look at the ways in which the various parts of the 'whole' both relate to each other and to the whole. We are encouraged to look at how each component of the organisation – its purchasing, technologies, marketing, production and so on – functions, in the same way that we might look at the part played in an animal's life by its brain, its heart, its lungs, and so on. Interrelated functioning is necessary if the organisation, as an organism-like thing, is not going to 'die'. Similarly we are encouraged to consider the effectiveness of the way in which organisational outputs are reviewed or monitored and information transmitted back to the input stage – ensuring, for example, that better quality raw materials are obtained if the customers report that the products they are buying soon fall apart.

In spite of the insights which this biological metaphor offers, it clearly has some major inadequacies as a frame of reference which managers might adopt for thinking about organisations. The most obvious one is that there is no role in the functioning of the organisation for the managers themselves. This, we might expect, would deter managers and managerially oriented thinkers from adopting systems thinking. Living creatures are simply there because they have survived through a process of evolution and they function through the operation of control mechanisms that are either built into them from birth or are learned by the creature itself. Work organisations, on the other hand, have not simply come about as a result of a process of biological evolution. Human beings have deliberately set them up. They have been consciously designed. Their construction and operation is dependent on human initiatives and choices and these initiatives and choices involve the pursuit of human purposes or goals. Use of the biological system metaphor encourages us to ignore all of this.

Given these problems with systems thinking in its basic biological form, we might have expected system frameworks to fall out of favour. But their attractiveness, it would seem, was too great. They have, in fact, become essential to the orthodox and dominant way in which we think about organisations. But this has only been possible because an alternative non-biological version of the model has become dominant. It is a version of systems thinking more in line with modernist thinking and modernism's emphasis on human control than the biological version. The older metaphor of a social entity as a living creature has been replaced with a metaphor of *the organisation as a big machine* (see Figure 2.3). The organisation can still be seen as a unified whole whose components, or sub-systems, function in an interrelated way to convert inputs into outputs. But now, this system, with its sub-systems and its control mechanisms, is conceived of as one that has been designed by managers and, furthermore, it needs to be driven, continually maintained, and, from time to time, re-engineered by managers.

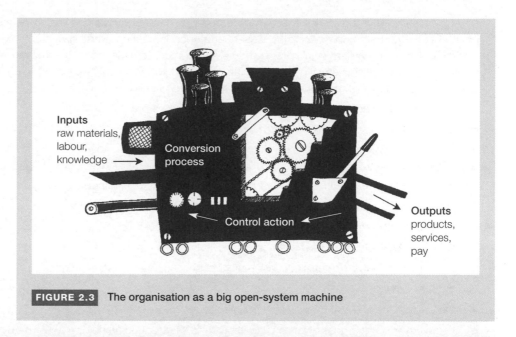

FIGURE 2.3 The organisation as a big open-system machine

Activity 2.2

Think of an organisation that you have come across or, if you prefer to keep it simple, a department or section of an organisation. Make a sketch of that organisation or organisational 'sub-unit' in open system terms. Identify the main inputs and outputs and some of the *control actions* that adjust *inputs* as a result of monitoring *outputs*. You may chose to do this before or after reading about Billy Daviot, the baker in Cases and Conversations 2.1.

Billy Daviot's bread, pies and lemonade   Cases and Conversations 2.1

Billy Daviot's bread and pie shop is an example of a very small organisation indeed. He makes a reasonable living in the rural community where his bakery and shop is based and he gives full-time employment to a baking assistant and a delivery girl and part-time employment to a cleaner and someone who 'helps with the books'. If we look at this small business as an open and living system, we can see it managing to survive through the conversion of a number of *inputs* into *outputs*. Among the inputs are:

- the flour and other ingredients which Billy buys to make his bread;
- the variety of pies which he buys from three different suppliers in the large town thirty miles away;
- the soft drinks which he buys from a long-established 'lemonade factory' in a small town fifteen miles away;
- Billy's own knowledge and baking skills as well as his reputation as a trustworthy member of the community who is an important source of information about what is going on in the community;
- information which is received by Billy and his staff from customers and others they come into contact with;
- the efforts, skills and knowledge of the employees of the business;
- the gas and electricity which heats the premises and fuels the oven;
- the loans which the local bank occasionally gives to help buy new equipment.

The outputs include:

- the bread, pies and soft drinks which people buy;
- the information and gossip which is contributed to the local community, not just by Billy himself when he sees people in the shop but also by Jane, the young woman who takes deliveries around the area;
- the wages and other benefits of employment which the small staff receive, some of which feeds directly back into the local economy;
- the well-being of Billy and his family who have the security of owning a business which has a reasonable value on the market.

The most obvious *transformation process* that occurs in this small organisational open system is the baking process whereby raw materials are transformed into bread and buns. But, alongside this, there is the transformation of cases of soft drinks and trays of pies, which are delivered to the shop, into commodities displayed on the shop's shelves. Also, the variety of items of information and gossip which Billy, his staff and his family come across are interpreted and converted into more coherent 'stories' or accounts which can be transmitted back into the community.

Although the shop supplies only a very limited range of products which does not vary a great deal over the year, Billy is very anxious to check continually that his customers are satisfied with what he is offering. The main control action that he uses to make adjustments within the business, as a system, is that of simply listening to what customers say. In recent times, for example, he has twice had to threaten the lemonade factory people with taking his business to a bigger national supplier because of complaints he has received about the poor quality of their cans. But his information from the customers also tells him that they like the idea of having drinks from a regional manufacturer rather than from a large multinational corporation. 'You've got to get the balance right', he tells the soft drinks company, 'between the appeal of a small local and traditional supplier and the exciting image of drinks marketed with a world image'. The problem was solved in this way. And this was a relief to Billy because Jane was telling him that there was also a problem with the freshness of some of the pork pies she was delivering. In this case, Billy was forced to change the supplier of this product. As Billy said to Jane, 'To keep this business going, we've got to keep our ears to the ground, and we've got to take notice of all the feedback we can get'. Billy did not speak of open systems, inputs, outputs, conversion processes or control actions but he understood very well, in his own terms, the logic of what others call 'open systems'.

This small case study illustrates the value of looking at work organisation in open systems terms. Such an analytical framework helpfully draws our attention to the ways in which the various components of an enterprise both relate to each other and relate to the 'environment' with which the enterprise *as a whole* transacts. However, there was a deliberate degree of irony in the selection of a small and traditional business to illustrate the application of systems thinking to organisational activities. This style of thinking about work organisation has been developed much more to understand the large-scale enterprises which have characterised modern industrialised societies, and, specifically, to come to terms with problems of controlling big complex undertakings. Systems analysis is really a creature of modernist thinking. Yet, although Billy Daviot is operating in what looks at first sight like a very traditional setting, it might be argued that he is very much dealing with a modern world. He is coping with the shifting tastes of the modern consumer society and he is handling competition from large modern corporations (including massive international soft drinks manufacturers). If he were operating in a fully traditional setting, people would tend to be satisfied with things staying 'as they always were' – the hallmark of traditionalism. He would undoubtedly need to take care with what he supplied, but the importance of the sensitive 'feedback mechanisms', control actions and the rest, that open systems thinking stresses, would be less critical than it is in the bigger and faster moving modern world. But, since Billy is operating in the modern world, systems analysis is a fitting way of looking at his activities. And, indeed, we might infer that Billy has not been completely untouched by such thinking. He did, after all, use the systems term 'feedback' in his conversation with Jane. Few people in the modern world are completely untouched by systems thinking. It has become a powerful orthodoxy across the worlds of practice and academic thinking.

Organisations and management: the systems-control orthodoxy

The widespread adoption of a systems way of looking at things, tied in with the central modernist concern of *control*, has given the modern period a set of orthodox and dominant assumptions about what organisations are and what management is (see Table 2.1). Although it has been used with varying degrees of consciousness and explicitness, it has given management academics and managers alike a style of thinking which has almost become a world view for many of them – a world view which is both taken for granted and is unassailable. We can characterise it as a *systems-control* framework for thinking about, and acting with regard to, the organising and managing of work.

TABLE 2.1 Systems-control views of organisations and management	
The systems-control view of organisations	**The systems-control view of management**
• the organisation is a system – a big 'social machine' • it takes inputs such as raw materials, knowledge and human effort through a conversion process utilising various technologies to produce outputs in the form of goods and services • it is designed and controlled by people who design, engineer and maintain it • it is controlled in order to achieve the organisational goals which it was designed to fulfil	• management is the design, control and maintenance of the organisation as a big social machine • managers are skilled and knowledgeable experts – the organisational designers, engineers and drivers • managing involves the application of a neutral technical expertise • managers do not further their own interests but work to fulfil the organisation's goals

The notion of a special activity of 'management' which is central to systems-control thinking would probably not be of particular interest to Billy Daviot. It is something much more relevant to the larger organisations and the complex corporations which play such a key part in today's societies. In the modern period, the division of labour in all but the smallest work organisations has come to include the specialised role of 'manager'. These are people required to step back from, and stand above, the basic operations and tasks of the organisation and, in the words of perhaps the most famous of all definitions of management, to 'forecast and plan, to organise, to command, to co-ordinate and control' (Fayol, 1916/1949, Reading Guide 2). Henri Fayol and Frederick Taylor, who coined the term 'scientific management' (Taylor, 1911, Reading Guide 17), pushed the notion that there should be a body of special knowledge and expertise which managers would apply to work organisation. This notion is utterly modernist. It gives a characteristically twentieth-century 'spin' to the eighteenth century Enlightenment principle of bringing about general human 'progress' and control of human affairs through the application of reason and scientific knowledge of them.

The powerful concept – sometimes explicit, sometimes implicit – of highly trained individuals *engineering* the big organisational machines that characterise modern societies has proved to be powerful and seductive. It offers a reassuring rationale to managers themselves and it provides a clear *raison d'être* to people engaged in educating and training managers. Not only this, but the belief in the possibility of a body of objective knowledge and politically neutral managerial expertise provides further comfort and reassurance by avoiding recognition that managing and *controlling*, in any field of human activity, is bound to meet resistance and is bound to involve managers in conflicts and power relations. The implicit modernist faith that all of this is being done for the sake of general human 'progress' helps avoid tricky questions of right and wrong or who might win and who might lose with regard to any particular organisational innovation or managerial initiative. Anything that is done in the name of reason, it is assumed, is bound to be 'for the best'. And a further tendency to 'neutralise' or de-politicise organisational and managerial work is encouraged by the wisely used concept of *organisational goal*. We need to look closely and critically at this notion.

Systems-control thinking and the problem of organisational goals

The concept of *organisational goal* lies at the heart of systems-control thinking. But closer examination of the idea tends to suggest that it is more its Achilles heel – its point of greatest weakness or vulnerability – than its beating heart. First, however, let us consider the central way in which it is typically used and reflect on just why it has become such an attractive notion to managers, teachers of management and, especially, organisational behaviour writers. Let's look, first, at how textbooks typically define organisations and make central use of the idea of goals.

TABLE 2.2 Ten textbook definitions of organisations
Organisations, according to ten different textbooks, are:

- systems of roles oriented towards securing a goal
- collections of people and structures controlled and coordinated to meet shared goals
- consciously created arrangements to achieve goals by collective means
- structures and behaviours devised to achieve agreed goals
- groups of people and resources being brought together and coordinated around the pursuit of specific goals
- social arrangements for the controlled performance in pursuit of collective goals
- goal-centred systems of coordinated human and technological activity
- planned and coordinated behaviours established to meet a set of common goals
- structured activities focused on the meeting of organisational goals
- sets of activities coordinated to achieve system goals

The list of definitions of organisations shown in Table 2.2 were quickly jotted down from a selection of management and organisational behaviour textbooks taken from the shelves of a business school library. The sample of books does not represent a formal statistical sample but what is striking about doing such an exercise is the immense popularity of this type of definition. It would appear that author after author relies on a notion of *goal* to give an overall coherence to the elements of organising that they choose to focus upon ('arrangements', 'systems', 'activities', behaviours', 'structures', 'groups' and so on). And, although the term '*organisational* goal' or '*system* goal' is only explicitly used in a minority of definitions, some notion 'organisational goals' seems to be implicit in all of these conceptions of the work organisation. Such goals are treated as qualities of the entity that is the organisation rather than as intentions of persons. A strong notion of 'system-ness' is thus implicit in all of these definitions. Clearly harking back to the biological origins of system thinking, the system is given 'a life of its own'. Further, it is effectively given a mind of its own – since goals, intentions or objectives are qualities of minds.

Another clear feature of these academic definitions – alongside the notion of an organisation itself having a goal – is that the goals seem to precede managerial action or initiative. Organising occurs in order to meet or achieve goals. Goals and objectives do not appear to be the decisions or intentions of managers – or any other human beings for that matter. They are taken-for-granted and pre-given, like the goalposts are in a football match. The players, referees, coaches or team managers involved in a football match have no freedom to choose what number, nature or shape of goals they are going to compete to score. So it would appear to be in the orthodox conception of organising and managing, at least as it is evidenced in textbook writing. It could be argued, though, that this type of thinking leaves real managers untouched. They may, sometimes, read this kind of thing when taking management courses. But does it go 'over their heads'? Or do they find it meaningful? These are not easy questions to answer but it is possible to get some indication of the ways in which management students tend to 'frame' management – by asking some simple questions. One way of doing this is through 'The Inquisitive Martian' game (Figure 2.4).

FIGURE 2.4   The Inquisitive Martian

Activity 2.3

Find a group of management students, organisation behaviour students, or perhaps managers who are not actually studying these subjects and ask them to play The Inquisitive Martian game. This entails pretending that the room has been entered by an armed Martian researcher. She points her ray gun at the group and demands that each person write down on a piece of paper the answer to her question, 'What is this "management" that you study/do here?'. Anyone failing to obey within ninety seconds will immediately be exterminated. Anyone writing what she takes to be a frivolous answer will be taken back to Mars to be experimented upon!

Gather in the pieces of paper and analyse the answers which have been given to the Martian and see if you can identify any common themes.

Table 2.3 has been compiled from the results of several 'inquisitive Martian' experiments. It presents a dozen answers picked out at random from a vigorously shuffled pile of a hundred or so responses taken from two postgraduate management classes and a class of undergraduate business students.

TABLE 2.3 A dozen management students' answers to the question, 'What is this "management" that you do?'

Various management students say that 'this "management" that they do or study' is:

- the controlling of human and financial resources towards achieving specific organisational aims and goals
- the bringing about of human cooperation to achieve stated objectives and goals
- the organisation and control processes involved in getting a group of individuals to achieve a given objective
- the organising of resources to obtain an agreed objective
- the organisation, control and utilisation of resources within a given operating environment
- clarifying the objectives of an organisation and planning how to meet these objectives
- the organisation and control of resources, human and financial, to obtain a specific objective or goal
- getting things done by and through the efforts of others to meet organisational objectives
- achieving results and objectives through the coordinated efforts of subordinates and others
- the control of groups of people to help those groups achieve common goals
- the organisation, controlling, monitoring and directing of resources to pre-determined goals
- marshalling and controlling resources to meet the objectives of an organisation

---

The theme of control is coming more to the surface here than it was in the organisational definitions. But there is a great deal in these hastily composed definitions of management that is reminiscent of the presumably carefully considered textbook definitions of organisations. The word 'objectives' or 'aims' is often used in place of, or alongside 'goals'. But some notion of 'goal' or 'purposiveness' seems to be the theme running through all the answers offered to the alien inquisitor. And this purposiveness is attached to the organisational entity itself rather than to any of the human beings associated with it. Why should such a conception of organisations themselves and of the managerial activities associated with them have become so dominant? Two main reasons can be suggested.

- Compared to other aspects of the broadly 'organised' nature of social life (in tribes, clans, classes, communities, nation states and so on), work organisations have been deliberately set up, to carry out relatively specific tasks. It has been convenient to represent this 'purposiveness' with the concept of 'organisational goals'.

● Attaching purpose or 'goals' to the organisation itself avoids awkward questions about the human interests and values which pervade all organisational activities. By suggesting that organisations themselves have goals and that management exists to achieve those politically-neutral 'organisational goals', we duck all questions about 'whose goals' the organisation exists to fulfil and we avoid any debate about conflicts over goals and purposes. Issues of human conflict, argument and debate are effectively pushed out of the picture. They stay outside of the frame of the systems-control perspective.

The incredibly popular and pervasive notion of 'organisational goal', then, can be seen as having two major attractions. The first is the attraction of convenience: giving some focus, direction or coherence to what might otherwise look incredibly messy and hopelessly complex. And the second is the attraction of keeping work organisation and management looking politically neutral. In the spirit of the critical study of organising and managing that was explained and justified earlier (pp. 21–6), it is vital to question both of these apparent virtues of the organisational goal idea, a notion which is at the core of systems-control thinking.

The first critical point to be made is with regard to the apparent convenience of giving focus or direction to the idea of an organisation by giving it 'goals'. It is simply unnecessary. Such a purpose could readily be achieved by the much simpler expedient of using the notion of 'tasks'. We could say that modern work organisations differ from other aspects of general social organisation by virtue of the fact that they are deliberately and formally designed to carry certain explicit tasks – make cars, treat patients, educate children, sell groceries and so on. This is quite different from saying that these are the 'purposes' or 'goals' of the organisation. Why? It is different because the notion of purpose and goal is much more complex and much more ambiguous than that of 'task'. There is immense ambiguity about the goals associated with the establishment of any enterprise. The setting up of a company to carry out the task of making cars, for example, may have involved a goal of enabling certain people to become rich, a goal of allowing engineers to exercise technical prowess or a goal of providing employment for local people. Such goals might be compatible. But, equally, they might not. For example, some of the founders of a particular school, established to undertake the task of educating the children of a town, might have been inspired by the goal of liberating the minds of those children. But others might, instead, have cherished goals of religious indoctrination of the children. At the same time, the goal of other founders might have been to produce compliant future employees for the local factories and that of yet others could have been to enable children to gain social advancement and leave the area.

The line of critical argument that is emerging here can also be applied to the other apparent attraction of the idea of organisational goals, that of its giving a seeming political neutrality both to the organisation itself as a social and economic arrangement and to the activities of the managers who try to control organisational activities. This justification of the idea of 'organisational goals' is open to criticism on the same grounds as the earlier justification (which says it gives focus or direction to the idea of organisation). The main reason we have to reject the notion of organisational goals is that it is only human beings that can have goals. Goals and purposes emerge out of the thoughts and wants of living beings – out of their minds, we might say. Organisations are not living beings and they do not have minds. To treat them as if they did (which we inevitably do if we talk of organisational goals) is to court the dangers of *reification* or *personification*: treating a relatively abstract notion like 'society' or 'organisation' as if it were a thing or a person itself.

It does not really matter in ordinary everyday life if we reify or personify some abstract entity for the convenience of mundane communication, saying for example, 'society makes people act in this way' or 'the organisation won't let me do this'. But if we are engaging in serious analysis of social or working behaviour, we are in danger of drastically over simplifying what are really complex matters. Even worse, we are leaving out of our analysis all the *human* actions, choices, interpretations, conflicts and value choices that must be taken into account if we seriously want to understand what is going on. To treat either 'society' or 'the organisation' as something that can itself take initiatives, make choices or impose its 'will' on human beings is to leave out of the analysis the fact that the social and organisational world is made – and is constantly being 'remade' – by human actions. And these are not politically neutral human actions: power, persuasion, resistance, knowledge, ignorance and ambiguity play a major part in every aspect of societal and organisational activity. They must not be left out of the frame when we try to construct an analytical picture of what is going on.

To argue that it is analytically unwise and politically naïve to think in terms of organisations having goals, and to argue that goals are features of human minds rather than of organisational systems, is not to insist that they only exist at the level of the human individual. It is perhaps reasonable sometimes to think in terms of social goals. If the members of a group willingly agree jointly to pursue certain outcomes of group activity, it would not be unreasonable to speak of a group goal or objective. It might even be possible to speak of an organisational goal or objective, in spite of everything we have said so far, *if, and only if, every member of a given organisation willingly agreed to work towards certain outcomes of organisational activity*. It might in fact be argued that it is part of the very task of those 'managing' organisations to try to bring about such a degree of corporate will. And, indeed, very skilled leaders throughout history can be seen, from time to time, to have persuaded people to commit themselves to shared goals. But such examples illustrate the very reason for not *starting off* any analysis with the concept of organisational goal – presuming its existence as part of the very existence of an organisation. Even if skilled managerial groups from time to time succeed in achieving unified commitment of all employees to certain objectives, those 'shared objectives' are the outcomes of human processes of persuasion, negotiation, manipulation or whatever. They are not characteristics of the organisation that can be included in the very definition of what an organisation is. To define organisations, as do some of the textbooks drawn on in Table 2.2, as if, by their very nature, they involved 'shared goals' (definition two), 'agreed goals' (definition four), 'collective goals' (definition six) or 'common goals' (definition eight) implies either blissful ignorance about the 'realities' of work organisations or a blind optimism about what can be managerially achieved.

It is naïve and foolish, then, to think of work organisations having, as part of their very nature, the sort of unity of purpose which is implicit in the notion of organisational goals and objectives. Managers will always talk in terms of corporate purposes, departmental objectives, organisational objectives and the rest. They do this as part of the process of persuading people to act in concert – to meet goals and objectives which might be better understood as the goals and objectives of whoever is in charge of the organisation, rather than objectives inherent in the organisation's very existence. The language of 'organisational goals', we might say, is the language of managerial persuasion. Such talk should be the *object* of our study of organisational and managerial processes, not part of the conceptual tool kit or 'framing' we apply to such processes. We need an alternative way of looking at the organising and managing of work. To help us do this, however, we need to reconsider the modernist assumptions which have produced the style of thinking that we want to move beyond.

From mainstream modernism to pragmatic modernism

The systems-control orthodoxy needed close critical attention precisely because it is an orthodoxy and, in the spirit of critical academic study, the value of any widely accepted body of ideas should not be taken for granted. To engage critically with an orthodoxy in this way is to accept and follow the important modernist or Enlightenment principle of subjecting any accepted tradition to rational scrutiny. Ironically perhaps, this involves turning certain modernist ideas back on modernism itself. This is indeed the case. A major critique of modernist social thinking developed in the latter part of the twentieth century, with some theorists adopting a *postmodernist* way of looking at the world. This rejects attempts to build systematic (or 'foundationalist') explanations of history and society and which, instead, concentrates on the ways in which human beings 'invent' their worlds, especially through the use of language or 'discourse' (see Reading Guide 1). The position to be adopted here – in the pragmatist spirit of seeking ideas, frameworks and theories that can usefully inform our practices in the world – takes up some key points from the postmodernist critique of modernism. But this is not done to reject modernism. Instead, it is done in the spirit of encouraging the development of a more 'modest' or *realistic* modernism. It is felt that the modernism which is inherent in the systems-control approach to understanding work organisations and their management is naïve and unrealistic. It has led, in particular, to a naïve and unrealistic belief in the possibilities of highly trained managers applying a body of organisational or managerial knowledge to the designing, engineering and 'driving' of work organisations as if they were big social machines incorporating uncontested goals or organisational objectives.

To enable us to move towards a more realistic or pragmatically reasonable way of 'framing' work organisation and its management, a shift has first to be made in our deeper assumptions about the social world. These are the modernist assumptions which inevitably underpin the whole edifice of work organisation and management thinking. Table 2.4 distinguishes between assumptions of *mainstream modernism* and those of a more modest *pragmatic* modernism.

TABLE 2.4 Mainstream and pragmatic modernism	
Mainstream modernism	**Pragmatic modernism**
Using science and other forms of rational analysis a body of knowledge about the social world (including scientific laws where possible) can be developed which will enable human beings to take control of their circumstances and make general progress in the quality of life and of human fulfilment	Rational analysis can yield important insights into and understandings of how social life works. This can enable improvements to be made in some aspects of the human condition. But because of the inherent complexity and ambiguity of the social world, the emotional dimension of human beings and their tendency to disagree and compete for scarce resources, there is no possibility of humans acting in concert, as a species, to improve the overall human lot
Human progress is visible everywhere as science, technology and large-scale organisations have made possible enormous improvements in human wealth, comfort, health, leisure, democratic choice and fulfilment. Parts of the world which have not achieved these, will do so as they undergo economic development and their citizens demand that they adopt the democratic practices of the developed western world	While much has been achieved in all of these respects in parts of the world, the same devices of science, technology and large-scale organisation have brought about wars on a scale never seen before and seen the systematic slaughter and domination of people to an extent previously unimagined. Improvements in the lives of people across the world have to be worked towards but no faith can be put in the inevitability of general human progress. It is even possible that the human species may destroy the very planet it lives on
Descartes' conception of rationality suggested that humans as *thinking beings* can stand back from the world around them – their own bodies included – to study it objectively. Such a principle not only made possible the Enlightenment and the 'modernist project' but also encourages us today to look at the social world as an objective reality outside and beyond us. In this way we can study, gather data on, measure and make predictions about human psychology, economic behaviour, social structures or systems of work organisation. This objective knowledge can be applied to human circumstances to bring them more under human control	While it is helpful to try to 'stand back' from time to time from the social world we live in to help us critically reflect on it, this can only be done to a limited extent. We can only partially separate ourselves from the social world we live in. We cannot gather 'objective' data about the social world. Although we can make measurements of certain things and offer limited predictions about the social world, we are ourselves part of what we are studying and must inevitably make sense of it from a particular perspective. We cannot 'know' the world other than through the concepts and languages we apply to it. The knowledge so gained can inform practices but those are shaped as much by human values and interest-based choices as they are by 'knowledge'

This pragmatic modernist approach encourages us to analyse the social and organisational world in a broadly scientific way. But it diverges from the mainstream modernist belief by denying the possibility of studying social phenomena in the same way that we scientifically study the physical world (a belief associated with what is often called *positivism*). Generalisations and theories about 'how things work' in the social sphere are still sought on the basis of rational and critical analysis of systematically gathered 'evidence'. However, these generalisations can never achieve the finality or completeness of what we normally take to be scientific laws. There is no possibility of reaching a complete truth or full understanding of the social world that is free from the limitations of the particular 'framework' we are using or that can ever enable us confidently to predict what people will do in particular circumstances.

A belief in a 'foundationalist' knowledge of this type has been a key tenet of mainstream modernist thinking. It is what some management academics hope for in the 'body of management knowledge' they want to create. But the possibility of any kind of coherent, complete and foundational knowledge resource has increasingly been brought into question. Growing recognition is given to the initiative-taking and choice-making nature of humans and their tendency to defy any 'laws' that might be constructed about their behaviour – in work organisations or elsewhere. To recognise this is not, however, to deny the possibility of developing social scientific knowledge about work organisations which is insightful and which we can *take into account* when we are dealing with them. As was established in Chapter 1, we cannot judge any of this as either categorically 'true' or 'untrue', as mainstream modernist 'foundationalism' would encourage us to do. The pragmatist principle of judging knowledge in terms of how effectively it informs our practices once again comes into play. And we need it to guard against some quite disturbing tendencies within mainstream modernism, ones with considerable implications for the role which management and managers play in modern societies. These are the dangers of *managerialism* and *managism*.

Managerialism and managism: twin pathologies of mainstream modernism and systems-control thinking

Although principles of democracy have played a central role in the way modern societies have developed, mainstream modernist ideas contain within them dangerous anti-democratic inclinations. And the systems-control conception of management and organisations plays a part in this. A belief in the possibility of a specially trained cadre of managers being able to apply their expert management knowledge to the design of rational work, governmental and administrative organisational systems which will further human progress, questions the need for what it would see as the amateurishness, emotionality and riskiness of democratic activity. This *managerialism* has been an ever-present threat to democracy throughout the twentieth century, and has had close connections to some of the totalitarian regimes which that century experienced. This was recognised in Burnham's classic account *The Managerial Revolution* (1945, Reading Guide 2). Why, the managerialist asks, allow all the debate, time wasting and inefficiencies of voting on how modern society should be run when we have experts with scientific knowledge about how affairs can be run – on purely rational grounds and for the benefit of everyone?

Managerialism, as a wicked child of mainstream modernism and of systems-control thinking, so to speak, is a threat to democracy and social debate. It is a danger to which critical management students must always be sensitive when looking at the part 'management' plays in the contemporary world. Managerialism amounts to 'rule by managers' and its relevance is mainly at the level of society and the political system.

Managerialism	Concept
A belief that modern societies, and the institutions within them, should be run by qualified managers who can organise society rationally on the basis of their expert knowledge – thus replacing the divisiveness and inefficiency of debate and democracy.	

Managerialism has a twin, whose relevance applies much more to everyday managerial practices. This we can call *managism*. It is an operating faith that managers themselves sometimes adopt when struggling with the pressures of managing in a complex and fast-changing world. In effect, it is an application of the orthodox systems-control thinking, organising and managing to everyday practice.

Managism	Concept
A belief that there is a distinctive managerial expertise based on a body of objective management knowledge which managers should apply to enable them rationally to design, maintain and drive organisational systems in the same way that expert engineers design, maintain and drive machines	

Both 'managerialism' and 'managism' follow the principle of *technocracy* – the principle of putting experts in charge of human affairs, whether it is at the societal or the organisational level. They can both be seen as 'operating faiths' – because, like religious faiths, they take a set of beliefs about how the world is and, on the basis of this, advocate what people *should* do. But faiths also have a psychological role in the lives of those who adopt them. They give comfort to people and reassure them in the face of the doubts, confusions, ambiguities and threats that they meet in their daily lives. And ambiguities, threats and confusions, we might say, are an everyday feature of the work organisations in which managers 'have to manage'. Their authority is regularly open to challenge, they are frequently faced with getting people to do things they do not wish to do and they frequently have to act on the basis of partial knowledge or inadequate understanding. It is therefore comforting to adopt a faith that teaches that managers actually can 'engineer' work organisations. Commitment to that faith is demonstrated every day in the mechanistic language so popular with many managers. This is the managist talk of 'putting in place' new structures or systems, 'delivering' strategies and 'driving through' changes. Such language is increasingly heard in the world of the modern corporate manager, and it is something we will return to in Chapter 5 (pp. 160–5) when we look at issues of managerial identity and angst.

Managerialism and managism both elevate the activity of management to a special status in human affairs. They give it a role in handling human problems which is utterly unrealistic as well as morally questionable. They do this in the same way that 'scientism' elevates science to an unrealistic and morally dubious role in human affairs. Rational calculation, scientific procedure and, indeed, management knowledge all have a place to play in how we manage our affairs and organise our work activities. But they can only ever play a partial role. And they must not be allowed to reduce everything to their own terms. The systems-control orthodoxy tends to do this. It *frames* work organisation as if it were a 'thing' that is amenable to rational control. It reduces the complex processes and relationships of organisations to systems or social machines with built-in (and therefore uncontestable) organisational goals. If we are going to understand organisational and managerial processes in a way that can more realistically inform our practices, then we have to frame these activities differently, and less simplistically. We need to frame them in a way that does not marginalise all the social, cultural, political and economic processes which go on within and between organisations. This means putting the notion of ongoing human relationships at the centre of the picture. In the spirit, then, of the *pragmatic modernism* which tries avoid the arrogance and pretentiousness of mainstream modernism, we turn to the *process-relational perspective* on the organising and managing of work.

Summary

In this chapter the following key points have been made:

- We can follow up the ways in which, in Chapter 1, three particular managers 'framed' managerial work by considering the more general (academic and 'applied') ways of talking about and understanding organisations and management that have developed historically.

- Orthodox or mainstream ideas about organising and managing can be understood as emerging from the *modernist* ways of thinking about human beings and the possibilities of their controlling their social, political and economic worlds. Such ideas came to the fore during the eighteenth century *Enlightenment*. These same developments were associated with the growth of industrialised economies, bureaucratic organisations and a highly rationalised or scientific way of thinking about the world and solving its problems.

- The modernist conception of managerial work sees managers as technical experts who design and run work organisations as if they were big social and technical machines.

- Systems thinking plays a major part in such orthodox or modernist ideas about work organisations and their management. Although this is sometimes a biologically based way of thinking, its more dominant version has been more mechanical: portraying the organisation as a big open-system machine. This perspective has become dominant, in part, because it gives a role to managers in organisations – a role as the 'organisational engineers' who design and drive the organisational machine.

- Systems thinking can be helpful to understanding organisations, up to a point. It can helpfully draw our attention to the role of organisations in processing inputs into outputs, and it draws our attention to the ways in which different parts of organisations, as 'sub-systems', relate (or fail to relate) to each other.

- The major weakness of systems thinking, however, is that it does not help much with understanding *how* these input–output conversion processes come about and how human goals, values and conflicts of interest play a part in 'what actually happens' inside and around organisations. The organisation is thus dehumanised and is a 'black box' whose internal life is left unexamined.

- The key weakness in systems thinking, as it is typically applied to organisations, lies in its dependence on the concept of *organisational goal*. The centrality of this notion to the academic study of organisations can be seen in the tendency for practically every textbook in organisational behaviour to define organisations as entities focused on meeting organisational goals. The idea is also central to the way management students define organisations, when they are asked to do so in the business school classroom.

- The notion of organisational goal gives some kind of purposiveness or intent to the organisation itself, as opposed to attaching purposes and intentions to the human beings who are associated with the organisation. The organisation is thus *reified* or *personified*. It is treated as if it were some kind of 'being' in its own right which has needs and intentions. This is not only nonsensical in a very fundamental way, it also diverts attention from all the human interests, goals and values which have to be understood if we are going to make any sense whatsoever of what actually happens in organisations.

- The concept of organisational goal is not only nonsensical and diversionary, it is also unnecessary. It can be replaced with the notion of organisational tasks.

- To move beyond these orthodox approaches to understanding organisations and their management we need to rethink some of the modernist assumptions on which they are based. Instead of wholly rejecting such assumptions, as postmodernist thinkers tend to do, we can move towards a more modest or 'realistic' kind of modernism: a *pragmatic modernism*. This continues with the modernist aspiration of seeking rationally and scientifically to understand the world to enable human beings better to cope within it. But it abandons mainstream modernism's unreasonable faith in the ability of human beings to achieve high levels of systematic control over their destiny. It comes to terms with the messy, muddled, ambiguous and contested world in which organising and managing occurs.

- Before an alternative perspective is developed (the purpose of the next chapter), it is necessary to be aware of two pathological creations of mainstream modernism and *systems-control* thinking. The first of these is *managerialism*, a technocratic belief that the best people to run societies are the trained and expert managerial elites. The second is *managism*. This is a much more common but no less insidious belief that managers can successfully operate as expert organisational engineers, applying a politically neutral technical expertise to solving all the problems that arise from the creation and distributing of goods and services by designing and engineering rational work systems.

Reading

Reading Guides 1 and 2, especially, contain material that supports and takes further much of what is covered in Chapter 2.

Organising and managing: a *process-relational* perspective

<table>
</table>

Objectives Having read this chapter and completed its associated activities, readers should be able to:

- Understand the *process-relational* way of looking at organising and managing which provides an alternative to the influential but inadequate *systems-control* orthodoxy which was critically analysed in Chapter 2.

- Recognise that we tend to use the word 'management' in three different ways and that we can exploit these different everyday usages to identify what can helpfully be seen as three different dimensions of the overall phenomenon of management.

- Appreciate the basic argument (to be developed in Chapter 6) that management is best understood as an essentially *strategic* matter – something concerned with the directing of work organisations as a whole.

- Distinguish between the *task* elements and the *social-status* aspects of managerial work and see how these influence each other.

- See how the *official structures and procedures* of organisations always operate in conjunction with the 'informal' or *unofficial* aspects of organisational life to produce what can helpfully be understood as an organisational *negotiated order*.

- Come to terms with the considerable degree of ambiguity and uncertainty which characterises organisational life and managerial action, appreciating how this limits what is managerially achievable and influences the way managers actually behave, as opposed to how the orthodox textbooks suggest they should behave.

- Make sense of what 'managers actually do' by seeing how the *process-relational* frame of reference helps us interpret research studies on what 'actually happens' in managerial work.

Going beyond the orthodoxy

There are considerable problems, as Chapter 2 has shown, with the orthodox ways in which work organisation and its management tend to be 'framed' in both academic and practical spheres. The systems-control frame of reference draws useful attention to some important facets of organisational activity. It requires us constantly to be aware that the organisation has to convert 'inputs' and 'outputs' in a linked way in order to continue in existence. It also draws attention to the ways in which the components of the organisation have to relate both to each other and to the organisation as a whole. The very idea of 'the organisation' is made easy to handle by imagining that it has an objective existence as a machine-like system. And by treating the organisation as a 'thing' in this way, managers are given the confidence to believe that they can *control* it. However, the role of the systems metaphor and the possibilities of controlling this objectively existing 'thing' can get out of hand, especially when the 'system' is treated as if it had a mind of its own and is understood to possess goals or objectives. To 'frame' organisations as if they were things or creatures with goals and objectives too easily leads to a forgetting of all the conflicts, arguments, debates, ambiguities and sheer guesswork that characterise the *processes* and *relationships* that what we might call 'real' managerial practice has to cope with all of the time.

The essential difference between the *systems-control* perspective and the *process-relational* way of understanding organisations is that the former gives central attention to a single, or perhaps to several, 'organisational goals' while the latter recognises that organisations, in practice, involve a *great multiplicity of goals*. And because these are the goals of human individuals and groups associated in some way with the organisation (as opposed to the goals of a fictional 'system'), they inevitably come into tension with each other and frequently clash. Systems-control thinking tends to ignore such matters because it focuses on inputs and outputs. Systems are thus often said to be 'black boxes'. What actually happens inside them, and how, is not attended to. Process-relational thinking, however, looks inside the black box. Its concern is more with *how things happen in practice* when people come together in work organisations.

 Link   The notion of the organisational 'system' as a black box is returned to in Chapter 8, p. 257, when we look at how organisational 'contingencies' are often treated in a 'black box' way.

Organisations and organising: a process-relational perspective

Because process-relational thinking is concerned with how things happen in practice, it attends to the range of social, technical, political, cultural and economic processes that make up the overall process of 'organising and managing'. And it looks at the patterns of constantly changing relationships that the organising of work entails – ones that both help and hinder the fulfilment of work tasks. The perspective is one that 'includes within the picture' the great variety of human processes and relationships that go on in every work organisation. But if it is going to be a useful frame of reference – one that can helpfully inform our practices – it must still take into account that 'purposive' quality of organisational activity that systems-control thinking somehow mystified into the notion of 'organisational goal'. The organisation must have some rationale or purposive logic. We saw earlier that the notion of 'task' can readily help us with this. The concept of 'task' is therefore at the heart of the process-relational definition of work organisations.

Work organisations	Concept
Work arrangements involving relationships, understandings and processes in which people are employed, or their services otherwise engaged, to complete tasks undertaken in the organisation's name.	

This concept of the work organisation takes us away from the systems-control tendency to treat the organisation as if it were a fixed or given entity or 'thing' with its own set of properties and priorities (including 'goals'). The orthodoxy gives to the organisation a quality of 'entitativeness', to borrow a term from Hosking and Morley (1991, Reading Guide 3), one that we will meet again when we consider some issues at the psychological level in the next chapter. The processual way of thinking looks at the organisation more in terms of relationships – hence we use the term 'relational', again taken from Hosking and Morley (and developed in Hosking, Dachler and Gergen, 1995, Reading Guide 3). But these relationships are not themselves to be taken as fixed things. A key feature of human relationships is that they are always 'in process', always changing. This is why processual analysts often follow the influential work of Weick (1979, Reading Guide 3) in replacing the word 'organisation' with the more processual or dynamic term 'organising'.

To talk of *organising* instead of 'organisation' helps remind us that, when making complex work arrangements, we never actually 'arrive'. We are always on the move. Organisation and management are never fully accomplished. Organising and re-organising goes on and on. And the focus of this is the struggle to achieve a level of *productive cooperation* that enables tasks to be completed, using various *technologies*. These are not simply pieces of 'hardware' like machines.

Every organisation will use a variety of technologies in different parts of its operation but every technology that is used – a particular production technology in a factory or a particular service technology in a shop, bank or classroom, say – requires a particular pattern or process of cooperative human activity.

Technologies	Concept
Technologies are the applications to task fulfilment of combinations of machines and other material artefacts with associated techniques of knowledge.	

The orthodox definitions of organisations that we looked at in Chapter 2 implied that cooperation was a 'built-in' or a taken-for-granted feature of the organisation (hence talk of common, agreed or shared goals in some of the definitions). But the process-relational perspective sees productive cooperation as something which has constantly to be fought for or achieved, through processes of negotiation, bargaining, persuasion and so on. This has to be the case because, in contrast to the systems-control view of goals and objectives as properties of organisations or systems, it is recognised that the people who get involved in it bring a whole variety of goals and objectives into the organisation. There will thus inevitably be endless differences, rivalries and conflicts over who does what and who gets what, with coalitions of interest constantly forming and re-forming.

Productive cooperation	Concept
The working together of people employed within, or otherwise involved in the organisation, to achieve the tasks that are undertaken in the organisation's name. This has to be achieved in the face of the tendency for people to pursue ends (often cooperatively) which are not consonant with efficient task fulfilment.	

Processes of persuasion, bargaining, manipulation, coalition formation, competition and the rest do not occur within the closed boundaries of any given organisation, regardless of the broader culture and political economy. The set of relationships and understandings which we identify as 'the organisation' is part of the scheme of relationships and understandings which make up the wider society, culture, class structure and economy of which, in effect, the organisation is part. And modern industrial capitalist societies share a key, and partly defining, institution: that of *employment*. Work organisations are *employing organisations*. They do not, like other systems of managing work that we have seen in history, depend on the ownership of workers as slaves, or the long-term binding of labour to ownership which characterised feudalism.

Employment	Concept
A characteristic institution of both modern industrial capitalist societies and modern work organisations which involves an *exchange* or trade between the employer and the employee whereby certain effort and commitment is offered by the employee to the employer in return for certain monetary and other rewards.	

In modern societies, then, people approach the work organisation to offer certain services in return for certain 'rewards'. There is a basic process of exchange, in the *employment relationship*, which is a defining feature of the modern work organisation. It is not an aspect of the organisation and management of work that we can delegate to a separate area of study such as 'human resource management' or 'industrial relations'.

Link

The employment relationship as one of the key exchanges which occurs in the organisation of work is especially in our later consideration of:

➡ implicit contracts, employee 'motivation' and work orientations in Chapter 9;

➡ human resource management in Chapter 11.

In what sense do organisations actually exist?

The biggest challenge that we face when trying to analyse organisations (and, indeed, to manage them) is that in the simple sense of the term *they do not actually exist*. They certainly do not exist in the same sense that the book you are currently looking at exists. You can see the book, touch it, smell it and, if you like, throw it up in the air. But the organisation in which you work or study is not something you can see, hear, touch, smell, kick, kiss or throw up in the air. And this is not just because you might be a relatively junior member of that organisation. The top managers of the organisation are no more capable than you are of relating to the organisation as if it existed in a straightforward way. This, in fact, is one of the most fascinating aspects of managerial work – and its essential ambiguity. Managers are there to manage, control or 'shape' something which one cannot 'put one's finger on', literally or even – much of the time – figuratively. This, of course, is partly why the 'reification' or 'personification' of organisations as machine-like entities or person-like beings with goals, which characterises systems-control thinking (Chapter 2, pp. 43–4), has proved so attractive.

In spite of the difficulties that arise with regard to what philosophers would call the *ontological status* of organisations (the sense in which it can be said to 'exist'), we have to find a way of relating to them. Organisations, we might say, have a *virtual reality*. To say this, however, is not to deny that this is a reality which can have a big impact on our lives: a 'reality' which can employ us, sack us, tax us, entertain us, feed us, teach us, kill us even. Not only this, but people employed as managers are paid to control the 'quasi-entities' which are work organisations. Systems-control thinkers aspire to achieving such control through 'setting up the right system' as if it were a 'thing' that can be designed and its basic shape realistically pictured on an organisation or a flow chart. Process-relational thinking does not turn its back on the notion of control, however. It recognises the aspiration of those 'in charge' of work organisations to achieve control over work behaviours. But it also recognises two other things:

● only partial control can ever be achieved. This is because organisations only exist through human relationships, and human relationships never allow the total control of some people over others (see our earlier discussion of the problem of aspiring to 'managing people', pp. 5–6). Power is rarely uncontested and, to a greater or lesser extent, attempts at control are typically resisted.

● Whatever control is achieved over work behaviour is brought about as much through processes of negotiation, persuasion, manipulation and so on, as through system 'devices' like rules and official procedures.

61

To speak of human relationships, then, is not to imply the necessary superiority of the warm-sounding and liberal exchanges typically associated with the term 'human relations'. No, human relationships can be manipulative, arm-twisting and intimidatory as well as involving deep mutual commitment or caring persuasion. While denying that organisations 'are' systems, process-relational thinking is able to recognise that some aspects of organisational control are experienced as 'system-like'. It can feel, in some organisational situations, as if the organisational 'system' is actually pushing us around. We can feel totally hemmed in by tight rules and strictly administered operating procedures. But these seemingly overpowering 'systems' are not the mechanical, dehumanised control systems that they seem to be. They are the achievement of certain human actors institutionalising their power over others. They are facets of *power relationships*, in other words. It might feel to the relatively powerless in the organisation *as if* they are being dominated 'by the system'. This, of course, is precisely what those attempting to control or dominate are trying to do. They want to say, in effect, 'It's not me who is making you do this – it's the system'. The process-relational way of framing organisational and managerial activities insists that we always recognise this aspect of organisational life. Political processes are central to managerial work as are meaning-making processes.

The way we defined work organisations earlier, incorporated this important aspect of organising: the making of meanings. It was what was being referred to when organisations were said to involve *understandings* as well as work arrangements and relationships. Another way of putting this is to say that organisations are *social constructions*. To use this term, however, is to risk the misunderstanding that often arises when sociologists and psychologists discuss the ways in which 'reality' can be said to be 'socially constructed'. The idea of social construction is used in a variety of ways within the social sciences. But the way it is understood and applied here is not as a specialised branch of sociology or social psychology. Instead, it is seen as the primary way in which social and organisational analysis is turning away from the principle that Descartes laid down and which has been the basis of so much orthodox social science. This is the belief, introduced in Table 2.4 in the previous chapter, that one can separate one's 'thinking self' from the objectively existing world – a world to which we can apply our rational minds.

The significance of Descartes' famous statement, 'I think therefore I am' lies in its definition of the human being ('you' or 'me') in terms of the thinking mind, as something which can be separated both from the body itself and from one's relationships with the world beyond that mind. Social constructionist thinking rejects this so-called *Cartesian dualism*. Cartesian thinking makes the fundamental error of ignoring the fact that we cannot know, think about or analyse the world without using concepts, language and 'frames of reference', and that these come from the social world that we are part of. When we relate to any part of that social world – trying to understand how a particular work organisation is managed for example – we can only do so by using concepts and terms which are part of that world. But we don't just passively *interpret* the organisational activities that we observe using some objective or neutral language or analytical scheme. Rather, we actively make sense of or *enact* that

Link   We will meet Cartesian dualism again in Chapter 4, p. 96, and in Chapter 5, p. 149.

reality, as Weick (1995, Reading Guide 3) so helpfully puts it. We do this by applying meanings, terms and concepts to what we observe and experience, taking these from the languages, stocks of knowledge, and ongoing interpretations of others to whom we relate. In this way, human beings 'socially construct' their realities: work together to make sense of their existence.

Because human beings are not part of one big unified social grouping in which everyone's interests coincide, there will always be a variety of social constructions available for making sense of any particular part of human existence. And new ones are always being developed and negotiated. Indeed, *Organising and Managing Work* is itself part of a social construction process. It is one in which the writer – in partial concert with certain other writers – is challenging certain 'orthodox' ways of socially constructing (or *framing*) work organisations and arguing for an alternative way of constructing, framing or making sense.

It is extremely important to avoid one major, and not uncommon, misunderstanding of the notion of social construction. This associates it with the claim, for example, that organisations only exist 'in people's minds'. Social constructionism cannot be labelled, as some writers mistakenly do, as a 'subjectivist' perspective. To engage in this kind of *idealism* (to give such a claim its philosophical name) would be to fall straight back into the grip of Cartesian dualism – by accepting that 'mind' can be differentiated from the world outside it in this way. Social constructionist thinking rejects such dualism. It rejects the separation of the 'subjective' and the 'objective'. This is not to deny that, in some sense, there is a world 'out there', beyond what we know. It is simply to accept that we cannot know it other than through socially produced categories of concept, language and perspective. Our knowing the world cannot be separated from our being in the world.

Organisations, we might say in the light of all this, are brought into existence or enacted through the ways in which those involved with them both think and act. The process-relational definition of organisations given above (p. 59) recognised the action aspects with its highlighting of the tasks which have to be done. Carrying out tasks, of course, involves 'thinking' as well as action. But the construction of the concept still required something more: something to give some focus to the conception that one has of any particular organisation. Systems-control thinking does this through the device of the 'organisational goal'. It would have been a mistake simply to replace the notion of a primary goal with the idea of a primary task. A range of tasks is performed in any given organisation. But what pulls these together, what is it that attaches these tasks to what we socially construct the organisation, as some kind of whole, to be? This is handled here with the notion of *the organisation's name*.

The naming of a work organisation is not the relatively minor matter it might at first appear to be. 'What's in a name?', it might be asked. 'Quite a lot', is the answer, if we use the word 'name' as shorthand for what is, in effect, an organisation's *formal identity*. We cannot easily 'know' an organisation by looking at it or touching it, as we discussed earlier. But anyone establishing an organisation would soon find themselves needing to give their enterprise some kind of 'identity' before any kind of trading or operating could take place. An organisation must have this formal identity to be able to buy or sell anything, rent premises, advertise goods and services and, especially, to employ people to get involved in any of these activities. And for many of these activities that identity needs to be a legal one – the organisation's existence has to be sanctioned by the state before the production of any goods or services whatsoever can occur. But this is only part of the story. The owners, sponsors and managers of work organisations typically face the problem of attracting people to use their services, work for them, trade with them or, otherwise accept what they do as socially legitimate (in the case of an armed force, a police force or a prison, say). This means that creating a 'positive' organisational identity, or an attractive 'corporate image', is an important managerial task. Thus the choice of a particular name – what the management actually call the organisation as well as the sort of 'good name' or image they attempt to build – is part of an engagement in social construction processes. The management of an organisation cannot simply construct this name unilaterally. The name that an organisation comes to have at any point in time will be the outcome of ongoing processes of social construction involving not only the organisation's managerial and public relations employees but numerous others, including clients, customers, journalists and possibly even academic writers.

Organisations can be said to be 'socially constructed', then. To use this terminology is not, however, to say that they do not 'actually exist'. It is to recognise that they do not have a 'being' which can be separated from the ways in which human beings make sense of them or *enact* them. Their reality, as was emphasised earlier, is nevertheless a powerful one that can even make life and death differences to people. But it would be a denial of the politics of human endeavour and a mind-numbing fatalism to say that such power is a quality of organisations themselves as objectively existing 'systems'. Organisations may often feel or look like they are 'systems' running themselves. But they are not: they are created and maintained by human beings. And what is done in their name, and how it is done, is always open to challenge. In practice, challenges of all sorts constantly arise and threaten the long-term continuation of organisational arrangements and understandings. The people who are employed as managers, as part of their working to create and maintain organisational relationships, understandings and processes, have to manage these challenges.

Management and managing: a process-relational perspective

In a general sense, the organisation and management of work are very similar things. Much of what has been referred to so far as 'organising' could be called 'managing'. Everyone in a work setting, however junior their status in the organisation, has to organise their desk, counter or workbench and manage the tasks allocated to them. But while it is always wise to remember that organising and managing work is something that most people do, at home as well as in employment, we are concerned here with activities that occur at a higher level. We are primarily concerned with how work tasks are related to each other and shaped into something that we can recognise as a coherent enterprise, undertaking or *work organisation*. Our focus here is on management in this sense: something that is a component of every modern work organisation. The process-relational view of the organisations sees them as 'sets of work arrangements relationships, understandings and relationships' (see above, p. 59) which involve human cooperation and the use of technologies to achieve certain tasks. But it has been heavily emphasised that these relations and patterns of cooperation do not automatically come about. They need to be shaped or 'managed'. What was called *productive cooperation* has to be worked for and 'won'. And, given that people (customers, clients, suppliers and others as well as employees) bring to the organisation a multiplicity of goals, interests and purposes, this can never be a straightforward matter. Shaping and re-shaping, negotiating and re-negotiating, mediating, persuading, exchanging and trading will continually have to occur if the organisation is going to complete the tasks undertaken in its name and to continue into the future.

There is thus an overall managerial task to be fulfilled, there are managerial activities that have to occur and there may well need to be roles in which certain people specialise in carrying out these activities. It is important to distinguish between these three dimensions of what we often treat as a one-dimensional phenomenon.

Three dimensions of management: management, managing and managers

One way in which we often unconsciously recognise the three elements of 'management' is in our language. We probably assume that we are regularly using the word 'management' to refer to a single aspect of organisational life. But we do not. There are three different usages of the term 'management' in which most of us engage. These relate to what usefully can be seen as three dimensions of 'management'. To begin to come to terms with this let us carefully consider what the consultant, Don Belivat, is saying to his clients.

Activity 3.1

When talking to people in Tradespark Gears in Cases and Conversations 3.1, Don Belivat uses the word 'management' three times. Look closely at what he is saying and consider the possibility that he is using the word rather differently each time he utters it. What different emphasis can you detect in each of his three uses of the word 'management'?

Don Belivat is the owner and main consultant of Belivat Consulting, a firm which works closely with companies to help them 'manage better for better success', as the firm's advertising slogan puts it. Don and his colleagues initially spent a week observing how the managers in Tradespark Gears go about their work. In the light of what they saw, they then set up and led various 'coaching workshops' in which managers were invited to get together and look closely at their own, and each other's, 'management habits and practices'. The purpose of the workshops was said to be to 'discover together' how 'you can manage more smartly for personal and corporate success'.

In the opening words of his talk to Tradespark's managers, at a mid-way 'review seminar', Don said, 'I am very grateful to the management of Tradespark Gears for inviting us to advise you on improving the management of your business. From what I have seen today, walking round the office, it's clear that the management is already being done quite differently from the way it was.'

Don Belivat opens his remarks by expressing thanks to 'the management' of the company. Here he is obviously thanking particular *people* who engaged him to do this work. Thus we have our first sense of the word 'management' – a set of people who hold managerial appointments. This usage is quite a common one and we come across it when we hear people in an organisation say things like, 'There's obviously a problem with the building we are working in. We'd better take this up with management.' We also hear people say, 'Management are on the top floor' or 'This business needs a new management'. But when Belivat goes on to refer to 'improving the management of your business', he is using the word differently. He is not suggesting that the people who make up 'the management' can in some way be 'improved'. What he seems to be referring to, instead, is the overall directing and shaping of the business so that it is successful (what his brochures call 'corporate success'). Here then, 'management' is not *people*, but a *function* of the enterprise that has to be performed. And it is the performing of that function that is being alluded to when Don Belivat, moving to a third meaning of the term, observes that 'management' is 'being done quite differently' from what he had observed earlier in the consultancy. Here, 'management' is action; things that *management as people* do to fulfil *management as function*. The set of concepts which is emerging here, a three-dimensional model of 'management' in effect, is set out in Table 3.1.

TABLE 3.1 Three dimensions of management	*Concept*
Management is the overall shaping of relationships, understandings and processes within a work organisation to bring about the completion of the tasks undertaken in the organisation's name in such a way that the organisation continues into the future	This is management as a **function**, something that must be fulfilled in every organisation. In principle, it could be carried out by just one person (in a small owner-managed enterprise, say), or by all the members of the organisation taking part (in a worker cooperative, say)
Managing is the activity of bringing about this shaping	This is management as **action**: things that are done to give coherence and direction to the range of activities that go on in the organisation
Managers are those people given official responsibility for ensuring that the tasks undertaken in the organisation's name are done in a way which enables the organisation to continue into the future	This is management as a **formal role** or office. It becomes necessary when organisational members are unable simultaneously to carry out basic work tasks and to think about how all the different activities and tasks of the organisation are to be 'brought together' to keep the organisation as a whole continuing into the future

A simple way of summarising the important distinctions made in Table 3.1 is to say that 'management' is *what* is done, 'managing' is *how* it is done and the 'managers' are those *who* do it. Although we will all undoubtedly continue to use the word 'management' in all of these senses, it is important to keep this three-way distinction in mind whenever we are thinking analytically about 'management'.

The relevance to managerial practice of this three-dimensional view of management can be illustrated by looking at the participant observation research circumstances in which the distinction was developed (Watson, 2001, pp. 33–35, Reading Guide 2). In a discussion with Ted Meadows, one of the most powerful managers in the company being studied, the researcher found it necessary to point out that, 'We need to distinguish between problems caused by us having ... the wrong managers, and problems caused by having the "right" managers who are, nevertheless, doing the wrong things'. This was necessary precisely because this individual had not been distinguishing between who the managers were (and how competent they were) and what the managers were doing. And, because he accepted that the overall management of the business (represented by the business performance of the company) was poor, he was contemplating 'getting rid' of these managers. The researcher's analysis was different from that of Meadows: it seemed that the managers in the company, generally speaking, were both capable and committed. However, the tasks that these managers were being given to do by the top management, and the priorities being imposed upon them, were such that their abilities were not being used to good effect. Here, then, were two analyses of a business situation, each of which had quite different practical implications (replacing managers on the one hand and getting managers to work differently on the other).

The simplistic inference that 'bad management' results from having 'bad managers' can be a very dangerous one, in practical terms, given the very real possibility that 'bad management' can arise from the 'misuse' of managerial talents as readily as from the appointment of incompetent individuals to managerial posts. We are once again reminded that conceptual or theoretical matters are very practical ones. And they can make a significant difference to people's lives. This is brought home by a comment made by a manager who lost his job with the company, after the research was published. 'I don't think', he said, 'that Ted ever really shifted from his view that the business problems all resulted from the company having too many of what he called "useless bastards like you"'. 'But', he pointed out, 'the company didn't exactly go from strength to strength as he got rid of more and more of us, did it?' Not surprisingly, this person's analysis of the company's managerial problems differed from that of Ted Meadows. He believed that his own analysis (which accorded in part to the one in the research study) was the correct one – one which would have led to better corporate management decisions. Whether or not the analysis was 'correct', we should note that it could not have been made had a distinction not been made between what Table 3.1 formally identifies as *management*, *managing* and *managers*.

There are two further implications of the three-dimensional model of management:

- management is a strategic matter and the logic of both the job of the manager and of the work of managing is one of contributing to the shaping and the directing of the organisation as a whole. Some managers are more directly involved with strategic matters than others but there is little point in identifying as managers people who do not concern themselves in any way with the overall direction of the organisation;
- while there cannot be organisations without management, it does not follow that organisations must necessarily have managers.

Management is being conceptualised very deliberately as essentially concerned with the *continuation of the organisation into the future*.

 Link   The theme of all managers having a strategic role is a key one in Chapter 6, pp. 173–7.

Taking a strategy-centred view of management accords with the pragmatist principle of choosing concepts that are helpful to human practice in the world. It would be less helpful to recognise as 'managers' people who are simply 'in charge' of a particular activity and who fulfil that function without any reference to how the activity relates to the overall shaping, directing and performance of the organisation. A manager is most usefully seen to be a manager by virtue of how they relate the particular tasks they do to the overall pattern of tasks and priorities of the organisation as a whole.

The second point, that organisations must have management but do not necessarily have to have managers, is a simple but important one. It is not being disputed that in the majority of organisations, other than very small ones, it is often sensible and practical to create posts within the organisation's overall division of labour whose incumbents involve themselves more in 'shaping and directing' work activities than in the direct work of producing goods or services. But we need to recognise that this is an organisational design *choice* and not something that automatically follows from some natural process of the 'growth' of enterprises. The smallest of organisations needs 'management' in the sense that the function of shaping and directing activities must occur. In small organisations, this can be done as a part of the work of one or two individuals. We can envisage, for example, the two owner-managers of a small building company spending some of their time digging trenches, laying bricks and plastering walls and some of their time seeking new contracts, allocating tasks to building workers and deciding what style and type of buildings to construct. In the smallest of building firms, 'management' in the sense of these latter activities would have to occur. If these two people then choose to increase the size of their business, they might at one point both cease to carry out any building work themselves. And, at another point of business growth, they might choose to appoint other individuals to act in a managerial capacity, on their behalf.

It has become normal in industrial capitalist societies for people to be appointed to managerial posts once an organisation reaches a size that makes it difficult for the managerial function to be carried out by people who are also engaged in mainstream work tasks. However, it should be noted that this is the particular way that has generally and historically been adopted in western societies to carry out the managerial function (Marglin, 1980, Reading Guide 2). This occurred in the context of historical changes in which shifting patterns of class, ownership and aspiration meant that individuals were seeking opportunities for new types of supervisory and 'overseeing' work – opportunities which owning interests were happy to provide. However, alternative ways of fulfilling the basic managerial function have been envisaged at various times since the early industrial revolution. Worker cooperatives and self-managed enterprises have come into and gone out of fashion at various times over a couple of centuries. And it is possible that some of their principles will be considered once again as new options are sought for organising work in a technologically and globally changing world.

Many of the difficulties experienced by employing organisations relate to issues of mistrust or resentment between people located at different levels of social status hierarchies within organisations. The question of the extent to which the carrying out of the managerial function has to involve a social status hierarchy must therefore remain an open question. The need to 'de-couple' conceptually the management function of the organisation and the existence of status-bearing managerial roles is a doubly important one. The relationship between the two is relevant to questions of the efficiency and effectiveness of the provision of goods and services, on the one hand, and to questions of the ethical and the political choices that exist with regard to social inequalities, on the other. We have to consider, first, the extent to which separating out certain people and labelling them as 'managers' is productive and the extent to which it is counterproductive. Second, we have to ask the closely related question of how far the various people involved in the organisation see differentials in reward and social status between managers and non-managers as 'right' or fair. These questions arise because all managerial jobs, in modern societies, have both a *task* and a *social–political* aspect to them.

Task and social-status aspects of management

The manager's job has a task aspect, involving the use of skills and knowledge to contribute to the overall management of the organisation. But it also has a social-status aspect: being a manager is a matter of *social-status* and prestige and something that is expected to give holders higher rewards and benefits than those generally received by non-managers. We can see how these 'task' and 'social' factors became closely intertwined in practice in the case of Andy Lethen's managerial changes at Meikle Printers. Activity 3.3 asks us to focus on this when reading the Meikle Printers case study. First, though, Activity 3.2 asks us to do a preliminary analysis of the case using the three-dimensional model of management.

Activity 3.2

Read the account in Cases and Conversations 3.2 of what happened when Andy Lethen took charge at Meikle Printers and try to analyse these events using the three-dimensional model of management set out in Table 3.1. Consider:

■ which aspects of the case relate to management as a function?

■ which aspects of the case relate to management as action and which relate to the phenomenon of their being members of the organisation who fill the official role or office of manager?

One step forward and one step back at Meikle Printers

Soon after Andy Lethen took over as general manager of Meikle Printers he found himself becoming very concerned about what he called the 'distance' between the firm's managers and the main workforce. He noticed on the first day he arrived that managers were immediately distinguishable from supervisors and other members of the workforce because they wore smart suits. Not only this, but they parked their cars in a separate car park and they used a separate dining room at lunchtimes. Also, managers' offices were designed so that anyone wishing to speak to a manager first had to speak to a secretary who was located in an outer level of the office.

Andy observed that whenever a manager walked through one of the working areas, there was a distinct change in atmosphere. 'It's just like when an officer visits a barrack room in the army', he said at an early managerial meeting. 'That's only because they respect us', said one of the longest serving managers. 'It means they take notice of us when we want to get things moving'. 'And it has changed a lot', he added, 'I can remember the days when everyone used to call a manager "Mr this" or "Mr that". Most of us are addressed by our first names these days. There's no real "distance", as you put it'. Another of the older managers responded to Andy in a different way, arguing that there was a 'degree of distance' but that this was necessary. 'If you didn't have a certain degree of distance, managers would have no authority. People wouldn't listen to you'. And another individual, who was well aware that Andy was considering removing many of the partitions between some of the offices and the main working areas, added, 'You would have no time to think or to plan work if every Tom, Dick and Harry could get hold of you whenever they wanted to'.

Andy strongly disputed all of these claims. He argued that much of the managerial conduct was 'years behind the times' and that it had 'more to do with social status than with managing the business'. 'People just don't treat managers with deference these days. They don't look up to someone just because they work in a suit and occupy an office with "manager" written on the door. I think this is a good thing. Social equality is something I believe in'. 'But we're running a business, not trying to change the world', one manager responded, 'and this does mean giving some standing to those who are taking on leadership roles'. 'All very well', responded Andy, 'but I think that the leadership which, of course, I want you all to show will be better coming from people who are much more accessible, both physically and socially. I want people to respect you, but I want them to respect you for how you can help them get out a better product and, that way, get themselves a better standard of living'. 'Aha', came back the first critic of Andy's promised new regime, 'And what about managers' rewards? All of us have worked hard and put in efforts over the odds to get to where we are. Why shouldn't we enjoy the standing and respect that comes from being seen dressed smartly, driving a nice car and having a secretary to manage our diaries?'. 'Yes, yes', replied Andy, 'I understand about rewards. What I am putting to you is that when we do away with these inaccessible offices, dining rooms and the rest, you will interact much more effectively with the staff. By working more closely together, solving problems and looking for creative ideas for improving performance, you will improve the business so that I will be able to improve your salaries. And you'll have the satisfaction of working for a leading edge company, rather than the social satisfaction of feeling that you, as a manager, are somehow a superior sort of being'.

Andy Lethen persisted with his intention to make changes to how managers and others related. But his battles to get rid of the management dining room, the separate car park and the office partitions were hard fought ones. Several of the younger and more highly qualified managers supported the moves but there was also strong opposition to them. The opponents of the changes used the term 'Lethen's social reforms', refusing to accept Andy's claim that 'more open management means better management'.

The price paid to bring about the 'reforms' was a high one. The bad feelings that developed between the younger and older factions led to several avoidable business mistakes occurring. Two of the managers left the company, one of them taking with him business contacts that Meikle Printers could not easily afford to lose.

Undoubtedly some important business was lost. Managers now parked their cars alongside everyone else and they went to the same dining room. They clearly spent more time talking with non-managerial employees and Andy believed that this was reflected in higher productivity figures and improved quality levels. But, at lunch times, managers sat exclusively with other managers within the communal dining room. In the early days of the 'open management' regime, Andy made a point of sitting with non-managerial employees at lunchtime. But, before long, he came to the conclusion that this was not appreciated and he started to bring sandwiches to eat at his desk. He felt that he could not compromise his stance by sitting with the all-manager group in the dining room. But he was very conscious of the fact that this was creating 'distance' between himself and the other managers. He had already had to react to this problem by conceding that several of the managers could go back to the closed office arrangement (reluctantly going along, for example, with one man's argument that he needed to talk to customers 'away from the noise and bustle of the works').

Andy tried to persuade himself that everything he had done would 'pay off in the long run'. But he could not help wondering whether all the pain had really been worth it. He found himself admitting this to his own secretary, one day. 'Look at what I've achieved', he frowned, 'one step forward and one step back!'. And, as he said this to his kind and helpful secretary, sitting back in his big leather chair, in his large and warm office, looking out over the river which ran beside the printing works, he came to terms with the fact that, like it or not, being a manager has a strong social component to it. It can never be just a matter of technical, professional or business expertise.

The three dimensions of management are readily identifiable in this story of managerial change. In fact the distinction between the three dimensions is indispensable to getting a good analytical 'grip' on what typically occurs, one way or another, in every organisation. If 'management' were a single undifferentiated phenomenon, the model would not need to exist and the problems at Meikle Printers would not have arisen. But the point of the model is not just that there is more than one dimension of management but that, more importantly, these three dimensions do not easily fit together. If there was not more than one dimension, then all the managers would straightforwardly have carried out appropriate managerial *actions* which would have led to the unproblematic and successful overall management of the company. This, however, was not the case. Andy Lethen wished to improve management in its *first*, or functional, dimension. He therefore tried to make changes in the *second* dimension by getting managers to act differently, in particular relating more closely and frequently with non-managerial employees. In some ways the changes made in the second dimension did improve 'management' at the primary level – at least potentially – in that there were productivity and quality improvements. But there were also negative developments in this dimension, with business being lost. These problems all arose as a result of 'social factors', ones that only existed because of the *third* dimension of management, the existence of the role or office of manager. As we pointed out earlier, the role of manager has both a task and a social status aspect. These two come into considerable tension in the case.

Activity 3.3

Reread the account of events at Meikle Printers. Then

■ Try to tease out the social-status aspects of the managers' jobs from the task aspects – the ones that relate to overall managerial effectiveness. Do not worry if you cannot easily do this. The case is a good illustration of just how mixed up these two things can become.

■ Consider what judgement you would make about Andy's attempted changes. Thinking of

what is better for the longer-term management of the firm, consider whether you would encourage Andy to be optimistic about his efforts or you would tend to sympathise with his more pessimistic feelings.

■ If you are able to, consider how these factors operate in an organisation you know about and consider what sort of changes, if any, you would make (and why) if you were to take a position in that organisation equivalent to that of Andy Lethen in Meikle Printers.

What soon becomes apparent as we look at the events in the Meikle Printers case is that the task element of the manager's job and its social status element are both closely interconnected and in tension with each other. One simple illustration of this is the matter of the manager's office. At first sight, this is a straightforward matter of task efficiency. To do their jobs – to fulfil the tasks of their posts – managers need a certain amount of peace to think and to plan and they need privacy at certain times to discuss matters that others in the vicinity do not need to know about. However, this immediately sets the manager 'apart' from others and to an extent, 'socially above' other people. And it can lead to resentment which, in turn, undermines the task-related reason for the existence of the office in the first place. It may also lead managers, in their physical isolation from everyday workplace events, to get out of touch with developments they would be better knowing about. But if managers' offices are taken away to overcome these problems, resentment might then grow between those managers and the more senior managers who insisted on their removal. Also, managers often argue that if they were not in some way 'set apart' from the rest of the workforce by such things as how they dress or where their desks are located, they would lack the authority to fulfil their managerial tasks. A common response to this is to argue that their authority might be greater if it were derived from demonstrable task competence rather than from symbols of 'status'. A whole range of social and cultural complexities thus arises – ones that are increasingly tackled by corporate attempts to 'change culture'.

 Link | Managerial attempts to 'change culture' are looked at in Chapter 7 and, especially, Chapter 8.

At this stage, we can move beyond the separating out of 'organising' and 'managing' and to observe a fundamental characteristic of both of these activities – ones which, in the process-relational perspective, are more or less the same thing. Organisations, in a strong sense of the word, do not actually exist. They exist, in the weaker sense of the word, as a 'useful fiction'. We all find it useful from time to time to talk about 'the organisation' and what it does. But what we are really referring to, in a 'shorthand' way, are numerous ongoing processes whereby social and technical arrangements, understandings, exchanges and productive actions are shaped and managed in order to fulfil complex tasks and meet the various goals and purposes of the multiplicity of people and groups who deal with the organisation. Most organisations have official organisation charts and official rulebooks of some kind. But the order that one actually experiences, on getting closely involved in any way with a work organisation, is more of a *negotiated order* than a set of practices that follow the prescriptions of the organisational blueprint.

Official blueprints and negotiated orders

Organisations are often initially presented to us as a set of procedures, rules and roles that are made explicit in the form of organisation charts, rulebooks and operating manuals. This aspect of the organisation is often regarded as having an existence separate from the people who are employed to fill the roles drawn up in the formal blueprint. People come and go, it might be said, but the organisation goes on. However, the big 'social machine' that is represented in the organisational blueprint cannot complete a single work task unless people are inserted into it as 'human cogs', so to speak. But human beings are not mechanical cogs. When they enter any organisation they inevitably bring with them their own priorities, interests, wants, values, assumptions, understandings and feelings. Not only this, but they are likely to want to organise certain aspects of their working lives and their working relationships for themselves. People joining the organisation will accept, up to a point, that they have to comply with rules and task requirements in the workplace. However, this is very much 'up to a point' and their engagement with corporate requirements is unlikely directly to satisfy every want, ambition or need that they bring with them into the workplace. A second aspect of organisational life thus comes into play. A whole set of relationships, games, arguments, status competitions, fun activities and task 'short cuts' emerge as people pursue interests and projects of their own, try to express and defend their private sense of self or simply try to get through the working day more easily. And this aspect of organisational existence sometimes fits in with the requirements of the official blueprint and operating manual and sometimes it does not.

All of this has to be coped with managerially. The work of managing organisations is thus a complex matter involving a whole range of processes and a vast number of ever-changing relationships. The process-relational perspective tries to do full justice to this, recognising that practices within organisations are unlikely to be successful if the people trying to manage work tasks are unaware of all of these complexities. Just a few of these complexities were seen in the case of Meikle Printers. However, the sorts of issue to which our attention was drawn in that case are ones that make many people uncomfortable, this discomfort being experienced both by people who study management and by people who practise it.

Managers and management thinkers alike have found it discomforting to have to accept that one cannot simply set up an organisation as a big machine and, having got the design 'right', expect organisational success to follow. Managism (see above, p. 53) represents a belief that such things are possible and such a faith, or aspiration, can comfort people facing the frightening complexities and ambiguities of organisational and managerial work (a point we revisit in Chapter 5, pp. 158–60). However, it is questionable whether any manager would survive in their job if they actually based their practices on a belief that successful management was essentially a matter of drawing up the right blueprints, plans, strategies, structures, rules and procedures and 'putting them in place'. They nevertheless frequently talk in this way even if, deeper down, they know that they have to involve themselves in endless processes of negotiating and renegotiating understandings and relationships with people across the organisation and outside it. The tendency is for managers to talk in terms of running the organisation as if it were primarily a big technical system while, intuitively, knowing that things do not in reality get done that way. This was recognised in one of the classic works of management thinking, Chester Barnard's *The Functions of the Executive* (Barnard, 1938, Reading Guide 2). This book represents the first serious attempt to apply broadly social science thinking to the management role.

Barnard looked closely at how organisations were coming to be understood in this period of history when the formalised management or 'executive' role was becoming a significant one in economically developing societies. His main worry was that there was an over emphasis on what he called the 'formal organisation'. This was the formal blueprint of the organisation and all its officially laid down rules, procedures and roles. This, he suggested, was widely focused upon, at the expense of paying attention to what he called the 'informal organisation'. Thus, 'major executives, and even entire executive organisations are often completely unaware of widespread influences, attitudes, and agitations within their organisations' (Barnard, 1938, p. 121). In spite of this, Barnard noted that 'one will repeatedly hear' executives commenting that 'you can't understand an organisation or how it works from its organisation chart, its charter, rules and regulations ...'. Nevertheless, managers still spoke as if this were possible in spite of recognising that, deeper down, to do so is equivalent to trying to understand how the government of a country works from reading its constitution, court decisions, laws and statutes. Barnard's position, in effect, was that managers need to come much more directly to terms with what many of them are intuitively aware of: that 'learning the ropes' in most organisations is chiefly a matter of 'learning who's who, what's what, why's why, of its informal society' (1938, p. 121). He therefore attempted to change the emphasis that was put on formal aspects of organisation and, indeed, to argue that the main task of the executive is to shape the informal organisation. Doing this fulfils three key functions: communication, the maintenance of cohesiveness 'through regulating the willingness to serve and the stability of objective authority', and the retaining of feelings of 'personal integrity, of self respect, of independent choice' (1938, p. 122).

In arguing this, Barnard was fully aware of the analysis which some of his associates at Harvard University were developing as a result of their study of factory life. In their own classic study of work organisation, *Management and the Worker*, Roethlisberger and Dickson (1939, p. 559, Reading Guide 1) challenged the common assumption that 'the organisation of a company corresponds to a blueprint plan or organisation chart'. 'Actually', they observe, 'it never does' and they pointed to the importance of understanding the 'informal organisation' which, as Roethlisberger later put it, 'evolved within this formal organisation' (Roethlisberger, 1968, p. 262, Reading Guide 1). This informal organisation was made up of 'the practices, values, norms, beliefs, unofficial rules, as well as the complex network of social relations, membership patterns and centers of influence and communication that developed within and between the constituent groups of the organisation under the formal arrangements but that were not specified by them' (1968, p. 262).

These two books, *The Functions of the Executive* and *Management and the Worker* can be regarded as two founding works of the managerially oriented tradition of organisational behaviour. In spite of their shortcomings, these books contain insights that are still vitally relevant. Although they represent an early move towards organisational systems thinking, their version of systems thinking is a 'natural systems' one which can still stand as an antidote to the 'organisation as big machine' orthodoxy of what has been called here the system-control perspective. The 'natural systems' approach of these Harvard thinkers is not something we wish to turn back to, however, given the tendency of all systems perspectives to view the organisation as more of a coherent and unified entity than it can ever be, in reality.

Rather than thinking of the organisation as a 'natural system' it is helpful to regard it as a *negotiated order*.

Negotiated order, in organisations · *Concept*

The pattern of organisational activities that has arisen or emerged over time as an outcome of the interplay of the variety of interests, understandings, reactions and initiatives of the individuals and groups involved in the organisation.

The concept of negotiated order was introduced in a study of a psychiatric hospital by Strauss *et al.* (1963, Reading Guide 1) but was extended in later work by Strauss where the earlier neglect of the part played by power relations and conflicts of interest was redressed by attention to conflicts which were, said Strauss, 'endemic, or essential to, relations between or among negotiating parties' (1978, p. 290, Reading Guide 3). In this, Strauss is giving full weight to the influence on his thinking of the classic participant observation study of managerial work carried out by Dalton (1959, Reading Guide 5). This showed how managers do not simply 'put in place' organisational arrangements and then ensure that they are complied with. They are shown by Dalton to be continuously involved in, as Strauss puts it, 'trading off, the paying off of accumulated obligations, the covert making of deals and other kinds of secret bargains, the use of additional covering negotiations for keeping hidden the results of previous covert arrangements, the bypassing of negotiations, and the mediating of negotiations; also, a very complex balancing of accumulated favors and obligations, along with the juggling of commitments within the negotiation itself' (Strauss, 1978, p. 139).

The official organisational charts and rulebooks, and all the formal operating procedures, roles and statuses that are associated with these, play a part in the patterns that emerge from the interactions that take place as work tasks are carried out and people's personal and sectional interests and priorities are played out. The organisational actors, in effect, interpret for themselves and make use of the official rules and procedures, in a way that both serves their own purposes *to a certain extent* and fulfils officially sanctioned tasks – but again, *only to a certain extent*. In what we might call the 'real world' of work organisations, neither the organisation's 'designers' nor the 'human cogs' that they employ get everything that they want. In all of this, the formal and the official aspects of organisational life on the one hand, the informal and unofficial aspects on the other – get intimately mixed up with each other in the negotiated and socially constructed order which is 'the organisation'. This occurs in the case of 'the board within the board' at Eagle Buses.

 Link

➡ The *official/unofficial* distinction will be used again in Chapter 7 when we look at the interplay between official and unofficial aspects of organisational structures and cultures.

➡ Both the *micropolitical* activities of managers and the various acts of organisational mischief discussed in Chapter 10 play an important part in the negotiated order of organisations.

Activity 3.4

Read the story in Cases and Conversations 3.3 of what happened when Suzy Findhorn was promoted to became chief executive of Eagle Buses and

■ identify elements which are part of the *official structure and culture* of the company;

■ identify elements which constitute the *negotiated order* that emerges, partly in line with and partly out of line with the official structures and procedures;

■ note ways in which these two aspects of the organisation's functioning are mutually supportive;

■ note ways in which these two aspects of the organisation come into tension with each other.

The board within the board at Eagle Buses

Cases and Conversations 3.3

Eagle Buses was a privately owned business which, some years ago, had been privatised. When it left the public sector its new board of directors established, for the first time, the post of chief executive. Previously, a director of transport services – a local government official – had been in charge of the service, although his decisions always had to be reached in negotiation with the chairman of the transport committee, an elected member of the local authority. The transport committee chairman who held this position for many years, up until one year before privatisation, had a warm relationship with the director of transport services. He took the view that his friend knew more than the elected members about buses and therefore ensured that the director was left to run the service as he thought fit. The committee chairman had a powerful personality and was able to overrule any councillor on his committee who tried to intervene in bus service matters. This was in spite of the growing number of complaints from the public and in the press about increasing fares and the declining quantity and quality of services.

A change of ruling party on the city authority then occurred, after many years of the same party being in charge. Consequently, a new transport committee chairman took office and he was determined to make the managers of the bus services, as he put it, 'be accountable to the electorate'. This was 'constitutionally required of him', he insisted. He therefore made sure that every decision that the director wanted to make was fully discussed with him and put before his committee for further discussion. The required negotiations between the council officer (the director) and the elected members (led by the chairman) were no longer the formality they had been under the previous regime. They were protracted and often heated.

The pattern of continual debate and often bitter argument between the transport officials and the politicians continued for a year. But initiatives at national level then led to the council selling off its bus service. It was at this point that the post of chief executive was established as part of the organisational design of the new company. The company chairman was a man with many years of experience in the retailing industry and, in establishing the new board of directors, he ensured members of it covered the full range of necessary expertise. A board of directors with twelve members was therefore established and it turned out that more than half of the members were former local authority employees – and these were all executive directors (as opposed to part-time non-executive directors). The chairman tried to balance this fairly traditionally minded group of individuals by appointing Archie Leven as chief executive. He was a very entrepreneurial man, also with a retailing background. On being appointed, he concentrated on competing with the other bus companies who had entered the now de-regulated transport 'market place'.

Before long, arguments started to happen at board meetings which were at least as heated and bitter as those which had previously taken place between councillors and bus managers. The rows tended to be between the supporters on the board of the chief executive, people who liked Archie's decision to paint the buses bright colours, his buying of a variety of different types of new vehicle and his encouraging of drivers to 'race' the drivers of competing buses to 'win customers'. The director of finance, who felt that he was investing recklessly, and the director of safety services, who was appalled by the fleet's increasing accident rate, led the opposition to him.

In spite of the fact that increasing numbers of people were travelling on the buses and the good profits that were being made, the disputes within the board of directors – at formal meetings and outside them in the offices and corridors of the company headquarters – reached such a level that Archie Leven resigned after one particularly acrimonious board meeting. After a couple of weeks with no one 'at the helm' and declining passenger numbers first beginning to become apparent (which Archie Leven may or may not have known about), it was decided to promote one of the especially well-regarded younger managers straight on to the board and into the chief executive role. Thus Suzie Findhorn found herself in charge of a bus company.

Suzie, on her first day in the new job, sat at her new desk and perused the job description that she had been given. It set out her duties in rather general terms and in a way which could probably be found in chief executives' job descriptions in any number of businesses around the country. Privately, however, the chairman had given her a brief. 'One way or another,' he told her, 'you have got to get the members of this raucous band of directors playing in tune with each other so that we can get on with growing the business. If that's not possible, you've got to work your way around the characters who are slowing us down and drive the business forward without them'. This was hardly any more precise than what her job description had said. But Suzie knew that the politics of the job were going to be at the forefront.

She already knew which directors were her 'friends' and which would be resistant to any kind of 'new broom'. At first, she worked hard behind the scenes, to get the support of each director (as well as the support of other managers) for her agenda of holding back expansion in the short term, building up the quality and

reliability of the service and giving it an image as 'the city's own bus service', prior to expanding the services to include taxi style minibuses and developing links with the rail services which served the city.

Once Suzie Findhorn was confident she knew who was going to support her agenda, and contribute actively to its development, she set up a group of five directors and three managers which she called the 'Serving the City Project Group'. Before long it became apparent that this was the forum where real strategy-development was occurring and that the company chairman, with Suzie sitting at his side, was managing the main board meetings so that they effectively backed whatever emerged from what Suzie sometimes called her 'ginger group'. But, in spite of the fact that the so-called 'project group' contained three managers who were not even board members, she had established a 'board within a board'. This, with the chief executive and the chairman in close partnership within it, was effectively directing the business, not its formally appointed board of directors.

This pattern of leadership and decision-making saw the hoped for improvements in every aspect of the company's performance. The business targets that the official board of directors had approved were being met. One day, however, an emergency board meeting had to be called. The share price had gone into rapid decline. It was unclear what was happening but Suzie began to suspect that one of the directors who had increasingly been showing resentment at the influence of what he called 'Findhorn's inner cabinet', had been briefing financial journalists and other business specialists to the effect that the business's growth had been too fast, and that it was not sustainable. 'So what are we going to do about this, then?', the chairman asked the chief executive, as he handed her a large glass of whisky the night before the emergency board meeting. 'What indeed?', mused Suzy as she stared out of the window into the dark bus park.

We first see the relevance of the distinction between an organisation's official structure and culture and its emergent negotiated order to events in Eagle Buses when we look back to its earlier existence as a public sector transport organisation. The official requirements were that the director of transport services should run the bus service under the supervision of the committee of the city council. The contact between the director and this committee of elected councillors was through the chairman of that committee. But, here, the actual order that operated in practice differed somewhat from what was 'officially' required. Partly because of a strong personal relationship between the two men, the director was left with more freedom to run the transport service than he should have officially been allowed. The committee chairman used his personal power to overrule any attempts by committee members to implement their proper stewardship (being 'accountable to the electorate', as his successor put it). On the evidence we have here of public complaints, it would appear that this set of circumstances was not conducive to organisational effectiveness. The official and the unofficial aspects of the organisation were clearly coming into tension with each other.

The official structure and culture of the organisation changes with the emergence of the Eagle business as a private company. Very soon the new set of individuals in important positions establish a working order which, in some ways, is 'in line' with the new official design and in some ways is not. In this case, as in the case of any 'actually existing organisation', we see human beings with unofficial goals, values and priorities establishing processes and practices which only *take into account* the official design they are meant to be implementing rather than *following* or fully implementing it. Orthodox organisational and managerial thinking tends to work on the assumption that the design is what primarily shapes organisational practices (albeit with deviations and failures of compliance). Process-relational thinking, however, sees such matters as just one factor in shaping the actual processes and patterns which emerge.

Suzie Findhorn could not completely ignore the requirements that she had to fulfil with regard to the board of directors. But she devised ways of operating which, in her view and in the view of the Company Chairman with whom she was informally 'allied', meant that the business could be operated more effectively than by following the official 'blueprint'. But no problem is ever finally solved and no set of arrangements can be made which do not, at some point, either face difficulties as circumstances change, or become challenged by individuals or groups who do not find those arrangements conducive to their own preferences or helpful to their unofficial projects. Accordingly, the 'board within a board' at Eagle Business seemed, at first, to be a very effective adaptation of the 'official system'. However, it appears that one of the main board members resented his exclusion from the group which, in practice, was 'in power'. He was determined to undermine the unofficial (or you might say 'partly-unofficial') arrangements and practices established by the chief executive and the company chairman. As these two individuals consider what is going to happen at the emergency board meeting and how they are going to handle what they suspect has been an act of sabotage on the part of their fellow director, they feel unsure of themselves. The ambiguities and uncertainties that are a normal part of managerial experience confront them in a particularly stark way this evening.

Coming to terms with uncertainty and ambiguity

The whole tradition of systems-control thinking is based on an assumption of the possibility of a high level of rational control of the complex behaviours that the organisation of work entails. This is an assumption that developed with the spread of modernism, which we looked at earlier (pp. 36–8). It is assumed that once it has been decided what human beings want to achieve (establish 'organisational goals' for example) and they have calculated the most appropriate means of achieving that end (designing the *official structures and procedures* of an organisation, for example), then those ends are likely to be met. The power of this principle of *instrumental rationality* cannot be denied, as its greatest theorist, Max Weber (1978, Reading Guide 16) pointed out in the course of explaining the growth of the bureaucratic form of organisation as a key feature of modern societies (see below, pp. 239–42).

 Link   The process of bureaucratisation of work activity is a central concern of Chapter 7.

The application of instrumental rationality, whereby systematic calculation of what method to use to achieve any given purpose, has enabled the human species to achieve immensely complicated tasks and enormously increase their control over aspects of their physical and social environment (sometimes for human betterment, sometimes for the opposite, as we noted earlier).

Instrumental rationality	*Concept*
The calculated choice of appropriate means to achieve specified ends.	

It enabled the customers of Eagle Buses to travel about their part of the country in a way that would have been unimaginable in earlier times, for instance. And one of the key features of managerial work is its continuous application of instrumental rationality – its constant concern with devising the most appropriate means of achieving specified objectives. The centrality of such a concern is indicated by the tendency of managers to answer the question 'What is this "management" that you do?' in the way that they did when challenged by the inquisitive Martian – 'the organising of resources to achieve an agreed objective', and the like (see above, p. 47). But if the application of instrumental rationality were as straightforward as 'mainstream modernism' (see pp. 36–8) would have us believe, then we would not see the sort of managerial 'realities' emerging that we saw in both the Meikle Printers and the Eagle Buses cases. It would not be necessary to separate out the 'official' and the 'unofficial' aspects of organisations at all. The official blueprint of the organisation, if it were carefully drawn on instrumentally rational principles, would simply be implemented in work practices and the intentions of the organisational designers would be met.

Experience of real life organisations, however, shows that a multitude of 'actual' processes and practices which are not specified in the original organisational plan invariably come into play. In part, as we have seen so far, this occurs because organisations only come into real existence when they involve human beings who bring with them to the organisational setting a vast multiplicity of private goals and interests. The human actors contributing to organisational task fulfilment thus devise their own practices and processes to 'get by', sometimes going with the grain of the official design, sometimes going against it.

A further reason that managerial work does not simply involve drawing up blueprints, plans and structures and overseeing their straightforward implementation is that the information and knowledge that goes into the calculative element of instrumental reason is always partial or 'bounded'. Rationality, itself, is always bounded (Simon, 1957, Reading Guide 6).

Bounded rationality
Concept

The human ability to calculate the most appropriate means of achieving a specified end is limited, or bounded, in two ways:

- only a small proportion of all the knowledge or information which is potentially relevant to any rational analysis can ever be obtained;

- the human mind would only cope with a fraction of all the relevant information, were it obtainable.

The concept of *bounded rationality* can be neatly illustrated by one of the comments made by Peter Brodie, the manager of a charity of whom we shall hear more below (in Cases and Conversations 3.4). He said 'I can only know a tiny fraction of what is going on in this organisation, in spite of the fact that I live and breathe it. And, anyway, my tiny mind struggles to cope with all the bits I do know about'.

To adopt a process-relational perspective is not to turn one's back on the principle of instrumental rationality – any more than one was arguing for the outright rejection of modernist thinking in Chapter 2. Instead it is, again, to adopt a stance of *pragmatic modernism*, and come to terms with the fact that instrumental rationality can only take us so far in helping us towards achieving our purposes, whatever they are. This means that in doing managerial work, or in trying to understand the managerial practices to be observed in 'real life' organisations (as opposed to textbook ones), we have to comes to terms with ambiguity in organisational situations and, with what follows from it: uncertainty about the future. Uncertainty could simply be defined as a state of being unsure about something. But it is generally used in organisation theory to refer to a lack of sureness or clarity about the future. Because managerial work is typically concerned with bringing about one future state of affairs or another, it is useful to conceptualise ambiguity and uncertainty along these lines.

Ambiguity
Concept

Ambiguity exists when the *meaning* of a situation or an event is unclear or confused and is therefore open to a variety of interpretations.

Uncertainty
Concept

Uncertainty exists when the *understanding* of a future situation or event is unclear or confused and is therefore open to a variety of interpretations.

To be realistic about organisational and managerial work – to be fully 'rational' about it, we might say – we have fully to come to terms with the pervasiveness and inescapability of ambiguity and uncertainty. And this may not be a comfortable thing to do. To put it in very simple terms, we can never *really know* precisely what we are doing in managerial situations any more than we can ever really know exactly where we are going. But this does not mean that we have to give up trying to organise and manage complex work tasks. It means that managers have to 'work at' organising their affairs while

- recognising that the world is a complicated, unpredictable and fickle place,
- accepting that the people that managers deal with are complicated, unpredictable and fickle beings,
- coming to terms with the fact that managers themselves are also complicated, unpredictable and fickle beings – like all other humans.

It is has to be admitted that the analysis of the problems of ambiguity and uncertainty presented here implies that the prospect of engaging in managerial work is a rather daunting one. This, in fact, may be the awkward but utterly realistic truth of the situation (a point to which we will return in the next chapter). To make sense of what this means in practice, however, we can turn to the body of research-based knowledge which tells us how managers go about their work. Since the days of Barnard we have seen a series of research studies which paints a detailed picture of 'what managers actually do'.

Link

The concepts of uncertainty and ambiguity play a major part in analysing:

- culture and human identity, see pp. 115–18;
- managerial anxiety, see pp. 158–60;
- strategy-making, see pp. 170–3;
- decision-making and managerial politicking, see pp. 328–9;
- employee selection and promotion, see pp. 404–12;
- ethics and morality in organisations, see pp. 455–62.

Making sense of what managers do

One of the first pieces of writing which attempted to apply broadly social scientific thinking to managerial activity was Barnard's *Functions of the Executive* (1938, Reading Guide 2), as we saw earlier. This work, like the associated Harvard studies of factory life (Roethlisberger and Dickson, 1939, Reading Guide 1), arose in part as a reaction to managerial thinking which looked at organisations primarily in terms of their official structure and culture side. Barnard argued that the executive's job was not to attend directly to this but to shape what he saw as the more 'informal' aspects of the organisation. But Barnard's book was not a research-based one. It was a later American study, carried out by Dalton (1959, Reading Guide 5) as a participant observer, that first produced systematic evidence of the centrality to managerial behaviour of what he also conceptualised as 'informal' relations (and which, as we saw earlier, p. 77, Strauss drew on in developing his notion of 'negotiated order'). Among all the conflicts and political rivalries that Dalton observed going on between various individuals and managerial groups, there was a constant process of negotiation, accommodation and trading which led to the creation of what he calls a 'web of commitments' and the negotiation of a myriad of 'workable arrangements'. In addition to this, research in Scandinavia, Britain and America, using a variety of investigative techniques varying from direct observation to diary analysis and interviews, produced evidence that paints a picture of management life that is very different from what one might expect from business or management textbooks. Many of these studies are brought together in Reading Guide 5. The picture which emerges from these investigations of 'what managers do' is one in which:

- Managers are endlessly on the move from one brief task to another. Their day is highly fragmented as they rapidly switch not only from issue to issue but from one social interaction to another.

- They spend a great deal of time *talking* with people. This occurs on the telephone, in formal meetings and in conversations that occur inside and outside the workplace, in offices, in corridors, when walking between buildings and when visiting people as they do their jobs. A large proportion of these conversations is with people over whom the manager has no authority.

- Managerial behaviour looks generally *reactive*. It rarely appears to follow a sequence of reflective planning followed by actions to implement specific decisions.

- Managers rely a great deal on gossip, hearsay and guesswork to keep informed. Formal reports and management information systems play only a small part in informing managerial thinking – and what is taken from these tends to be contextualised by more informal sources of knowledge and insight.

- They thus spend little time analysing formal information in the quiet of their offices or systematically planning how they are going to spend their time.

- Managers are rarely seen getting their way or getting tasks done by giving direct commands to subordinates.

These studies, taken as a whole, suggest that managers rarely behave in the ways we might expect – as planners, as designers and implementers of systems or as instruction-giving 'people managers'. Instead, they are *handling their dependence on other people* through endless talking, listening and persuading . They do this primarily by negotiating, trading and exchanging with all the parties upon whom they rely to achieve the tasks for which they have responsibility.

There is logic behind this apparently frenzied managerial whirl of activity, then. But there is still a risk of misunderstanding what is going on. It is easy to allow this evidence of the seemingly reactive, fragmentary, speculative and chaotic wheeling and dealing to blind us to what it all 'adds up to', in organisational or corporately strategic terms. Such a danger arises at times when this evidence about managerial activity is used to debunk the earlier or 'classic' definitions of management. The most famous of these is Fayol's identification of five elements of management (Fayol, 1949, Reading Guide 2). Management, Fayol said, consists of:

- *planning*: devising a plan of action for utilising the organisation's resources to achieve the organisation's 'objective';
- *organising*: making sure that materials and labour are available when needed;
- *commanding*: directing people so that they carry out required activities;
- *coordinating*: ensuring that all the activities support each other and combine to contribute to the overall fulfilment of the organisational objective;
- *controlling*: checking that activities following their planned course and correcting any deviations that are found.

Fayol's characterisation of management as 'planning, organising, commanding, coordinating and controlling' has been taught to endless cohorts of management students. And numerous management students, down the years, have tried to memorise Gulick's mnemonic, POSDCORB – a device to help them remember that management is about 'planning, organising, staffing, directing, coordinating, reporting and budgeting' (Gulick, 1973, Reading Guide 2). Fayol's and Gulick's lists have functioned, in effect, as slogans for the systems-control orthodoxy in organisational and managerial thinking. The process-relational perspective on management dispenses with the concept of a single 'organisation objective' which Fayol and other such 'classical' writers use, of course. But it nevertheless recognises that many of these 'elements of organisation' must be present if the organisation, as a set of task-oriented relationships and understandings, is going to continue into the future. There has been a tendency to debunk 'classical' conceptions of management on the grounds that managerial activities do not look *at first sight* as if they are fulfilling the functions of planning, coordinating and so on. We need to go back to the earlier distinction between *management as a function* and *managing as an activity* (Table 3.1, p. 67) to see that there is a fundamental organisational logic behind all the frenetic activity that the research studies report. The research should not therefore be used to justify treating classical thinking about management as a 'myth' to be rejected (Mintzberg, 1975, Reading Guide 5). Instead, it should be read as showing that the functions of management which people like Fayol were concentrating upon are carried out, in practice, in a much more complex and subtle way than Fayol and other early writers on management were willing to acknowledge.

This point can perhaps be most clearly illustrated by considering the case of Fayol's 'commanding' element. It is indeed true that study after study has found little evidence of managers directly 'commanding' subordinates to act in certain ways. But just because direct orders are rarely seen being given, the same end (or 'function') has to be achieved, albeit by other means like persuasion, manipulation or trading. Paradoxically, then, commanding may not be *seen to be done* but command nevertheless has to be *achieved*. Similarly, we may not see managers directly controlling activities, or coordinating them. But control and coordination does have to occur. Without a degree of control and without a certain level of coordination, there would be no organisation. This, we can infer, is what Peter Brodie is getting at when he says, 'I may look like a crazy man, dashing about the place all day – but there is method to my madness'. Before we hear more about what Peter Brodie has to say about his managerial day, it is helpful to look in a little more detail at one of the studies of managerial behaviour which was drawn upon in the generalisations made earlier. This is a detailed study of the lives and the work of fifteen general managers who were deemed to be especially successful in their work – on the evidence of the business results that they achieved and the judgements made of them by other managers, by their subordinates and by the top managers who employed them – by Kotter (1982, Reading Guide 5).

Kotter observed that these very successful managers not only looked 'less systematic, more informal, less reflective, more reactive, less well organised' than we might expect of effective performers but indeed looked 'more frivolous' than the stereotype of such people might lead us to expect (1982, p. 59). When he was able to recognise behaviours that he thought he might classify as involving 'planning' or 'organising', they appeared to be 'rather hit or miss, rather sloppy' (1982, p. 85). Kotter makes sense of this, at first sight, puzzling situation by recognising the inevitability of what we have been emphasising as the immense ambiguity and uncertainty that surrounds the manager's job. Decisions, therefore, cannot emerge from the cool calculating analysis of clear and objective data. The world is not like that or, as Kotter puts it, the decision-making environment is 'characterised by uncertainty, great diversity, and an enormous quantity of potentially relevant information'. And, correspondingly, decisions could not, in the 'real world', be implemented by the straightforward issuing of orders to subordinates. Instead, they have to be implemented through a 'large and diverse group of subordinates, peers, bosses and outsiders', people over whom, effectively, the managers have 'relatively little control'. The methods that these managers used to get things done were therefore much more about 'influencing' people than commanding them. They used a great deal of face-to-face contact and were constantly encouraging, cajoling, manipulating and persuading people. They were demanding of others and used a range of ways to reward people for producing what was required.

Much of the 'influencing' work of the managers studied by Kotter was done indirectly. The networks established by the managers were such that their members would influence each other to work towards fulfilling the agenda around which the network had been developed. In fact the series of 'agendas' that managers identified for themselves mediated between the longer-term strategic priorities of the business as a whole and the day-to-day activities orchestrated by the general manager. We could perhaps see these 'agendas' as mental maps that the manager used to make sense of what was happening and to help them understand how unfolding events might be linked to the overall directing of the organisation. Various activities and projects encouraged by the manager could thus, in their different ways, contribute to the meeting of such agendas and the achievement of the multiplicity of objectives that the agendas contained. These agendas, however, were not schemes conceived away from the day-to-day hustle and bustle. The constant monitoring of information coming from the range of sources available to the manager (gossip, rumour and hearsay included) contributed to the development of the agenda and the managers were skilled and assertive when it came to questioning people and obtaining relevant information.

Once we recognise the 'method behind the madness' or the 'efficiency of seemingly inefficient behaviours' of managerial activity, we can see a series of seemingly disparate processes occurring which, when taken together, add up to a certain degree of organisational 'system-ness'. The process-relational perspective draws our attention to the range of social, political, cultural, economic processes that managerial and organisational work involves. It rejects the systems-control assumption that the organisation *is* a system, and should be looked at as a system from the start. Yet it does not reject any notion of there being systematic features to what *emerges* from all the processes that go on. The problem with systems-control thinking is that it assumes a system-like quality of the organisation as a given. Process-relational thinking sees it, instead, as emergent, fragile and temporary. It has to be won and re-won by skilful managerial action.

Activity 3.5

Peter Brodie, is the manager of the Youth Links charity and he is widely regarded as an especially successful voluntary sector manager. Read what Peter has to say in Cases and Conversations 3.4 about his working day in conversation with the researcher who has been shadowing him throughout the day. Consider:

■ how far this account of a working day fits with the pattern of research findings made by researchers on 'what managers do', summarised on p. 85;

■ which activities mentioned here can be related to organisational

■ social processes,

■ political processes,

■ cultural processes,

■ economic processes;

■ how these various processes and practices, when taken together, contribute to meeting Peter's responsibility for successfully directing the organisation as a whole so that it continues into the future. In other words, consider the strategic significance of all this activity. What does it add up to, what is the 'method behind the madness'?

Peter Brodie reviews his day	Cases and Conversations 3.4

So, Peter, can we take a few minutes to review what you've done today? I feel pretty exhausted just trying to keep up with you.

Yes, let's have a break. But I can't stop for long. I need to change to go to the reception at the town hall.

What's that about?

Well, at one level it's just a matter of showing my face, you know, representing the charity. I was pleased to get an invite, given that the present mayor is not too keen on what we are doing. Any chance I can get to encourage her to see that we really are helping rehabilitate young offenders, rather than encouraging 'rough elements', as she calls them, is welcome.

You'll get a chance to talk to the Mayor?

Probably not. But I'll try – you know how charming I can be. One of the council members who is very helpful to us will try to get me into conversation with the mayor. It was him I eventually got through to on the car phone earlier.

Yes, I was wondering what that was all about. I couldn't really see the point of the conversation. It seemed to be about the wisdom or not of going on skiing holidays at this time of the year. It didn't appear to have much to do with rehabilitating young offenders.

That's right. But it's all part of 'smoothing the way', as you might say.

Is that a big part of your job?

It has to be.

Because this is a charity?

Partly I suppose. But it wasn't really different when I was in business. You're always keeping this person right, then that person. You've got to put a lot into winning people over if you're dealing with some of the difficult things that we get involved in as a charity. But it's not that different when you are dealing with people who are committed from the start.

For example?

Well, do you remember this morning? You'll notice that the first thing I do every day is wander round the staff in the office, passing the time of day and all that. I think that's important for any manager – building the relation-ship and all that. But one particular thing I was doing this morning was checking up on young Mary. I am worried that she has got too committed to the clients. I wanted to find out – not too directly of course – whether she was out with some of our clients again last night. When I was joking to her about trying out more of our 'sophisticated night club life' I was trying to get a message over that she should switch off more often – get away from the job, mix with people more of her own background. But, of course that phone call from the police interrupted me before I really finished the conversation.

That sort of thing seems to happen a lot.

Tell me about it. It's a struggle sometimes to keep a tab on just what I am doing from minute to minute. But, at the end of the day I add all the bits up and manage to paint for myself some sort of picture of what's going on – not that it's ever a complete picture. I can only know a tiny fraction of what is going on in this organisation, in spite of the fact that I live and breathe it. And, anyway, my tiny mind struggles to cope with all the bits I do know about. But if I keep good relationships with all the people I deal with, I feel I can trust them to do the right thing when my eye is off the ball.

It didn't sound like you have a very trusting relationship with the police officer I heard you talking to?

No, not with that one. The politics of it are complicated. He's a young graduate officer who wants to get on fast and, somehow, he thinks that taking a tough line is the way forward. And that means, if possible, driving out of town the sort of people we are trying to help fit back into the community. I've got the senior police people on my side though and I'll eventually get him to see the light – when he comes to understand better which side his bread is buttered on.

You were very tough with him, I thought.

Yes, I judged that was the right way to play it. You see, people get the idea that we charity types operate in a soft, caring sort of culture and are therefore vulnerable to be being bullied. But that's no good. You have to have a culture where you're caring, but tough with it. And that applies to clients especially. This is something that I'm always trying to teach the younger staff. It is also partly why I took Darian with me when I went to talk to the landlords of the new property we want to rent. Given our funding – or the lack of it – I've got to drive a hard bargain over everything we spend. This property company seems to think that we'll be a soft touch when it comes to bargaining over rents. But they also know that we are not rich. I've got to play that up when trying to beat them down on rents. But, at the same time, I can't imply that we're in danger of going insolvent. It's a tricky game to play, balancing all the politics and the economics of it.

How do you manage to do that?

I do wonder sometimes, as I go dashing about from one crisis to another, one bit of fixing to another piece of fixing. I've got to pay attention to detail but, at the same time, keep my eyes above that detail.

You are not just reacting to events, then?

It often feels like that. But I know I've got to do something more, at the same time as rushing hither and thither. I may look like a crazy man, dashing about the place all day – but there is method to my madness. I am determined to get this organisation recognised as part of the life of the town, and one that is here to stay – at least as long as there is a problem of youth crime. We are called Youth Links because the charity makes links with the youths that it serves. But it does this in order to make links between those youths and the community to which, as I see it, they very much belong. I feel strongly about this. I left a promising business career, as my old company pointed out to me when I left, because I wanted to take on a real challenge and I wanted to show that I could use my management skills to serve values that I deeply believe in. I think that I am getting the people within the charity, and most of those outside it, to support and further my agenda. And, personally, I am getting a lot of satisfaction out of doing something I feel is really worthwhile and does more than simply please the people who run the stock market.

That's interesting, can I ask you . . .

No, another time. We've got to dash. A bit of reflection's all right. But too much of it and I'll be late at the town hall. At the moment, getting across the town is what is important.

We cannot know the details of everything that Peter Brodie did on this typical day in his working life. We can, however, get quite a good idea of how he manages his job from this conversation. The picture that emerges fits with that painted by the body of research reviewed earlier. Peter's day is fragmented and his 'dashing about' from one task to another is apparent from his account of interrupted telephone conversations and from his own need to interrupt the very conversation in which he reflects on such matters. Talking is clearly the main behaviour that he engages in through the day, this occurring with a considerable range of people. And there was no evidence of Peter systematically planning his time or sitting in his office analysing formal information. It would appear, however, that there is a rationale behind all of this. Peter is gathering scraps of information from all of these conversations, as well as developing relationships and trying to influence people through them. We can see this in the conversation with Mary, for example. At first sight this is simply a 'What did you do last night?' type of conversation. But he is also checking up on her at the same time as trying to persuade her to behave differently in her job. He does not do this, however, by instructing her. Although, as Peter agrees, his managerial behaviour looks reactive, he is working to an 'agenda' and is co-opting people inside and outside of the organisation – all of whom he is dependent upon in some way – to help him fulfil it. All these disparate activities, and the social, political, cultural and economic processes he involves himself in, relate to a clear strategic direction in which he is moving the organisation.

The strategic direction in which Peter Brodie is taking the charity is one of getting it established as 'part of the life of the town' for as long as it is needed. He doesn't give this the grand title of a 'strategy'. But he does use the word agenda. He is nevertheless fulfilling the key strategic task of an organisation's management – that of taking it forward into the long term and carrying out the tasks which are done in the organisation's name. This rationale of fulfilling the principles implicit in the charity's name of 'Youth Links' gives 'method to his madness'. The logic of what he is doing reveals the efficiency of behaviours that, at first sight, look inefficient. We thus see how, in this case, there is a linking of management as a *function* and management as an *activity*, in the terms introduced earlier (p. 67). But, remember, there was a third dimension to the general phenomenon of 'management' – management as *people*. Peter was the only person in this small organisation to occupy the formal role of manager. And we can see that his personal agenda, his personal values – what we might call his personal life strategy – is also an important factor in what goes on in this organisation. We will look at the 'strategic exchange' between Peter Brodie and his organisation when we meet him again in Chapter 5 (p. 127). In the next chapter, however, we will develop a more general process-relational way of understanding human beings that we can subsequently apply to their involvement in organisations and managerial work and to the *strategic exchanges* they make with the organisations that employ them.

Summary

In this chapter the following key points have been made:

- To go beyond the orthodoxy of *systems-control* thinking it is necessary to 'get inside the black box' of the organisation as a system. To do this we can focus on how things happen in practice when people come together to work in organisations. The *process-relational perspective* enables us to do this.

- Organisations can most usefully be seen, not as goal-seeking entities as in systems-control thinking, but as sets of ongoing human relationships, understandings and processes. Organisations involve the use of various technologies and people are employed within them to cooperate towards the completion of whatever work tasks are undertaken in the organisation's name.

- Organisations involve attempts to control human behaviours but this can only ever be partially achieved. What control is achieved has to be 'won' through processes of negotiation, persuasion and manipulation.

- Management can most usefully be seen as the overall shaping of relationships, understandings and processes which enables tasks to be completed in such a way that the organisation can go on existing into the future. This is the *functional* dimension of management. It is the essentially *strategic* dimension of organisational management. The term 'management' is also used, however, to refer to the processes and activities whereby this function is fulfilled. This is the action dimension of management. We can refer to it as 'managing'. And the third dimension is management as a *formal role* – the dimension whereby people designated as 'managers' typically (but not necessarily) carry out these activities.

- The three dimensions of 'management' – management as strategic direction, 'managing' and 'managers' – need to be distinguished from each other whenever we are analysing managerial processes in any organisation.

- It is necessary, when analysing processes of work management to look at the interplay between the *task* element of managerial work and the *social-status* aspects. These sometimes work together but often work against each other, with serious consequences for the achievement of productive cooperation.

- It is also necessary when analysing organisations to distinguish between the official blueprint (or formal organisational chart) and the *negotiated order* which emerges in practice as the formal and official aspects of organising work mix together with the informal and unofficial.

- Uncertainty and ambiguity are endemic in organisational life and one has to come to terms with both of these things, and with the fact that the human capacity for reasoning and making decisions is severely limited, if one is going to understand how managerial processes occur in 'real life' as opposed to 'in textbooks'.

- Studies of what managers actually do in 'real' organisations indicate that managers operate in a fragmented, conversation-based and apparently reactive way. They do not act, as we might expect, as cool, calculating and reflective planners who rationally decide what is to be done and then instruct others to do what is required.

- A *process-relational* analysis of this pattern of behaviour helps us see that there is a clear rationale behind this pattern of behaviour, at least in the case of managers who are 'effective' in their work. There is 'method' behind the apparent 'madness' of the typical managerial day, this involving negotiating, trading and exchanging with the great range of people upon whom the manager is *dependent*.

Reading

Reading Guides 1, 2, 4, 5 and 6 contain material that supports and takes further much of what is covered in Chapter 3.

People, identity and culture

Having read this chapter and completed its associated activites, readers should be able to:

- Recognise that to understand organisational and managerial processes we have to come to terms with the complex relationship between the human individual and his or her social and cultural context.

- Appreciate that orthodox approaches to organisations and management tend to apply a systems-control perspective to understanding human individuals, one which partly parallels that which is applied to organisations.

- Identify the ways in which we have to go beyond the systems-control way of looking at human beings in societies and organisations.

- Understand the advantages of viewing human 'individuality' as both *relational* (only existing in relation to others) and *emergent* (always in a process of 'becoming').

- See how an understanding of people and behaviour in the specific circumstances of modern work organisations needs to be rooted in a general awareness of 'what it is to be human'.

- Recognise how our individual 'humanness' cannot be understood without relating it to basic issues of how human beings manage their existence and how, as a species, they have developed *cultures* to help deal with these existential challenges.

- Understand how industrial capitalist forms of economy and society fit into this broader pattern of social patterning and how, in turn, modern work organisations and the occupation of management are elements of that type of political economy.

- Appreciate the importance of narratives and discourses in the patterning and functioning of human cultures and individual identities.

Individuals and organisations: beyond 'either or' thinking

It was argued in Chapter 1 that one of the biggest challenges of studying the organising and managing of work is that of doing justice to how individual human characteristics and actions, on the one hand, and social or structural patterns, on the other, both 'play their parts in social life'. The two aspects of human existence, the *individual* and the *structural* as they might simply be labelled, do not work separately but are 'inextricably intertwined'. It seemed that Sadie Rait in Cases and Conversations 1.3 had a strong intuitive appreciation of this and based her understanding of doing managerial work on her appreciation of the fact that the individual and the structural are not readily separable. She assumed that to influence the way work was carried out in her hospital ward she had to attend to individuals in a direct way ('chasing people up', as she put it) as well as making use of the closely connected structures and procedures ('rules, systems, procedures' and the rest). The other two managers we looked at in Cases and Conversations 1.1 and 1.2, Mark Merryton and Harry Carse, tended to focus on just one side of things. But how useful is it to make a distinction between these two 'things': individual matters on the one hand and social/organisational/structural matters on the other? Several different dualisms are in danger of getting mixed up in all of this, but they all come back to difficult questions about the relationship between:

● that part of each of us which we regard as our unique individuality and our freedom to make choices about our lives;

● that part of us which makes us a social animal, shaped and influenced by the groups and societies to which we belong.

These are complex matters – but one has to sort them out before one can effectively analyse any organisational or managerial process. Just because these issues are complicated, they cannot be ducked in the way traditional 'organisation behaviour' ducks them, with its tendency to divide its courses and texts so that matters at the individual level tend to be covered in one section (perception, motivation, learning, say), group factors in another section and structural issues in yet another. However, our considerations do need to be organised in some way and it is difficult to turn our backs completely on dualisms like the individual–structural one. It is related to a basic dualism that has occupied the minds of thinkers throughout history. This is the dualism which philosophers, and theologians (as well as many a public house debater) have typically conceived in terms of individual free will, on the one hand, and determinism on the other.

The ancient free will/determinism debate was carried over into the modern social sciences as they tackled questions such as whether human actions and behaviours derive from our individual characteristics and inclinations or are determined by 'society' or 'culture'. This is no abstract and esoteric debate of limited relevance to the study of work organisation and management. One of its crudest manifestations, for example, has been the discussion that one still hears about whether leaders are 'born or made'. Is it our individual characteristics, inherent in us as unique beings, that leads us to be good leaders, or is it something that can be developed in people through social processes like training and personal development? At a more sophisticated level, we might consider the extent to which how we behave in organisations, as individuals, is a matter of what each of us 'is like' as an individual and the extent to which our behaviour is determined by the rules or the 'culture' of that organisation.

To some extent, social scientists have moved away from a simple dichotomising of 'the individual and society' or 'nature and nurture'. Inevitably, there has been a trend towards seeing the two as influencing each other. It might be said, for example, that it is a particular mixture of individual characteristics and social experience that makes some people more effective leaders than others. Similarly, we might argue that the way people behave in a particular workplace is the outcome of an interplay between what they are 'like' as individuals and what the organisational structure, culture or managerial authority pushes them towards. To argue this way might seem like a simple solution to the problem. But it is only a start.

What we need to understand better, in any given organisational or social setting, is just how the interaction between the 'individual' and the 'social' operates – if indeed it is realistic even to separate the two. Some theorists see the interrelationship between human individuality and structural context as so intimately related that we should abandon even trying to separate them. The position taken here is clearly that there is an immensely strong relationship between our individual natures and our social involvements. In organisations, for example, the behaviours of organisational members cannot be understood separately from the organisational circumstances in which they are acting. But – by the same token – these 'organisational circumstances' (rules, structures, cultures and so on) cannot be understood in isolation from the human actors that make them and are otherwise caught up in them. Neither the 'organisational member' nor the 'organisation' itself, in the final analysis, exists separately from the other. Without an organisation there cannot be an organisational member (or employee) any more than there can be an organisation without any employees or other organisational members.

While it is accepted here, however, that human individuality and social or structural circumstances are so intimately related that, in practice, they each shade over into the other, it is felt worthwhile *analytically* to separate the two. This is equivalent to analysing a so-called 'black and white' photograph. In practice, few such photographs actually have any black or white in them (technically, they are 'grey-scale' images). However, it is *analytically useful* to have in our minds the concepts of 'black' and 'white' when we are studying how the image is made up – or 'works'. So it is when we study the organising and managing of work. No human act exists separately from the organisational context in which it occurs and no organisational circumstance exists separately from the human actions that occur with regard to it. But it is helpful to analyse organisational processes by treating human agency and organisational influences *as if*, for the moment of analysis, they were separate. The precise way in which they *come together as a singularity* can only be appreciated if we treat them

FIGURE 4.1 Descartes and the 'thinking self' as the ghost in the machine

analytically as a *duality* (a 'duality' being a pair of essentially inseparable things – 'two sides of the same coin' perhaps, whereas a 'dualism' implies the existence of two separable things – two coins).

These matters take us back to the important influence on western modernist thinking of René Descartes which we encountered earlier, first, when looking at the origins of modernist thinking and how it has shaped the way we think about work organisations (p. 137) and, second, when we looked at how organisations are, in a certain sense, socially constructed (p. 62). In this latter discussion we introduced the idea of *Cartesian dualism*, where the thinking mind, which to Descartes was the essence of the human individual ('I think therefore I am'), is seen as something separate from both the human body and the rest of the world 'outside' that mind. The essential being of each of us, in this view, is the *deus ex machina*, the ghost or spirit inside the machine of our physical frame (Figure 4.1).

The influence of Descartes' way of thinking about human beings has been enormous and has been at the heart of the orthodox psychology that has been widely applied to the study of people in work organisations. However, Cartesian dualism not only encourages us to go too far in separating the organisation as a relatively autonomous *entity* from its constituent members and from the world in which it exists. It also splits the human individual from their social world and their culture. It sees humans as relatively free-standing entities (forgetting

Donne's poetic reminder that 'no man is an island entire of it self'). This contrasts with the process-relational perspective, which sees a human's 'being' as in large part defined by his or her *relations* with others in the social world and as always in a *process* of 'becoming'. Before we develop this perspective, however, we need to note the ways in which the systems-control frame of reference is applied to human individuals in ways that parallel its applications to organisations. It is based on the either–or dualisms of modernist thinking.

The systems-control view of people – dualisms in action

The systems-control view of the individual in orthodox thinking about work and organisation sees the individual, in effect, as a little machine-like system in which goals or 'motives' operate as a motor 'powering' the human entity so that it *behaves* in a particular way. Like the systems-control notion of the organisation, the individual is an entity with 'goals' which converts inputs into outputs. Every human individual has built into it a set of needs, to which these goals or motives are related, and if opportunities are offered that might satisfy these needs, the individual is 'motivated' by the prospect of need satisfaction. Thus, need-satisfying *inputs* of food, water, or pleasure, say, (or cash with which to purchase these) are converted into *outputs* of need satisfaction for the individual and task completion for the employer. The employer, in effect, *fuels* the

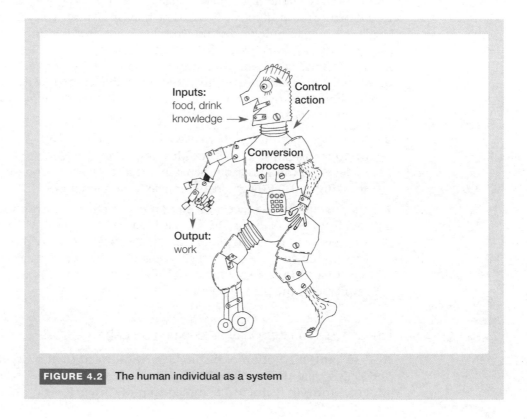

FIGURE 4.2 The human individual as a system

employee to get work done. To put it like this, of course, is to caricature the perspective, but such a caricature can be justified as a means of getting us critically to reflect on the assumptions which are so easily taken for granted in managerial thinking about people and work. We can visually caricature these assumptions, in fact, by applying to the individual, in Figure 4.2, a combination of elements from the two organisational systems pictures, the biological and a mechanical one, which we saw in Chapter 2 (p. 39 and p. 41).

 Link   An alternative way of understanding what is traditionally called 'motivation' in organisation behaviour will be developed in Chapter 9.

The notions of 'motive' and *motivation* are clearly central to this way of thinking about working human individuals and the concept of motivation is probably the one most remembered by people who have studied organisational behaviour. However, it is not the only psychological concept used in conventional organisation behaviour thinking. *Personality* is the key concept used to recognise differences between human individuals and other concepts like *perception*, *communication*, *attitudes* and *learning* are used to look at the way the individual-as-entity relates to the world around them. As was noted earlier (p. 30) different concepts can relate to the same word – 'communication', 'personality', 'learning' and so on are conceptualised in different ways at different times. Generally speaking, however, orthodox thinking about human individuals and work has conceptualised these facets of human existence in ways which stay close to the systems-control assumptions outlined so far. It also stays faithful to the Cartesian dualism that emphasises the separation between the individual, as an entity, and the individual's social existence.

The dualism inherent in orthodox modernist psychology – and in the systems-control perspective – works in two ways:

- It divides up human experience and splits human beings from their worlds by applying various dualisms. Most importantly, it splits the individual from society and thinking from behaving. It also makes strong divisions between speaking and acting and between reason and emotion.
- Having split these facets of human experience (treating useful analytical 'dualities' as 'dualisms', as we put it earlier) it typically treats the relationship between them in a *linear* manner. Hence, the individual first exists and then becomes social (or is 'socialised', as the jargon has it). And the individual first thinks (or 'plans' or 'makes a decision') and then acts (or implements the plan or decision).

Linearity and dualism in analysing human behaviour

At first sight, the notion of distinguishing between such processes as thinking and acting, and then looking at how one precedes the other seems wholly reasonable. Indeed, it might be argued that an intention or a plan precedes an action or a motive comes before an action, by definition. We start with a *reason* to behave. And we then behave. However, if we think more deeply about this, and apply *critical* common sense to it (Chapter 1, p. 20) we can see that things are not as simple as this in practice. Assumptions of *linearity* of this kind can be very misleading if we wish to understand human behaviour in a way that is actually helpful to us when confronting the 'realities' of human practice. Although it is true that we sometimes think carefully and make plans about what we are going to do before we act on a particular matter, it is equally often the case that we operate in a much more complex way. Regularly, in our every-day lives we 'find ourselves doing something' without actually identifying a motive or a reason for doing it.

Activity 4.1

Read the story of Grant Park leaving his desk to buy a cup of coffee in Cases and Conversations 4.1. Then

- try to remember something like this that you have done recently at home or at work (or something you *might* do, if you prefer). It needs to be a case of where you could be said simply to have 'found yourself' acting in a certain way;

- think about the relationship between your thoughts and your actions, and consider whether either one came before another or whether they were completely mixed up with each other;

- think about the rational aspects of your actions (where means are clearly chosen to meet specified ends) and the emotional dimension to the behaviour (where feelings came into the matter), and consider whether either was dominant or whether the two were jointly involved;

- consider in what ways your actions can be seen in 'individual' terms and in what ways they had a 'social' dimension – in the sense that either the behaviour itself or the thinking associated with it took into account your relationship, or possible relationship, with other people.

Grant Park gets thirsty, or does he? Cases and Conversations 4.1

Grant Park was sitting at his desk in the publishing company where he worked. He had been trying all day to finish a rather difficult management report that he had to do for Marjorie, the editorial executive. The report was already two days late. Grant had only been back from his lunch break for thirty minutes when he found himself wandering away from his desk in the middle of compiling a table of figures on book sales. He then found himself putting money in the vending machine down the corridor and pressing the button for a cup of his usual brew of white coffee with extra sugar. As he turned away from the coffee machine and looked down at the cup of muddy liquid which was burning his hand, he paused and asked himself, 'Just what am I doing here with yet another cup of this awful stuff?'. For a moment, he thought he heard Marjorie coming out of her office. He wondered just what he would say to her if she questioned his being away from his urgent task. Marjorie did not appear. But Scott found himself wondering what he would say to her. What indeed was he doing visiting the coffee machine at this time? He asked himself,

'Now, did I do this because I was thirsty?

No, I've been drinking coffee all morning.

It might just be a habit I've got into.

Or, then again, it might be because I was hoping to come across that bloke from management accounts I need to speak to.

But perhaps it was to reward myself for having written two whole pages.

On the other hand, it could have been to cheer myself up for having written so little in four hours.'

What Grant Park is doing, in envisaging being asked to explain his actions, is trying to *attach a motive* to his behaviour *post hoc* – after the event. The action has preceded the motive, goal or purpose, we might say. This is not to say, however, there were absolutely no reasons or motives behind his actions, even if he can't remember them subsequently. In practice, then, thinking and acting are often muddled up, and not only does this lead us to question the thinking/acting Cartesian dualism, it also makes us aware of the inadequacy of the rationality/emotion dualism. In the processes, whatever they were, that involved a walk from the desk to the coffee machine, there were clearly emotions at work just as much as analytical reasoning (implicit in the notion of reward and, even more so, in the notion of cheering oneself up). But a further dualism also has to be abandoned if we are to understand what is going on here – that of the 'individual' and the 'social'. The issue of why the desk was left only arose because Grant contemplated how he might explain himself to someone else. Thus *motives* in human behaviour – things that at first would seem to be very individual matters – are actually *social* or *relational*. Their logic is as much one of making an act seem sensible to another person (real or imagined) as it is a logic of behavioural causality.

To make this point about the social aspects of individual motives even more forcefully, we might say that the 'motive' in a murder case is as much, or more, a social matter (something to be established by police and in a court of law) as it is a cause or a straightforward 'reason for' the murder having occurred. Although we all take for granted that crimes have 'motives', just think for a moment about any murder that you might have read about in detail at some time. Then ask yourself if it was really likely in that case that there was a 'motive' acting as a single 'mainspring of action'. Although our society and culture would tend to demand that such a 'cause' be identified for such a horrid event and put in the public records, it is difficult to believe that things could normally be that simple or that 'mono-causal'.

We are therefore better placed to come to terms with the complexities of how thinking and planning (cognitive aspects of human functioning), on the one hand, and acting or doing on the other relate to each other if we move away from anything resembling simple cause–effect sequences. There is a multiplicity of motives and goals relating to any given human act, whether it be going to buy some coffee at work or murdering someone. Also, the cognitive and action aspects of behaviour tend to work in a process where we think, act, think, act, think act in a complex and iterative way – with the process potentially starting with *either* a thought or an act. This *processual* way of looking at thoughts and behaviours is contrasted with the typically modernist *linear* way in Figure 4.3.

At its simplest, this means that human beings are typically thinking about or planning their activities as part of the same process of actively dealing with the world. We think as we act, we act as we think. Sometimes managers give emphasis to the thinking side of things before they act ('shall I go to visit customers today or shall I stay in the office?'). And sometimes they prioritise actions ('I just had to deal with the letters, e-mails, phone calls, knocks on the office door

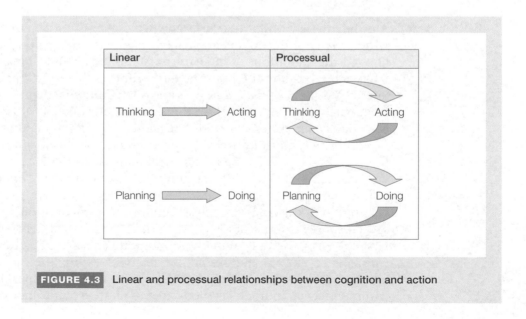

FIGURE 4.3   Linear and processual relationships between cognition and action

that *came at me* through the working day'), reflecting or 'thinking' after these events just what might have been achieved ('have I wasted my time today or have I helped move the business forward?'). These latter thoughts, which might pass through a manager's mind as he or she drives home at night, could be thought of as the manager identifying the 'goals' or 'objectives' which they can attach to what we did that day – to make sense of that day.

We have illustrated these rather basic matters about human behaviour and social activity with fairly simple and relatively individualistic behaviours. But the insights that we are trying to crystallise with Figure 4.3 are ones that are relevant at other levels of analysing work and its organisation. It is highly relevant to assumptions we tend to make about many areas of our personal lives and about how decision-making and strategy-making occurs in organisations.

Link

The processual way of looking at how thinking/planning relates to action and behaviour helps us understand

← the patterns of managerial behaviour looked at in Chapter 3, pp. 84–91.

→ Processes of strategy-making in Chapter 6, pp. 189–91.

→ Processes of decision-making in Chapter 10, pp. 338–41.

There is one more very important dualism that we have to consider before we move towards setting out a frame of reference that is less 'either–or' than typical modernist ways of thinking about human beings and their social existence. This is the separation that is made between what we think and what we say (or write) – the separating of *language* and *action*.

Language and action

A different view of *language* and how we use it is fundamental to the way in which many philosophers and social scientists are encouraging us to move beyond the limitations of modernist assumptions about human behaviour. In what is often called the *linguistic turn*, thinkers like Austin and Wittgenstein questioned the idea that what we say is something that can be separated either from what we think or what we do (see Reading Guide 3). It is normal, within everyday common-sense thinking (Chapter 1, p. 20), to assume that when we say or write something we are reporting what is 'in our heads'. We have a thought, in the privacy of our individual mind, so to speak, and then we express or 'externalise' it. The only exception to this normal way of communicating that we recognise is the lie – a deliberate attempt to deceive people. However, if we apply critical common-sense thinking to the common assumption that speech simply externalises what is 'in the head', we will recognise two things. First, we recognise that thinking cannot happen separately from language-use (speaking or writing) and, second, we realise that thinking should not be separated off as something which either precedes or follows speaking. Speech (or writing) is action in itself. Let's look at each of these points in turn.

First, let us deal with the argument that thoughts cannot precede language. We need words as concepts to form our thoughts in the first place. We cannot think, 'I shall go and serve that customer' without the concepts or linguistic devices of 'go', 'serve' and 'customer'. In a sense, then, we are already talking when we are thinking – talking to ourselves in a sense. This means that no thought is totally personal, private or 'individualistic' – it has to use concepts taken from the culture or 'language community' to which the thinker belongs. Not only this, but we must also recognise that one is not only 'talking to one-self' when this thinking occurs. In a sense, all thinking is *relational* – one is rehearsing what one might say, or has said previously, to another person. Sometimes this happens more clearly than at other times and the thinking process in which Grant Park engaged is a clear example of how one can, in effect, enter a dialogue with oneself *in one's head.* In this case Grant is prompted by the prospect of a particular person, Marjorie, arriving on the scene. But he might have considered other people, too, and imagined having dialogues with them. Grant might well move on from thinking what he might say to Marjorie to imagine himself mentally 'debating' with the writer of the article in a magazine he read about how too much coffee can be harmful. We might also imagine him 'arguing' with a colleague who recently accused him of being incapable of concentrating for long on a work task. We might even picture him 'disputing' in his mind with his mother about her suspicion that Grant is becoming addicted to coffee. Thought, then, is very much a social, relational and indeed *rhetorical* matter (Billig, 1987, Reading Guide 3). Arguments are set one against another as we engage with the world mentally; the decisions that emerge from any thinking process have to be understood as having this social or *relational* nature.

Activity 4.2

Reread the story of Grant Park and his coffee drinking activities (Cases and Conversations 4.1). Envisage him continuing to ponder upon why he has left his desk yet again to visit the coffee machine, and try to imagine other people he might 'bring to mind' and what they might 'say' to him and what he might 'say' to them in his thoughts.

Second, we have to abandon the Cartesian dualism between *speech* and *action.* At the heart of the *linguistic turn* in philosophy was the recognition that *speech is action.* When we speak to someone we are *acting with regard* to that other person, not simply reporting our thoughts to them. This was always understood with respect to some speech acts like attempts to persuade or command someone to do something. What we need to recognise is that all communication has this dimension to it, even where it is not immediately obvious. No speech act is a simple 'reporting' of what is in the speaker's mind or a simple 'description' of what they have seen or done. We can turn to philosophers like Austin (1962, Reading Guide 3) to tell us that language is action or to social scientists like

Goffman (1958, Reading Guide 3) to point out that all communication involves a 'presentation of self' dimension ('how will I be regarded if I speak this way rather than that?'). But the application of critical common sense will remind us that we learned this kind of thing for ourselves when we were children. In fact, we all learn early in life that when people speak they are not straightforwardly describing what is the case, or straightforwardly reporting the world. When a parent tells us something so seemingly straightforward as, 'It is warm outside – the sun is shining', we put these words in context and think to ourselves 'Aha, I wonder if it is really warm enough for me? Could it be that my father is trying to get me to get out of the house?'. We all operate in this way when we listen to people. 'She would say that, wouldn't she?', we think to ourselves when some-one tells us that they are the best qualified person in the office to undertake a certain job. In ordinary life we put into context whatever we hear, endlessly applying the proverbial 'pinch of salt' to what people say.

In spite of our all having this very commonsensical understanding that when people speak to us they are 'acting towards us', it is often suspended when we do social science research, engage in market research surveys or try to interpret employee questionnaires. Typically, when we carry out surveys or get people to complete psychological questionnaires, we take what they say as if were 'the case'. We take it that if 70 per cent of people tick a box to indicate that they enjoy their work, then it is the case that this proportion of people take pleasure in what they do at work. Little thought is given to the possibility that, for some reason, some of these people might have decided that this would be a 'good' or an impressive thing to say, or that they might be attempting to persuade the sponsor of the investigation that this is so (or persuade themselves, for that matter). Why do so many of us become dopes in this way once we move into an allegedly 'scientific' type of activity? Why do we suspend our critical faculties?

A possible answer to this question is that people tend to hope, against their better judgement, that these seemingly scientific procedures can produce a degree of certainty about other human beings that, in normal everyday life, we know to be impossible. This parallels the hope for certainty, predictability and control that probably lies behind the faith that many managers have in organisa-tional or managerial 'systems' – a faith connected with the systems-control orthodoxy or, indeed, to managism (see above, p. 53). They aspire to manage-ment becoming a science or at least, a systematic activity similar to engineering. In our ordinary lives we are well aware, in the words of Mark Merryton (in Cases and Conversations 1.1), that trying to manage or control people is like trying to herd cats. But such are the pressures on many people in managerial work to achieve the near impossible, that it is comforting to take up a faith in the various sorts of quasi-scientific devices that involve asking people questions and then assuming that their answers 'reveal' the attitudes or beliefs that exist 'inside their heads'. It becomes too easy to forget that what people say in any situation is an act taking place within a social and cultural process. We need to remember that what people say or write cannot be interpreted without regard to those processes and the relationships between the people involved in that situation. Statements must never be 'taken out of context', we might say. This pushes us towards adopting a process-relational perspective for looking at people and organisations.

A process-relational view of people, work and organisations

It is now possible to outline a broad process-relational perspective for applying to the more individual side of the individual/structural duality (duality not dualism!). Table 4.1 sets out its main features, alongside the systems-control orthodoxy that it tries to go beyond.

TABLE 4.1 Systems-control and process-relational views of the human individual	
The systems-control view of individuals	**The process-relational view of individuals**
The individual is a more-or-less fixed entity with a given *personality*	The individual is always in a process of becoming with an *identity* which is always 'emergent', never finalised
People *perceive* the world which is external to them and cognitively process the *data* which this perception 'inputs' to the brain to enable a *decision* to be made about how to behave	People *enact* the world. In the light of the *language* and understandings of their *culture*, the individual actively *makes sense* of the *ambiguous* world of which they are a part, and then acts in the light of these *interpretations*
Behaviour occurs, in the light of data gathered, as the individual is *motivated* to fulfil *needs and wants*	Actions take place, in the light of interpretations made about the world, to *enact* whatever *projects* individuals are undertaking *strategically* to *shape their lives* and to manage *existential challenges*
Knowledge and information which people hold as data about the world can be acquired from others or communicated to others	Knowledge and understandings about the world are negotiated as people work together at sense-making about the world – with some people being more influential than others in establishing 'how things are'
Learning involves acquiring knowledge or skills through experience and acquisition of knowledge from others	Learning is a process of changing – through experience, dialogues and 'negotiation of realities' with others – understandings of how the world 'works' and how one can skilfully operate within that world
Individuals acquire *attitudes* towards various aspects of the world as they are influenced by other people in society to be predisposed to act in certain ways with regard to those aspects of the world	Individuals have continuously *emergent orientations* towards various aspects of the world, these shifting as individuals come to terms with changing situations and make sense of them in the light of their life-shaping and situational projects and in light of the *discourses* and *linguistic resources* available to them in the culture
Remembering involves *recalling* information from the memory – where it was recorded when the individual acquired it from direct experience or communication by others	Remembering involves *reconstructing* experiences or knowledge in the light of current circumstances and the *narratives* about the world which are available in the culture with which the individual engages
Individuals have both *emotions* and a capacity to reason; they are capable of putting emotions to one side to enable rational analysis and decision-making to occur unaffected by feelings and values	Rationality and *emotion* are simultaneously involved in all thought and action; rational analysis and decision-making cannot occur unaffected by feelings and values – but *reflective reasoning* is possible which takes into account that feelings and values are part of it

It could be argued that what are outlined in Table 4.1 are simply two ways of talking about human psychology. This is true in part. There are words in the process-relational column like 'sense-making', 'enactment', 'orientation' and 'narrative' that do not play a part in systems-control language. And some of the terms that are widely used in orthodox psychological language, especially 'personality', 'attitude' and 'motivation', do not play a part in the process-relational way of speaking about human beings and their behaviour. In other cases, similar words are used, but they have undergone a conceptual shift – with 'memory' or 'reason and emotion' being spoken of in different ways across the two 'languages'. While it is reasonable to talk of these two perspectives as two languages, it would nevertheless be profoundly wrong to suggest that they are *merely* two languages – just two ways of talking about the same thing. To take such a line would be to ignore the fundamental point that language – how we talk and write about the world – cannot be separated from what we *do* in the world in this way.

To conceptualise the world in different ways is to *frame it* in different ways – to position ourselves with regard to it differently. Such a connection between the way we 'frame' the world and how we act within it has been central to this book from the very first pages, when we looked at three people's ways of 'framing management'. These frames of reference had clear implications for how the work would be approached in practice. Mark, Harry and Sadie in Cases and Conversations 1.1, 1.2, and 1.3 saw managerial work differently, and did that work differently. Managers who adopt a systems-control frame of reference and think about their staff as people who are motivated by certain needs which they bring to the workplace are likely to develop a particular understanding of those people when considering how to influence their behaviours. However, managers who work with a process-relational view of their staff are likely to take into account the more subtle aspects of their staff and, hence be better placed to influence employee behaviour. Their greater awareness of how each individual has their own identity, emotions and personal projects inside and outside of work makes them better placed when it comes to influencing staff behaviour. Also, they are more likely to recognise the extent to which people change, as their life circumstances change. And they will be more aware of the extent to which understandings and behaviours are things to be negotiated within the employment relationship, as opposed to matters imposed by a system or by managerial command.

The process-relational view of human individuals suggests that the most helpful way for us to understand our fellow human beings is as

- *emergent*: people's identity is always in the process of becoming; the person is not a fixed entity with an 'essence' and a given 'personality'; they are continually adjusting to the world and learning;
- *social*: a person's distinct individuality is only possible through their relating to others ('I am only me and you are only you because you see me as me and I see you as you', we might say);
- *strategic* and *situationally sensitive*: people always act with regard to their specific context, given their broader projects in life and what they currently regard their identity to be;

- *exchanging*: people's physical and their psychological survival both depend upon give-and-take exchanges with others; they exchange meaning-giving and emotional resources as well as material goods or necessities;

- *rational and emotional*: people's reasoning capacities and their feelings mutually influence each other in everything they do; to relate to others and to influence others they must take into account the feelings of others as well as their rationality;

- *culturally, linguistically and discursively located*: people are both enabled and constrained by the cultural and discursive resources available to them; they can only deal with what they can speak of as they struggle to come to terms with the potentially disabling ambiguities of existence; cultures (which individuals both take from and contribute to) contain discourses and narratives which provide resources to be used in sense-making about both self and the world;

- *story users*: they tell and listen to narratives about people and the world as a primary way of coming to terms with the world.

Identity	Concept

Identity is a notion of who a particular person is – in relation to others. It defines in what ways the individual is like other people and in what ways they differ from other people. It has a *self-identity* component (the individual's own notion of self) and a *social-identity* component (the notion others have of who the person is).

The view of the human being that is emerging from all of this is one of someone who has to 'work at' their identity and their material survival throughout their lives. A person has continually to make adjustments in their thinking and their actions as they come to terms with the changing circumstances of their existence. They can be seen as *strategic* because they must actively shape their lives, their identities and their biographies. Survival depends on this. Without making arrangements to take care of their physical needs they would die. And without developing an identity – some consistent sense of who they are, where they have come from and where they might be going – they would lose their sanity. And this would displace them from 'society'. A sane person is someone who has sufficient consistency of 'self' to enable them to relate to other people and for other people to relate to them. Identity is simultaneously individual and social. The person has their own notion of who they are – their *self-identity* – and they are identified by others through the attribution of a *social-identity*. However, these are really two parts of the same thing (a 'duality' as opposed to a 'dualism', as we put it earlier). You can only hold a concept of 'who you are' in the light of how other people act towards you. And who others 'take you to be' will be influenced by how you present yourself to them.

Orthodox psychology deals with the issue of each human being having certain consistencies or an 'existential integrity' with the concept of *personality*. This is something which is typically treated as a 'given', as fairly fixed and even as measurable. Process-relational thinking also gives recognition to the notion of a consistency and an integrity to each individual's 'being' (as they see themselves and others see them). However, it treats this as something that is 'worked at' or 'achieved' rather than given, and as something liable to change over time as the person shapes and re-shapes themselves in changing circumstances of age and circumstance. And this does not deny a role to genetic make-up or the nature of one's 'given' body. One may inherit a range of characteristics, from a tendency to depression, say, to a very tall stature, or a black skin. But these will not *determine* who one is. A self-identity and a social-identity will still have to be negotiated with the others to whom one relates in life and to the material and emotional exchanges one makes with others both in one's private and working lives. Those processes of negotiation and exchange will take into account an individual's propensity to be depressively ill from time to time, say, or they will deal with the fact that someone is much taller than everyone else in the office where they work, or they will assist with handling the pressures of being one of the few black managers in an organisation.

Activity 4.3

Read what Colin Darnaway says in Cases and Conversations 4.2 about his 'fragility' and some of his life experiences:

- Consider how this relates to the notion of one's identity being something which is not fixed.

- Consider the relationship between Colin's two aspects: his *self-identity* and his *social-identity*.

- Try to think of situations in your own life when you found your sense of 'who you are' threatened by something which happened to you.

- Try to think of situations in your own life when you found your sense of 'who you are' being enhanced by something which happened to you.

Colin's ups and downs

Cases and Conversations 4.2

When I was told out of the blue just before Christmas that the company I had been with for ten years was going to make me redundant I took the experience very badly. To come to terms with what was happening to me I found myself looking back to some experiences I had when I was quite young.

When I was about twelve my parents moved house and I had to go to a school which was completely different from the one I had previously attended. In the first school I was top of the class and the teachers used to point to me as an example to other kids. I liked this. It made me feel good. It was almost too good to be true, with the teachers, the other pupils and my parents all reinforcing my idea of myself as somebody a bit special. I came to earth with a crash when I arrived at the other school. There were other kids cleverer than me and I was rather looked down upon. This bothered me a lot. I began to feel like a stupid person. This got so bad that one day when we were doing mental arithmetic in class I found that I couldn't even answer the simple questions. I was laughed at by the class and by the teacher. I went home that night humiliated. And for months after that I was simply a different person from what I had been before we moved. The bright and lively kid was now

the dull and stupid kid. But my parents were very good about this and they kept pointing out that, to them, I was the same person I had had always been. They persuaded me that I should think of myself the way they did, and the way my grandparents did. I suppose that they persuaded me to 'believe in myself', whatever others tried to make out about me.

So this was something that went through my mind a lot when I lost my job. My company, who had always rated me very highly, had now decided that I was surplus to requirements. I took this to mean that I was useless. It certainly reminded me of those experiences at school. 'Pride before a fall', perhaps. But I also realised that I had to come to terms with this personal 'fragility' which seemed to be part of my life. I had thought about this a lot when I was in my final year at school and I was beginning to go out with girls. I remember so clearly an occasion when I made a date with a girl who I thought was the most magical creature I had ever seen. For a whole week before the Saturday night I was to go out with her I was on top of the world. I felt tall, handsome – the epitome of male desirability. But when Saturday night came I not only tripped over and spilled beer down my new shirt within minutes of meeting the girl, I later got my face slapped by her when I tried to kiss her as we were queuing to get into a club. I tell you, I never felt so small and useless in my life. The next day I couldn't even get out of bed. For months I was, as my friends kept saying, 'a different person'.

I know all this sounds a bit pathetic, but I don't think I am desperately more fragile than other people I know. I got over the late teens uselessness like I had got over the early school experience. At that time I got support from my family and a couple of good mates at school. And with this redundancy thing I realised that I had to re-invent myself yet again. At first my wife was very strange with me and, let me tell you, if this had continued I would have been finished. If she had followed through the threat to leave me, which she made at one point, I would definitely have become a pisshead – a useless unemployed drunk. But I persuaded myself that I was really still the person I had thought myself to be. I made sure that I presented myself to potential employers as a really good worker whose previous employer had been foolish enough to let go. This wasn't easy. But here I am now. I have got an even better job. They've given me a company car, after only six months with them. I am a successful man. I have a great marriage. That's who I am now.

In looking at how there are 'ups and downs' in Colin's self-identity, we can see situations in which the identity he is 'given' by others influences his self-identity (his teachers at one school 'building him up', the teachers at another, 'taking him down' for example). At other times, we see his self-identity influencing the social-identity he persuades others to attach to him (the way he negatively presents himself to the girlfriend, for instance, or the positive way he 'presents himself' to later employers). But, in spite of the fact that Colin is implying that he is one person at certain times of his life and another person at another, we should not treat this as denying any consistency of 'self' over his biography. While it is wise to move away from the orthodox psychological notion of a fixed personality, we still need to recognise that there is something of the 'same Colin' running through his biography. This partly comes from matters external to him – the body he is born with and the parents he is born to for example. But it is also something that he achieves by the way he *strategically* shapes his own life and his sense of self. The very act of speaking about his post-redundancy reflections is part of this shaping. He is both telling us and telling himself 'who he is'.

 Link   The 'emergent' aspects of people's lives is especially relevant to understanding their orientations to work – a key concept in both Chapter 5 and Chapter 9.

Coming to terms with the shifting or *emergent* nature of identity is vital to the understanding of work and managerial behaviour. However, some of the key features of the process-relational perspective on human beings and their behaviour still need more explanation. Most important here is what was referred to in Table 4.1 as the shaping of lives to 'manage existential challenges' and, subsequently, as the 'struggle to come to terms with the potentially disabling ambiguities of existence' (p. 105). It is only by recognising the importance of this fundamental aspect of the human predicament that we can appreciate the role in our lives of *culture*, *discourse* and *narrative*. And these are immensely important because they provide vital resources which enable people to cope at work and with every other aspect of their existence.

Individuals, societies and the role of culture in the managing of human existence

Our main concern in *Organising and Managing Work* is with the management of work and, as has been emphasised from the beginning, the activities of those formally designated as 'managers' are just one part of this. But managing work is itself part of something even more fundamental – the managing of human existence. It could be argued that a book such as this one should not engage with such deep matters and should confine its attention to processes of work behaviour and management. But this is not possible. The processes by which work tasks are managed in human societies cannot be understood separately from the processes by which we manage our human existence – processes of which work organising and managing are a part. When we are at work we are doing much more than just doing work tasks. We are also 'working at' or 'managing' our basic humanity. Managing life and managing work are inextricably connected. We cannot properly understand one without understanding the other, and we cannot understand either without an appreciation of where humans differ from other animals. Here, culture, discourse and narrative have a vital importance.

What separated the human species *homo sapiens* from other animals, as its uniquely large brain evolved, was its capacity for language. Accompanying this, as an eminent anthropologist put it, was the 'possibility of making value judgements and exercising moral choices' (Leach, 1982, p. 104, Reading Guide 3). Humans now had the capacity rationally to analyse the situations they found themselves in and to choose how to act in those situations. But humans did not lose their instincts. Whereas other animals continued to be more-or-less completely driven by their instincts (patterns of behaviour being 'wired into their brains', so to speak) humans found themselves facing choices about how those instincts would be channelled, directed or suppressed. As humans evolved they found themselves confronting the fact that what they should eat, for example, how and when they should eat, with whom they should eat, and so on, was a matter of choice. Once this possibility of discrimination and choice was recognised, it became inescapable. What also became inescapable was the potentially high level of *angst* that arose from the terrifying recognition that everyone is going to die. Such a realisation was only possible once there was language and the capacity to conceptualise such matters. Thinkers at various times in human history have marked the start of human culture (or religion, or art, or philosophy) as the point at which humans first confronted the ultimate existential angst: anxiety about their own mortality. This, together with the challenge of the potentially vast range of value choices confronting the human individual, had to be handled socially. The choice-making dilemma and the fear of mortality had arisen in the first place along with the essentially social phenomenon of language.

Human beings' capacity for language and their highly social nature were intimately tied up with each other from the start. For reasons varying from the way they acquired and processed food to the fact of the immense and long-lasting vulnerability of their babies and small children, human beings were dependent on each other and had to develop patterns of exchange between them. These exchanges might be simple ones of task responsibility: 'You make a bonfire, I'll cook dinner'. They might be straightforward barters: 'You give me an axe head, I'll give you a necklace'. Or they might be matters of complex commitments: 'You join our community and we'll protect you from marauders' or 'You live and sleep only with me and I'll live and sleep only with you' or 'You be an obedient child and I'll be a gentle parent'.

To manage these patterns of *reciprocity* – of give and take exchanges – which brought human societies into existence, there had to be shared understandings of what should and should not happen, what was right and what was wrong. Rules and moralities are at the heart of the sets of shared understandings and meanings that we conceptualise as human *culture*.

Culture

The set of meanings shared by members of a human grouping which defines what is good and bad, right and wrong and consequently defines the appropriate ways for members of that group to think and behave.

Without culture, each human being would be left without guidance on how to handle the choices that occur at every moment of one's waking existence (when to get up, what to wear, what to say to one's lover …). Without culture, we would simply go mad. Without guidance on choices ranging from when we should get out of bed to whom we might marry or how we should bury our dead, we would spin into a state of ontological chaos – a very breakdown of 'being'. Without help in making sense of what the obligations are between man and woman or parent and child, without help in making sense of our bodies and our sexuality, without help in making sense of sickness, pain and death, we would become psychologically overwhelmed and collapse. We cannot handle such matters on our own. Our species therefore worked, and continues to work, to construct cultural resources to assist us. Culture provides a degree of order (*nomos*) instead of *chaos*, predictability instead of crippling ambiguity, sanity instead of madness. It guides us on how to balance instinct and social commitment, to balance rationality and emotion and to balance our sense of a unique self and our sense of membership of society.

Activity 4.4

Make a list of the instincts that human beings have – drives that come from the animal aspects of our existence.

For each of these instincts, think of the ways in which 'culture' plays a part in their expression, satisfaction or suppression.

As humans, we do not swoop on the first piece of edible material we see when we feel pangs of hunger. Neither do we leap upon the first body we see when we feel a desire to mate. Culture has to be 'referred to' in every case. Even when the human being finds themselves facing a wild beast or a human enemy threatening to kill them, they are likely to think – however fleetingly – of cultural notions like courage or cowardice, before fighting or fleeing.

If human evolution and the invention of culture by human beings had straightforwardly developed along the lines we have suggested here, human social existence would be a warm and comforting experience with a high level of social reciprocity giving a life of mutual and universal love and care. It has not worked out like that, however. The cruelties and unhappinesses we see occurring every day in our homes, streets, workplaces and across the globe testify to this.

But might it have turned out differently? We do not know. But it seems likely that if complete mutuality and reciprocity had been achieved at any stage in human evolution, then social and economic development would have ceased at that point. It is hard to imagine a society with any dynamic aspect whatsoever that did not contain human rivalries, conflicts and a determination for some to have more than an equal share of whatever goods were currently scarce and socially desired. It is likely that, from the start, human cultures were developed both to encourage human assertiveness and competitive acquisition and to keep it under a degree of control to prevent what the philosopher Thomas Hobbes called 'a war of all against all'. Yet from as far back as we can know from the historical and the archaeological record, humans have mobilised themselves into coalitions of interest and engaged in *social closure* practices.

Social closure	Concept
The process whereby a group seeks to gain or defend its advantage over other groups by closing its ranks to those it defines as outsiders.	

All societies have their own patterns of inequality and divisions into groups, factions, elites, tribes, classes, races and the like. And conflict and competition has occurred in every social order, both between and within these groupings, for scarce and desired resources.

Much of what we have established so far is represented in Figure 4.4, this being a rather audacious attempt to pull together a lot of social science thinking in a single diagram. It is not an attempt at grand social theory however. It is, rather, an attempt to outline the theoretical thinking that has informed the writing of *Organising and Managing Work*. It is a conceptual scheme using the rather crude devices of overlapping circles (or 'ellipses', to be accurate) and double-ended arrows to emphasise that the *individual* aspects of human existence must be seen as intimately related to the *structural* aspects. It takes as its starting point the fundamental human problem of having to manage existential dilemmas. The structural aspects of how these are handled are identified in the 'societal' and the 'organisational' ellipses in the figure and these are seen as mediated by the *industrial capitalist* patterning of contemporary societies and the institution of employment (p. 60). The more individual aspects of the 'individual–structural duality' are covered in the ellipses labelled 'the individual' and 'managers'. The issue of managers' identities and self-shaping identified in the 'managers' ellipse are to be discussed in Chapter 5 and the organisational exchange processes identified in the 'organisations' ellipse will be central to the concerns of Chapter 6. What remains for us to clarify at this stage is the reference in the 'individual' circle to there being a 'dialogue between self, others and culture' which utilises 'narratives and discursive resources' and the reference in the 'societal' circle to 'discourses which contribute to and emerge from socially constructed realities'.

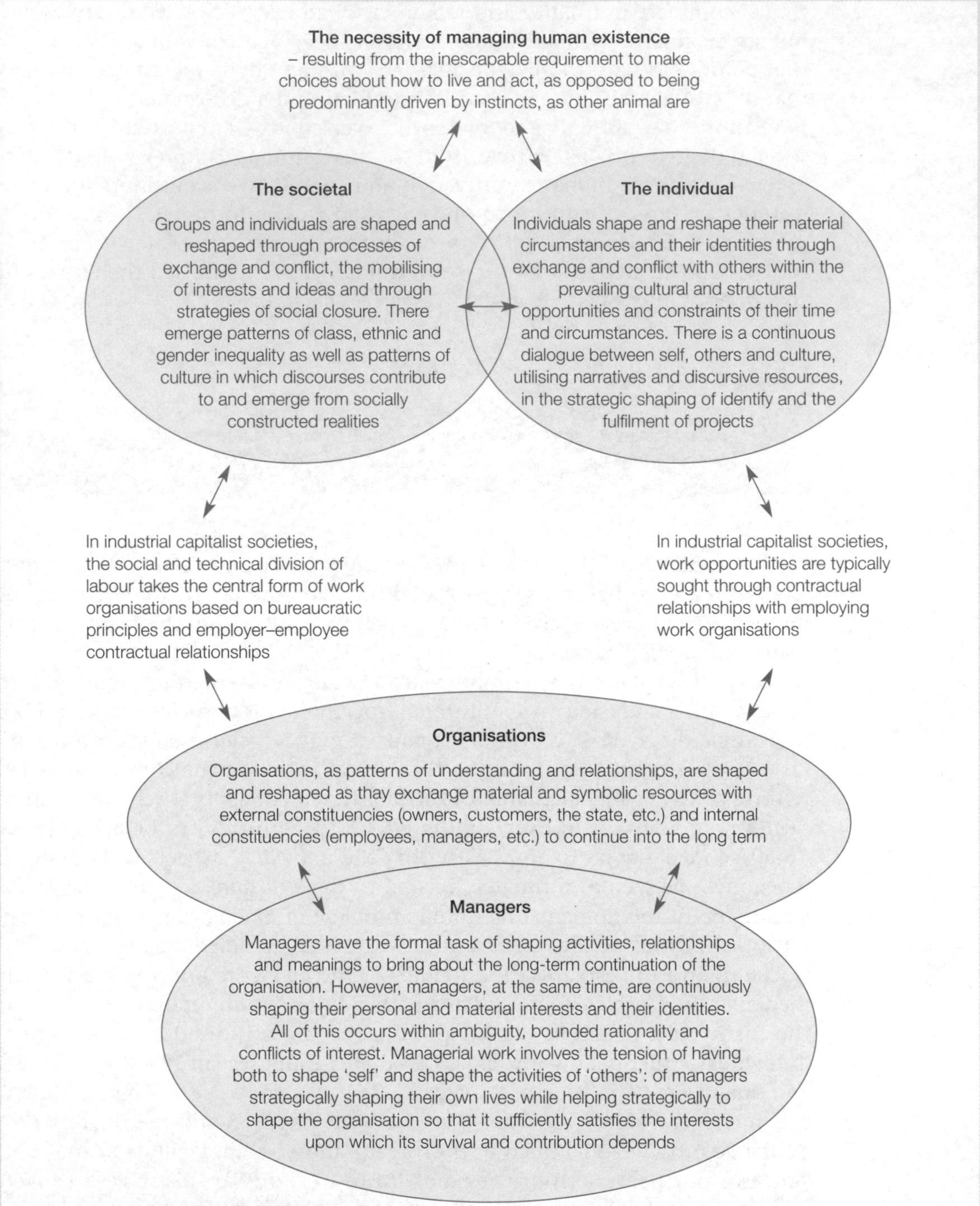

The necessity of managing human existence
– resulting from the inescapable requirement to make choices about how to live and act, as opposed to being predominantly driven by instincts, as other animal are

The societal

Groups and individuals are shaped and reshaped through processes of exchange and conflict, the mobilising of interests and ideas and through strategies of social closure. There emerge patterns of class, ethnic and gender inequality as well as patterns of culture in which discourses contribute to and emerge from socially constructed realities

The individual

Individuals shape and reshape their material circumstances and their identities through exchange and conflict with others within the prevailing cultural and structural opportunities and constraints of their time and circumstances. There is a continuous dialogue between self, others and culture, utilising narratives and discursive resources, in the strategic shaping of identify and the fulfilment of projects

In industrial capitalist societies, the social and technical division of labour takes the central form of work organisations based on bureaucratic principles and employer–employee contractual relationships

In industrial capitalist societies, work opportunities are typically sought through contractual relationships with employing work organisations

Organisations

Organisations, as patterns of understanding and relationships, are shaped and reshaped as thay exchange material and symbolic resources with external constituencies (owners, customers, the state, etc.) and internal constituencies (employees, managers, etc.) to continue into the long term

Managers

Managers have the formal task of shaping activities, relationships and meanings to bring about the long-term continuation of the organisation. However, managers, at the same time, are continuously shaping their personal and material interests and their identities. All of this occurs within ambiguity, bounded rationality and conflicts of interest. Managerial work involves the tension of having both to shape 'self' and shape the activities of 'others': of managers strategically shaping their own lives while helping strategically to shape the organisation so that it sufficiently satisfies the interests upon which its survival and contribution depends

FIGURE 4.4 Organisations and managers in their societal and human-existential context

Narratives and stories in culture and identity-management

The challenges that face us as human beings as we develop our identities and come to terms with what we ought or ought not to do in our lives are almost infinite. But if we tried to reflect deeply on everything we do and to agonise over every choice facing us – from how to cut our hair and what clothes to wear, to how to treat our families or other people at work – we would go crazy. To give too much thought to the risks we take every time we cross the road or to dwell too long on how we will eventually die could drive us to distraction. How do we cope with all of this then? In part, we cope through our direct relationships with people around us. As children, for example, a lot of help and guidance comes directly from our parents and teachers. But this is not enough.

The resources of meaning that are needed for each of us to work out who we are, where we are going and how we are to handle the normal fears of human existence are far too great for them to be supplied by our families or close associates. The guidance, comes, instead, from a vast range of 'others' who exist in the culture of the society in which we live – albeit guidance that is mediated by those to whom we directly relate. We tend to know about these cultural 'others' from the stories we hear, see and read about. We constantly make reference, throughout our lives to 'cultural others' – people who may be living or dead, 'real' or fictional. We exchange with the culture we live in by listening to and telling stories.

Narratives and stories   *Concept*

Narratives are accounts of the world which follow a basic form of 'this, then that, then that' and which, when applied to human affairs, typically take on a more developed *story*-like form involving characters with interests, motives, emotions and moralities.

How the world 'is' is not a given. We have to 'make up' our understanding of it. Hence, we learn about it, and teach others about it, to a large extent through narratives. From the stories our parents tell us about their past or what they have been doing at work to the fairy tales they tell us and the stories we read in comics or see on television, we find resources to use in working out who we are and how we might live our lives. This goes on throughout our lives as we engage with gossip at work, read murder stories in novels and newspapers, watch soap operas on television or read case studies and tales of business heroes in management books.

This process of working out our identities and how we are going to act in the world through engagement with the 'cast of thousands' who inhabit the cultures we relate to is only partly a conscious one. We 'use' stories as an alternative to engaging in the sort of continual and exhausting rational decision-making which would undermine our sanity. To be a cultural being is to be a user of stories – someone who comes to terms with the world by listening to and telling stories. The clearest example of the non-conscious functioning of stories in our lives is the role they play in dealing with our fear of death. Most of us, most of the time, do not consciously worry about death. But this has not been handled by the evolving human species managing to 'forget' about mortality – quite the opposite in fact. In modern societies, most of us confront death several times a day, albeit through stories. Our engagement with 'the news' is typically an engagement with death and agony as is much of our novel reading and film watching. Stories give us a way of confronting horrors (the horror of marital infidelity, the horror of our house burning down, the horror of being murdered or the horror of losing our job) by taking us into the experiences of 'others' (real or fictional) and then reassuring us by giving the comfort of leaving the cinema, switching off the television or closing the newspaper. The archetype of all of these stories is, of course, the child's fairy tale. This is typically structured so that it frightens the child with its cast of giants, monsters, ghosts, devils and goblins before seeking a resolution in the victory of good over evil and an assurance that everyone 'lived happily ever after'. It would seem that countless cultures have recognised that the use of the story to frighten and then reassure the child enables the child to sleep better at night than it would if the horrors of the world were denied. The same explanation can be offered of why most of us, as adults, read news stories, watch films, pass on 'urban myths', tell jokes – and all the rest – that deal with the worries of adult life. There are, of course, narratives of joy, fulfilment and delight in all cultures. But typically stories make sense of these by setting them against their possible or actual loss.

In the process of the narrative-based engagement with culture, human beings are helped to negotiate a social order and work out a morality. And they are offered sense-making resources that help them work out an identity for themselves and help them make choices about the sort of work they want to do. Jane Cawdor gives us some insight into this when she talks about how she came into managerial work.

Activity 4.5

Read Jane Cawdor's account in Cases and Conversations 4.3 of some of the stories which helped her shape a notion of who she is and influenced her career interests. Ask yourself whether:

■ you can think of any stories which you heard or read in childhood, or since, which have played a part in the shaping of your identity or your career interests;

■ the stories you tend to hear about managers and managerial life would tend to encourage or discourage somebody contemplating becoming a manager themselves.

Jane Cawdor, heroine and engineer

Most of my friends from school went into the health service or into teaching and they thought that I was strange becoming an engineer. I don't know what they would think of me now being the chief executive of an engineering company. But I must admit that when I was at school I got tired of hearing all those stories about how girls had gone on to university and then came back to the town to teach in one of the local schools. And I definitely took offence at the stories that some of my friends' parents used to tell about girls who had gone into nursing and then ended up as doctor's wives. Yuk! Come to think of it, though, there was a time when I thought I might like to be a doctor. I think that was something to do with a story my own parents told me – to counter these other tales of soppy nurses I think – where a friend of theirs had got really good exam results and, instead of going to be a nurse like her friends, went to medical school and became a doctor herself. I wonder if they made that up to persuade me to do more homework?

I suspect my parents had noticed that I always liked stories and books about women who were outstandingly successful in some way. However, that was only part of what got me on the track of becoming an engineering manager. I think the stories that influenced me here were my father's stories of when he was in the army; a lot of stuff about building bridges and mending tanks under enemy fire. This appealed to me and sometimes when I feel that I am 'under fire' in this present job, I think back to those stories and try to see myself as the heroic figure who is going to win through. I'll be the woman that leads the company through its battles, beats the competition and defends people's jobs.

Managers, then, can be seen as 'users' of stories in their personal identity management or 'self-shaping'. However, stories have a further significance for many people involved in managerial work. In all societies there are people who make a bigger input into the shaping of cultures than others. The politicians, priests, generals and business leaders – whoever the most powerful happen to be in any society – will play a major role in shaping a culture so that the culture's norms and values are supportive of their power and advantage. The powerful within any culture will prefer the stories that are told to be ones which go with the grain of their interests. Story telling, we might say, is neither politically nor economically innocent. Managers are inevitably caught up in structures and processes of power, with many of them being required to shape the meanings that employees attach to their involvement in an organisation or that customers attach to the products or services that they buy from the organisation. Thus story-telling skills are likely to be relevant to the work tasks of many managers – not least when they are trying to shape the cultures of the organisations in which they work.

 Link The role of stories in organisational cultures is examined in Chapter 8, p. 270.

When culture was defined earlier, it was said to involve a *system* of meanings. This was meant to recognise that the cultural aspects of societies are in some ways patterned, with the various elements of that patterning being related to each other. We should not go too far with this, however. We must remember, for example, that certain stories told within any culture will contradict other stories in what they encourage people to believe. Cultures provide a multiplicity of sense-making resources on which we draw as we choose our own preferred identity or way of life (to be a social worker, say, rather than the manager of a massage parlour). Nevertheless, the sense-making resources upon which we draw when we 'exchange' with our cultures are patterned in significant ways. We have already alluded to this in noting certain patterns that can be found across seemingly different forms of story telling. Narratives as diverse as nursery tales and television advertisements, for example, 'play upon' existential anxieties – with monsters threatening to devour children in one case, perhaps, and germs threatening to take over our happy homes in the other – before giving reassurance through the closure of the story or advertisement and the child falling asleep or the viewer contemplating buying the cleaning product. Another form of patterning can be seen in the range of *discourses* which exist in any given society at any particular time in its history.

Discourse, language and human practices

The concept of *discourse*, as it is increasingly used in the social sciences, is one that bridges the concepts of culture and language. The basic idea of discourse, in this sense, has been implicit from the beginning of *Organising and Managing Work*.

Discourse   *Concept*

A set of connected concepts, expressions and statements that constitutes a way of talking or writing about an aspect of the world, thus framing and influencing the way people understand and act with regard to that aspect of the world.

Link

The references to different ways of 'framing' reality, early on, for example, with the analysis of how Mark Merryton, Harry Carse and Sadie Rait spoke in Cases and Conversations 1.1, 1.2 and 1.3 about management and, later on, with the analysis of systems-control thinking or of 'managism' all relate to the notion of discourse. These are all ways of 'discursively framing' certain aspects of the world.

Discursive framing
Concept

The process whereby human beings draw on sets of discursive resources (concepts, expressions, statements, etc.) made available in their culture to make sense of a particular aspect of their lives and are thereby influenced in the way they conduct themselves in that part of their life.

At this stage we are formalising this notion of 'framing' or 'discursively framing' with the concept of *discourse* as the set of linguistic resources – concepts, terms, statements, expressions, sayings and so on – that are used to provide a frame of reference for applied sense-making in the world. The concept, as it is used here, has some similarities to that developed by Michel Foucault in his influential and controversial historical and social writing (Foucault, 1979, 1980, Reading Guide 3). However, the notion is used here within a conceptual scheme which differs in some significant ways from Foucault's. A powerful illustration of the concept's value is nevertheless seen in Foucault's account of how, over a particular period of western history, the notion of 'being mad' was re-framed (as we might say) to one of 'being mentally ill'. Foucault goes further than simply pointing out how various aspects of social life become re-defined or re-labelled at different times. A whole set of ideas, terms and practices – a system of talk belief and action, we might say – *sometimes* comes to replace another. Where, at one time, people spoke of someone being 'possessed' by demons which needed to be 'cast out', they later framed the problem as one of that person being 'ill' and needing 'treatment'. It is clear that we have both a shift in language and a shift in practice. There is a shift in *discursive practices*, as it is sometimes put. Deranged people are not only spoken of differently, they are treated differently. Not only this, but they are given a different 'subjectivity' – a different identity.

The danger in this type of thinking is that we can come to treat discourses as determining our practices or dictating to us what our identities are. But this is the same danger – that of *cultural determinism* – which threatens all forms of cultural analysis and encourages us to see human beings as *cultural dopes*. To avoid this, we need to recognise that people are *active* sense-makers whose identities and understandings of the world are not *determined* by culture. People are nevertheless powerfully constrained in terms of what they can 'be' and what they can do by the discursive patterns of their culture. There is a mixture of choice and constraint. Because there are varieties and variations in the discourses which are current in any given social order at any particular time, people can, to some extent, draw on different *discursive resources* when shaping themselves, their lives and their practices. If, today, one found oneself regularly going berserk and out of control one could choose to define oneself as mad and either seek a priest to drive out one's demons or try to channel that madness into some creative artistic activity. Alternatively, one could define oneself as mentally ill and go to seek medical treatment. However, if one was living in an earlier age, when the discursive resources of mental illness, psychiatry and so on had not yet been devised, one would not face the option of defining oneself as a mentally sick person, let alone going to seek treatment.

Activity 4.6

Look closely at what Mike Kilrock has to say in Cases and Conversations 4.4 about himself to support his application to be promoted in his organisation and

- identify as many as you can of the discursive resources which Mike draws upon to make his case to the interviewing panel;

- try to identify any of the discourses that Mike draws these ideas from.

Mike Kilrock promotes himself

Cases and Conversations 4.4

'I am sure that you have all carefully read my CV and that you can see how I have developed myself over the past few years to make myself worthy of promotion to this important post. The first thing I want to draw your attention to are my leadership qualities. You can see how I have built up successful teams who really have delivered and have increased business in their areas. I think that if you speak to any of the people who have worked for me, they will tell you that I am someone with vision and someone who really can make a difference.

I am not just someone who gets things done, though. I am very much an entrepreneur. I know that this organisation has got to find new opportunities and find new markets. The world does not owe us a living and you will be aware that I was responsible for several of the new initiatives that have occurred in my region. And I hope that my professionalism is also apparent in everything that I do. I have all the technical qualifications that are important in our area of activity and I know that all my clients feel that they benefit from the discretion and confidentiality I apply in all my dealings with them.

I will now be pleased to answer any questions you wish to put to me. Do tell me if anything is unclear in my application or if there is anything further that you want to know about the contributions that I have already made to developing this firm into one of the most successful in the country. My vision and ambition is to see us being recognised as the country's leading funeral directing business.'

Almost every concept that Mike uses is, inevitably, a discursive resource that is related to one or another of the discourses that makes up the culture in which both he and his interviewers live. But three discourses, or clusters of discursive resources, are drawn upon in particular in this piece of self-promotion occurring in a promotion interview: discourses of leadership, enterprise and professionalism. The discursive resource of 'leadership qualities' is clearly part of a set of concepts and terms that constitutes a particular discourse about *leadership* which exists in modern cultures. In fact Mike uses several other discursive resources from that cluster of concepts: 'building a team', 'vision', and 'making a difference'. He then moves on, with his claim to be an entrepreneur, to a discourse of *enterprise*. He uses from that particular 'language game' (as the philosopher Wittgenstein might label it) concepts of opportunity, initiative, market and the notion of the world 'not owing one a living'. He then, ingeniously, moves from this discursive realm to one that is often seen as a rival to the entrepreneurial one – that of *professionalism*. Here he draws on that set of cultural ideas which recognises certain occupations as being special, by virtue of their control of specialist knowledge and their rules of treating *clients* with confidentiality and with discretion. We should note here that the discursive resource of 'client', which is a key concept within the discourse of professionalism, is used rather than the concept of 'customer' – a discursive resource which plays a correspondingly key role within the discourse of enterprise. Mike Kilrock, in fact, is showing great skill and cunning in carefully selecting elements from different, and partly rival, discourses to help construct a case for his own promotion. Such a skill has been identified elsewhere as one of *discursive ingenuity* (Watson, 2001, Reading Guide 21).

Mike Kilrock is working to construct an occupational identity to sell to his employer a notion of himself as a businessperson, a leader and a 'professional', all at the same time. It is interesting to note that he does not use the discursive resource of 'manager'. As our Chapter 3 account of the emergence of modernism suggested, the concept of 'manager' is very much a product of a particular historical period – as were Foucault's 'mad person' and his 'mentally ill person'. In modern times one can choose to 'become a manager' only because there is a discourse current which makes such a self conception or occupational identity possible. But if one were living in fifteenth century France or seventeenth century Britain this would not have been possible. There were undoubtedly people in those times and places who earned a living of some kind through 'organising work activities', as we might put it in twenty-first century terms. But to try to understand what somebody was doing in that period when they were directing the efforts of others in a field or farm by applying the concepts of a modern management discourse would not give us much insight into either the practices or the thinking of those people. We would have to consider what discursive practices and resources were used in that setting: concepts of *master* and *servant* being an obvious starting point.

It is convenient to demonstrate the value of the concept of discourse by looking at fairly clear historical examples of how thought, language and practices change over time in a closely associated way. But this concept is equally valuable for looking at contemporary situations. In the first place, it can help us understand how power and authority is being exerted in both societal and organisational settings. The politician or manager who can influence how others frame the realities they experience is going to be well placed to exert authority over them. In the second place, the concept of discourse is helpful because it gives us a tool for understanding patterns of contemporary change. We might point here, at one level of analysis, to discourses of workplace *empowerment* appearing in some organisations (Chapter 9) and, at another level, to a discourse of *globalisation* (Chapter 12) being used to come to terms with, and shape behaviours within, changing international patterns. In the third place, we are sensitised to the contested nature of the social and organisational arrangements that we make. We are, for example, prompted to be aware of the existence of alternative or rival discourses which might be current at the same time – even within the same organisation. We might see, for example, a contest within a single organisational management over whether a 'worker empowerment' discourse should be developed or a discourse of 'management's responsibility to manage' should continue to prevail. Similarly, we might see the senior managers of a police organisation taking different views of whether the discourse of a 'police force' should be replaced with a discourse of a 'police service'. The managers in these cases do not themselves use the concepts of *discourse*, *discursive framing*, *discursive practices*, or *discursive resources*. These are nevertheless invaluable conceptual tools that we can use to analyse in a process-relational manner the issues that are arising and the events that are occurring in these organisations. And, were it the case that these managers themselves had this conceptual equipment to hand, it can be argued, they too would be better placed to make sense of the challenges with which they are dealing.

In the next chapter we shall be using some of the concepts that have been introduced in recent pages to look at a variety of individuals and their organisational and managerial involvements. Focus will be given to the application of concepts we have developed here – ones like emergent identity, narrative and discourse – with the use the key concepts of *work orientation, implicit contract* and *strategic exchange*. There will then be a return to the issues of *emotion* and *stress* and the roles these play in work experience generally and managerial work specifically.

Summary

In this chapter the following key points have been made:

- It is very common to talk and write about human individuals as entities that can be understood separately from the society or the culture of which they are a part. It is also common to analyse societies or cultures as if they had an existence in some way independent of the people who live within them. By the same token there has been a tendency to speak of individual organisational employees as if their actions could be separated from the organisational processes in which they participate – and vice versa. This kind of either–or thinking needs to be avoided and, although it is useful to distinguish between 'individual' and 'structural' *aspects* of any aspect of social life, neither of these should ever be looked at in isolation from the other. To understand any human activity or organisational event we have to look at the interplay between factors of human individuality, choice and sense-making on the one hand and the structural and cultural setting in which it occurs on the other.

- Orthodox thinking about work and organisational behaviour has tended to treat the human individual in systems-control terms – as a miniature machine-like system which is 'powered' or 'motivated' by need-satisfying 'fuels' to behave in a certain way. This maintains either–or thinking and encourages an unhelpful separation between the individual and their social/organisational context, between thinking and acting, between reason and emotion and between language and action. It is assumed, for example, that people reason before they act – whereas it is just as possible that a person will act, and then attach a reason, or a motive to that action. Human thinking processes and human behaviours can be better understood by abandoning both this kind of *linearity* in our thinking and the 'either–or' *dualisms* with which it is associated.

- A process-relational perspective has considerable advantages over conventional systems-control thinking when trying to understand human behaviour. It recognises that human individuality is always *relational* (only existing in relation to others) and *emergent* (never becoming fixed – is always in a process of 'becoming').

- Within a process-relational frame of reference, common psychological concepts such as personality, perception, motivation, needs, attitudes tend to be avoided. Instead, key concepts are identity, enactment, culture, dialogue, negotiation and sense-making. Even where terms are used which sound similar to those used in systems-control language – learning and emotion, for example – they are used in a rather different way in process-relational analysis.

- The behaviour of human beings in contemporary situations can only be fully understood if it is seen in the context of how human beings, as a species, have developed *cultures* and *cultural resources* to help them handle fundamental problems which are unique to the species.

- Within the variety of cultures and institutional arrangements which human beings have devised over their history as a species, the specific institutions and cultural priorities of *industrial capitalism* have come to dominate recent human history. Modern work organisations and the occupation of 'management' are to be understood as elements of this modern form of economy and society.

- The cultural resources which people draw upon (and, to a certain extent, themselves create) to help with both everyday sense-making and the handling of existential anxieties are patterned in various ways. First, there is the key part played in all cultures of *narratives* and *stories*. Second, there are *discourses* – ways of framing particular aspects of human reality that involve both specific ways of using language and associated patterns of action. Realities are not handled as 'givens' but are framed by people using the discursive resources which are available to them in their culture or which they themselves develop. The fact that some people in societies and organisations are more active than others as 'story-tellers' and some are more *discursively ingenious* when it comes to processes of *discursive framing* than others has important implications for power relationships in general and managerial authority in particular.

Reading

Reading Guides 3 and 4 contain material that supports and takes further much of what is covered in Chapter 4.

CHAPTER 5

Experience and work: orientation, emotion and managing to manage

Objectives

Having read this chapter and completed its associated activites, readers should be able to:

- Recognise the importance of the *implicit contract*, which is made between the employee and the employing organisation, to an understanding of work behaviour and organisational relationships.

- Apply the concept of *work orientation* to people's involvement in work organisations, appreciating that organisational employees are better understood not as 'motivated' to work in particular ways but as 'oriented' to their work circumstances by the meanings they both bring to the organisation in the first place and by the way these meanings change as they move on through their life and work careers.

- Understand the importance of matters of *emotion* and *feelings* in the work context and come to terms with the fact that these permeate every aspect of organisational activity.

- Recognise that an emotional dimension is sometimes deliberately built into the design of certain kinds of work and that people in various kinds of work, including management, find themselves engaging in *emotional labour*.

- See how emotional matters are involved in situations of individual stress and how the experience of stress, or work-related distress, can best be understood in terms of an interplay of factors in the organisational circumstances and factors in the individual's own life – especially their 'personal resources'.

- Appreciate that managerial work itself has significant emotional dimensions to it and that managers can both be helped with and hindered by some of the *discursive resources* which are offered to them in, for example, managerial writing.

continued

● Understand how managerial work involves people in a *double control problem*, whereby managers experience the pressure of both trying to control the activities – and even sentiments and values of others – while having to manage their own lives and identities.

● Be sensitive to the ways in which managerial work often leads those engaged in it to adopt forms of language use which differ from normal or straightforward language.

● Form a judgement about the extent to which the peculiarities of language among some managers, and others involved in work organisation matters, might reflect attempts of individuals to accommodate that dimension of managerial work which requires people to try to 'control the uncontrollable'.

Strategic exchange, work orientations and implicit contracts

A useful concept that can be developed out of the general analysis of Chapter 4 is that of *strategic exchange*. People can be seen to be, insofar as they are active shapers of their lives, striving to come to terms with the circumstances in which they find themselves. Their 'biography' does not just write itself. People, in part, have to be the authors of their identities and biographies. They therefore pursue their projects in life and manage their continuously emerging identities through exchanging meanings and resources with others and through a 'dialogue' with their cultures. And, here, there is a parallel with organisations. Organisations are most certainly not people. But their future existence, just like the future existence of the human individual, depends on their making exchanges with others – in this case with customers, suppliers, employees and so on. Both organisations (as sets of understandings and arrangements), and the people involved in them (as individuals with identities and biographies) are shaped and shape themselves to continue their existence into the future. This shaping may be relatively deliberate ('planned') or it might be very reactive, haphazard even.

Strategic exchange
Concept

As both individuals and organisations shape themselves and are shaped to continue their existence into the future, the exchange of material and symbolic resources occurs (a) between individuals and others in their social worlds (including employing organisations) and (b) between organisations and their internal and external constituencies upon which they are resource dependent (including employees).

The concept of *strategic exchange* draws attention to the interplay that occurs between how people involved with work organisations shape and make sense of their lives and the way organisations themselves are strategically shaped. An important strategic exchange that many people make in their lives is with an employing organisation. And vitally important strategic exchanges that organisations make are with the people they employ. This 'interplay' between individual and organisational exchange processes was illustrated in the story of Peter Brodie and the strategic direction being followed by the Youth Links charity which he manages (Cases and Conversations 3.4). Peter was shaping his life and identity and was also shaping the Youth Links organisation *in ways that tied into this identity*. The organisation was being shaped, and taken forward into the future, through processes of economic, political and social exchange. These exchanges were managed by Peter to ensure that the resources of effort, support, accommodation and so on, needed by the organisation to survive and continue into the long term, were obtained from employees, politicians, police officers, landlords and the rest. He did all this in a way that shaped and expressed his own life and identity at the same time as it shaped the enterprise he was running.

 Link   Further examples of the link between the strategic exchanges at the personal and at the organisational levels are made in the final part of Chapter 6 when the role of corporate strategists themselves in strategy-making is examined (pp. 213–18). Earlier in that chapter, the ways in which organisations exchange strategically to cope with 'resource dependency' will be an important theme (pp. 200–7).

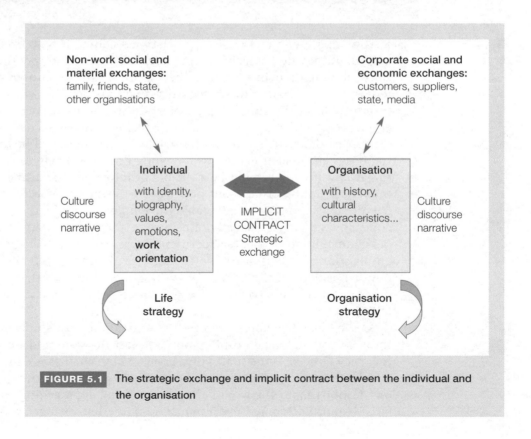

FIGURE 5.1   The strategic exchange and implicit contract between the individual and the organisation

The focus at this stage is on the exchange that occurs between organisations and their employees. This exchange can helpfully be seen as taking the form of an implicit contract between the two parties, as Figure 5.1 illustrates. The normal way for people in a modern society to join a work organisation is to enter into an exchange with that organisation whereby they trade their application of skills and capabilities for a bundle of 'rewards' including cash, security, status, work satisfaction, opportunity for advancement and so on. Certain elements of this exchange are formally agreed and a very limited proportion of it is written in a formal contract of employment. However, the bulk of the 'understanding' that comes about between the employer and the employee is unwritten and is, in large part, unstated. The concept of implicit contract first started to be used (Levinson *et al.*, 1966, Reading Guide 22) at about the same time as the work orientation concept, to which we shall shortly connect it, and is related to the concepts of *effort bargain* (Behrend, 1957; Baldamus, 1961, Reading Guide 22) and *psychological contract* (Schein, 1978, Reading Guide 22).

Implicit contract	Concept
The tacit agreement between an employing organisation and the employed individual about what the employee will 'put in' to the job and the rewards and benefits for which this will be exchanged.	

The implicit contract is clearly a relational matter. It is an exchange between an individual who is seeking employment as part of the way they are strategically shaping their lives to take them into the future and an employer who requires their services to strategically shape its activities to take it into the future. It takes the form of a set of understandings negotiated between the employee and the employer, much of which is unlikely to have been explicitly stated, let alone written into a formal contract. There will be unstated understandings about such matters as how long the job is likely to last, what sort of career advancement might be available or how much overtime can be earned. Inferences will be made about how willing the employee will be to take orders from managers and how adaptable the employee will be if organisational circumstances change. What all of this means is that the employment relationship (a key institution of modern societies, as was stressed in Chapter 3) is a highly ambiguous one. It is also a potentially fragile one, given the very different power positions of the employee, on the one hand, and the employer on the other (an observation central to Marx's classic critique of class relations in capitalist societies).

As the individual approaches the organisation to seek employment, they take into the potential relationship more than just the skills and working capacities that they possess. As the strategic exchange notion emphasises, the individual also takes with them an identity and a biography as well as various values and feelings or emotions about the world. The human being approaching employment is a whole human being, not just a human resource. But, as they approach an organisation, many of these aspects of their lives and identities will, in the light of their particular life circumstances at the time, inform a particular meaning which they attach to the work and the job they are going into: a *work orientation*.

Work orientation	Concept
The meaning individuals attach to their work which predisposes them both to think and act in particular ways with regard to that work. There is an *initial orientation* at the point of entry to work and this is liable to change as circumstances and interests change within the continuing employment relationship.	

At the stage of approaching employment we can refer to an initial orientation to work, in recognition of the fact that it is liable to develop and change once they have joined the organisation. The concept of orientation to work has its origins in sociological studies that were carried out in the 1960s in Britain. Goldthorpe, Lockwood and their colleagues (1968, Reading Guide 22) developed the concept as they recognised the inadequacy of need-based motivational analyses for understanding the groups of employees that they studied. The concept of work orientation was seen as a more realistic tool for analysing what employees were seeking when they took certain jobs. The researchers argued that to understand the way different groups of workers behaved one should examine what those workers' jobs meant to them and what calculated choices they were making when entering that particular employment. Some people had an orientation to work that caused them to seek jobs which offered promotional opportunities or the opportunities to apply manual skills, for example, while others sought simply to maximise the money they could earn and *discounted* opportunities, say, for job interest or career advancement. Clearly these choices were made in the light of the abilities and aptitudes which people possessed as well as their value preferences. Most famously the study showed that many of the people working in the car assembly factory had chosen this work to maximise the income they could then spend on their families. And this meant forgoing the potentially more satisfying, but lower paid, work that they could have taken, should they have so chosen.

A way of linking the concepts of work orientation and implicit contract, as well as identifying some of the elements of the employment bargain is suggested in Figure 5.2. This puts the individual's 'understood employment trade' or *perceived implicit contract* at the centre of their work orientation (see Figure 5.2). It does not exist 'in the head' of the employee in isolation from their relationship with the employer but it does play a key part in how they *enact* their work roles and their relationships with the managers in the employing organisation. Every employed individual, in the light of their current circumstances, their self-identities, life projects and the rest, has a notion of what they are exchanging with the employer: what mix of *inputs* of physical and mental efforts, the taking of responsibility, willingness to take risks of accident, stress and acceptance of managerial control is being traded with the employer for a particular mix of money, job satisfaction, social reward (satisfaction of serving the community, say), employment security, status, and opportunity to wield power, develop skills and advance a career.

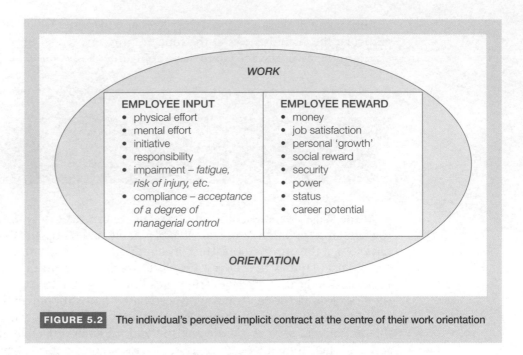

FIGURE 5.2   The individual's perceived implicit contract at the centre of their work orientation

This way of looking at people's work meanings and behaviours takes us a long way from the old fashioned debates about whether people generally 'go to work mainly for the money' or seek employment for some other reason. Such 'either–or' thinking is simple minded and of little value in understanding either work behaviour generally or the behaviour of particular groups of worker. In practice, every one of us has our own bundle of expectations and wants that we take into the strategic exchange we make with an employing organisation. There may be times in the life of each of us when we prioritise, say, money over job interest or security over high pay. But such a situation is recognised in this process-relational focus on orientations and implicit contracts as something which is particular to a particular person at a particular time and in particular circumstances. This is not to say that the concept cannot, to a certain extent, also be applied to groups, however.

A pattern of similar orientations may be seen across groups of employees who are similarly placed in the organisation or have come to the organisation from similar situations. It would tend to be the case that highly qualified senior staff would have different orientations, as a group, from unskilled and temporary manual workers, say. And it is possible that a different pattern of orientation might be found amongst people coming from one ethnic grouping, age or gender group rather than another, within the same organisational area of activity. Clearly, the cultural or age-group expectations of different groups of employees will vary as will the bargaining strength which different types of prospective employee will take into their negotiation of an implicit contract – these varying with the skills, competencies or experiences they have to 'trade'. And, in circumstances where there is a formal trade union or other group representation, the bargaining over some aspects of the contract of employ-ment will actually take place collectively. Nevertheless, even where there are clear patterns of orientation across groups of organisational members, it is nec-essary to recognise the variations that occur between individuals, albeit within these group patterns.

To understand any individual's or group's work behaviour we have to look at how they are predisposed to act in certain ways in the light of their orientation at that time and their perception of the deal they are making with the employer. We have to consider how they *enact* their role within the organisation, in other words. This, however, has to be set in the context of the employees' lives before they enter the organisation. We can see the importance of this in the case of Ravi Barr and how he came to be in the management job that he now does, by looking at the *initial orientation* which he brought to his present employing organisation. To look at processes of work entry and 'occupational choice', as it has traditionally been called, in the process-relational way, which a focus on work orientation involves, means once again turning away from the kind of *serial thinking* which was criticised in the previous chapter. Orthodox thinking tends to see the process of work entry as one in which we develop our interests, values and aptitudes as we grow up and go through education and then make a *choice* of occupation or career to fit this. Thus 'choice' precedes entry into a job or occupation. But, in practice, it does not work as simply as this, as Ravi Barr's story illustrates. What is the out-come of choice and what is adventitious, or a matter of circumstance and chance, is far from straightforward when we look at how people come into the sort of work we find them in at any point in their lives, in practice.

Activity 5.1

Read the conversation with Ravi Barr in Cases and Conversations 5.1 and consider the following questions:

- To what extent did Ravi 'choose' his career? Did he 'make a choice' of career and then enter it. Or did he 'find himself' in a job and then give this the rationale of a choice? Or was it a combination of these two?

- How has Ravi's work orientation changed over time, from the work he did in the family business, to the part-time jobs he took as a student, to the jobs he has done in the organ-isation he joined when he left school?

- How has Ravi 'managed' his identity? Because he has lived 'between two cultures', as he puts it, he is especially conscious of how identity is not a 'given' or fixed thing.

Ravi Barr gets oriented

Tell me how you came to be a human resources manager, Ravi?

It was pure accident really. I was working as a supervisor in one of our shops, a job which I took when I got chucked out of university in my second year. I had always liked playing with computers, would you believe, and when a job came up in the home electrics department, as it was then called, I jumped at the chance. They said they wanted someone to build up that side of the department's business and I thought this would suit me. In fact it built up quite fast and I was soon spending a lot of my time recruiting new staff and training people on the computing side of things. I was training myself as I went along but I persuaded the general store manager that I was much more expert than I really was. The consequence of this was that he promoted me to a store-wide training job, getting managers and supervisors across the departments up to speed with computing. This went so well that when a personnel officer's job came up, I got it and then when the top human resources job become vacant I chose to go for that. I found I enjoyed the status I was building up and I liked the power that went with it. So here I am.

But you said, a moment ago, that it is 'pure accident' that you are in this job. And a few breaths later, you are telling me how you 'chose' to apply for the job. Can you explain this seeming contradiction to me?

Sorry about that. I suppose what was in my mind is that I originally wanted a career in marketing. This is what I hoped to specialise in on my degree course. So it's a sort of accident that I am now firmly in an HR career. I suppose that, on the other hand, there is consistency in that I am in a managerial sort of career. I wanted something that would give me seniority in an organisation – although I never thought of retailing as the industry I would end up in. And it is true that I enjoyed the human resources module I did in the second year at university – even if I failed it like all the others because I was enjoying myself too much pubbing and clubbing to do any academic work.

So why did you take the risk of not getting into a managerial career by not working at university?

Believe me, that is something I thought hard about at the time. In part, it was me sorting out who I was. You see my parents are in retailing and I was brought up to be a 'good hard-working Indian boy' who would eventually run the family business. And through my school years, I accepted this. Well I more or less did. I worked enthusiastically in the family business whenever I had got my homework out of the way. I simply fitted into the business, like my older brothers, and did whatever my father asked me, whether it was delivering orders or sorting out the invoices. I didn't think of myself as cheap family labour. At home I was their dutiful Indian boy. At school I played that down and was just 'one of the lads' who were particularly interested in computers and computer games. Some of that group were Asian, others weren't. And it didn't matter. Asian identity was something for home. I was just another of the 'computer boys' at school. I sort of shifted my identity about across the two cultures I lived in. But I didn't really think about it at the time. I only started to think about all of this when I was at university. It was when I came home on the first vacation and found that I was expected to carry on the same as before. I started to see myself then as cheap family labour. I began to resent this and I got more and more awkward with my father and brothers – doing the minimum amount of work and refusing to take any kind of initiative at all. This all ended up in a big row and for the next few vacations I got work near the university, refusing to go home. I resolved never to have anything to do with retailing again. Apart from that, I did any work I could get, my main concern being to earn as much money as I could as fast as possible. I did labouring, worked in bars. I even did some horrible work in a chicken factory.

You just worked for money?

Exactly. The work was a means to an end.

And the end was?

Having a good time. And the money I made enabled me to carry on partying in term time too. I was sort of shaking off all those years of being the quiet conscientious boy. And I was also refusing the plan my parents had for me, as the first one in our family to go to university and, hence, the one who would eventually run the business (something I knew my elder brothers really resented).

But now you are a senior manager in a retailing business.

Funny isn't it? I am very career oriented now. I am making sure that I am learning about every aspect of this business so that I can eventually be a chief executive of a large retailing outfit. My parents have now accepted that I do not want to work in the family business. I think they are proud of what I have achieved and I suppose I want them to be even more proud of me when I really get to the top. My wife, who comes from a similar background, thinks similarly about her career as an accountant. I think my marriage, in fact, has been an important factor in my approach to career. Her family wanted to arrange a marriage for her and she had to fight them to marry me. So we have both had to make our way, and establish who we are, by sort of escaping from our families. So we are both making careers away from the Asian community. But, as we have both realised, we are still very much the products of the community and families that, in part, we turned away from. Yes, funny, isn't it. There are so many reasons for what you do, aren't there?

Ravi Barr's closing words rather neatly summarise the story he has told. But what is really interesting about his story is not just the large number, or even the variety, of the factors that have shaped his life and career. It is also the fascinating way that they interact with each other – home factors with work factors, family pressures with school priorities, ethnic influences with individual assertiveness, and so on. So complex is this interplay, in fact, that Ravi finds himself, rather paradoxically, talking of his career 'choices' since leaving university in terms of 'accident' one minute and 'choice' the next. This is not unusual when one interviews people about their work histories. The work biographies of most of us involve a complex interplay of choice and chance factors and when we report them to others we find ourselves, at certain points, drawing on all those stories in our culture which have the theme, 'Isn't it strange what things happen to people in life?'. And at other points in the narratives or biographies we present to people interviewing us, we draw on the discursive resource of the 'rational man or woman' who carefully plans a career to make the best use of their talents in the labour market. The 'either or' dualism of choice *or* chance is not in fact helpful to understanding people's biographies. The two aspects of the duality do, however, interact with each other in different ways in different people's biographies. As we shall see in Chapter 11 (pp. 404–12), the way we present that biography to employers or potential employers can have important consequences for recruitment and promotional decisions made by employers.

Ravi Barr's orientation to work is clearly tied up with his family and his ethnic background and with the process of managing his identity. He is making choices about his own life but those choices are very much made in the context of the structural situations in which he has found himself – whether these be the family and community structures into which he was born, or the structure of opportunities he later found himself within in the company for which he is now working. In different work situations in which he has found himself he has made different *implicit contracts* with the people employing him. When he first worked in the family firm he exchanged hard work and a willingness to be flexible for personal security and the social reward of belonging to a family and a community. Once he had left home and he felt that this reward was not what he was seeking, he was less willing to 'put in' so much effort or, as he points out, show so much initiative. The orientation to work and the implicit contract had changed, albeit with the same person and the same work situation. Ravi's changing concept of who he was and what he wanted from life led to a change in his work orientation. And when he sought employment while at university he thought of it in terms of a very simple trade – he wanted to maximise the money he could earn.

After the shock of having to leave university, Ravi approached his employment in the department store with a different kind of orientation. He was clearly willing to put more into that job than he had into the temporary jobs. And one of the rewards which was important in his understanding of the implicit contract with the company was the opportunity to work with computers. We can see then his orientation shifting further as he discovered his abilities in recruiting and training people. The ambition which then developed meant that the 'career potential' element of the reward side of Figure 5.2 was becoming more salient. Undoubtedly it was not replacing an interest in monetary reward, because we can presume that this was increasing at the same time, as were the rewards of status and power. We can see him trading a particular bundle of work inputs for a particular bundle of rewards. And this exchange is not just influenced by his relationship with the employing organisation. His current family life plays an important part in his emergent identity and his shifting work orientations. And this current family situation is itself related to his own and his wife's biographies. They are still working out their pasts as they work on the present and on their futures. Their exchanges with their present employers and with all the other people in their lives are indeed *strategic exchanges*. We each make strategic exchanges in our lives in our own ways.

Activity 5.2

Moving your attention away from Ravi Barr's story to your own, ask yourself the following questions.

● In what ways have both choice and chance played a part in your own unfolding work career or career ambitions?

● What different implicit contracts have you made in different work situations at various stages of your life? Use the employee input/employee reward boxes in Figure 5.2 to chart the perceived 'trades' you made in different jobs you have done.

● To what extent have you ever changed your orientation to work (and, of course, the way you perceived your implicit contract) within the same job? If you wish to be prompted on this question, you may choose to give a quick initial glance at what Sacha Boath has to say about how 'people change at work' in Cases and Conversations 5.2.

Sacha and the seven dwarves

Cases and Conversations 5.2

Yes, you will hear several of the managers here refer to me and my department as Sacha and the Seven Dwarves. As Director of Corporate Affairs, I am the only woman in the company's top team and they like to tease me about being tall and fair-haired. That's OK, I can handle the banter and I suppose being compared to the fairy tale Snow White is not really uncomplimentary. I do get bothered sometimes, though, that they are rather diminishing my team by referring to them as dwarves. Only one of them is really a small person, even if they are all shorter than me. In fact some of them have actually 'grown' in the job you might say. I think it's really interesting how people can change at work. Let me tell you about them; Smithy, Biffy, Sniffy, Snippy, Chippy, Iffy and Sparky, as the managers call them.

Smithy, Biffy and Sniffy are my three public relations officers. Biffy and Sniffy are amazing cases of people who have changed. When I came here I was told they were simply miserable types. It was also said that they both had 'chips on their shoulders' because they had lost their jobs when the second of the town's papers closed down. They felt they were demeaning themselves by working in public relations. Both were well on the way to becoming alcoholics and they ruined their marriages, largely because of the drink. However, about a year ago there was this amazing change. In part, it was down to my giving them the most almighty shouting at – 'Shape up or ship out' is what I basically said. But it was also to do with some kind of conversion experience they had, as our managing director put it. They had both joined Alcoholics Anonymous and, at the same time, they discovered the delights of line dancing. Somehow the smartening up that went on with getting off the booze and their meeting women at the dancing sessions translated into their work. It was amazing. Almost over night they changed from lazy and uninspired individuals who were in danger of letting the company down to smart and reliable characters who I can happily allow to speak for the company. Smithy, on the other hand, is somebody I increasingly can't trust. In her case, the change seems to have come about after moving in with a new partner, as opposed to losing a partner. She is my languages person and used to be brilliant at dealing with almost any issue where we needed to deal with Europe. It seems that her bloke has been getting resentful about her travelling abroad for us and this has led to her taking it out on all of us in the office. She's managed not to go abroad for six months now and the other day she rushed out of the office screaming, 'Oh, sod the French'. One of my best people has become a complete liability for reasons which, it seems, have nothing to do with the company.

Changes at work do seem to be the source of the changes we've seen with Snippy, however. Her job is to monitor press coverage. She used to be the life and soul of the office. She would sit over there, snipping away at her press cuttings and joking with everybody who came into the office. But since we've rearranged the office and her desk is less central to what is going on, she seems to have completely dropped her role as the office wit. I shall have to re-think the office layout, I think. But, for some reason, she's recently taken up smoking and keeps disappearing to the smoking room across the road to have a cigarette. In the past, I could have spoken to her about that, but the way she is just now would make that difficult.

In some ways Snippy's social role in the office has been taken on by Iffy. She is my secretary, sorry PA – personal assistant. She used to be a total misery. She was a graduate trainee with the company. She said she didn't mind taking on a 'graduate secretary' role but she resented the fact that it was only female graduates who did that. They called her Iffy because she was always saying things like, 'If a man were asked to do that, he'd refuse'. So what's made the difference? I don't really know. The job title change might be a factor, but I don't think it was that important. And it might be that she became aware that I was never going to ask her to make me coffee or go out to buy flowers for me to give to my mother on Mother's Day (something she says happened to her before I came). Actually, I think it is simply that she and I have become good friends. We do meet socially but, at work, we really enjoy working together. There's no doubt that I am 'the boss', as anyone will tell you ('the blonde Tsarina', Iffy called me the other day, when I stormed into the office generally threatening murder all round). The simple truth is that Iffy enjoys working with someone she gets on with, and that has led her to take on more and more tasks which she then finds she really enjoys.

I wish I could bring about a similar change in Sparky. He runs the computing and IT side of the department – our web site and all that. When he was here first I think he felt that he was a pioneer and that he understood things none of us had a clue about. He was a cheerful chap to have around – a really sparky character in fact. It seems now that everything has settled down and his work is more routine, he is a bit bored. Consequently he is not helping people as much as he should be. He's well paid though and I think that he has got himself locked in here by the salary. He has taken on a mortgage on a new house recently and doesn't want to risk a job change. He's pretty secure too, given the relevance of his skills to our work. I can't see what promotional opportunities we can offer to 'turn him back on'. I'll have to look for some exciting new project.

Chippy is someone for whom everything is a new project. I have rarely seen anyone so positive about his job. He came to us from the maintenance department who 're-deployed' him when that operation was down-sized. His resentment of moving into here was palpable. He thought he was simply going to be some sort of odd job man who would only occasionally use his carpentry skills when we needed a display preparing. However, once he realised that he could make the job an important one, by seeking opportunities to make exhibition stands and by being the key person at out-of-company presentations, he really changed. He regularly travels abroad now – which he had never done before, and I often think he has developed better public relations skills than some of the professionals. The job is very much what he has chosen to make it. After that first miserable couple of weeks here he just seemed to decide, 'Right, let's make something of this'. The MD – ever the joker himself – actually asked me the other day, 'Is that Chippy of yours still a chirpy chappy?'. Indeed he is.

These brief portraits painted by one manager of the staff in her department very effectively illustrate the foolishness of looking at the demeanour or the behaviour of any given person at work and concluding, 'Aha, that is the sort of person they are'. Although there will be certain consistencies which could be perceived over time in the lives and identities of each of these individuals, the orthodox psychology categories of 'personality type' hardly seem relevant to the complexities of what is going on in these seven lives and to the work orientations of Smithy, Biffy, Sniffy, Snippy, Chippy, Iffy and Sparky. The concepts of emergent identity, work orientation and implicit contract are far more helpful than any concept of personality type.

Activity 5.3

Carefully examine each of the individuals that Sacha Boath talks about and, using the model in Figure 5.2:

- note what factors appear to have led to their changed orientations;

- given that Sacha has only a partial picture of what has happened in each case, speculate about what other kinds of factor might also have come into play (i.e. things you might

'look into' if you were trying to do a research project on the orientations of people in this Corporate Affairs – or 'public relations' – department);

- try to think of any examples of people, other than yourself, whose work orientations appear to have changed during their employment within a particular job.

A complex multiplicity of factors seems to be relevant to the workplace identities and the work orientations of each of these people. Numerous factors influence how they see the implicit contract they have with their employer. Sacha Boath has clearly tried hard to understand each of these people and, indeed, she gets close to analysing how they might perceive the implicit contracts they have with her and the company. Notice, for example, the way in which she analyses how Sparky might be thinking about the rewards he is getting from the company: he has got security and good pay but he is not getting any intrinsic rewards or fulfilment from the job itself. He is bored. This might be compensated for by promotional opportunities, but that is not really a possibility. Sacha is therefore considering what she might do to give him more excitement in the job. She is not getting the work 'inputs' she wants, given what rewards she is offering. She therefore needs to act to get a better trade. And this takes us into that area of management often called 'motivation'.

Link   Chapter 9 shows how managerial attempts to 'motivate' employees can be understood in terms of *manipulating* their perceived implicit contracts with the employing organisation.

For the present, however, we simply want to give full recognition to the extent to which a person's identity is always *emergent*, their work orientation is always liable to change and their involvement at work has to be seen in the context of the strategic exchanges which are going on in their lives and biographies as a whole. And if we are going to look at people in this holistic way, then we have to recognise that they do not simply go to work to act as task-completing biological machines. The 'whole person' goes to work, as we recognised earlier. And that means that they approach the organisation with feelings, preferences, beliefs and the whole range of human vulnerabilities, as well as the skills, aptitudes and willingness to follow instructions that the employing organisation is buying from them.

Feelings, emotions and the experience of stress

Work organisations are parts of an institutional pattern which has developed at a very recent stage in the overall evolution and history of the human species. It is part of *modernism* which, as we saw in Chapter 2 (pp. 36–8), involves a concerted attempt to apply rational thinking to human activities and institutions in order to increase humans' control over their circumstances. The principles of *reason* and of *control* are thus central to the work of trying to shape modern organisations – the work of managers. As we established in Chapter 3 (pp. 8–14), the form which this reason takes is that of 'instrumental rationality', whereby calculated choices are made to find the best means for achieving given ends. We are not meant to perform a work task in the way we *feel* like doing it at a particular moment. We are not meant to carry out a task in a particular way because we *guess* that this is how to do it. And we are not meant to do a job in a particular way because that is the *traditional* way in which it has always been done. To act in these ways is to go against the principles of carefully, or scientifically, calculating the most efficient way of carrying out work tasks.

Max Weber, the key theorist of these matters, pointed out that this would mean that if modern organisations or 'bureaucracies' were to exist in a pure form, they would have no place for 'love, hatred and all purely personal, irrational and emotional elements which escape calculation' (Weber, 1978, p. 975,

Reading Guide 16). The key phrase here is 'which escape calculation'. Weber was recognising the aspirations of those building and leading the large organisations of the modernising world and, as Albrow (1997, Reading Guide 8) points out (in contradicting a common misreading of Weber), he was well aware that they were not seeking to *exclude* an emotional or affective dimension from organisational life. We might say that what they were seeking were ways of harnessing the 'humanness' and the emotional involvement of human labour. This was indeed the logic of the attention given to 'informal' aspects of organisational functioning in those classic 1930s studies by Roethlisberger and Dickson and by Barnard, which we looked at in Chapter 3 (pp. 75–7). Managers should pay heed to the 'sentiments' of workers in shaping factory activities, argued the former, while the latter put the management of 'informal activities' at the centre of the executive's job. In effect, Barnard was recognising the need of organisational managers to appeal to employees' hearts and sentiments as well as to their minds. His social-science influenced analysis of all of this, and the advocacy which follows from it, can itself be seen as part of what Weber recognised as a trend not to allow 'emotional elements' to 'escape calculation'. Emotions are all very well in the modern work organisation, in this view, but they must be kept under control and, wherever possible, harnessed to the ends being pursued by the organisation's controllers. Hatred for an enemy would probably be a managerially desirable emotion to be felt by soldiers in a modern army during a war. And passion for the product being sold by a commercial enterprise could be very welcome to those in charge of that enterprise. However, if either of these got 'out of hand' – beyond calculation and control – the soldiers might disastrously run amok and the over-passionate sales person might frighten away some of their customers.

It has recently been recognised that the bulk of management and organisational texts attend too little to the emotional side of organisational life and work involvement. Where it is given recognition in standard texts, it is dealt with in an indirect, and often rather 'bloodless' way. Sometimes it is seen as a dimension of gaining employee compliance – rewarding people with *self-actualisation* or overcoming their *resistance to change* for example. At other times it becomes pertinent because of an interest in overcoming tendencies of individuals to break down through *stress* or the inclination of certain groups over enthusiastically to pursue *grievances*.

We can usefully reflect on why there has been little direct attention to the emotional aspects of working lives. The subjective states of the individuals whose feelings and emotions make up the 'emotional side of organisational life' are not easy to understand and, partly as a result of the ambiguity and unpredictability that such matters involve, people can readily become quite uncomfortable when trying to address them. It might also be the case that when we are working as researchers, or as thoughtful managers, in specific organisational situations, we feel uncomfortable about invading the privacy of the people we come across. We might ask whether we have the right to enquire too deeply into the emotional states and the private feelings of the people we meet in work situations. This would be a proper ethical question to ask. Yet if we want to understand the full complexities of organising and managing work, we need to attend to matters of feeling and emotion in the workplace. The ethnographic style of research, in which the researcher gets closely involved with the people living or working in the particular setting being studied, enables such factors to be looked at. An ethnographic episode which demonstrates the type of insight that can be gained in this way is that of Ken Steary's collision with his office desk (Cases and Conversations 5.3). At this stage we have not formally conceptualised the issues that arise in this broad area of the 'emotions and feelings'. This is deliberate. We will look at some events occurring in Ken Steary's hotel and then consider how we might bring some conceptual rigour to bear on them.

Activity 5.4

Read the researcher's conversation with Ken Steary in Cases and Conversations 5.3. Then

- list all of the ways in which issues of emotion and feeling come into these events
- identify any way in which those running this hotel organisation – represented in this story

by the regional manager – appear to have taken account of the emotional dimension of what goes on in hotels.

Ken Steary laughs, cries and falls over
Cases and Conversations 5.3

You don't look good, Ken.

I don't feel good, mate.

You look altogether stressed.

Stress is supposed to be a mental thing, isn't it? Well, you see this black eye. That's stress for you. It's physical and it hurts. And I know what you think. You think that I am going to tell you that I got so stressed last night trying to manage this bloody hotel that I got into a fight with a customer. Well that isn't what happened.

Did a member of staff thump you, then?

No. I didn't get into a fight with a member of staff. It was my office desk what did it.

I see.

No you don't. I was at the end of my tether last night, stressed up, tired out and on the point of laughing and crying at the same time. But I am the manager and I am meant to be in control. I can neither afford to let the staff see me crack up nor let the hotel guests see me fall apart. So I went up to my office and drank myself stupid. And then I fell over, catching my eye on the corner of the desk. I thought I was doing really well, keeping up the façade of the man who is always in control – dealing with my pathetic grief in private. And now I've got to explain to everybody how I got the black eye. I've already told three different stories to explain it away. I am really losing the plot.

OK, tell me the plot then. What is the real story?

The problems started yesterday with the visit from the regional manager. She comes round every month to look at 'the figures' with me and generally to keep me on my toes. I really hate her, the officious cow. She has a go at me for things that she couldn't do. She really likes to wind me up.

How do you mean?

Well, yesterday, I started off in a good mood. I was feeling good because I knew the figures were OK. Our occupancy figures have been really excellent, the bar and restaurant turnovers are on the up and up and the staff turnover figures are slightly down. I've even got the wages tightly under control. But guess what? Did they thank me? Did they congratulate me? Did they hell. No, what I got from madam was, 'Region are perturbed about some complaints they have received'. They had got a couple of complaints about the sullen behaviour of my reception staff. I'd like to see her try to deal with a problem like that.

You recognise that this is a problem, then. I must admit that I was put off earlier by the rather surly manner of one of your barmen. I felt most unwelcome and would have walked out if I hadn't been meeting you.

Don't you start. I thought you were my friend. But, yes, you are right. This is an issue that has been bothering me. I just didn't like the idea of my bosses sitting around their boardroom table tut tutting about poor old Ken Steary not being able to make his staff smile at the punters. And that cow of a regional manager wouldn't be able to make a drunk on his honeymoon smile. So who is she to lecture me?

But you accept that there is a problem?

Oh yes. And I could do with some help handling it. But who do I turn to? I am the boss here. And you can get very lonely, even in big hotel full of people like this one was last night. I've got to show a smiling face to the world and my staff know damn well that they need to do the same. Even on my way up to my office last night I smiled at a grumpy guest who refused help with his suitcase and then complained that the steps on the stairs were too steep. 'What's wrong with using the lift, you stupid bastard?', I said under my breath as I felt my skin burning and my colour rising. But my expression was a picture of genuine sympathy. And since I've had this black eye, I have smiled a hundred times at one member of staff and one hotel guest after another.

But you can't get all of your staff to act in this way?

Most will, they know their jobs depend on the hotel doing well and that it won't do well if the guests are not treated hospitably. That doesn't seem unreasonable. And they have chosen to work in the hospitality industry, for God's sake. They are paid to be hospitable.

But are they paid to be actors?

Would you like a black eye too?

Matters of feeling and emotion come into this story from the beginning. One of the first things Ken says is that he does not *feel* good. He talks about how his black eye 'hurts' – suggesting that the abstract phenomenon he calls 'stress', itself 'hurts'. His reference to his hotel as 'this bloody hotel' is clearly emotionally loaded, as is his worry that one might infer that he had fought with a customer. He loads his account of his feelings the previous evening with terms like 'the end of my tether', 'tired out', 'crack up', 'fall apart', 'drank myself stupid', 'pathetic grief' and 'losing the plot'. The description of his 'laughing and crying at the same time' involves the use of a discursive resource commonly used in the wider culture to give a picture of somebody who is so out of control that they have gone beyond the cultural norm of crying to express sadness and laughing to express happiness. He talks of hating the regional manager and, twice, uses another common discursive resource which is applied to express strong antipathy to a woman, as does his ironic use of the term 'madam'. Positive feelings are expressed when Ken looks back to earlier the previous day when he 'felt good' and was, it seems, feeling that he deserved thanks and congratulations. These are aspects of the sort of reciprocity we referred to earlier when discussing culture and social exchange (pp. 110–13). His looking for these endorsements and the manager failing to provide them reveal significant *relational* aspects of the emotional temperature which built up for Ken. Also, the regional manager's use of language in saying that the 'region is perturbed' is interesting. She is mystifying exactly who is worried by *personifying* 'Region' (see above p. 49), something which, if Ken is reporting her verbatim, we might take to be slightly provocative. It implies that some power greater than any nameable human individual is looking down upon the insignificant figure of Mr Steary. The formality of the word 'perturbed' rather than the more obvious 'worried' has been taken by Ken, we can infer, as a further attempt to 'wind him up'.

The alleged 'sullenness' of the reception staff, and the researcher's mention of the 'surly manner' of a bar worker, are clearly matters of emotional interpretation made by customers of the apparent emotional state of these hotel employees. The researcher speaks of *feeling* unwelcome and Ken goes on in the conversation to paint a picture of a very emotional state he was in the previous night and the equally emotional state he is in at present with the use of one emotionally loaded expression after the other. He also makes a bitter joke about the regional manager's demeanour, one that has all sorts of sexual and sexist undertones (couldn't 'make a drunk on his honeymoon smile') and he even threatens the researcher with violence, even though (as it happened) he says it with a smile on his face, echoing back to the pathos of the earlier 'I thought you were my friend'.

This episode is packed with emotionality and it could be argued that an exaggerated picture of the role that feelings play in organisational life is being painted by the selection of an episode in which there has been a crisis in the life of one particular individual. There is some truth in this. But it can be argued that critical events like this simply reveal factors and issues that are present all the time but only come fully to the surface when circumstances arise in which the normal controls of social life are weakened and conventional courtesies are strained. For example, if the regional manager had been polite to Ken and thanked him for his good work before diplomatically raising the question of the customer complaints, there would still be emotional factors in play. The regional manager would have been taking Ken's feelings into account and he might have 'felt good' about being thanked and he might have appreciated the senior person's 'sharing' a managerial problem with him. This kind of social exchange process and the maintenance of reciprocity is so common or 'normal' in social and organisational life that we tend not to be consciously aware of it. It is when there is some breakdown in it that the presence of feelings and emotions in the work context become starkly apparent. They are, however, never absent.

The emotional issues raised by Ken Steary's tale go beyond ones of staff relationships. The issue that triggered Ken's distressing experience was one of how the organisation, as a business, relates to its customers. It does not apparently stay in business simply by selling food and renting beds to customers. It provides *hospitality* to its *guests*. The very tasks which are done 'in the organisation's name' (above pp. 63–4) are ones with a strong emotional dimension. Ken is fully aware of this. And one can reasonably infer from his outburst, 'they have chosen to work in the hospitality industry, for God's sake', that a key source of frustration to him is the difficulty he is having in getting some of the staff to *engage emotionally* with their work, by acting in a friendly and smiling way towards 'guests'. We notice that he stresses how the regional manager would be unable do this. And we note that he emphasises how he is willing to 'make his face a picture of genuine sympathy', even when he is in a bad mood and is provoked by a 'stupid bastard' and 'grumpy guest'. Where we heard Mark Merryton complain about the difficulty of trying to 'herd cats' in Cases and Conversations 1.1, we can imagine Ken Steary complaining here about the difficulty of making cats smile! A concept which we will use to look at the issues that arise here is that of *emotional labour*. But, before we can properly deploy that concept, we need to conceptualise the more general phenomena of emotion and feeling.

It has been possible in the above analysis to refer in a broad way to 'feelings and emotions', as if they were more or less the same thing. This is what we tend to do in everyday life. We talk about 'feeling happy' on one occasion, for example, and refer to the 'emotion' of happiness on another. It has been normal, in the history of human reflection, to link feelings and emotions. So why should we consider splitting them – distinguishing between the two? The only justification for doing this would be the pragmatist's one of developing our conceptual tools to enable us to analyse something more effectively than we would otherwise do, with a view to better informing our subsequent practices. On these grounds, it is useful to conceptualise feelings and emotions as separate, but closely linked, phenomena.

Emotions and feelings   *Concept*

Feelings are sensations felt bodily which relate to a psychological state. *Emotions* are the way these sensations are made sense of with reference to culture, either privately or socially.

It is helpful to follow Fineman in separating *feelings* – the 'subjective experience' in which 'we are aware "in" ourselves of some bodily state, peturbation, or more diffuse psychological change' (Fineman, 1999, p. 546, Reading Guide 8) from the more culturally mediated *emotions* with which they are associated. Fineman, however, treats emotions as *displays* of these feelings. He does this to enable him to distinguish between, say, the way someone might express the *emotion* of anger in a situation, by shouting and raging, while actually *feeling* pleasure in what they are doing. There is clearly an important distinction to be made here (to understand situations like the one Ken Steary was in when he *felt* angry with the grumpy customer while he *displayed* sympathy). However, it is felt more analytically useful here to say that the *feeling* was the physical sensation Ken describes when he says 'I felt my skin burning and my colour beginning to rise'. And the *emotion* is the cultural label of 'anger' that might be attached to this feeling when we try to make sense of it. The two are closely linked but the 'animal' sensation that Ken experienced does not automatically read across to the cultural interpretation of 'anger'. Ken himself, or somebody else hearing about his experience, might choose to interpret or 'construct' that experience as one of 'going mad', 'being disgusted', 'getting furious' or 'being appalled'.

The distinction between feeling and emotion, then, is a way of taking account of both the 'animal' and the 'cultural' aspects of our natures – our humanity. As we said earlier, with regard to instincts (p. 112), everything in the human being, is culturally mediated. Animal 'things' are 'there in us', as indeed our body is ontologically 'there'. But they are always subject to processes of social construction, to cultural interpretation, to enactment. The situation is not as simple as, say, good *feelings* first being 'there', or being 'experienced', and then being *enacted* in a particular way as happiness, joy, contentment or whatever. To assume this is again to fall into the trap of the 'linear' type of psychology we rejected in the previous chapter (pp. 98–102). It might be possible, for example, for one to start off sad and then, with the cultural notion of happiness in mind, to lie back on a pile of comfortable cushions, smile to oneself and actually experience the sensation we label 'happiness'. It has been widely observed, in fact, that choosing to smile can make one 'feel happier' than one was before the smile appeared on our face.

We are getting ourselves involved here in matters which philosophers and psychologists have agonised over for centuries. Why should we trouble to engage with such matters? It is to sharpen our conceptual tool kit in order to come to terms with the issues that were raised in Ken Steary's story. If we are going to require people like Ken and his staff to perform in ways which involve emotional labour, then we need to understand the relationship between the feelings these people might have and the emotional face they are required to present to the world. What are we asking of people who we require to smile at – and 'make feel good' – hotel guests, airline passengers, hospital patients, shop customers and a multitude of other consumers of services in modern societies?

Emotional labour

Emotions and the way these are presented play a key part in all the exchanges we make with other human beings. We smile at a child to show our approval of its behaviour or we frown at a friend who fails to notice the new clothes we are wearing. This is an exchange, in the sense that we are suggesting certain emotions on our own part in order to elicit certain emotions in the other person, ones that will take the relationship forward in the way we wish it to go. This kind of emotional management, which characterises much of our private lives, is called *emotion work* by Hochschild (1985, Reading Guide 8) and she contrasts it with *emotional labour*.

Emotional labour	Concept
An element of work activity in which the worker is required to display certain emotions in order to complete work tasks in the way required by an employer.	

Here, emotional work on the part of an organisational employee is carried out to further the interests of the employer who is buying their services. There is a close relationship between the emotion work which is a normal part of everybody's lives and emotional labour. In the workplace, one does 'emotion work' all the time, simply in order to relate to the other human beings with whom we come into contact. But this overlaps with those efforts that we feel obliged to make as part of our implicit contract with the employer. In dealing with other people at work we would generally be unaware of any tension between our 'natural' inclination to interact, say, in a warm and friendly way with colleagues or customers and what our employment entails. However, once our 'private self' (our self-identity as we are experiencing it at that moment) finds itself in some tension with our self as an 'organisational representative' (a manifestation of our social-identity, as required of us by our employment) we are likely to experience discomfort. We tend, then, to become aware of that which we conceptualise as emotional labour. Such an awareness is reported by Ken Steary when he describes the friendly and sympathetic demeanour he presented to the grumpy guest. He felt obliged to behave in this way because of his understanding of his contract with the hotel company. As a hotel manager and a representative of the organisation he had to behave in this way. His private self, however, was silently addressing the customer as a 'stupid bastard'. He could not show this to the guest because, to do so, would be to break his implicit contract with the employer. And he believes some of his staff are doing precisely this. The reception staff who were complained of were forgetting, or ignoring, what Ken takes to be implicit in the agreement made between employees and employers in the *hospitality* industry: that employees should act hospitably.

A useful distinction that Hochschild makes when examining emotional labour is that between *surface acting* and *deep acting*. Ken Steary's behaviour was an example of surface acting, because he was aware that he was 'putting on a show'. He might be deceiving the guest, but he was not deceiving himself. With deep acting, the employee either 'works up' a feeling in themselves which fits with the emotion they are expressing in doing their job or, as Hochschild puts it, they train their imaginations to achieve the same effect. We see an example in some of the experiences of Cindy Sutor, a sex worker who is reflecting on her work and what it requires of her 'self'.

Activity 5.5

Cindy Sutor's work (Cases and Conversations 5.4) takes her towards the more extreme end of the 'emotional labour market'. Consider:

- how the concepts of *deep acting* and *surface acting* can be applied to Cindy's experiences;

- how the implicit contract she used to make with the clients or with the employer she now works for contains limits on what can be expected emotionally;

- having looked at this relatively extreme case of emotional labour, how many relatively 'normal' jobs can you think of which involve *emotional labour*;

- what elements of *emotional labour* there have been in any jobs you have done and to what extent (a) this involved deep and surface acting, (b) there were limits built into the implicit contract, as you perceived it, which helped in the managing of the emotional demands of the job.

Cindy sets the limits   Cases and Conversations 5.4

I have recently stopped working as a prostitute on my own account and I now do just five shifts a week for the sex phone line company. It pays less but it's safer. It's also different because I now just *talk* about what I actually used to have to *do*. But there are lots of similarities. In both kinds of work, you have got to protect your own idea of who you are. You must not sell your whole self. When I was working on the street I knew that I had to show a certain level of interest in the punter – but not too much. I'd say something like 'Come on, big boy', without really implying that I thought that he was a big boy. You train your clients to know what they are paying for. You show a certain amount of interest in the man, especially if you are hoping for repeat business, but what you don't do is show any kind of excitement and, certainly, absolutely no hint of passion. I'd demean myself if I let that happen. And if I felt myself getting interested I'd damn quickly shut that off. The only exception to this was when I got into the posh call girl game for a while. You get paid a lot more then. So you play it just a little more positively.

Working on the telephone line is really an acting job. You sometimes put on a sexy voice and tell the punter that you are dressed in a skimpy nightie. But, as you tell them this, you make sure you keep a blank face and you look down at the dirty old jeans you are wearing.

Sometimes, though, I get bored with this. If I then find myself talking to someone who sounds really nice I let myself imagine that he is someone that I would actually like to go out with. Then I close my eyes and let myself stop pretending. Sometimes I quite enjoy this, get genuinely excited even. It helps the shift go a bit faster. It's only daydreaming, though. But perhaps those punters do get a better deal – something more genuine. I doubt it though – a proportion of our calls are monitored by the management and I would not want that creep in the 'control room' to think I was giving more than I am being paid for.

As Cindy Sutor is engaged in activities which potentially have deep emotional significance yet which occur within a framework of instrumental economic transaction, she has to work hard to manage boundaries and to 'set limits'. The public or temporary social-identity she is paid to adopt must not be allowed to take over her private self-identity. Such issues arise for workers in an increasing number and variety of occupations, ranging from the airline workers to whose work Hochschild first applied the *emotional labour* concept, to sales staff, call centre workers, entertainers, medical workers, and the 'greeters' who welcome customers as they walk through the entrances of some supermarkets. The more work organisations attempt to develop internal cultures which follow the 'quality management' principles of treating fellow workers as 'internal customers', the more we will see a requirement for most employees to go beyond the 'emotion work' which is a normal and spontaneous part of all human exchange and to be monitored for the quality of the *emotional labour* they put in.

It might be argued that issues of this general kind have to be handled by all workers: protecting themselves from what has often been called the *alienation* of self or, in a more recent formulation, the 'corrosion of self' (Sennett, 1998, Reading Guide 8). The notion of alienation is more a philosophical than a social scientific one and it adopts an *essentialist* view of the human individual, instead seeing 'humanness' *processually* as something which people 'work at' and 'achieve'. But the notion has played a major part in critiques of modern work institutions and the effects they have on the integrity of the human individual. It is consistent, however, with the process-relational recognition of the need of each human being to manage their identities. Identity has to be managed and a logic found or created which links people's self-identities and their social identities to keep them sane and capable of competently playing a part in social life.

Alienation
Concept

The destruction of the integrity of the human self – a splitting of one part of a person's 'being' from another.

Cindy Sutor's management of identity involves a high degree of 'distancing' of her 'self' from her work and this means that much of her 'acting' is of a surface kind. However, she does talk of occasionally moving over into some 'deep acting' when she decides to use her imagination and let herself 'daydream'. But even that is circumscribed by the contractual setting in which she is operating – and by the constant reminder of this in the form of the monitoring manager in the 'control room'. Just as she did not want her prostitution clients to get more than they were paying for, she was not willing to exceed the 'inputs' she was making in her implicit contract with the phone line company. We can well imagine Ken Steary's unsmiling hotel workers in Cases and Conversations 5.3, in the same spirit, arguing that for the money they are paid they cannot be expected to put 'heart and soul' into their jobs. They cannot be expected to treat hotel guests in the way that they would treat guests in their own houses, any more than Cindy would treat her 'punters' as if they were lovers. We might not expect Ken, as a manager, to go along with such an argument. But if Ken were to point out that he always treats customers as if they were his personal guests, we can imagine his reception staff pointing out that Ken is much better rewarded than they are for continuously presenting a positive 'face' to customers. Implicit contracts are not only perceived differently by different parties to them. They are also frequently contested.

Stress
Concept

A sense of distress arising because of pressures experienced in certain social or economic circumstances that render the sufferer emotionally, and sometimes physically, incapable of continuing to behave in the ways expected of them in those circumstances.

Stress, strain and distress

The stressed executive, falling apart under the strains of heavy responsibility, has been one of the clichés of modern life for some time. But this image is coming to be replaced by the one of employees of every kind afflicted with the pathology of *stress* in every corner of the pressured and increasingly competitive organisational world. We hear of people being 'off work with stress', in the same way that they might be off work with mumps or measles. But stress is not something that one 'has' in this way. The notion simply implies that someone is suffering in some way under the strains of their work situation to the extent that they are becoming unable to perform satisfactorily in that work. Stress is a reaction to circumstances and it can arise in situations other than work. A poor single parent with several energetic and demanding children could well find themselves approaching an emotional state where they no longer felt able to act as a parent is expected to act. A husband or wife, oppressed by the nature of their relationship with their spouse, could well find themselves emotionally unable to continue to act as a husband or wife is expected to behave. Similarly a teacher, office cleaner, social worker, factory worker or manager might reach a stage of emotional agitation within their work experiences in which they become incapable of fulfilling the tasks required of them.

What characterises the state of being 'stressed', in work or elsewhere, is clearly being in a position where the person *feels* they cannot continue to perform as they are expected. It is a subjective state – it is not just a matter of being incapable. Someone who found that they simply did not have the patience to look after children, that they were no longer attracted to their spouse or that they were no longer physically strong enough to continue in their current job could *rationally decide* to abandon their children, leave their spouse or resign from their job. Stress – as the etymology of the word suggests – implies something oppressing, pressurising or 'drawing tight' around one. This leads to a feeling, a subjective state, in which one cannot tolerate these pressures. And that subjective state may be accompanied by one or more physical afflictions in which there is a breakdown of some part of the body. No sense can be made of the many experiences of stress if one persists with the Cartesian dualism which separates body and mind and tries to suggest that suffering has to be *either* in the body *or* 'just in the mind'.

While there is no denying the 'reality' of stress, as something which people experience and which can be manifested in physical symptoms, it is important to recognise that this reality is nevertheless one which involves processes of social construction (see above, pp. 62–4). People are making sense of their situation through the use of discursive resources which are available in their culture (p. 120). In another place and time, a worker suffering from what we would nowadays label stress might simply be dismissed as a 'weak character' and a soldier who would, today, be recognised as undergoing stress might be shot at dawn as a coward. But to recognise the importance of processes of construction, interpretation or enactment in how stress is experienced and handled is not just a matter of how we are socially labelled. The sufferer from 'stress' will make sense of their situation in their own way, albeit in the context of the discursive resources which are available to them. Each individual will also be better or worse placed with regard to personal resources such as experience, physical strength, intelligence, intellectual ingenuity and a self-identity which entails their defining themselves, say, as a relatively robust or vulnerable person. They will also be better or worse placed with regard to friends, relatives or advisers to whom they can turn for advice and emotional support. All of these resources, cultural and personal (not that in the final analysis these can be separated – to decide that one is a 'fighter' rather than a 'quitter' is clearly both a personal and a discursive matter), are drawn upon to deal with whatever pressures, strains or 'stressors' are being experienced. Thus, in any workplace or occupational stress situation we choose to look at, we have to consider the interplay of two sets of factors: the *pressures of the work circumstance* and the psychological, emotional and *social resources of the worker* facing those circumstances.

Activity 5.6

Look at the experiences of Tim Dyke and Con Tessock in Cases and Conversations 5.5 and

- note the ways in which the personal resources of the two individuals made a difference to the ways they experienced and dealt with the stress of handling the pressures of the work circumstances they faced;

- identify any work or organisational situation you have witnessed, experienced or can envisage in which different individuals react differently to the same potentially stressful situations, noting which factors you think were the most important in leading to these different reactions.

A tale of two deputies

Cases and Conversations 5.5

We were seen as a team over the several years we worked together as classroom teachers – Tim Dyke and Con Tessock, the dedicated teacher twins. Then, when the school got into trouble and they put the new head teacher in to sort it all out, it wasn't seen as strange that we were both appointed as deputy heads. I was to look after the lower school and Con the upper school. In some ways mine was the more difficult job because I had a higher proportion of disruptive pupils. By the time you reached the senior classes, which were Con's, the worst troublemakers had left. But we had both been pretty good at classroom control and we both had managed to get reasonable examination results with the sort of pupils which we had to handle. What I am saying is that we both started off the managerial stages of our careers similarly placed, similarly matched – not that there was any competitiveness between us, as far as I could see at the time anyway. So it's really interesting to try to work out why I am now about to become a head teacher and Con is a retired teacher at 48, 'put out to grass' on ill health retirement because he couldn't take the stress.

Because the school had been inspected and deemed by the inspectors to be an officially 'failing school', the local authority got rid of our old head teacher and put in Winnie Knowe with a brief to act as a 'super head' and 'turn the school around'. So, from Winnie's arrival and the appointment of Con and myself as deputies, we were being constantly watched and monitored. We knew that everything we did was in order to get a clean bill of health when the Ofsted inspectors came back in. Every little success had therefore to be recorded, every little failure had to be explained and we had to write policy documents for every single aspect of school life – from a careers advice policy to a buildings maintenance policy. The workload was enormous, with all these tasks being piled on top of what was thrown at us by daily events in the school. Con and I seemed to cope well with this, not least because, as mates, we were able to work together. We had each other's shoulders to cry on, if we needed it. So far, so good. But, after a while Con started to get bad tempered with me and he increasingly failed to meet the deadlines we agreed to set each other. I first realised that things were really going wrong one day after he'd had a meeting with Winnie. He came into the staff room absolutely fuming. Winnie Knowe had failed to support a decision that Con had made about disciplining a girl who had been found with a pocket full of illegal pills. Not only had she not backed him, but Winnie had apologised to the girl's parents for the school not being 'sympathetic enough' to a girl 'going through a difficult time'. I couldn't blame Con for getting angry. What sort of time did Winnie think we were all having? I had got angry with the Head on a couple of occasions, for exactly the same reasons. She was clearly unwilling to back Con and me in any risks we took. When we were successful she used to take the credit, and when something went wrong, she blamed us.

Having a boss who does not back you when you are doing an already difficult job is a real strain, believe me. And not only was this made worse by her not giving us any kind of reward or thanks for good work done, she was always sneaking around asking the other staff about us. So, all of the time you felt you were being watched and that you would get slapped if you fell short. The stress of all this was made worse by the press, who seemed to be very keen to see us fail again. Anything negative they could get hold of, they would make a fuss about. You began to feel the whole world was against you. The kids in our school always were difficult. Con and I both knew that before we went there. But somehow the parents were now getting even more of a problem than they had been before. They had never been wonderfully supportive but, now, they seemed to take the attitude that we should sort out their kids all on our own. Disciplining these obstreperous teenagers was our job, they seemed to think. When we asked for their help they tended to look at us and say, 'Just because you are useless – a teacher in a failing school – don't expect us to do your job', and all that.

At times I thought the job was too much. At one point I came out in this rash. The doctor just laughed this off and told me that she knew it was just a stress symptom that I should 'shake off' – because she got exactly the same problem when she found her workload beginning to get too much for her. After that visit to the doctor, I decided that there wasn't much else I could do but will the rash to go away. That didn't work exactly, but once I got into the habit of a glass of good malt whisky every night, it slowly disappeared. Poor old Con, on the other hand, was down at the doctor's all the time. He developed an ulcer, which tended to make him even more evil tempered than he had already become. And he started to talk about a blood pressure problem too.

With all of this he became more and more unpredictable, failing to turn up to meetings and one day he actually hit a pupil who, he said, had come out of a French lesson and called him 'Con the con'. It was his final downfall. So they got him out: a 'victim of the government, the head teacher and of stress' he said at the embarrassing leaving party we held for him.

Why, I ask myself, did I cope and my pal didn't? We were both able and confident teachers. We both had exactly the same stress problems at work. In a sense, I probably just made up my mind I was going to cope and realised that both of us couldn't go under. I sort of took responsibility for him as he started to break down. I needed to do that because I knew he was getting no support from his wife. She's a successful fashion designer who could not see how he couldn't deal with what she saw as the simple problems that face teachers. My wife, on the other hand, was once a teacher and she used to 'talk me down' some nights when I got home. And the kids used to take my mind off things. Con doesn't have kids, just a temperamental dog which is more unpredictable than our worst pupils. I thought at the time that Con had support from his parents, who are both ex-teachers, whereas my parents show no interest in my work. But I rather think, in retrospect, that his parents were just another source of pressure, always telling him what he might do in his job, without realising just how different a school like ours was from the old grammar schools they had taught in.

I also think that Con was starting to be troubled by his association with a notorious and rough school. 'Doesn't it damage your self esteem, having people know you work in such an awful place?', Con asked me one day. 'Self esteem, what's that?', I thought. On reflection I have come to the conclusion that I had no problems in this area. I had convinced myself that the world was a rough old place and that perhaps I was a bit of a hero taking on the challenge of working at the rougher end of the educational service. Con, on the other hand, convinced himself that things shouldn't be the way they are and that the world was somehow against him personally. 'The whole effing world, and this ulcer, is against me' he sobbed one day into his empty coffee mug, the one with the slogan 'A good teacher can make a world of difference' painted on it.

These two individuals involved in managing a large problem school were faced with considerable sources of stress. Not only did they have an enormous amount of work to do, at both the operational and the policy levels, but they also received very little support in the job. Even worse, they tended to get criticised from every quarter – by the head teacher, by journalists and by parents of pupils. Stress, as an emotional and physical reaction to these circumstances was something that Tim and Con both experienced. But Tim was better placed in terms of personal resources to manage the symptoms. Just at the physical level, it would seem that Tim was fortunate in that his body did not react as negatively as Con's did. But, we must be careful not to de-couple the physical and the emotional or mental aspects of human functioning in a Cartesian manner. We cannot assume that there was an initial physical difference between the two men. The mental state of each could itself have been a factor in the physical state that each found himself in, just as the physical state of each of them could have been a factor in their respective emergent mental and emotional states. However, it would seem that Tim was better placed in terms of social and family resources, and the support and opportunity to relax that he could find at home, than Con.

On top of all of this, we can see Tim actively adopting a certain orientation towards his work which helped him manage his situation. He opted to define himself by applying a particular culturally available discursive resource to himself: the notion of a 'hero' who takes on a challenge. He also takes his relationship with Con into account in trying to explain his emergent orientation to events – suggesting that taking some responsibility for his friend was a factor in his adopting a positive stance towards the difficulties of their shared circumstances. Notice also that he adopts a positive characterisation of the school, as 'rough' as it was, as part of an educational *service*. And where Tim takes a stoic philosophical view of the world, seeing it as a generally 'rough place' that one has got to make the best of, Con adopts a different view of the world as one which 'ought' to be better than it is. Whereas Tim is willing to try to take control over circumstances, Con seems to be adopting an orientation in which he resigns himself to losing control, because the world is against him.

In looking at this case study in occupational stress and how individuals manage it, we must remember that we cannot read it as if we were actually seeing into the minds of these two individuals. Tim is creating an account of what happened, rather than neutrally 'reporting' it. He is constructing a plausible tale which helps make sense of things both for himself and for the researcher that he is speaking to. The only account we have of Con's experience is that which his old friend gives us, on the basis of what he remembers seeing and hearing. We might also note that Tim Dyke is taking part in the ongoing social construction process, whereby work researchers, and others, analyse the sort of events that happened here in terms of 'stress' factors and personal resources for 'managing stress'. Nevertheless, in pragmatist terms, there is value in using an analysis of this kind. It is invaluable in helping us to understand and, potentially, to manage stressful situations.

We are making use here of a process-relational style of analysis in which exchanges and reciprocities – positive ones and negative ones – are seen to play a part in the way two individuals manage their identities, their work and their lives. We have a framework that we can apply to situations of stress and stress management generally. It suggests that we should not regard stress as something that necessarily results from having either heavy responsibilities in our jobs or being faced with a heavy workload. The emotional and physical difficulties which we label 'stress' arise when the individual does not have the personal and social 'resources' to enable them to define the pressures of this responsibility or workload as *manageable*. Occupational stress, or *distress*, is avoided when the occupational or organisational circumstances are ones over which the individual feels they can assert control, rather than ones which will swamp them or lead to their 'breaking down'.

One of the ways in which stress at work can be handled is by having a home or family life that enables ones to balance the stresses of work with the pleasures and recreation of home life. However, the growing problem of a 'long hours culture' in work organisations has made this increasingly unlikely for many professional and managerial employees – even if it were true in the first place that home life is the haven of peace and relaxation that we often would like it to be. In spite of employers claiming to be concerned with helping employees to find a 'work–life balance', organisational restructuring and the associated insecurities have increased the pressures on managers to spend long hours at work (Worrall and Cooper, 1999, Reading Guide 9). For many people the stresses of family life and the stresses of work have come to be mutually reinforcing, leading to a situation when, as Hochschild (1997a and 1997b, Reading Guide 22) has put it, 'work becomes home and home becomes work'.

Managing and not managing

Stress can arise in any kind of occupation and at home as well as at work. But there may be particular ways in which the formal role of 'manager' involves stresses, or potential stresses, for the person filling it. Such a suggestion was made in Chapter 2 (p. 53) when the notion of 'managism' was introduced. This is a discourse based on a view of management as a specialised occupation with a body of objective knowledge which enables managers to design, build and run organisations in the same way that one might engineer and drive machines. It was seen as having a possible psychological function for people in managerial jobs. It can function as a comfort in the face of the doubts, ambiguities and threats that managers face in their work. It can give some security in the face of finding that one's authority is regularly challenged, that one has to get people to do things they do not wish to do and that one frequently has to act on the basis of partial knowledge or inadequate understanding. In many ways, one might say, such pressures exist in a range of occupations other than that of management. This is undoubtedly the case, but the dominance of the systems-control view of work organisations and the foundations of this in the modernist faith that human beings can rationally control their world and their destiny, has created expectations of what managers should be able to do which are wholly unrealistic. Much of the management literature, in book and magazine form, on offer to the aspiring manager is based on tales of management heroes – of super-men and superwomen who make and break the big corporations that make the world go round. The rising manager is encouraged to aspire to *mastery* of their domains, whether or not they choose to certify this with that badge of advanced competence, the *master* of business administration (MBA) degree.

There is no reason to see anything *inherently* stressful in managerial work. But it is possible to argue that there is a particular danger of managers becoming stressed if they find that they are not in a position to behave or 'perform' in the ways expected of them as *managers*. This is especially likely to become a problem if they are influenced by a dominant discourse that portrays managers as strong, cool, reflective planners who see further ahead than everyone else and are able to exert control over all those around them to ensure that their visionary strategies and plans are implemented. This is where the 'managism', which we have recognised as being a potential *comfort* to managers faced with all the ambiguities, anxieties and unpredictabilities of their work, can also become a *threat* to them. It can create unrealisable expectations of managers as supermen and superwomen. It demands that they should constantly be demonstrating their high level technical (engineering-like) skills. It demands that they regularly demonstrate their possession of near mystical personal virtues like 'vision' and 'leadership qualities'. And, of course, it demands that they prove themselves all the time by achieving the ever more demanding 'results' that the increasingly pressured and competitive political–economic context encourages their employers to require of them.

Much of the discursive material that is available to managers to enable them to frame their work and the occupational pressures they face incorporates elements of 'managist' thinking. And it incorporates the 'double-edged blade' of that discourse. It can help managers cut through the vines and creepers that impede them as they make their way through the jungle of corporate life. But it can come back on the wielder of the blade and do them an injury. In stress terms, it can help in handling the sources of managerial stress but it can also make this more difficult. It is worthwhile looking at some of the material written for managers to see how this works.

Activity 5.7

'Popular', as opposed to academic, management literature can be seen as both trying to reassure or assist managers and also as something which puts heavy pressures on them by creating unrealisable expectations or ambitions. Look for evidence of each of these tendencies (*potentially reassuring and potentially disturbing*) in:

- books in shops, including high street bookshops and those in railway stations or airports;

- articles and advertisements in management magazines and the business pages of newspapers;

- recruitment advertisements for management jobs.

In performing this exercise, it might be noticed that much of this documentary material contains the potential to reassure and to frighten, at the same time. Process-relational thinking would encourage us to recognise that there is no unambiguous meaning or message in any piece of text, however. The reader actively makes sense of what the text was intended to imply – they 'make their own reading' in the light of their own past experiences, current concerns and future aspirations. Thus one can note the potential for the reader of the book club brochure quoted in Table 5.1 to be given confidence, or to be frightened off – or a combination of these two possibilities – by the array of books offered.

TABLE 5.1 Books to help you manage: excerpts from a book club brochure

Books get you Skilled

- Financial Engineering: tools and techniques to manage financial risk
- The Handbook of Skilful Management
- The Shorter MBA: a practical approach to business skills . . .

Books get you Ahead

- Corporate Strategies of the Top 100 Companies of the Future
- Focus: the future of our company depends on it
- Profitable Purchasing Strategies: a manager's guide for improving organisational competitiveness through the skills of purchasing
- The New Dynamics of Goals Setting: flextactics for a fast-changing future
- How to be a Better Problems Solver
- How to be a Better Decision-maker . . .

Books get you Success

- Management Masterclass: a practical guide to the new realities of business
- Re-inventing Leadership: strategies to achieve a new style of leadership . . .
- The Master Marketeer . . .
- Imagination Engineering: the toolkit for business creativity . . .

Books get you Noticed

- Emotional Intelligence: why it can matter more than IQ
- 10-Minute Time and Stress Management . . .
- Super-learning 2000: new, triple-fast ways you can learn, earn and succeed in the twenty-first century
- Great Answers to tough Interview Questions
- The Perfect CV . . .

Books get you Heard

- Assertiveness at Work: What to Say When you are Dying on the Platform
- Dealing with Difficult People: proven strategies for handling stressful situations . . .
- How to Write Proposals and Reports that get Results
- The Handbook of Communication Skills . . .

Books get you Results

- NLP for Trainers: communicating for excellence
- Managing Change Through Training and Development
- The Success Culture: how to build an organisation with vision and purpose . . .

This advertising material can be understood as functioning like many stories do (p. 116). It builds up anxieties in the reader and then implies that these anxieties will be overcome by the purchase of the product. The writers of the book club brochure have worked hard to remind the reader how frightening the managerial (or 'business') world is. We are told that a very uncertain future is facing us and there are many skills that we must acquire if we are to be success-ful. We are reminded that we have to solve problems and make decisions, deal with markets and manage our time and the stress that our work takes us into. We are not allowed to forget any anxieties we might have about how assertive we are, how capable we are at communicating generally and, especially, how confident we will be when we have to get up on a platform to give a speech. We are presented with the horrific prospect of 'dying' in front of an audience. And we are confronted with the spectre of the 'difficult people' we have to handle and nudged to remember that we are likely to face tough questions in the inter-views we will be put through. Not only that, but we are also prompted to believe that these interviewers will expect a 'perfect' curriculum vitae to accompany any application we make for the jobs we want to get. We have a lot to cope with if we are going to travel upwards and onwards into the sunny uplands of the 'suc-cess culture'.

To reassure us that all of this can be handled, the copywriters make use of a whole range of 'managist' discursive resources in presenting their wares. Work organisations can be *engineered*, if we acquire the right *skills*. Not that we should worry too much about acquiring these skills: they are available in a 'handbook' or a single volume MBA. Not only can the potentially terrifying world of finance be 'engineered', so can our very imaginations. We need not worry therefore about whether we are creative or not – we simply have to buy the 'toolkit'. What we can achieve is *mastery* (available in the 'Masterclass' if not in the shorter MBA). That means that we won't be ordinary marketing managers. We will become master marketers. And, we won't just be ordinary management learners. We will become 'superlearners'. But if we do not want to be 'masters', then we can become gener-als or field marshals, devising strategies left, right and centre: corporate strategies, purchasing strategies, strategies for becoming leaders and strategies for handling stressful situations. And, if the role of strategist does not appeal, then we might resort to what the author of one of these books calls, 'flextactics'. For some, this might be 'neologism too far' (to borrow a phrase applied by a friendly critic to the present author's invention of the word 'managism'). But maybe the term has something to offer as a new discursive resource for managers who want to be highly adaptable, dynamic and fast on their feet – managers who are more excited by the prospect of being the guerrilla fighters of the fast moving twenty-first cen-tury rather than the crusty old generals of the slow moving past.

Kurt Delnies, whom we shall meet shortly in Cases and Conversations 5.6, tries to summarise the problems that these materials are attempting to address when he observes that 'managers are expected, in principle, to control that which, in practice, cannot be controlled'. The search for control, whether explicitly spoken of or not, is the *leitmotif*, the slogan, the war cry of all these management books – and of many more, academic ones included. Control was something Ken Steary spoke of directly when he was referring to his difficulties in the hotel company. He was 'meant to be in control' he said, and he felt that he could not afford to be seen to drop what he referred to as the 'façade of con-trol' (p. 140). Even when he felt out of control of the situation (and, hence, laughed and cried at the same time), he kept the manifestations of this collapse private. The hotel manager was not in a position to reveal too much of his humanity. On top of that, he had no one to turn to for help, he said. This, of course, is not to say that he might not have friends, advisers or family to help him in this respect, as Tim Dyke did in Cases and Conversations 5.5. But Ken is suggesting something particularly 'lonely' about the position of the manager, someone who has to be an exemplar to the rest of the staff in many ways. Again, it is something of a pressure to be more than human – taking on the role of the manager as the hero, superman or superwoman of the popular management literature. And these pressures are added to, not just by the monitoring of the managers by more senior managers, but by the career-competitive environment that many managers work in.

Jackall (1988, Reading Guide 22) provides an especially disturbing research account of the pressures faced by managers in certain American corporations. He observes managers continually expressing excitement and enthusiasm for what they are doing while covering up the profound anxieties they are experiencing. They display cheerfulness and 'iron self control' in the face of recurring fears of losing their jobs or losing the chance of career advancement. They see constant threats from the capriciousness of the corporation and from the contingencies of the corporation's circumstances. This means they must constantly be on the watch for re-organisation or recession. They feel as if they are all the time 'on probation' and are in constant danger of being caught out making mistakes or of being blamed for the mistakes of others. They worry about being evaluated against performance criteria to which they cannot make a difference and they get anxious about simply finding themselves in the wrong place at the wrong time.

How generalisable Jackall's rather extreme account is to other corporations or to organisations in other societies might be debated. There has certainly been evidence to suggest that many people in 'middle management' have been made increasingly insecure and pressured by trends to remove layers of management from organisations and from general pressures for increased performance. One study suggested that a high proportion of British managers could be characterised as 'reluctant managers' (Scase and Goffee, 1989, Reading Guide 9). Other studies, however, have suggested that the same restructuring of organisations can lead to an increase in the sense of autonomy and job satisfaction for *some* managers in such organisations (Dopson and Stewart, 1990; Thomas and Dunkerley, 1999 and other references in Reading Guide 9). The *extent* of the pressures to show control in the face of the uncontrollable which were put upon the managers studied by Jackall may be especially high and may be particular to the corporate settings concerned. But the general nature of those pressures and anxieties is something that we can expect to see, to a greater or lesser extent, in many other organisational and managerial situations. The closer the researcher gets to managerial activity, by adopting an ethnographic or participant observation style of investigation, the more apparent this kind of thing becomes. What also becomes apparent are the various ways in which these underlying worries manifest themselves in managers' behaviour, as the following observations made in a British research situation suggest:

The more I saw of the managers at Ryland, the more I became aware of the extent of human angst, insecurity, doubt and frailty among them. I observed managers being rude to their staff, refusing to listen to advice given to them within their departments, curtly announcing unexplained decisions, losing their tempers with people from other departments, creating rows with fellow managers. I came across numerous examples of managers offending others by failing to reply to telephone calls or by writing curt memoranda or electronic mail messages rather than explaining decisions face-to-face to people, of managers spreading malicious gossip about others, of managers failing to turn up to meetings where their presence was important. On a number of occasions I found myself mediating between managers who had fallen out with each other and were unwilling to meet to sort out difficulties. And on three occasions, I actually found myself having to persuade a manager that it would not be advisable to go and exert physical violence against another

(Watson, 2001, p.178, Reading Guide 2)

It was suggested in the study at the Ryland plant that a number of the managers were tending to fall in with the assumptions of classical management thinking which required managers to be the rational planners and the analytical designers of corporate systems. They were thus setting themselves above and apart from many of the daily organisational actions and 'shopfloor problems' in which more junior people in the company felt these managers should have involved themselves. Managers were tending to spend more and more hours in management meetings, as business difficulties became increasingly apparent. They were risking knowing less and less about what was going on in the factory and amongst the sales force – at the same time as they had to continue to give an impression of knowing everything. Not only did the anxieties that this created lead to various emotional outbursts and illogical and over-personalised clashes between managers, it seemed to encourage them to work even harder at devising new 'systems', new organisational structures and an endless stream of fashionable 'new initiatives'.

Managers' attitudes to new management fashions, fads and consultant-led initiatives (see Reading Guide 12) were not straightforward, this research suggested. They tended to be ambivalent about them – loving and hating them at the same time (Watson, 1994, Reading Guide 12). The same managers who would complain one day about 'the launch of yet another new management idea' (usually something given an acronym or abbreviation like PDP, TQM or BPR) would, another day, be heard talking enthusiastically about some equivalent manifestation of 'new management thinking' which they felt was relevant to the problems faced in their own area of management. The initiatives undertaken and the consultants' reports commissioned were sometimes recognised as managerially effective, but often they were not. They all, however, functioned in part as a means of managers handling the pressures and anxieties of the type of work they were in. They gave some kind of emotional reassurance. They were all ways of helping with the *double control problem* that all managers have to handle. This is the challenge that every manager faces of having to handle the requirement to control the activities of others (and increasingly the sentiments and values of others) at the same time as they have to control their personal identities and manage their own lives.

Double control problem

Concept

That pressure that is put on managers to manage the activities and thinking of others at the same time as they have to manage and shape their own identities, lives and personal projects.

A further manifestation of the behaviours that arise when all of this becomes difficult is resorting to tortuous language.

Manager talk and controlling the uncontrollable

It is often observed how the management world increasingly requires its inhabitants to talk in an unnecessarily jargonistic way. There is nothing wrong with jargon in itself, of course. Every specialist activity, from engineering to psychology and cattle breeding has its own technical language. However, the question arises as to why people in managerial work often speak in ways that depart from normal language when, in practice, they are talking about matters where normal language would be more than adequate. It might be done to impress people, inside and outside of management, but a more likely explanation of the phenomenon that we will shortly hear Kurt Delnies call 'management bollock speak' is that it can give emotional reassurance to managers in the light of the anxieties and pressures that they are having to handle. The manager feels that little bit better revealing a worry about coping with a new job by telling an interview panel, 'I am cognisant of the steep learning curve I shall confront' instead of perhaps saying, 'I know I am going to have to learn a lot rather quickly'. This kind of talk might be dismissed by a cruel critic of managerial 'bollock speak' as a matter of 'whistling in the dark'. But we should remember that when we are out on a very dark night and feeling unsure, whistling a bold melody can make us feel a lot better and a lot more confident about the possibility of reaching our destination. The sound produced might not mean much to anyone who hears it but the whistler copes better with the darkness and feels less afraid of the unknown world through which he or she is travelling. But, should they be fooling themselves in this way? Kurt Delnies thinks not.

Activity 5.8

Read Kurt Delnies' story in Cases and Conversations 5.6 of how he changed his approach to his job and avoided 'falling over the edge of the cliff', paying particular attention to the role that 'managerial language' played in this. If you are in a position to listen to, or read, some of the 'pseudo jargon' (or 'bollock speak', as Delnies calls it) that is used in work organisations,

- note down as many words or phrases as possible that you only hear in a managerial or organisational context – ones you would not expect to hear outside the workplace;

- think about why such language is used in this context;

- consider how much validity there is in Jill Gollanfield's theory – her idea that the use of such language might be a sign that someone is 'losing it'?

Kurt crawls back from the edge

Cases and Conversations 5.6

How long have you been in charge of the company, Kurt?

I have been chief executive here for nearly a year now. It's good, yeah.

You seem very pleased with everything.

I am. The business is going great. The chairman puts that down to me. And if you're implying that I sound pleased with myself, then I confess to that. But this is not a confession of smugness or complacency, let me reassure you.

What is it then?

I am pleased with myself precisely because I know all about becoming smug and self-satisfied. I therefore consciously avoid – avoid like the plague – getting complacent.

I notice that you say you 'consciously' avoid this. You've thought hard about these things?

If your career goes really well, like mine did in my first ten years, you get the idea that you know it all. Then you don't see the dangers creeping up on you. You become blind to the cliff edge that you are getting close to. Or perhaps it would be truer in my own case to say that I half sensed that I was getting near to the edge of a precipice. But all I did, in practice, was to run faster towards the edge. I just held my head up in the air, looked over the heads of all the people round me and, I suppose, talked over the people who might have warned me.

What was this precipice?

It was the appearance of a competitive product that could easily have smashed our market share. But let me tell you first how I got into this position. I got a first class degree in electronic engineering and joined the company's design department where they treated me as a bit of a star. They sent me to the States to get an MBA. I thought I was popular with the other design engineers but, I now recognise, this was only because they could come to me for help with difficult problems, ones that I always seemed able to solve faster than most of them. I was promoted very fast and, before I knew where I was, I was Director of Business Development. The RAE 3000 was my baby and with the sales force working their socks off and the engineers making regular upgrades on the software side, we got the bulk of the European market. My personal knowledge of Germany was a big factor in that. Anyway, I was tasked to grow the US market. So I developed a marketing plan and I invented a way we could build up the functionality of the unit in the future. Following this?

Yes, I think so.

Well, never mind the technical details. I can't be sure about all this but, looking back, I think I was half aware that the sales people were looking less confident when I addressed them at our monthly meetings. And I was sort of conscious of the engineers being edgy with me at the team briefings. They seemed to have nothing to say and I found I was more and more talking at people. But being the determined chap I was, I brushed this off. However, I am told that my 'speeches', as my talks and briefings were referred to, were becoming increasingly – what was the word? – yes, 'convoluted'. That's what I was told. What this apparently meant was that I was not just rambling but that I was using more and more pseudo-business jargon, you know, management bollock speak. Looking back, it appears that as I got more and more anxious (inwardly or subconsciously, I suppose), the more I gabbled out this stuff. Anyway, I realised what I was doing. I stopped thinking that I could mastermind all the engineering and all the marketing and I started to listen to my colleagues. I related much better to people generally and I crept back from the edge of the cliff. After a brilliant team effort, we managed to get out an RAE 5000, and beat the competition. So now I am in the top job. That's the story. We re-engineered our best product and I re-engineered myself. That sounds good, doesn't it?

Very good. But it does sound a bit, a bit unconvincing. I don't mean the outcomes but how you came to have this epiphany. You can't tell me that you saw a blinding light on the road to Damascus sitting here in this corporate office block? How did it happen?

I'm not sure I want to talk about that. It's, er, sensitive.

It's completely in confidence. I won't write anything that anyone will pin down to you.

I am not sure. It was all to do with my having an affair with my secretary, you see. Well, you know Jill. It wasn't a sordid affair, let me tell you.

But will you tell me?

OK then. Yes, I feel I have to, having said what I have. I was happily married, and I still am. So is Jill. But I was obviously getting in something of an emotional state at work. Jill Gollanfield is a wonderful person as well as a great secretary and she understood far better than I did what was happening. Anyway, I noticed that she was increasingly altering the letters I was dictating to her. I mentioned it on one occasion. Apparently, like a lot of the other managers in the company, I kept using the world 'substantive' when I should have used 'substantial'. She thought this was pompous as well as ignorant. But she said nothing. It was only when the topic came up again at breakfast in a German hotel, after the first night we spent together would you believe, that she really put me in the picture about myself. It was amazing. You couldn't make it up.

What couldn't you make up?

She even had shorthand notes in her handbag of some of the things I had been saying at briefings. That's when she used the word 'convoluted'. And she had this idea that the more people in organisations, and in management especially, start to 'lose it', the more they descend into affected language. I call it bollock speak, but she wouldn't use such a term. Anyway she realised that I was 'losing it' and, bloody hell, she was monitoring my progress to the cliff edge by the extent to which I was burbling.

So you've reverted to plain English?

Oh yes, I call a cock up a cock up and not a 'contingent operating difficulty', if that's what you mean. But it's not getting rid of the old bad language – the pompous bollock speak I mean, not the good old Anglo-Saxon – that is important. Jill helped me see that. For all the stuff I did in the past, and the Wharton MBA I took, Jill has been the best management teacher I have had. What I now realise is that the manager, and the more senior you are the more this is the case, is dependent on other people. Business circumstances, organisational and engineering matters as well, are too complex for any manager to control. It seems that managers are expected, in principle, to control that which, in practice, cannot be controlled. However clever you are, you've got to learn the importance of using the people around you, using their eyes and ears and using their knowledge.

And you and Jill, are you…?

Er, only now and then. But Jill, I think, is cleverer than me. She has weaned me off depending on her emotionally. But she and I are a great team.

This story is relevant to many of the issues we have considered in this chapter, but let's concentrate for the moment on the issue of what Kurt calls 'bollock speak'. Kurt Delnies tells us that Jill Gollanfield has a personal theory about the connection between how managers talk and their confidence in their jobs. Indeed, the less confident Kurt became, the more he resorted to what Jill calls 'convoluted language'. There is probably a valuable insight here, something that Kurt seems to appreciate when looking back to when he was beginning to 'lose it', and was using such expressions as 'contingent operational difficulties', rather than plain English. A similar insight is offered by Hoggart, as he chronicles in his parliamentary sketches the ways in which government ministers borrow from 'modern management-speak' and 'have a special love for buzzy words such as "delivery", "best practice" and "excellence", as illustrated in a minister's statement that "we are putting in place the job search programmes which have already had considerable success at the pilot stage, offering practical help, and are delivering people into the jobs which are there"' (Hoggart, 2000a, Reading Guide 3). Hoggart suggests that no minister could bear to say 'we're doing three things to tackle this'. Instead they announce a 'three-pronged integrated strategy'. He calls this 'Lego language' because it works like the children's building blocks: 'start fixing it together and you soon have something sturdily built but quite impossible to recognise'. In a sense, government ministers are facing some of the biggest managerial challenges of modern societies and Hoggart gets close to the Gollanfield theory that people involved in managerial work are showing signs of panic (or 'losing it') when they resort to convoluted pseudo-jargon. 'You know when things are bad', he says, 'when ministers start to hammer on about "rolling out new cross-cutting initiatives at local level"' (Hoggart, 2000b, Reading Guide 3).

But how relevant is this type of explanation to the language examples that you have collected or to the expressions included in Table 5.2? There appear to be two kinds of language, both of which one would be unlikely to hear outside the work organisation context – the relatively formal and the informal.

TABLE 5.2 Organisational expressions heard being used by managers	
Relatively informal expressions	**Relatively formal expressions**
● We'll run it up the flagpole and see how it flies	● We are becoming much more client-centred and less finance driven
● Shall we put that on the back burner?	
● I would appreciate more input and a lot more feed-back	● The executive away-day envisioned a bolder strategic emphasis for the division
● Run it past me again – are we really talking telephone numbers?	● Downsizing is not our preferred option, we must smartsize
● Would you rubber stamp that scenario?	● We have the strategy in place to deliver our vision
● Put some feelers out while I see if there's a window in my diary	● Our premier market position has been achieved through the unflaggingly professional delivery of quality services
● Let's touch base	● Having bottomed it out and made the appropriate and timely interventions domestically, we made several strategic withdrawals on the global side
● Shall we take that on board and offer them a ballpark figure?	
● We can suck it and see, and perhaps float the idea elsewhere if it works	● Resource deployment will be highly leveraged in this instance
● If we do lunch I can share my thoughts with you	● You will be the prime mover on the development of a platform of sustainable and robust strategies for the delivery of the core business activities of the portfolio
● Let's see if we can get them to buy into the mission	
● We'll ditch the offer if we find it's dead in the water	● What we can offer is an integrated management development experience and the benefits of buying into the achievements of an internationally recognised centre of excellence
● It's a matter of deliverables and walking the talk – so get real	
● They tell me that the management information system will be rolled out in August – and the human resources information system will be off the ground by Christmas	● The business has the right architecture in place to ensure the delivery of sustainable competitive advantage

A variety of factors might encourage people to speak and write in the rather artificial, unspontaneous or 'convoluted' ways we often come across in organisational contexts. For example, it is obvious that much of the language reported in Table 5.2 is the result of people simply mimicking others. The tendency of managers across Kurt's organisation to misuse the word 'substantive', for example, can be taken as a simple matter of people imitating whoever it was who first committed this error, consciously or otherwise. It might be that the first person to speak in this way was simply being pompous for the sake of being pompous, as Jill implies, as opposed to being pompous in order to handle any managerial angst. The question arises, however, of why rather unnatural language forms seem to arise in the context of the management of work in the first place. Even if much of the transmission is a matter of imitation, how did such strange language come to be there to imitate?

It might be that the cultural pattern whereby people involved in managerial processes adopt language that differs from 'normal' ways of speaking has something to do with the difficulties of handling the rather abstract and ambiguous matters that they are faced with. We noted in Chapter 3 (p. 61) how common it is to 'reify' or 'personalise' the organisation to be able to deal with a reality that is a virtual rather than a concrete one. We cannot see, hear or touch an organisation yet we often speak about it as if it were a concrete entity. We speak of it as something that has goals or missions and as something that acts in particular ways. To say that 'the organisation decided to move out of that market', for example, is easier and more convenient than to try to talk about all the complex events, arguments and negotiated understandings that amount to this change in business activity. Perhaps we do something similar in everyday organisational talk, constantly using metaphors to make abstract matters seem more solid – and thus more manageable. We thus get all the talk of rubber stamps, feelers, ballparks, windows, drivers, levers, movers, cores and deliverables. The abstract is made concrete, the vague is made solid, the ungraspable is made graspable, and the uncontrollable is made controllable. Or is it?

How effective any of this bizarre language actually is when it comes to successful communication is surely questionable. Perhaps we can see some point in Jill Gollanfield's suspicion that managers and others who resort to this kind of talk are losing touch with reality rather than grasping it. There could, however, be a rational motive behind a manager's choice to talk in this way. They might, for example, have calculated that it would help them in their work by impressing the people they are dealing with. Or the language might be part of a deliberate attempt to avoid communicating – to avoid being challenged perhaps. Hoggart suggests that such an effect comes about in parliament when, for example, government ministers refer to 'new job retention pilots', 'better regulation taskforces' and endless 'rollouts'. People, he suggests, do not challenge this kind of thing because nobody 'knows exactly what it means' (Hoggart, 2000a, Reading Guide 3). One suspects, however, that there is a much greater emotional significance to the choice of such language. Again, it is to do with the emotional pressure of being in a job where one has to try to control that which is not readily amenable to control. There is a degree of 'whistling in the dark' about all this peculiar talk, but the emotional and the rational should not be separated too much. As was implied earlier, there is a degree of rationality in choosing to whistle or sing in the dark. If we know it will make us feel better and less afraid of the dark, then we might be wise to handle the emotions of fear or insecurity by holding our heads high and singing in the loudest voice we can manage about 'sustainable competitive advantage', 'robust platforms' and 'timely interventions' – or whatever other catchy numbers we hear belted out by other singers who are also making their way through the murk of the organisational, political or managerial jungle.

The challenge of managerial work

Encouraged by his lover and mentor, Kurt Delnies clearly concluded that he should fully come to terms with the challenges of managerial work and not hide behind pretentious or affected language. In many ways he was coming to terms with the complexities and subtleties of managerial work that we examined in Chapter 3 when looking at how both research on managerial behaviour can help us make sense of what managers do.

Activity 5.9

Look back to Chapter 3, pp. 84–91, and consider:

- how well Kurt Delnies' account of his managerial practices in the present chapter fits what we learned in the earlier chapter about managerial behaviour from the research studies on managerial behaviour;

- what similarities and differences you see between Peter Brodie's account of his working day and what Kurt says about the way he manages his chief executive job.

The story that Kurt Delnies has to tell about his almost 'losing it' and falling over a precipice brings together many of the themes of this and the previous chapters. Kurt very effectively illustrates how an individual's *orientation to work* can change, as a result both of changing circumstances and the way the individual makes sense of or *enacts* those circumstances. In changing his orientations he has modified his own *self-identity* as well as adjusting in a significant way work aspects of his *social-identity*. The pattern of *reciprocities* in his relationships with others in the organisation has changed and, as his general appreciation of *strategic exchange* issues has become more sophisticated, he has succeeded in his personal career project of becoming a chief executive. This success has happened in large part as a result of a personal and *emotional* relationship that developed between Kurt and Jill. From Kurt's account, it appears that careful *emotional management* is occurring here. He has been weaned off 'emotional dependence' on Jill and, it would appear, they are both happily married to their respective spouses.

Kurt's story illustrates the key point made in Chapter 4, that an understanding of people and behaviour in the specific circumstances of work organisations or managerial work has to be rooted in a general awareness of 'what it is to be human'. And, as Activity 5.9 will have shown, to get a full understanding of what was occurring in Kurt's life and work experience we need to set it in the context of the sort of research evidence and theorising about the nature of managerial work which was presented in Chapter 3. In that chapter it was argued that the most useful way in which to make sense of managerial work is to relate it to matters of the strategic shaping and directing of the work organisation in which it occurs. The *strategic exchange* thinking does this theoretically by drawing a parallel between the exchanges which human beings (and managers in particular) make as they shape their lives and the exchanges which are made between organisations and the range of constituencies with which they 'trade'. We now turn to these matters of organisational strategy in Chapter 6.

Summary

In this chapter the following key points have been made:

- At the heart of the relationship between the employee and the employing organisation is an *implicit contract* whereby it is understood that the employee will make a particular set of contributions, at a particular level, to the organisation's work in return for a particular mix of rewards. This bargain has to be understood in light of both the life situation and projects of the employee and the strategic direction being followed by the organisation – it is thus central to the *strategic exchange* relationship between the individual and the organisation.

- The implicit contract, as it is understood by the employee, forms part of that employee's *orientation to work*, the meaning they attach to their employment and which influences the ways they act within that employment.

- Individuals' entry to work or to an organisation can be understood in terms of their *initial orientation to work*. This, however, is likely to change as both the organisational and the individual's circumstances (inside and outside work) change. The process of change continues as the individual's personal life and projects move on and as their employment career develops.

- Feelings and emotions play a central part in all work and organisational situations. They cannot be seen as incidental and peripheral to the rational task-based activities with which people are involved.

- In various kinds of work, service work and managerial work especially, there is an emotional dimension built into what is required of the worker. This *emotional labour* can be handled in different ways; by the worker choosing to engage in either 'deep' or 'surface' acting, for example.

- *Stress* is an emotionally related phenomenon. It involves an experience of distress which leads to an individual being incapable of performing the tasks that are required of them. It is not something that is inherent in either the individual or the work. It can only be understood by looking at how the circumstances of the individual interrelate with the organisational circumstances and pressures.

- People vary in how they cope with potentially stressing circumstances and the psychological, emotional and social resources that they can draw upon influence how well they cope.

- Stress is not inherent in managerial work any more than it is in any other kind of occupation. However, there are particular emotional pressures upon people in this kind of work which can be understood as deriving, in part, from the expectations which are attached to particular managerial appointments and, in part, from *managist* discourses which tend to frame managerial activity in modern societies. Paradoxically the *discursive resources* of 'managism' can function both to reassure managers faced with the challenge of 'controlling the uncontrollable' and to increase their sense of insecurity in the face of the *double control problem* which characterises managerial work. This results from the fact that managers are required to shape and control the activities and even the feelings and values of others at the same time as they have to cope with controlling their own lives and identities.

- Managerial and organisational work often involves people adopting a pseudo-jargonistic style of convoluted language that can be understood in part as reflecting a struggle to handle the anxieties and unpredictabilities of organisational work. The often-bizarre expressions to be heard in managerial and organisational situations may have other functions too and any particular organisational practitioner would need carefully to consider both the advantages and disadvantages of talking in a way which departs from normal language use. They would be wise to bear in mind the possibility that resorting to 'managerial bollock speak' is not just an indication of possible communication breakdown but a sign that a manager is beginning to lose their grip on what they are doing.

- A manager's reflection on such matters as the type of language they use would entail their reviewing their basic orientation to managerial work, as well as judging how well they are performing the tasks allocated to them. It would also relate to how they were managing their own emotions, their identity and the general strategic exchange processes in which they are engaged.

Reading

Reading Guides 8, 9, 12 and 22, especially, contain material that supports and takes further much of what is covered in Chapter 5.

Organising and strategy-making

Having read this chapter and completed its associated activites, readers should be able to:

- Recognise the limitations of treating strategic thinking as a search for organisational 'competitive advantage'.

- Appreciate the advantages of seeing strategy-making as a component of managerial activity generally and see the relevance to managerial practice of treating all managers, in part, as strategists.

- Identify the characteristics of the 'rational', 'serial', 'linear' or 'strategic planning' orthodoxy about strategy-making and understand how this suffers from many of the same limitations that were identified in earlier chapters with regard to systems-control ways of thinking.

- Understand how process-relational thinking can be applied to strategy-making, recognising the advantages of regarding strategies as the *patterns to be seen emerging over time that enable an organisation to continue into the future*.

- While noting how all organisational strategies are 'emergent', see that there may be variations across them in the balance that exists between attempts to plan ahead, on the one hand, and incremental adaptations, experiments and opportunistic moves on the other.

- Relate the process-relational thinking to some more broadly processual thinking that is developing in the broader managerial literature, recognising how this reflects certain changes in organisational practices.

- Appreciate how the term *directed evolution* can be used to characterise this broad shift in thought and practice and see the relevance of this to concepts of *logical incrementalism*, *strategic intent*, and *the learning organisation*.

continued

● Relate strategy-making processes to the concept of organisational effectiveness by appreciating the centrality to managerial and strategy-making work of the logic of working towards the survival of the organisation into the long term.

● Analyse the strategic issues facing any particular organisation by identifying the organisational *strategic exchange* processes necessary for handling the perceived patterns of resource dependence that are relevant to survival into the long term.

● Understand the two-way relationship of the identities, orientations and personal strategic exchanges of strategy-makers themselves and the emergent strategies of the organisations within which they work.

Strategy-making and managing in an uncertain world

Various ways in which *Organising and Managing Work* seeks to 'go beyond' the traditional business school subject of 'Organisational Behaviour' were identified in Chapter 1. And one of these was the avoiding of OB's tendency to look inwards – focusing on behaviours and patterns within the organisation and leaving to the separate subject of 'strategy' issues of how organisations relate to the larger environment of which they are a part. It was also noted that strategy courses tend not to draw on the social and behavioural sciences in the same way that OB does and that their central concern seems to be with how predominantly commercial business organisations, as entities, behave or 'perform' within their social and economic context. This means that trying to combine social scientific and strategic management thinking is by no means a straightforward matter.

Trying to bring together these two traditions of thinking about organisations and their management is also made more difficult because of differences in the basic discursive framework within which each 'subject' operates. They operate in what are practically two separate languages – with social scientists talking about 'how organisations work' and strategic management people talking about 'how organisations can be made to win'. The language of the strategic management 'subject' seems to be one in which the key *discursive resource* is the idea of 'competitive advantage' and the main focus is on finding ways in which strategists can achieve this. It seems to be taken for granted that the main concern of people in charge of every kind of work organisation is with getting an advantage over other organisations that might otherwise take business away from them. This is not an entirely unrealistic way to look at the situation in which many people in managerial roles in modern organisations find themselves, of course.

It will be argued later in the present chapter that achieving the survival of their organisation is central to the logic of the work of all people involved in strategic management. But to reduce this insight to a notion that survival is primarily a matter of winning battles with competitors is to simplify corporate managerial activity to an extreme degree. It is not only to ignore the fact that survival can as readily be worked towards through cooperation and alliances with other organisations (yes, even with ones that the organisation is also in competition with). It is also to privilege the interests of those managing commercial and highly market-oriented organisations over those struggling to manage organisations involved in the provision of services of health, welfare, education, justice, defence or public safety. Again, this is not to deny that competitive pressures are experienced by organisations in all of these areas. But it is to argue that pressures of competition should not be regarded as the 'be all and end all' of strategic management and corporate shaping. This means taking care not to frame issues of strategic management in a way that suggests support for a particular market-oriented ideological view of the world. A *critical* study of the organising and managing of work must be sensitive to the dangers of limiting one's perspective on strategic issues in this way. This is not to say, however, that a social scientific discourse can readily find discursive resources that are free of ideological overtones. The very word 'strategy', for example, has a very particular history and set of associations.

The term *strategy* derives from the realm of war and military leadership and it is perhaps unsurprising that a discourse centred on such a concept should be one which attends so passionately to the idea of *winning* – the idea of defeating one's competitive corporate enemies. However much one might dislike the militaristic connotations of the notion of strategy, it has the virtue of resonating clearly with the challenges that are faced by all of those managing work organisations. Fighting for the survival of the set of relationships and understandings which make up every organisation is something experienced by all of those trying to shape and direct organisations – be they operating in the sphere of commerce, welfare or public administration. But it is not simply 'competitors' that strategists are battling with.

 Link

Any consideration of the problems facing organisational strategy-makers must confront the issues of ambiguity, bounded rationality, uncertainty and unpredictability which were examined in Chapter 3 (pp. 81–4) as pervading all aspects of the organising and managing of work.

As we recognised in Chapter 3, those running organisations have to cope with all the challenges thrown up by a world which is ambiguous, complex, unpredictable and fickle. And they have to trade, literally and figuratively, with an enormous range of individuals, groups and institutions, all of which are similarly complex, unpredictable and fickle. They are operating in a world of bounded rationality (p. 83) and confronting the potentially terrifying reality that the managers can never really fully understand what they are doing or be fully aware of precisely where they are going. They are struggling to 'control the uncontrollable', as Kurt Delnies put it in Cases and Conversations 5.6.

On top of all this, organisations themselves cannot be regarded as tight battle units – as unified military forces that are forever ready to move quickly and effectively on the command of their strategic commanders. The human beings who involve themselves with any given organisation all have their own purposes and, as our *strategic exchange* framework recognises, their own personal strategic projects. Each employee, each manager, each supplier, each investor is making their own strategic exchanges with the world and their particular exchange with the organisation is just one element of this. They each give something to the organisation they deal with – but they also want to take something from it, something that will not necessarily fit in with what the multiplicity of other parties involved with the organisation will be seeking. Within and around organisations, then, there are multiple interests, competing priorities and conflicting groups. It is for this reason that research on managerial behaviour shows managers engaged in what often looks like a frenzy of activity – as somewhat 'embattled' one might say. The metaphor of 'strategy' seems far from inappropriate and one that can help us make sense of the challenges that this entails for those trying to give overall shape and direction to a work organisation.

When we looked closely at what managers do, in Chapter 3, we saw that the apparently frenzied activity that typifies the managerial day may nevertheless have a clear logic behind it, even if that logic is not immediately apparent.

 Link   In the process of considering the nature of managerial work in Chapter 3, three dimensions of management were identified (p. 67). The key dimension was said to be the *strategic function* of managerial work. Strategy-making was thus established at that stage as being central to all managerial work.

In terms of the three dimensions of management which were identified in Table 3.1 (p. 67), *managers* engage in certain *actions of managing* in order to fulfil the *function of management*. These actions may look illogical or frenzied at first, but, with various degrees of success depending on the manager's general competence and commitment, they contribute to the basic function of the corporate management to which they relate. This is the function of the overall shaping of relationships, understandings and processes in order to bring about the completion of the tasks undertaken in the organisation's name in such a way that the organisation continues into the future. Herein lies the strategic element of every manager's work. It is the basis of what Kotter (1982, Reading Guide 5) called the 'efficiency of seemingly inefficient behaviour'. It was what Peter Brodie (Cases and Conversations 3.4) was referring to when he talked about the 'method to his madness'. When we examined how Peter Brodie talked about a day in his life as the manager of a charity we inferred that the 'strategic direction' in which he was taking the charity was one of getting it established as 'part of the life of the town' for as long as it was needed. He used the word 'agenda' rather than strategy, but he was nevertheless referring to what we can understand as the key strategic role of the charity's management, that of taking it forward into the long term so that it can continue to carry out the tasks done in the organisation's name. This suggests a conceptualisation of *strategic management*, one that is concerned not so much with local or day-to-day task fulfilment as:

- issues at a corporate level – the level of the organisation as a whole;
- issues relating to the long-term future of the organisation.

> ## Strategic management
> *Concept*
>
> The element of managerial work that concerns itself with taking the organisation as a whole forward into the long term.

Peter Brodie, Kurt Delnies and the general managers whom Kotter studied are all people occupying senior management posts. We would therefore expect all of these people to be centrally concerned with the performance of the organisation 'as a whole' and with the long-term activities carried out in its name. But to what extent are such matters a concern of managers whom we might not immediately expect to be concerned with strategic matters in this sense?

Strategy-making and the work of all managers

It has been assumed throughout earlier chapters that it is helpful to see the work of all of those designated as 'managers' in work organisations as *strategic* to some degree. In the pragmatist spirit of the whole of *Organising and Managing Work*, this is not a matter of trying to provide a final or a perfect definition of what management or strategy is. As was argued earlier (pp. 68–9), managers can *most usefully be understood* to be managers by virtue of how they relate to the organisation as a whole. The manager is treated in this book as an officer of the corporation that employs them. The reason for their being appointed is to contribute to the performance of that corporation as a whole. They will typically be given specific responsibilities within the managerial division of labour but their role is to fulfil those responsibilities in the way that best serves the strategic priorities of the organisation. This means in practice that:

- the manager needs to be knowledgeable about the priorities and strategic direction of the organisation and be influenced by that knowledge when deciding how to carry out any specific task or reach any particular decision when fulfilling their particular or 'local' aspects of their responsibilities;
- the manager must be willing and able to make inputs into policy debates at the corporate level, bringing together their knowledge of current strategic priorities with the specialist knowledge and insights which they develop in the process of carrying out their specialist or local tasks.

Thus we have a link between the way we conceptualise managerial work and the ways in which managerial responsibilities might be defined in practice, in an actual organisation. The relevance of linking theory and practice in this way is demonstrated in the words of Mats Clunas, a strong managerial advocate of the view that all managers should be strategists. In looking at what he says we must remember that he is arguing a *managerial case* for building on the *analytical* insight that the work of all managers can usefully be looked at in the light of the overall strategic situation of an organisation. He is building on that insight by consciously adopting a policy whereby he wishes all his managers to work actively and knowingly in a strategically relevant way.

Activity 6.1

Carefully consider the arguments that Mats Clunas makes in Cases and Conversations 6.1 for defining all the managers in his company as strategists and

- identify both the advantages and the disadvantages of an employing organisation expecting all its managers to be concerned to some extent with strategic matters;

- consider whether there are any organisational situations in which it might be reasonable for an employer to label as 'managers' certain people would who not be expected either to be aware of matters of organisational strategy or to contribute to thinking at a strategic level.

Mats and the reluctant strategist
Cases and Conversations 6.1

Clunas Wholesale is really quite a successful international business now and, as the chief executive, I feel confident that we will continue to expand. This is not an easy business to be in and you can lose quite a lot of sleep worrying about whether you are going to get the right goods in the right place at the same time. I started the business on my own and did not find it too worrying when I had to start appointing managers to share the running of the business. But I had a different understanding of what a manager is, then, compared to how I see things nowadays.

My original idea was that managers should be given carefully defined responsibilities for a certain patch of the business and that they should get on with doing whatever was required in that patch, as laid down by me. I would look after strategic matters and they would deal with the operational side – basically implementing whatever I decided as the way I wanted the business to go. But as time went on I realised that the better managers I had working for me could be quite helpful to me beyond their just doing the job as I had set it up. I found myself going along to a couple of these people for a chat whenever I was considering developing a new line or moving into a new area. Their experience on the ground was very relevant to a lot of the business matters I was agonising over. Also, I found that these two people were actually performing better and better on the ground, the more they knew about the way I was trying to develop the business. Because I had read a lot of business strategy stuff I had been confident that I could do all the strategy side of management myself. Early on I decided that I would not be employing any strategic management specialists, business analysts or whatever, however large the business got. I would do all this myself. But what I found happening, without my intending it, was that Jacques and Carole were part of my little strategy team. They've both been promoted to run bigger territories but they still act as key advisers to me. But they are not the only managers I use in this way. It is my policy to treat all my managers as members of what I call my 'corporate team'. I only give somebody a management title if they are interested in what Clunas is doing as a business and if they are willing to relate what they do in their personal area of responsibility to the 'bigger picture' of Clunas as a growing enterprise. I regularly get all the managers together for business conferences as well as going out to visit them whenever I think any one of them might have an input to my thinking.

Arthur Hilton was very much a test case in all of this. He was an early managerial appointment and he was, and is, an excellent warehouse manager. But when I tried to get him to join in the approach I had developed with Jacques and Carole, he wanted nothing to do with it. It was difficult to argue with him because he 'ran a really tight ship', as he used to boast. He built up a really good team of workers and all the goods came in and went out exactly as required. The whole place was immaculate and it was rare for even the slightest damage to goods to happen. Losses from the warehouse – 'shrinkage' and all that – were lower than any other warehouse across Europe. So Arthur felt confident telling me that he wanted nothing to do with 'strategic matters'. 'I am just not interested in business in that way', he said. 'Just let me get on with running the warehouse and I'll do a good job for you. You run the business. You've got all the expertise that's required.'

There wasn't a lot I could do to persuade Arthur to change. And he was too good at running the warehouse for me to risk losing him by taking away his 'manager' title. 'I am managing the warehouse so you can call me Warehouse Manager, Region 3, can't you?', he kept saying. However, three things happened that changed all of this.

The first thing that happened was when we got into a rather bad cash flow problem a couple of years ago. This was the result of problems of growth rather than problems of failure. But it meant that we could not meet promises that had been made to workers on improving pay and conditions, at the time we had said we would do this. Other managers understood what was going on and found ways of explaining it to their staff. But Arthur hadn't got a clue about what was going on and found himself unable to explain the situation to his people. As a result, we lost some really good people to a competitor and the general quality of people's work fell off. The second problem arose when I got a new contract that increased the throughput in Arthur's area of the country. We needed to expand the warehouse and it turned out that if Arthur had been aware that this was likely to happen, he could have bought up a chunk of land next to the warehouse at a really good price. But by the time I came to tell him that we needed this land it turned out that a builder had just bought it. And I had to pay that bloke double the earlier price to be able to expand the warehouse. Arthur's lack of interest in strategy cost me a lot of money.

Arthur was aware that I was pretty cross about these two things. But it was the third thing that happened that persuaded him to change his view of what a manager should be. And it was less a matter of my persuading him to change as one of his discovering a strategic dimension of his role for himself. It all started when he noticed that there were problems with the lorries of one of the firms that delivered to the warehouse. Arthur started to ask the drivers what was going on. It turned out that the owner of the lorry company was in failing health and was not managing to organise the servicing of the lorries. The owner was interested in selling the business but had no clue about how to go about this. Arthur himself, would you believe, got in touch with this chap and suggested that he might have lunch with me when I was due to visit that area. And the outcome of all of this was that Clunas made its first entry into the lorry side of our business. Of all things, it was old Arthur who instigated the strategic shift whereby we expanded into the transport business. He has now got a taste for this sort of thing and is one of the liveliest contributors to our management conferences. Once upon a time he refused even to attend them. He tells me he enjoys his job more than ever. He says he likes to think of himself as a businessman as well as a manager now. And I say that this is how I want all my managers to think of themselves.

All the managers still spend most of their time managing their own patch but they regularly feed information and suggestions to me. This is useful for the development of the business as a whole. Carole gave me some very useful warnings recently about problems that were developing with one of the companies in her area, a company we do a lot of business with. She picked up some rumours about them over-stretching themselves and I was able to follow these up. Without her early warnings I could have signed a contract with that business which could have got us into a severe bad debt situation. But I also think that these managers do the job on their local patch better as a result of being able to relate everything they do to the bigger picture. Arthur discovered this, for example, when he found himself short of warehouse space before we got the extension built. He got into a situation in which he had to be really awkward with some of our suppliers about when they could deliver to us. But because he was now 'strategically aware', as I would put it, he knew which of these suppliers we wanted to maintain a long-term relationship with and which we were thinking of dropping, he could decide who to favour and who to make suffer because of our shortage of space. One of the companies in particular had proved to be increasingly unreliable. So it was them who were asked to make inconveniently smaller and more frequent deliveries to us over the period before we increased our space. This was just before, it so happens, we stopped doing business with them altogether.

Mats Clunas clearly feels that it is to the advantage of both his company and the managers who work for the company for all managers to be involved in business level matters as well as detailed operational matters. They make an input into corporate management and they are better able to do their main day-to-day job as a result of being aware of corporate priorities and direction. It would also seem that the Clunas Wholesale managers find this way of doing their job satisfying. But this is not to say that all managers, everywhere, would have the same *orientation to work* that Jacques and Carole had always had and which Arthur Hilton eventually developed. We might expect to see managers in many organisational situations seeking the same sort of relationship with their employing organisation that Arthur had originally wished to maintain. We note that Mats was very concerned not to lose the services of Arthur as a 'local' manager. If an organisation finds itself with a large number of managers like the 'old' Arthur, then there could arise serious questions about whether the difficulty of changing them all to the more strategic style of managing would be cost effective. There could also be disadvantages in very large organisations that have a large number of managers of such a policy of involving all managers in regular strategic discussions. The cost and the difficulty of organising this could well lead the central management of such an organisation to leave its operational managers to concentrate on carrying out their specific and local responsibilities. This would involve making sure that what they did linked into strategic priorities by clearly instructing them on what to prioritise in their work and on what to communicate to their staffs and the other people with whom they deal. We might well imagine this being an option adopted by, say, a large retailing organisation with a large number of shops selling a relatively straightforward range of goods into a market which did not vary from one manager's patch to another.

What is becoming clear is that there are options about how *in practice* any given organisation involves its range of managers in strategic issues. Analytically, it is equally clear that it is wise always to look at the activities of managers across the organisation in terms of the relationship of these activities to the organisation's strategic direction. The practical choice which has to be made in any given organisation is over the extent to which the link between managers generally and those in senior and manifestly strategic roles is a one-way or a two-way one. But this is just one of the variety of *strategic choices* which those in charge of a work organisation are faced with.

Strategic choices	*Concept*
Managerial choices about the basic way an organisation is shaped and the relationships it has with the parties with whom it exchanges and which influence the long-term future of the organisation.	

We will later look systematically at the strategic choice that organisations are faced with and we will consider what factors might encourage one choice to be made rather than another. To do this, however, we need first to establish a clear process-relational frame of reference for looking at strategic issues. And this means moving beyond the orthodoxy that has tended to dominate thinking about strategic management. This is an orthodoxy that tends to see strategic choices in terms of *plans* made by senior corporate managers on the basis of cool rational analysis.

The systems-control view of strategy-making

The orthodox approach taken to writing and teaching about strategy has been one of presenting strategies as the basic policies or plans which the people in charge of work organisations rationally devise and which they direct the rest of their managers to implement. These policies and plans provide the basic blueprint for how the organisation is to be shaped and the key actions which are to be taken to ensure that it has a successful future in its social, political and economic environment. The strategic position that is adopted is a matter of both the organisational objectives that the organisation is to follow and the key means by which these objectives are to be fulfilled. These 'means', in turn, include both the structural and cultural *arrangements* that compose the organisation and the *actions* which are taken by those working within these organisational arrangements.

The basic assumptions behind this fit into systems-control thinking about organisations explained and criticised in Chapter 3. The biological metaphor of organisations as living creatures (out of which systems thinking originally emerged), encourages us to envisage organisational strategists as playing the part of the organism's brain. They continually analyse what the organism is doing well and what it is doing badly. They continually reflect on what strengths and weaknesses the organism has, in the light of its need to stay alive in the circumstances in which it finds itself. They continually pay attention to whatever threats might be facing the organism and they also look out for opportunities that might present themselves to the organism, so enabling it to thrive in its environment. As long as one remembers that this is only a metaphor and that work organisations are not actually unitary organisms, it usefully draws attention to the same basic 'realities' of organisational existence. It points to the reality that no organisation is likely to stay in existence and produce a living for those working in it if attention is not constantly paid to the relationship between the organisation and the context within which it operates. It would be as relevant to a group of people running a window-cleaning business in a big city or a charitable voluntary organisation collecting money for the homeless in a small town to do regular SWOT ('strengths, weaknesses, opportunities and threats') analyses of their situation as it would be for a thoughtful urban fox, coping with life in a busy suburban district. The question arises, however, about how systematically strategic managers can gather unambiguous 'data' about these strengths, weaknesses, opportunities and threats. Organisations do not have the instincts of the fox and the ability to make intuitive decisions based on sniffing the wind. The organisational system thus requires 'inputs' of detailed information which its strategic sub-system can systematically and analytically work upon. Systems-control thinking looks for a high degree of objectivity in the information that the organisation 'inputs' and aspires to a consequently high level of predictability and managerial control.

As we saw in Chapter 3, the biological metaphor has tended to be superseded in management thinking by one of the organisation as a big machine. It was not the problem with the organic metaphor's naïve and unrealistic view of organisations as unitary entities that encouraged management thinkers to move away from it, however. It was the relatively limited role it left for managers themselves that weakened the appeal of the biological metaphor. It might be appealing for managers to think of themselves acting as the organism's brain, monitoring the environment and choosing to act adaptively in the light of opportunities and threats. But animals' brains do not have a function that enables them to choose the shape and structure of the animal itself, though this is a function that managers often do want, with regard to their organisations. Managers have therefore tended to embrace instead the notion of themselves as the designers and drivers of enterprises as big organisational machines. And as the designers and drivers of these vehicles, expecting to be in command and in control, they could also look for inspiration to military commanders. They could model their approach on the generals who lead armies – armies that the generals knock into shape and armies for which they devise strategies. Managers as strategists would thus be the top soldiers, sitting on the highest hills, working with the best available intelligence, logically and rationally devising plans which are passed down to the 'line' officers and their supporting 'staff' officers for implementation. The strategic manager works *at the top* and ensures that his or her organisation comes out *on top*.

Following these system-control assumptions, what has been variously called the 'rational', the 'serial', the 'linear' or the 'planning mode' approach to strategy-making, has provided a template which managers are encouraged to follow. Strategy-making, in this formula,

- is done by top managers, sometimes with the help of internal strategic analysis experts and sometimes with the advice of external expert consultants;

- is informed by as much systematic evidence as can be gathered about the organisation's own capabilities, the capabilities of competitors or rivals, the requirements and potential requirements of clients or customers and the general political–economic environment in which the organisation operates;

- involves the analysis of this information using whatever quantitative and formally rational techniques are available, avoiding emotion, bias and prejudice;

- follows a clear sequence of steps on the basic logic of *analyse, plan, implement, evaluate*. Within this, the strategists decide where the organisation currently is, where they want the organisation to be in the future, and what strengths and weaknesses the organisation has with regard to these objectives, and what options might help it meet the objectives. Having decided which option is most likely to succeed, it is then necessary to decide what structural arrangements have to be made and what actions have to be taken to implement the option successfully. It is also decided what measures of successful implementation will be made so that evaluations can later be made in preparation for a further cycle of analysis, planning and implementation;

- assumes that the plans which emerge from this 'top-down' strategy-making process will be acceptable to those involved in their implementation, on the grounds that they have been carefully and rationally devised by people with appropriate expertise on the basis of full information.

Activity 6.2

Read the story which Dina Budget tells in Cases and Conversations 6.2 about the strategic changes made to the Tigermill company as Steve Dallas takes over running this former family firm and then

- identify the ways in which the approach adopted by Steve Dallas fits with the systems-control view of strategy-making outlined here;

- identify the strengths of this approach, as it is applied to the Tigermill company;

- identify any weaknesses of the approach which you feel are identified in its application to this company.

Tigermill goes strategic

Cases and Conversations 6.2

Tigermill was a ramshackle family firm that had grown and grown as my father and his brother tried out one business venture after another. When my father died, only a few months after my uncle was killed in a car crash, there were about six different activities which the business covered. The largest profits came from the range of cookery books that we published. The gardening books did quite well but were really beginning to look rather dated in their style. Our printing works had once printed most of our books but now they were largely involved in doing brochures and catalogues for other businesses. Our books were generally printed elsewhere. There was a reasonable income from this activity whereas our taxi company was largely out of control and didn't give much of a return. The bookshops were scattered all over the country and had this strange mix of second-hand books and displays of our own range of new books – cookery and gardening only of course. These books were also sold in our three large garden centres and I think that these provided the main outlet for our gardening books. My cousin Ali ran one of the garden centres and he had developed a mail order section for certain of the lines that the centre stocked. I think it was the success of this part of the business in selling our gardening and cookery books that attracted the venture capitalists who bought us after my father's death six years ago.

The new owners of Tigermill put in charge of the company a man they had recruited from a large publishing company. Steve Dallas had taken a year out from that company to study for an MBA and, before he got round to going back to them, he found himself running Tigermill. At that stage I had just left university and was rather naïve about modern business ideas. I was quite happy to stay on in the former family business as an employee because it was what my mother wanted me to do. I was open-minded as to what my long-term future would be so I happily accepted Steve's offer of a supervisory job in the main office. I had little directly to do with the management of the business but I was in a good position to watch how Steve went about changing it. 'I am basically a strategist', he told me, 'and I am going to get Tigermill sorted'. After this I did not see a lot of Steve. For the first few weeks he was with us he seemed constantly to be in his office with the finance director that he recruited (from the same course he had been on, I think) in his first week here and with the marketing director whom he also brought in very quickly. She had worked in a senior position in a big national bookshop and stationery chain and she brought with her huge amounts of market research data on trends in consumer tastes and a series of forecasts of likely future leisure and consumption patterns which that company had commissioned.

Most of the managers from across the firm came along to the main offices and spent some time with Steve's strategy team (or 'stradegy team' as I noticed the three of them tended to say). But the strategic plan that eventually emerged from the group was clearly their own production – with some help from a professor

from the business school Steve had attended. He acted as a consultant to the group. I was genuinely impressed by the presentation they gave to the managers when introducing the plan. They talked wisely about how certain lines had reached the end of their product life cycle and they made a lot of sense when they differentiated between 'stars' and 'dogs' in our product portfolio. Their diagram of where each of our activities stood with regard to five 'market forces' was especially helpful. Their view of where we were weak and where we were strong more or less accorded with my own view. And I thought that the 'value chain analysis' which they had done of each activity was a much more systematic version of what I had seen my father do on several sheets of paper when he had talked of 'sorting out the business' only a few months before he died. I was amused by their repeated use of the rather homely phrase 'sticking to the knitting'. I thought this contrasted with some of the more technical language – some stuff about configurations and environmental matches was completely beyond me for instance – and 'sticking to the knitting' sounded not unlike my father's unrealised resolution to 'get back to what we're best at'.

What the strategic plan amounted to was a sequence of actions that would lead to closing the taxi business, selling off the printing works, the bookshops and the garden centres. They had considered the option of keeping the printing works and the bookshops but felt that these still made the company too diverse, too liable to distract it from the book publishing 'knitting' they had judged it to be best at. The same logic applied to the garden centres. The mail order activity would be separated from the garden centre where it was currently based before the centres were put on the market. The plan had the virtues of simplicity, said Steve, and I agreed with this. The idea was to 'grow' the cookery books, which were seen as the most successful of our current activities and to 'develop' the gardening books on the model of the cookery books. And the same model, in terms of book design and presentational style was to be applied to a new, and third, line of books, 'leisure and travel'. These were both to be distributed through the normal retail trade and sold by the mail order section. There would be a significant increase in advertisements placed in the targeted magazines which a big 'market research exercise' would identify as those most likely to have readers who would also like our books in the three areas of food, gardens and leisure/travel.

These activities would be financed by a combination of returns from the sale of unwanted areas of the business and by promised investment by the company that had purchased us in the first place. That company, we were told, 'loved the stradegy' (sic) and were 'sold on every aspect of the detailed business plans'. There would be no problem with investment and we would immediately go ahead with signing up new writers and illustrators for the books, employing editors, and recruiting a 'small but dynamic high-flying sales force to inter-face with the retail trade'. There would also be investments in a 'dedicated call centre' to deal with the increased mail order business. This would be in a new building which would also contain the new Tigermill offices and a 'packing and despatch facility' which would send out our books.

All of this amounted to a considerable investment and Steve felt confident enough to tell us all that the strategy amounted to a 'plan that cannot fail'. This was because the strategic plan was based on 'high quality data about the trends in consumer interests' and because 'a team who had identified all the key drivers for success' was leading the company. A number of 'control systems' were 'put in place' so that any difficulties with the implementation of the plan would be readily identified and appropriate corrections made. Steve and his colleagues showed us graphs of how business was likely to increase in the various areas as established activities would 'grow' and as new activities would 'come on stream'. He and the investors had confidence in all of these projections because they were based on an approach to business and management that was a 'proven and winning formula'.

One of the first actions that Steve's team took had not been included in this plan. This was the appointment of a human resources director. Some gossip had it that the man appointed was an old contact of the marketing director who had been persuaded to retire earlier from the very large organisation in which he had worked for years. But his appointment was justified on the grounds that the strategic plan clearly involved considerable recruitment work, to find the 'best available' people to bring into the expanding areas of the business. He would also be 'tasked' with devising an 'HR strategy' that would enable all of these people and everyone else too, to 'personally grow' and 'add increasing value' to the business. This new HR department replaced our old Personnel office and was soon very active in bringing in new people to work on commissioning and developing books across the three areas. The HR director was also personally instrumental in getting Tigermill to sign up a well-known television cook, who seemed to be a close friend, to do a series of books. This caused a great deal of excitement among all the staff and this increased further when this 'TV chef' persuaded a fellow television presenter who worked on gardening programmes to sign a similar deal for gardening books.

Partly as a result of these very lucky signings, the cookery and gardening books divisions developed very much as the strategic plan had projected. However, the third division, which had been projected to be the largest area of growth proved very difficult even to get started. The category of 'leisure and travel' seemed to be too vague and a ragbag of projects were started and abandoned. A series of managers joined the company to run the division, before quickly leaving. It soon became apparent that this division was absorbing most of the profits from the two successful divisions. And the profits that remained were more than soaked up by the generally increased employment costs and the costs of the new buildings that were going up. A number of the managers tried to persuade the 'top team', as Steve now called his little strategic group, to consolidate activities into the two divisions. They not only suggested that Tigermill abandon its 'leisure and travel' aspirations, but that they also halt the building works, renting space until the physical expansion could properly be justified. However, the strategic team argued that it could not depart from its 'bold growth strategy' just because the 'going was a bit rough'. It must persist and 'meet the challenge'. One of the ways it did this was to recruit a manager from the United States to head the division, at great further expense. The woman appointed spoke of 'strategic focus' and put the focus of the division on travel guides. As soon as these appeared on the market it was clear that they were going to fail. She had taken into account the fact that she was entering a crowded market but she had underestimated the extent to which the largely American writers she was using would fail to appeal to European book buyers.

This head of the leisure and travel division also ended up having a tremendous row with my cousin, Ali Budget, who was still running the mail order side from the garden centre. This, like the other two garden centres (and in line with the strategic plan), had not yet been sold off. The argument was about a book on digital photography which Ali believed one of his garden centre departmental managers could write. This individual was a very active amateur photographer who also had considerable expertise with computers – an expertise that was applied to great advantage to the running of the garden centre. However, the 'bloody American woman', as Ali called her, thought it was ridiculous to get an amateur to write a book. Also, it would not accord with her notion of 'strategic focus'. Steve and the marketing director backed her on this and Ali soon fell out with the whole 'top team'. This created a serious problem because, according to the plan, Ali was going to take control of the expanded mail order business, an area of activity in which he was obviously very skilled. But as a result of the row, Ali said he would leave the company as soon as the garden centres were sold off.

Ali did leave Tigermill. When the garden centres were sold off it transpired that Ali was a partner in the new company that had bought the garden centre he had been managing. And partly because of his general fury with the Tigermill top team, and partly because it would enable him to publish his colleague's digital photography book, Ali kept a books mail order business within the garden centre. It also transpired that he had managed to buy the bookshops from the people who had originally acquired them from Tigermill. Steve Dallas refused to let Ali sell any of Tigermill's books. As a consequence of this he became an even more determined promoter of the gardening books of rival publishers. And the considerable success of what became a series of digital photography and camcorder books meant that his business expanded. Tigermill found itself losing some of its best employees to Ali. Before long Ali saw the need to expand physically, while Tigermill found itself with an excess of expensive space.

Steve Dallas and his top team continued trying to make their strategy succeed. They argued that the problems were all 'operational' and not strategic ones. 'Adjustments' were made 'within the strategy' and these were generally of a cost-cutting nature. A proportion of staff from each department was made redundant and the morale of the remaining staff generally declined. And as Steve and his colleagues became more remote than ever from other managers and from the staff generally, I contemplated leaving the company myself. So did several other managers. I had become a manager in what had once been my father's company. But this company was now in trouble while an offshoot from it, led by my father's nephew, was thriving. Steve and his 'strategist' friends were eventually summoned to a crisis meeting with the investors. And I decided I would go and visit my cousin in his cramped office in the garden centre.

What happened here suggests that the senior management team taking over Tigermill had a view of strategy-making which closely fits the systems-control model which was outlined earlier. If we follow the concept of strategic management as 'that element of managerial work that concerns itself with the taking forward of the organisation as a whole into the long term' then it is clear that Steve Dallas believes that such work should be the preserve of the senior managers of an organisation. He recognises that such a 'top team' may need external expert help and, accordingly, makes use of the consulting services of a business academic. The information 'inputs' which are made into the strategic process, as far as Dina is able to tell, includes a lot of systematic data which the marketing director has brought with her from her previous employment. It is impossible for us to know how far they followed the principle of avoiding bias and emotion in analysing the material which they had gathered. However, we get some idea of the 'rational techniques' that they applied from some of the phrases that Dina picked up when listening to the presentation of the plan to the staff. They obviously used the SWOT – strengths, weaknesses, opportunities and threats – framework, which every business student who has ever attended a strategy class will be familiar with. But the strategy group has also brought into their deliberations other frameworks from the academic literature. Use has been made of the popular 'product life cycle concept' and the reference to 'stars' and 'dogs' suggests they have applied the famous Boston Consulting Group's 'growth share matrix' approach to portfolio analysis (Henderson, 1970, Reading Guide 14). Talk of five 'market forces' and 'value chain analysis' indicates that they have been adopting analytical frameworks associated with one of the 'guru' figures of academic strategy courses, Michael Porter (1980, 1985, Reading Guide 14). The 'sticking to the knitting' prescription, which amused Dina somewhat, is very much associated with the writing of Peters and Waterman (1982, in Reading Guide 14). All of this is applied within the sequence of analyse, plan, implement and evaluate which we noted earlier and part of the analysis was the standard one of assessing strategic options (whether the printing works and bookshops be retained, or not, for example). The 'control systems' mentioned by Steve Dallas are presumably part of the strategic evaluation process, although one suspects that a more significant process of evaluation was going on in the crisis meeting with investors that Dina mentions at the end of her account.

The final characteristic of a systems-control model for strategy-making which was identified earlier was that it separates the plan-making aspect of the process from the *implementation* of the plans to which it leads. It is assumed that people will find the expert strategists' plans acceptable because experts who have taken into account the best possible systematic evidence have devised them. Legitimacy of the strategy is seen as deriving from its technical rationality. Implementation should follow smoothly after the careful explaining of the logic and rationality of the strategic plan to those who are expected to implement it. This, we can reasonably infer, was the thinking behind the presentation that Steve Dallas gave to the staff at Tigermill.

A reading of Dina Budget's account of strategic management at Tigermill strongly suggests inadequacies in the prescriptive model for doing strategy-making which derives from systems-control thinking. Systems-control thinking is a perspective or a frame of reference for understanding organisations. But any frame of reference, as our discussion of discourse in Chapter 4 stressed (p. 119), influences the practices which are engaged in by people who look at the world within that framework. Hence, a systems-control view of what organisations and managements are suggests certain behaviours that strategic managers should follow. Steve Dallas and his close colleagues, we can infer, operate with an implicit view of organisations as machine-like entities that can be designed and 'driven' by expert managers. They do not think of Tigermill, or any other organisation, in a process-relational way. They do not see it as a pattern of understandings, relationships and exchanges that are negotiated in a world of ambiguity, unpredictability and conflict of interest. They therefore see it as feasible for senior managers to make complex and detailed plans for an organisation on the basis of private analytical reflection on objective 'data'. And they see it as reasonable to expect this to be smoothly implemented regardless of the feelings and reactions of others involved with the organisation, not least the feelings and reactions of managers and employees within the organisation and the customers outside the organisation who are expected by the strategic plan to want its products.

The weaknesses of this orthodox systems-control approach to strategy-making are the weaknesses of systems-control thinking about organising and managing in general which have been identified in previous chapters. These are both *analytical* weaknesses (the approach is an inadequate way in which to understand how things work in the social world) and practical or *prescriptive* weaknesses (the approach provides inadequate guidance for practice). Once again reiterating the pragmatist stance of this book, it must be stressed that this is not a matter of saying that such an approach is totally wrong or totally useless. It is, instead, to say that a more adequate approach can be found, one that is more helpful both analytically and as a guide to practice. This takes us towards outlining a process-relational frame of reference for looking at strategy-making.

The process-relational view of strategy-making

The starting point for devising an alternative way of thinking about organisational strategies and processes of strategic management is to concentrate on what concept of 'strategy' we are going to work with. Orthodox approaches to strategic management tend to follow the ordinary everyday or dictionary meaning of the term. If someone tells us that they have a strategy for taking a holiday we simply assume that they have sat down and planned a series of actions involving getting some time off work and perhaps finding a warm and comfortable place to take some leisure. We also expect to see them eventually put this plan into action – to see them implementing their strategy. This seems unproblematic, and such a simple concept of 'strategy' appears reasonably useful for making sense of what people do in areas of life such as this. It might seem equally reasonable to see such a concept of strategy being useful for understanding military campaigns. An army general sits down and works out a strategy for winning a campaign, calculating what numbers and types of soldiers are to be deployed, how they are to be armed and provisioned, when and where they are to attack and so on. If we were interested in studying wars and how they are won or lost, then we simply focus on what strategies – in this sense of war leaders' campaign plans – were implemented in different wars. We would then study how different types of strategy, and different approaches to implementation, have historically led to different types of outcome. But is this really going to be useful – in the sense of helping us understand wars? It is not. If we look at almost any detailed account available to us of how wars have been conducted we find that most formal 'plans' or strategies that can be recognised were unlikely to have been the product of an expert strategist working solely on the basis of rational calculation. It is much more likely that the strategy *emerged* from a process of argument, dispute and compromise involving not just line generals but politicians, staff officers, intelligence advisers, allies and even junior officers with relevant information or insights. Not only this, but we would typically find that as the 'strategy' was put into operation it actually changed. If unexpected numbers of enemy aircraft appeared at a key stage of a campaign or a battalion of allied troops failed to turn up or the weather suddenly changed, adjustments might be made of quite considerable proportions.

If we really want to make sense of how wars are 'actually' conducted, it would be helpful to think of 'strategy' not so much in terms of campaign leaders' prior plans of action but as the broad pattern to be observed in the overall way the campaign was conducted. Even in the military context, where the word 'strategy' comes from, it is useful to conceptualise strategy in terms of processes or patterns emerging over time rather than as plans. This takes us back to the Chapter 3 argument that we should generally replace 'linear' ways of analysing human behaviour in 'plan–act' terms with a more incremental or cyclical view of humans as typically following an 'act–plan–act–plan' pattern (p. 101). It also fits with the Chapter 4 claim that it is useful to see a strategic pattern in every human being's life – a pattern that emerges over time as the individual shapes his or her life and is shaped by circumstances. That pattern may involve quite a lot of deliberate planning of, say, career or family, or it might be a pattern of relatively haphazard moves and opportunistic shifts. So it is with organisations. The most useful way to understand organisations and how they are managed, over a period of time, is to look at strategies as emergent patterns. All strategies, in this view, are 'emergent' with this emergence sometimes involving a relatively high degree of deliberate planning and sometimes involving a high degree of incremental adjustment, trial and error experimentation and opportunism.

Organisational/corporate strategy *Concept*

The pattern to be seen emerging over time as actions are taken that enable an organisation to continue into the future.

Activity 6.3

Return to Dina Budget's story about Tigermill (Cases and Conversations 6.2) and reread it in the light of the claim that all strategies are emergent, in spite of the fact that they vary in the extent to which they follow a relatively pre-planned pattern or a relatively incremental or opportunistic one. Clearly the 'strategy team' favoured a 'top-down' strategic planning approach. Yet what actually happened was not altogether *determined* by this 'strategy-as-plan'. Their analyses and plans were, rather, contributors to the strategy that *emerged*. But so were various other circumstances and opportunities. Therefore:

- identify any circumstances, events or opportunities which 'arose' (rather than being part of the strategic plan itself) and which contributed to the emergent general strategic direction of Tigermill;

- consider whether your analysis raises any questions about the balance that Steve Dallas and his team are making between acting 'according to strategic plan' and acting incrementally and opportunistically.

Even when setting up the strategic planning process, Steve Dallas shows a tendency to act opportunistically by appointing one of his former MBA student colleagues to his top team and by using as a consultant one of the teachers from the university where he did his course. It appears that he did not follow the more formally rational procedure that we might expect of such an analytical character of engaging in a systematic executive search and a competitive selection and appointment process. Perhaps a realisation that a more formally rational approach to recruitment might be appropriate for future appointments is indicated, however, by his later decision to appoint a human resources specialist. There appears to be some clear incrementalism here because this was not a need identified in the strategic plan. However, the appointment itself appears to be another case of choosing 'someone they knew' rather than someone formally selected (he was a 'contact' of the marketing director, Dina tells us, and he was someone who was in need of a job). But one of the most strategically positive pieces of opportunism in the whole story is that of the HR director using his own personal friendship to get the television chef (and subsequently a television gardener too) to do deals with Tigermill. These two 'pieces of luck', as Dina regards them, helped bring elements of the strategic plan to emerge successfully. But such good fortune did not help fulfil the 'leisure and travel' part of the strategic plan. In fact, a falling back to some incrementalism of a 'muddling through' nature is suggested by Dina's statement that 'a ragbag of projects were started and abandoned'.

An eventuality that the strategic plan did not take into account was the loss of the skills and experience of Ali Budget (as well as the loss of employees who subsequently went to work for him). Personal feelings and loyalties clearly played a part in this – factors which no strategic plan can readily handle. But the events that occurred here suggest that Steve and his senior colleagues were unwilling to balance their fondness for strategic planning with recognition of the virtues of opportunism and experimentation. The clash with Ali could indeed be seen in part as a clash of strategy-making philosophies. The determination of the 'strategy team' to stay 'on plan' made them unwilling to go along with Ali's keenness to treat an employee's fortuitously relevant hobby as a business opportunity. They also turned their faces against those more incrementally-oriented managers who urged the dropping of the leisure and travel part of the strategic plan and the postponing of building plans. Their faith in their preferred style of making strategy led them to work on 'adjustments' *within* the strategy rather than any serious modifications of it and this, it appears, pushed them into the dangerously vicious circle of cost-cutting, morale loss and increasing managerial 'remoteness'. Dina suspends her story telling at the stage when these problems reach crisis point. We will take up the tale again later. For the present, we can treat her account as a very effective illustration of the value of looking at strategy as an emergent pattern in which both a degree of planning and a degree of incrementalism tend to play a part. It also suggests that the balance achieved between these two things in any given set of organisational circumstances has a key practical relevance for organisational managers.

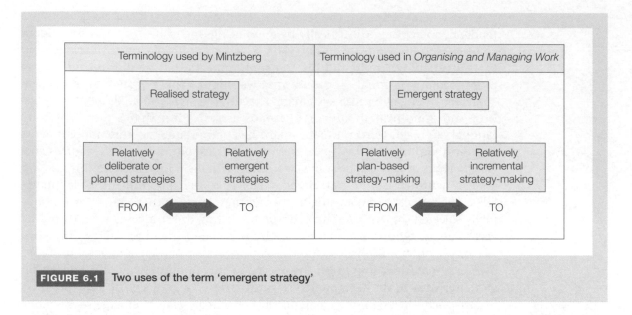

Terminology used by Mintzberg

Realised strategy

Relatively deliberate or planned strategies

Relatively emergent strategies

FROM ⟷ TO

Terminology used in *Organising and Managing Work*

Emergent strategy

Relatively plan-based strategy-making

Relatively incremental strategy-making

FROM ⟷ TO

FIGURE 6.1 Two uses of the term 'emergent strategy'

The view of strategy which we are developing is one very much associated with the influential writing of Mintzberg (1994, in Reading Guide 14) and the concept of strategy offered corresponds with his formulation of strategy as 'the pattern in a stream of actions' (1988, p. 14, Reading Guide 14). What we concentrate on, in this view, is the strategy which is 'realised' when we look at how any given organisation is shaped and those involved in the organisation act with regard to it over time. However, the language being used in *Organising and Managing Work* differs from that used by Mintzberg. He applies the term 'emergent' to realised strategies that have involved relatively low levels of planning. Hence Mintzberg sees actual ('realised') strategies as varying from being relatively 'deliberate' to being relatively 'emergent'. Here, on the other hand, we refer to all strategies as 'emergent' but recognise that these emergent strategies will vary in the extent to which they involve deliberate long-term planning. This is clarified in Figure 6.1. In spite of the variation in terminology, there is the same acknowledgement that actual cases of organisational strategy varying from ones where there is a relatively high degree of 'deliberate' or 'pre-planning' to cases where the strategic pattern has developed as part of a step-by-step or incremental process.

The reason it has been decided here to use different language from Mintzberg's is not in order to confuse matters or to be different for the sake of being different. It is done to be consistent with way the term 'emergent' is generally used in the broad style of social science thinking which is being drawn upon in *Organising and Managing Work*. This sees all aspects of social life – from one's personal identity to the way societies are structured, as 'emergent' – as patterns arising from complex processes of continuous human interaction and change. In this perspective, therefore, strategies – as patterns to be looked for by the observer examining an organisation over time – are always and inevitably emergent. Yet within this emergence it is recognised that 'actual' strategies are likely to vary in the extent to which some formal deliberation or planning plays a part. Mintzberg argues the same way, in spite of his use of different terminology. And we would agree with him that we are nevertheless unlikely to find 'real life' cases of organisational strategies that fall near the ends of the two continua show in Figure 6.1. Because of bounded rationality, unpredictability, human resistance and all the other unintended consequences which tend to follow from organisational initiatives, no organisational leadership is ever likely to tightly and completely plan an organisation's future and then find it working out as planned. Correspondingly, no organisation is likely to survive over a long period of time if those running it indulge in totally random decision-making and unthinkingly spontaneous action. But in saying this we are again allowing our theoretical analysis to guide us towards certain styles of practice.

Directed evolution: a general trend in strategic thinking and practice?

The process-relational frame of reference being used in *Organising and Managing Work* draws attention to the complexities of strategy-making processes. It is, however, a perspective and not a prescription for practice. It is a way of *looking at* the processes whereby organisations are shaped and their activities are patterned over time. In itself, then, it does not say how any given strategist *should* go about making strategies in order to be 'successful'. However, it is clear that some advocacy or prescription along these lines has come out of the move towards a broadly 'processual' way of looking at organisations and their management that is becoming increasingly apparent in the academic literature on strategy. In effect, this increasingly processual way of thinking about strategy-making is suggesting that certain strategy-making practices are more likely to 'work' than others, because the world, organisations and human beings 'work' in a certain way. The 'big strategic plan' approach to strategic practice which the older systems-control way of thinking suggested would 'work' (because of the way it assumes the world, people and organisations 'work') should, for example, be advised against. A processual perspective on people and the world suggests that what is more likely to 'work' in practice is something which gives fuller recognition to all the ambiguities and uncertainties and conflicts of interest that are part of 'the way the world works'. Researchers like Mintzberg (1994, Reading Guide 14) and Quinn (1980, Reading Guide 14), for example, following studies of the managerial practice carried in broadly processual terms are therefore able to advocate or prescribe particular styles of strategic practice.

The research that has been carried out by these and by other researchers who have looked at the ways in which strategic processes appear to relate to corporate success (defined in conventional business terms) supports the view that neither tightly planned strategies nor random strategies of 'muddling along' are either common or successful. Most organisations are found to be located in the middle range of the planned-incremental continuum in the way corporate managers go about strategy-making. Mintzberg's studies, which 'tracked' a sample of organisations, 'found strategy making to be a complex, interactive, and evolutionary process, best described as one of adaptive learning' (1994, p. 110, Reading Guide 14). He suggests that rather than use metaphors of architectural design or the steering of a ship to characterise the making of strategy, it would be better to see it as a process of 'crafting'. Like creative potters shaping their pots, strategists shape their organisations as part of the process of making them.

A crafting approach does not, of course, in itself guarantee success to the strategy makers in whatever it is they want to achieve over time. But Quinn's study of the practices of organisations that are relatively successful in conventional business terms suggests to him the advantage of taking a relatively incremental trial-and-error approach, as long as it is carried out within a strong managerial sense of direction. He calls this alternative to both muddling along and rigid strategic planning *logical incrementalism*.

Logical incrementalism	*Concept*
An alternative to top-down strategic planning in which strategic development happens in incremental and experimental steps that are taken within a sense of a broad organisational direction or strategic logic.	

There is, Quinn says, 'a process of the gradual evolution of strategy driven by conscious managerial thought' (1980, p. 38, Reading Guide 14). He suggests that successful strategists have a strong sense of the direction for the enterprise but then follow a relatively piecemeal, step-by-step or experimental approach to getting to where they want to be. 'The most effective strategies of major enterprises', he argues, 'tend to emerge step by step from an iterative process in which the organisation probes the future, experiments and learns from a series of partial (incremental) commitments'. Successful strategists are aware that the environment is ambiguous and uncertain and that they must be flexible in how they relate to it. And the strategy that emerges is not just the creation of the senior managers in the organisation. These people draw from the thinking and experiences of the different groups who make up the organisation and its management.

Activity 6.4

Re-visit Peter Brodie's reflection on his working day running a charity (pp. 88–90) and reread what Mats Clunas tells us about his way of making strategy in his company (pp. 174–6) and consider the extent to which these two individuals are approaching strategy-making in the *logical incrementalist* way identified by Quinn.

If we look back at the words that have been used in the preceding few para-
graphs to characterise this more 'thoughtfully incremental' type of
strategy-making practice, we will notice that the notion of 'evolution' seems to
play an important role, as do the notions of adaptation, experimentation and
learning. The terms evolution and adaptation echo back to the biological
metaphor which sees organisations as living creatures (pp. 38–40). The danger
therefore arises of implying that some kind of natural selection occurs with
regard to organisations whereby they 'adapt to their environment', independently of human decision-making and political contest within the organisation.
This would be wholly unacceptable within a processual style of social science
analysis. Yet the notion of adaptation to circumstances over time, implicit in
the word evolution, is worth retaining. Organisations obviously must change
as they face changing circumstances. But this change is the outcome of how
human actors interpret and argue about those circumstances and act on the
basis of their negotiated understandings. There are attempts at human direction (or 'management') involved in all strategic processes. The concept of
directed evolution perhaps usefully brings together the two aspects of strategy-
making which are always in tension with each other, those of *managerial
initiative* on the one hand and *pressure of circumstances* on the other.

Directed evolution	Concept

A style of strategic management in which continuous organisational adaptation occurs through
processes of trial and error, opportunism, exchange, negotiation, experimentation and learning
within a clear sense of general organisational direction and managerial priority.

Activity 6.5

Read the second part of the Tigermill story (Cases
and Conversations 6.3), as the cousins Dina and Ali
Budget take the company back 'into the family' and

- note the ways in which the approach to
strategy-making can be characterised in
terms of directed evolution;

- consider whether or not this changed
approach to running the business involves a
complete rejection of any notion of 'strategic
planning'.

Ali and Dina come into their own

The day that Steve Dallas and his fellow members of the Tigermill 'strategy team' went to see the investors for what we were all aware was to be a crisis meeting, I went to visit my cousin, Ali Budget, at the garden centre. As soon as I walked through the door of the small hut that he used as an office I was aware of a sense of jubilation on his part. 'I think you know something I don't', I confidently speculated. 'Well, sort of', he responded, 'I was going to talk to you tomorrow once things have been confirmed'.

'What things? I guess it's got something to do with the Tigermill crisis meeting today. Am I right'.

Ali went on to explain that he had been determined for some time not to accept the loss of Tigermill from some significant level of family involvement. He saw this as a matter of pride and some kind of recognition of what my father and his father had achieved. They had started as penniless immigrants and had gone on to build up a good business. He saw the early deaths of both of our fathers as a cruel co-incidence and was convinced that had my father not died Tigermill 'would have got sorted out and never got into the hands of Dallas and those other strategy fanatics'.

'I don't think you should knock strategic thinking', I pointed out to Ali, 'I get the impression that you're about to reveal some pretty shrewd strategy work of your own'. 'I suppose you could say that', he admitted with a grin before going on to explain how he had been closely watching the difficulties that had developed in Tigermill following his own departure. 'I've been looking for opportunities in every little mishap they've had', he revealed. 'I was even tempted to use you as a Trojan horse – or at least asking you to act as a spy reporting back from occupied territory. But I didn't want to compromise you. It's different now. You and I can come into our own.'

Ali went on to explain how he had been in touch with the investment company who had put Steve Dallas in charge of Tigermill and, 'carefully felt my way with them over several months'. He was confident that Steve would resign at the end of the crisis meeting that was occurring that day. Once that had happened there would be immediate talks between those investors and Ali and his current business partners. 'The ground is laid for it all to be put back together and, now that you've got the necessary experience, I'd like you to join me in running Tigermill. We can't take the company back into complete family ownership. But we Budgets will be running it.'

It turned out that Ali had taken part in a series of 'very informal' meetings with the various parties to this hoped-for merger and that he had 'laid out a number of tentative business plans'. He said that he had done this 'to demonstrate to the people with the money' that 'I mean business and that I know about business'. He had argued that he was not committing himself to any particular plan. 'But I don't think they would have accepted that position, he said, 'if I had not been able to point out that the difficulties that Steve and his friends had got the company into were because they were too keen on sticking to their big strategic plans. You've got to be flexible and free to go with the flow of how things work out. You've got to be free to take advantage of what things might come up. They bought this line, I'm relieved to say'.

Steve Dallas did resign the next day and within a week Ali was appointed managing director of the new Tigermill. In line with Ali's scheme, the two main elements of the business that had been split off under the Dallas regime were brought back together. Both the finance and the marketing directors felt bound to follow Steve Dallas. The human resources man also felt he should go. However, I persuaded Ali that it would be wise to 'keep him on board'. This was partly because he had a lot of expertise in the various technicalities of personnel management and had acquired a lot of personal experience of managerial politics in his career. This latter matter was something that Ali and I were only just getting to grips with. But I also believed we needed him because of his relationship with the TV chef and the other important contacts that had followed from this relationship. 'It's not just what he does, it's who he knows', I put to Ali. He readily endorsed this thought. 'Also', I admitted, 'I quite like him'. 'So do I', said Ali, 'and I think that sort of thing is important too'.

I took over the finance position and we recruited my younger brother, who had recently qualified as an accountant, to work with me. But Ali was not keen on too tight a division of labour among his management team and he and I decided that we would both work on marketing and business development issues. The other person who came to work closely with us on developing Tigermill was Archie Kingsteps. He was the character who had started as the manager of the aquatic section of Ali's garden centre and had gone on to develop the series of digital photography and camcorder books because of his interest and hobby-oriented expertise in these areas. But he was also very good with computers and had set up the excellent information technology systems that had helped make the garden centre he worked in such a success. Archie started to talk one evening, only weeks after we had been running the new Tigermill, about a 'wheeze' that had occurred to him. 'What about Tigermill using the internet and trying a 'spot of e-commerce?'. This had not occurred to Ali or to me. We felt slightly stupid about this and, by the end of that evening, we had decided to make Archie a director of the business. We asked him to try out selling one or two of our lines over the internet.

Within two years we were a flourishing e-commerce enterprise, a possibility that had not crossed our minds when we took over the management of Tigermill. The new warehouse and office space that had been an embarrassment to Steve Dallas was soon filled and had to be expanded further. As this occurred we found ourselves wondering about whether we should keep the five shops. Steve's talk about 'sticking to the knitting' came back to us and I even risked Ali's ire by mentioning 'strategic focus'. However, it was at a meeting of bookshop managers that one of their number decided to 'just throw into the discussion' the possibility of making the shops 'cyber shops' as well as bookshops. He was keen on the internet and soon was in earnest discussion with Archie Kingsteps about how this might be done. After a period of experimentation in the one shop, the other shops were equipped with computers – and high quality coffee machines too.

There was also reflection on the role of the garden centre. Ali did not want to listen to suggestions that we should sell it to 'concentrate on what we are best at'. His reasons, he confessed, as its former manager, were 'purely sentimental'. However, much to Ali's amusement, I argued that I 'could find a strategic argument' for retaining the garden centre. I pointed out that, just like the shops on a smaller scale, the centre could be a place where we could meet some of our customers face-to-face and where we could talk to them about what we were selling and what they thought of the service we were providing. We were going to have to learn a lot as we developed the business and some of the most important people we ought to learn from were our customers. This thought led to our developing the idea that we would offer special gardening or photography 'hobby days' at the garden centre. After two of these, most of the tickets for which had been sold over the Internet, we decided to invest in a lecture theatre/demonstration room and make such events a featured activity on our web sites.

A further new line of business emerged as a result of a conversation that occurred at one of these events. A customer asked us whether we had ever thought of organising tours to 'interesting gardens' around the country or 'even abroad'. He had retired from a tour organising company and we persuaded him to act as a consultant to Tigermill and try the idea out. The consequence of this was that both gardening and photography tours became another key feature of our business and a further source of our rapid business growth.

Another retired person whose skills we made use of was my husband's father. We were getting dissatisfied with the service we were getting from local taxi companies when it came to collecting groups of visitors to our hobby days from the local station. We therefore bought a minibus and put my father-in-law in charge of it.

'Well, well', my father-in-law said to Ali and me, as he drove off in the vehicle for the first time, 'I know it's some time since Tigermill sold off its taxis, but don't forget that it was with taxis that your fathers started off.'

'So we're back where we started are we?', laughed Ali.

'Oh no, not exactly.' I replied, equally amused, and rather touched.

Throughout this story of the revived Tigermill company we get an impression of its new managing director, Ali Budget, as someone who has a strong urge to shape or direct events. Yet he is clearly an opportunist and a believer in a flexible approach to organisational management, a flexibility that enables continuous adaptation to occur, as circumstances change and opportunities arise. His willingness to spot and exploit opportunities was demonstrated in his previous role in the garden centre, when he first used Archie Kingsteps' hobby interests to develop a line of books and his computer expertise to make the garden centre efficient. He was even looking for opportunities within Tigermill when he was outside the company watching from afar the mistakes that he believed were being made. His inclination towards a *directed evolution* style of strategic action is clearly one that Dina shares. Their decision to retain the services of the human resources director is an interesting example of mixing together cold rational analysis (he has valuable expertise and experience), political shrewdness (recognising the importance of who he knows) and sentiment (Ali and Dina both like the man). The role of ongoing negotiation in the strategy-making process is visible from the beginning in the deals that make the new Tigermill a reality. It is further seen in the exchanges that are made with one party after another over time. A good example is that which sees Archie being made a director, in recognition of his identifying a new line of business and to encourage him to take charge of that new line of experimentation. Experimentation seems to be a key characteristic of how the new company works, with the hobby days and the cyber shops being good examples of the 'let's try it out' principle as, indeed, was the very notion of trying out e-commerce in the first place. All this experimentation occurs, it would seem, in a spirit of learning, and Dina (who, we might remember, originally entered the family firm with a commitment to personal learning) is explicit about the importance of learning from customers. She is also explicit about relating learning to the concept of strategy: it is part of her 'strategic argument' for retaining the garden centre.

The starting point for the decision to retain the garden centre was, on Ali's account, a sentimental one. But Dina is aware that decisions like this need to be related to some strategic logic or broad sense of direction, as the concepts of *logical incrementalism* and *directed evolution* both recognise. Hence Dina's relating of the decision to the basic managerial priority of moving forward and growing the business through continuous learning and, especially, paying direct attention to customers. Such a practice was so effective that the tours element of the growing business developed from an idea put forward by a customer (who, again in the spirit of opportunism and experimentation, was asked to try out the idea). Strategic learning and negotiation can also be seen in the way another area of adaptation, the development of the cyber shops, emerged from discussions with managers. This was a development we can imagine Mats Clunas (Cases and Conversations 6.1), with his belief in treating all managers as contributors to strategy-making, strongly approving of.

Although Dina and Ali retain a flexible approach to strategy-making, one which Ali would say allows them to 'go with the flow of how things work out' and be free to exploit 'what things might come up', this does not mean that all notions of strategic planning are abandoned. Ali admits to Dina that he had been doing some 'shrewd strategy work' in planning his return to Tigermill and we notice that Dina refers to 'Ali's scheme', just as he talks about 'ground being laid'. The reference to Trojan horses and spying in 'occupied territory' suggests sensitivity to the military origins of the very notion of strategy as well as considerable cunning. Yet Ali is very conscious of not going too far with planning ahead. He has learned from the mistakes of Steve Dallas. Yet he is also aware that one will not be given credibility unless one can talk of plans. He compromised in his negotiations with the investing interests by using the concept of 'tentative business plans'. Considerable wisdom is suggested here. This is not just wisdom about the symbolic and legitimising functions of being able to talk of plans – or finding a 'strategic argument' for a specific idea, as we see in Dina's justification for keeping the garden centres without risking the danger of losing 'strategic focus'. It is also wise because it recognises that business opportunities might arise that one might not have even thought of in a 'planning ahead' mode of strategy-making. In just two years, we note, Tigermill had become a 'flourishing e-commerce enterprise', and this was a possibility that had not 'crossed the mind' of either Dina or Ali when they took over the management of the company.

The notion of *directed evolution*, one that is so well illustrated in the Tigermill case, can be helpful in making sense of a broad shift that has occurred in much 'applied' strategic management thinking. Such a shift has partly come about as a result of theoretical moves in the direction of what is called process-relational thinking here. However, the shift in applied thinking has only partly been influenced by such theoretical trends. The influential writing of Peters and Waterman (1982, Reading Guide 14), for example, was shaped to some extent by their reading of processual styles of organisation and management theory. They also claim to be learning from how they observed the managers of 'excellent companies' increasingly practising what they call 'intentionally seeded evolution' (1982, p. 110). The authors say that the successful organisations that they have observed are learning organisations.

Learning organisation	Concept

An organisation in which experimentation, reflection and mutual learning are normal aspects of the work of all organisational members and in which learning provides a key source of satisfaction for individuals as well as enabling the organisation to be innovative and productively adaptive.

Learning organisations 'experiment more, encourage more tries, and permit small failures … encourage internal competition and allow resultant duplication and overlap … maintain a rich informal environment, heavily laden with information, which spurs diffusion of ideas that work' (Peters and Waterman, 1982, pp. 100–111, Reading Guide 14). The overall analysis that Peters and Waterman develop is only partly a process-relational one, however. It over-estimates the extent to which the management of an organisation can achieve a sense of unity and common purpose and it ends up offering what is, in effect, something of a modified form of systems thinking. The similarly influential writing of Senge (1990, Reading Guide 15) on learning organisations is explicitly rooted in systems thinking with both the naïve idealism and the unitary assumptions about organisations of his approach being apparent in his characterisation of learning organisations. These are organisations where 'people continuously expand their capacity to create the results they truly desire, where new and expansive patterns of thinking are nurtured, where collective aspiration is set free, and where people are continually learning how to learn together'. The utopianism implicit in this type of utterance has not undermined the popularity of this work however.

The notion of the learning organisation is a powerful one. In spite of the danger of its being drawn into a systems-control style of thinking, the concept appears to be consistent with process-relational thinking. If we see all organisations as sets of ongoing human relationships, understandings and processes that are continuously negotiated and are continually *emergent*, then it is possible to regard all organisations as learning organisations. It is only as a result of a degree of continuous and mutual learning, about what is going on and what is expected, that any pattern of activities worthy of the description 'organisation' becomes possible. But what is aspired to by managerial advocates of the special type of enterprise they call 'learning organisations' is a situation in which continuous and high level learning about the world inside and outside the organisation is *harnessed to the organisational purposes of those in charge of the organisation.*

One cannot complain about managers of organisations aspiring to such a managerial utopia, but a naïve belief that it is actually realisable could be highly counter-productive for them. And such naïvety is something against which an understanding of process-relational thinking should inoculate both practitioners and analysts. At the same time, process-relational thinking recognises that part of the managerial task is to try to achieve as much corporate unity and common purpose as employees can be persuaded to go along with. Much of the managerial interest in 'learning organisations' derives from an interest in achieving a degree of such unified action by getting as many employees as possible to 'share' in the strategic management of the organisation. It is, in effect, trying to involve all employees in strategic thinking in the way Mats Clunas was trying to involve all his managers in strategic matters (pp. 174–6).

Its advocates see the achievement of this sort of 'learning organisation' as possible if each employee can be persuaded to see their engagement in continuous learning at work as directly and personally rewarding. Particular stress tends to be laid on the reward of 'personal growth', something that is said to result from such learning. It can also be presented as indirectly beneficial to the employee, on the assumption that everyone will benefit from the improved performance of the organisation. And if organisational success is increasingly going to require skilful *knowledge management* (Nonaka and Takeuchi, 1995, and other references in Reading Guide 15), then continuous learning *with reference to the organisation's overall strategic direction* by a high proportion of organisational members is something that organisational strategy-makers are likely increasingly to encourage.

Knowledge management   *Concept*

Practices which encourage the acquisition, creation, sharing, manipulation and developing of knowledge (recognised as ways of understanding the world as well as having information about it) within an organisation in order to enhance the effective performance of that organisation and, hence, its strategic success.

It is in the spirit of both knowledge management and learning organisations that so much attention has been given to the account by De Geus (1988, Reading Guide 15) of his attempt to convert the planners in his organisation from acting as the producers of plans that others would follow to being facilitators and accelerators of learning processes across management teams. The same applies to Hamel and Prahalad's (1989, Reading Guide 14) argument that, instead of devising strategic plans, managements should gain commitment across the organisation to a *strategic intent* which is related to the organisation's 'core competences' (becoming the leading supplier of management textbooks in Europe within five years, say). They then create the conditions in which employees generally are encouraged to learn, innovate and act creatively in ways that those employees themselves judge to be appropriate as means towards fulfilling the strategic intent to which top managers have persuaded them to be committed.

Strategic intent   *Concept*

A statement of a clear and specific strategic position that an organisation's management aspires to reach at a specified time in the future and to which employees are persuaded to commit themselves and actively work towards.

The high level of employee commitment towards a managerially conceived corporate direction that is implicit in the notions of strategic intent and of the learning organisation is something that managers frequently aspire to and many try to bring about. This is not unreasonable. But a fully developed process-relational understanding of organisational activities emphasises the unattainability of anything approaching the managerial ideal of complete unity. Every organisation contains a multiplicity of interests and an enormous range of individuals and groups all seeking to make *strategic exchanges* with the organisation that fit with their own sectional priorities – these existing *within* management as well as across the rest of the workforce. Negotiations, compromises and attempts to win commitment and some degree of unity therefore become part of the strategy-making process itself. They are not something that occurs at a later 'implementation' stage. Strategies are better not seen as the creations of 'strategic managers' to which commitment from others is *subsequently* sought. It is more helpful to see negotiation, bargaining and exchange with the range of parties concerned with the organisation as part of the overall and ongoing strategy-making process from the beginning. Indeed, organisational effectiveness itself is seen, in the process-relational perspective, as a matter of enactment, negotiation and exchange. And the most useful and straightforward way of conceiving of *organisational effectiveness*, if we want a concept that can be applied to all and to every type of organisation, is to see it in terms of survival of the organisation into the long term.

Strategy-making, organisational effectiveness and survival into the long term

Over the years, business writers, economists and organisation theorists have suggested a whole range of criteria which might be used to judge how effective – or otherwise – any given organisation is. We all work with a variety of such criteria as we go through life, reflecting on how well or poorly we would judge the organisations we come across, as potential employers, say, or as users of whatever services an organisation might offer us.

Activity 6.6

As quickly as possible, list all the criteria that come to mind by which we might judge the effectiveness of an organisation.

The first and most obvious criterion of effectiveness that comes to mind, at least with regard to business organisations, is profitability. But as soon as this is suggested, the questions tends to be raised as to whether this is short- or long-term profitability. The slightest knowledge of how the business world operates will make us aware that a business that is likely to fail in the medium term can easily get a reasonably high level of profit squeezed out of it in the short term by shrewd managers and accountants. Long-term profitability might seem like a better option. But would we still judge an organisation that was profitable in this way to be 'effective' if its very profitability was leading it towards takeover by another business? We tend not to. If we turn to economists' thinking on these matters will we find some of them arguing that a better criterion for judging how 'good' an organisation is, is to look at its share of the market or perhaps its rate of growth. Some commentators, though, will balk at this emphasis on purely economic factors and argue that a business organisation should not be judged as effective unless it is, say, giving a high quality of goods or service to its customers, or a high level of satisfaction to its employees. Alternatively, they might point to something more general like its contribution to the welfare of society as a whole. Criteria like this have in their favour the advantage that they can be applied to all sorts of organisations, and not just to business ones.

The problem with this kind of reflection is that it brings a whole series of competing value judgements to bear on the matter. One person's idea of what 'benefit to society' is, will not be the same as another's, for example. The way this kind of problem is typically avoided is to suggest that we simply look at what the goals of any particular organisation are, and then judge that organisation to be effective if it is successful in achieving its goals. Such an approach would have the virtue of being as applicable to business and non-business organisations alike. And, associated with this type of thinking is the distinction that is often made between *effective* and *efficient* actions.

Effectiveness and efficiency
Concept

An action is judged to be *efficient* if it uses the most appropriate known means to achieve a given end but it is only judged to be *effective* if the action fulfils the intentions behind it.

Efficiency is said, in the cliché, to be about 'doing things well' while effectiveness is about 'doing the right things well'. An organisation that is only efficient might be one with very streamlined and cost-effective procedures for fulfilling smoothly and effortlessly goals that the organisation was not intended to meet. We might imagine a very efficient airline that flies from a place nobody wants to leave to a place nobody wants to go, for example, or a hospital that was very well organised to deliver babies in an area of the country with a negligible birth rate. But if we say that an effective organisation is one that does the right things well, we are left with the problem of what the 'right thing' is (assuming that by 'well' is meant 'efficient' in the sense of using the most appropriate means to achieve given ends). To use our airline example again, we would tend to answer this by saying that an effective air service would be one which efficiently took people from where they wanted to leave to where they wanted to arrive – at the right price, at the right time and so on. This should satisfy the passengers. But would it be the 'right thing' if it meant that the noise of the aircraft ruined the peace of all the people living near the two airports or that the popularity of the service led to calls for airport expansion and the loss of hundreds of homes?

We are back to the problems of thinking of organisations and of their performance in terms of organisational goals and to the vexed question of whether it is not sometimes the case that actions happen before reasons or causes are attached to them.

Link   Issues of organisational effectiveness inevitably take us back to the problems of organisational goals and goals in organisations that were examined in Chapter 3 (pp. 45–50) as well as to the difficult relationship between intentions and actions discussed in Chapter 4 (pp. 98–102)

We are confronted by the difficulties we looked at earlier of there being multiple, ambiguous and conflicting goals present in every organisation. How, for example, would we possibly judge a prison service to be 'effective' in straightforward 'goal achievement' terms, given that the likely purposes associated with it by those judging it would range from goals of treatment and rehabilitation on the one hand to ones of retribution, deterrence or even revenge on the other? It is impossible. Not only this, but those actually having to manage organisations find themselves facing a whole range of pressures on them from a multiplicity of parties in addition to those from the direct users of the organisation's services or from its owners (be these public or private). In practice the managements of organisations – the makers of their strategies – tend to be judged as 'effective' or otherwise, in terms of how well they handle this range of constituencies with which they have to deal. The management of the airline will not just be judged simply in terms of how efficiently they fly people to desirable destinations and the management of the prison service will not be judged simply in terms of how many prisoners go on not to re-offend or how many escapes occur. They will be judged by how well they deal with all the pressures that are put upon them from the great variety of people who have an interest of any kind in the airline or the prison service. More specifically, they will be judged in terms of how effective they are at preventing these pressures forcing the demise of the airline or the prison service.

What all of this suggests is that we can cut through all the complications and value judgement problems by using a relatively simple criterion. It is the one that tends to be used in practice across the organisational world for judging organisations and their managements. The most helpful way of judging an effective organisation, and hence an effective organisational management, is to judge how well that organisation is placed to survive into the long term. It follows from this that the *basic logic of strategic managerial work is one of keeping the organisation 'fit and healthy' so that it will survive into the long term*. And the term *basic logic* is used here very deliberately to avoid the language of 'purpose' or 'goal', with all the metaphysical or logical difficulties that such terms can get us into. The logic that is being pointed to here is the logic to which all strategic managerial work necessarily works in the world of contemporary organisational practice. The approach being taken is one that does not involve any *moral pre-judgement*, about, for example, whether it is morally right or wrong for a particular organisation to survive, although such value judgements are immensely important and we shall consider them later. For the moment, our concept enables us to judge the effectiveness of the management of a contract murder business in the same way we would judge the management of a charity devoted to spreading love and happiness. Moral judgements about what is going on in these organisations are no less important – in fact one might argue they are more important – than judgements of managerial or strategic effectiveness. But they are judgements of a different kind.

Organisational and managerial effectiveness

Concept

The ability to satisfy the demands of the range of constituencies inside and outside the organisation so that continued support in terms of resources such as labour, custom, investment, supplies and legal approval is obtained and the organisation enabled to survive into the long term.

 Link Chapter 12 will look at the ways in which organisational effectiveness can be pursued as well as closely examining the issues of ethics and morality that arise.

We will shortly look more closely at the notion of strategy-making being to do with satisfying the resource demands of multiple constituencies. For the moment, a few more points about the logic of long-term survival need to be made and how these relate to human behaviours and meanings that we tend to observe in the world of organisational practice.

People's involvement in organisations, especially the involvement of those taking a managerial role with them, is rarely a matter of simple short-term instrumental engagement. Meaning tends to get invested in the organisation and it is most unlikely that people with a 'strategic' involvement in an organisation are likely to be happy about being associated with its demise, or its 'breaking up'. When the Microsoft Corporation was first threatened by the American state with being broken into two parts, the first reaction of business commentators was that this was a death threat, a defeat for the corporation's management. Leaving aside the economic and business logic of what was at stake here, massive managerial pride informed the fight to 'save the organisation' – the organisation in the form, that is, that the management believed in. Even at the level of shrewd career calculation – leaving aside matters of pride and identification with an enterprise – a manager is unlikely to want to be seen as someone who took part in the demise of an employing organisation. But what if an organisation has clearly completed the tasks that it was set up to fulfil? Would that not change the situation so that, for example, a management team running a charity established to fund the discovery of a cure for a particular disease would be quite happy to close that charity on the discovery of a successful cure?

What we have tended to see historically in situations where organisations have completed a relatively specific set of tasks for which they were explicitly established is a search for another role that such an organisation can take on. A whole set of relationships, practices and habits of working will have developed and people involved in such undertakings often seek other tasks that their organisation might undertake. Also, the more successful such an enterprise was, the more it is likely to be argued that its potential for further successes, in an associated area, should not be lost. However, if we turn our attention to what people might regard as failing organisations, we see there too a tendency for people involved with them to 'fight closure'. And this commonly observed tendency makes us aware of a further general reason why the survival principle is so central to organisational and managerial work. This is the simple and straightforward fact that people's employment in an organisation does not just mean a certain degree of association with the enterprise at the level of meaning or sentiment. It also tends to be accompanied by a set of associated attachments and investments in housing, children's schooling, social networks and employment in the area of other members of one's family. All of these tend to influence managerial interests in maintaining the organisation they are involved in as a 'going concern'.

In addition to these factors, which are largely ones associated with managerial interests and motivations, there are some rather more fundamental factors that are relevant. There is little realistic possibility whatsoever of anyone running an organisation of any significant size or complexity as a short-term operation. To carry out tasks at all, in the short term, a level of perceived confidence or security on the part of investors, employees or customers with regard to the longer term is required. Little support or commitment, especially on the part of people working within it, is likely to be given to an organisation that is perceived as lacking a secure future. And similar pressures exist with regard to all the other parties with which the organisation exchanges or 'trades'. Hence working towards survival into the long term and exchanging with a multiplicity of constituencies to bring about that longevity are central to strategic managing of organisations. It is to these processes of organisational strategic exchange that we now turn.

Strategic exchange and the managing of resource dependencies

Strategy-making involves strategists in making sense of the world and acting in the light of the sense they make of it. The 'environment' in which an organisation exists and in which its management works towards its long-term survival is not a simple 'given'. It is not an objective set of conditions about which strategists can gather unambiguous 'data' which they then process in order to reach strategic decisions and predictable survival outcomes. In process-relational terms, the world 'outside' the organisation is *enacted*, just like the organisation itself.

Enacted environment   *Concept*

The environment of an organisation exists for members of an organisation by virtue of the interpretations they make of what is occurring 'outside' the organisation and the way their own actions influence or shape those occurrences.

In very simple terms, the world to which the organisation relates is very much a matter of what those dealing with that world 'make of it'. This is not to say, of course, that strategy-makers can bring about anything whatsoever that they would like to see happen. Far from it: realised actualities can only emerge out of potentialities. This point, as well as the basic notion of an enacted environment, can be illustrated with the very simple case of a market and a product. A business organisation does not go out and 'find' a market which it then satisfies in order to stay in business. Instead, its managers first strategically identify the *possibility* of a market relationship with certain would-be customers outside the organisation. They then work at their product in the light of the possibilities and potentials that they *envisage*. Next, they present their product to the would-be customers in a way that will *persuade* them to trade with the organisation, again in the light of their *interpretation* of the inclinations of these potential customers. Active sense-making is central to all of this. Marketing is an active, creative and sense-making organisational process. It involves skilful trading and the establishment of exchange relationships.

To bring together the two emerging key themes of sense-making and exchange, we can suggest a particular model of strategic enactment. This *organisational strategic exchange* model is an attempt to represent schematically how strategic managers enact exchange relationships with the range of parties with whom they have to deal, inside and outside organisation, to enable the organisation to survive into the long term.

All organisations (as sets of patterned understandings, relationships and practices) have to trade with a range of parties or *constituencies* to survive into the future. They are dependent upon these constituencies for resources. Such resources vary from the labour, applied knowledge and the commitment obtained from the organisation's employees and the raw materials obtained from its suppliers to the revenues it obtains from its customers and the legal approval it obtains from the state. To receive such resources it enters exchange relationships with each of these constituencies. It trades with them. It provides employees with such resources as pay, job interest or status. It pays the bills of its suppliers and it provides its customers with the products or services they seek. It pays its taxes to the state and 'gives' the state compliance with the law. These 'resources', it is important to note, are both *material* resources like raw materials or cash and *symbolic* resources such as work satisfaction or job security, in the case of employees, or satisfaction with and confidence in the product, with regard to customers. Meanings are traded in all of this as much as objects and cash are traded. Matters of satisfaction, security, trust or commitment across the range of exchange relationships are as relevant to long-term survival as are the artefacts that change hands. Figure 6.2 represents a possible set of constituencies for an organisation – in this case a business organisation operating in a market-based political economy.

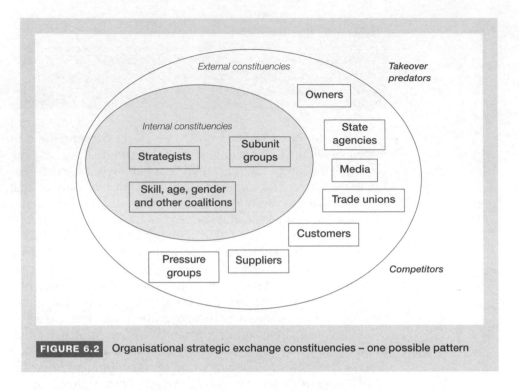

FIGURE 6.2 Organisational strategic exchange constituencies – one possible pattern

The inner circle of Figure 6.2 contains parties and constituencies that are part of the organisation itself. A tiny fraction of the multitude of individuals and groupings with which the organisation trades are identified here. The outer circle covers a typical set of parties with which a commercial organisation might externally trade. Outside the two circles are forces that are *not* resource-dependent constituencies. They are both presences, however, that the external constituencies might deal with, possibly with profound consequences for the organisation if, say, the owners sell their shares to a takeover 'predator' or customers take their business to a competing company.

In a sense, the picture painted in Figure 6.2 can be understood as a mental map with which anyone thinking strategically about an organisation might work. The map that applies to every individual organisation will be different and each one will change over time, sometimes changing from day to day. However, strategic managers who are continually mentally mapping the current strategic situation of their organisation, cannot take into account every party with which the organisation trades. To go that far would be to give attention to every single employee and every single customer, as well as to countless other people in the other organisations with which the enterprise exchanges. In practice, there has to be a prioritising of the attention paid to constituencies, with priority being given to those constituencies that are perceived to be the most significant, at any given point in time, for the long-term survival of the organisation.

Strategic constituencies   *Concept*

All the parties with which an organisation exchanges are strategic in the sense that the exchanges made with them contribute to long-term survival. At any point in time, however, some constituencies are more strategic than others insofar as they create a greater degree of uncertainty with regard to the organisation's long-term future.

To put this argument another way, strategy-makers give priority of attention to areas of exchange where there is the greatest degree of uncertainty with respect to the supply of resources necessary for future viability. If it transpires, for example, that the only person who understands the coding of a key product of a software company is threatening to leave, then that person becomes the key focus of strategic attention.

 Link

The exchanges that an organisation makes with its internal constituencies are typically centred upon the *implicit contracts* made between organisations and employees. These were discussed in Chapter 5 (pp. 126–38)

Similarly, if a government agency finds that the only senior official that the current relevant minister of state finds credible is about to retire, his or her replacement becomes a key strategic concern. Strategic constituencies, then, are sometimes single individuals, but, more typically, the constituencies with which strategy-making concerns itself will be groups of people or other organisations. These will nevertheless often be exchanged through relationships with representatives of such groups or organisations, people like trade union officers or the managers of other companies. The focus will be on the whole constituency, however. Thus, if it transpires that medical general practitioners are discouraging their patients from attending a particular hospital for treatment, then these GPs become a strategic constituency that the management of that hospital will come to focus their attention upon. If, say, the younger customers within the 'customer base' of a clothing company appear to be turning their backs on that company's fashion offerings, strategic attention will tend to turn upon these youths and attempts will be made to make sense of what is happening to their tastes.

Activity 6.7

Try to draw a rough sketch, along the lines of Figure 6.2, of the key constituencies that you understand are relevant to the strategic management of any organisation that you know about.

This might be an organisation you are, or have been, employed in or it might be one that is currently in the public eye and is being discussed in the business press.

Any strategic exchange map that one might draw for an organisation will inevitably be very sketchy indeed. This is bound to be the case unless the person doing the 'mapping' has a close and intimate knowledge of the internal processes of the organisation they are looking at as well as a good understanding of the organisation's wider business or institutional context. Strategy, in practice, is a matter of considerable detail as well as of broad direction. And, of course, it never stays still. The strategic exchange view of organisational strategy-making is one of a dynamic and an emergent process, consistent with everything that has been said from the beginning of the present chapter. And, as is suggested by the illustrations that have been used here so far, there is a continual relating of the immediate to the long term. It implies the necessity of a managerial 'scanning' of the events of each day in terms of their significance for the long-term viability of the enterprise as a whole. This emphasis on scanning across a range of contacts and sources of insight and information fits with the patterns that we saw in managerial work generally when we reviewed research on managerial behaviour in Chapter 3.

In spite of this emphasis of the strategic significance of everyday events, the strategic exchange model should not be taken to suggest that strategic thinking always starts with attention to the immediate and short term, and then moves up to longer-term thinking. Nevertheless, the longer-term thinking about how things might be in the future and what general direction the organisation might follow can only occur in the light of how strategy-makers project forward from their understanding of the current patterns of resource exchange to envisage how these *might change* in the future. In the case of the clothing company, for example, managers concerned with strategy can only do their best to interpret young people's fashion preferences, as they are currently able to make sense of them. But this is done in order to envisage what preferences these potential customers might have in the future or, more significantly, what preferences they might *be persuaded to adopt* by shrewd marketing and advertising. It is because no strategist can ever find out about the future from reliable forecasts, or from a magic crystal ball, that all strategies are necessarily *emergent* and effective strategy-making always depends on imagination as well as analysis, creativity as well as reactive sensitivity.

Organisational strategy-making, then, operates in a world of multiple constituencies and ambiguous demands, but it also takes place in a world of scarce resources. Strategy-making can be seen as an imaginative, a creative and a political activity. But it must also be understood as an economic activity. The strategic exchange model very effectively relates the issue of scarcity and competition for resources to the issue of taking the organisation forward into the future. It does this by recognising the logic whereby strategy-makers reduce the satisfaction of the resource demands of constituencies upon whom they are resource dependent to a level which is as low as is possible but which does not threaten long-term organisational viability. This is not a logic whereby the organisation pays its staff as low a level of pay as it can get away with at that point in time, however. But it does mean that it pays as low a range of wages as it can, while still getting the employees to provide the commitment and the quantity and quality of labour it needs to enable it to continue into the long term. In some circumstances this could mean paying a very high level of wages indeed (if that is what was necessary to attract and keep the quality of labour needed for long-term viability). Similarly the logic is not one of providing the lowest quality of goods or service that the organisation can get away with. But it does mean keeping quality down to the lowest level at which customers or clients will still continue to buy those goods or use those services into the future, to the extent and with the frequency that the healthy long-term future of the organisation requires. In some circumstances – where the market was for expensive luxury goods, say – this could mean an extremely high level of quality. It would be an unwise producer of luxury goods, however, who supplied gold fittings on a product when supplying items with silver fittings would fetch the same price and would encourage customers to buy from that producer again in the future.

Strategic economising (minimised resource outflow within long-term viability)
Concept

The principle whereby organisations allocate to constituencies upon whom they are *resource dependent* the least costly level of demand compliance that is possible without the constituency withdrawing the level of resource support that is necessary for long-term survival.

If this broad principle of minimal resource outflows within the dictates of long-term viability were not followed by a commercial enterprise, operating in an industrial capitalist political economy, then a competitor that managed its costs more effectively would push it out of business. Alternatively, it would be acquired by the first takeover 'predator' to catch sight of the economic fat on such a prime takeover target. If a public service organisation similarly failed to follow the economic imperative of cost sensitivity, it too would suffer censure and punishment. This would happen the moment the guardians of the public purse discovered that a university's students were being taught in one-person tutorials, the books in a public library were being bound in vellum and decorated with gold lettering or the patients in a national health service hospital were being fed a diet of champagne and caviar. Although they were not on this level, issues of quality were relevant to the strategic issues facing Strath Guitars, and this was only one among a range of issues that were pertinent to the long-term future of this organisation at the point at which we investigate it.

Activity 6.8

Examine how Donna Dulsie and Willie Cose in Cases and Conversations 6.4 reflect on the strategic position of Strath Guitars in a way that follows the logic of the organisational strategic exchange model, noting down:

- what you understand the basic 'resource exchange' currently to be between Strath Guitars and each of the constituencies about which information is given;

- what changed terms of exchange you think Willie and Donna hope to bring about between Strath Guitars and each of these constituencies in the fairly near future, in the hope of ensuring the long-term future of the organisation.

Also answer the following three questions:

- To what extent does the notion of directed evolution (see above, p. 191) apply to the way strategy-making appears to be going on here?

- In what ways do we see evidence of these strategy-makers following the strategic economising principle of minimising resource 'outgoings' in the context of trying to ensure long-term organisational viability?

- How typical do you think it is of organisational strategy-making in general to involve the sort of personal and emotional factors that Willie and Donna are bringing into their strategic thinking and decision-making?

In doing this analysis, note how Figure 6.3 is a version of Figure 6.2 that has been drawn to represent the basic analysis that the two strategy-makers are developing for their organisation. Also, take care not to treat either takeover interests or competitors (those falling outside the two circles in Figure 6.2) as if these were resource-trading constituencies like all the others. Neither of these are constituencies in the model, because the focal organisation does not trade with them, in resource exchange terms. The relationship between these other organisations and Strath is an indirect one, mediated by constituencies like Willie Cose himself, the company's customers or the wood suppliers – with whom direct exchanges do occur.

Crunch time at Strath Guitars

Willie Cose started playing electric guitars when he was barely old enough to get his hands round the neck of a half-sized instrument. While still at school he started making his own guitars and was able to make enough money from this part-time activity to be able to set up his business, Strath Guitars, when he was only eighteen. He combined the establishment of this business with performing in his own band, Crunchtime. The band featured Willie's very distinctive style of playing, one that involved a variety of different open tunings and a finger style of playing. His own guitar had been especially designed to accommodate this relatively unusual approach to the playing of electric guitars and as the band became more and more popular so the demand for these guitars from Strath grew. Early on, Willie realised that he was not going to be able to combine running the guitar-making business himself at the same time as doing concerts, making records and broadcasting. Fortunately, his girlfriend, Donna Dulsie, was interested in the business and was very happy to manage it for

him. Within five years she had built the business up into a sizeable concern. Important to this growth was the expanded range of models that were made possible from the investment arising from the success of the original guitar called, in fact, the Strath Original. The expansion of the model range was also made possible by Donna's recruitment of Ben More, a brilliant young instrument designer. This happened at about the same time that Donna ended her intimate relationship with Willie. With the break up of this relationship, which happened very amicably, Donna took on the formal role of managing director of Strath Guitars, and Willie agreed that he would very much leave the running of the business to her, in spite of the fact that he owned 80 per cent of the shares – with Donna owning the other 20 per cent.

Seven years after the company had started, a series of strategic issues are facing Strath Guitars and one of the most complicated aspects of the company's situation is that there is no single strategic manager, or strategic managerial group, to sit down and try to sort out the difficulties. This is because one of the key strategic threats to Strath Guitars, as it currently exists, is the possible retirement of Donna herself at the age of 28, to start a family. She is also anxious to get away from the increasingly irritating interference of Willie in business matters, a sort of interference he always promised he would avoid. But Willie himself is not interested in coming in to help sort out the difficulties. In fact, he is himself providing another significant threat to the continuation of the business. He is tempted to take up an offer from Bigsounds Corp to buy it. This multinational corporation produces his records and they publish his music. They have a musical instruments division and would like to bring the two most popular Strath models, the Strath Original and the Strath Crunch, into their portfolio of instruments.

Donna found herself very unsure about what to do with both her own life and the company to which she had become very attached. Ben More told her that he was also considering leaving to set up his own business and Donna was worried about the dissatisfactions being expressed by most of the company's craft workers, the people who did the more skilled part of the guitar construction work. All of these matters had considerable implications for the long-term future of Strath Guitars. There were also several other issues, of a more external nature, that needed thinking about. Eventually, Donna persuaded Willie to spend a day at the company going over all of these matters. It was the nearest they had ever got to an attempt explicitly and systematically to look at the strategic situation of the company. What could be perceived as a smooth and successful pattern of strategic development up until now had occurred without any deliberate policies ever having been laid down. All the key parties to the company had a similar understanding of what was possible and they all were happy to see things working out the way they did. Now, however, serious threats to the business had arisen and some strategic decisions needed to be made. First, however, Donna and Willie needed to do a strategic analysis of the company and the situation it was in.

If the analysis that Donna and Willie did on the morning of their meeting were to be represented in organisational strategic exchange terms it would look like Figure 6.3. The picture here is a version of the more general model show in Figure 6.2. Very roughly, the various constituencies have been represented in a font size judged to be proportionate to the size of the strategic threat arising from each of them. That is, the larger the font size, the more uncertainty Donna and Willie believe is currently created for the organisation's long-term survival.

Willie and Donna went through what they thought were all the major issues facing Strath Guitars.

- It first agreed that the most significant issue was that of Donna herself. There was nobody inside the company who could replace her, and there was nobody outside it that they were aware of. She is clearly the key internal constituency in the organisational strategic exchange model.

- Willie was a vital external constituency, of equivalent importance to Donna internally. He said he would definitely sell out to Bigsounds if Donna were to stop working. While agreeing that this was a possibility that they both might settle for at the end of that day, Willie and Donna also agreed that they were both very unsure whether this is what they really wanted. Before returning to this fundamental decision they would examine all the other strategic issues that they felt were relevant.

- The loss of Ben More would certainly be serious. The trade were expecting new models from Strath in coming years and the excitement connected with this expectation was very much based on what it was believed Ben might achieve as an important innovator in electric guitar design. It did seem, however, that Ben wanted to develop his interests beyond the design work itself. Donna had noticed that Ben was showing more and more interest in the business side of Strath but she had felt less able to involve him in this than she otherwise might have, because of her problems with Willie interfering in everyday business issues. If a way could be found of bringing Ben into business issues more, however, perhaps he might be more willing to stay.

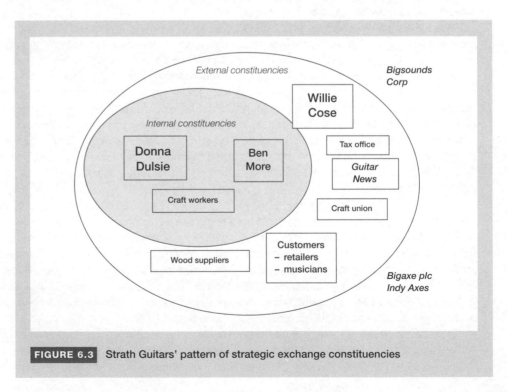

FIGURE 6.3 Strath Guitars' pattern of strategic exchange constituencies

- The craft workers were the only other area of concern within the organisation, Donna felt. The area of dissatisfaction was about managerial pressure to reduce the extent of individual variations from guitar to guitar. Several of the craft workers felt that it was important to their identity as instrument workers to have a degree of discretion about how each instrument was made. They did not want to be seen as 'mere assemblers'. This however was causing the sales team problems. The problem was one of perceived variation of quality 'out in the market place'. The workers insisted that every guitar was of equally high quality. But because the guitars varied, the retailers often argued that certain guitars delivered to them were better than others. Some way of handling the workers' requirements for opportunities to work at an appropriate craft level had to be found that would not cause marketing problems.

- An external constituency that was relevant to the dissatisfactions of some of the craft workers was that of their trade union. The union's regional full-time official was seeking a meeting with Strath management. Precisely what issues he was going to raise were not known at this time.

- The retailers who were complaining about quality variations fit into the organisational strategic exchange model as part of the customer constituency. But these people also complained that their own customers ('end users of Strath Guitars', as Donna chose to call them) were becoming unhappy about what they perceived as 'inconsistencies' in the instruments that Strath were producing. Something clearly needed to be done about this to avoid losing customers to competitors. All the other major guitar makers were competitors but the two that customers of Strath were most likely to turn to were Bigaxe and Indy. Each of these was offering instruments that were similar to the Strath models but were significantly cheaper. Their quality was not so high, but retailers perceived their quality as consistent. This tended to encourage retailers to see Bigaxe and Indy as generally more reliable organisations to do business with than Strath.

- The type of wood that Strath used was becoming increasingly expensive and Donna suspected that this was because Bigaxe and Indy were buying from the same suppliers, quite deliberately hoping to get a 'Strath sound' by using similar materials. There was a threat, then, with regard to the wood supplier external constituency in that the cost of these materials was approaching a level where it might have to lead to dangerous price increases in Strath Guitars. Because the prices of the rival instruments were significantly lower, the competitors had more scope to increase their prices as a means of getting hold of the same type of wood that Strath used.

- An external constituency that Donna was worried about but which had no direct connection with music or guitars, was part of the set of state constituencies that every organisation has certain exchanges with. In this case, there appeared to be some problem with the tax authorities. Donna had been summoned to the local offices of the Inland Revenue to discuss what she had been told were 'serious problems with how Strath had been dealing with the PAYE of its staff'. Donna had little idea what the problems might be. She was worried that this might be just one of the problems that had been created by the company's accountant, a man who was nearing retirement and who Donna knew she urgently needed to talk to (this potentially making him another 'problem constituency').

- A further external constituency that was worrying Donna was the influential magazine, *Guitar News*. She was aware that they were going to do a large feature on Strath Guitars and was anxious to find a way of influencing what they wrote, without being seen to be trying to bribe or otherwise illegitimately influence them. At the moment there was a danger of some of the threats to Strath becoming attractive journalistic material to the magazine. Both Donna and Willie, however, wanted to see a positive story, not just because of its important strategic significance to Strath as a business, but because of the sense of personal pride that each of them had in the company. They were also worried that the magazine might bring their former personal relationship into the article, something that neither felt would be helpful in their current private lives. What would be helpful, in every respect, would be if a 'good story' of some kind could be offered to the magazine. Was there any way in which Strath could exchange with the magazine some 'good copy' in return for a 'good write up' that would enhance the reputation of the business, as well as giving personal satisfaction to both Willie and Donna?

● The final constituency that was discussed was a rather ineffective pressure group calling itself the 'national acoustic society'. This was dedicated to getting rid of electric and digital musical instruments and encouraging all musicians to play only acoustic instruments. The group had picked on Strath as a special target, because it only made electric instruments. Was there any way of conceding something to this group to encourage them to direct their negative publicity stunts at company's other than Strath?

After many hours of discussion Donna and Willie came to a decision about how they would proceed. At an emotional level they not only realised that neither of them really wanted to end their involvement in Strath Guitars, they also realised that they could still have a good personal relationship. It was one they wanted to continue, as long as they could formally clarify the responsibilities that each of them had with regard to the running of the business. They decided on what they called a 'broad strategic direction', one that included some new organisational arrangements as well as a distinctive approach to developing their products and markets.

Willie would take on a role as the non-executive chairman of Strath, leaving the clear executive leadership role to Donna. To take some of the pressures off Donna, and to allow her to think about starting a family without giving up work, she would chair a small 'operational executive group'. This would comprise herself, Ben More (as a director of design and marketing), the head of sales and a new finance and administration director. Somebody to fill this post would be recruited urgently to replace the company accountant, who would be offered immediate early retirement. Donna would try to persuade the tax authorities to postpone their meeting until she had made this new appointment.

It was hoped that Ben could be persuaded to stay with Strath and take on this expanded role (and the 'considerably improved benefits, of course', as Willie put it). If he agreed, he would be asked to start discussions with the craft workers about the possibility of the company offering 'custom guitars', special editions that would allow those workers who were especially concerned about utilising their craft skills to gain a higher level of job satisfaction. In return for involvement in this development, however, it would have to be accepted that standard models would be built to a single set of standards and characteristics. Moves in the custom-building direction would be experimental, however, and Ben, together with the head of sales, would talk to as many retailers and their customers as possible to 'test the water' with regard to it. Also, while talking to the craft workers about these possibilities, Ben would 'sound them' about why they had asked their trade union official to visit the company – with a view to settling whatever was worrying them informally and without union involvement. He would also be asked to consult them about an idea for an altogether new model that Donna knew he had in mind. This was an electro-acoustic instrument. Such a development might help persuade the 'nas' pressure group to take some pressure off Strath. Together with the possibility of producing custom guitars, this departure would form the basis of a really 'good story' that could be offered to *Guitar News*. Donna and Ben would invite both the editor and the lead journalist to lunch at the best local restaurant as soon as possible to talk to them about the 'new direction' for Strath and their 'fight back' against the competition.

At the end of the evening, Donna and Willie decided they would telephone Ben so that they could outline their ideas to him while it was all 'fresh in their minds'.

'The sooner we get him on board, the sooner we can get this show on the road', said Willie, excitedly.

'Oh yes,' responded Donna, with a note of caution in her voice, 'but what if it turns out to be too late and Ben's committed himself to going? Or what if he doesn't like what we're offering?' 'Well, we'll just have to start again. Without Ben, though, it really could be crunch time for us all.'

One of the first things that becomes apparent when trying to analyse the nature of the various exchanges that go on between an organisation and the constituencies involved with it, is that our knowledge is very limited. In part this is inevitable because those of us reading this story are given only a fraction of the information and the insights that Donna and Willie have themselves. Closer reflection will remind us that there is also a great deal of ambiguity in the understandings that they too are likely to have of such matters. How much do they understand about what Ben More is looking for in his career, what is bothering the craft workers or what products are likely to appeal to the potential customers of Strath Guitars? Their knowledge is bound to be incomplete. Speculation, guesswork, working to hunches and simply trying out 'hypotheses' about what might 'work' are inevitable parts of all strategy-making. The almost mind-boggling extent of the ambiguity that faces analysts and decision-makers in this area is exemplified by the fact that neither Willie not Donna are even sure of what it is they themselves 'really want' with regard to the future of the organisation at the start of their meeting. In fact, what they *decide* they want, tends to *emerge* within the very process of analysis. What happens in the future will equally be a matter of what emerges in the complex circumstances that Strath Guitars will have to deal with – even if things go as closely 'to plan' as Donna and Willie are hoping they will. They know only too well that uncertainty is always present, however confident one may come to feel at certain times. This recognition becomes apparent in their closing conversation, before they telephone Ben More. He could tell them that he is not interested in their proposals that very evening. Then what do they do? A key feature of all strategy-making is inevitably the wants, interests, commitments, understandings of all of the human beings who are parties to the organisation's existence – present and future. By treating the people working within organisations, and their managers especially, as strategically significant constituencies, we are recognising that the strategic exchange aspects of organisations are intimately related to the strategic exchange aspects of the human beings employed to manage them.

The influence of strategy-makers themselves on strategy (and vice versa)

To deal with organisational and managerial activities we inevitably speak, at times, as if organisations have an existence of their own. In the above discussion, for example, we have talked of organisations exchanging resources, even of them having inputs and outputs, in a way that is reminiscent of systems-control thinking. This, however, is only a shorthand device. The organisation is not an entity equivalent to a person. It is a pattern of activities and understandings involving a range of human constituencies, all of which have their own interests and strategic priorities. It is only for convenience, then, that we talk of an organisation as if it actually were a trading entity. As long as we remember that we are only talking metaphorically (and in a sort of verbal shorthand) then we can from time to time talk of organisations *as if* they were traders, resource exchangers, themselves. In practice, we always have to remember that the actual 'organisational' exchanging is done by people employed by the organisation. This involves organisational members at every level and in a whole variety of roles – from the retail sales assistant to the purchasing assistant to the chief executive. But those who are employed as managers have the formal responsibility for the general direction of these exchanges and the role of overseeing them all so that they contribute to long-term viability. The more 'senior' the manager is the more they involve themselves with this kind of work and this matter of 'seniority' also differentiates the types of exchanges that employees themselves make with 'the organisation'.

The more senior a person is in the hierarchy of the organisation the greater will be the strategic significance of their particular exchange relationship with it. In organisational strategic exchange terms we recognise that organisations are dependent for their existence on the whole range of employee or 'internal' constituencies. However, the significance for the organisation's strategic direction of the nature of the exchanges (or 'employment trades') that it has with those in positions of authority will obviously be greater than exchanges made with people in more junior positions.

 Issues of relative power across individuals and constituencies will be considered in Chapter 10 (pp. 329–31) in the general context of organisational *micropolitics*.

Although, from time to time, a relatively 'junior' person may acquire power because of some capability that the organisation is strategically dependent upon, it is normally the case that the general strategic direction of an organisation will be more influenced by those people given formal managerial and strategic responsibilities. It is therefore vital to look at the nature of the strategic exchanges that exist between senior managerial strategy-makers and the organisation. These can have a considerable influence on the general strategic direction followed by the organisation. Figure 6.4 is a simplified representation of this and it relates back to the general discussion of the exchanges or implicit contracts that employees generally make with the organisation.

 The analysis here derives from the more general one presented in Chapter 5 and Figure 6.4 is derived from Figure 5.1.

If we look back at some of the senior managers we have come across in this chapter we will see a number of ways in which the priorities and interests of managerial involvement in strategy-making has implications for that strategy – and, indeed, vice versa. Mats Clunas in Cases and Conversations 6.1, for ex-

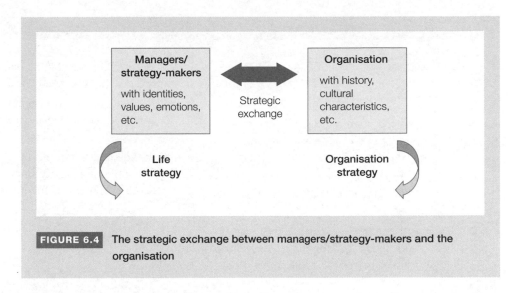

FIGURE 6.4 The strategic exchange between managers/strategy-makers and the organisation

ample, tells us that because he personally started the business he initially felt that he should deal with all strategic matters himself. But he learned to change his understanding of the managerial roles in the business as time went by. We could say that he shifted his managerial identity from one of his being the sole strategic decision-maker to one of being the leading member of a team of strategy-makers. Insofar as this appears to be leading to the success and growth of Clunas Wholesale, we can expect this emergent organisational strategy to have an effect on Mats' own identity by attaching to him the label of 'successful businessman'. This, in turn, is likely to have significant impact on his overall personal life strategy – how he generally develops his life and his relationships outside of work, as well as within it.

Arthur Hilton's case is perhaps even more significant as an illustration of how identity and aspects of 'life strategy', with regard to a managerial role, can change. After persuasion by Mats Clunas, and after certain learning experiences, Arthur came to see himself 'as a businessman as well as a manager'. This was a significant change in work orientation and it not only means that he has found a new source of satisfaction in his work (so increasing what he 'gets out' of his employment). He also contributes to a greater extent to the strategic directing of Clunas Wholesale (thus increasing what he 'puts in' to the organisation). Arthur's overall orientation to work has changed – work orientations being the meaning that individuals attach to their work which predisposes them to think and act in particular ways with regard to that work (Chapter 5, p. 129). We should also note, his work orientation has come into line with those of other managers in Clunas Wholesale, people like Jacques and Carole, for example. This suggests that we need to look at general patterns of work orientation among groups of strategy-makers, as well as considering each individual separately. We need to look at the shared meanings and approaches to strategy-making that exist among the strategy-makers in any particular organisation.

Activity 6.9

Reread both the episodes of the Tigermill story, Cases and Conversations 6.2 and 6.3, and answer the following questions:

- What was the shared approach to strategy-making adopted by Steve Dallas and his 'strategy team'?

- How did this relate to their identities as managers – to their shared orientations to managerial work?

- What implications did these shared orientations, and hence the common approach to strategy-making adopted within this group,

have on the strategic direction which emerged in Tigermill during their regime?

- How does the general orientation shared by Dina and Ali Budget differ from that of the Dallas team?

- What factors in Dina and Ali's identities and backgrounds appear to be influencing their broad approach to strategy-making?

Steve Dallas tells us explicitly that he is 'basically a strategist' and his notion of what this entails seems to be very influenced about what he learned at the business school he attended. His approach to strategy-making is one of undertaking detailed formal analysis and planning, with implementation being expected to follow from the expected perceived legitimacy of these plans among other managers and employees. His personal investment in and personal identification with this view of strategy-making appears to be shared with the other members of the small 'strategy team' that he has appointed. The strength of their shared orientation is suggested by their reaction to the difficulties that are later encountered. They argue that they persist with their 'bold growth strategy' and they are not going to be deterred by the 'going' becoming 'a bit rough'. This lack of flexibility leads Tigermill into considerable difficulties and, as a general approach, it contrasts strongly with the one later adopted by Dina and Ali. This is much more akin to the 'directed evolution' style of strategising. It would appear that whereas the Dallas team were influenced by their shared business school backgrounds in adopting their preferred style of operating, the Budget cousins are influenced by their family backgrounds. Their whole orientation to the organisation as well as their style of management is coloured by the fact that their fathers created Tigermill. As shrewd and rational as their thinking appears to be, they are happy to recognise a role for sentiment in the decisions they make and, although they have not taken financial control of the business, they clearly like to think of it as still, in part, the family firm. Family relationships also come in to specific decisions that are made – the recruiting of Dina's younger brother, for example, and the employment of their uncle. Here is sentiment and opportunism combined in a way that fits into a broad directed evolutionary approach.

The two-way relationship that exists between the way key managers shape their lives, sometimes purely personally and sometimes as the member of a group, and the way the organisation is shaped is very effectively illustrated in the Tigermill case. The same applies with the Strath Guitars story. As a result of the strategic negotiations Donna Dulsie has had with Willie Cose, and is about to have with Ben More, certain significant strategic outcomes are likely to follow for the Strath organisation. At the same time, however, Ben's personal life and career is going to be very different from what it was or what it might have been. And Donna's personal life direction is going to be very different from what she was envisaging prior to the meeting with Willie Cose. If her life works out as she is now hoping, she is going to be both a mother and a managing director. This is very different indeed from the life of being a full-time mother that she had been contemplating. How all of this will work out, neither they nor we know. This has to be the case with all plans. But, whatever happens, the pattern that arises in Donna and Ben's lives will be closely influenced by the strategic pattern that emerges in Strath Guitars. And the pattern that emerges in Strath Guitars will be very influenced by the pattern that Donna and Ben's personal lives and orientations follow. In this way, the *individual* strategic exchanges made at the level of the manager are closely connected to the *organisational* strategic exchanges made at the corporate level.

The implication of this analysis is that whenever we want to understand the strategic direction taken by any particular organisation we must always take into account the assumptions, values, backgrounds and orientations of the human beings working to shape those strategies. These, of course, are only one element in the vast range of factors that play a part in how any organisation strategically emerges. But their role can be quite significant, as Erica Schoenberger (1994, 1995, Reading Guide 14) has shown with regard to some major American corporations. She observes how the power interests and identities of groups of managers heading large business enterprises can lead to the development of particular managerial cultures and corporate identities. These 'frame the kinds of knowledge that can be produced and utilised by the firm in the creation and implementation of competitive strategies' (1994, p. 449). An illustration of what this can mean is provided with the story of how the giant Lockheed Corporation avoided for years what would have been a competitively advantageous entry into the market for missiles. The key managers in this corporation defined themselves as aircraft makers, rather than 'aerospace' people. This shared self-identity and the strategic orientation that followed from it had significant influence for some years on the direction taken by the organisation – with all the implications that this was bound to have for people's employment and the economic well-being of the area in which the organisation was located.

It was argued at the very beginning of *Organising and Managing Work* that the way managers 'frame' their activities will influence the way in which they go about them. We should not be surprised to see this happening at a corporate or strategic level, as well as at the level of the departments and the hospital ward where we saw Mark Merryton, Harry Carse and Sadie Rait working in Cases and Conversations 1.1, 1.2 and 1.3. Just as the way Sadie Rait 'discursively framed' the notion of 'managing' and was oriented to her work influenced how she went about her work, so we could expect to see the strategic direction of her hospital as a whole to be influenced by the orientations of its senior managers. We might imagine, for example, the hospital's management coming to be dominated by people who define themselves primarily as administrators and as the pursuers of high rating in terms of governmental performance indicators. Such people might structure the hospital in a particular way, develop a certain working culture and generally move activities in a particular strategic direction. But a group of hospital strategy-makers primarily defining themselves in terms of service to the local community might work to shape a rather different kind of structure, culture and emergent strategy.

Chapter 7 will not turn away from matters of strategy and strategy-making. It will, however, have its focus on the notions to which our attention has just been drawn: those of organisational *structure* and *culture*. These are concepts that further help us with connecting the strategic level of organising and managing to the level of everyday organisational operation and task performance.

Summary

In this chapter the following key points have been made:

- A focus on the pursuit of 'competitive advantage' is not the most useful means of trying to understand strategic processes and patterns in organisations. A more useful focus is upon the more general struggle for organisational survival. This allows for recognition to be given to alliances and collaborations between organisations as well as competitive relationships. Within this focus, full recognition can be given to the conflicts and multiple interests that pervade all organisational work as well as to the ambiguity and unpredictability that characterises every aspect of organisational and managerial activity.

- Strategic work can usefully be regarded as an aspect of the work of all managers, even though some managers are more heavily or directly involved in strategic work than others.

- The orthodox way of thinking about strategic management treats strategy-making as a matter of senior managers devising strategic plans on the basis of cool rational analysis. It tends to be assumed that implementation of strategic plans will follow smoothly as long as the rationality of the strategic plans is demonstrated to organisational members generally. This thinking encourages a 'rational' or 'linear' approach to strategy-making practice but tends to ignore all the problems of bounded rationality and conflicts of interest that, in practice, limit the wisdom of the overall approach. It also fails to attend to the role of sentiment and emotion in the devising of strategies.

- A process-relational view of how strategies come about does not deny the place of a certain amount of planning in strategy-making. However, it takes into account the various complexities and ambiguities of organisational life that orthodox thinking tends to play down. All of these complexities are better taken into account if a strategy is seen, not as a plan, but as the pattern to be seen emerging over time in the ways an organisation is shaped and enabled to continue into the future.

- All organisational strategies should be understood as 'emergent', with this emergence sometimes containing a significant amount of formal planning and sometimes being much more a matter of incrementalism and experimentation. There will nevertheless always be a mixture of some kind of planning with some kind of incrementalism.

- Research evidence suggests that strategic 'success' appears to be related to the adoption of a style of strategic management that can be characterised as *directed evolution*. In this, continuous adaptation occurs through processes of trial and error, opportunism, negotiation, exchange and learning within a clear sense of organisational or managerial direction. Concepts of *logical incrementalism*, *strategic intent* and *the learning organisation* are related to the notion of directed evolution.

- Organisational and therefore managerial effectiveness can most usefully be seen as the ability of the organisation to satisfy the demands of the range of constituencies inside and outside the organisation so that continued support in terms of resources such as labour, custom, investment, supplies and legal approval is obtained and the organisation enabled to survive into the long term.

- Processes of exchange between organisations and the constituencies upon which it is resource dependent are part of the way in which organisational environments are *enacted*. Organisational environments are not objectively existing contexts to which organisational managers react. Instead, they come to exist for members of an organisation by virtue of the interpretations that those members make of the world outside the organisation and the way their own actions influence or shape aspects of that world – by 'creating' a market, for example.

- Exchanges of resource occur between the organisation and constituencies internal and external to it so that 'resource dependence' is managed and the organisation enabled to continue into the future. At any one time, certain constituencies are more 'strategic' than others. They are more or less strategic according to the extent to which they create uncertainties with regard to the organisation's long-term survival. The directing of resources towards constituencies, as part of this trade, is always done at the lowest level that is compatible with retaining the long-term support of that resource-supplying constituency.

● The strategic exchanges made between organisations and their managers significantly influence, and are influenced by, the strategic exchanges made with all the
other constituencies it deals with. We therefore always need to consider the role
played in the strategy-making process of any given organisation by the interests,
emotions, preferences and identities of its key managers.

Reading

Reading Guides 14 and 15 contain material that supports and takes further
much of what is covered in Chapter 6.

CHAPTER 7

Structure, culture and the struggle for management control

Objectives Having read this chapter and completed its associated activites, readers should be able to:

- Recognise that structural and cultural aspects of the managerial pursuit of control over organisational activities do not simply *follow* from strategic decisions and are not therefore most usefully seen as aspects of the 'implementation' of strategies.

- Appreciate that organisational structures and cultures are not features that organisations 'have' but are closely related aspects of the general processes of organising and managing work which also connect organisational activities back to the way society as a whole is organised.

- Recognise that the basic logic behind managerial attempts to change organisational structures and cultures is one involving bringing official and unofficial aspects of structure and culture into line with each other.

- Understand that all organisations are based upon principles of *bureaucracy* and that there is no managerial option of 'getting rid of bureaucracy'.

- See how bureaucracy is nevertheless a fundamentally problematic way of organising and managing work because of certain contradictions built into modern employment and work institutions and because of a general 'paradox of consequences' in human affairs.

Structure, culture and the struggle for control

In moving on to issues of organisational structure and culture in the present chapter we are not turning away from the strategic issues considered in Chapter 6 to ones of strategy 'implementation'. To do that would be to follow the orthodoxy that we wish to go beyond. In the orthodox style of management thinking and business education, strategy tends to be seen as being about *ends* while structures and cultures are regarded as the *means* by which those strategies are achieved. Such a seemingly logical approach is quite appealing – at first sight. A moment's reflection soon reveals its adequacies. For a start, strategy-making tends to happen in organisations which already exist and which, therefore, already have structural and cultural characteristics. These pre-existing structural arrangements and cultural assumptions are likely to have an influence on the strategy-making that occurs within those arrangements, as was apparent in the various cases of strategy-making that we examined in the last chapter. This is the case even though such strategy-making often involves making structural and cultural changes in the organisation. And, as we saw in the previous chapter's discussion (p. 217) of Schoenberger's research (1994, 1995, Reading Guide 14) the pre-existing culture and the managerial notions of both personal and corporate identity may sometimes preclude consideration of structural and cultural changes that might well have been to the advantage of everyone concerned, had there been sufficient cultural openness for them to have been considered in the first place. Managerial control in organisations is thus no straightforward matter. It can only ever partly be achieved, yet it is something that managers are employed to strive for.

How reasonable is it to talk about attempts to achieve a degree of managerial control in terms of striving or struggle? It is very sensible. While there is a general expectation in managerial circles that such control is achievable, experience soon makes it apparent to any reflective manager that only a very limited degree of control over circumstances and events is ever achievable in practice. This point was strongly made in our earlier discussion of the nature of organisations (Chapter 3, p. 61). It was also very effectively expressed by Kurt Delnies in Cases and Conversations 5.6 when he said that it seemed that 'managers are expected, in principle, to control that which, in practice, cannot be controlled' (pp. 161–3). It is in the context of this rather extreme occupational challenge that, at the level of the organisation as a whole, strategy-making occurs and managers concern themselves with making strategic choices.

Strategic choices were defined earlier (p. 177) as choices about the basic shaping of the organisation itself and about the shaping of the relationships the organisation has with the parties with whom it exchanges resources. Chapter 6 focused on the latter part of this strategic choice-making process. It looked at the shaping of the relationships with constituencies with which the organisation has a resource-dependent relationship. The present chapter turns to the other aspect of strategic choice identified earlier: the shaping of the organisation itself. This shaping of the organisation, structurally and culturally, then, is as much part of the process of strategic emergence as is the network or trading relationships that go on between the organisation and the variety of internal and external constituencies with which it deals. To continue with this emphasis on the emergent nature of organisations and their strategies in the present chapter will again require us to turn away from the linear modes of thinking that we earlier rejected both generally (pp. 98–102) and with specific regard to conventional 'rational' or' linear' models of strategy-making (p. 179). Figure 7.1 demonstrates this non-linear way of looking at the relationship between 'strategy' on the one hand and 'structure' and culture' on the other.

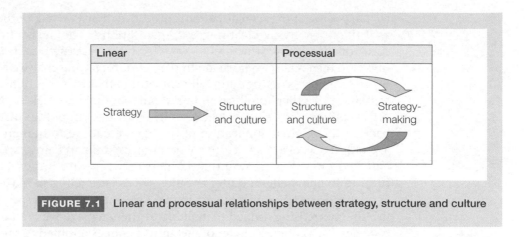

FIGURE 7.1 Linear and processual relationships between strategy, structure and culture

In making the important point about avoiding simplistic 'planning then doing' linear thinking, we must also avoid the trap of treating structural and cultural matters as if they were 'things' – simply because we find it convenient to draw them on a diagram joined together with arrows. Just as we constantly have to be on guard not to *reify* or *personify* the organisation (as we reminded ourselves when talking of organisations 'trading', in the previous chapter), we must be careful not to treat structures or cultures as if they were fairly solid 'things' that exist separately from the processes and relationships that the two concepts are intended to help us make sense of. Thus Table 7.1, as well as defining the concepts of structure and culture that are to be used here, shows how the very notions of organisational structure and culture are essentially metaphorical.

The patterns of thinking and acting that we call cultures and structures are all rather vague and abstract phenomena and we have to create metaphors to help us 'get hold of them' mentally. We saw how this was the case with the notion of organisation itself in Chapter 3. But where the notion of 'organisation' derives from an analogy with a living creature and its system of biological 'organs', the notion of 'structure' involves an analogy with buildings and 'culture' originates in an agricultural analogy (Barnhart, 1988, Reading Guide 16). Thus when we try

TABLE 7.1 Organisational structure and culture			
Organisational structure	*Concept*	**Organisational culture**	*Concept*
The regular or persisting patterns of action that give shape and a degree of predictability to an organisation		The set of meanings and values shared by members of an organisation that defines the appropriate ways for people to think and behave with regard to the organisation	
A concept originally deriving from a metaphor of the organisation as 'something built'		A concept originally deriving from a metaphor of the organisation as 'something cultivated'	
Official roles, rules, hierarchies, technical procedures, etc.	Unofficial roles, rules, hierarchies, technical procedures, etc.	Official norms, values, beliefs, symbols, rituals, etc.	Unofficial norms, values, beliefs, symbols, rituals, etc.

to make sense of the regular patterns of work activity we talk of them one minute as if they were living creatures, as 'organisations'. The next minute – when we speak of their being 'structured' – we effectively treat them as if they were buildings. We then realise that we are in danger of forgetting that we are dealing with something that is 'living', and with something that involves human thought and aspiration. We therefore turn to talk about 'culture' and make a parallel between organisations and fields that have to be cultivated. In doing this we are looking back to the original application of the idea of culture to human affairs and the aspiration of educators to cultivate or 'improve' human beings (make them 'more cultured') in the same way that farmers cultivate and improve their crops. In turning to one metaphor after another, we are struggling to make sense of some very complex and ambiguous matters. There is an almost desperate resort to the use of 'concretising' mixed metaphors in the language we are forced to use ('all mixed up in a concrete mixer of metaphors', one is tempted to say).

In denying that organisations are literally 'things' that 'have' a structure and arguing instead that they are sets of practices, relationships and processes, we nevertheless have to recognise the need to talk about them much of the time *as if* they had this more concrete existence. This is why we continually turn to metaphors from biology, building, engineering or agriculture when trying to understand organisational activity. We need a degree of predictability about organisational patterns to be able to deal with organisations and this is recognised in the process-relational conceptualisation of structure used here which suggests we can most usefully think of structure *as the regular or persisting patterns of action that give shape and a degree of predictability to an organisation*. This definition follows mainstream social science thinking, rather than managerial thinking, in treating the structure of the organisation like everything that regularly goes on in it, as opposed to restricting the notion of structure to arrangements drawn up in the organisational blueprint or organisation chart. This is simply a more realistic way of looking at things. The 'shape' referred to in the definition is, of course, a perceived shape. Without our perceiving an organisation as having a particular 'shape' we would be unable to relate to it. We need a structural map to guide us as to who is in charge of what, who is responsible for what and with whom we talk to deal with this or that issue. Thus an awareness of a shape or a structure of an organisation produces a degree of predictability and actually enables organising to proceed.

When we involve ourselves in organisations, however, we soon learn that just coming to terms with the patterns of 'what regularly happens' is not really enough. We find that we also need to know something about the patterns in the way people in the organisation think and feel about what they are doing. We want to know what people in the organisation take to be the right and the wrong ways to think and behave in their dealings with the organisation. We thus have the concept of culture to 'fill out' the picture provided by our notion of structure. It brings meanings, interpretations and values into the picture and we conceptualise organisational culture here as *the set of meanings and values shared by members of an organisation that defines the appropriate ways for people to think and behave with regard to the organisation*. Clearly manifest in this conceptualisation is the central issue that arises in practice when we talk of organisational cultures: the issue of the extent to which any set of meanings is ever likely to be *completely* shared by all the people in an organisation, in reality. It is never going to happen. What this means is that an organisation is never actually going to achieve a 'complete' organisational culture. It could only do so if people came to live their whole lives within the organisation. There could only be a full corporate culture if every member took their morality from that corporation, worshipped its Gods, spoke its language. For any employee fully to embrace an organisational culture would be for them to drop their notion of being French, British or American or of being a Muslim, Christian or agnostic. Conceptually, then, it would probably be much better to talk of 'cultural aspects of organisations' rather than of organisational culture. This would recognise that employees only partly live their lives in organisations that employ them and relate in only a partial way to the beliefs and values that are distinctive to that organisation.

Link   Just how profound a part *culture* has played in the development of the human species and in the lives, identities and moralities of every human being is discussed in Chapter 4, pp. 110–18.

We will see in the next chapter that an important trend in managerial thinking in recent decades has been one of encouraging managers to try to *create* strong organisational cultures. It has been recognised that it would help managers enormously in the struggle for control if they could get all their employees to subscribe to the beliefs inscribed in a corporate bible – especially if they themselves could write this bible. The concept of organisational culture is therefore one we need to continue to use, recognising always that it is something that tends to be managerially aspired to and can only ever exist in a partial way. We also have to recognise that any organisational culture is likely to have elements to it that have arisen other than through managerial 'cultivation'. We will deal with this as part of the official/unofficial distinction that is identified in Figure 7.1 shortly. First, however, we have to come to terms with the full extent to which both cultural and structural issues in organisations must always be understood in the light of structures and cultures outside the organisation.

Organisational and societal structures and cultures

Organisations do not, as we have stressed on various occasions, exist separately from the world of which they are part. The societies, economies and cultures in which we all live are not best understood as the environments or the 'contexts' of work organisations. As institutional theories of organisations emphasise, the cultures that prevail in organisations are the culture of the societies of which the organisations are a part (Scott, 1995; Tolbert and Zucker, 1996 and other references in Reading Guide 1). The same point can be made about the structures of organisations. To be a manager in an organisation is to be a member of the middle class of a society, for example, just as to be an unskilled manual worker is to be a 'working class person' in the world outside the organisation. Societal structures both contribute to and result from 'organisational structures'. Yet organisational structures are typically discussed in 'non-critical' OB texts as if they were simply and directly the outcome of managerial 'organisational design'. By the same token, 'organisational cultures' – the whole set of values, norms, symbols, visions and missions that managers increasingly say they have 'put in place' in their organisation – are often spoken of as if the organisation's employees leave their normal Chinese, Welsh, male, female, young, old, illiterate or highly educated 'cultural selves' in the locker room as they arrive for work and change into the organisation's cultural uniform and pin onto their chests their corporate identity badge.

Activity 7.1

Read the account given by Mohammed Croy in Cases and Conversations 7.1 of the experience of himself and his wife in Mountains Components and consider how possible it is to distinguish between an organisational culture and structure and the culture and structure of the society in which the company is located.

Jan and Mohammed come to Mountains
Cases and Conversations 7.1

I was very happy when I arrived from the middle east and got a job as a driver at Mountains. Although I was not given a job that reflected the qualifications I had, it was good that my wife and I both got employment in what seemed like a very modern and enlightened organisation in the part of the world Jan had grown up. She started off in a quite ordinary job doing telephone sales but we both were very impressed with the 'culture of equal opportunities' that they told us about. And we liked the idea of the 'non-hierarchical skill-based structure' that they said we would be part of. Indeed, Jan very soon got a decent promotion and she used to joke that she would 'now be called a manager' if the company was not so anxious to avoid such labels for all but the most senior people. She was a 'team leader' at work but she used to tell all her friends, and especially her mother, that she was a 'sales manager'. I think some of her staff – sorry, team members – see her as a manager as well. She certainly gets tarred with the management brush when she has to press her people about meeting the production targets. It's amazing how quickly the 'them and us' attitudes emerge when business gets tough. These go back generations in this country, Jan says.

Generally speaking though, Jan does feel quite 'empowered' as she calls it, and her boss is really quite good at letting her use her initiative in the job. And so is my boss. In fact it is left up to me when to get the car I use serviced and Donald is very good at turning a blind eye to my using the car sometimes at weekends. So neither of us has got anything to complain about, you could say. But it's not as simple as that. I wouldn't like to talk about racism too much, for example, but I admit to getting tired of people asking me if I've got a prayer mat in the boot of my car. And the blokes here are always trying to get me to drink alcohol with them. They quote the company's 'culture of colleagues' propaganda at me and say that part of the culture around here is having a drink after work. But I know that what they are really looking for is the satisfaction of getting me to

break the rules of my religion. But, would you believe, they are touchier about their own religions than I am, especially when it comes to their football obsession. I know some of the production 'teams' where, at certain times, the Catholic colleagues won't even talk to the Protestant colleagues. Yet the company culture tells us we're all part of one big family, all 'focusing on the customer'.

As it happens, Jan was just quoting the 'one big family' part of the company's culture statement the other day. Her boss wanted some problems sorted out with one of the customers she was dealing with. But he said that he would deal with it himself because he didn't think that a woman would have enough 'clout'. She yelled at him about 'empowerment', equal opportunities and the non-hierarchical structure. But he just calmly warned her not to 'get above herself'. Such behaviour would not surprise me in my own country. But I didn't think it was meant to happen at Mountains.

Mountain Components is clearly an organisation where a managerial attempt has been made to shape a particular structure of relationships and a distinctive culture that will help it succeed with its customers. Mohammed and Jan both seem to welcome aspects of this and identify with what is *meant to happen* in the company according to its 'official' position. Mohammed's concerns do not appear to be about bad faith on the company's part, however, although there is perhaps an implicit criticism of this kind with regard to Jan's 'boss'. Jan and Mohammed seem to recognise that they are as much experiencing the culture and a structure of relationships of the society that Mohammed has moved into and Jan moved back to, as they are working in a particular 'organisational' structure and culture. Mountain Components appears to have been officially structured in part on principles of team working. The official language of 'non-hierarchical skill-based structure' implies that rewards are tied into the skills that people apply to their tasks rather than to any 'status label' that is applied to them. In accordance with this they do not give people like Jan a managerial label. But notice that the term 'boss' nevertheless seems to be used quite readily in the company. Both Jan and Mohammed have 'bosses'. To what extent is this insistence on hierarchy a matter of organisational or societal culture? One simply cannot say.

The discrimination that Mohammed experiences, both at the hands of the company (he has a job below the level that his qualifications apparently fit him for) and at the hands of his work mates, are obviously related to wider patterns of racial attitude prevailing outside the organisation. The same can be said about the religious dimension of the production workers' behaviour and the gender discrimination that Jan experiences. But can we really say that these factors are not, in practice, part and parcel of the structure and culture of Mountain Components – even if they are contrary to the official position taken by the management of the organisation?

 Link

One of the key features of a critical study of organisations and management identified in Chapter 1 (pp. 21–6) was that it locates work practices in the wider society and culture of which they are a part and recognises the way societal patterns of conflict, inequality and discrimination are partly reproduced within work organisations.

These matters are very important ones both analytically and managerially. No realistic managerial innovation or effective strategic shaping of organisations can ever be achieved if such efforts are based on a naïve belief that organisations can have structures or cultures that will function according to corporate priorities and not be massively influenced by the wider social structure and culture of which they are inevitably a part. What goes on in the world outside the organisation means that whatever 'official' structures or organisational cultures managers devise when drawing up their corporate blueprints will soon find themselves existing alongside the 'unofficial' patterns that arise as employees bring into the workplace their own identities, projects and priorities. People in work organisations will inevitably draw on discursive resources (p. 120) from outside the organisation as well as from within it to make sense of and deal with what goes on in work organisations

Official and unofficial aspects of structure and culture

An important element of the struggle for managerial control is one of coming to terms with the fact that the formal or official arrangement that the managers make when they 'design' organisations do not work out as expected, in practice.

 Link

We now build on the analysis developed in Chapter 3 (pp. 74–81) where the distinction between official and unofficial aspects of the organisation's *negotiated order* was introduced and applied to Eagle Buses.

Systems-control thinking about organising and managing tends to engage with just one of these two 'sides' of the organisation – the 'official' side. It focuses on the organisational structures and the corporate cultures that managers choose or design. It tends to take it for granted that managerially designed structures and cultures more or less make organisations what they *are*. Such thinking has become so deeply ingrained that people often tell us what the structure of an organisation 'is' by pointing us to the organisation chart. And they tell us what the culture of an organisation 'is' by reporting to us what is said in a set of management documents outlining corporate values and missions. It is absolutely normal for managers to claim to be telling us what the structure of their organisation *is* or what the culture of their organisation *is* when what they are actually telling us is *what they would like these to be*. This might be reasonable if they were simply acting as official spokespersons for their corporation, but if they are actually unable to see the inevitable gap between what they are managerially trying to bring about and what is actually the case, they are likely to get into severe difficulty. Process-relational thinking, which uses such a distinction, thus has vital practical and analytical value. It sees organisations as continuously emergent and its managers as always having to cope with the multiplicity of interests and understandings associated with the people involved in it. Process-relational thinking therefore recognises that there will always be a gap between the official structure and culture and the prevailing structures and activities that make up the actual negotiated order of the organisation.

Official and unofficial aspects of organisations *Concept*

Official aspects of organisations are all the rules, activities and values that are part of the formally managerially sanctioned policies and procedures. *Unofficial* aspects are the rules, activities and values that people at all levels in the organisation develop but which do not have formal managerial sanction.

The process-relational perspective gives priority of attention to the negotiated order of the organisation: to the emergent organisation that can be observed when we pay attention to the totality of what goes on. It subsequently considers the *official structure and culture* as only a contributor to the pattern of activities and values that actually prevail in the 'emergent organisation'. It recognises that alongside all this formally sanctioned managerial 'input' are all the unofficial aspects of what occurs in organisations. These are rules, understandings, practices, languages, games and processes that members of the organisation devise or develop in order to meet whatever purposes they bring to the organisation – including the purpose simply to 'get by'. And *official* and *unofficial* practices can relate to each other in various different ways.

- Sometimes unofficial practices support the official ones – where a manager regularly takes days off to play golf, for example, and, in the process, makes business contacts that help fulfil the organisation's official policies.
- Sometimes unofficial practices undermine official ones – where organisational members follow a rule of never sharing information with people from outside their own department, for example.

- Sometimes unofficial practices make very little difference at all to official ones. An example here might be the custom for most people in an organisation to do very little work on a Friday afternoon but where this was always preceded by a Friday morning of intensive effort which 'earns' for them a relaxed final few hours of the working week.

Activity 7.2

Think of as many examples as you can, from an organisational situation you are aware of, that fit these three categories of the relationship between official and unofficial aspects of organisations:

- where unofficial practices support the official ones;

- where unofficial practices undermine official ones;

- where unofficial practices make very little difference at all to official ones.

The closeness and overlap of structure and culture

It might be noticed that these examples of official and unofficial processes and practices do not readily fall into the categories of 'structural' or 'cultural'. This is important. It relates to the point made earlier, that structures and cultures are not two separate 'things' that organisations have. Instead, we suggested that the two concepts refer to different aspects of the overall phenomenon of 'the organisation'. But they are two aspects that are closely related. Many of the processes and practices that we observe in an organisation could as readily be said to be part of the 'structure' of the organisation as part of its 'culture'. A further simple example would be the case of an organisation where there was a regularly observable pattern in which male rather than female members of the organisation took all the important business decisions. We can readily envisage this organisation being described as having a 'male dominated *structure*'. There is indeed a 'regular and persisting pattern of action' to be seen which might be characterised as an 'official structure' if the organisational rules kept women out of key decision-making roles and as an 'unofficial structure' if these rules were ones never written down or otherwise formally acknowledged. Equally, however, one could characterise the organisation as having a very 'male oriented *culture*'. It could be called this because the 'set of meanings and values' prevailing in the organisation valued men's decision-making as worthier than women's and consequently defined the exclusion of women from important decisions as appropriate – as the 'right thing' to happen. Whether or not this was to be regarded as a matter of official or unofficial culture would be a matter of the extent to which these meanings and values were formally espoused by the organisation's management.

Why then do we need the two concepts of structure and culture? It is arguable that we do not necessarily need either of them. A fully process-relational perspective would simply look at the processes and practices that make up an organisation, always paying attention to both the regularities within activities (which the concept of *structure* emphasises) and the patterns of meaning associated with them (which the concept of *culture* emphasises). However, the concepts of structure and culture – and a tradition of treating them as separate facets of an organisation's functioning – are firmly established in the languages of both social scientists and organisational practitioners and it would be difficult to try to communicate without them. But what can be done here, to do full justice to the considerable overlap between what is called the structural and the cultural, is to consider the two facets of organisational life alongside each other whenever this is possible. Thus we might look at the pattern of male dominance in the organisational case we have just considered in terms of a male 'power structure'. However, to understand that we would have to attend to the question of how this 'power' of the men involved has been made 'legitimate' (on the assumption that it is not all down to crude coercion), which takes us into the area of meanings and of 'culture'. Correspondingly, if we prefer to analyse this organisation in terms of, say, a 'culture of masculinity', then we would need to attend to regular patterns of activity through which this set of meanings is manifested at the level of practices. And this would bring us back to 'structural' matters. We can't look at the one thing without looking at the other. In fact, it is in recognition of the need to look at both the 'structural' and the 'cultural' when trying to understand organisations that the present chapter is about both structural and cultural matters. There are good reasons for abandoning the convention followed by most textbooks of having separate chapters on organisational 'design' and organisational culture.

Activity 7.3

You might be concerned that this discussion of what is structural and what is cultural and about how we might use both concepts, but in a very linked way, is rather 'academic' and not relevant to practice. Therefore, ask yourself:

- What relevance would the insight that 'structural' and 'cultural' factors are inevitably and closely linked have for managers setting up an organisation – or re-organising an existing one?

- How far do your conclusions agree with those reached by Walt and Roger in Cases and Conversations 7.2 as they think about the green field site they are to develop?

Walt and Roger go into the country

I was the first manager appointed here when Wyvis moved into the UK. For the first year I was meant to be second-in-command to Walt, the man who was to be seconded over from the USA to establish the business here. When he went home I would take over as chief executive.

The first task Walt and I undertook was to acquire the green field site we were going to build on. We then sat down to think about the buildings we were going to commission and to 'design the organisation', as Walt put it. This is where Walt and I had something of a disagreement. He wanted to get the building designed first, and then work out what sort of organisational structure we would have. Once these two sets of decisions had been made, we would give some thought to the type of culture we would want to develop when we started recruiting people to work in the buildings and to fill the slots in the organisation structure. I said that I didn't like the idea of doing things in this order. You had to think about buildings and structural and cultural things all at the same time. I argued that these were all equal and interacting facets of what our organisation would be, and that each had to be thought through with reference to the other.

To begin with, Walt overruled me on this. There was real urgency about getting architects to work on designing the buildings and he therefore insisted that we should get on with sketching out what sort of buildings we required before we thought about anything else. Walt obviously relished this task and he was soon sketching on the white board in our office the site scheme and the buildings he had in mind. He drew the central management and administrative block at the end of a gravel drive. This was to have a Palladian style porch on the front of it and to one side of it would be an ornamental pond. A small car park for managers and visitors was sketched alongside this pond. One the other side of the first building was a row of trees and behind this were the call centre building and the two warehouses. A separate road came into the site to take lorries up to the warehouse and staff cars up to the main staff car park, which was behind the call centre.

Walt drew all this up on the board at great speed and with great relish. I think he expected me to be excited by his design. I'm sure that he thought that, as an Englishman, I would like the idea of driving up this gravel drive, across the lovely countryside surrounding the site, and walking from the executive car park into the mock classical doorway of the central building. In fact, I was appalled. And this quite shocked Walt. But in explaining my reaction I had a good opportunity to explain to him my approach to thinking about buildings, organisational structure and organisational culture as interrelated issues.

My obvious starting point was to persuade him that he was doing more than just shaping the physical site with his proposals. He was shaping the culture from the start: a culture that would privilege managers and administrators over warehouse and call centre workers. The separate car parks alone would suggest a culture of first and second class citizens. The site design would also limit us in terms of organisational structure – not least in making the structure from the start a sort of class structure (Walt was very impressed by this point, I'm pleased to say). By putting warehouse workers, call centre workers and the rest in separate physical locations, we were constraining the sort of communication structure we would have on the site. We were also implying that warehouse, call centre and administrative staff were very separate categories of employee with little chance of promotional movement across the categories. My pointing this out convinced Walt of my case. 'All along,' he said, 'I envisaged us having everybody here dressed similarly, eating in the same place and all that. I want them all to be company associates, rather than staff'. 'There you are,' I laughed, 'You had ideas about the sort of culture that you wanted from the start. Yet you said you were going to think about culture later'. Walt joked that perhaps he had risked getting seduced by his ideas of Englishness and being diverted from his belief in 'Good old American values of opportunity for all' and his personal conviction that 'all structures should be structures of opportunity in any outfit that I run'.

Walt wiped the white board clean and gave me the pens. I then sketched a single building that would have the warehouse at its centre with all the offices and the call centre desks being located around it. This was done so that everyone would regularly see the goods we traded in coming in and out of a single workplace – it would make the point that we are all in the same business. And everyone would easily be able to communicate with everyone else, whatever their current tasks were. I wanted to develop a flexible task structure for the business and I needed a physical set up that would fit with this. To make this possible I wanted to avoid cultural symbols of status and privilege being built into the site and the buildings. Walt saw the point, 'so it's goodbye to the separate car parks, the pond and the screen of trees'. 'Indeed it is,' I agreed, 'and it's goodbye to your Palladian columns – very un-American!' 'Whoopee', came back Walt, 'I think we're going to be a great team'.

In some ways we have an unusually straightforward situation here in which two managers are able to think about setting up an organisation practically 'from scratch'. But this 'green field' case demonstrates with unusual clarity how the structural and the cultural cannot be separated in managerial practice any more than they can in social science analysis. Even at-first-sight neutral matters of site and building design have considerable and closely interconnected implications for both organisational structure and culture. Roger clearly takes the view that you cannot think about structures (whether physical ones or organisational ones) without thinking about cultures, and vice versa. He very neatly, and very easily, persuades Walt that it is managerially wise to think about structures and cultures at the same time when making strategic choices. And Walt and Roger, together, remind us that matters of national culture also come into organisational decisions that are made, thus reiterating the point made with the Mountains case that organisational structures and cultures connect closely with societal patterns and preferences.

Walt and Roger are very clearly thinking about the structures and the culture they want in the organisation they are developing. At this stage they are thinking directly about what we have termed the official side of structure and culture. However, it is reasonable to infer that this is being done in the hope that any unofficial patterns that emerge once the organisation is operating will be compatible with these official arrangements and values. Ideally, from a managerial point of view the official and the unofficial aspects of culture would be one and the same. This could never be the case in the plural and ambiguous world of actual human activity, however. Nevertheless, the pursuit of such an ideal can be seen as giving logic to a lot of what managers do when trying to manage through structure and culture.

The logic of managerial attempts to shape organisational structures and cultures

The official/unofficial distinction is very helpful to us as a means of identifying the logic underlying managerial efforts to shape or reshape organisational structures and cultures. Systems-control thinking would see the logic of structural or cultural design as one in which managers simply design the most appropriate structure or culture and then implement it. But process-relational analysis more realistically sees managers, in their struggle for control, as trying to push forward their own preferred structural and cultural arrangements in the face of all the 'contrary' values and practices that they are bound to come up against. And they can only go so far with this. The logic behind what they are trying to do can therefore be understood as one of attempting to make the official and the unofficial aspects of their organisation become one and the same. Should this dream of perfect management control come true then what the employees of the organisation would want to do and what they would do would be the same as what the management of the organisation wanted them to want to do.

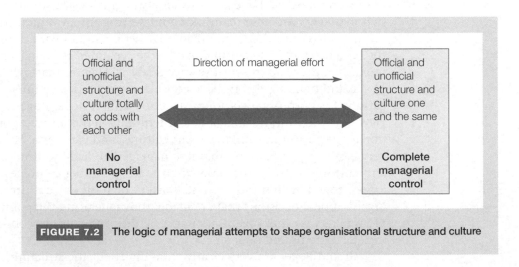

FIGURE 7.2   The logic of managerial attempts to shape organisational structure and culture

The positions at the two ends of the continuum drawn in Figure 7.2 are ones that are never going to exist in practice. The left end of the continuum represents a situation in which the bulk of what goes on in the *negotiated order* of the organisation tends to undermine the *official structure and culture* to such an extent that survival becomes impossible. And the situation at the other end would only be possible if there were complete unity of purpose across all the organisational members and a willingness of everyone to cooperate with everyone else in a spirit of complete harmony. Such a situation is hard to envisage. However, it is the image that seems to inform the organisational design aspirations of many organisational managers as well as the intentions behind much of the 'management of culture' thinking that we will consider later in the next chapter.

Activity 7.4

Accepting that the situation represented at the 'complete managerial control' end of Figure 7.2 would never come about in practice, ask yourself:

- How close, in your view, it is possible for the managers of an organisation to get to that degree of control?

- What sort of organisational circumstances would need to apply before this could happen?

Then, if you are feeling sufficiently imaginative (and possibly doing this as a group activity):

- Try to paint a picture of an imaginary organisation that would be as close to this managerial utopia as possible.

- Try to imagine the managerial dystopia that would take us as close as possible to the opposite end of the continuum.

You might choose to read Charles Cawdor's stories in Cases and Conversations 7.3 before or after attempting these activities. His granddaughter, Jane (whom we met in Cases and Conversations 4.3), tells us how he reported experiences to her of organisational situations which take something from close to the right-hand end of the continuum in Figure 7.2 and something from more towards the left-hand end.

Charles Cawdor at war and peace

Cases and Conversations 7.3

As I told you, I was very taken with my grandfather's stories about when he was an engineering officer in the Second World War. Well, I took him back to these tales when I was at university studying engineering and management myself. I particularly remember him telling me about a business that he and some of his ex-army friends set up after the war. This, he claimed, was as close to a perfectly managed organisation as you could get – for its first two years of operation. But, after that, it declined into the very opposite. Let me tell you the story, as I remember him telling it to me.

When Charles and some of his friends from the engineers were demobbed from the army after the war they saw an opportunity, in the need to rebuild the bombed roads and bridges of parts of Europe, to continue working together and to make some money. They therefore set up a business called Freeheight and employed a number of the soldiers that they had commanded in the war. They designed an organisation structure for Freeheight that was based on the skills they had rather than on the ranks they had held during the war. They drew up an operating manual and a disciplinary code that contained all the best procedures that they had found worked well when they were in the army. This, my grandfather emphasised, was different from the army's engineering procedures and code of discipline. It was completely based on what they had found worked in practice. Apparently, every single individual joining the firm read all of these in detail and was only taken on if they indicated that they wholeheartedly agreed with them.

The pay system was a simple one. There were just four levels of pay; these being based on four levels of responsibility that everyone thought were reasonable. The *actual* amount of pay that people got each month was a simple sharing out, according to this differential, of whatever profit remained from that month's work (after costs had been covered and a certain amount had been put aside to buy whatever was necessary for the next project). Charles insisted that the culture (or 'spirit of the enterprise' as I think he called it) was one of comradeship with every member being someone who, first, was keen to work for the firm and, second, was thought to be acceptable to everyone else. 'We couldn't go wrong', Charles claimed, 'We had what amounted to a band of volunteers, all of whom knew each other very well. It was practically a cooperative of self-selecting members I suppose. We had been careful to reject anybody we thought might rock the boat and we had agreed ways of working that we had tested out in every imaginable circumstance. In addition to all of this, we were making a lot of money, faced no real competition, and when we finished work we had a damn good time. We built into our system generous breaks and holidays for chaps with families at home and we paid for most of their travel'.

The way my grandfather described the management of the firm was that the 'operation managed itself'. 'The rules and procedures we had were ones we had all had a hand in devising and, to be honest, these were so logical and sensible to us that we rarely needed to look at what was written down. When we faced a new circumstance we simply used our common sense to overcome it, and we absorbed into our future working practices whatever it was we had found to work'. He also argued that there was no 'slacking' and that nobody cheated or kept secrets from anyone else, because 'in such an open atmosphere and where everyone was making such a good living, nobody felt the need to pull a fast one'.

As I said to my grandfather, this all sounded too good to be true. 'Yes', he agreed, 'But it does show what is possible, in principle'. He accepted that it was too good to continue in the longer term. After a couple of years, and after a vote of all members of the company, it was decided to move the business out of Germany and France and back to the UK. There was growing competition in Europe and most of the men wanted to settle down to a normal home life with their families. But things soon went into decline with FreeheightUK, he felt. The decline was in terms of what he felt the managerial process turned into, rather than a significant decline in profitability. To buy new equipment in the UK, which would replace the extremely cheap army surplus machines they had used in Europe, they had to seek investors. These insisted that the business grow and, to help this growth, adopt employment policies and pay differentials more in line with what other businesses were following. Civil engineers, office workers, supervisors, skilled and unskilled manual workers and managers were recruited on the normal labour market.

In spite of a declared intention to work within the same values and culture of the original Freeheight, it was not long before the UK version of the organisation was displaying what Charles called all the normal 'pecking orders, jealousies, class prejudices and fiddles' that he felt characterised much of the civil engineering and building industry of the time. He found that his own engineering interests became subordinated to his senior management responsibilities. A high proportion of his time was spent 'checking up on people to make sure they were doing what they should be doing' and 'catching people out that were trying to cheat the firm or steal from us', these as often being employees as people outside the company. 'We basically turned into a low trust outfit', Charles explained. 'At times I felt as if we were losing all managerial control over what was going on. Getting any contract completed on time to the right standard was just one bloody great battle'. 'Ironic, isn't it?', he observed, 'that I felt I was much more involved in organisational warfare in this peacetime situation than I ever was in the wartime period'.

The first organisational situation that Charles Cawdor described to his grand-daughter takes us as close as we are ever likely to get to the managerial situation in which the official and the unofficial aspects of organisational functioning are practically indistinguishable from each other. Perhaps the clearest example of this is with regard to the Freeheight 'operating manual' and the 'rules and procedures' that it contains. These are written down and are therefore very much an 'official' element of the way the organisation is structured. However, what 'actually goes on' appears to fit with this – to such an extent that people in the organisation 'rarely needed to look at what was written down'. Similarly, if we accept the claim that there was no slacking and cheating, we can say that the official rules written down in the disciplinary code were indistinguishable from the 'unofficial' rules that guided people's day-to-day behaviour. It would also appear that the hierarchical structure, officially expressed in terms of the 'four levels of responsibility' that also gave the firm its pay structure, was what operated in practice. The 'official' and the 'unofficial' were, again, one and the same. There was no unofficial 'pecking order' existing alongside and potentially undermining this official order – something that did develop in the FreeheightUK version of the firm. Where the original Freeheight could be said to have a single shared culture (official and unofficial aspects being one and the same), which Charles characterises in terms of 'comradeship', FreeheightUK appears to have an everyday operational, or 'unofficial', culture of low trust, task avoidance, cheating and stealing. This was utterly at odds with the official culture of the transplanted enterprise – the declared intention to 'work within the same values and culture of the original Freeheight'.

Charles Cawdor, in describing his experiences as a manager in FreeheightUK, gives an account that resonates strongly with the notion of managers 'struggling' to achieve a degree of control. He refers to 'organisational warfare' and talks of getting the organisation's major tasks completed as a 'battle'. So why was it so different in the original Freeheight? What sort of conditions need to apply before one can get close to the pattern of official and unofficial practices that Charles believes applied to the original firm? It has to be said that these are very rare circumstances. We have a situation where an organisation was established by people who already knew each other and had already discovered how to work together harmoniously. They also trusted each other, and made sure that they excluded any individuals who might 'rock the boat'. In effect, the official structure and culture of Freeheight was based on the aspects of the unofficial structure and culture that 'worked' when these people worked together in the army. Charles also makes it fairly clear that 'official' aspects of army life that were felt to be unhelpful were avoided. We are left to infer that the rank structure was one of these, with Freeheight going for the fairly radical four-level command and pay structure based on principles of skill or responsibility, as opposed, presumably, to anything along class or social status lines.

Freeheight was almost able to 'manage itself' we are told. Indeed, Charles characterises it as 'practically a cooperative of self-selecting members'. The *function* of management was most certainly being carried out, in the sense identified in Chapter 3, as the overall shaping of relationships, understandings and processes to fulfil tasks in a way that allows the continuation of the enterprise. But it was also observed in that chapter that such a function could, in principle, be carried out by 'all the members of an organisation (in a worker cooperative, say)' (p. 67). That is practically what was happening in Freeheight. This suggests a rather interesting paradox. It would appear that a situation approaching 'total managerial control' is only likely to arise in an organisation when there are no managers or, rather, where everyone is a manager.

Link

The issue of who does the 'managing' that occurs in every organisation was first raised when the three dimensions of 'what management is' were identified in Chapter 3, p. 67 (especially Figure 3.1).

It would appear from historical experience that it is only in very particular circumstances within industrial capitalism that such organisational self-management is likely to be successful. Charles Cawdor gives us some idea of what those circumstances might be. But the circumstances he described were short lived. The lack of competitive pressures and the high levels of reward were temporary circumstances of a reviving post-war mainland Europe. Once the organisation found itself operating in the UK within a much more normal set of multiple internal and external constituencies and resource dependencies – with all the competing and conflicting interests and priorities that this entails – it took a great deal more time and effort to 'manage'. In the rare circumstances in which Freeheight was originally established, the organisation was practically able to operate on its own terms, structurally and culturally. It was, in many ways, isolated from the societies and cultures within which it operated in the unusual, artificial and temporary circumstances of early post-war Germany and France. Once back in Britain, FreeheightUK had to come to terms with being an integral part of the ownership, investment, labour market and class structures and the culture of that society. FreeheightUK was a normal pluralist and conflict-riven work organisation, no longer the relatively unitary band of insiders and comrades it had once been.

We will return shortly to managerial efforts to shape organisational structures and cultures but, at this stage, it is necessary to focus one of the key principles that has been behind the general shaping of organisations throughout the industrial capitalist period of human history. This is the structural and cultural principle of *bureaucracy*.

The ubiquity and inevitability of bureaucracy

Bureaucracy is frequently treated in the academic literature as a type of organisational *structure*. It is recognised as the basic type of structure that has been used to shape work and administrative activities since the industrial revolution. However, it is just as much a cultural phenomenon. This tends to be recognised in everyday organisational talk. It is quite usual, for example, to hear someone in an organisation speak of 'the bureaucratic structures we work in'. Equally, these days, we will hear people referring to 'the bureaucratic culture of this organisation'. Perhaps the mention here of 'these days' is a clue to what is happening. The concept of culture was rarely used in either academic or managerial circles when looking at work organisations prior to the 1980s. It was *structure* that was mainly focused upon until that late stage of the twentieth century, when growing international competition coming from Asia made western management thinkers and strategic managers aware that seeking 'better' structures to help them compete with countries with different cultures was not enough. It was recognised that there might be other 'variables' to think about and these might be 'cultural' as well as structural ones – the values and assumptions within which people worked as well as the procedural arrangements and reporting relationships.

There is an irony in this focus on the 'structural' at the expense of the 'cultural' throughout much of the twentieth century. The irony arises because the major analyst of bureaucracy who identified its centrality to modern industrial and capitalist societies very early in the century, Max Weber, theorised it in a way that attends to the 'cultural' as much as to the 'structural' (Weber, 1978, Reading Guide 16). But perhaps this relates to an even greater irony; the irony that textbook after textbook has treated Weber as if he were a managerial writer who advocated bureaucracy. In the crude and bizarre narratives that are central to so much management teaching (and reappear every year in the examination scripts of management students) we even see him portrayed as 'the father of bureaucracy'. Instead, Weber was a sociologist, historian and economic thinker trying to make sense theoretically of what we characterised in Chapter 3 as 'modernism'. He saw bureaucracy as a central institution of modernism and he was as aware of its negative side as he was of the advantages it could give to organisers in terms of machine-like precision, unambiguity, speed and impersonality.

A key part of Weber's analysis of what was happening to societies and economies in the late nineteenth and early twentieth centuries was a recognition that their cultures were becoming less and less centred on traditional values. Modern cultures were replacing traditional cultures. Tradition as a criterion for decision-making – following how things had always been done, to put it very simply – was being replaced in many areas of life, and in the economic and technological spheres especially, by criteria of *instrumental* (or *formal*) *rationality*. This, as we saw earlier (p. 81), is the calculated choice of appropriate means to achieve specified ends. People were thus moving away from simply following the practices of their parents and grandparents when wanting, say, to solve problems of ill health or the problem of how to cross a wide river. Instead, they were looking to scientists and engineers *systematically to work out* how to cure or eradicate a disease or more easily or enable them to get quickly from one side of a wide river to the other. The same instrumental rationality that led to new drugs and hygiene practices being developed and few feats of bridge and railway engineering achieved was being applied to the organising of complex work tasks and to the administration of public affairs. Out of this major cultural shift came *bureaucracy*. And *bureaucracies* are what modern organisations are.

This latter point explains why we can write of 'the ubiquity and inevitability of bureaucracy'. Dissatisfaction with certain aspects of modern organisations often leads people to complain about 'bureaucracy' or criticise structures and cultures that they say are 'too bureaucratic'. We have to take these concerns seriously, but what we cannot contemplate is the abolition of bureaucracy. To *remove* bureaucracy from an enterprise would be to remove 'organisation' itself. To *modify* bureaucracy in a rational and calculated way, however, is what a great deal of managerial effort is increasingly devoted to, as we shall see shortly. For the moment, though, we need fully to appreciate the point of regarding all modern work organisations as bureaucracies, in the sense of the term established by Max Weber.

Bureaucracy

Concept

The control and coordination of work tasks through a hierarchy of appropriately qualified office holders, whose authority derives from their expertise and who rationally devise a system of rules and procedures that are calculated to provide the most appropriate means of achieving specified ends.

Modern organisations all have a hierarchy of offices and office holders (hence the term *bureaucracy* or 'rule by office'). These days, the majority of such officials are called 'managers' and, in principle, they obtain their posts on the basis of the appropriateness of their expertise, an expertise that is increasingly obtained by systematic training and is indicated by their possession of a formal qualification. This expertise on the part of the office holder or manager gives them authority over people lower in the hierarchy. The legitimacy of the office holders' power over others resides in their recognised expertise and in their always following formal rules and procedures. These rules and procedures are the codified ways of proceeding that officials themselves have devised, through their expert application of rational calculation of the most appropriate ways to fulfil specified tasks. The authority (or legitimate power) that officials or managers possess is thus, in Weber's terms, *legal-rational authority* (it follows rules that have been rationally and instrumentally devised). Authority does not derive, as it does in non-modern types of society or organisation, from either *charisma* ('I follow you because you have magical qualities') or *tradition* ('we obey you because we've always obeyed people like you').

In identifying the essential features of this distinctive way of organising work and administration, and in contrasting it to other approaches, Weber was not arguing that bureaucratic principles were being applied everywhere in a pure form. He fully recognised that all kinds of non-rational criteria would continue to inform human decision-making and that tradition and charisma would still influence people. However, to bring out clearly how bureaucracy differed in essence from other forms of administration he constructed an *ideal type* of the phenomenon, a model of what it would look like if it were to exist in an utterly pure form.

In a pure ('ideal typical') bureaucracy:

- every operating rule and procedure would be formally written down;
- tasks would be divided up and allocated to people with the formally certified expertise to carry them out;
- activities would be controlled and coordinated by officials organised in a hierarchy of authority;
- all communications and commands would pass up or down this hierarchy without missing out any steps;
- posts would always be filled, and promotions achieved, by the best qualified people;
- office-holders' posts would constitute their only employment and the level of their salary would reflect their level in the hierarchy;
- posts could not become the property or private territory of the office-holder; the officer's authority deriving from their appointed office and not from their person;
- all decisions and judgements would be made impersonally and neutrally – without emotion, personal preference or prejudice.

The unfortunate use of the word 'ideal' to label this sort of model, a type of analytical device that Weber used widely in his comparative sociological studies, has led generations of students of organisational behaviour to misunderstand his work. They have inferred from the use of the term 'ideal' that Weber was suggesting that bureaucracy was ideal, in the sense of 'perfectly desirable', as a way of organising human affairs. In this, they are utterly mistaken. Weber recognised the enormous advantages that bureaucracy has over other ways of administering complex activities – advantages that would, he correctly envisaged, make its growth and spread across the world inevitable. He also saw the enormous dangers that would arise if all decisions in the world came to be based solely on rational calculation and instrumental analysis. Value debate would disappear as people found themselves imprisoned in a *stalhartes Gehäuse,* a 'steel hard house' or 'iron cage' of modernity and unfreedom. The 'iron cage' is not a structure, of course. Weber is contemplating a culture, one from which values other than those of instrumental calculation and formal procedure have been removed. It is a nightmare world of the type envisaged by Franz Kafka in *The Trial* and portrayed in numerous science fiction novels and films.

Bureaucracy, we might say, plays the part in the modern world that fire played in the world of the ancient Greek gods. Fire was a gift bestowed on humanity by Zeus. But the benefits of the gift were balanced by the box of evils that Zeus also sent down, in the hands of Pandora. If that comparison sounds far fetched, one only has to look at the benefits that bureaucratic organisation has made possible in the hospitals, schools and institutions of democratic administration in which it is applied and in the manufacturing and service organisations that have provided goods and welfare on a scale previously undreamed of. One then sets this alongside the ruthless bureaucratic efficiency seen in the death camps and gulags of the twentieth century. Bureaucracy, like fire, can be used for the benefit of human beings or to their detriment.

 Link — The analysis in Chapter 2, pp. 52–4, of the 'twin pathologies' of managerialism and managism, is closely related to the worries that Weber had about bureaucratic or managerial criteria threatening to displace other value-based judgements about how the world should be.

A critical study such as *Organising and Managing Work* has to be sensitive to this dark side of organisational and managerial achievements in the modern world, but it also has to attend to the various ways in which bureaucracy, in its normal and everyday manifestations, has a tendency to 'go wrong'.

The failings and contradictions of bureaucracy

If we examine closely the various characteristics of the pure or 'ideal type' of bureaucratic organisation outlined above, we realise that a bureaucracy could never work out in this way in reality. If it did so, it would become the big dehumanised organisational machine aspired to in systems-control thinking and in what we have called 'managism'. Both of these closely associated ways of thinking about organisations and their management have been shown, in Chapter 2 especially, to be unrealistic about the extent to which organisations can be either designed or run like big corporate machines. There is an underestimating of the extent of the differences and conflicts of interest that exist between human beings and about the role that emotion and bounded rationality plays in people's lives and relationships. All of this means that any scheme drawn up by the designers and managers of organisations will never work out fully to plan. We can say that there is a *contradiction* built into the logic of work organisations; one whereby they depend on the passive controllability of employees and resources and *at the same time* require employees willingly to take initiatives and actively commit themselves to organisational tasks. What this means, in practice, is that the variety of interests, sentiments, orientations, projects, preferences, priorities and differences that people bring into the organisation preclude organisational members ever simply becoming cogs in a corporate machine.

People are employed to act as means towards organisational ends. But people, being people, have ends of their own and will only go along so far with what is required of them. This is why we see so many of what we have called the 'unofficial' activities that arise in organisations and have been discussed already in this chapter and were identified earlier both in the discussion of the multiple and conflicting goals that are always present in organisations (pp. 48–50) and in the analysis of the *negotiated order* of organisations (p. 77). This can be related to a general tendency in social life for *unintended consequences* of deliberate actions to arise.

A recognition of the role that a *paradox of consequences* plays in social life was central to Max Weber's thinking. The means that are adopted to achieve certain ends often turn out to subvert rather than fulfil those ends. Weber distinguished between the *formal or instrumental rationality* that was increasingly being used in the modern world – applying systematic calculation, science, technology, accounting and so on to human problems and projects – and *material rationality*, whereby those problems would actually be solved or those projects fulfilled. This is not dissimilar to the efficiency/effectiveness distinction mentioned in Chapter 6 (p. 199). Weber pointed out that formal or instrumental rationality, which is typically undertaken as a *means* of achieving material rationality, often fails in practice to bring about materially rational *ends*. Means all too often become ends in themselves. We acquire a computer, say, as a means of writing novels. But we then get so caught up in learning how to use new software, acquiring new pieces of hardware, and so on, that we end up simply becoming a 'computer nerd', who never writes a word. At a more structural level, a political party might be set up to bring about social reform in a society but ends up primarily as a vehicle to give careers to the politicians who run the party.

We can even use a simple domestic example to illustrate the general tendency in social life for means to defeat the ends that they were meant to serve. Imagine the members of a family arranging a holiday that will enable them all to take a rest. But the means of getting that rest – getting away from work, booking tickets, arranging lodgings for the cat, cancelling the milk, obtaining foreign currency, getting injections, packing bags, travelling to the airport, finding the hotel at the end of a long journey and so on and so on, lead the family to feel more exhausted after the holiday than it was before it. Arguments within the family, differences of opinion with airline staff and rude behaviour by hotel staff might all be things that contribute to the failure of the holiday as a rest. The means adopted to meet certain ends have completely undermined the achieving of those ends.

The paradox of consequences can happen in any aspect of social life, then, but nowhere do we see this type of social 'sod's law' applying more than within bureaucratic work organisations.

- We can see it in the case of a database that was set up to help control certain activities in a government department, for example, but where it transpired that the database was simply being maintained for the sake of maintaining the database. An individual had taken this on as their job. It gave them a living, and they made sure that they held onto the role even though the database was little used. Organisationally, the means (the database) had become an end in itself, and the reason this came about was that it was serving the ends of one of the human beings who has been employed to operate this 'means'.

- A similar process is occurring when managers in an organisation build personal 'empires' that serve their own private purposes more than they serve corporate ends of achieving long-term organisational survival. An example of this was the head of computing services of a large financial services company. What this man really aspired to was running his own information technology company. But he was reluctant to leave the comfort of the company with which he had spent most of his career and which paid him a large salary with an excellent pension scheme and a cheap mortgage. Consequently, he built up his department with experts in every branch of computing and information technology – often when that expertise was of little relevance to the main business. This man persuaded the chief executive that all this was necessary to 'cope with the future'. But eventually the cost burden of the department became too great in the eyes of the board of directors. The IT man was removed with half of his staff with the consequence that the costs fell dramatically and the computing and IT service improved considerably. The IT function had been subverting the ends for which it was set up.

- The same danger arises where departments of organisations are run more in the interests of the members of that department generally than they are run with the intention of contributing to the effectiveness of the organisation as a whole. An example here might be the case of the marketing and advertising department of a pharmaceutical company who became much more concerned with building their reputation for creativity and innovative marketing techniques with other marketing and advertising people around the world than with helping the sales of their own company's products.

- It is not just work roles and departmental structures that lead to means becoming ends in themselves. It can happen with systems and procedures too (perhaps as it was doing with the above case of the database which lost its original purpose). Budgeting arrangements are a good example of this. It is not unusual to see budgeting procedures established to manage costs but where the system of annual budgets, in which money saved cannot to be 'rolled over' into the next financial year, leads to frantic and even frivolous expenditure towards the end of the financial year. Why does this happen? It is again because human beings and human interests are involved in the procedure. The budget holder does not want their budget for the coming year to be less than it was for the current year. An underspend on the budget in the current year would be seen as a cost-saving achievement on the part of the budget holder, and the budgeting system would thus be a 'means' of successfully working towards intended 'ends'. Equally, the budget holder might interpret the new and lower budget likely to be allocated to them as likely to make their job more difficult in the coming year. The current budget is thus urgently 'spent up'. This means that the budgeting system was, in practice, leading to unnecessary costs rather than encouraging people to avoid them. Means again have got in the way of the ends for which they were designed.

TABLE 7.2 The organisational paradox of consequences and its relationship to a fundamental organisational contradiction	
A fundamental organisational contradiction *Concept*	**The organisational paradox of consequences** *Concept*
Organisations use people but people also use organisations. Organisations depend on the passive controllability of employees as resources but at the same time (and in a way that is potentially incompatible with this) they have to allow employees the freedom to take initiatives and apply discretion to the performance of organisational tasks. A tension thus exists between pressures to make people controllable and pressures to allow them discretion	The means chosen in organisations to achieve certain ends have the tendency to undermine or defeat the very ends for which they have been adopted. This arises as part of the tension between two contradictory principles of modern work organisations and the associated institution of employment. This is the tension whereby people accept a degree of control but always insist, to some extent, on doing things 'their own way', a way that will not necessarily fit in with organisational priorities

In each of these cases, the bureaucratic hierarchy, the bureaucratic division of labour and bureaucratised procedures chosen as *means* have, in one sense, become *ends* in themselves. In another sense they have come to be means to the ends of people employed in the organisation, rather than means to corporate ends. This is happening because of the 'human element' and as a result of people diverting bureaucratic means to the fulfilling of personal or sectional ends. Or, to put it another way, a contradiction in the basic principles upon which work organisations in industrial capitalist societies are based manifests itself in various specific ways that can be understood as expressions of the organisational paradox of consequences, as we see in Table 7.2.

From this arises a particular paradox whereby too much attention to bureaucratic means results in the purposes to which they were originally attached inevitably being undermined. Thus:

- organisations have rules, procedures, structures and cultural features that must be followed for the organisation properly, or efficiently, to complete work tasks (the rules etc. are the means to certain ends);
- if those rules, procedures, structures and cultural features are fully followed by the people working in the organisation, the tasks will not be properly or efficiently completed (the means defeat the ends they were supposed to meet).

This sounds illogical at first, but once we bring what we have just called the 'human element' into the calculation (personal and sectional interests, feelings, class differences, bounded rationality and all the rest), it makes sense. Indeed the power of the paradox of consequences is recognised by workers who deploy a 'work to rule' sanction against a management with whom they are in dispute. Nothing slows an organisation down faster, and frustrates managers more, than members of an organisation following 'every letter of the law', or doing everything 'completely by the book'. A number of much more common examples of the contradiction or 'paradox of consequences' that is behind practices like these can be seen in Ronnie Brackla's account of the problems he encountered when becoming the new manager of a large public house.

Activity 7.5

Read Ronnie Brackla's account in Cases and Conversations 7.4 of his becoming the manager of the Seaforth Arms and note down:

- as many examples of the paradox of consequences – the ways in which means get in the way of the ends for which they were chosen – as you can find in this story;

- as many examples you can think of from your own experiences of organisations, as a worker, customer, manager or whatever.

Ronnie falls into the Seaforth Arms
Cases and Conversations 7.4

I remember the first time I arrived at the pub. I literally fell into the front door. This is why I can joke that I 'fell into the job' when people ask me why I became the manager of such a large and busy pub.

What happened?

It was simply that some idiot had polished the floor of the entrance area so much that anybody wearing the wrong sort of shoes was bound to slip over when they walked in.

Why did they do this then?

Well, it was actually quite a good introduction to the problems that I had to sort out. The area manager had told me that the staff had developed what he called a 'hyper jobsworth culture'. I had no idea what he meant – until I got here that day. I arrived at the pub a few minutes before opening time but, rather than wait for them to unlock the doors, I went up to one of the open windows and waved to one of the staff who was setting tables to let me in. He just ignored me at first. I eventually got his attention and asked him to unlock the doors. You can guess what he said.

Yes, I suppose he said something like 'It's more than my job's worth, mate'.

Exactly. Well you're nearly right. But he called me 'pal' rather than 'mate'. It's interesting because when I tackled this bloke later on about his behaviour he not only told me that he was following 'management instructions' about the opening time of the pub – as you would expect with one of these 'jobsworth' types. He also told me that he was following the 'culture that management had brought in' by calling me 'pal'. You see, I not only

pointed out to him that he was being unnecessarily inflexible by refusing to open the doors before 11.00 am precisely. I also told him that calling a customer 'pal' was being a bit too 'familiar'. 'Oh no', he insisted, 'I was following the "customer friendly culture" that management brought in'.

So he was being unfriendly in a friendly way – refusing to break opening time rules but doing so in a nice way?

No he wasn't. There was actually nothing friendly about the way he spat out 'pal'. He was simply expressing contempt for the pub's management by taking two of their instructions very literally – one about punctuality of opening and closing times and another about friendly behaviour towards customers – without paying any attention to the spirit of those instructions. He was 'going through the motions', paying no heed whatsoever to what the management were trying to do by issuing those instructions.

So did this chap have a particular grievance against the management?

No, he didn't. My first reaction to what happened was to think about sacking this individual once I was settled in. I'm glad that I went easy on him though, because I soon came to realise that he was simply acting out this 'jobsworth culture' that I had been warned about. Many of the staff behaved similarly. In fact, that is how I had come to slip over when I did get through the doors that morning. It turned out that a cleaner had been told in a rather officious manner to polish the floor 'until you can see your face in it'. The resentful floor polisher got his revenge by doing the job to such an extent that someone was bound to have accident. Believe it or not, you actually could see your face in this highly polished floor. This is not what you want in the entrance to a pub. But the cleaner had taken the supervisor's instruction absolutely literally. Instead of working with the spirit of what was required – a clean and smart environment in this case – the staff tended to say, 'so this is what management say they want, this is what management will get'. Closing time was the best illustration of this culture. It was a ritual almost like a military ceremony. They would sound the bell to indicate the end of drinking-up time and the bar staff would instantly dash out from behind the bar to collect glasses and clean tables, practically knocking over any customer who got in their way.

Not very customer friendly, then?

No, but they would always say 'very sorry, madam' or 'I beg your pardon, sir', as they were taught to do on the 'customer friendly culture' course. But they said it in a way that bordered on the sarcastic. Again it was a matter of carrying out orders without paying any heed to what the point of those orders was.

So why did this sort of thing happen?

With some of the staff it was simply a way of getting through their shift, with as little effort or attention to others as possible. The fact that it was so prevalent – a cultural rather than just an individual thing – was because there was a general resentment of the management, I think. Much of this was down to the man I was replacing. He was an ex-military type, as you might have guessed. His manner to staff was overbearing and I think that he resented the way the pub company's management required him to implement the corporate 'head office fads', as he called them – the customer friendly culture training programme especially. So he put across these values to staff in a way that undermined them from the start. You could say that he himself, 'went through the motions' when doing the staff training, and this came through in the way the staff applied this training – or, rather, failed to apply it. And, of course, they just didn't like him anyway. So you got similar behaviour over the jobs people would do. Bar staff refused to serve meals when the waiting staff were under pressure and the bar wasn't, for example. And the waiting staff themselves would never be flexible about the order in which they got meals done in the kitchen. All customers had to 'wait their turn' for their orders, regardless of whether they were in a hurry to get back to work or were there with plenty of time to spare. If tackled they would simply say, 'we're following company procedures', and the manager was not subtle enough himself to explain that all procedures and rules have to be flexibly interpreted, in a spirit of making the pub a place people wanted to eat and drink in.

I'm surprised they had any customers left.

Exactly. Well that was a real issue. And it was why I was put in there to change things.

And have you?

I am getting there. I had to build a different type of relationship with the staff and I had to get away from this 'two cultures' thing – a situation where the company claims it has a chain of friendly pubs and restaurants, while the culture in reality is a 'hyper jobsworth' one that would eventually have taken the pub out of business.

You say you are 'getting there'.

Yes, I have changed things a lot. I'm not stupid enough to think that I'm going to get it all right though. OK, I am a much better manager than my predecessor. I am getting the culture of the pub sorted out. I am getting it in line with the strategy and the culture of the business that owns it. But, when it comes down to it, I am a boss and a lot of the people I employ are never going to earn half of the salary I'm on. I've got to make sure that the shareholders get a good profit out of what goes on here. That's what I get the salary for. And the staff know that. They respect me, but they're never going to love me. However hard I work at getting everyone to 'share the corporate values', situations regularly arise where I have to discipline people for falling short. And I do sack people for fiddling and stealing. I am flexible about rules and the staff, I am pleased to say, are a lot more flexible and helpful than they were. But, at the end of the day, the company has its structures, its rules and its 'bottom line'. People have to fit in – or else.

The sort of person who is colloquially known as a 'jobsworth' was identified early on by organisational theorists as a 'bureaucratic personality' and the existence of such people was labelled a 'dysfunction of bureaucracy' (Merton, 1940, Reading Guide 16). However, it seems rather doubtful that organisational involvement could be powerful enough to influence someone's 'personality'. Ronnie Brackla's suggestion that some people were rationally adopting a 'jobsworth' approach to their work to make it easier to get through their shift and to avoid having to pay too much attention to other people seems a more realistic analysis. But Ronnie goes beyond identifying the problem as one of individual motivation. He sees it as part of a broader pattern of actions and meanings – as something that has become *structural* and *cultural* within the pub, in effect. And this, in part, relates to conflict between staff members and the manager that Ronnie is replacing. This conflict is manifested in a series of ways in which *means* that the organisation has adopted to meet certain organisational *ends* have come to defeat rather than serve those ends. This has happened with the rules about opening and closing times, the procedures for fulfilling customers' food orders, the division of labour between bar and waiting staff and even the instructions given to cleaning staff about polishing the floor. It has also happened with the 'culture change' training programme that was meant to encourage staff to make customers feel welcome. All of these things were intended to be a means to making the pub operate efficiently and attracting and keeping customers to a level whereby the owners of the pub would produce a satisfactory profit for shareholders. Instead, all of these 'means' were tending to lose customers and to make the pub unprofitable. The contradiction or paradox of consequences also applied to the interests of the staff themselves. Those workers who were making life easier for themselves by acting in a perfunctory way or in a 'jobsworth' manner were risking their jobs in the longer run. The former manager himself, who seemed to take a leaf out his staff's book when it came to doing the 'customer friendly culture' training, actually did lose his job.

Ronnie captures quite well the idea of 'means becoming ends in themselves' with his description of both the staff and his managerial predecessor 'going through the motions' when doing certain tasks. He sees them as applying company rules or following organisational procedures in a way that is not 'in the spirit' in which those rules and procedures were established. This is an effective way of describing the tendency of organisational members to detach the means from the ends to which they were intended to be attached. Staff were not meant to say 'very sorry, madam' or 'I beg your pardon, sir' in the spirit of simply 'following instructions'. They were meant to 'follow instructions', but they were meant to follow them in a spirit of making customers feel welcome in the pub. Here Ronnie talks of the sort of *flexibility* in rules and procedures following what he was trying to bring about. He was trying, in effect, to bring official and unofficial aspects of the pub's structure and culture more into line with each other than his predecessor had managed to do. Hence we can see his actions as an attempt to move further to the right-hand end of the continuum shown in Figure 7.2. Ronnie is not, however, naïve enough to think that he can turn everything into complete harmony and achieve total managerial control. He can move things further in this direction by doing an exchange or a 'deal' with the staff that differed from the one his predecessor had done. This is a deal in which Ronnie will be 'flexible' towards staff in return for staff acting flexibly with regard to bureaucratic rules and procedures in their actions. However, he recognises that this exchange is occurring within a set of unequal social and economic relationships and that cultural devices like the 'sharing of corporate values' are inevitably compromised by their location within the structures and priorities of the capitalist economy in which the pub operates. Ronnie speaks of himself as a boss who is working, in part, for shareholders. His staff, he acknowledges, have to fit in to the priorities that follow from this – 'or else'. Structures and cultures in organisations are again seen as elements of the structure and culture of a wider social, economic and political order.

Summary

In this chapter the following key points have been made:

- The design of organisational structures and the development of an appropriate culture are sometimes seen as aspects of the *implementation* of organisational strategy. This means that they are seen as involving choices that *follow* strategic decisions about the general direction to be followed by the organisation in the future. In practice, however, strategic decisions made about the direction to be followed by an organisation (the focus of Chapter 6) are significantly influenced by the existing structure and culture of the organisation. Thus the basic 'shaping' of the organisation, structurally and culturally, should be seen as a process which can as readily precede the 'directional' aspect of strategy-making as follow from it.

- Organisational structures and cultures are not separate features of organisations. The concepts of structure and culture are most usefully used as two different ways of looking at the same thing – the way the organisation is 'shaped' – with *structure* being seen as the regular or persisting patterns of action that occur in the organisation and *culture* as the associated set of meanings and values shared by organisational members. When it comes to managerial efforts to shape organisations, attempts to change 'structures' and modify cultural patterns cannot readily be distinguished one from the other. Changes regarded as primarily about the organisation's structure inevitably have cultural implications and attempts at cultural change correspondingly have structural ramifications.

- Both the structure and the culture of an organisation cannot be understood separately from the way the society in which the organisation is located is structured and cultured. This means that no organisation will 'have' a culture of its own. It is better therefore to talk of the cultural aspects of an organisation, always recognising that these often derive as much from cultural features of the broader society than from particular circumstances of that organisation. Managers may try to change certain cultural aspects of their organisation but, because many cultural aspects are ones deriving from the wider culture and are beyond managerial influence, managers have to *work with* culture as much or more than they can ever expect to 'manage culture'.

- Whatever efforts are made by managers to design structures or develop cultures, there will always exist alongside the *official* structural and cultural arrangements that follow from these managerial initiatives a pattern of *unofficial* activities and priorities. Sometimes unofficial beliefs and practices support formally and managerially sanctioned official ones, sometimes they undermine them and, on other occasions, the official and the unofficial co-exist without affecting each other too much.

- The logic underlying managerial attempts at cultural change or structural modification in organisations is one of working to bring together official and unofficial patterns of structure and culture. If a circumstance ever arose in which managers' aspirations to complete managerial control over an organisation were to be met, the official and the unofficial dimensions of that organisation's structure and culture would be one and the same. In this managerial utopia, what employees actually believed, said and did would be identical to what the organisation's policies, rules and operating procedures said they should believe, say and do. In spite of the fact that such a situation is unachievable, managers frequently strive in their strategic shaping of organisations to get as close as they can to such a state of unity, harmony and total cooperation.

- Strategic attempts to shape organisations have to find ways of taking advantage of the bureaucratic principles of work organisation while avoiding the problems that bureaucratic structures and cultures inevitably create. All bureaucracies are prone to failing as the *paradox of consequences* comes into play and means chosen to fulfil certain ends come to undermine those ends. Modern work organisations *are* bureaucracies and there is no possibility of 'getting rid of bureaucracy'.

Reading

Reading Guides 16, 19 and 20 contain material that supports and takes further much of what is covered in Chapter 7.

CHAPTER 8

Choice and constraint in the shaping of structure and culture

Objectives

Having read this chapter and completed its associated activites, readers should be able to:

● Realise that, although bureaucracy cannot be abandoned, there are nevertheless strategic choices to be made about whether any given organisation is more or less 'bureaucratic', structurally and culturally, and that this choice can be understood as one between *direct* and an *indirect* means of attempting to achieve managerial control of organisational practices.

● Appreciate that in spite of the fact that *contingency thinking* about organisations tends to be based upon systems-control assumptions about organisations, it contains valuable insights that can be related to the issues of managerial choices about *direct* and *indirect* controls.

● Understand how structural and cultural strategic choices are made in a context of managerial argument and negotiation in which both personal or group values and *enacted* contingencies play a part.

● Analyse the cultural features of an organisation and understand the various ways in which managers concerned with shaping organisations attempt to change or manipulate the various cultural elements.

Direct and indirect options in the pursuit of managerial control

A basic contradiction applying to all organisations was identified in Chapter 7. Two of the basic principles upon which organisations are based are, in the final analysis, incompatible. There is a logic to work organisations whereby people are employed in order to be exploited as resources. They are there to be *controlled*. But there is another logic existing alongside and in tension with this one.

This is a logic whereby people have to be *coopted* or actively involved in the enterprise. They have to be allowed discretion. This happens because:

- human beings are not passive resources easily open to exploitation or readily amenable to control;
- rules or instructions are never 'politically neutral devices' that will be received by organisational members without question or potential challenge;
- no rule and instruction could ever be sufficiently precise to ensure that employees will do exactly what is required of them.

These two logics of needing to control and needing to allow discretion, we have said, are incompatible 'in the final analysis'. But, in practice, this potential incompatibility has to be handled by managers. It can never be resolved, but the tensions we have identified have to be dealt with if the organisation is going to continue into the long-term. Consequently we can see the history of attempts at managerial control as a constant switching back and forth between efforts to control organisational members in a relatively and straightforwardly *direct* way and efforts to seek that control in a more sophisticated, subtle or *indirect* way. In its most basic form, direct control management would give us an organisation in which people were hired to do closely specified tasks and were rewarded for doing exactly what they were told. In an organisation characterised by *indirect controls*, however, we would see people hired to use their discretion and decide for themselves how best to carry out tasks in a way that would help the long-term survival of the organisation.

With direct controls we would tend to see a culture involving a low level of mutual commitment between the organisation and its members while indirect

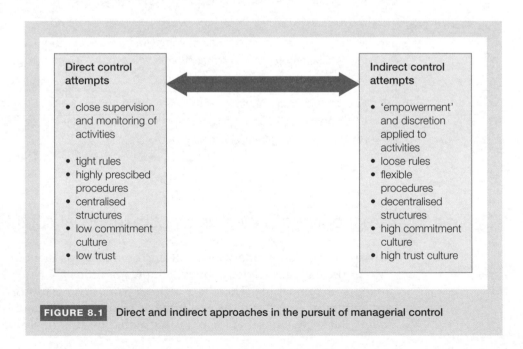

FIGURE 8.1   Direct and indirect approaches in the pursuit of managerial control

controls would be associated with a culture of mutually high-level commitment. These two types of organisation are very much 'ideal types' in the sense of that term used by Weber (1978, Reading Guide 16). Neither of them is ever likely to exist in anything like a pure form. In practice organisations will tend to lean towards one of these broad approaches or to the other. Typically, each organisation will contain a mixture of the two styles of striving for control and each one will fluctuate back and forth between the two over time. Figure 8.1 locates the two approaches to seeking control on a continuum along which this variation and tendency to fluctuate occurs.

The two basic ways of seeking managerial control within organisations that are characterised here as *direct* and *indirect* control attempts have been recognised and characterised in numerous different ways by organisational and managerial writers over a long period. A common thread can be seen running through the following examples:

- In the 1950s, Jaques (1956, Reading Guide 17) pointed out that every job has *prescribed* and *discretionary* elements and the proportions of these vary across different kinds of work. McGregor (1960, Reading Guide 17) famously differentiated between 'theory X and theory Y' managerial thinking. Managers who worked with theory X assumptions about human beings and regarded people as inherently reluctant to work and generally keen to avoid responsibility were inclined to adopt what are called 'direct controls' here. But managers thinking in a 'theory Y' way would favour controls of a more indirect kind. Looser controls of this kind would encourage people to apply their inherent inclinations to involve themselves creatively in work tasks and fulfil themselves through taking on responsibilities.

- In the 1960s, Burns and Stalker (1994, originally 1961, Reading Guide 16) showed how highly bureaucratised mechanistic organisational structures differed from *organic* ones which were much more informal and flexible and had lower levels of task prescription. Each of these two types of organisational structure was said to be appropriate to a particular type of organisational circumstance (as we will see below). Hickson (1966, Reading Guide 17) related Burns and Stalker's study to an emerging tendency for organisation and management writers to focus on the 'structural variation' between organisations – whereby 'role expectations' varied between ones of specific and precise *role prescription* and ones allowing legitimate discretion.

- In the 1970s, at a time where there was particular concern about bad industrial relations, Fox (1974, Reading Guide 16) related patterns of industrial conflict to variations in organisational structure and culture. He differentiated between 'low discretion' work role patterns and 'high discretion' work role patterns, pointing to the ways in which the former tended to be associated with *low trust* work relations and the latter with *high trust* relations. Patterns of industrial conflict would tend to be reduced by moves towards higher discretion work design and the development of high trust cultures. Friedman (1977, Reading Guide 17), at about the same time, distinguished between the *direct-control strategies* that managers would adopt in certain employment circumstances and *responsible-autonomy strategies* that they would favour in other circumstances (see Chapter 9, p. 309).

● The 1980s saw a growing interest in changing patterns of 'human resource management' and Walton (1985, Reading Guide 21) influentially wrote about a move away from 'control-based HRM systems' to 'commitment-based HRM systems'. As well as this giving employees increased discretion over work tasks it saw a cultural shift coming about as managers moved away from adversarial relationships with employees towards 'mutuality' and the adoption of joint problem-solving and planning.

● The growing talk of a shift towards 'postmodern' forms of culture and social organisation in the 1990s saw some writers contrasting the 'rigidity' of the modernist organisation with the 'flexibility' of the postmodernist organisation (for example, Clegg, 1990, Reading Guide 1). This was done in a way highly reminiscent of the mechanistic/organic distinction made decades earlier by Burns and Stalker (1994, originally 1961, Reading Guide 16). It was almost as if the old 'theory Y-based practices', 'organic structures', 'high-trust' work relations, 'responsible-autonomy strategies' and so on had to be relabelled *postmodern* for the late twentieth century. And various writers combined the postmodern label with the label 'post-bureaucratic'.

The labelling of more flexible forms of bureaucratic structure and culture as 'postmodern' or 'post-bureaucratic' is unhelpful. It is unrealistic to suggest that there is something new occurring to work organisations at the level of the basic organising principle. There is no postmodern or post-bureaucratic organisational form available to us that is *essentially* different from the modernist bureaucratic organisation. We are indeed seeing different mixes of direct and indirect management control attempts as the world changes. But the world was always changing. Probably from the very beginning of industrialisation there has been a mixing of direct and indirect controls with emphases in one direction and then the other being made at different times. Even before the push towards systematic direct controls at the production level of industrial enterprises led by F.W. Taylor, around the turn of the nineteenth and twentieth centuries, for example, there were variations between *strong* 'hire and fire' direct control strategies and *weaker* direct control efforts incorporating paternalistic relationships between employers and employees that follow the principle of indirect control attempts (Watson, 1986, Reading Guide 17).

 Link Taylorism or 'scientific management' will be looked at in Chapter 9 as part of an analysis of this alleged historical fluctuation between direct and indirect controls on the parts of employers.

The various ways of differentiating between relatively direct and relatively indirect attempts at managerial control are most usefully understood as ways of recognising that organisations can vary between a tendency to be *tightly bureaucratic* and a tendency to be *loosely bureaucratic*. Strategically, managers have the option to shape their organisations in a broad *tightly bureaucratic* way or broad *loosely bureaucratic* way. Hence the comment in the previous chapter that we cannot remove or dispense with bureaucracy. We can only modify or 'loosen' bureaucratic principles when trying to shape organisational structures and cultures. But what factors are likely to influence them when it comes to leaning one way or another?

Enactment, contingency and argument in structural and cultural shaping

An obvious starting point for considering the choices that managerial strategists might make when considering how to shape the organisation they are working in would be the values held by those managers. They will clearly be influenced by their ideas about what is right and wrong, good and bad in organisational activity and employment relationships. Some managers will agree with each other that it is a 'good thing' to give people responsibility at work and that it is wrong to subject other human beings to close supervision or to monitor their behaviours tightly and in a way that implies they are not trusted. These people will tend to look towards indirect control measures rather than direct ones and establish a loose rather than a tight bureaucratic regime. Managers' *beliefs* about 'human nature' are obviously connected to such values and to the *theories* they hold about 'human motivation', as McGregor (1960, Reading Guide 17) pointed out when distinguishing between theory X and theory Y managers (see above p. 252).

The theories and beliefs of managers may well be influenced by their education and training but they are also likely to be influenced by the cultures of the societies to which they belong (see Reading Guide 20). The values prevailing in this broader culture will also influence other members of the organisations that the managers are trying to shape. This means that societal values will be relevant to what is likely to 'work' with employees as much as it is likely to influence managers' own preferences. Helpful insights into these influences are to be found in the research-based analysis by Hofstede (2001, Reading Guide 20) of how managers in one large global company varied in the values for which they expressed support. Especially relevant is the extent to which a particular national culture encourages or discourages its members to accept high degrees of *power distance*. If members of a given culture tend to dislike large disparities in the inequalities of power within social and organisational arrangements, for example, we might expect a tendency to favour indirect and loosely bureaucratic arrangements. On the other hand, if members of a society tend to favour as much *uncertainty avoidance* as possible, there exists a pressure to keep bureaucratic arrangements relatively tight. Differences over inclinations towards individualism or collectivism in values or differences between an orientation towards the long-term or the short-term will also play a part in the approach to structural and cultural shaping that managers attempt.

Managers' own values and their 'theories' about what will 'work' in the managerial context have been shown to be very closely connected: morality and pragmatism are tightly interrelated in the way managers 'think' (Watson, 1996, Reading Guide 25). But there are other circumstances that are likely to be relevant to the sort of organisational structure or culture that is likely to 'work' in managerial terms.

Organisational contingencies	Concept
Organisational circumstances like size, main technology or environment with which organisational structures and cultures need to *fit* or *match* if the organisation is going to function successfully.	

A whole series of research projects that form an important strand of organisation studies and have come to be labelled as *contingency thinking* or 'contingency theory' have shown how particular organisational arrangements match or fit different organisational circumstances or 'contingencies'. Burns and Stalker's (1994, originally 1961, Reading Guide 16) immensely important case study research is often put in this category, even though they did not use the language of 'contingencies'. Their research showed that the companies they studied which manufactured products for a stable market requiring little innovation in product or method tended to perform better in business terms if they worked in a *mechanistic* or 'tightly bureaucratic' manner than ones which did not. Companies in which there needed to be much more innovation because of 'changing conditions, which give rise to fresh problems and unforeseen requirements for action' (1994, p. 121, Reading Guide 16) found it necessary to adopt *organic* or loosely bureaucratic 'management systems' if they were going to succeed in the relatively turbulent business environment with which they were faced.

Much of the research that followed up what we might call this early 'contingency insight' pays less attention to processual matters like managerial politics and to cultural issues within organisations than did Burns and Stalker. It tends to use rather general survey-based research methods rather than the detailed case-study techniques used in their *Management of Innovation* (1994, originally 1961, Reading Guide 16). Also, it is much more firmly set within the systems-control tradition and pays little attention to how organisational circumstances, like the organisation's size, its environment or the key technologies actually influence strategic choice processes. It tends to present research that identifies patterns whereby one type of structure, say, is associated with 'successful' organisations more frequently than with another type. Woodward's (1994, originally 1965, Reading Guide 16) study of smaller manufacturing organisations showed, for example, that businesses in their sample using unit or small batch production technologies tended to be more successful, in standard business terms, if they had relatively flat organisational structures (fewer levels of authority and wider 'spans of control' – numbers of people supervised by one individual) than if they had tall structures. Companies working with process-flow technologies, like petro-chemicals, performed better if they had tall and narrow organisational structures rather than the short and flat ones that worked with simpler technologies. However, little was said here about how these 'fits' between structure and circumstances came to be made in some organisations and not in others. The same applies to the range of studies (most famously the Aston studies – Pugh and Hickson, 1976; Pugh and Hinings, 1976; Pugh and Payne, 1977, Reading Guide 16) that show a general necessity for larger organisations to be more 'tightly bureaucratic' (in our terms) than smaller ones. This type of research demonstrates some important associations. But we need to go beyond the limitations (Chapter 2, pp. 43–50) of the systems-control tradition to understand how they come about.

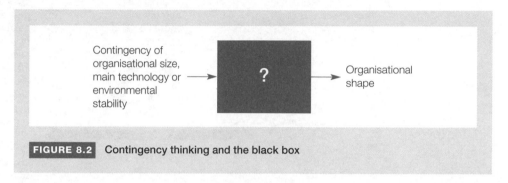

FIGURE 8.2 Contingency thinking and the black box

Generally speaking, contingency thinking leaves us in the dark about the nature of the connections that come about between contingencies like those of organisational size, technology or environment and the structural 'outcomes'. This is represented in simple terms in Figure 8.2. It is because so much is 'left in the dark' in the black box that it is preferred here not to call this strand of organisational analysis contingency *theory*. To warrant the label 'theory' we would need to pay attention to the part played by human actions and choices in creating the shapes that contingency thinking only vaguely links with contingent circumstances. This takes us towards developing a process-relational analysis that incorporates the contingency *insight* into fuller processual understanding of how strategic choices come to be made in varying organisational circumstances.

Figure 8.3 is a model that brings the contingency insight into a process-relational way of thinking. The insight that the strategic shaping of an organisation needs to take into account various contingencies or circumstances if it is going to help move the organisation forward to achieve long-term survival is incorporated into this more sophisticated frame of reference. It is one that puts processes of enactment and negotiation at the centre of strategy-making processes.

Link The notion of enacted environments was central to the analysis of strategy-making processes in Chapter 6, p. 203.

The contingencies of the organisation's size, technology or environment are not given 'things' that directly and straightforwardly 'affect' the organisation. Managers always interpret them and 'what they are' is partly an outcome of the interpretations that managers make. For example, an organisation is not unequivocally and objectively 'large' or 'small', and therefore needing to be

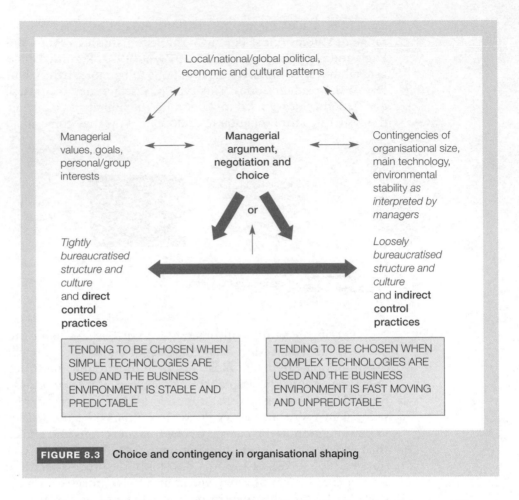

FIGURE 8.3 Choice and contingency in organisational shaping

pushed towards a more or a less bureaucratic structure and culture to achieve a 'fit' between contingencies and organisational shape. In the first place, managers will typically differ on just what a small, medium or large organisation is. For example, an argument was witnessed in a management meeting along the lines:

'We are becoming a rather big business now and need to think of the implications of this for our efficiency' . . .

'Oh no, I wouldn't say that. We have a long way to go before we start to worry about size'.

In the second place, managers may choose to act upon the perceived 'contingent factor', and change it rather than make some structural change to accommodate it. The first manager in the above conversation, for example, went on to argue that what he took to be the 'bigness' of the organisation meant that some more 'formal operating procedures' were going to be needed to avoid 'things getting out of control'. The other managers disliked his ideas, one of whom expressed a personal 'hatred of big bureaucracy'. The discussion then proceeded along the lines that it would be preferable to try to 'keep things small' than move in the direction of tighter bureaucracy. They therefore discussed ways of splitting the organisation into two smaller ones. The contingency of size had thus been tackled rather than a structural arrangement made to 'fit' with that contingency.

This tiny case study illustrates the process that is at the heart of Figure 8.3, the process of *managerial argument, negotiation and choice*. The managers start off by identifying a possible 'contingency' of large size – a circumstance that does not fit with what we can take to be currently a fairly loosely bureaucratised structure and culture. But their interpretations of the salience of this contingency differ. Some personal values, like one person's 'hatred of big bureaucracy', are then brought into the argument. It does appear, though, that the discussion then proceeded in a direction whereby the managers agreed that there was an issue about size. But instead of *reacting* to the 'contingency' of larger size, they considered acting upon the contingency itself. In effect, they were contemplating 'getting rid' of 'bigness' by splitting the organisation and retaining 'smallness'. This possibility is recognised by the double-headed arrow between the managerial *argument* and the *enacted contingencies* 'boxes' in Figure 8.1. This avoids the linear thinking (see above, pp. 98–102) tendency of systems-control contingency thinking represented by the one direction arrow in the black box in Figure 8.2.

The double-headed arrow between the *managerial argument* box and the *managerial values* one has a similar intention – recognising, in effect, that managers' values or interests are themselves emergent and enacted phenomena. It recognises that managers *develop* their values, goals and interests within the arguments and negotiations they have with other managers and do not simply bring them pre-formed into those debates. The other pair of double-headed arrows is intended to reinforce the point made throughout this chapter that organisation structures and cultures must always be seen in the context of the wider social and economic and political context. But this context is not just one that makes an 'input' into processes of organisational shaping. The way the managers of organisations generally attempt to shape organisations is equally an 'input' into the shaping of the societies and changing global relationships of which organisations are a part. Organisations make societies and societies make organisations, we might say, to put it very simply.

The strategic choices about shaping the organisation in a way that can be located somewhere along the continuum between direct (tightly bureaucratised) control attempts or indirect (loosely bureaucratised) control aspirations emerge from the managerial argument, negotiation and choice process. But even here, Figure 8.3 includes an arrow pointing back the other way. This recognises that a perception of the *status quo* in an organisation (its current shaping) will have an influence itself on the managerial strategic debate about strategic shaping for the future. To put this another way: ideas about 'what we have already got', structurally and culturally, typically act as significant 'inputs' to managerial discussions about what is to be done henceforward about structural and cultural shaping.

Complex as it might seem, the model represented in Figure 8.3 is necessarily an over simplification. It does, however, identify the basic processes that are involved in the part of the organisational strategy-making process that deals with the 'shaping' of the enterprise. It can be put alongside the model of strategy-makers trading or 'resource exchanging' on the organisation's behalf with internal and external constituencies that was central to Chapter 6's concern with the organisation's broader strategic exchange involvement. These two aspects of strategy-making relate to each other of course. This is, first, because the organisational shaping aspect of strategy-making pays particular attention to that element of strategic exchange relationship that deals with employee constituencies. And, second, both parts of the strategy-making process share a logic of working towards the survival of the organisation into the long term.

Activity 8.1

Read the story in Cases and Conversations 8.1 of the attempts led by Mick Moy and Joy Petty to get Motoline 'on track' and

- consider whether this account suggests Motoline are moving in the direction of tighter bureaucracy and direct control attempts or in the direction of looser bureaucracy and indirect control attempts;

- analyse Mick and Joy's story using the model shown in Figure 8.3 by finding as many points

as you can that illustrate each of the elements of the model: local/national/global patterns; managerial values; managerial arguments and negotiation; enacted contingencies, and strategic changes taking the organisation in the direction of either increased direct control attempts or increased indirect control attempts.

Getting on track at Motoline
Cases and Conversations 8.1

Mick Moy is the chief executive of Motoline, a company that manufactures rail-buses, trams and rail–road buses. The latter product is a public transport vehicle, largely sold overseas, that can travel on both rail and road. Joy Petty is Director of Quality and Corporate Development.

When I joined the company as chief executive I was, to be honest, quite terrified of what I was taking on, wasn't I Joy? I knew that I had to change an old fashioned inward-looking company with an engineering-led culture into one that was much more customer-led.

Yes, I remember meeting Mick a week after he had arrived here and how he expressed sheer wonder at the attitudes and values he was coming across. In fact, his shock cheered me up because after ten years of this kind of thing I was thinking of leaving the business. Since joining as a graduate ten years earlier I had to put up with a macho culture that did not recognise that a woman – and a social science graduate at that – could say sensible things to engineers. But, worse than that, everything was focused on getting the engineering of the product right and no attention was paid to either the end users that might travel in our vehicles or the transport authorities that would buy them. For most of its history the company developed and produced rolling stock for governments.

These state customers were very undemanding and they seemed not to mind if the development of a product went on years longer than was intended. And they paid on what was called a 'cost plus' basis. This meant that the company was guaranteed a basic price for what they were to produce and if the costs of either the development or the manufacturing went beyond what was originally budgeted, the customer then paid the costs. This led to an engineering-led mentality with engineers working hard to get the product 'right' in their own terms – and not in terms of what end users might prefer or in terms of what customers could afford. The assumption ran deep that the world out there owed the company a living – because they were very good at rail and vehicle engineering. Although nobody spoke in terms of the world owing the firm a living, I did have almighty rows with some of the older board members about their attitudes. To them 'engineering excellence' was everything. They deplored the idea that customers might know better what they wanted than the 'true transport experts' at Motoline. The individual who actually used this expression was one of two men I had to get rid of. It wasn't just his personal values that I disagreed with, however. He was clearly trying to defend his personal empire within the organisation. I was happy to have managerial arguments and debates but not continuous rows about what a business exists for. Nor am I the sort of bloke that can tolerate individuals putting their own hunger for power over the interests of the wider working community that they are supposed to be part of. And it was because I was beginning to realise the continuing currency of assumptions like the ones this bloke held to and the strength of these generally outmoded values across the firm that I promoted Joy to the job she is still doing, a job with the funny title that she chose for herself.

It's not a funny title, Mick – 'Quality and Corporate Development'. You and I agreed that it would be highly symbolic of the cultural direction we wanted to move in if we put quality in my title as well as the key word 'development'. Up until then 'quality' was little more than an extension of the old inspection function that monitored production output. Although the function was headed by a man with a commitment to modern ideas of 'total quality management' it was still dominated by individuals who saw their role as one of catching out and punishing people who did not come up to their high standards of engineering quality. By appointing, with a 'quality' responsibility, a board member who had a marketing background who was also charged with running the series of 'change programmes' we called 'Getting On Track', we were sending out important signals. And Mick announced my appointment with heavy emphasis on the importance to Motoline's survival of getting everybody to think about quality as a matter of producing what would suit customers rather than as something that fulfilled engineering pride. We needed new passenger-centred values that would be shared by all employees, not just ones to be taken up by the immediately 'customer-facing' staff. This would mean harnessing everybody's skills and insights to work towards this end. For this to be possible we would be empowering employees to take responsibility for their own contribution to the business – we would be moving away from the culture of supervisors telling people what to do and inspectors catching out production workers who fell short. There was a culture of blame that ran from top to bottom in the old culture. Mick and I worked hard to persuade other managers that this had to change completely. Even the old marketing director used to blame the production director for his failures and the production director regularly attacked the marketing function for its failure to agree with customers 'enough time to iron out teething difficulties' when a new product was going into production. And whenever complaints were made about the lack of flexibility on the part of employees across the business, it was standard practice to blame the trade unions.

Yes, I was endlessly telling managers that you 'get the unions you deserve' in management. If unions adopted a totally adversarial stance towards managers, they ought to ask why the union people thought this was necessary. We had one massive row, which spread well beyond board level, after I had been here a few months. They thought that my 'new broom' role would mean that I would work towards de-recognising trade unions. I agreed that I would challenge very hard much of what the union representatives did but that I wanted to work towards 'bringing them on board' the new ways of working that were going to be vital to saving the jobs of their members.

Privately, I was influenced in my arguing for working in partnership with trade unions for the benefit of everybody concerned by my own background as the son of a trade union official. But, at the same time, I did feel that it was easier to persuade employee reps of the wisdom of becoming more flexible than it was to persuade some of the older managers that their own unionised employees were not 'the enemy'.

I think, Mick, that this related to the generally defensive culture here where nobody trusted anybody else. The whole structure was heavily bureaucratic with managers, and technical experts becoming obsessed with their slow climb up the bureaucratic ladder. There was no tolerance of anybody by-passing anyone in the 'chain of command' (yes, they actually used this term) and each department's territory was jealously protected.

That's right. The research and development department was a brilliant example of this. They were a sort of sub-culture within the organisation. They were actually much less bureaucratic than the rest of the business in their internal way of working and they even had a degree of quite flexible project-group working long before the rest of the plant had heard of this. But when it came to their relationship with design and with manufacturing it was quite different. Here, they were heavily into the main culture. All communication between the R&D and design people had to be written down and it got so bad that they used to bring what they called 'independent witnesses' from other departments into some of their meetings. And the relationship between design and manufacturing was little better.

I saw this particular relationship – or the lack of a relationship one might say – as a key problem, from the point of view of 'quality', as I understand quality. It was clear to me, for example, that production people had a lot of expertise about how the product was actually going to be put together that ought to be taken into account at the design stage. But the designers would have none of this. As a consequence, we frequently got problems in production that could easily have been avoided if the design process had taken into account just what was feasible and was not feasible in manufacturing terms.

In the early stages of our 'Getting On Track' programme, Joy tried to tackle this by arranging joint seminars for research, design and manufacturing people. The idea was to try to get them to value each other differently – as each other's 'internal customers' for example.

While this was certainly a cultural problem, Mick and I came to the conclusion that it would only be possible to change values if we also changed structures.

Yes, I had been reluctant when I joined Motoline to do the all-too-common thing of a new chief executive restructuring a business. I felt that it would be better to take time and let any necessary structural changes come about as people came to see for themselves that such changes were necessary. In fact, I don't think I could have won the argument with the other senior managers for the sort of changes we have made if they had been the result of me, as chief executive, just telling them that this was going to happen. They might have gone along with these ideas grudgingly. But this would have been no good – without enthusiastic buying into the new ways, little of significance would have happened.

And this is where my 'joint seminars' of design and manufacturing people were helpful. We got more and more individuals, at all levels, to see that relationships were not going to improve significantly if people were located in separate 'boxes'. At first, Mick had been thinking of splitting the business into three divisions: railcars, trams and railroad cars. He felt it was the considerable size of the company that led to its being so rigid and bureaucratic. Splitting it down into three more reasonably sized companies that were of a size that people could identify with seemed a good idea at first. But we would have lost so many economies of scale, as several of the board members persuaded us. To have to set up three separate marketing functions, three separate procurement functions, three separate personnel functions, and so on, would have been very costly. If the three products had been more fundamentally different, using very different materials, techniques and relating to very different product and labour markets, then this might have been worth it. But this was not the case. The three lines are different but not that different. And the problems of change that they face are all very similar. All three products are no longer ordered by 'tame governments', as in the past. We are competing with manufacturers globally and the customers increasingly want a product tailored to their own needs, rather than simply accepting what our own engineers think they ought to want.

There is also a similar pressure from technology on each product area. As a management team we tend to differ on how much the technology in our type of business is changing. Some colleagues argue that we are simply doing the same things better than before. But I think it adds up to more than this. New materials are increasingly coming along that we need to consider and electronics is playing a bigger and bigger part on the control systems side. Engine technology could change radically in the next few years, I believe. Our growing expertise in areas like these has to spread across all the products – as does our changing approach to the manufacturing process itself, the use of robotics being just one example here.

So what we have done structurally, instead of splitting down into three divisions, is to get away from the problems of the 'big bureaucratic monster' mentality and the functional myopia that went with it by grouping as many activities as possible into 'product teams' or 'project groups'. The idea is to get people relating to units that are of a more meaningful size and to enable them to see that they are contributing to a whole task. For example, we recently set up a project group to work on a rail–road bus for more hilly countries where there is more frequent snow and ice than in the areas where our current models sell. This group has its own R&D, design, and manufacturing people attached to it and we are about to allocate to them their own personnel officer and a marketing manager. All of these people still relate to the specialist department that they originally belonged to. That is important – it makes sure that they share insights and develop their skills with people having the same specialist expertise.

This can be messy though – with people having one loyalty to their function and one to their product or project group. And it can be awkward when we want someone to move from one group to another because their expertise is needed in another setting. It is therefore very important to me that this structural arrangement is balanced by a strong corporate culture and sense of corporate mission that reminds people that whatever their group or team is working on, it must contribute to the business as a whole. To do this I spent a lot of time, when Joy was on holiday a couple of years ago, writing a beautiful mission statement and devising a set of posters that would set this out together with 'value statements' and slogans about 'delighting passengers'. I thought Joy would be proud of me. But she tore it to pieces when she got back.

Yes, Mick, but you understood why, didn't you? That sort of fancy propaganda stuff just would not go down with our people with all their local traditions of being plain-speaking northerners. And I think you have proved the wisdom of doing things more subtly. I think the T-shirt story illustrates this beautifully.

Oh yes, that's where I noticed a ritual in the project group I have just told you about of them wearing T-shirts on Fridays that had printed on the front the legend 'Mission Impossible', below a cartoon of a rail–road bus hurtling down a ski slope. I was visiting the group one Friday and they tried to persuade me to put one on. The excuse I found was that the shirts had neither the Motoline name nor the company logo on it. But they called my bluff and asked if I would wear one if it had the logo on the back. I not only said I would but I also promised to pay for new shirts which had the company logo on the back and an improved version of their cartoon on the front. I felt a bit daft the first day I wore one of these T-shirts. But Joy persuades me that this is an indication of what a brilliant manager I have become!

Well flattery has its place, doesn't it? But, seriously, what that shirt symbolises is considerable. However, if the shirts were just a stunt they would be nothing. What is much more significant than the cash Mick put into a few T-shirts is the money he has put into sending our employees at all levels out to meet customers and end users of our vehicles, all round the world. They bring back lots of ideas that are put into practice and, to quite a sur-

prising extent, they do act as sales people for us or, if you like, informal ambassadors for the company. These days I notice that people tend to tell stories of things they discovered about our products from, say, talking to tram drivers in South America. These are rather different from the sort of stories they used to tell. These were largely stories about how stupid people were in departments other than those of the storyteller. So this policy seems to be having a real cultural impact across the business. The travel and accommodation side of it is certainly an extra benefit to staff (even though the unions refuse to have it mentioned when they are engaged in wage bargaining). But its real significance is one that, of all people, the convenor of shop stewards pointed out to me one day. It showed, he said, that Mick means it literally when he says he wants everybody in the business to 'get close to customers'. This, he went on, suggests that the company these days actually trusts its employees. We've a long way to go but . . .

We are 'Getting On Track at Motoline.

Yes, I think we are.

This is an account of what is happening at Motoline provided by two senior, and closely allied, managers whose personal and career interests are clearly tied up with changing the organisation. There is a clear intention to give the company a more secure future than it had prior to Mick Moy's arrival as chief executive and Joy Petty's subsequent promotion to the new post of Director of Quality and Corporate Development. We must therefore treat cautiously what they say, bearing in mind that others might have a much less positive picture of what is occurring than these two people. Although there is apparent sincerity and a degree of modesty alongside significant pride in what they have to say, we have to remember that we are hearing something of an 'official story' of events in the company. There may be unofficial aspects of this that we are not likely to hear about from these senior corporate officials. Nevertheless, their account gives us an invaluable illustration of how the sorts of process we identified earlier, and represented graphically in Figure 8.3, can work out in practice. It is fairly clear that their strategy-making work involves loosening the bureaucratic structures and culture that prevailed in the 'old' Motoline. They are in no way loosening managerial control over activities in the company, however. They are, instead, making those controls more 'indirect' ones. They want to abandon the old regime of supervisors telling employees what to do and inspectors monitoring workers and even 'punishing' those who fall short. People are being given more discretion but the closer involvement of people in project-oriented work and their mixing more with customers and 'end users' is intended to ensure that this discretion is to be used to ensure the long-term future of the whole business.

We are told of the changing national and international pattern of culture and economy where there is much more competition and where governments are no longer willing to make 'cost plus' agreements with suppliers or to accept late delivery. In this way, Motoline is part of the culture and structure of the world it lives in and not a separate structural and cultural entity in its own right (as we have emphasised repeatedly with regard to all organisations). The local cultural context is something that is also seen as relevant by Joy when she talks of people from the area in which the plant is located tending to be resistant to anything but 'plain speaking' from managers. This led her to discourage Mick from the type of mission and value statement that plays a part in many culture-change programmes in contemporary organisations. Rightly or wrongly, she thinks these would be managerially counter-productive in this 'northern' part of the world.

These contextual factors, and the way they require a 'customer-led' or 'passenger-led' culture rather than an 'engineering-led one', take us into the *enacted contingencies* element of our model. The type of environment, as it is interpreted by Mick and Joy, is one that the Burns and Stalker (1994, originally 1961, Reading Guide 16) research considered earlier suggests 'fits' with an organic or loosely bureaucratic structure and culture rather than a mechanistic or tightly bureaucratic one. We have to stress that this is a managerial interpretation of the business environment rather than a straightforward 'fact'. Undoubtedly, the market is more competitive than it was previously, but it might be argued that with large expensive products like those of Motoline, there is not the same degree of turbulence in the business environment requiring employee flexibility and high levels of innovation that one might see in, say, a consumer electronic goods business. Similarly, we can see that the contingency of technology is one that Mick is choosing to interpret in a particular way. He acknowledges that others see changes here as less significant than he does himself. Indeed his words about this take us immediately over into the area of 'managerial argument, negotiation and choice'.

This connecting of contingency considerations with processes of argument and negotiation applies even more to the interpretation put upon the technological differences between the three products that discouraged Mick from his idea of dividing the organisation into three divisions. He makes powerful use of the 'contingency insight' that there needs to be a degree of 'fit' between structural arrangement – like whether or not the organisation is divisionalised – and the degree of technological variation between different parts of the organisation, when he recognises that divisionalisation would have been appropriate if there had there been more technological variation between the production of rail-buses, trams and 'road–rail buses'. But in the argument and negotiation that typically goes on within strategy-making processes, managers persuade Mick that the loss of economies of scale that divisionalisation would entail would not be justifiable.

In spite of the non-viability of the divisionalisation option, Mick seems convinced that the contingency of size is an issue. He associates it with the rigidity and heavy bureaucracy that he believes has been dogging Motoline. Hence an effective 'psycho-logical' reduction in size (in which people are in units they can more readily 'relate to') is *enacted* instead, with the move of emphasis onto smaller product and project teams. But this enactment itself came out of managerial debate and negotiation. This debate and negotiation, like that between Mick and Joy over such matters as having or not having mission statements and posters, presumably came about once more fundamental differences within the senior management of the company had been overcome. Mick tells us openly of some basic disagreements over values that he had with one of the two directors that he 'got rid of' early in his regime. This individual, Mick tells us, had values and worked with business assumptions that clashed with his own. But this man was also bringing to the processes of managerial debate and argument personal and group interests associated with what Mick labels his 'empire building'. Mick strongly objects to people who put their own 'hunger for power' in front of what he calls 'the interests of the wider working community'. Here we see personal values and beliefs playing a key role in strategy-making processes, as we indeed also see the role of power in the negotiation processes that go on. Mick does-n't just disagree with two of his fellow directors. He had the power to remove them. Some of this power undoubtedly played a part in his retention of the relationship with the trade unions and his commitment to a 'partnership' relationship with them. He gives a good pragmatic managerial argument for this element of his stra-tegy – as indeed he did for sacking the two directors – but he is quite explicit that his own family background and values also influenced him. We are back here to the importance of the personal values and interests on the part of strategy-makers that was emphasised in the last part of Chapter 6 (pp. 213–18).

 Link The changes being made in Motoline involve a significant shift in the *human resourcing strategy* of the organisation, as well as a modifying of its culture and structure. We will therefore return to Motoline later, in Chapter 11, in connection with HR strategy-making generally and the notion of part-nership relations with trade unions specifically.

Cultural analysis and manipulation

The part played by managers' personal values and beliefs in the strategic shap-ing of organisations is yet again shown by the Motoline case to be more important than has traditionally been recognised in the academic literature on strategy-making. But values play a part in every aspect of an organisation's functioning. Values are central components of every culture. This is recognised in the way cultures are conceptualised in *Organising and Managing Work* as sets of meanings and values shared by members of a social grouping (societies in Chapter 4, organisations in this and the previous chapter) that define how people should think and act with regard to their involvement in that social grouping. Given that cultures are very much about what *should* happen, it is not unreasonable to see cultures having at their hearts *moralities* ('systems' of values, that is). And managers wanting to analyse the culture of their organisations therefore find themselves having to make inferences about the moralities and values that are influencing behaviours in the organisations, as well as trying to work out the basic assumptions about the world that underpin these. This is challenging but even more challenging is the notion that managers might try to change or manipulate cultural elements of the organisation.

Link The connection between cultures and people's 'need for meaning' is central to the analysis of human identity and culture in Chapter 4, pp. 110–18.

Link Ethical questions about management were raised early in Chapter 1 (pp. 5–6) and will be returned to in Chapter 12, pp. 447–63.

The notion of cultural manipulation is challenging ethically because it raises the question of what right managers have to engage with the deeper beliefs and conceptions of right and wrong held by organisational employees. An implicit answer to this, and a justification for managers manipulating values and meanings in the workplace, is given in the book which first encouraged managers to try to change organisational cultures – Peters and Waterman's *In Search of Excellence* (1982, Reading Guide 16). These authors built upon the general anthropological argument that people have a strong *need for meaning*. They argued that if an employing organisation were to become an important source of meaning in the lives of their employees, then these employees would be willing to do a great deal for that organisation in return. This raises some serious ethical questions, given the considerable difference in power between corporate employers and individual employees. It is nevertheless a managerially attractive argument. It sees 'meanings' as part of what is 'traded' or strategically exchanged between the organisation and the employee. And this is the logic followed in cases like that of Motoline where managers attempt both to analyse and manipulate cultural aspects of life in the organisation as part of their strategic attempts to shape and control organisational activities.

Trying to manipulate cultural factors is, then, a challenging task ethically and practically. But the analysis of what the state of the 'organisational culture' is in the first place is also challenging. People's beliefs and, especially, their *values* (ideas about what is good and bad, right and wrong) are not easily identified when we are trying to analyse the cultural dimension of any given organisation. Just what values, let alone deeper assumptions about the world, are playing a part in an organisation at a particular time is only something we can *infer* from what we hear people say, from what we see people doing and from what we read into objects

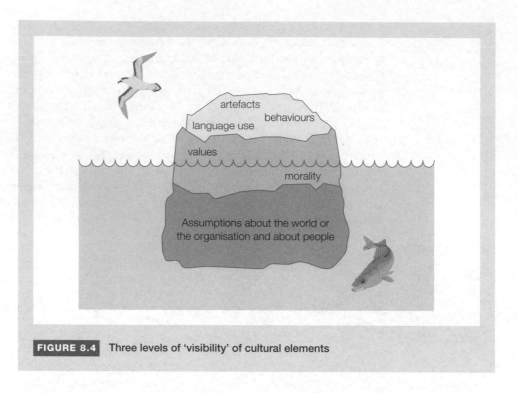

FIGURE 8.4 Three levels of 'visibility' of cultural elements

ranging from documents and the shape of buildings to signposts and the content of notice boards. And on the basis of the inferences that they make in this way about current values, people like Mick Moy and Joy Petty attempt to manipulate or change the cultural dimension of the organisations they are struggling to control.

The patterns of values, beliefs and assumptions that make up the 'culture' of a particular area of social life like a work organisation are not 'things' that we can readily analyse. But there are objects, behaviours and what people say or write that we can observe. Schein (1985, Reading Guide 19) pointed out in his influential writing on organisation cultures that some components of a culture are more visible or, we might say, 'readable' than others. Figure 8.4 is based on his analysis of three levels of culture, using the analogy of an iceberg to suggest that some elements are more visible than others because they are nearer to, or above, the surface of the sea in which the iceberg floats. One cannot see or hear the basic assumptions that people make about the nature of the world or about 'human nature' and one cannot touch or measure a morality. Values are not actually visible, of course, but values are perhaps a little more 'readable' than assumptions or moralities (moralities being 'systems' of values) in that one soon learns on entering any cultural context at least a little about what one should or should not do in that setting and what is regarded there as 'good' and 'bad'.

The main way we can try to analyse values, moralities and underlying assumptions is to pay attention to the top layer in Figure 8.4 – to artefacts, language use and behaviours. To analyse culture we look at these objects, words and activities and try to work out what they *symbolise*.

Symbol

Any act, word, sound or object acts as a symbol when it stands for 'something else' that is not visible, audible or tangible.

Although a manager's desk is, in one sense, 'just a desk', it can at the same time symbolise the authority of that individual. And the physical distance it puts between the manager and subordinate who sits in front of the desk can symbolise the social distance between the two people. An office cleaner's overall is, in one sense, just a garment that keeps the dirt off the rest of their clothes. At the same time, however, it symbolises their relatively low status in the organisation as well as the fact that by the time most of the main office workers have arrived at work this individual will have disappeared from view as they end their very early working shift. All of these symbols contribute to the overall culture or pattern of meanings that can be said to constitute an organisational culture.

Again, it is important to stress that an organisational culture cannot exist separately from the wider culture to which it relates (one in which office cleaners, say, have lower general social standing than the people who work in the offices they clean). And it is equally important to stress that there is unlikely to be a single monolithic culture to which every group and individual in the organisation subscribes. Not only are there official and unofficial dimensions to every organisation's cultural pattern but different sections of an organisation may have *subcultures* or even *contra-cultures*. We notice, for example, that Mick Moy refers in Cases and Conversations 8.1 to the research and development department of Motoline as 'a sort of subculture within the organisation'. He refers to them in this way because they were less 'bureaucratic' and worked more 'flexibly' than people in what he calls the 'main culture'.

Subculture/contra-culture

A *subculture* may be identified where a section of an organisation follows a cultural pattern that is a variation of the main organisational pattern of meanings and values. When such a pattern includes values that contradict the main organisational ones it is sometimes called a *contra-culture*.

Some of the concepts that can be used when analysing the culture aspects of an organisation are shown in Table 8.1, organised under the three categories that are shown in the top level of Figure 8.4 – artefacts, language use and behaviours. And, as we look at each of these and some of the examples that are given, we need to recognise that all of these can contribute to either the official aspects of the organisation's function or the unofficial aspects. Following the model represented earlier in Figure 7.2, however, we would expect strategy-making managers to aspire to a situation where all artefacts, language uses and behaviours contribute to one overall corporate culture in which official and unofficial aspects of the organisation have become 'one and the same' (p. 234).

TABLE 8.1 Elements of organisational culture to be considered in cultural analysis

Made objects

Artefacts *Concept*

Objects that have been created by human hands	Artefacts to analyse for symbolic meaning include tools, machines, documents, clothing, signs, badges, logos, building layouts, furnishings and décor

Language use

Jargon *Concept*

Language use and terms that are peculiar to a specific cultural setting	This can vary from the technical language of a group of specialist workers ('multi-platform support') to abbreviations and acronyms ('the DOD building') or organisational local slang ('the knobheads upstairs' or 'the pipe benders across the road')

Discourses *Concept*

Sets of connected concepts, expressions and statements that constitute a way of talking or writing about an aspect of the organisation, thus framing and influencing the way people understand and act with regard to that aspect of the organisation (see Chapter 4, p. 118)	It was observed in a study of managerial transition in a telephone systems manufacturing company that two competing discourses were being drawn on by managers. First, there was a *control, jobs and costs* discourse in which managers spoke and acted in the way favoured by an earlier regime in the company. Employees were regarded as having specified jobs that managers should try directly to control while all the time seeking opportunities to cut costs. Second, there was a newer way of 'framing' managerial activities (a *skills, empowerment and growth* discourse) in which employees were to be treated as people with bundles of skills who should be given discretion so that they act both to help their 'personal growth' and the growth of the business. Confusion arose as people swapped back and forth between the two discourses (Watson, 2001, Reading Guide 2)

Stories *Concept*

Simple narratives in which particular characters are reported to have acted in particular ways with certain effects	It is often noted that in organisational cultures which tend not to support high levels of cooperative activity stories are told that express cynicism about the organisation's management whereas in cultures that help further long-term organisational survival the stories that are told tend to illustrate and uphold practices that are 'positive' for the organisation as a whole

Jokes *Concept*

Humorous stories or pranks engaged in to cause amusement. Jokes and humour will be looked at again in Chapter 10, pp. 358–65	Taken on their own these may simply represent organisational members amusing each other at work. But the overall pattern of what is most joked about can be very significant. It was observed, for example, in a large shop that the jokes told by shop workers and the practical japes they indulged in frequently had a theme of the gullibility of the customers who used that shop. The management was aware of this and were disturbed that their employees valued the customers so negatively

Legends *Concept*

Narratives about events that might or might not have happened in the organisation's past, which have a sense of wonder about them and which point to activities that the listener is encouraged to admire or deplore	In a military unit, which had a reputation for high levels of morale, the tale was regularly told of the legendary soldier who had saved the lives of all of his comrades when a military exercise had gone badly wrong and their amphibious vehicle capsized when crossing a deep river. In another military unit, where morale was very poor, the legendary figure about whom admiring tales were told was a man who had gone absent without leave for more days than he had actually served. There was also a legend in this unit about a former sergeant major who regularly punished soldiers by setting them utterly impossible tasks (like climbing a vertical rock face in full battle kit). Officers and soldiers alike deplored his behaviour

Myths *Concept*

Narratives about events that are unlikely ever to have happened but which illustrate some important 'truth' about life in the organisation	There was a myth frequently referred to by the employees of an airline that told of an event in which both the pilot and the co-pilot were taken ill when the aircraft was in mid-Atlantic. Several of the cabin staff worked together, it is said, each drawing on their partial knowledge of cockpit procedures and closely guided by air 0traffic controllers, to bring the aircraft safely to land. Sometimes the story was told with the aircraft landing in the USA, sometimes in Hong Kong and sometimes in Australia. No names or times were ever specified

Language use (*continued*)

Sagas *Concept*

Narratives with a series of events that are said to have unfolded over time and which constitute an important part of the organisation's history

Part of the learning experience of every individual joining a certain bank was to be told the story of how the bank's founder was a poor refugee who came across the border into the country with a small sum of money that his dying father had given to him just before he started the long journey on foot to escape repression. Later this man had two sons and a beautiful daughter who married the son of another bank and … and … and so on

Heroes and villains *Concept*

Characters referred to in stories, jokes, legends, myths and sagas who are used either as inspirational figures ('role models') that current employees are encourage to emulate or as extreme indulgers in behaviours that employees are meant to avoid

The three soldiers, the airline cabin crew and the founder of the bank are all examples of heroes or villains. In a timber yard the employees picked out certain lorry drivers who delivered loads of wood to the yard as heroes and others as villains. These designations were related primarily to the care with which the lorry drivers had loaded their vehicles at the docks and, secondly, to how willing they were to help the workers do the unloading. A badly loaded lorry could be very dangerous for the timber yard workers who were unloading them. A myth existed that the timber yard's management paid a lower price for the dangerous deliveries. 'Good' lorry drivers were those who put fellow workers' safety before their own pockets. Villains were selfish individuals who also had 'traitorous dealings' with timber yard managers

Behaviours

Norms of behaviour *Concept*

Regularly recurring pieces of behaviour that become accepted in the organisation as 'the way things are done'

It was normal and unquestioned in a particular government agency for managers at all levels to call non-managerial staff by their first names. They also, like the rest of the staff, called junior and middle-level managers by their first names. But everyone gave senior managers the title Mr, Mrs or Miss (even if, before promotion, they had been addressed by their first names). A new senior manager joined the agency and asked to be addressed as Joyce or, if they felt awkward about this, Ms Smith. Everybody insisted on calling her 'Miss Smith', however

Rituals *Concept*

Patterns of behaviour that regularly occur in particular circumstances or at particular times in an organisation

In a large joinery workshop the joiners would start every morning after clocking in (and therefore officially starting their working shift) by putting on the kettle, making tea and drinking it. After precisely twenty minutes they would wash their cups and start to work. Supervisors followed the associated ritual of staying in their offices, with their backs to the working area, reading their newspapers for twenty minutes

Rites *Concept*

Rituals that are more formally (though not necessarily officially) organised and pre-planned

Every worker in a printing works, upon becoming fully qualified as a printer, would be stripped naked by the other workers and intimate parts of their bodies blackened with ink. There was considerable consternation across the organisation as the day approached when the first women printer was to end her apprenticeship. She insisted on receiving the traditional treatment, in spite of strong management objections. She believed she would never be fully accepted by her fellow workers unless she underwent this ordeal

Actions leading to reward and punishments

Actions either complying with or failing to comply with the values or rules of the culture (the official or the unofficial culture) so leading to either positive or negative sanctions

In one university department promotions always went to people whose research was in the same area as the head of the department, regardless of whether they were making a good or bad job of their teaching or administrative responsibilities. In another department, promotions typically went to staff members who were the longest serving, regardless of their performance. In a third department it was staff who achieved a balance between good teaching, significant research output and administrative efficiency that were favoured when promotions were available

Each of the elements or indicators of organisational culture (or organisational subculture) identified in Table 8.1 can be used analytically to try to understand the cultural characteristics of any given organisation. However, the organisational examples given in the table prompt us to recognise that all of these dimensions can also be seen as 'variables'. They are factors that managers attempting to shape the culture of the organisation often try to manipulate. The point of doing this is to try to influence managerially the artefacts, language usages and behaviours in the organisation so that they symbolise values and encourage activities that fit with, rather than undermine, the strategic direction that the managers want the organisation to follow. Again following the logic of managers trying to bring official and unofficial thinking and practices into line with each other, we would expect to see managerial attempts to manipulate the 'variables' categorised in Table 8.1. To enhance managerial control, managers might thus be expected to try to make artefacts, language usages and behaviours work *for* the organisation's long-term success, as they interpret this, rather than *against* it.

Certain strategic managers in the company referred to under the 'discourse' entry in Table 8.1, for example, were trying to make the *skills, empowerment and growth* discourse the official and dominant one. There were, however, managers (some of these in very senior positions) unofficially still trying to frame company activities in the *control, jobs and costs* terms that key organisational strategists were trying to move away from. The result of this was a degree of cultural confusion and perceived inconsistency in values and practices across the plant (Watson, 2001, Reading Guide 2). The airline's myth referred to in the table would seem, on the other hand, to be one where an element of culture has simultaneous official and unofficial currency. And the saga of the bank's founder is clearly one that is transmitted as part of the official culture of the bank – with an aspiration that it will not be unofficially resisted we might assume. The initiation ritual that occurs in the printing works is clearly an unofficial cultural phenomenon, however. But the company's management is becoming worried about it because, we can assume, they feel that its continuation will clash with official values about the 'decent' and fair treatment of all its employees, male and female.

Activity 8.2

Re-read the Motoline story (Cases and Conversations 8.1) and note:

- what *assumptions* Mick and Joy have analysed as underpinning the existing Motoline culture (the bottom level of Figure 8.4);

- what values or matters of organisational morality do they provide us evidence about (the middle level of Figure 8.4);

- what artefacts, language usages or behaviours are referred to in their account (the top level of Figure 8.4).

Having completed this analysis, turn your attention to the extent of cultural manipulation that is going on at Motoline. Using both Figure 8.4 and Table 8.1, note down:

- any ways in which Mick and Joy have already attempted to bring about some cultural change with regard to any of these elements or indicators of the organisational culture;

- any ways in which you think they could go further into trying to shape the cultural aspects of the Motoline company.

Mick Moy tells us that he has detected an assumption among people at Motoline that the 'world owes us living' and he sees this as a legacy of a time when governments were rather undemanding customers who paid whatever it cost to produce what they ordered. Mick clearly wants to change this assumption and suggests that he must move to a culture based on the assumption that customer and passenger ('end user') requirements are more important than 'engineering excellence' for its own sake. To do this he is going to point out that such a change is vital to Motoline's very 'survival'. To be successful in this he will have to tackle the defensive attitude of employees. Joy, in referring to a 'defensive' culture implies that there is a basic assumption operating at Motoline that people cannot be trusted. This is presumably connected to what she calls a 'culture of blame'. Mick and Joy see it as vital to change this together with changing the way people tend to value their own area of activity above their involvement in Motoline as a company. They wish to bring about shared values that not only focus on customers but also value the organisation as a cooperative entity. This presumably would include valuing women as well as men – moving beyond the 'macho culture' that Joy mentions.

At the level of behaviours there are clearly numerous norms of behaviour associated with this cultural pattern that Joy and Mick want to change. One ritual in particular is noted as symptomatic of the culture that has to be changed – the practice of including 'independent witnesses' in meetings between people from departments whose members do not trust each other. The 'Getting On Track' seminars are clearly a key tool that Mick and Joy are using to change this pattern and Joy speaks of getting people to value each other differently – as 'internal customers'. Here is a piece of language use that they are encouraging as part of the cultural change or manipulation work they are undertaking. This is something also seen in the 'Getting On Track' title given to the change programme as well as illustrated by the job title that Joy chose for herself. She says explicitly that her title as Director of Quality and Corporate Development was chosen to be 'highly symbolic of the cultural direction' in which they want the company to move. Joy seems to have a high level of sensitivity to symbolism in the organisation that perhaps suggests that there was an anthropological element in her university social science studies. This sensitivity leads her to counsel Mick against the type of language he uses and that many managers develop when trying to manipulate cultures – mission statements, posters, values statements and slogans about 'delighting passengers', as Joy puts it. She judges that this kind of managerial talk would be counter-productive within the local culture that employees relate to.

A very interesting and subtle piece of conscious cultural manipulation occurs with the ritual of certain workers wearing a project-group T-shirt on Fridays. This particular clothing artefact, with its project-based logo on the front, was presumably welcome to Mick and Joy, because it recognised a high level of team commitment and the use of humour to support group solidarity. Yet there was a worry on Mick's part that the corporate logo was missing. He was keen on high group morale, but he wanted this to be tied into a corporate consciousness. Hence his willingness to pay for replacement shirts that included the company logo. Here is a highly sophisticated example of a manager trying to bring unofficial and official aspects of culture together through a minor alteration to one relatively minor artefact. Joy clearly admires Mick for the subtlety with which he has done this. 'What that shirt symbolises is considerable', she points out. But perhaps the most significant way in which Mick and Joy have acted to change the cultural pattern of the organisation is through the policy of sending employees out to meet customers and passengers. The union convenor clearly sees the symbolism of this when he tells Mick that he wants employees to get literally 'close to customers'. The implication is that more than lip service is being paid to ideas of people becoming actively committed to furthering the Motoline business. Cultural change attempts are recognised by these strategy-makers, Mick Moy and Joy Petty, as being about changing how people are rewarded, changing task structures and changing relationships between different parts of the organisation's overall structure. Again, structure and culture come together as closely related aspects of managerial attempts to shape organisations to take them into a long-term future.

In Chapter 9 the focus moves towards more detailed aspects of how tasks are structured in organisations and how people are 'motivated' to do these tasks.

Summary

In this chapter the following key points have been made:

- There is managerial scope about how tight (or direct) or loose (or indirect) the bureaucratic controls applying to any given organisation are.

- Some circumstances or *contingencies* that organisations face tend to 'fit' with stricter or more directly ('mechanistic') bureaucratic controls while others fit better with looser or more indirect ('organic') ones. However, contingencies such as those of organisational size, technology or business environment do not determine or directly influence the type of structure and culture to be found in any given organisation. Structural and cultural decisions result from the way strategy-making managers interpret and *enact* these contingencies in a context of managerial argument and negotiation in which personal and group values and interests play an important part.

- It is possible to analyse the cultural situation of any organisation and make inferences about values and assumptions through examining organisational artefacts, behaviours and language uses – both 'official' and 'unofficial'. The cultural factors that one looks at when doing a cultural analysis – from artefacts, discourses, stories, legends and myths to rites, rituals and norms of behaviour – can also be seen as 'variables' that managers attempt to manipulate. This is not something that can be separated from attempts at structural manipulation, however. The organisation-shaping aspect of strategy-making typically involves simultaneous attention to cultural and structural matters. Both of these need to be seen as part of the general, and only ever partially achieved, striving for control that all managerial work entails.

Reading

Reading Guides 16 and 19, especially, contain material that supports and takes further much of what is covered in Chapter 8.

Shaping tasks and winning cooperation

Objectives

Having read this chapter and completed its associated activites, readers should be able to:

- See that those aspects of the organisation of work at the level of basic task performance that are often treated as separate matters – motivation, leadership and job design – are better understood as closely related aspects of managerial task shaping and the winning of employee cooperation.

- Recognise the advantages of considering organisational members' *orientations to work* and the *strategic exchanges* that occur in the context of the employment relationship rather than focus on people's general 'motivation to work'.

- Recognise the advantages of focusing on the managerial manipulation of employees' perceived *implicit contracts* rather than on managerial efforts to 'motivate' employees.

- Understand the extent to which there is negotiation and bargaining within the associated processes of 'motivation', 'leadership' and job design.

- Appreciate the importance of the *indulgency patterns* that arise – the implicit 'give and take' practices that can be observed in the relationships between workers and supervisors or managers.

- Question the value of concentrating on leadership and, especially, motivation theories.

- Appreciate that so-called 'process' theories of motivation like 'equity' and 'expectancy' theories nevertheless contain important insights that fit with the basic *strategic exchange* analysis developed in this chapter.

- Apply the concepts of *direct* and *indirect* managerial control attempts that were developed in the previous chapter to the *principles of work design* that have influenced the *job design practices* which have developed over the history of industrial capitalist economies.

continued

● Understand how the application of different types of work design principles at different times can be related to the basic managerial problem of handling contradictions in the basic industrial and organisational system.

● Appreciate the ways in which values, choices and contingent circumstances influence the enactment of specific job designs – and are an element of the more general and strategic organisation-shaping processes that were identified in Chapter 8.

Beyond motivation, leadership and job design

In one sense, the organising and managing of work can never 'go beyond' issues of motivating organisational members, asking some organisational employees to play a more leading role than others in the workplace or giving thought to what sort of tasks are to be allocated to different people. The issues are always there and have to be tackled. However, where we need to move forward in our thinking (as many already have done in their managerial practice) is to go beyond treating matters of motivating, leading and shaping tasks as separate matters. Indeed, we must be careful not to go too far in separating these from the questions of broader organisational culture and structure that were considered in the last chapter or from the policies and practices in what is increasingly called 'human resource management' that will be considered in Chapter 11. One cannot write a book on organising and managing work without some kind of separation of issues into chapters any more than one can produce an educational programme without some kind of division of material into 'subjects' and 'modules'. However, as our earlier critique of much management education suggested (pp. 11–15), there is a tendency to go too far in treating separately different facets of organising and managing ('organisational behaviour' and 'strategy', for example), and we will typically find that a book with an 'organisational behaviour' type of title will have separate chapters on 'motivation', 'leadership' and 'job design'. Yet ask any manager trying to direct the activities of an organisational section, department or function where the 'motivating' aspect of their work stops and 'leadership' starts. Even if they accepted the value of these concepts for understanding the work that they do, they would be hard pressed to explain how they differed in practice.

One might similarly ask any manager tackling issues of how tasks in an organisational department are going to be shaped and allocated whether this 'job design' work is simply a matter of the efficient sharing out of work tasks. No, they are likely to reply, a key consideration has to be how effectively different patterns of tasks and roles will 'motivate' or fail to motivate the people undertaking them. To choose whether, on the one hand, to ask employees to tackle the same simple task day in, day out or, on the other hand, to give each individual a variety of challenging tasks to do, requires giving thought to how those employees are likely to react in 'motivational' terms to such arrangements. If 'job designers' find themselves deciding to group people into work teams, it is unlikely to be long before they are talking about the need to design into the teamwork arrangements a role for a team *leader*. In practice, then, those matters that are typically treated as separate issues within orthodox managerial/academic discourses are closely interrelated.

The general meanings of the words that are used in this area would suggest this close interrelationship. When managers 'lead' people, our dictionaries suggest, they are getting people to 'go along with them'. When they 'motivate' them, they are providing 'a stimulus to some kind of action'. These two things are clearly closely interrelated, and both are relevant to the work managers do when they design jobs – when they lay down the patterns of tasks that people are required to undertake. The cluster of tasks that any particular individual is asked to undertake will typically have been designed by managers to get their workers to 'go along with them' and to contain 'stimuli to action'. But managers do not do any of these things in their own departments or sections in isloation from what is going on more generally across the organisation in which they are involved. All of this motivating, leading and patterning of tasks happens in the context of the broader structural and cultural patterns that were looked at in Chapters 7 and 8. And, especially important as we shall see, is the extent to which the structure and culture of the organisation tends towards the use of *direct* or *indirect* attempts to achieve managerial control (pp. 302–5). Managerial control is something that will never be completely achieved however hard managers work in *attempting* to achieve it. And the *productive cooperation* that managers are required to pursue will never be complete. Whatever productive cooperation is achieved has to be worked for. It has to be 'won'.

Motivating, leading and job designing are facets of this attempt to 'win cooperation' and they are often indistinguishable from each other in practice. We could say, though, that:

- when people speak of 'motivation' they tend to focus on aspects of the *people doing work tasks*;

- when people speak of 'leadership' they tend to focus on aspects of the *person trying to influence the carrying out of those tasks*;

- when people speak of 'job design' they tend to focus on the *tasks themselves* and in using the word 'design' are perhaps linking activities at the local level back to the way the organisation as a whole is structured, particularly in terms of either a *direct* or an *indirect* control emphasis.

Motivation, leadership and job design need to be regarded as closely interrelated aspects of patterning of activities and understandings across the whole work organisation. And this means remembering that no manager works outside the basic structure and ethos of the organisation that employs them. The present chapter nevertheless tends to concentrate on activities at a more 'local' level within the organisation. It looks at those issues that are traditionally tackled under the traditional headings of motivation, leadership and work design as different facets of the overall processes that occur within task management practices and within the patterns of relationship, rivalry, adjustment and negotiated order that enable productive co-operation (p. 60) to occur to a level that allows the organisation to continue in existence into the future. This means operating in the spirit of process-relational thinking that has been developed over the earlier chapters and focusing, specifically on processes of strategic exchange that make productive task performance possible. Already, the development of this way of thinking about work and its management has questioned the value of the social science concept of 'motivation' as a tool for analysing and understanding why people do what they do at work – or anywhere else for that matter.

Link   The problems with an emphasis on motives and motivation in understanding human behaviour were discussed in Chapter 4, pp. 98–104.

'Motivation' was shown in Chapter 4 to be a concept that is rooted in systems-control thinking about human beings and their behaviour in which the person is seen as 'a little machine-like system in which goals or "motives" operate as a motor "powering" the human entity so that it behaves in a particular way' (p. 97).

The story of Grant Park and his coffee drinking activities was used in Chapter 4 to demonstrate that motives are not usefully seen as things that people 'have' which *precede* behaviour (in the modernist tradition of dualism and linear think-ing) (pp. 99–100). Instead, it was argued, 'motives' have to be seen as social rather than purely individual phenomena – often acting as justifications of a piece of behaviour made after the event rather than as causal springs of action or 'triggers' of behaviours. What people do (whether it be to commit a murder or to work hard at a desk all day to please a boss) is an outcome of a multiplicity of factors going way beyond the straightforward fulfilling of motives or the meeting of needs. Whereas systems-control thinking sees human behaviours occurring as individuals who are *motivated* to fulfil *needs* and *wants*, process-rela-tional thinking sees actions taking place 'in the light of interpretations made about the world, to *enact* whatever *projects* individuals who are undertaking *strategically* to shape their lives and to manage *existential challenges*' (Table 4.1, p. 105). Thus, if we want to understand what is 'motivating' a particular individual to behave in a particular way at work we would look at their overall *work orienta-tion* – the meaning that they currently attach to their work. And this orientation has emerged in the light of their idea of 'who they are' (their identity) and 'where they are going in life' (their personal *strategic shaping*). It is also an aspect of how they are handling life's anxieties and the pressures of their circumstances – matters ranging from how their family is to be fed to ones of values and, say, of conscience about what one 'ought to be doing with one's life'.

Link   'Work orientation' as an alternative to the idea of 'work motivation' was introduced in Chapter 5, pp. 126–38 . At the centre of the individual's orientation to work was shown to be the way they perceive the *implicit contract* they have with their employer.

From 'worker motivation' to work orientations and strategic exchange

What all of this implies is that we need to stop focusing on people's 'motives' and look at what people are thinking and doing within the broader context of the *strategic exchange* relationships between employing organisations and employees. People going to work in organisations are involved in strategically shaping their lives and organisations themselves have to be shaped strategically to trade with a whole range of constituencies. Employers and employees come together in an exchange that helps both parties fulfil their respective strategies. And the 'strategy' of the employee can be understood as their basic *orientation to work*. This is something much more subtle, much more complex and much more dynamic than 'motives'.

Activity 9.1

Reread the stories of Ravi Barr (Cases and Conversations 5.1) and Sacha and the seven dwarves (Cases and Conversations 5.2)

- to remind yourself of the extent to which people's orientation to work (their overall 'work motivation' as it might be called) varies

at different times of their life and in different circumstances,

- to recognise that the efforts of managers and supervisors in the workplace to 'motivate' their staff are only one factor in the resulting 'motivational' state of those staff.

In considering these two stories and what they tell us about the variations that can exist between how people are oriented to (or 'motivated within') their work it readily becomes apparent that we tend to use the notion of motivation in two ways when we look at work behaviour and meaning, as is noted in Table 9.1.

TABLE 9.1 Two ways in which we talk about 'motivation' in the work context	
Motivation as *the factors leading a person to behave in a certain way at work* (this is similar to the *strategic-exchange* notion of a person's orientation to work)	Motivation as *managerial action to influence the people's behaviour at work so they perform as managers require* (in *strategic-exchange* terms, this entails managerial manipulation of the implicit contract to get people to behave in a way that leads to productive cooperation)
We say, for example, that a person's 'motivation' has changed when their orientation to work has shifted from one where they sought to maximise their cash return from the employer while showing little interest in the employer's business to one where they concentrate on making a conscientious input to developing the business with a view to building up to a high salary level later in their career	We often say that part of a manager's job is to 'motivate' their staff: find a way of getting them to act in a way that fits with organisational requirements. A manager might observe that his or her staff is primarily interested in short-term cash reward and prefer to be told exactly what to do. However, the manager decides that it is necessary for these staff to involve themselves in finding new ways of doing the job. They might therefore talk of 'motivating my people differently'. This might involve persuading them they will find taking more initiative within their jobs rewarding

In the case of Ravi Barr in Cases and Conversations 5.1 we notice how a variety of factors in his life experience and his changing notion of identity led to changes in how he was broadly oriented towards work at different times. This could be expressed in terms of how his 'motivation' varied from circumstance to circumstance. The term 'orientation' is preferred, however, because it suggests the relevance of a wider variety of factors influencing the way an individual thinks and behaves at work than something as simplistic as a set of 'motives'. It might be reasonable to use the notion of motive to label a simple interest in maximising one's income. However, it is less helpful when it comes to considering such matters as the way in which one expresses one's identity in one's work or the way one develops a working career to fit into a changing set of life priorities or circumstances. We can see the same problem when we look at the staff who work in Sacha's public relations department in Cases and Conversations 5.2. The original 'poor motivation' of Biffy and Sniffy, for example, simply cannot be put down to something as simple as 'motives'. Their problems appear to Sacha to be related to problems of identity arising from the loss of their jobs as journalists. Complex problems of marital disharmony and alcoholism were related to this. But their changed work orientations (to a 'positive motivation', as some would put it) seem to have come from changes that they made in their private lives rather than from direct managerial efforts to 'motivate them'. Sacha does claim a part in this change by pointing to her threat to them that they would have to 'ship out' if they did not 'shape up'. For all we know this might have been crucial in getting both men to reconsider what they were doing with their lives, but it can hardly be recognised as a case of a manager 'motivating' a member of staff. Sacha has made a significant managerial intervention, it would seem, but it was an intervention rooted in a subtle consideration of a range of factors influencing the men's lives. It was also risky: the men could have been alienated even more from their work as public relations officers and descended even faster into personal and work troubles.

Trying to influence employees' work orientations is a much more complex matter than simply seeking to 'motivate' them by trying to 'meet their needs' – as much of the standard motivational thinking has it (and to which we will return shortly). One reason for this complexity is the fact, demonstrated in Ravi's case as well as in the case of Smithy (Sacha's third public relations officer), that work orientations are highly influenced by aspects of people's lives outside the workplace. This is not to say that organisational influences are not themselves of enormous importance. And here, what might seem at first sight like fairly simple changes can have considerable effects. Sacha tells us how Snippy's approach to her work and to relationships in the office have changed significantly since her desk was moved from a relatively central position in the room. The office re-arrangement can be understood as a matter of change in job design – the pattern of tasks and work roles and how these relate to each other is inevitably changed whenever one changes the physical layout of a workplace, however minor this may be. But this has changed the 'reward' side of the perceived implicit contract at the heart of Snippy's work orientation. The pleasure of being at the centre of the office's social life and being able to joke with everybody that entered the office has gone away. And Sacha is thinking about how she can intervene in this. We can infer that she is considering trying to bring something of this back into the informal contract with Snippy when she tells us that she is going to have to 're-think the office layout'.

From 'motivating people' to the manipulation of implicit contracts

By manipulating Snippy's work orientation Sacha is, in orthodox terms, trying to 're-motivate' her. But equally one could say she is attempting this shift in orientation by engaging in some minor job re-design. One might even say she is displaying a degree of subtle 'leadership'. The same might be said of the case of Sparky. Sacha recognises that his job has changed – it has become more routine and is thus less intrinsically satisfying for him. But Sparky is happy with his salary and his job security. Such are the complexities and the multiplicity of factors that come into the work orientation of any individual and the implicit contract between them and the employer. Sacha has considered manipulating this by promoting him but, given that this is not feasible, she is talking of finding 'some exciting new project' that will turn him on. Again we can ask whether what is going on here is 'motivation', 'job design' or 'leadership'. It is hard to separate these out. And it is unnecessary. It is more helpful simply to recognise that:

- managerial work involves getting employees to do things that they might not otherwise do;

- to do this managers have to understand the complexities of employees' work orientations;

- any attempt to change these must involve making some adjustment in the individuals' perceived implicit contract – the way employees understand the relationship between what they are 'putting in' to the job and what 'they are taking out' of the employment relationship;

- to change an implicit contract there is bound to be a degree of bargaining, but all negotiations over the 'employment trade' always relate to all the *strategic exchanges* which both the individual and the organisation are making and occur within a relationship involving power differences. The managers, as the employer's agents, with all the organisation's resources behind them, typically having a power advantage over the employees.

Manipulating employees' perceived implicit contract   *Concept*

This is at the centre of all motivational, leadership and job design work done by managers. Tasks are shaped and rewards are offered as part of a bargaining process in which managers try to persuade employees to work in the way they want them to work.

TABLE 9.2 An 'input – reward' representation of how employees perceive their implicit contract with the employing organisation

Employee input	Employee reward
● physical effort	● money
● mental effort	● job satisfaction
● initiative	● personal 'growth'
● responsibility	● social reward
● impairment – *fatigue*, *risk of injury etc.*	● security
● compliance – *acceptance of a degree*	● power
of managerial control	● status
	● career potential

All motivational, leadership and work design efforts made by managers attempt to influence employee behaviours by influencing the employee's perception or understanding of the contract that is at the heart of the *employment relationship*. How people behave in the workplace is fundamentally influenced by their understanding of the 'employment deal' which, following the analysis provided in Chapter 5 (p. 130), is represented in Table 9.2.

Managers, in 'leading' or getting workers to go along with them, in 'motivating' or giving them incentives to act in a certain way and in shaping their tasks are necessarily involved in complex processes of negotiation. Recognition of this is central to process-relational thinking. It is not just a matter of negotiating with workers what tasks they do or how much they are to be paid for doing those tasks. It is a negotiation over the basic 'realities' of the employment relationship. Within the power relationship within which the employment relationship is always set ('if, in the end, you do not do what we ask, you will lose your job') the manager has to establish a pattern of workplace relations and understandings. Within this, the employees have to be persuaded that there is a fair and reasonable return for the efforts and initiatives that they make, the risks to health and mental well-being that they take, and the degree of managerial authority over them that they accept. That return will be a complex mix of monetary, psychological and social rewards. It will be a mix of so much pay, so much security, so much opportunity for career advancement, so much social 'standing' and so on, that makes a fair balance, in the employees' mind with what is being asked of those employees by the employer.

Activity 9.2

Read the story that Dal Cross tells in Cases and Conversations 9.1 about the foundry yard gang and

- use as many as possible of the elements or 'headings' in the model of the general 'implicit contract' identified in Figure 9.2 to make sense of the yard gang's perceived implicit contract with their employer – the one that prevailed before Dal Cross arrived;

- consider what actions Dal might consider, in terms of manipulating the perceived implicit contract, to change the yard gang's way of working, and stop it being necessary to have a foreman or manager sitting in the office all day turning requests from across the site into direct orders to be given to the 'yardies'.

Dal Cross and the recalcitrant yardies

Cases and Conversations 9.1

I think I learned everything I know about the management basics from that six months when I was put in charge of the people who do the outdoor work in our foundries. I had only been with the company for about eighteen months and was coming towards the end of the management-training programme. My final 'attachment', as they called them in those days, was to work with the foundry works manager. This man turned out to be quite different from what I expected. He was a highly qualified metallurgist and he prided himself on being an educated and cultivated individual who, at the same time, had a 'common touch' when it came to his relationships with foundry workers. I'll never forget the words he used when I went to see him to discuss the assignment he was going to give me. He said, 'I can give you a job which, if you succeed with it, will teach you all the basics about managing in this sort of business', and he then used this unforgettable phrase, 'I want you to sort out my recalcitrant yardies'. That night, as you might guess, I looked up the word recalcitrant in my dictionary. It said something like 'not susceptible to control or authority'. What was I taking on?

I had not, in those days, heard of Jamaican 'yardy' gangs and immediately recognised who he was talking about when he pointed out of the window at a couple of men who were slowly – incredibly slowly – sweeping up a section of the factory yard opposite the works manager's office. Their foreman was about to retire and I was to take over from him for a six-month period. The brief was to 'sort things out' and recommend to the works manager what should be done about a permanent replacement for the foreman who, the works manager said, he was 'damned glad to see the back of'. I have to admit that I was rather nervous about taking this on. But I had been complaining to the training manager that I wanted a 'real management assignment' in which I would not only learn about doing management but 'prove myself' as a manager. I'd asked for everything I was going to get, hadn't I?

The foundry site had been developing over 30 to 40 years and it had become a complex jungle of buildings and workshops with all sorts of alley ways leading off the twisting main road that ran through the site. The role of the dozen or so yardmen was to keep these ways clear, clean and safe. They were also responsible for moving materials and 'work in progress' about between buildings on the various motorised trucks and hand pushed carts that they controlled. The responsibility for scrap handling was also theirs.

The work was very hard and often very dirty. One minute they were shifting foundry sand, the next minute carting heavy castings from the furnace room to the fettling shop and soon after that they were having to sweep floodwater away after a heavy rainstorm or shovel snow or ice off the roadways. The work could be dangerous, especially given the cramped areas they often worked in and the heavy and awkward material they

sometimes had to handle. And there was a degree of responsibility with this work. Some of the moulds or patterns that they moved about were very fragile, as were some of the ceramic cores that they handled. One slip with these items and not only was money lost but the production schedule could be completely blown. On top of that, the scrap was often quite valuable and the security people were always anxious that no one with a criminal record or with criminal contacts should be in the gang. Scrap thieving can be quite a lucrative activity around engineering works, you know.

What was obvious to me from the moment I began meeting members of the gang was that they took no initiative whatsoever. They wouldn't even sweep up a broken beer bottle in the middle of the car park without being instructed to do so, I discovered. The foreman had insisted that no work be done unless it was under his instruction. Members of the gang had to do exactly what he told them. If any one of them disobeyed him they would find themselves spending a disproportionate amount of time cleaning lavatories. When I looked at the wages that the blokes got they seemed fairly reasonable to me. They compared well with other manual workers who did not have a skilled trade. It seemed that the relatively dangerous and physically uncomfortable aspects of the job were well compensated for by the fairly high security of employment that the job gave them. The foreman might have been a bossy so-and-so but he made sure that his blokes stayed in work if they went along with him. Nevertheless I was quite puzzled at first that they were willing to put up with the heaviness of the control that he exerted. But after a few days I realised that this was balanced by the space he gave them for 'having a laugh together', as they put it. He allowed them longer tea breaks than any other workers took and he turned a blind eye to their practice of 'taking it easy' for the last half-hour of each working day. I knew that other supervisors across the site resented all of this, both because it undermined their own authority with their workers and because they often found themselves unable to get things moved towards the end of a shift or when the yardies were finishing off their card game during a protracted tea break. But few complained too loudly to the yard foreman because he would 'punish' them by ensuring that their 'breakages' increased for a few days or by saying that he had no truck available to move their goods.

There seemed few satisfactions for the yardies in the tasks that they did but I think they nevertheless enjoyed coming to work. And although, in one sense, their status was low as an unskilled group who had some pretty unpleasant tasks to do, they did carry a certain perverse status among the workforce. This was because of the informal privileges they enjoyed as a result of their foreman's power to protect them from any disciplines that might come from another direction. Nobody, including the works manager, dared question what went on. Too much boat-rocking would follow from upsetting the yardies.

Some of the other supervisors used to call the foreman the 'yard führer' and one of them, who had an Italian background, simply called him 'Il Duce'. This name-calling was obviously more than a matter of people with a knowledge of languages using the German or the Italian word for 'leader'! And if I was going to follow my own beliefs about good leadership in my six months with these men, I was going to have to make some big changes. I had to run things the old way at first, however. If I hadn't, the foundry would have ground to a halt. No man was willing to move from the rest room until he had an instruction from me. When I suggested that they all surely knew 'what needed doing on a Monday morning if they thought about it', they responded that they 'were not paid to think'. That was the foreman's job. But after a couple of days sitting at the old fore-man's desk receiving phone calls from around the site asking for a truck here, a lavatory cleaner there, a bin emptied somewhere else and an oil leak cleared up outside the main waxroom – and then despatching the appropriate yardy for that job – I was even more convinced that I had to change things.

The implicit contract between the company and the yard gang members, as Dal Cross understands it, is as complex as one we might find with any group of workers. On the employee 'input' side of the trade there is clearly a high level of physical effort required and the yardies subject themselves to a degree of 'impairment' by getting quite dirty and risking accidents in some of the danger-ous conditions they meet. They do not appear to make much input by way of initiative-taking, however, and the responsibilities they bear are of a relatively passive kind. They simply have to take care not to damage fragile items that they are moving about. But this is a heavier responsibility than it might at first sound, since damage to some of these goods could harm the overall perform-ance of the foundry as a business operation. We might imagine, though, that the foreman himself would take formal responsibility for such damage, given that he exerts so much direct control over the yard gang's work. The approach he takes to his job means that anyone working in his gang has to surrender a significant amount of personal autonomy while at work. For the rewards that they receive, these men have to submit to a high level of direction from a 'boss'.

The pay that the yardies received, Dal infers, was not an issue. Taken together with the other rewards, an acceptable balance between the two sides of the effort bargain had been struck. Security of employment was clearly a significant factor on the reward side. There appeared to Dal to be little reward in terms of job satisfaction, personal growth or career potential. But we can imagine that they felt some degree of power through their being identified with the power that the foreman himself had over other supervisors and managers. Dal cer-tainly notes a degree of 'perverse' status coming from certain advantages that the yardies had over other foundry workers. They had a greater opportunity to enjoy leisure at work than any other group, for example. It can be inferred that these lengthy card-playing tea breaks and the winding-down time provided the yardies with a degree of 'social reward' in the workplace. It was a fairly distinc-tive factor going into the mix or balance of 'inputs' and 'outputs' that makes up the implicit contract of this particular group of workers with the employing organisation. It was at the core of their work orientation and is thus something that anybody would need to appreciate – Dal Cross included – who wanted to understand why the yardies thought and behaved in the way they did with regard to their work.

The implicit contract has just been referred to as a trade that goes on between employees and the employing organisation. But, of course, 'the organisation' is not literally a trader itself. The bargain that we say, in a short-hand way, 'the organisation' is making with its employees is in fact made in the organisation's name by the various managers, personnel recruitment staff and supervisors with whom the individual deals at different stages of their entry to and continuing involvement in the organisation. And where there is a manager or supervisor directly involved in shaping the everyday activities of any individual or group of individuals there will necessarily be a degree of day-to-day negotiation or *give and take* about what work is done and how and when it is done. The works manager clearly saw the yard gang as an especially 'recalcitrant' group – clearly thinking of the yardies and the foreman together as a group that had managed to get itself in some ways 'above the law' that applied to other groups under the works manager's authority. However, we could say that all employees – all human beings indeed – are recalcitrant to a degree (see the earlier discussion of this, pp. 6, 74–5). Every manager, schoolteacher or parent knows that the employees, pupils or children formally 'under their control' will never follow every instruction that they are given or submit totally to every rule that is meant to shape their behaviour. There has to be a degree of 'give and take' which allows the person in authority to get 'some of their own way' in return for allowing those subject to that authority to 'get away' with infringing some of the rules which, if followed in every detail, would turn the individual into a puppet or a robot rather than a human being with free-will and personal autonomy. Gouldner, in a classic study of factory life (1964, Reading Guide 16), conceptualised as an *indulgency pattern* the tendency he saw for supervisors to 'turn a blind eye' to certain rule-breaking activities. The supervisors did this as part of an implicit understanding that the workers would, reciprocally, indulge the supervisors when they sought compliance over matters that the workers might reasonably refuse to go along with.

Indulgency pattern   *Concept*

The ignoring by supervisors or managers of selected rule infringements by workers in return for those workers conceding to requests that, strictly speaking, they could refuse.

The joiners' shop ritual reported in Chapter 8 (p. 271) whereby the joiners always used the first twenty minutes of their shift to take an 'illegal tea break' while the supervisors deliberately kept their backs to the working areas for the same period of time is an example of a ritualised expression of an indulgency pattern. In this case a particularly assertive manual work group is ritually demonstrating that it only cooperates with 'management' on its own terms, and the supervisors are ritually displaying their acceptance of this. A more typical indulgency pattern, however, is one in which a manager ignores their staff taking an extra long lunch break once a week to do their shopping, in return for those employees complying with the occasional short notice request to do some overtime or to cover for another worker who has not turned up for work. The yardies' foreman clearly indulges his staff by allowing them to take long breaks and to stop working well before the official finishing time. This, we can reasonably infer, is a trade. It is a conceding of free time during working hours in return for the workers allowing the supervisor to have an unusually high level of task control over them.

It is clear that implicit contracts have some very subtle aspects to them. The very fact that they involve a range of formally unstated agreements makes the managerial 'motivational' task quite a subtle and challenging one. The manager is constantly bargaining with the people that in traditional 'organisation behaviour' terms he or she is said to be 'motivating' or 'leading'. And, given that managers are frequently required to take initiatives to make changes in work behaviour, they face the considerable challenge of having to re-negotiate the ongoing work exchange or *contract* with the people whose behaviours they are trying to change. Dal Cross refers to his foundry assignment as a 'change management' one and he uses the analysis of the yardies' work orientations and perceived implicit contract that we have just reviewed to make the changes he sees as necessary. And the *processes* that he engages in to negotiate these changes are ones where, once again, we see the overlapping of so-called motivational, leadership and job design initiatives.

Activity 9.3

Read Dal Cross's continuing story in Cases and Conversations 9.2 about his managerial experiences with the 'yardies' in the foundry and

- using Table 9.2 again (p. 282), analyse the new implicit contract that makes possible Dal's reorganising of the yard gang;

- consider the extent to which Dal has made changes to 'job design' in setting up the modified 'site services' function;

- consider whether you can see a 'theory of leadership' behind Dal's working towards these changes;

- identify the extent to which it might be said that there is now a new 'indulgency pattern' within these 'site services' arrangements.

Dal and the yardies' 'triumph of change management'   Cases and Conversations 9.2

I had talked of 'proving myself' managerially by taking on this assignment with the foundry works manager and I knew that I was either going to fail miserably or that I was going to pull off a triumph of change management. I had been on a change management course and read all the stuff on choosing the 'right leadership style', motivating people, enriching jobs, empowering staff, quality circles and goodness knows what else. As I read through all this stuff again on the Monday evening after my first day with the yardies, I struggled to make it all add up. I had to fall back on what I believed in about being a manager. When I had been interviewed for the management traineeship in the first place it seemed that I had said very much the right thing when I had argued that managers were going to have to initiate a lot of changes to make businesses successful in an increasingly competitive world. But managers would not be able to – nor should they morally – unilaterally impose these changes on the organisation's employees. The interviewing panel had been wary of my suggestion that this might involve negotiating work organisation changes with trade unions. But they warmed to my theme that managers and their staff had to 'work together' – with those being paid to be managers taking the lead – to find new ways of working that would give benefits to the organisation and the workers alike.

All these fine words came back to me on that Monday night. Although this was rather idealistic sounding, it did feel to me to be the only way I could *realistically* go about tackling the problem of the yard gang. The works manager was simply unwilling to allow the continuation of an operation led by a gang boss who bullied other managers and supervisors into a situation where they could neither question the level of service he gave them nor challenge the way he indulged his staff. What was clear to me was that I could not simply order the yardies to work differently and to start using their own initiative to provide the site with a fast and efficient service that didn't always have to be mediated by a gang boss.

Ever since my early reflections on what being a manager should mean, I knew that my preferred personal style of leadership would have to be one of establishing a relationship of trust with the men and then negotiating with them a new way of working. That Monday night I decided that I would 'give a lead' by proposing a working principle of 'providing a service to the site' and that this would entail treating people in the various foundry departments as 'internal customers'. I was fully aware that I could not simply foist these ideas onto the men as a cynical act of pushing management fads that I had heard about on a course. I was very tempted to use the 'empowerment' word in my discussion, for example. I think the word describes well what I wanted to do. But I thought that the pretentious overtones of this word would not go down well in the foundry context. If I was going to work with them in a trusting relationship I had to be subtle and establish with them that the 'new order' I had in mind would be one in which they would all be better off than under the old regime, in one way or another.

I called a meeting with all the men in their 'winding down' time on the Tuesday evening, promising overtime payment to cover time spent in this or subsequent meetings that might go beyond the end of the shift. I took time to listen to what each of the men felt about the good and the bad aspects of the job and I worked hard to get them to see where, as a bloke, I was 'coming from'. I think this worked out quite well, partly because I think I am quite good at presenting myself as a sincere sort of person. But it was equally because all of this was set within a promise that nobody would 'lose out' if they 'went along with me'. Pay would certainly not suffer and I would look into ways in which an 'improved service to the foundry' might lead to an improved pay level. As I pointed out, the company had a job evaluation scheme which would ensure that if they were to 'increase the thinking or initiative element' of their work then they should move to a higher pay band.

Above all, though, I argued that they would surely be much happier to be 'getting out from under the thumb' of the boss man who had pushed them around for so long. And surely it would be better to get proper job satisfaction from providing a service to people across the foundry that would be genuinely appreciated than to carry on taking whatever satisfaction they had been getting from long tea-breaks and card games. Taking my managerial life into my hands – or so it felt at the time – I added to this that whatever pleasure they took in the 'fun time' that they had at work was surely undermined by the disgust that other workers felt at what they were 'getting away with'. A stony silence followed that particular input to the discussions. But I got out of the impasse that I had backed myself into by pointing out that if members of the new 'site services' department were to be given discretion over how they went about providing services then they would also obviously have to be given discretion over when they might need to rest or otherwise recover after carrying out a particularly onerous or exhausting task. All of this, I argued, would have to be part of the trust that would need to exist between the members of the department and whoever would be in charge of it.

I hope all of this doesn't sound too glib. It was all very hard work and I found myself fluctuating between elation and depression as I worked towards the new department that I wanted to establish. Without going into all the details, the 'gang' were now to be a 'team' who would meet each morning to allocate among themselves the areas in which each of them were to work through the day. Sections of the team would be allocated each day to an area of the foundry and the members of that section would themselves agree who would do what task – lavatory cleaning and bin clearing included – as the need for it arose within any given area of the site. I got the jobs upgraded and this was helped by a deal I did with the security department whereby the 'site services staff' carried out certain routine security tasks as part of their work. I also got the works manager to agree that it might be possible to appoint a team leader from within the group when I came to the end of my six months. I told the team that this was simply a possibility but that if any of them was interested in future promotion in the company they might like to talk to me about this idea. I felt it was important that the yardies should have the incentive of personal development and a career available to them, just like elsewhere in the organisation. Site services, and everybody in it, were on the 'up and up', I was proud to say.

The new implicit contract does not involve any less physical effort or risk of impairment than the old one. The major changes are with regard to the increased degree of initiative that the men are being asked to show in organising their own work schedules and task allocations. This can be seen as an increased 'input'. Alongside this there is what might be seen as a reduced input: the removal of the old requirement to surrender a high degree of personal autonomy by submitting themselves to a foreman's tight and direct control. It is sometimes argued by managers in situations like this that the only change in reward that this requires is one that automatically follows from the workers being freed to take charge of their own working practices: the reward of increased job satisfaction. Such people argue that 'empowering' workers by giving them increased freedom to choose how to work is a reward in itself. However, it is far from unusual for employees to reject this line of bargaining. They are quite likely to respond in the way the yardies did and raise the principle of 'being paid to think'. Employees are quite likely to observe that their 'empowerment' involves them taking on tasks that managers or supervisors previously carried out. They argue that taking on such work should be recognised with a higher rate of pay. Dal Cross is well aware of this type of argument, it would seem. Consequently he has sought ways of getting their pay increased: using the company's formal job evaluation scheme, one that incorporates the principle of paying for initiative and responsibility. To ensure that such an upgrading occurs he also adds a security-guard dimension to their work. This has the potential tacitly to improve the status element of the reward side of the implicit contract. Dal also explicitly addresses the status issue by suggesting they will be better off without the rather questionable sort of status they gained by getting more leisure-in-work time than other employees.

Dal seems to be very aware that taking away the opportunity to enjoy unofficial social rewards in the extended tea breaks is not going to be easy. He therefore seeks to redefine it as implicitly a little shameful and unfair to other workers. It is not an untainted reward. But he goes even further to deal with this potentially tricky issue. In effect, he suggests his own version of the indulgency pattern that was part of the old regime. We can understand in this way his statement to the yardies that they would 'obviously have to be given discretion over when they might need to rest or otherwise recover after carrying out a particularly onerous or exhausting task'. This offer is subtly connected to the principle of mutual trust that he speaks of as inherent in their generally increased discretion.

There is a lot of subtle 'motivational' work going on in the meetings of Dal and his staff and he shows considerable rhetorical skill in drawing on discursive resources like 'trust', 'service', 'internal customer' and 'team' to paint a very positive picture of the new world into which he wants to lead them. He was wary of using the discursive resource of 'empowerment', however. We might see this reluctance to use a possibly pretentious term as a reflection of Dal's skills of persuasion and leadership. He certainly seems to have worked out his own theory of leadership; one that incorporates a belief that one cannot impose changes on employees (or 'foist ideas' or 'management fads' on them). He sees negotiation as an important part of his 'personal style of leadership' and believes this should happen after establishing a trusting relationship with those with whom he is to negotiate. For Dal, this means allowing the men to get to know him personally and 'where he is coming from'. He also mentions taking time to listen to the views of the group before putting his ideas to them. To be a leader is nevertheless still a matter of initiating actions for Dal. He talks of 'giving a lead' by proposing the site service idea. However, that assertion of leadership is balanced with a clear recognition that is occurring within what is an essentially negotiated relationship of exchange – the employment bargain.

Dal is 'motivating' and 'leading' then, but he is also engaging is some significant job design work. By incorporating much of the foreman's old role into the work of the yard gang members themselves he is significantly redesigning the tasks away from the former *direct* control principles towards one in which control is much more *indirect*. Dal is not moving to a situation where the foundry management abandons control over the yard workers. It is asking them to control themselves, in the interests of the employing organisation as well as for their own benefit. He is utilising work design principles of *job enrichment*, *team-working* and the *semi-autonomous work group* (concepts we look at below, pp. 309–11). He does recognise, however, that the group might not satisfactorily work in an entirely 'leaderless' way when he ends his involvement with them in a few months time. He therefore talks of the possibility of a team leader being appointed. And in talking of this he is making yet another adjustment to the implicit contract with the group – he is putting into the bargain for the first time a possibility of career advancement.

Breaking the bounds of motivation and leadership theories

It was possible when examining what Dal Cross had to say about his leadership approach to recognise something of a personal 'theory of leadership'. But if we look closely at the way he presented his ideas we will notice that he relates these principles to his 'early reflections on what being a manager should be'. This suggests that it was more a theory of management that he was trying to articulate than a theory of leadership as such. Indeed, his reflection on what is likely to be successful in managerial work is quite consistent with the way managerial and organisational activities generally have been theorised in *Organising and Managing Work*. His thoughts fit well with our theorising of organisational and managerial work in processual terms – as work that involves *strategic exchanges* in which individuals and groups negotiate arrangements to ensure tasks are done to suit a variety of different constituencies so enabling the organisation as a set of understandings, relationships and activities to continue into the future.

If we can develop a sufficient understanding of all of these processes, do we need a theory of motivation or a theory of leadership? It is arguable that we do not. A moment's reflection on just what people are really doing when they try to develop such theories might well lead us to conclude that the whole idea was somewhat wrong-headed from the beginning. If 'motivation' is basically a matter of why people do what they do – which is what it seems to amount to – then the aspiration to a 'theory of motivation' is an aspiration to something ridiculously grand. It is nothing less than an aspiration to develop a general 'theory of why people do what they do', and this amounts to nothing less than a general theory of human behaviour! If this is the case, then motivation theory is something that could not be covered in one chapter of an organisational behaviour textbook. Even less, is it something that can be separated from other dimensions of human behaviour like leadership, identity, culture, social structure and the rest. What this means is that anyone wishing to understand the processes of organising and managing work has got to theorise the broad process of the shaping of human activities that goes on in the modern institution of the complex work organisation. And doing this *necessarily involves engaging with the general psychological, sociological, anthropological, economic and political theories that can help us make sense of the specific activities that go on in modern workplaces*. It is for this reason that the present book has located its analysis and theorising of managerial work and organisational processes within a much more basic consideration of how we can most usefully understand what it is to be a human being, what it is to live in society, and what the dilemmas are of managing our identities and material existence in a particular type of society and economy at a particular time in history.

Theorising 'leadership' – which amounts to theorising the way some people get other people to 'go along with them' – needs to be located in the wider consideration of how organised behaviours come about just as much as 'motivation' does. Various insights into what might be called the 'leadership dimension' of managerial work have been developed in the present and in previous chapters. We will return to them later when we consider what makes some managers more *competent* than others. Those parts of the manager's job that might be called 'motivational' will continue to be of concern, as they also have been throughout our analysis so far regardless of whether or not that particular term has been used. Does this mean, however, that we can now move on and avoid saying more about the 'theories of motivation' that seem to play such a central part in the orthodox study of organisational behaviour? No. We cannot, because 'motivation talk' is such a central part of the discourse of modern management thinking. It is therefore necessary to look more closely at that thinking and see how we can relate it to the broad *strategic exchange* approach taken in the present work. But there is one 'theory of motivation' in particular that has to be engaged with first. This is Maslow's 'hierarchy of needs' theory of motivation – a piece of pseudo-social science that has mysteriously come to play an iconic part in the study of organisational behaviour and courses on management.

A central place has been given for half a century or so in management education to certain thoughts of this particular mid-twentieth-century American writer, Abraham Maslow (1943, 1954, 1968, Reading Guide 22). Typically utilising the triangular diagram shown below in the illustration accompanying the conversation with Cam Toon, countless teachers and students of a whole variety of areas of human endeavour ranging from management to consumer behaviour have regurgitated Maslow's highly suspect notion that human beings in their lives and activities generally work *upwards* through a particular sequence of 'needs'. People are said generally to seek to satisfy 'lower order' *physiological* and *safety* needs before moving upwards to satisfy 'higher order' *social* and *esteem* needs. At the top of the hierarchy is an idealised notion of perfect human fulfilment called '*self-actualisation*'. This is something that people allegedly seek to satisfy once they are well-fed, safe, socially integrated and 'well thought of' by others. At the level of a truism perhaps, there is some sense in this. If we wish to motivate a starving worker running away from a hungry lion it is not unreasonable to consider giving them a loaf of bread and protection from predators in return for them performing as we require. Once the worker is getting plenty to eat and has had his or her 'safety needs' met, it seems reasonable to expect it to be necessary to offer some further incentives to gain workers' cooperation: giving them the satisfactions of sociability with other human beings and making them feel esteemed or 'highly thought of'. Perhaps, beyond this, the only incentive that the worker can be offered is an opportunity to self-actualise or somehow to 'become everything that they would most want to be'.

The so-called 'hierarchy of needs' theory has some appeal at the level of a general truism about human beings then. It plays on some simple and obvious truths, but its original popularity probably came about more because it resonated with a truism that applied, at a sociological level, to certain increasingly affluent parts of the world. In settings like Maslow's own, within the increasingly comfortable middle classes of the USA, it was plausible to expect people who were 'doing well in life' to seek to 'get even more out of life'. The message from Maslow's popularisers to employers in the increasingly affluent sections of certain mid-twentieth-century societies was, in effect, 'if you want to get more out of your increasingly comfortable employees you had better think of some extra things to give them'. The ultimate 'extra' that successful industrial capitalism could offer people was the opportunity to achieve the total opposite of the 'alienation' that so many social commentators had worried about as a consequence of industrialism and capitalism. Maslow's message was corporate capitalism's answer to the Marxist fear of work under capitalism leading to dehumanising or *alienation* of people (p. 147). Instead of people being separated from their essential humanity, as Marxists and other radical critics of capitalism feared, they could be rewarded not just with the material and social rewards of economic success but also with the chance to become everything that a human being could possibly become – the chance to realise their essential humanity, whatever that might be. This was self-actualisation.

Any critical study of organisational and managerial behaviour must pay attention to these ideological implications of what is probably the most frequently taught and most commonly remembered single 'theory' in the business and management studies curriculum. Beyond that, it must apply the normal social scientific critical rigour to the Maslow theory itself. Each of the three types of 'truth claim' that can be made for knowledge, set out in Chapter 1 (pp. 26–9), can be applied to the hierarchy of needs theory's claim that people only seek to satisfy 'higher order' needs once they have satisfied the lower level ones. The *correspondence* criterion for judging the 'truth' of a theory might be applied by testing whether the sequence of 'need fulfilment' posited in the theory accords with what we see to 'be the case' if people are systematically studied meeting their needs in a research laboratory. Research psychologists have attempted to do this and found that people simply do not follow the sequence suggested by Maslow (Rauschenberger, Schmitt and Hunter, 1980, Reading Guide 22). On these grounds, then, the theory fails.

On the *plausibility* criterion, which would judge the theory to be true if it fitted with everything else we know, we have already seen that there are some grounds for acceptance, given the truisms in which Maslow trades. But the plausibility of the theory soon drops away once we move beyond the everyday common sense mode of thinking (p. 20) in which truisms play an important part ('it's obvious isn't it?' we often say when thinking at the unreflective *everyday common sense* level). The *critical common sense* advocated in Chapter 1 requires us to step back and critically put our minds to what at first seems credible. In applying our critical common sense to the Maslow theory we can also turn to the pragmatist principle of judging truth claims (Chapter 1, pp. 27–9).

This would entail our asking how helpful the theory would be in informing our practices were we to find ourselves in the situation of trying to 'motivate' people at work. Cam Toon was a manager and a management student whom we see applying both critical common sense thinking and the pragmatist principle of judging truth claims in his reflections on how his learning about the hierarchy of needs theory influenced some of his managerial work – not that he actually uses either of these terms.

Activity 9.4

Read Campbell Toon's conversation with the researcher in Cases and Conversations 9.3 and his experience-based rejection of the Maslow theory of motivation and reflect on:

- why you think so many people seem to remember the 'hierarchy of needs' theory (or the triangular representation of it at least) and not the more complex theories that deal with 'motivation';

- the extent to which the hierarchical sequence of need satisfaction is followed in your own life (following the approach that Cam takes to analysing the place of different aspects of need satisfaction in his personal life).

Cam Toon confronts the magic triangle

Cases and Conversations 9.3

During a management class the researcher had reported the outcomes of some 'ethnographic experiments' he had done with other management students. During one of these events, a year or more previously, a student had uttered what the researcher took to be the very significant words, 'Motivation, that's Maslow isn't it?' (Watson, 1996, Reading Guide 22). Most of the current class reacted positively to the researcher's argument that these words perfectly captured the sort of 'surface learning' that can occur in management education when the topic of study becomes what 'this or that American professor wrote years ago' rather than how academic theorising relates to the actual practices of people involved in organising and managing work. Cam Toon, however, was especially vocal in his attack on what he called 'Maslow's bloody magic triangle', arguing that he had been 'foolish enough to think that what he studied on management courses should be relevant to his practice as a manager'. When he visited the researcher's office after the class to collect a copy of the journal article reporting the study, he agreed to a tape recording of a conversation with the researcher. The researcher speaks first.

I hope, Cam, that I wasn't going too far in the class in asking the course members to be critical of both themselves and the material they have to study.

No I don't think so. I think that you are right that too many lecturers and too many students simply go through the motions of drawing that dreaded triangle as an alternative to engaging with serious attempts to understand what it really means to have to motivate people at work. I'm not sure, though, whether you are right that people keep reproducing the triangle in their lectures and in their assignments as a magic ritual or a magic charm because they are actually frightened by – what was it you said?

'The frightening realities of managerial work', or some such thing, probably. No, I was just speculating that per-haps the endless drawing of the triangle by teachers and students is equivalent to people crossing themselves when they see a funeral pass by. You know, it's a sort of whistling in the dark when you are frightened because you don't really know what you are doing. But, leaving all that aside, I'm interested in your point that you did try to apply this thinking in your work.

Yes, I was facing some big problems in the packaging business where I work. It was made clear to me that the productivity levels in my part of the factory were not good enough. I knew I had to get more out of people. I had no sticks to beat people with – they were all doing a reasonable job, even if they rarely showed any kind of initiative and hardly ever helped each other out with problems. Generally, people seemed to me to be compla-cent. The firm was ostensibly doing well and people were reasonably paid and were secure in their jobs. When I tried exhorting people to speed up a bit, to work together a bit more when problems arose and to look for smarter ways of doing things, they just smiled at me and carried on in the same way. So you can see that when it came to the classes on motivation I was dead keen to see what these 'theories of motivation' would have to offer. The Maslow thing clicked with me when we covered it. The lower level needs of my people were all satisfied, I concluded, and therefore to motivate them to do more I had to offer them something at the 'higher order' level. I saw that Herzberg's job enrichment principle ('Herzberg spelled without a "t"', I remember the lecturer saying) was a way of applying the Maslow theory. I therefore set about re-arranging the jobs of my people so that there was more variety in their tasks and, by taking away a level of supervision, that they were given more freedom to choose how to do the work. In introducing this I really played up the 'social needs' bit by pointing out that they would need to work more closely together and would find this socially rewarding. I gave even more emphasis to the 'esteem' need by making the point very strongly that I had a high opinion of my staff and that the firm had perhaps been insulting their abilities by supervising them so closely and prescrib-ing every little detail of how to do things.

And did this work?

Did it hell. After only a week and a half I had to get some tight supervision back. The simple truth of the matter is that my people *did not want to have their jobs enriched*. Well, this is not entirely true. Two or three of them were persuaded by my arguments. I had a sort of post mortem talk with two of these. They told me that they agreed that people ought to find some of the fulfilment in their work that they tended to get with their families or in their hobbies. However, I inferred from what they told me that most of their work mates were happier get-ting their social, esteem and fulfilment needs satisfied outside of work and that they were happy 'cruising along' at work. But when I put it to them that 'money was not a motivator' they just laughed at me and said that had the new system lasted a little longer they were all going to put in a wage claim. When I expressed some shock they said, 'Sod money as a motivator. First, there's no way any factory worker is ever going to feel that they are paid enough. And, second, it would simply be unfair to leave people on the ordinary factory rate when they were now doing some of the old supervisor's job'.

One might argue that you had just been naïve here as a manager and that you can't really blame old Maslow for your naïvety.

I accept that. But your class last week made me think a lot about why, as management students, we often fail to test the material we are offered against our own work experiences, let alone common sense. Somehow, with me though, the confrontation with Maslow's magic triangle had encouraged me to *switch off* my common sense. When you think hard about the so-called hierarchy of needs, it doesn't stack up, does it? I am Jewish and I get a good deal of my self-esteem and an awful lot of the social rewards in my life from belonging to my culture. The meeting of these social and esteem needs, I have to say, comes before I meet my need to eat or my need to make love to whoever I fancy. The rules of my religion and my community define what and when I eat and who I can have sex with. If I was in the Israeli army, like my cousin recently was, I would put the need to belong to my community and my personal prestige needs, as a fighter for freedom, way before even my need for safety. Yet Maslow's simplistic scheme has us all working up through the satisfaction of the more basic physiological and safety needs towards the higher social or esteem ones. It is nonsense – there is simply no straightforward sequence how people pursue their needs. And Maslow's whole notion of human beings seems to be one in which people live outside of culture. What I said about being Jewish would apply, in various ways, to members of any other culture of course.

Well, I'm sure he wasn't unaware of all of these things but the 'theory of motivation' that has been extracted from his writings and presented to generations of management students does seem to do just this. It reduces people, with all their choices, preferences, values and cultural influences to need-led little machines.

So this doesn't say a lot for business school education does it.

Well perhaps not. But to be fair, I am sure that you covered other motivational theories that would be closer to your own commonsensical thinking and would helpfully, in my favourite phrase, 'inform your practice'. Do you not remember coming across something called 'expectancy theory' – an approach which stresses the importance of finding out just what your own particular employees actually want, rather than wasting time reflecting on human 'needs' in general? And did you not look at 'equity theories' and their emphasis on how ideas about fairness influence people's motivation (as happened with your people). All of that would have been very useful to you as a manager, I suggest. And, of course, I would argue that the ideas about work orientations and implicit contracts that some of us use in this area are even more useful.

I confess that I just didn't take in these other theories – 'process theories' I think they called them. They just seemed to be more complicated – and more difficult to remember.

Well, you're not alone there. In the research paper you will see evidence that the vast majority of the three hundred or so students who took part in the events covered in the project, one year on, could remember practically nothing of the 'process theories' they studied.

For them motivation was Maslow?

Something like that.

On pragmatist grounds, then, it would seem that very weak truth claims indeed can be made for Maslow's theory. What Cam Toon has to say, however, has a significance way beyond the hierarchy of needs theory specifically or to motivational theories generally. The conversation raises serious questions about the role that traditional management education plays in the management learning processes of those who take the courses and use the standard textbooks. This connects back to Chapter 1 and the arguments developed there for applying critical common sense to the questions that arise whenever we really want to understand the complex issues that arise with organising and managing work. Both parties to the conversation reflect on why the particular motivational theory of which they are so critical should be given such massive attention within management education. Cam recognises the relevance of information (and images) being easy to remember. The researcher speculates, at an anthropological level, about a possible symbolic role for the 'magic triangle' as some kind of talisman that helps management tutors and management students alike cope with the ambiguities and anxieties involved in studying something as complex and daunting as managerial practice (see Watson, 1996, Reading Guide 22). This echoes back to the discussion of managerial angst in Chapter 5 and the 'controlling the uncontrollable' aspect of the expectations that are put on managers.

Cam's thoughts about how he does not move through a sequence of need satisfaction that remotely resembles the hierarchical models in his own life are especially significant. As he points out, every one of us lives within a culture. This means that satisfying 'needs' that can be characterised in social, esteem or 'self-actualisation' terms could be seen as having precedence over the satisfaction of so-called lower order ones – contrary to the hierarchical model. Is there anyone who could say that they regularly satisfy their physiological needs for food, drink, sex or to excrete without first considering the norms of the social groups to which they belong or prior to reflecting on what sort of esteem they will be held in if they prioritise their hunger, thirst, lust or full bladder over a need to 'belong' or a need to be admired? Of course not. One's 'motivations', in work or elsewhere, are matters of one's cultural location, personal identity, work orientation, values and life priorities and how these lead to exchanges in particular circumstances – like the exchange that people make through an implicit contract with a particular employer at a particular time.

Furthermore, it is unlikely that any of us would be able to point to any kind of sequential pattern at all in the way we go about managing our lives and handling our 'needs'. Maslow's desire to impose a particular order on people's need satisfaction behaviour is a further example of the type of *linearity* in theorising about human behaviour that was rejected in Chapter 4 (pp. 98–102). But those earlier criticisms of conventional systems-control thinking also questioned the usefulness of the concept of 'needs' when studying behaviours in the first place. Matters of work motivation and orientation simply cannot be reduced to something as simple as 'needs'. While it is reasonable to talk of people 'needing' food and water, it becomes much more difficult to use the language of needs when considering matters like pursuing promotion to a high status position or trying to obtain a company car. 'Wants' would be a more realistic notion here, as would be the concept of *expectancy*, as it is used in some of the more process-oriented motivational theories. The concepts of *expectancy* and *equity* were mentioned in the conversation with Cam Toon as something that Cam is likely to have met in his studies, even if he has forgotten about them.

Equity, balance and expectancies in work orientations

Although it is now common for motivational theories that use ideas of equity or expectancy to be referred to as 'process theories' they go only a part of they way towards the full process-relational thinking that has been developed over the chapters of *Organising and Managing Work*. Their insights do parallel much of what has been said about orientations to work and implicit contracts however. An early process-oriented contribution to what has variously been referred to as 'balance', 'social comparison' or 'equity' theorising in this area was a classical study of American soldiers (Stouffer *et al*., 1949, Reading Guide 22). The researchers observed that there was a greater dissatisfaction with promotional opportunities in the Army Corps than in the Military Police. This was in spite of the fact that, objectively, there were better opportunities in the former part of the military than in the latter. The dissatisfactions and the 'demotivating' influence of these were not the outcomes of what was objectively the case but arose out of the expectations of the people involved with regard to promotional opportunities. A general sense of unfairness had developed in large part as a result of individual soldiers comparing their own prospects with the way that others had been treated. Developments in this kind of thinking were pulled together into an 'equity theory of motivation' by Adams (1963, 1965, Reading Guide 22). This sees people balancing what they put into their work with what they get out of it in the light of what they see other people putting in and taking out in similar situations.

> ### Equity or balance theories of work motivation *Concept*
>
> These theories show how work behaviour is influenced by how people perceive their situation after comparing their work/reward exchange (or 'implicit contract') with the employer to that of other members of the organisation.

The basic insight of so-called 'equity theory' is a vital one and it is wholly consistent with how the *work orientation* and *implicit contract* concepts have been used here. The central attention given in strategic exchange thinking to how people perceive or understand the contract they make with an employer is the same as in balance and equity thinking. The stress on how this perception involves comparisons with other people is implicit but clear in, for example, the earlier reference to employees having to 'be persuaded that there is a fair and reasonable return' for everything that those employees 'put into' their work (p. 282). None of us can decide how 'fair or reasonable' we can regard anything that we are asked to do or anything that we are offered without making comparisons with other people and their circumstances.

Activity 9.5

Consider how far matters of 'equity', 'balance' or perceived fairness come into the stories both Dal Cross in Cases and Conversations 9.2 and Cam Toon in Cases and Conversations 9.3 have to tell us about:

- the way Dal first analyses the work orientations and perceived implicit contracts of the yard gang and, later, enters negotiations with the men;

- Cam's attempts to increase the productivity of the packaging workers in his part of the factory by 'enriching' their jobs.

When Dal Cross was trying to make sense of the work orientations of the members of the yard gang in his early involvement with them he looked at the balance between what they were 'putting in' and 'getting out' – as far as he could understand it as an observer. He is explicit about the fact that he is talking at this stage about his perception of their perceptions, so to speak, when he says that their wages 'seemed fairly reasonable to me'. In effect he tries to put himself in their position, and makes the sort of comparison with others that he thinks that they would make – with 'other manual workers who did not have a skilled trade'. Some more subtle thinking along these lines is done as he goes on to look at what he calls the 'perverse status' that they enjoy in the foundry. This analysis emerges from his trying to make sense in 'balance' terms of the fact that the yardies get more free time for their own leisure during working hours than do other workers. All of these complexities are later taken into account during the bargaining that he enters with the gang as he works to move them towards a new implicit contract. He tries to get them to redefine this 'privilege' by effectively suggesting that it is not really a reward at all.

Dal is well aware that worker perceptions of inputs and outputs have an important economic dimension. He appreciates that a pay increase is going to be vital in shifting the exchange relationship. It is interesting that the company's 'job evaluation' scheme that he makes use of is a device similar to that which many employers use to deal openly with matters of comparison and perceived fairness in wages or salaries paid to different groups within an organisation. Job evaluation schemes are used in deciding pay relativities in many work organisations. They use measurements of work 'inputs' and 'outputs' that are believed to be acceptable to everyone as the basis for pay comparisons. Such a scheme could also be a help to Cam Toon if he wishes to try again to redesign the work tasks of the members of his department. He reports how his workers were comparing the new tasks that they were doing with what they believe supervisors do. In principle, a job evaluation scheme would enable their new jobs to be measured, compared to the work that a supervisor typically does in similar areas of the organisation and a 'fair' wage for the new employment trade identified.

Expectancy theories of work motivation

Concept

These theories show how work behaviour is influenced (a) by the particular wants and expectations which particular employees, in particular circumstances, bring to the organisation and (b) by the extent to which these are met by the employer.

The concept of *expectancy* has been utilised by various theorists to deal with these matters of employee perception or 'understanding'. The concept has played a central part in the turning away of motivation theorists from the focus on 'needs' towards use of the much more realistic 'wants' and expectations that employees bring to particular jobs. Instead of indulging in generalisations about the needs that human beings generally are said to bring to the workplace, it encourages managers to look at the specific work circumstances of whatever group of employees they are concerned with and at the specific expectations that they bring to their employment relationship with a particular employer. The 'expectancies' referred to by psychologists and motivation theorists like Vroom (1964, Reading Guide 22) or Lawler (1971, Reading Guide 22) correspond to some extent to the 'work orientations' notion that has emerged out of the industrial sociology tradition. We can draw out of expectancy thinking some highly commonsensical guidelines that can be applied to the various facets of work organisation and bear on the input–output bargain at the centre of the employment relationship management – from pay systems and promotional policies to job design and management style. For successful 'motivation' to occur several conditions have to be met.

- Employees must see that the effort they put in will, in fact, cause effective performance. It would be inappropriate for an individual output bonus to be paid to someone operating a machine that had a fixed rate or level of output, for example.

- Employees must see that appropriate performance will lead to their receiving the rewards claimed to be linked to them. Promotion would not be a good motivator, for example, if the individual either sees people being promoted for reasons other than effective performance or if they see cases of such performance failing to lead to promotion.

- The rewards available to employees must be ones in which they are actually interested – or can be persuaded to become interested in. The offer of the rewards of intrinsic job satisfaction (that Cam Toon offered his staff, for example) or increased job status would be poor motivators for employees who simply wanted a quiet life at work in a secure job with a good level of pay to take home.

- Employees must have both the technical skills and knowledge to do the job.

- Employees must understand the broader implications of the role they are taking on – the sort of relationships they are expected to have with managers themselves and with other people in the organisation for example.

These practical managerial guidelines emerge from what textbooks label 'expectancy theories of motivation'. The theory behind these highly common-sensical recommendations is consistent with strategic exchange thinking and its emphasis on the interpretations and understandings that people bring to their employment. Expectancy thinking's focus is on the employees themselves, as we would expect from work emerging from the psychological tradition of 'motivational' theorising. In this respect, it is a more narrowly focused analysis than the strategic exchange one. Strategic exchange analysis is broader and deeper in its locating of managerial attempts to manipulate the implicit contract within both the social and cultural location and priorities of the employee and the strategic position and priorities of the employing organisation (whose exchanges with employees are just one resource exchange among many, as we saw in Chapter 6.

 Link

The importance of recognising that the modern employment relationship is a distinctive institution of industrial capitalism was stressed in Chapter 3 (p. 60) and the fundamental contradictions that arise from this and with which managerial work has to deal were considered in Chapter 7, pp. 242–9 .

Strategic exchange analysis and the way it uses the concepts of work orientation and implicit contract is also broader (more fully process-relational we might say) than expectancy theory in its attention to the ongoing processes of negotiation and re-negotiation that occur in the relationship between employers and employees. This is a relationship that exists within a political–economic context. And the nature of that context means that significant managerial efforts have to go into the constant handling of the basic tensions and contradictions that characterise the employment relationship in industrial capitalist societies. These tensions are always there in the background of every 'motivational' situation in the work organisation. Sometimes they are more obvious than at other times, however. They could be understood as manifesting themselves, for instance, when one of the two workers with whom Cam Toon discusses the issue of whether or not 'money is a motivator' in Cases and Conversations 9.3. He rejects the language of motivation and contextualises the proposed pay claim with the words, 'there's no way any factory worker is ever going to feel that they are paid enough'. Issues of social class and basic employer–employee conflicts are clearly playing a part here.

Work motivation, then, cannot be considered in isolation from a whole range of other issues that impinge on the negotiated relationship between the employing organisation and its employees. And there is no particular aspect of a manager's job that can be separated out from the rest of what they do as the 'motivational element' of their job. It has been clear throughout this chapter, not least in the reported managerial experiences of Dal Cross and Cam Toon, that to 'motivate' people (getting employees to do what they otherwise would not do) managers lead, build relationships, develop understandings, train people, devise promotional schemes and design jobs. Both Dal and Cam are, for example, engaged in a degree of job redesign work in their attempts to 'motivate' their staff to work more effectively. These were personal initiatives applying to their own departments. But, as was stressed earlier in the chapter, we cannot separate out what any manager does in their own department from the wider cultural and structural arrangements of the organisation as a whole. Each of these managers was attempting a move from a relatively *direct* approach to seeking managerial control to a relatively *indirect* one. In this, we can assume that they felt that such a move was not inconsistent with the broader cultural and structural trends in their companies. Broad considerations of job design are an important element in the strategic shaping of the organisation as a whole.

Direct and indirect control principles of work design

Organisational structures, and the task shaping and task allocation that is part of them, are very much 'emergent' phenomena – outcomes of the balance of managerial initiatives and employee acceptance. Process-relational thinking draws attention to the negotiated, political and emergent aspects of organisations. Organisations, as they emerge out of the processes of cooperation and conflict, rarely resemble their official managerial blueprint or organisation charts when we look at them in action. But this does not mean that managers are not continually working to design – or *re*design – the activities that are carried on in the organisation's name. To understand this, it is useful to look at certain work design principles that have played a part in shaping the practices of organisational managers throughout the history of the modern work organisation.

Work design/redesign principles   *Concept*

General principles about how narrow or broad the tasks associated with jobs should be and the extent to which jobholders should use discretion in carrying out those tasks.

Job design/redesign practices   *Concept*

The shaping of particular jobs, especially with regard to how narrow or broad the tasks associated with those jobs are and the extent to which jobholders exercise discretion in carrying out those tasks.

The terms 'job design' and 'work design' are often used interchangeably but, here, we will use them to represent two different, but closely related ideas. The actual task pattern that emerges in any particular part of an organisation (the new version of the yard worker job introduced by Dal Cross in Cases and Conversations 9.2, for example) is referred to here as a matter of *job design* (or redesign). The broad principles that are drawn upon when designing or redesigning jobs are, however, referred to as *work design* principles. The former, then, are matters of actual practice and the latter matters of prescription or intent.

Work design is clearly something closely related to the broader structural and cultural 'design' of the organisation as a whole. It was argued in Chapter 7 that there is a basic choice that managers can make in trying to achieve managerial control through this design – through the shaping of the organisation as a whole. This is a choice between *direct* control attempts and *indirect* ones.

- An organisation leaning towards direct control principles would be a highly centralised one with a tightly bureaucratic structure and culture. There would be an emphasis on tight rules and closely prescribed procedures in which a relatively low level of psychological commitment would be sought from the employees. Because these arrangements imply that the management are not putting a lot of trust in employees to do what is required of them of their own accord, a 'low trust' culture emerges in which relationships between employer and employees tend to be adversarial. Differences of interest between parties to the employment relationship thus become manifest and visible at a surface level.

- The organisation leaning more in the indirect control direction would be less centralised and have a loosely bureaucratic structure and culture. Rules would be relatively loose and procedures left flexible because employees would have discretion about how to carry out those tasks. They would, however, apply this discretion in a way that fitted with managerial requirements and the strategic priorities of the organisation because of their high level of psychological commitment to the organisation. This commitment is made possible, in turn, because of a culture of high trust between members of the organisation – one in which common or mutual interests between different parties to the employment relationship are emphasised. Differences of interest between parties to the employment bargain tend to remain below the surface of on-going activities and are not expressed through overt confrontations.

Within these two basic approaches to what we might call *organisational* design there are two basic sets of *work* design principles and these are outlined in Figure 9.1.

The two sets of work design principles outlined in Figure 9.1 are *ideal types* – constructs created by the social scientist to help make sense of the much more complex and potentially confusing picture that emerges when we go out into organisations to see what is happening 'on the ground' (as we saw with Weber's 'ideal type of bureaucracy' in Chapter 7, p. 241). No actually observable job designs have ever fully followed the descriptions set out as two ends of the continuum in the diagram, and job designs can be found that are close to the basic work design principles set out in the two columns without following every element of the above characterisation. Within teamworking, to take an example from the 'indirect' side, it might be that the team allocates its own roles from day to day but is still subject to external monitoring of the resulting performance. Sometimes teamworking involves a 'team leader' who retains certain of the roles of the supervisor who plays an important role on the 'direct' side.

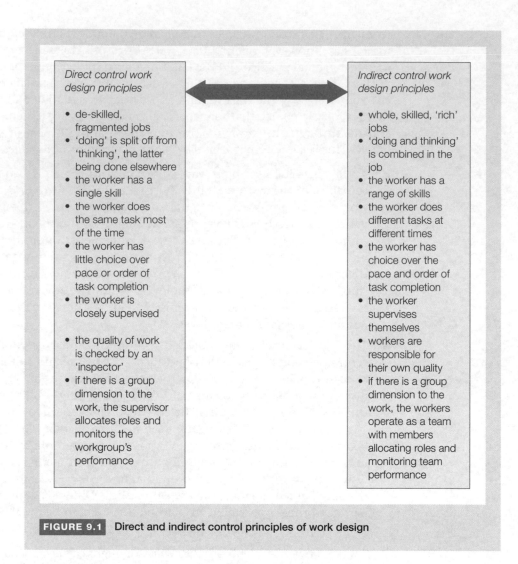

FIGURE 9.1 Direct and indirect control principles of work design

In practice, the actual job designs we are likely to come across in organisations will fall somewhere along the continuum outlined in Figure 9.1 and may even combine elements from both ends of it. The model is nevertheless valuable because it represents in a clear way the scope of choices open to managers when they embark on designing jobs in particular organisational settings. We might imagine some scheme like this having been in the minds of both Dal Cross and Cam Toon when they set out to make changes in the designs of jobs for which they had managerial responsibilities. Both, as we noted earlier, were interested in making moves towards more *indirect* ways of controlling the work done in their departments. Each of these two managers were influenced by 'newer' work design ideas that they had come across. Dal tells us how he had been on a 'change management course' and amongst the 'stuff' that he had read was material on 'enriching jobs', 'empowering staff' and 'quality circles'. Cam refers to his 'classes on motivation' where one of the things he learned about was Herzberg's 'job enrichment principles'. Although these men mention different bits of 'management thinking', they do not closely follow any of the texts or manuals on any of these specific techniques. Instead, they pragmatically apply the basic principles that underlie all these specific innovations ('job enrichment', 'empowerment', 'quality circles' for example). These are the basic principles being characterised here as *indirect control* principles. Within these, Dal pragmatically devises his own form of 'teamworking', that in the longer run may or may not have a team leader role within it. Cam speaks of 're-arranging the jobs of my people so that there was more variety in their tasks'. He also tries to give them 'more freedom to choose how to do the work' by removing a level of supervision.

We shall shortly review some of the more significant managerial innovations and fashions that have been put forward in different guises and under different labels over the past half century. But it is more important to see what all of these have in common than to try to look for distinctions between, say, 'job enrichment', 'vertical task integration' and 'empowerment' or between 'semi-autonomous work groups' and 'teams'. Exactly that has been done here by clustering many of the features of these managerial innovations and identifying them as 'indirect control attempts' which, at the level of job design, are used to handle, in effect, the basic contradiction that all managerial work has to deal with. This is the contradiction whereby managers need to control what workers do while, at the same time, recognising that every managerial attempt at control is liable to be challenged. Organisational members, to varying degrees, will demand 'freedom' or autonomy in the workplace. But managers must make sure that this freedom is a freedom to do what, in the end, the managers want them to do. Loose control, in effect, is stronger than tight control: That is the basic principle of indirect control work design thinking.

Modernity, industrialism and the hesitant embracing of direct control work design

There is a powerful irony behind the fact that we typically treat the principles of *indirect* work design principles as managerial innovations, as 'new thinking', or in terms of progressive or enlightened management ideas. This is ironic because, in the larger historical scheme of things, it was the shift in industrialising societies towards *direct* forms of work control that was one of the fundamental innovations of the new industrial capitalist order. One has to take care not to romanticise the pre-industrial past but, generally speaking, the division of labour that operated in pre-industrial societies was a *social (or general) division of labour*.

Social or *general* division of labour
Concept

The allocation of work tasks across society, typically into occupations or trades.

The key work design principle was an occupational one: the working individual played their part in society as a farmer, brewer or shoemaker and would be expected to develop the cluster of skills that went with their particular craft or trade. They would be able to handle what work design experts later came to call 'whole tasks' – the planting, nurturing and harvesting of a crop or the production of a pair of shoes. In practice there were undoubtedly numerous people who did little more than sweep floors or carry trade workers' tools. However, something along the lines of what we have characterised as indirect work design principles were the ones that were generally seen as desirable and at the centre of the pre-industrial social order. The rise of industrial capitalism, the growth of the institution of formal employment and the rationalising force of bureaucratisation saw a splitting down of many of the occupational roles within the old social division of labour into de-skilled jobs. There was now to be a *technical* (*or detailed*) *division of labour* whereby many work activities in factories and offices were split down so that individuals only did one specialised part of what had previously been the 'whole task' associated with an occupation.

Technical or *detailed* division of labour	Concept
The breaking down of 'whole' occupational roles into specialised and generally unskilled jobs.	

We can envisage the seventeenth or eighteenth century violin maker working on each instrument all the way from the initial woodcarving stage to the varnishing and the adding of the bridge, pegs and strings. But we would find the typical worker in a modern violin factory only able to work the wood cutting machine, glue the front, sides and backs of the instrument together or varnish the violin when it reached the varnish shop. The work would have been de-skilled. Many more violins could be produced at a much higher rate of profit for the employer, but for this to occur, those with the expertise have to take on the role of instructing and monitoring the rest. The managers have to control the workers. Thinking is separated from doing (an important direct control design feature identified earlier in Figure 9.1) and the implications for human beings of this trend were recognised from the start. Adam Smith in his massively influential work *The Wealth of Nations* of 1776, in which the new industrial order was both chronicled and boosted further, provided an analysis of the splitting down of the process of making tacks ('pins' as he called them). This showed that if you fragmented the job of the craft pin maker, who was able to do every stage of pin making, so that each stage of the process became the specialised task of a different worker, a vastly greater number of pins could be produced per day. However, in an industrial order based on this principle, with all the increases of general wealth that would accompany it, these new specialised labourers would be serious 'losers'. 'Those who labour most get least' he observed. What he had in mind was what we might nowadays call the quality of their lives. Someone whose life 'is spent in performing a few simple operations', he observed has 'no occasion' to 'exert understanding' and hence 'becomes as ignorant as it is possible for a human creature to become'.

Smith's reservations about this aspect of modern industrialised labour have come forward and then retreated again at various times ever since he first expressed them. However, the growth of the de-skilling and direct control trend in the ninetenth century was significantly boosted by Charles Babbage (1832, Reading Guide 17). Babbage powerfully demonstrated to employers just how much cheaper de-skilled labour was compared with skilled or craft-based labour. F.W. Taylor in the later part of the nineteenth century codified and systematised these direct control principles of work design and proselytised passionately for their introduction across the workshops of the fast growing industrial enterprises of that time (Taylor, 1911, Reading Guide 17).

Scientific management (Taylorism)	Concept
Work design principles that maximise the amount of discretion over task performance given to managerial experts, who calculate and precisely define how each job is to be carried out.	

Taylor's so-called called *scientific management* entailed:

- managers and experts systematically or 'scientifically' analysing every work task;
- each job being fragmented to achieve the highest possible technical division of labour, on the basis of this analysis;
- the planning of work being separated from its execution;
- skill requirements and job-learning times being reduced to the minimum;
- materials handling by operators being minimised to avoid distraction from the worker's focal task;
- work performance being closely 'time-studied' and monitored;
- pay being tied directly to individual output to encourage each worker to maximise their efforts;
- the relationships between employers/managers and employees remaining formal and distant.

Although Taylor's principles were rarely followed in their entirety, the basic scientific management approach to work design was widely embraced in the industrial and industrialising world as it moved into the twentieth century. This included communist countries where one might have expected some resistance to what many saw as the dehumanisation of working people. But there was also controversy and resistance to the de-skilling and close control trend. We should perhaps note, however, that although Taylor can be seen as pointing to a way forward for large areas of industrial activity, his thinking was rooted in solving problems of workshops in the late nineteenth century American steel industry where much of the labour was unskilled and the workers unfamiliar with the English language. His system might have been more viable in that context than in others where workers might have expected more than monetary satisfactions from their employment. The same argument may apply to the innovations introduced into the car factories of Henry Ford where the 'robotising' of the worker implicit in Taylorism was extended by the placing of the worker on an assembly line. Ford was very conscious of the costs that could follow from treating workers in this way, however. He therefore departed radically from Taylorism in paying a fixed and relatively high wage and called for the worker to show a long-term loyalty to the employer and live a sober and responsible life fitting for a Ford worker. In this way, there was a shift away from the arms-length type of employment relationship recommended by Taylor.

Fordism	Concept
A combining of mass production de-skilled job design in the industrial workplace with employment and state welfare policies that develop workers as both fit workers and willing consumers of the products of industry.	

Ford, we might say, set out to manipulate the work orientation of the industrial worker in the more sophisticated way called for by the changing circumstances of the twentieth century. But his innovations also actively influenced the way employment and indeed whole economies and societies were to develop. He recognised that industrial workers could also become the consumers of the products they made. The implicit contract was now to be one which might be expressed by managers as, 'Work hard in our factories in the way we direct you and in return for that you will be well paid and will be able to afford to buy one of the cars you make. And the more cars you buy, the more work there will be – and the better off you will become'. Fordism thus goes way beyond work design. As Fordist work design practices spread in industrialised societies they were supported by the state, whose economic, welfare and educational policies were increasingly aimed at developing a healthy workforce who would also be the consumers of the products and services they produced.

At the same time that Fordism was spreading, attention was beginning to be paid to the arguments of Roethlisberger and Dickson (1939, Reading Guide 1) and Elton Mayo (1933, Reading Guide 17) arising from the research in the Hawthorne plant in Chicago. This research was said to show the importance to them of people's social involvement at work and it was alleged that employees worked more effectively when managers 'showed an interest' in them. These arguments kept alive in some managers' minds an awareness that employees' expectations at work were complex and would not necessarily be straightforwardly satisfied by monetary rewards alone. Such awareness did not detract, however, from general managerial recognition of the immense benefits to employers that Taylorism and Fordism offered by way of both cost efficiency and the tightness of managerial control. A widespread recognition of these benefits meant, and continues to mean, that a powerful de-skilling logic runs through many work design efforts across a multiplicity of different types of employment. As Marxian analysis suggests, the *labour process* in a society based on capitalist principles is one where de-skilling is frequently the option that most effectively enables the employer to exploit the labour power of their employees (Braverman, 1974, Reading Guide 17).

Capitalist labour process	Concept
In Marxian analysis this is the process whereby managers design, control and monitor work activities in order to extract surplus value from the labour activity of employees on behalf of the capital-owning class who employ them.	

However, de-skilling always has its costs – as observers from Smith onwards had pointed out and as many managers themselves discovered. In some circumstances it was not the most effective way of utilising the efforts of employees (Friedman, 1977; Edwards, 1979, Reading Guide 17).

Continuing doubts about de-skilled and tightly controlled work and the recognition of its inappropriateness to many work and labour market circumstances brings us back to Maslow and the significance we noted earlier of his recognition of the changing expectations that would be coming forward for workers in increasingly affluent sections of fast developing economies. As Cam Toon remembered from his management classes, Herzberg turned the Maslow principle into some specific job design practices: *job enrichment*.

Job enrichment	Concept
The expansion of the scope of jobs by such means as the re-integration of maintenance or inspection tasks; an extension of the work cycle; an increased degree of delegation of decision-making by job holders.	

Herzberg (1966, Reading Guide 17) argued that what were frequently taken to be work incentives or 'motivators' – pay, good working conditions and good relationships with supervisors – were no longer motivators at all. They were, rather, 'hygiene factors' – conditions that had to be fulfilled before motivation would actually happen. And the rewards that would lead to this 'motivation' were ones such as achievement, recognition and, especially, the satisfaction coming from the job itself. Jobs should thus have more variety and responsibility built into them. Job enrichment would see the scope of jobs increased. The argument, in effect, was that managers should 'redesign' jobs along these lines to meet the rising expectations of modern employees.

But what about the social or group dimension of work design? The Hawthorne research referred to earlier (p. 308) had stressed the importance to employees of the social aspects of work and Maslow included 'social needs' in his scheme albeit at a lower level than the rather idealised 'self-actualisation' notion that Herzberg tried to turn into something practicable. Mayo saw workers being 'tied into' the employing organisation via their location in meaningful groups of fellow workers. Maslow argued that people would look for social needs to be met at work once their lower level needs had been satisfied. However, other advantages of making groups or 'teams' central to work (re)design were stressed by British researchers working with the Tavistock Institute of Human Relations (Rice, 1958; Trist *et al.*, 1963, Reading Guide 17). It was argued that work organisations should be regarded as *socio-technical systems*.

Socio-technical systems

Concept

An approach to work design in which the technical and the social/psychological aspects of the overall workplace are given equal weight and are designed at the same time to *take each other into account*.

The Tavistock researchers noted that, typically, the technical aspects of a work enterprise tended to be designed first: the buildings, hardware and the layout of both of these is 'blueprinted' first and a set of social arrangements then designed to slot into it. What would be more effective, the Tavistock writers argue, would be for the technical and the social components of the overall system to be designed simultaneously and for them to take each other into account.

Activity 9.6

Reread the story 'Walt and Roger go into the country' (Cases and Conversations 7.2) and consider the extent to which it could be said that Roger is following socio-technical system principles in suggesting how he and Walt should go about designing both the physical/technical aspects of their new organisation and the social/cultural aspects.

Roger closely follows the principles that socio-technical thinking would suggest appropriate for both organisation and job design. He very effectively persuades Walt that organisation design should consider social and cultural factors, on the one hand, and technical and physical factors on the other hand *at the same time* – the one taking the other into account. This would mean that when the 'system' is operating these two aspects of it – the 'socio' and the 'technical' – would *fit* with each other. Walt's approach of setting up the 'technical' aspect first and then 'adding people onto it' would lead to real difficulties once the site was operating, Roger persuaded him. At the level of job design, the same principles should be followed according to the Tavistock researchers. In setting up an office or workshop, the technical tasks (together with the desks or machines associated with the tasks) should be grouped together to form a logical 'whole task' that can then be performed by members of the group with minimal supervisory interference. We thus get a *semi-autonomous workgroup* in which a group of people possesses all the necessary skills and all the necessary equipment to manage themselves in, say, the assembly of a motor car. Or, we might see a group of staff take charge, as a team, of producing a company's in-house magazine. Members of the team would share out among themselves and jointly coordinate tasks ranging from the collection of stories to the assembling of the pages on a desktop publishing system.

Teamworking/semi-autonomous workgroups   *Concept*

The grouping of individual jobs to focus work activities on a *whole task*, with team members being fully trained and equipped so that they can be given discretion, as a group, over how the task is completed.

With this example of the 'self-managed' group of staff who produced their company's house magazine we see something that might be labelled 'a semi-autonomous workgroup' or put forward as an example either of 'teamworking' or 'high performance work design'. Labels change in the managerial world as fast as they do in the world of fashion clothing. Something close to what we see modern companies celebrate as highly innovative 'high performance teams' or 'cellular manufacture' might well have been seen in certain craft groups producing goods way back in the middle ages, albeit producing much simpler products or services. A detailed division of labour and tight direct control managerial supervision and surveillance has played a central part in the vast increases in wealth and welfare that industrial capitalism has brought about. But to de-skill and tightly control work task performance is to wield a double-edged sword. It can cut both ways: sometimes helping the managers of employing organisations to fulfil their agenda, sometimes hindering them because of the counterproductive 'de-motivating' or 'alienating' tendencies of de-skilled and directly controlled work.

Dilemmas and choices in shaping work tasks and gaining cooperation

Implicit in our review of changing work design principles and job design practices since the industrial revolution is a recognition that there may be circumstances in which certain work design principles are more successful, from a managerial point of view, than in others. For example, it is very likely that Taylor's scientific management practices would be more viable with the unskilled immigrant workers he came across in the nineteenth century steel mills than they could ever be with well educated and articulate workers in a modern aerospace company. Similarly, we are not too surprised to see principles very close to those articulated by Taylor proving satisfactory to the managers of a modern company hiring (and firing) relatively young and transient workers to serve hamburgers to a highly standardised recipe in fixed service format across the world (Ritzer, 1993; Royle, 2000, Reading Guide 17). But we would be surprised to see the motivational and job design practices that prove profitable to the high street hamburger restaurant proving to be managerially successful in, say, a university or a city architect's department. There appear to be 'contingencies' that are relevant to managerial decision-making in the job design area. These are the circumstances of the organisation, like its size, technology or environmental situation, which have a better 'fit' with certain types of organisational arrangement and culture than with others.

When we applied the contingency insight to general organisational arrangements earlier, it was emphasised that contingencies do not *determine* organisational arrangements. Managers take into account their interpretations of contingent circumstances when arguing about and negotiating what patterns of organisation they will work towards. So what are the contingent factors that might be relevant to managerial debate within any given organisation about the work design principles that are to be applied when specific jobs are designed?

 Link   The relationship between organisational contingencies and how organisations are shaped was a central topic of Chapter 8.

Activity 9.7

Review the model in Figure 8.3 'Choice and contingency in organisational shaping' (p. 258) and how this was explained in Chapter 8. How do you think the contingencies represented there might be built upon to bring out circumstantial factors directly relevant to job design issues?

The contingency of *organisational size* might be relevant to job design in that having a large number of employees increases the scope for making people's jobs more specialised, whether this is specialisation of the type that leads to the appointment of a company lawyer, say, or the de-skilling type of specialisation that fragments the job of a pin maker. However, the other two contingencies shown in the model are perhaps more significant – those of technology and environmental stability.

The organisation's *technology* is a key job design factor in two closely related ways. First, it defines the tasks that are to be done and the extent to which those tasks are amenable to fragmentation or de-skilling. The technology of brain surgery, for example, does not lend itself to a detailed division of labour in which a succession of single-skilled individuals take their turn at wielding different types of scalpel for different stages of an operation. The technology of high street hamburger cooking and serving, however, lends itself well to such an approach.

The nature of the *environment* within which the organisation operates is also immensely important. We saw in the last chapter that a fast-changing and highly competitive business environment, one that requires frequent innovative action on the part of employees to enable it to survive, finds an 'organic' or loose structure more appropriate to its situation than a tightly bureaucratic one. This clearly implies a need for job designs that do not involve the sort of tight prescription and standardisation that goes with direct control types of job design. There is a tendency therefore for managers to choose indirect control types of job design where there are environmental pressures requiring high levels of innovation or adaptability on the part of employees. There is an obvious incompatibility between asking people to apply high levels of discretion and innovation in their work and expecting them to take detailed orders from a manager and be continually checked up on by a supervisor.

A concept that is often used in this context is that of *flexibility*. It is frequently argued that a move towards indirect control job designs are necessary if workers are to perform flexibly so that an organisation can quickly change what it is doing to cope with competitive pressures. This, however, is only partly true. There are two types of flexibility that managers of organisations look for: flexibility for long-term adaptability and flexibility for short-term predictability.

Flexibility for long-term adaptability *Concept*	Flexibility for short-term predictability *Concept*
The ability to make rapid and effective innovations through the use of job designs and employment policies that encourage people to use their discretion and work in new ways for the sake of the organisation – as circumstances require.	The ability to make rapid changes through the use of job designs and employment policies that allow staff to be easily recruited and trained or easily laid off – as circumstances require.
This fits with *indirect control* work design principles and high trust relationships.	This fits with *direct control* work design principles and low trust relationships.

Sometimes organisations will have a predominant need for just one of these types of flexibility. A consultancy organisation would mainly need flexibility for long-term adaptability, for example, and would therefore tend to follow indirect control work design principles across the firm. An organisation in the sugar beet processing industry, with inevitably seasonal patterns of working, on the other hand would need flexibility for short-term predictability. It would therefore find it more fitting to adopt predominantly direct control job designs. This would not only suit the seasonal need to hire at one time and fire at another. It would also fit with the generally low levels of skills required to apply the technology. And it would fit with the almost non-existent need to innovate and develop the product.

These two cases are relatively straightforward. But, in many organisations, managers find both types of flexibility are required. Sometimes one type of flexibility is relevant to one area of the organisation and the other to another area.

This is a circumstance that will be considered later when we look at issues of how job design issues relate to overall issues of how an organisation is to be 'resourced' with inputs of human skill, knowledge and labour. Researchers on innovations in work design have frequently commented on the tendency for the managerial success of these initiatives at a local level to depend on whether or not they were supported by appropriate human resourcing policies at the level of the wider organisation (Buchanan and Preston, 1992, Reading Guide 17, for example).

 Link   The possibility of organisations needing *dual human resourcing strategies* to cope with different types of flexibility being required in different parts of an organisation will be looked at in Chapter 11, pp. 396–8 .

Human resourcing policies inevitably have to cope with the fundamental contradiction that work design initiatives are always faced with. They must gain commitment and consent from the same employees that they need to 'exploit'. In recent decades of increasing international competition, we can see various employers desperately seeking new ways to handle this tension in order to stay in business – or rather to find new combinations of established work design principles. This has led to work design and human resourcing practices that incorporate novel mixtures of direct and indirect control principles. The *lean production* practices seen in the car industry are an example of this (Womack, Jones and Roos, 1990, Reading Guide 17). 'Leanness' means that no time, effort, or resources are wasted and high psychological commitment to this ruthlessly tight regime is also expected from a workforce that is also expected to use its discretion in the spaces where this is allowed, always with the benefit of 'the customer' in mind.

Lean production   *Concept*

The combining, typically within car assembly, of teamworking with automated technologies. Workers are required both to initiate 'continual improvements' in quality and to ensure that every task is got 'right first time' and completed to a demanding 'just-in-time' schedule.

A similar combining of direct and indirect control work design and human resourcing principles is seen with *business process re-engineering* (BPR) (Hammer and Champy 1993, and other references in Reading Guide 16). BPR has seen

Business process re-engineering (BPR)   *Concept*

The restructuring of an organisation to focus on business processes rather than on business functions. Advanced management control information technologies are used together with team working and employee 'empowerment'.

organisations across a range of industries restructured to focus on business *processes* (getting a product designed, manufactured and sold, say). This means turning away from an emphasis on business *functions* (where a design function focuses just on design, a manufacturing function focuses on production and a sales function concentrates just on selling, for example). A clear and integrated flow of processes is thus made possible by the use of advanced information technologies. Employees can be *empowered* and given new degrees of freedom to manage themselves in teams. They are no longer trapped in the separate boxes of functional organisation where managers, planners and schedulers have to direct and coordinate people's efforts to ensure that all the separate tasks and operations 'add up' to the provision of a successful product or service. The clearer logic of the basic process flow means that workers can 'make things add up' for themselves, as Roberto Auldearn's managing director put it when explaining the 'embracing of business process reengineering' at Dovecot Components in Cases and Conversations 9.4.

Activity 9.8

Read Roberto Auldearn's account in Cases and Conversations 9.4 of how Dovecot Components 'embraced' business process re-engineering.

- After looking back once again at the model set out in Figure 8.3 (p. 258), note the ways in which a part was played in this exercise in 'organisational shaping' by:
  - contextual political, economic and cultural patterns,
  - enacted contingencies,

- managerial values, goals and interests,
- managerial argument, negotiation and choice.

- Consider the extent to which we are helped to make sense of this story by the notion of a basic contradiction whereby managers have to gain commitment and consent from the employees at the same time as they are required to exploit and manipulate them.

Re-engineering the Doocot   Cases and Conversations 9.4

Dovecot Components has been an important employer in this town for a long time. Most people around here just call it 'The Doocot'. For over twenty years now the workforce has been steadily falling as we have increased investment in newer technologies and found a whole lot of ways of making the work less labour intensive. Productivity was steadily rising over this period and, as a management, we felt freer to make changes without having to fight with trade unions over every little detail. Government policies were partly responsible for this, but the unions – indeed the workforce generally – recognised that we were struggling in an increasingly difficult and increasingly international market place. Almost every year would see some redundancies and there was not a great deal of argument about this. I think people regarded these job losses as a sort of unfortunate fact of life and I don't think they affected morale within the company to any real extent. But people did not realise just how difficult things were going to get as we saw the auto companies that bought our components increasingly looking across the whole global economy to source their production.

About five years ago we realised that we needed to make radical changes in the business. We had been developing our technologies incrementally over the years and had introduced at different times a variety of innovations ranging from quality improvement groups to cellular and team working. A lot of our production is now done on a just-in-time basis. Components go out of the door just a few hours before the car plant two hundred miles away needs them to stick in its cars. It was becoming clear to us, however, that there were increasing numbers of other suppliers who could get their products to the factories just as promptly. And not only could they supply at significantly lower prices but several of them were much faster than us at developing and improving their products. Our customers were facing increasing global competition just as we were and were constantly looking to improve the quality and functionality of the components they put in their vehicles.

At the first executive meetings where we talked seriously about making radical changes I put forward a plan to set up a completely new 'Research, Design and Manufacturing Innovation' department. This would be a crack team that I would recruit by head hunting from my quite extensive contacts across the engineering world. It would combine product development and the improving of production methods – making sure we designed for ease of manufacture as well as to delight our customers. Immediately I suggested this I was shot down. The first bloke to 'have a go' didn't bother me. As a management accountant, our finance man was right to look critically at my plans and question how we could possibly afford this. But, like every one else, I knew that he personally disliked me and would attack anything I put forward. It was the MD, Jerry Penick, who really put the boot in however. This did bother me. In the first place, he said, 'there is certainly no way we can afford to do that'. And, 'secondly', he went on, 'your whole philosophy is out of date'. That made me wild. I ranted on about how advanced my 'design for manufacturing' ideas were and that I would easily get a job with one of our competitors if he had so little respect for me. In fact I did slam out of the meeting at one point. I think it was when the manufacturing director – a blinkered and territorially-minded idiot if ever there was one – made it clear that he wasn't keen for me to get involved in manufacturing issues. The MD came and found me puffing a cigar in the directors' lavatory and persuaded me to go back into the meeting and hear his thoughts on 're-engineering the Doocot'.

It turned out that the consultants that Jerry had brought in six months earlier, 'just to look over things' as he told us, had in fact come up with this scheme to 're-engineer' the processes in Doocot 'from top to bottom'. 'We have got to jump out of our functional boxes and our obsession with departmental boundaries', he said, looking directly at me and then at my manufacturing colleague. 'Everything has got to be stripped down to the basics and everyone will make their contribution to the basic processes of getting ideas quickly and efficiently through from the drawing board to the customer's delivery bay. The bloke on the drawing board will be as interested in that customer's needs as the driver of the delivery wagon will – or as I will'.

At this stage we were all looking at each other a little shocked. Most of us had heard of this 'business re-engineering' thing, but had not really related it to our situation. Molly, our marketing woman, ventured to say that all the re-engineering cases that she had come across had been more exercises in 'blood letting' and 'axing people as well as departments' than improving processes. 'Well', came back Jerry, 'I don't want any talk like that. But the re-engineering exercise will mean taking quite a big axe to our management structures. Levels will be taken out.' He accepted that 'delayering' and 'becoming leaner' would be painful. The consultants, together with a small senior management team, would 'look at everybody's job' and nobody 'whose job doesn't serve our core processes' would survive. This would be hard and it would 'hurt everybody involved', Jerry said. But those who survived would be much better off. It wasn't just that their jobs would be more secure. Their 'prospects with the firm' would also be better. Above all, people would benefit by being 'more empowered'. He explained that, at present, all the efforts that people put in and all the operations across the plant had to be 'made to add up' by managers, supervisors and other 'functionaries'. By taking a lot of these out, people would be given the satisfaction of 'adding it all up' for themselves. And, he added, by 'taking away all the managerial buffers that exist between the workforce and the market place' people will see the need to 'work hard, conscientiously and cooperatively *for the business and not for their department* because they will know that if they don't we all go under'.

The whole thing seemed sensible, if rather terrifying. For six months the 'Re-engineering Action Group' (RAG), comprising four senior managers and four consultants, were to work 'day and night' with Jerry to 'completely re-shape the business'. The business was to be more 'focused' than at present and this basically meant making it smaller. 'We have got too big and unwieldy', Jerry argued, 'so we'll cut the less profitable lines and try to stay at a size where a smallish top management team can keep their eyes on everything'. There would be a major investment in ICT, with the savings made on labour costs more than covering the 'costs of the new computer systems'. The 'software and hardware that are available now for management control', he insisted, 'were sophisticated enough now to cover the work of all the people who will be leaving us – and more'.

So, all of this went ahead. I was lucky to be kept on. But both my finance director and manufacturing director colleagues – and enemies – got the push. I was on the RAG – the action group charged with 'implementing' the re-engineering. At first I felt privileged. But this feeling soon went. I began to realise quite early on that the whole thing was doomed from the start. We had embraced business process re-engineering in a big way. But we had embraced a monster. In principle, I thought, it was wise. It was harsh. But harsh measures were necessary. And all of those who stayed with the business would experience a much higher level of empowerment and involvement with the core processes of the enterprise. They would clearly benefit. But as we all quickly learned, it wasn't to happen like that, and it's so easy to see why, in retrospect.

In one voice, we were saying that people were to be empowered, to be trusted and were to have their 'energies' released to do 'really meaningful work'. But in another voice we were asking people to kneel down to have their heads chopped off. This is where the massive catch in the whole thing lay. On the one hand we were asking people to be empowered, to manage themselves and be committed to the business. The logic of de-layering was one of saying that an empowered and committed workforce could, in many respects, manage things better than managers could. But on the other hand, we were a group of managers and consultants acting as if we were mighty gods who knew better than anyone how things should be done.

As you can imagine, the whole thing was treated with deep suspicion and bitter hostility from the beginning. And that's just among the managers! We RAG members were treated with utter disdain and mistrust as hypocrites and axe wielders. Because nobody would cooperate with us or give us any information we could trust, we simply could not do the work we were meant to do. But how could we back down? Consequently we made lots of cuts and we re-organised the place from top to bottom without really knowing what we were doing. And, yes, the business has survived. But we are running it through a regime of terror with most of the best staff we had having moved out to other jobs. I give the business a couple more years at most. And I shall be out of here well before that. When you see me next time, I'll have flown the Doocot.

These events at Dovecote Components would not have come about if there had not been major changes in the global economy. The most important contextual pressure is the growth of competition from producers of motor components across the world and the combination of this with car manufacturers choosing to 'source' themselves from a global market place. Relevant nationally is the state's role in reducing the ability of trade unions to resist managerial initiatives. And, at the local level, there appears to be a degree of goodwill towards 'The Doocot'. This goodwill might have helped managers make incremental changes which involved loss of employment over the years. Equally, it is possible that a sense of betrayal of this goodwill may have increased the level of resentment towards management when it came to the radical cuts associated with the business process re-engineering initiative.

These contextual matters influenced the particular *contingencies* that Dovecote managers *enacted* (interpreted and acted with regard to). The instability of the increasingly competitive business environment is obviously the major contingent factor. Jerry Penick has also acted on the basis of his view of technological contingencies. He believes that significantly more effective 'management control' hardware and software is now available to the company, and he has views about the contingency of organisational size, arguing that Dovecot is 'too big and unwieldy'.

Although the big decisions about how to handle the company's difficulties have largely been made by Jerry Penick alone, arguments taking place between the senior managers seem to reflect different value positions and interests among them. Roberto himself puts forward a solution that fits with his personal area of expertise and it is a solution that would have increased his personal influence in the company, we can reasonably infer. It was obviously one that clashed with the interests of the manufacturing director, an 'enemy' of Roberto who, apparently, was very 'territorial'. This individual was keen to 'fight his corner' as was Roberto's other 'enemy', the finance director. It is difficult to separate the values and the personal interests of the protagonists to these arguments. But it would appear that the marketing director brought certain values of concern for human beings into the discussions. It would seem that Jerry, in speaking of the inevitability of 'hurting' some people in order to benefit others, has gone through some internal value debate.

It is Jerry's choice, as the most powerful actor within the management team, to adopt business process re-engineering. However, the resistance to the way this was implemented, especially from other managers across the company, turned out to be so great that the initiative was seriously undermined. What Jerry Penick appears not to have realised was that strategic management has to cope with – or 'manage' – the basic contradictions that underlie all employing organisations. The contradiction between the requirement that managers must exploit or 'use' employees as resources and the requirement that they must win commitment and consent from employees as human beings is badly misman- aged here. The Dovecote management is saying that the changes will benefit the 'survivors' of business process re-engineering. People should therefore commit themselves to the changes. But it is making it clear at the same time that, for the moment, every individual is being considered for possible removal from the firm. Roberto expresses this by referring to the company as speaking with two voices. In one voice, he says, it talks of trust and empowerment, but with the other voice it is effectively asking every individual to 'kneel down' to allow the management to cut off their heads, should the 'Re-engineering Action Group' not see them as fitting into the new, re-engineered scheme of things.

Many organisations have in recent years reacted to the sorts of pressure faced by Dovecote Components by adopting business process re-engineering. And, even by the accounts of leading proponents of the practice, many of these have achieved nothing like the dramatic changes expected. Given the radical nature of the initiative and the way it tends to bring to the surface major underlying tensions this is not surprising.

Matters of the basic structure of economies and of global economic change cannot be separated from managerial efforts to 'motivate' and 'lead' people within organisa- tions or from the initiatives they take to design or 'redesign' jobs – whether they involve minor initiatives or larger radical ones like business process re-engineering. The managerial shaping of tasks and managerial attempts to win the cooperation of employees always occurs in a context where interests both coincide and clash, where people both make agreements and dispute with each other, where people both strive to advance themselves and have to defend themselves from each other. In the next chapter we will look further at a variety of ways in which all of this influences how decisions are made, how people adjust to the situations they find themselves in and how they generally both 'behave' and 'misbehave' in work organisations.

Summary

In this chapter the following key points have been made:

- What are often seen as separate 'topics' in the study of organisations and their management – 'motivation', 'leadership' and 'job/work design' – can better be seen as closely related to each other and, also, as closely tied into the wider struc- tural and cultural features of the organisation in which they occur and as influenced by the whole way in which modern societies and economies are organised.

- It is more helpful to look at people's general *orientations to work* rather than to consider their 'work motivation'. A focus on orientations allows a wider range of relevant factors to be taken into account and makes us more aware of how people think about their work, and what they are prepared to do, and can change as circumstances change.

- Both the 'leadership' in which managers engage in the workplace and the actions they take to 'motivate workers' can better be understood as aspects of *strategic exchange* and as involving managerial attempts to manipulate the way employees perceived the *implicit contract* which is at the heart of the employment relationship.

- The strategic exchange processes that occur as tasks are shaped and as managers strive to win the cooperation of employees involve a great deal of detailed and ongoing negotiation and often lead to the emergence of *indulgency patterns* whereby 'give and take' relationships develop between managers and workers.

- In spite of a growing interest in processual thinking, an almost fetishistic level of attention is given to 'motivation theories' in business and management education and, especially to Maslow's 'hierarchy of needs' theory. This latter theory has enormous weaknesses and has little value as a guide to human practice. But it nevertheless has an important ideological significance in how employment relationships have been thought about in more affluent societies over the past half century. It may also have a symbolic role in the handling of managerial angst.

- The very notion of a 'theory of motivation' is a questionable and potentially unrealisable one. Such a theory would, in effect, be a theory of 'why people do what they do'. However, useful insights have been developed about the role of perceptions of 'equity' and the role of 'expectancies' in shaping work behaviour under the 'motivation theory' banner. These insights can be incorporated into a process-relational way of thinking.

- There are two main principles of *work design* – direct control and indirect control principles – which can be drawn on when managers engage in specific *job design* work. These two sets of principles, the first of which operates with a logic of de-skilling and the latter with a logic of 'enriching' jobs in skill and responsibility terms, have been applied in different ways at different times across the history of industrialised societies.

- The application of these principles, and how it varies with circumstances and the ways in which managers 'enact' contingent circumstances, can be understood in terms of managerial attempts to cope with the underlying contradictions in the organisation of work and employment in modern societies. Managers need to control and manipulate employees as resources and, at the same time, win a degree of consent and commitment to the enterprise from them as human beings. Problems that can arise with the recently popular managerial initiative of *business process re-engineering* can be understood in terms of managerial struggles to handle these fundamental tensions.

Reading

Reading Guides 17 and 22, especially, contain material that supports and takes further much of what is covered in Chapter 9.

CHAPTER 10

Power, decision-making and organisational mischief

| Objectives | Having read this chapter and completed its associated activites, readers should be able to: |

- Apply the concept of *power* to various aspects of everyday organisational functioning, recognising that power operates at several levels.

- Recognise the importance of *micropolitics* to organisational and managerial processes, noting the various ways in which the power of specific individuals or groups can vary, albeit within a basic pattern of power relations.

- Appreciate how the relative amount of power or influence exercised by an individual or group within an organisation relates to their involvement in the handling of *uncertainties* or perceived threats to the organisation's future continuation.

- Understand how processes of managerial decision-making involve much more than the rational analysis of situations and the choice of optimum solutions to given problems.

- Analyse decision-making processes as 'garbage cans' in which a multiplicity of issues and differences of power and perception are thrown together and help shape outcomes.

- See how practices that can be characterised as *organisational mischief* – from fiddles and sabotage to sexual, joking and 'play' activities – all relate to matters of power, identity and negotiated order in the workplace.

- Recognise the particular significance of sexuality and humour in both challenges and adjustments to organisational controls.

Power and exchange at interpersonal, organisational and societal levels

When looking at managerial attempts to 'motivate' or 'lead' people in the previous chapter, the notion of *getting people to do what they would not otherwise do* was used. A 'leader' is someone trying to get others to 'go along with them'. Left to their own devices, we can assume, the people towards whom the leader directs their attention would go off in their own direction. Someone a manager had failed to 'motivate' would presumably 'do their own thing' and not perform in the way the manager required. Much managerial work is therefore about getting people to do what they would not otherwise do. And, interestingly, words like this have often been used by social scientists to define 'power'. One person is said to have power over another to the extent to which they can get them to do things they would not otherwise do. Power, in the human context, has long been recognised by thinkers as involving much more than the simple coercion of one person or group by another. If one person has a large sum of money, for example, and exchanges some of this money for several hours of labour from another person who has very little money, the first person is exerting power over the second – regardless of whether that second person is keen and willing to do that labour. But even if this case were one of a very rich person employing a very poor one, the power does not necessarily all flow one way. If, for example, the poor worker is the only person around with the ability to mend the hole in the rich person's roof then the poor person can exert some power when making the exchange with their rich employer. The rich person's dependence on the worker's unique skill makes them liable to the exertion of power over them by the poor person. These two people are not equals in power terms, but each has some power to exert over the other. Power and exchange, dependence and bargaining are always intimately related.

Discussions about power are often cast in terms of what power 'really is'. The approach here is rather different. As was explained in Chapter 1, concepts should not be regarded as more or less 'correct' definitions of phenomena. Instead, concepts are regarded as more or less helpful devices that we use to understand the world and hence act in a certain way with regard to it. In this spirit, we can draw on a whole tradition of social science thinking to help us come to terms with the power aspects of work organisation and management. Especially helpful here is the recognition that the power aspect of human relationships and social orders has several levels or dimensions. For our purposes, we can identity three dimensions:

- The *interpersonal* dimension of power: the ways in which some people are able to get other people to do things they would not otherwise do. I might feel disinclined to sweep your floor but you might nevertheless get me to do it. This could be because you are bigger than I am; you have a gun and I don't; you dazzle me with your 'charisma'; you persuade me with your silver tongue; you have money to offer which I would like to have, or I have entered a contract accepting you as my 'boss'.

- The *organisational structural–cultural* dimension of power: the pattern of relationships within an organisation whereby rules, hierarchy and cultural norms that people have 'signed up to' by joining the organisation make it normal and 'reasonable' for some people to get others to do what they would not otherwise do. The rules and cultural norms also mean that it is only certain people who define what can and cannot be spoken of – people who say what is put on an agenda and what is left off it, for example. It is the existence of this level of power that makes it possible for you as my 'boss' to get me to sweep your floor. Also, you are one of the people who effectively 'wrote the agenda' which said that manual workers like me can be asked to sweep floors but which rules out my even thinking of asking you, a boss in a smart suit, to sweep a floor.

- The *societal structural–cultural* dimension of power: the pattern of relationships and understandings generally prevailing in a society that mean, first, that certain groups have the material capacity to exert pressures on others (the possession of wealth or weapons, say) and, second, that there is legitimacy given to practices whereby certain people get others to do what they would not otherwise do. The society in which you and I live incorporates a system of ownership of wealth. It also incorporates the institution whereby managers administer some of that wealth on these owners' behalf. This means that you can offer me money to sweep the floor. The culture that we live in identifies some organisational members as bosses and others as workers. Without this, I would be unlikely to accept your right to get me to sweep the floor.

This complexity might seem to rule out the possibility of developing a single concept of power that we can use. But it does not. We can develop a concept by looking at what is common to each of these dimensions. What runs through all of them is the capacity of individuals or groups to affect *outcomes* of situations to their advantage. These outcomes typically relate to the distribution of whatever 'goods' or resources are scarce and are valued in the society. Without 'scarcity' there would be no need for anyone to exert power.

Power	Concept
The capacity of an individual or group to affect the outcome of any situation so that access is achieved to whatever resources are scarce and desired within a society or a part of that society.	

If everyone could obtain anything they wanted without reference to other people (from a large country estate to a clean office floor, say) they would never need to act towards others in power terms at all. This is unimaginable of course. Not only are many desirable things inevitably in short supply but sometimes what one person wants necessarily precludes another person from having it. I might want music playing in the office, for example. But you do not.

Negotiation is called for. But whichever of us is generally the more 'powerful' in the office is the one who is likely to get their way over this matter.

Even where a piece of 'power behaviour' occurs in private between just two people it cannot be understood as something separate from the culture, structure and patterns of advantage and disadvantage prevailing in the society and culture to which these individuals belong. A concept (or 'working definition') of power must therefore recognise the societal or structural–cultural dimension of power as well as the fact that it is often manifested at the level of individuals and groups. If we really want to understand specific actions and practices in work organisations, we need to consider power factors that go beyond the immediate and the local. This has been done in our consideration of many of the organisational and managerial cases we have looked at in previous chapters. We can look back to the most recent story put before us, for example.

Activity 10.1

Revisit Roberto Auldearn's story about the business process re-engineering of Dovecote Components (Cases and Conversations 9.4) and try to identify 'power factors' operating here which can be understood in terms of each of the three dimensions of power set out above:

- the interpersonal;
- the organisational structural–cultural;
- the societal structural–cultural.

The boardroom events that Roberto Auldearn told us about involved interpersonal power rivalries between Roberto and two other senior managers. There seemed in this to be elements of both material interests ('territoriality') and emotions (personal dislikes are mentioned). Also at this level, we see Jerry Penick very clearly wielding power over all the other managers. He is exerting his authority as the managing director of the company – not just to 'put the boot in' to Roberto's ideas or to say who will and will not be involved in the 'action group'. He actually sacks the manufacturing and the finance directors. Jerry's use of his chief executive's authority to act towards these individuals in this way is connected to the interpersonal dimension and to the organisational structural and cultural dimension of the power that is operating here. And that dimension would not exist unless it, in turn, was embedded in a set of cultural institutions and wealth-ownership patterns at the societal level that gives chief executives the right to act in this way. But Jerry's power behaviour with regard to the re-engineering of the business also has to be understood in the light of the global changes in the way wealth and power is being restructured in an increasingly international market place. The power relationships between major corporations are shifting. And formal governmental politics are also playing a part in the power plays occurring in Dovecot Components, as Roberto's mention of government industrial relations policies suggests. However, the outcomes of all of this go way beyond the boardroom. The access to scarce and valued resources of all of those who lose their jobs as a result of the restructuring of Dovecote will be seriously affected. Power and politics in the boardrooms of work organisations create winners and losers both within those boardrooms and in the communities within which the organisations are located. Micropolitics must always be understood in the context of 'macropolitics'.

The inevitability of organisational politics or 'micropolitics'

A distinction was made in Chapter 3 (pp. 68–9) between an organisation's *management* (the function of shaping and steering of the organisation into the long term), its *managing* (the actions taken to bring about this long-term survival) and its *managers* (the people whose actions 'take forward' the organisation strategically). This view of the nature and purpose of managerial work recognises that *in principle* the managers working in an organisation are employed to work together to ensure the continuation of the organisation as a whole. First and foremost, managers are there to contribute to the organisation's general performance. They attend to their specific departmental or specialist role within the organisation as a means to the continuation of the organisation and not as an end in itself. The value of operating like this in practice was illustrated in Mats Clunas's story about his company and the strategic role played by all the company's managers (Cases and Conversations 6.1). However, such a principle is not as easy to put into practice, as Mats himself was well aware.

Link   The discussion of the inevitable failings and contradictions of bureaucracy in Chapter 7 shows various ways in which sub-sections of organisations, which are meant to be *means* to a corporate end, can become ends in themselves or come to be run more for the benefit of members of those sub-units than for the corporation as a whole.

It has repeatedly been stressed in *Organising and Managing Work* that people in organisations tend to have goals, priorities and ambitions of their own. All employees, managers no less than any others, are there to use the organisation just as much as the organisation is there to use them. This is fundamental to the employment exchange that all employees make with their employer. Inevitably, managers will at times see that attending to functional or departmental priorities rather than corporate ones can more readily further their personal interests. Most managers below the level of chief executive are located within one of the many 'sub-units' of the organisation – a function like finance, marketing or human resourcing, perhaps, or a department like a university's history, physics or education department. This inevitably risks managers prioritising the interests of their own sub-unit or their own personal interests, as people whose reputations are attached to that department. This tendency is made even greater if their sub-unit location is related to their occupational or 'professional' identity as an accountant, a personnel manager, a historian or a physicist. Whatever their commitment to the larger entity of the organisation might be, the members of any sub-unit – the manager included – are likely to find themselves coming into competition with members of other sub-units. They will typically find themselves competing with other sections of the organisation for the scarce resources that they might want, sometimes to carry out their sub-unit function successfully and sometimes to satisfy other personal or group wants.

Micropolitics/organisational politics	Concept
Processes occurring within work organisations as individuals, groups and organisational 'sub-units' compete for access to scarce and valued material and symbolic resources.	

The *micropolitics* that go on in organisations are not all to be understood in terms of sub-unit commitments, however. Neither are they only indulged in by managers. It is possible that coalitions of women might form within part of an organisation to compete with groupings of men who have been trying to exclude them from certain rewards, for example. Or younger employees might get together to challenge certain older individuals who have tried to maintain a monopoly over particular resources. Equally, we are likely to see competition between individuals for scarce and valued resources varying from car parking spaces or sunny offices to salary increases and career promotions.

Micropolitical conflicts often occur over obviously material resources like budgets, floor space or salary increments, but almost every material resource also has a symbolic value. To have the biggest office in a building means more than simply having the most office floor space, for example. For a person or a group to be given better material resources than others is typically associated with their being afforded higher prestige or respect. It is not unknown for an individual to feel that their whole working life and standing in the organisation has improved simply because they have been allocated a reserved parking spot, for example.

Micropolitics, or the competition between organisational members for scarce resources, is far from a trivial matter. It is much more than a 'side-show' to the main organisational performance of producing goods or services. One frequently hears people complain that the organisation in which they work is 'very political' and implying that this might not be the case in another organisation. Although it might well be the case that the 'politics' in some organisations are more vicious and potentially destructive than in others, there is no possibility whatsoever of discovering, this side of utopia, an organisation in which politicking was not a significant fact of life. But are micropolitics necessarily counterproductive to organisational effectiveness? Competitive behaviour between members of organisations may indeed undermine productive cooperation between organisational members. Yet it can also contribute to successful organisational performance (for reasons we shall see shortly). Either way, micropolitics are an inevitable and intrinsic part of organisational life and activity. This is so for a number of reasons.

First, micropolitics are inevitable because human beings, by virtue of being human, are 'strategic animals'. They continually strive to establish who they are and they seek to meet the material requirements of themselves and their families. To do this they will inevitably have to cooperate with others, both at work and outside it. But they will just as inevitably come into competition with others – given the scarcity of many of the things that human beings tend to want, as we recognised earlier. We could say, then, that a degree of competition and rivalry between people is a normal part of the human condition and is as likely to manifest itself in work relationships as anywhere else in people's lives.

Micropolitics are inevitable, second, because of the way organisations themselves are set up. This relates to the point made above that the division of labour in an organisation and its allocation of people to organisational 'sub-units' tends to encourage people to act in the interests of that grouping rather than in the interests of something much more difficult to identify with – the 'organisation as a whole'. And if a group does not have this 'bigger interest' or 'wider loyalty' to discourage them from acting sectionally then they are likely to find themselves competing with other sub-units, given the scarcity of many of the resources that each sub-unit will be seeking. These are resources varying from budgets to premises and from able new organisational recruits to prestige within the corporate status hierarchy. At the level of the sub-unit managers, such tendencies are exacerbated by the fact that managers across any particular level of an organisation's sub-units are often in competition with each other for posts at the next higher level on the organisation's narrowing managerial career ladder. Figure 10.1 illustrates this. In a classic analysis of micropolitics, Burns (1961, Reading Guide 7) pointed out that organisational members 'are at one and the same time co-operators in a common enterprise and rivals for the material and intangible rewards of successful competition with each other'. This is a key feature of the institution of bureaucracy – a defining characteristic of every organisation (Chapter 7, p. 240). The bureaucratic structure works both as a control mechanism and a reward ladder. These two aspects of the structuring of all organisations are bound to come into tension with each other.

In the case of a school, for example, this dual control/reward aspect of organisational structure might mean that all the teachers of science would be required to cooperate with each other to gain a good assessment of science teaching in that school by the visiting quality inspectors. One of the 'motivators' to positive and cooperative behaviour for each of these teachers is the possibility of future promotion to the better-paid and more prestigious post of head of science. But only one of these teachers can become the head of department. Thus cooperators are simultaneously competitors. This is competition *within* a sub-unit or department. What about *across* sub-units? If we look at the next level of hierarchy in this school, we see the post of deputy head teacher, and the potential competitors for this are all the heads of department across the school. So here we see departmental managers being required both to cooperate with each other to make the whole school

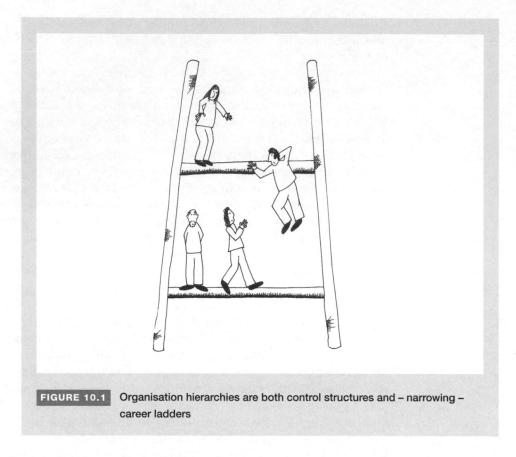

FIGURE 10.1 Organisation hierarchies are both control structures and – narrowing – career ladders

successful at the same time as those sub-unit leaders are put into competition with each other. Career pressures are thus added to pressures of which department is to get the better classrooms, the better book budget, and so on.

 Link Ambiguity and uncertainty are shown in Chapter 3 (pp. 81–4) to be inherent in organisations and to be major factors influencing the way managers behave as they do in their work.

The third set of factors making micropolitics inevitable relates to the high degree of ambiguity and uncertainty that runs through all organisational situations. It is impossible for anyone to have the 'full facts' of any situation, for them to understand fully what is going on at any given time or for them to be able to predict the outcome of any action taken. This characteristic of organisational life helps explain how managers come to depend on other people in their work situations and why they need to make trading, negotiating and influencing others so central to their work. Political processes play a significant part in the handling of all of this, but the concern here is with how ambiguity both makes possible and encourages competitive behaviour between organisational members. Such micropolitical behaviour is something that managers are liable to engage in on their own account

– promoting their own careers, for example. They will also get involved in micropolitics as they find themselves having to handle the political activities of other employees – ensuring that the career competition between members of their own department is channelled is such a way that it does not prevent productively cooperative work being done by those individuals, for example.

Ambiguity exists, we said, when the meaning of a situation is unclear or confused and is therefore open to a variety of interpretations (p. 83). Given the considerable scope for people to offer different interpretations of what is going on, it is not surprising to find individuals and groups exploiting such situations to their own advantage. There might be ambiguity, for example, about whether a new and influential job would be best done by one of my friends and allies or by one of your friends and allies. In such a situation it is quite likely that you and I will compete in arguing for giving the job to our own respective friend and political ally. In doing so, we would be acting micropolitically. In doing so, we might be acting to further personal and private interests (helping a personal friend along in their careers). Equally, we might be acting to further the interests of our respective departments (ensuring someone is appointed who will favour my department rather than yours in future contests between your departmental interests and mine). What is most likely, though, is that we will be acting to further or defend *both* our personal situation *and* that of our departments. We might even be politicking to get an outcome that we believe will benefit the organisation as a whole as well as serving our sectional interests. Alternatively, though, we might be acting to bring about something that will favour our sectional interests at the price of corporate ones. Which of these is the case in any particular circumstance will always tend to be ambiguous, of course!

Uncertainty is closely related to ambiguity and was conceptualised in Chapter 3 by treating it as an aspect of ambiguity that is related to the future. Uncertainty exists when the *understanding of a future situation or an event* is unclear or confused and is therefore open to a variety of interpretations (p. 83). This brings strategic matters into the picture – strategy being essentially about how the organisation is to develop into the long-term future. One of the key tasks of organisational strategists is to know, at any point in time, which of the constituencies with which it trades or 'exchanges' are most 'strategic' at that time – in terms of the degree of uncertainty they are creating for the organisation's long-term future. If a group of workers in an organisation without which the organisation cannot survive are threatening to leave, for example, it might become a strategic priority to find an inducement to keep them 'on board'. At another time perhaps, the managers of that organisation might discover that they are desperately short of funds to invest in a new product that is vital to long-term survival. Faced with this uncertainty, the search for investment funds is likely to become a strategic priority.

Link   The notion that certain of the constituencies with which an organisation exchanges resources are, at any point in time, more strategic than others as a result of the degree of uncertainty they are creating was central to the organisational strategic exchange analysis of Chapter 6, pp. 188–213.

> ## Strategic contingency theory of power   *Concept*
>
> A sub-unit of an organisation will have greater relative power or influence within the organisation the more it (a) is central to the organisation's workflow, (b) cannot be substituted by another unit, (c) reduces uncertainties perceived to be of strategic significance to the organisation.

The fact that strategic priorities change over time in the light of changing organisational uncertainties has considerable implications for micropolitics. One of the main sources of relative power enjoyed by any person or sub-unit – in the sense of having relatively good access to scarce and desired resources – is the role it plays in handling uncertainties thought to be facing the organisation with regard to its future. Thus, the person who persuades the vital group of workers to stay with the organisation will be well placed the next time a promotion comes up or a smart new office becomes available. Also, he or she is likely to find themselves being listened to by managers at senior levels on subsequent matters. Their influence and the likelihood of their further succeeding in micropolitical activity has thus been enhanced by dealing with a strategic uncertainty. They are well placed to repeat such successes and generally advance their power and gain further rewards in the future. Similarly, if a particular department were seen to be solving the problem (overcoming the uncertainty) that had arisen with regard to new product investment that department or function would be likely to rise up the departmental 'pecking order' of the organisation. The relative power of the sub-unit is enhanced and, again, its members are better placed to succeed in subsequent micropolitical manoeuvrings. This would only be the case, however, if that sub-unit was regarded as substitutable by another sub-unit, as is pointed out by Hickson *et al.* (1971, Reading Guide 7) in their analysis of what they call 'strategic contingencies' (strategically important uncertainties) as key sources of sub-unit power. Power would not go to either the individual keeping the key workers in the organisation or to the department obtaining the investment funding if, in either case, it was seen that another party could just as readily solve such problems. Neither would this happen if that individual or sub-unit were not, in the first place, seen as relatively 'central to the workflow of the organisation'. One is not likely suddenly to acquire power and influence by dealing with an uncertainty if one is generally regarded as peripheral to the key operations of the organisation.

It is important to note here that process-relational analysis treats all these contingencies as matters of interpretations (or 'enactments') made by members of the organisation and not as objectively existing circumstances – as they would tend to be regarded in more systems-oriented contingency thinking about organisations (Chapter 8). Thus, an important element of the political behaviour of an individual or a sub-unit within an organisation wishing to increase their relative power would be the *persuading* of people with the greatest relative power that a certain contingency, such as a shortage of investment funds or the likely loss of a key customer, should be regarded as a serious strategic threat. If they wish to persuade the 'powers that be' that they are the people to solve the problem they will have to work on the way they are themselves perceived. Their being 'central to workflow' or as 'unsubstitutable' is always a *perceived* centrality or an *understood* irreplaceability. To 'politick' successfully one has to persuade the people in charge that one is both central to operations and that one's role cannot be played by anyone else. Bearing this in mind we can turn to the example of a person who sees himself as an especially successful organisational politician.

Activity 10.2

Look at the account Derek Duffus gives in Cases and Conversations 10.1 of his 'rise and rise' in the newspaper industry and identify:

- the 'rewards' of micropolitical activity that come to Derek or to any other of the people in the story (i.e. what 'scarce and desired resources' we see anyone obtaining as a result of politicking);

- the micropolitical moves or 'tactics' that are mentioned by Derek;

- situations where the handling of strategic uncertainties perceived to be facing the newspaper were relevant to the obtaining of 'power' (i.e. the winning of access to scarce and desirable resources) either by individuals or by organisational sub-units.

The rise and rise of Derek Duffus
Cases and Conversations 10.1

I've heard you say a couple of times that you are a particularly 'political animal'. You've also said that every newspaper editor has to be 'a consummate politician'. How do you relate these two things?

In the obvious way, I suppose. I think it is true that to do a job like that of an editor of a big paper you have got to have a lot of cunning and a great deal of skill at getting what you want from people. And I have both of these things. That's why I have got to the top here much younger than I would if I'd been a less political animal. And I have beaten others to get where I am. There's no denying that. I wasn't the only candidate for the editorial chair.

OK, then. Can we first just look at you and your career and then come back to the editor's job? Take me back as far as you can with your life as a 'political animal'.

Gosh, I suppose I should try to remember some playground stories to tell you. I can't remember much beyond the fact that I once did a deal with a teacher. I gave her some strong hints about where the smokers were going at break time for their illegal fags. In return, she helped me become a school prefect. That had some quite nice perks which made my last year at school more comfortable than it might have been – nothing special, just things like having a chair to sit on at assembly instead of having to sit on the floor with all the rest.

And when you were at college?

Yes, I suppose I developed that sort of knack further. Making friends with a couple of the journalism lecturers certainly helped me – you know, allowing me more generous deadlines for assignments and all that. In fact,

yes it's coming back to me now, there was this tutor who'd once had a glorious career on a national Sunday before being ruined by the drink. I used to go down the pub with him. And on several occasions he gave me an assignment mark for telling him, over several pints, what I would have written if I had got around to putting things down on paper. That was a good deal. We both saved time – I didn't have to write the essays and he didn't have to read them.

Did you feel you were cheating?

Only occasionally. I mean I did actually learn a lot in my chats with him. I am sure I would have got good marks if I had put in proper assignments.

And were you in this on your own?

Oh gosh yes. I wouldn't have trusted more than a couple of my best mates with that secret. I probably did tell them about it, but they did the assignments like everybody else. I do remember, though, conspiring with these two friends to make sure that, every year, two out of the three of us got elected as year representatives. We always made a point of praising the quality of the teaching, even when it was crap. I'm sure that helped us get better marks than we might have got, especially from one of the really bad lecturers. He particularly had to – how shall I put it? – look after me and my mate so that complaints about his incoherent lectures didn't get to the course committee.

It sounds like you were training yourself in more than journalism at college then?

I'd never thought of it like that before. But I suppose you are right. I certainly looked around pretty quickly to work out which of my fellow reporters I could team up with when I got my first proper job. I had just one mate there and he and I decided to take up golf, just to get in with the news editor, who was obsessed with the little rubber ball. I think it worked for a while. We both got allocated to more interesting stories than the other younger reporters, I think. But it nearly backfired on us. The others recognised what we were up to. They didn't like our little alliance. They sarcastically called us the 'super cubs' and they made life so difficult for us that I decided to drop the golf thing. But I made up the ground I'd lost by taking on a sort of informal leadership of the younger reporters. Most of us disliked the older clique, who looked down on us with contempt. We called them the 'old farts'. And sometimes, when we met as a group down the pub we would devise tricks that would get one or more of the old farts out chasing non-stories.

How did you do that?

The best example is where we got one of the girls to ring up one of these blokes and pretend she was a councillor who was worried about corruption on the local authority. We had a couple of the old journos chasing their tails for weeks on that one.

And did they realise they had been tricked.

Oh yes. They caught us out eventually. After that it was real war.

Who won?

They did. Generally speaking. It turned out that they were much better at that sort of thing than we were. They wiped the floor with several of us 'pathetic cub reporters', as they called us. But I turned things round to my personal advantage, I must admit.

How?

In the end, this battle between the 'old farts' and the 'young ones' was doing real harm to the paper. The editor called us all in and put it to us that if things didn't change the paper might be sold and merged with another one. 'You had all better get your eyes back on the ball, or your jobs are at risk', he said. I decided to go and see the editor a couple of days later. I told him that I wanted some personal advice from him on my long-term career and whether it was a good idea to try to become an editor. I didn't really want such advice from him. But I did want to find out whether the paper was under real threat. It turned out that it really was. The news operation had to be sharpened up or else. At the end of the meeting he asked me if there was anything I thought I could do to mend fences between the factions on the paper. 'Of course', I said 'I will do my utmost'. And indeed I did – using all the charm I could muster to persuade people to work together rather than work against each other. And in the process of this I became a sort of protégé of the editor. A bit of patronage here and there never does any harm, I always say. I used to see him regularly for what he called 'our mentoring chats'. And, in the process of discussing his advice I used to drop in little bits of information that might be useful to him and the management of the paper. And, guess what? My salary went up rather nicely. My expenses got queried much less than anybody else's. And when the news editor retired, guess who replaced him?

You did.

How did you guess? Yes, the rise and rise of Derek Duffus was really under way. I was heading for the editor's chair.

But you were just news editor at this stage?

That's right. But I saw that as just a step to the top job.

And was it?

Not as directly as I had calculated. It turned out that, of all people, it was the sports editor who was the most powerful baron at court. He was even more influential than the financial and the marketing people. I saw straight away that he was someone I had to sort out.

Why was he so influential?

It all turned on one particular sports writer. Francis Khyber was immensely popular with readers and everybody knew that several nationals were courting him. He was a natural networker. He had a network of contacts across the sporting world, and indeed well beyond it. He basically named his own salary here. But the sports editor argued that it was his relationship with Francis that kept him on the paper. The editor himself, the finance and the marketing people therefore tended to allow the sports editor first say on all sorts of things. Through his relationship with just one of the newspaper's best assets, Francis Khyber, he made himself indispensable. Whether it was true or not, the whole editorial and management team assumed that the loss of this one writer would do real damage to circulation. With the editor just a few years away from retirement, I had a serious rival for his job. Sport, in effect, counted for more than news.

I can't wait to hear how you dealt with this.

Think about it. It's dead simple really.

Well, assassination comes to mind, but I'm sure . . .

Well I did consider a bit of character assassination when I discovered that the sports editor had a minor criminal record – years back. Only I had this killer information. But no, I calculated that if I played things that dirty I would risk my own integrity. I didn't want to risk being seen as that ruthless. Papers do want their editor to be seen as a person of integrity.

So you . . .

Yes, I worked out that if one asset, one writer, was the source of a rival's power, then perhaps I should try to acquire that asset for my own department. It turned out that this was much easier than it might sound. I made a point of getting to know Francis Khyber and soon discovered that he was quite keen to 'develop out of sport'. He had done one or two feature articles with only tenuous sporting links and was quite close to the features editor. He'd been thinking of moving in that direction but was having doubts. The affair he was having with the features editor was becoming a problem to him. So you can see where I saw my chance. I started discussions with him about joining my team. I persuaded him that his networking abilities could be exploited in news journalism much better than anywhere else, which was absolutely genuine. I discovered that he already knew several key politicians very well and that a couple of very senior police officers were amongst his family friends. He'd met all these people schmoozing at sports events apparently.

And that's what you did?

Yes, after an almighty fight I was allowed to recruit Francis to my team. There was blood on the carpet, I can tell you. The sports editor bitterly fought me over my claim that Francis would be an even bigger asset to the paper if he featured more on the front pages. And he nearly went berserk when I said that moving him to my area would be the only thing that would keep him on the paper. In the end, as you can guess, Francis said what he wanted to do. And nobody could argue. Consequently, I moved to the top of the pecking order, below the editor. And when Jack retired? Well here I am.

Editor and 'managing editor' I notice.

Yep, king of the castle – a power in the land.

We must be careful not to take this example of a self-proclaimed 'consummate politician', as typical of managers and others who engage in the everyday micropolitics of the average work organisation. However, this man's exceptionally frank and colourful story is full of insights into the way power and conflict can manifest themselves in organisations. The language used here is very much the language of power, power clashes, ambition and political intrigue. Scanning the account gives us terms like 'cunning', 'beating others', 'alliances', 'conspiring', 'war', 'battle', 'barons at court', 'influencing', 'networking', 'sorting someone out', 'killer information', 'sources of power', 'blood on the carpet', 'pecking order' and, of course, 'king of the castle' and 'a power in the land'. But such language is far from unusual in the discussions of relationships and activities that occur everyday in corporate offices and the 'corridors of power' of organisations ranging from banks to breweries, government departments to opera houses, schools to newspapers. The micropolitics that occur in all these settings are part and parcel of how bureaucratic enterprises operate and the ways in which individuals, groups, 'sub-units' pursue power – in the sense of seeking or maintaining access to whatever resources are scarce and desired.

We hear of various types of 'resource' being pursued in the school and the newspaper that feature in Derek Duffus's story. Promotions and good salaries were resources we are not surprised to hear mentioned and these were clearly central to much of the politicking in the newspaper organisation. Derek's career advancement is the central theme of this slice of autobiography but, on the way, he makes sure to mention that his salary was 'going up nicely'. We also hear that Francis Khyber had got himself into a position whereby he could 'name his own salary'. Political advantage can also mean that one's expenses are queried less than those of others, it would seem. And the rewards of power or influence can include 'perks' as modest as having a chair to sit on at school assemblies. They can also include having a greater amount of 'free' time, as we saw in the case of the alternative to a written assignment that Derek negotiated with the college lecturer. Later, one of the rewards that Derek receives as a result of his cultivating the news editor is his allocation to news stories that were 'more interesting' than the ones given to other young reporters.

An impression that we tend to get, not just from this story but from other accounts of organisational politics, is that power and influence *themselves* are rewards that power and influence can bring. At a simple level, this can be understood as a matter of the sense of achievement that accompanies the possession of power and influence. The very tone of Derek's story-telling suggests that this might be the case with him. But there is another level at which the 'power as a reward of power' phenomenon operates. People pursue power not just to obtain the immediate resources that come from having power – money, status and general 'comforts of life'. They also pursue it to put themselves in a position whereby they will be able to obtain whatever they might turn out to want in the future. To have power is to have the potential to 'do better' in the future. We don't know what Derek might want in the future – wealth, lovers, opportunities to travel, career advancement for his children or even entry into national politics and government. But his current position as 'king of the castle' at his newspaper puts him in a better position to obtain these things than he would be in if he were just one of the underlings at court.

The outcomes of micropolitical success are clearly many and varied. But the methods or tactics used to achieve micropolitical success are equally numerous and varied. We hear of numerous tactics and stratagems in Derek's story.

- *Doing deals and making exchanges*. Derek actually refers to the 'good deal' that he made with the college tutor. It was a trade from which both benefited. One party to the trade had less assignment writing to do. The other party had less marking to do. All the exchanges that Derek makes across the range of his politicking activities, can be understood as *strategic* exchanges. They are trades, sometimes minor and sometimes major, that play a part in advancing his career or life strategy.

- *Seeking patrons.* Derek learned of the advantages to be gained by establishing relationships with more powerful people when he was still at school. We see him doing something similar at college. Early on at work, we see him seeking the patronage of the news editor to help advance his situation. Later, he manages to get the editor himself to be his patron. He initially flatters the editor by pretending to be seeking career advice. He then builds up the relationship, and creates a degree of dependence, by trading 'little bits of information' that might be useful to the editor and to 'the management'. He does this for both immediate material reward and for a crown prince role – the position of heir to the throne.

- *Making alliances.* Derek sought to 'team up with' selected colleagues as soon as he got his first job. He soon found a 'mate' to join him in gaining advantage over the other reporters.

- *Conspiring.* Derek uses this term to describe the earlier alliance at college when he and two friends exploited their position on a course committee to get higher marks than other students.

- *Mobilising groups and assuming informal leadership roles.* This type of alliance-making is seen in Derek's mobilising of younger reporters into what might be called a 'cabal' to oppose the older 'clique' he labelled the 'old farts'.

- *Lying and cheating.* This is seen both in the 'praising' of bad teaching at college and the effective blackmailing of certain lecturers. It also comes into the 'tricking' of the older journalists into pursuing non-existent news stories.

- *Making strategic retreats.* Derek is willing to take a step backwards if he perceives an immediate advantage potentially compromising longer-term success. He 'dropped the golf thing' when he found other reporters getting hostile about his cultivation of the news editor. He recognised the disadvantages of fellow reporters 'making life difficult' for him and his fellow 'super cub'. He made a further strategic retreat when he sought to end the war with the 'old farts' who were proving too clever for Derek and his gang.

- *Using charm and skills of persuasion.* It appears that Derek uses such skills regularly. He explicitly mentions them when telling us about his efforts to repair relationships between the factions in the news office.

- *Networking.* We can assume that Derek himself will have built up a network of contacts that he can 'trade with', especially as a means of obtaining news and information. However, it is Francis Khyber's networks that he tells us about, and he paints a picture of Francis 'schmoozing' with influential people at sports events. Derek sees this aspect of Francis's skills as a key resource he can draw on to assist in his own personal advancement.

- *Talent spotting, selective recruitment and adopting protégés.* A key method many managers use to advance their own or their department's interests is to look out for talented people outside their own sub-unit that they can bring into their fold. This often leads to competition between unit heads, as we see when Derek 'poaches' Francis from the sports department. Francis may be too established a figure to be a protégé of Derek, but we can expect Derek to be as adept at adopting able junior people as protégés as he was earlier in his career when he sought to become the protégé of more established people himself. The patron–protégé relationship is a form of strategic exchange in which the more junior person gains a 'push up the ladder' in return for loyalty given and favours done for the patron.

- *Gathering information that may actually or potentially be used against a rival or otherwise to advance one's interests.* At some stage Derek has clearly researched the sports editor's background and found potentially damaging information that, as it happens on this occasion, he does not use. He also seems keen to let us know that he also has 'dirt' on the features editor in the form of knowledge of her affair with Francis Khyber. To what extent he used this to advance his interests when negotiating with Francis we do not know. What we can infer, however, is that he regarded this piece of knowledge as politically advantageous. We also see Derek gathering information that he can trade with others to gain advantage in other ways. This happened early on at school with the information about where other boys smoked on the school premises being traded for help in 'promotion' to a prefect's position. The information he supplies to the editor and the management of the newspaper in the period prior to his inheriting the editor's throne is clearly an important key that helped him unlock the throne room.

Throughout his career, Derek Duffus strategically exchanges in a variety of ways with people around him. He gives something here, he takes something there – all to help with the shaping of his life and his work career. But he most significantly advances his interests (increasing his relative organisational 'power') when he links his *personal strategic exchanges* directly to issues of the newspaper's *organisational strategic exchanges*. This is where the strategic contingency insight is helpful to our understanding of what is happening on the newspaper. We hear of the newspaper facing perceived strategic uncertainty on two occasions. The first is when the in-fighting between news reporters is beginning to threaten the quality of the paper and, hence, its circulation figures and long-term survival. And what does Derek do? He is already regarded as central to the workflow of the paper when he puts himself forward to the editor as the person who can reduce this uncertainty. Given the shrewd political operator that he is, we can assume that he will have put himself forward as the only person who can do this. He will have ensured that he is perceived as unsubstitutable.

The second time Derek reveals his understanding of the strategic contingency principle is over the uncertainty created for the paper's future by the possible loss of Francis Khyber. It would appear that Francis himself has some grasp of this principle. He has made himself central to the paper's journalistic work. He has made himself a unique and therefore unsubstitutable 'star' reporter. He has control over the strategic uncertainty he himself creates: he can choose to go or stay. Derek sees in Francis's position an opportunity to increase his own power and influence and to make the news department a more powerful sub-unit than the sports section. By taking Francis into his own department and making it more likely that Francis will stay with the paper, he – and his sub-unit – is handling a strategic uncertainty for the paper. Both he and his department thus move up the micropolitical pecking order. The paper is better placed to exchange strategically with its readers, advertisers and all the other constituencies with which it deals if Francis stays on board. Francis, Derek and the news department are thus rewarded for their contribution towards this strengthened strategic position of the paper.

Activity 10.3

Look back over all your own organisational experiences, whether in school or college or arising from managerial activities (or possibly in books, films or TV programmes with an organisational setting that you have seen), and

- note down examples of some of the micropolitical tactics reported by Derek Duffus that you have personally observed;

- if possible, note down any further types of politicking activity that you might have come across;

- consider whether you are able to point to any examples of the 'perceived strategic contingency' factor playing a part in the organisational politicking you have observed.

Organised anarchy and decision-making in the garbage can

Within the micropolitics that occur in all organisations we see numerous goals and purposes being pursued by individuals, organisational sub-units and the coalitions or alliances that are always forming and re-forming. There are inevitably winners and losers in every political engagement and, sometimes, the outcomes of these engagements will strengthen the strategic position of the organisation and sometimes they will compromise the organisation's long-term survival. The resulting *negotiated order* that, in effect, constitutes 'the organisation' at any point in time is not just an outcome of random human efforts to advance or defend their sectional interests, however. The official structure and culture of the organisation – the formal blueprint or 'organisational design' – contributes to the negotiated order of the organisation as much as do the calculations and actions of organisational actors.

 Link   There is clearly a close relationship between the concept of organisational micropolitics being examined here and the notion of *negotiated order* examined in Chapter 3, pp. 74–81.

The way the hierarchical structure of organisations functions as both a control system and a narrowing career ladder is an important illustration of this. The outcome is that whenever we look at an organisation we see, at one moment, a pattern of order in which things seem 'very organised' and, at another moment, something that is much disorganised' – anarchic even. The term *organised anarchy* was used in a study of several universities to capture this quality of organisational life (Cohen, March and Olsen, 1972, Reading Guide 7). The term usefully brings out the rather paradoxical quality of all organisational processes: their tendency, at the same time, to be both very organised and very disorganised. Similarly, the *garbage can model of organisational choice* developed by these same researchers can usefully help us see how this 'disorganised-organisation' quality of organised life manifests itself in decision-making situations in organisations generally.

Garbage can model of organisational choice	*Concept*
Organisational decisions are influenced by the various problems that are around at the time of the decision; the various available solutions which might be attached to these problems; the people who are around at the time; the amount of time these people have available.	

The 'garbage can' concept can help us understand further the way that the general *negotiated order* of an organisation comes about by focusing on the specific processes that occur in particular decision-making or organisational choice events. The model is invaluable in sensitising us to the complexity of 'what is going on' in the typical decision-making meeting that occurs daily in work organisations.

Our consideration of micropolitical processes has already made us aware of the variety of different goals and interests that are brought into play when managers make organisational choices. But the garbage can model makes us aware that there are plenty of other factors 'at play' when managers meet to make decisions. It is the idea that a complex mixture of items is thrown together in the big vessel of the decision-making event that leads to the use of the metaphor of the garbage can. The model could just as easily be called the 'big suitcase' or 'loaded shopping trolley' model. Figure 10.2 represents the garbage can of the decision-making event.

We can immediately see in Figure 10.2 a departure from conventional conceptions of decision-making situations and processes. We normally assume that a decision-making process is a linear one (pp. 98–102). It starts off with the identification of a problem that requires solving. People with relevant interests and knowledge are then brought together to discuss all the relevant information they can gather. Out of this emerges the solution to the problem – one that is best for the organisation. Such an approach is eminently sensible, and most of us who work in organisations regularly try to follow such a sequence to help us make 'good decisions'. However, if we are shrewd, we will be aware that there is a great deal more going on in the typical decision-making event. The garbage can model points out how complex the mix of factors is.

● There is typically more than one problem 'floating around' at the time. A meeting may have been called to tackle a specific problem, but people will tend to bring along further problems that might be dealt with at the same

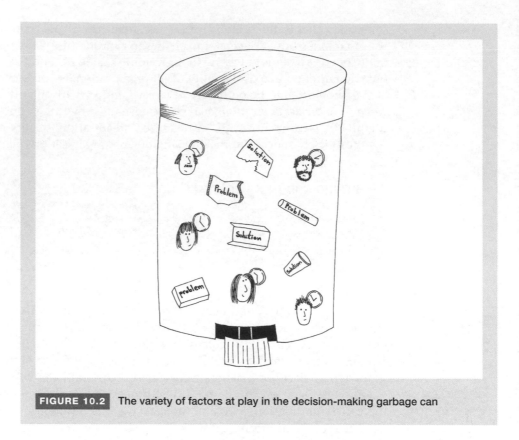

FIGURE 10.2 The variety of factors at play in the decision-making garbage can

time. A meeting is called, for example, to tackle the problem of the ineffective heating system in a building, but the problem of the shortage of car parking spaces is 'brought along' by several of the meeting's members.

● Solutions are rarely 'created' in the decision-making process. People will bring along various already-existing solutions to a problem-solving event. Sometimes these are solutions to problems that are quite different from the focal one on the official agenda. There is nevertheless the possibility that pre-existing solutions might be attached to the problem the meeting is tackling. A decision-making event might be organised to decide where to place a contract for the replacement of a heating system, for instance. Several participants come along to the meeting, however, with the 'solution' that the building itself should be demolished and replaced (perhaps by a building with a large underground car park!).

● The people who turn up to contribute to the decision-making process, and those who fail to turn up, will affect outcomes. The outcome of a decision-making event about the heating of a building might be very different if the individuals with some knowledge of heating engineering fail to turn up.

● The amount of time the people who are involved have available – or, indeed, the extent to which they are willing to concentrate on what is going on – will make a difference to the decision that is reached. If the heating engineer present at a meeting has just arrived back from holiday, is sick and jet-lagged and has to leave early for a doctor's appointment, a different decision might be made about how to improve the heating system from the one that might have emerged if this individual had been fully alert and present to the end.

Our awareness of the importance of micropolitical processes encourages us to pay close attention to the 'variables' of who is present and what amount of time or concentration each of them is going to devote to the event. But it is not just the personal or sub-unit interests that each person brings with them that are important. People will certainly act to defend or further their personal or departmental interests. They may also act to support a 'friend' (or someone to whom they owe a favour), or they might act to undermine somebody they dislike. Alternatively, they might support someone to whom they are physically or emotionally attracted. Sometimes people will speak up simply in order to impress others or make a lot of interventions because they enjoy taking centre stage wherever they go. We should not underestimate the 'play' element that comes into organisational decision-making events. It is far from unknown for people to pursue a certain line in a meeting to amuse themselves, to reduce boredom or simply to create a 'good story' to take home to tell their husband or wife over supper. This might merely waste a certain amount of time without affecting the decision that is eventually made. On the other hand, such activity might make a material difference to the organisational choices that are made. All these matters are ones that any individual who tries to lead a decision-making process or manage a choice-making meeting has seriously to take into account. Godfrey Nairn is well aware of this.

Activity 10.4

Read Godfrey Nairn's account in Cases and Conversations 10.2 of the meeting that he called to make organisational choices about surveillance systems for the Links Leisure Centre of which he is the general manager. Then identify:

- what problems are floating about in the garbage can, in addition to the one that the meeting was intended to focus upon;

- what solutions are available in the bin to be attached to any of these problems;

- how the meeting is affected by the particular mix of who is there (and who is absent) and by the variable levels of time and attention that people are willing to pay to the main issues;

- what conflicts and key alliances come into play;

- how anyone's interest in 'play' influences events.

God, Todd, Plod, Wad, Bods and Oddjob in the garbage can   Cases and Conversations 10.2

I think that chairing meetings is one of the most difficult aspects of a manager's job. This is especially the case if you're trying to get to a decision that is important for the business. It should be straightforward. But it isn't. Everybody always seems to have their own idea of what is best. You have to cope with all the different characters who each want to have their say. And you have to work out where every one of them is coming from. That's not easy. Everyone has their own agenda, whatever the topic is meant to be. I've never yet run a management meeting where everybody was willing to follow my agenda – let alone sing from the same company song sheet.

Yes, I can give you an example of what I am talking about here. I organised a meeting last week that went on from lunchtime into the middle of the evening. And it got me nowhere. The basic problem that I had in mind, as the general manager of the Links Leisure Centre, was that of how we are going to cope with security problems in next year's busy season. I am conscious that the new motorway into the town and the improved rail service are going to bring us a lot more customers. And I think that the customers will be much more socially and generationally mixed. We are going to be catering for older people, for families with children and for youths who tend to come along in gangs, all at the same time. We have got to think hard about how we are going to maintain order so that one type of customer doesn't spoil things for another. Des Cromarty, the chief executive of the company that owns the Links Leisure Centre is keen on our security measures being 'tight but low profile'. That's company policy he says and he suggested that I call a management meeting to consider introducing an electronic surveillance system – visible and hidden cameras, secret microphones and all that. So that's what I did. I got together Todd, our head of marketing and publicity; Plod, the security manager;

Wad, our accountant; Bods, the personnel manager and Oddjob, the technical services manager. I also invited a police crime prevention officer along and arranged for a security consultant to join us.

The first thing that went wrong for me was that neither the police officer nor the security consultant actually turned up on the day. The absence of people like these, with specialist knowledge and with some independence from all the political crap that goes on within our management team, was a blow. I also thought that my colleagues might be more polite to each other than usual if we had guests at the meeting. But there was no sign of either of these. And, on top of this, Todd was late. We really needed his marketing and publicity input and I wanted his personal support, as the most senior person in my management team.

The second disaster was an extremely rude intervention from Desmond Cromarty, the chief executive. I knew he was calling into the Centre that day to show around an important investment analyst. But just as I was halfway through outlining the key issues to the meeting, in pops Des. He walks over to the plate of Danish pastries I had sent out for in case people got hungry later in the afternoon. He picks up two of these, says 'Good afternoon ladies and gentlemen' and walks out again. My colleagues laughed half-heartedly about this and someone said, 'Oh we all know about Desmond and his ability to sniff out food wherever he goes'. Nice as my colleagues were trying to be, I felt humiliated. I am sure Desmond did it to show off to his guest, at my expense.

I was just getting back into my stride and was ready to open up the debate when in marches Todd, munching a Danish pastry. 'I just bumped into Des and look what he gave me', he announced, grinning broadly. I was furious. In retrospect I am sure he deliberately came into the meeting late. I also wondered, in retrospect, whether one of this group was responsible for deterring the police officer and the security consultant from joining us. Todd had turned up late like this several times before. It was a ploy, I think, to show that he was too important to turn up on time like the others. He just has to show that he is 'different'. I wonder too if he hadn't been deliberately hanging around in the hope of 'bumping into' Des Cromarty.

I think my one-time close friend, Todd, is getting rather jealous of my success in this job. We go back a long way. We worked together at the same level in another company – 'God and Todd' they called us (which is partly why we use these silly Plod, Bods and Wad nicknames here now). He increasingly seems to like the sound of his own voice at meetings and at this one he seemed quite indifferent to the issues being discussed. I think he was intent on spending the afternoon getting in as many of his little jokes as he could and taking pleasure in needling Oddjob, whom I think he hates. Without Todd, we would have got on much better, I regret to say. And he left, too, well before the end of the meeting, claiming that he had to make an important phone call. I had been hoping that, at the end of the meeting, he might make up for all his nonsense and use his considerable skills to help me push people toward some kind of clear conclusion. He has done that before and showed that he and I can still be a good team. But he didn't this time.

Plod, I think would have been willing to stay all night. His priority was clear. He didn't want the surveillance system at all. He wanted the money to be spent on increasing the number of his security staff. He also wanted their rate of pay to go up so that he could 'recruit a better quality of person' which, in turn, would enable him to put a proportion of his security people on plain-clothes patrol. Nothing could more perfectly fit company policy than to have 'tight but discrete security', he argued. This sounded reasonable and was discussed at length. Bods, our personnel manager, was utterly opposed to this however. She argued that her 'labour market research' showed that such a policy was doomed to failure. Plod got very angry with Bods and very nastily accused her of taking the line she was simply because she had been instructed by the company human resources director to get the 'indirect headcount' down 'at all costs'. Surprisingly Bods didn't argue with this. She just coldly suggested that she knew that Plod had boasted to his staff that he could get them all a wage increase and that he would 'do anything to bring this about'. She also said he had problems about his status, believing that he could 'only feel important if he had a large workforce'. 'But size is not what counts', she said with a sly grin on her face.

Wad then came in and tried to calm things down a little by saying that he was 'neither for nor against the proposal'. If a system could be bought which would be covered by the budget that he was putting forward, he was happy. But if the price were anything more than a 'gnat's whisker above my figures', it was 'not on'. Bods said that she fully supported everything that Wad was saying. This led Todd to make some unpleasant insinuations about accountants and personnel people always wanting to 'get into bed together'. He saw me glare at him when he'd said this and he explained that he had noticed a general tendency for these 'so-called expert types of manager in personnel and accounting always to stick together'. I had, in fact, noticed something like this myself. But I had put it down to the fact that both Bods and Wads were university graduates and knew that this made the other managers, none of whom had degrees, rather wary of them.

At this point, Oddjob spoke for the first time. I was surprised that he had stayed quiet for so long. We all knew that he loved anything 'high tech'. It was central to his personal image in the leisure centre world that he be associated with a 'state of the art' centre. Sophisticated surveillance systems were nowadays 'state of the art' he said. Although he 'respected the need to be cost conscious' he felt that a 'top notch' system would be an excellent investment that would release us from the pressures of having to 'recruit clapped out retired police officers and train them as security officers'. In response to this, Plod went into a long and boring account of the virtues of every security officer he had ever recruited or trained. I should have stopped him but I knew I had to keep him on board. Passions were running much higher than I had ever imagined they would and I had to keep things going if I was ever to reach a conclusion.

In fact I never reached a conclusion that night. Well, there was some conclusion to the meeting. But it was what I have always felt is a coward's conclusion to such an event: I set up a working party to look into the advantages and disadvantages (with special reference to costs) of all the surveillance systems on the market. This, I knew, was just buying me time. But before calling any other meetings of this group, I was going to spend time with each of these individuals and try to get a fuller understanding of exactly what agenda each of them was working towards. If I could reach a decision on the security and surveillance issues without having to get all the protagonists into the gladiatorial arena at the same time I might end up deserving the title of general manager. In the meantime, I had better drop my little joke of introducing myself to people as 'Godfrey Nairn – just call me God'.

Godfrey Nairn's story is an excellent illustration of how 'messy' managerial relations and decision-making processes can get. Perhaps it justifies the 'garbage' element in the title of the garbage can model, though no model is going to resolve the messiness of this situation and it is not a simple matter to apply the categories of the model to these events. We can attempt to do this, however, by first looking at what *problems* are floating about in the bin. There is the initiating problem, of course, of how order is going to be maintained in the leisure centre when both the number and the variety of customers increases in the new season. The slightly more specific problem identified by Des Cromarty is one of developing security measures that are 'tight but low profile'. However, contributors to the problem-solving process inevitably bring along their own problems to the party. Not surprisingly the person from the accounting function, Wad, brings along the ever-present organisational problem of keeping costs under control. Bods, from personnel, keeps on the table the related problem of keeping the organisational 'headcount' under control. Problems with a more departmental (as opposed to functional) focus are brought into play by Plod who has a problem of his staff's pay, as he sees it, being too low. It also seems possible that he has a personal problem; one involving the relationship he is alleged to see between his status in the organisation and the number of people he employs. Oddjob's interventions also seem to be influenced by a personal problem of self-identity; the problem of maintaining his image and reputation as someone involved with 'state of the art' initiatives.

When we turn to the *solutions* that are floating about in the bin, a corresponding variety of positions is visible. It was Des Cromarty, from outside the meeting, who first threw in the solution of buying an electronic surveillance system. Oddjob's version of this solution is to buy the most sophisticated one of these available, but Plod's solution, of course, is completely contrary to this. He argues that a bigger and better paid security force would perfectly fit the bill of 'tight but discreet' security. Bods presumably favours the technological solution and, given the tendency of Bods and Wad to support each other, we can assume that they would both support the purchase of an electronic surveillance system that did not exceed Wad's budget limit.

When we come to consider who was present at the meeting, we inevitably recognise that the particular mixture of God, Todd, Plod, Wad, Bods and Oddjob – without the calming influence of any external or more neutral characters – was a volatile one. It seems reasonable to assume that things might have gone differently if the police and the consultant experts had been present (and note how Godfrey speculates that one of his managers might have discouraged them from attending). It is also possible that Des Cromarty, who initiated the whole process, might have been present. His seniority would possibly have led to a more positive debate. But perhaps not. His very brief presence on the occasion undermined Godfrey and his rudeness left his mark on the proceedings, as Todd's late arrival and early departure may have done too. Godfrey is clearly of the view that Todd could have helped him significantly if he had been willing to devote more time and attention to the business in hand. There is clearly a degree of conflict between God and Todd, in spite of their long friendship, and we are told that Todd 'hates' Oddjob for some reason. The tensions between Oddjob and Plod are clearly based on certain diametrically opposed interests (the former seeming to prefer 'high tech' solutions and the latter labour intensive ones) and the reference by Oddjob to 'clapped out' retired police officers suggests that a degree of passion to the conflict exists here. Something similar is suggested by Bods' barbed reference to Plod's interest in 'size'. In fact, given all these crosscutting conflicts, it is almost warming to see one case of people supporting each other, but the others do not necessarily see the alliance between Bods from personnel and Wad the accountant as benign.

Todd's suggestive remark about Bods and Wad 'getting into bed together' certainly implies that their alliance is not generally approved of. It is hard to say, however, just when a remark like Todd's is a straightforward piece of work-related or political behaviour and when it is just a matter of someone having fun – making a joke to pass the time or to impress other people. The serious and the playful frequently overlap in organisational behaviour and it is often difficult to judge precisely what is 'meant to' happen in certain circumstances and what is 'not meant to happen'. It is possible, however, to identify a broad category of activities that are 'not meant to happen' and which provide a channel for people to challenge the organisational hierarchy. These we can label as *organisational mischief.*

Workplace mischief and the organisational underlife

There are both 'official' and 'unofficial' aspects to the negotiated order of every organisation. It was shown in Chapter 8 (pp. 229–30) that, in different circum-

 Link The notion of *official* and *unofficial* aspects of the organisation was introduced and related to the organisation's *negotiated order* in Chapter 3, pp. 74–81, and was further developed and utilised in Chapter 8.

stances, unofficial or 'informal' practices can contribute either positively or negatively to the long-term survival of the organisation – towards officially approved ends, we might say. Some of the micropolitical behaviour we have looked at in the present chapter functioned 'positively' for the organisation in which it occurred, for example. The poaching of the star sports reporter by Derek Duffus in Cases and Conversations 10.1 to further his personal empire building might be an example of a corporately 'positive' piece of managerial politics, given that it was likely to lead to an increase in circulation. But other examples of politicking were potentially destructive to the organisation concerned. The instigation of a war between younger and older reporters threatened the newspaper's circulation and hence its future, as the editor had to point out to Derek.

Organisational mischief   *Concept*

Activities occurring within the workplace that (a) according to the official structure, culture, rules and procedures of the organisation, 'should not happen' and (b) contain an element of challenge to dominant modes of operating or to dominant interests in the organisation.

Although we are now focusing our attention on something explicitly called *mischief*, the same ambiguity arises with regard to its likely corporate effects. *Organisational mischief* is a category of unofficial workplace activity that involves some kind of challenge by organisational members to the dominant order of the enterprise. It clearly has the potential to undermine a dominant order or to thwart dominant interests. However, there are *unintended consequences* of mischievous actions just as there are unintended consequences of formal and official corporate initiatives (Chapter 7, pp. 242–9). This is illustrated by the story of the man who set fire to the premises where he worked as an extreme expression of the contempt he and his workmates felt for the company that employed them. After initial resentment at this act of sabotage, the senior management came to see it as an immense piece of good fortune. The building completely burned down, but it was old, inefficient and awkwardly located. New premises that were much better suited to strategic managerial priorities were built with the insurance money that the company received and a new, much more compliant, workforce was recruited to work on the new site. The challenge had misfired. An act of gross organisational mischief had the unintended consequence of reinforcing the order and the interests that it had been intended to undermine.

Much of the mischief that routinely occurs in the unofficial or informal *underlife* of an organisation challenges the dominant order much less directly, and often less deliberately, than was the case with the aggrieved arsonist. An employee might, for example, falsely claim that they were taking a day off work because they were ill when, in fact, they simply wanted to avoid the pressures of a typical Monday morning in their office. Such behaviour, especially if it becomes widespread or persistent, will have the effect of challenging organisational interests. The worker has prioritised their own interests over those of the employing organisation – in spite of the commitment they have made to the employer through their employment contract.

The *implicit contract* that employees make with employing organisations is the most useful starting point for any attempt to understand what is going on when people go absent from work, engage in sabotage, steal from the workplace, or 'misbehave' at work in any of the variety of other ways we will shortly be considering. A key element of the implicit contract between the employee and the employer is the employee 'input' of *compliance*, the acceptance of a degree of managerial control over the worker. This means that whenever someone joins an organisation as an employee they *surrender a degree of personal autonomy* but, as we have frequently observed, human beings do not readily give up control of their circumstances or their 'selves'. This is especially the case in modern democratic societies, where the concepts of human rights and the autonomy of the 'free citizen' are culturally significant and people are only willing to submit to the control of others to a very limited and closely circumscribed extent. When one takes a job, for a certain level of pay, job security, opportunity for fulfilment, and all the rest, one accepts that certain people, to a certain extent, may tell one what to do. Such an acceptance is typically loaded with reservation, reluctance and caution. Resistance to any attempted control that falls short of total legitimacy in the employee's eyes is to be expected in every workplace circumstance. And where that resistance cannot take the direct form of a straightforward refusal to comply – which often it cannot – we can expect the employee to seek one means or another to maintain their pride or otherwise protect their identity.

To defend their sense of 'self' and, in effect, to restore some balance to a threatened implicit contract, people engage in activities ranging from burning down their workplace to stealing a pencil from their desk; from circulating rude cartoons round an office to playing practical jokes on people. To point to this 'defence of self' aspect of such activity is not, however, to deny that people at work often joke with each other simply for the sake of enjoying a joke or take a pencil home simply because there is no one looking and the pencil from the telephone pad at home has worn out. However, this should not stop us recognising that there is often a further and a deeper significance to many of these acts – a significance that we must always take into account when trying to understand behaviour in organisations.

Many of the studies of workplace resistance to organisational control have focused on manual workers in industrial situations and deep insights into the importance of acts of defiance and anti-authority cultural gesture have been gained by close studies of the experience of working class employment. It is unfortunate, however, when managerial workers are excluded from analyses of organisational mischief, as is done in the review of what they call 'organisational misbehaviour' by Ackroyd and Thompson (1999, Reading Guide 24). Managers are themselves employees of organisations and the majority of them are subject to controls over their behaviour by more senior managers – controls that may be experienced by a manager as a 'threat to self' no less significant than the threat felt by a non-manager. Indeed the controls to which managers are subject can be far more sophisticated or even insidious than those experienced by more junior employees. Managers frequently invest more of their 'selves' in their work than do ordinary employees. Consequently, 'defence of self' gestures and acts of 'resistance' through mischief are to be seen from the top to the bottom of the organisational hierarchy. Todd's late arrival and early departure from Godfrey Nairn's meeting in Cases and Conversations 10.2 is not essentially different from that of an ordinary leisure centre worker cutting short their working day. Plod's suspected discouraging of the police officer and the security consultant from attending the meeting is not essentially different from a gym assistant's persuading a maintenance engineer not to repair an exercise machine that she does not like working with. Bods' insulting of Plod by referring to his worry about 'size' is little different from the teasing we might hear the cook in the leisure centre's kitchen inflicting on one of the kitchen porters.

Mischief at any level of the organisation is likely to involve a mixture of the more 'psychological' *defence of self* and the more material pursuit of *self-interest*. A day 'illegally' taken off work may, for example, benefit a worker by giving them the satisfaction of upsetting a supervisor who has been overloading them with work. The worker's pride and sense of autonomy is thus defended and if they use that day to paint a room in their house, they also save the money they might otherwise have had to pay someone else. Their material self-interest has thus been served at the same time as they were protecting their sense of self-integrity and personal autonomy. Now, returning to the leisure centre case, while Todd might have felt some psychological satisfaction at making life difficult for Godfrey, the erstwhile friend who was now his boss, he might well have helped his career forward at the same time by having a chat with the chief executive whom he was able to 'bump into' by being late to Godfrey's meeting.

Some forms of mischief are relatively individualistic and involve just one person defending their sense of self, engaging in an act of personal resistance or otherwise furthering their personal interests. We might include here:

- *Spontaneous individual acts of absenteeism.* The shop worker staying away from work on the day that it is rumoured the company's 'mystery shopper' will be visiting the store to check up on the quality of service.

- *Inattentiveness through day-dreaming or chatting to work colleagues.* The counter staff in a council office failing to notice someone entering to pay their rent because they are too busy discussing rumours about their manager's private life; the police officer allocated to a particularly boring beat failing to notice a street crime because he is re-playing in his mind the football match he watched the night before.

- *Minimal compliance with instructions.* The activities of the 'jobsworths' or 'bureaucratic personalities' we came across in Chapter 7 (p. 248); the warehouse labourer who was told to 'get those boxes moved out of the gangway before you go home' moving a pile of cardboard boxes containing fragile goods out into the yard so that heavy overnight rain destroys their contents.

- *Keeping information to oneself.* The maintaining of a strong sense of indispensability and 'being in control' by a bank's branch manager who gives staff only minimal information about the headquarters' guidelines to which the branch is meant to be working.

- *Bullying.* The regular tormenting of the weakest member of a work team by a supervisor who feels aggrieved that he himself has to take orders from a manager who is 'half my age and barely out of college'.

- *Sexual harassment.* The repeated commenting on the sexual characteristics of women colleagues by a male employee who also pinned photographs of naked women to the wall above his desk and who only modified his behaviour when the women took to decorating another wall of the office with pictures of naked men.

- *Opportunistic pilfering or embezzlement.* The taking of a couple of new books from a library by a library assistant who feels that he is too poorly paid to afford to buy books and who finds himself left alone to lock up a local library one evening; the regular siphoning-off of amounts of money by an accountant who finds that a particular very rich client rarely checks the figures with which they are provided.

- *The sabotaging or breaking of goods or equipment in a moment of individual frustration.* The throwing of a crate of bottled beer down the cellar stairs by a bar manager whose staff had failed to turn up for work, leaving him to cope with a rush of customers.

- *Using work premises or equipment for private purposes, both within and sometimes out of working hours.* The use of a production machine to make a toy for one's children; the photocopying at work of invitations to an employee's birthday party; the sending of flirtatious or aggressive personal e-mails to other employees.

- *The punishing of an awkward customer who has offended the worker.* The waiter who spits in the third plate of soup to be taken to a customer who has sent back a first plate of soup because it was too cold and a second plate of soup because it was too hot.

- *Leaving the organisation at an especially inconvenient time.* The university professor falling out with the faculty dean and resigning from their post so that their departure coincides with the beginning of the vital and difficult report-writing stage of a major research project which they have led and which only they fully understand.

All of these relatively individualistic pieces of mischief still have a social dimension. They all relate to problems in the employment 'trade' with the employing organisation. And it is likely that individual acts such as going absent from work will develop into a more general pattern of absenteeism, as more and more people see staying away from work as a defence against work overload. This possibility needs to be recognised when we identify some of the more social and group-oriented types of organisational mischief:

- *Acts of absenteeism or inconvenient resignation that accord with unofficial norms which have developed in an organisation or a sub-unit of an organisation.* The standard practice of people claiming to be ill when allocated to the shift in a restaurant when the most difficult customers tend to turn up.

- *The setting of group work-output norms that suit group members but are managerially defined as 'restrictions of output'.* The refusal of a group of machine operators in a garment factory to allow any of the group members to produce more than 15 garments per hour or fewer than 13 garments (because that is deemed a 'reasonable and fair' work rate by most of the group) in spite of the fact that the management want a higher output and indeed operate a bonus system that would give higher pay for higher output.

- *Organised fiddles.* The standard practice among staff in a public house of overcharging customers who are thought unlikely to check their change; shop staff giving extra change to customers to whom they are related.

- *'Dehumanising' or 'putting down' customers or clients – typically behind their backs but sometimes 'to their faces'.* The practice of referring to all customers as 'punters', 'marks' or 'Johns' rather than customers; the norm among motor mechanics in a garage of telling customers that the fault with their car is something different from what the customers say they believe it to be; the labelling by workers in a fish and chip shop of all customers into categories like FOBs (fat overeating slob), TLTCs (too lazy to cook) and SUBs (soaking up the beer).

- *Using work premises for group-sanctioned non-work purposes.* The use of a medical room by nightshift workers taking turns to snatch an illegal hour's sleep during the shift; the playing of competitive computer games involving several workers during office hours.

- *Workplace games.* The weekly competition between senior managers in a company to collect as many as possible management 'buzzwords' used by the managing director, both orally or in documents; the throwing of an item such as a chicken leg from worker to worker in a food factory whenever supervisors or managers are not looking.

- *Practical jokes, organised 'piss-takes' or 'wind-ups'.* The pinning of a large sheet of paper bearing the legend 'pompous bastard' to the back of a manager's jacket, unknown to him, before he shows a group of visitors around a new building; the nursing tutors in a hospital always ensuring that they send at least one member of each new intake of nurses to the medical stores to collect an item such as a 'bronchial tube' or a bottle of 'mild infarction'.

- *Organised bullying and harassment.* The persistent persecuting of black men and women workers in a textile factory, involving name-calling and the damaging of work in progress, by a group of white male maintenance workers whose supervisor not only encourages such behaviour but discriminates against men in his team who do not join in these practices by giving them fewer overtime opportunities and by allocating them to more than their fair share of unpleasant jobs.

- *The organised sabotaging of goods or equipment.* The regular damaging of an assembly line to give all the workers on it a break from machine-pacing; the deliberate overloading of an organisation's e-mail system by people widely and unnecessarily circulating copies of lengthy documents and large attachments.

- *The mobilising of groups to take sanctions against management as a means of resolving a grievance.* The decision of a group of design engineers, after taking a vote, to work on only one design at a time – this sanction to continue until the company brings the department up to its official full staff strength; the agreement by a group of van drivers that their union representative should tell management that no overtime will be worked until the pay is brought up to the level of a rival delivery service company; the refusal, after a brief lunchtime meeting, of all the departmental managers in a large retail store to attend meetings called by the general manager after the 6pm closing time.

In each of these more group-oriented types of organisational mischief, we again see people protecting or advancing the material aspects of their implicit contract with the employer. The van drivers want more pay, for example, and are disrupting the overtime arrangements to achieve this. The cheating of drinkers in the public house is a means of maintaining a higher level of income than the employer provides in the pay packet. A certain level of pay – part legal, part illegal – has become part of the implicit contract associated with their employment, in effect. The machine operators who fix an output norm are also working to shape their implicit contract (as were the workers in the famous Bank Wiring Observation Room study at the Hawthorne plant reported by Roethlisberger and Dickson, 1939, Reading Guide 1). There is, then, a degree of informal bargaining between employers and employees occuring in all of this misbehaviour. Does this mean we should reject the 'mischief' label, then? It does not. All of these behaviours are, to some degree, taken against the dominant order of the organisation. They constitute a refusal simply to accept the roles and rewards laid down for them by the employer. Just as with the more individualistic types of behaviour, these group-oriented actions have a 'defence of self' or protection of autonomy dimension for the members of the groups. This works in conjunction with the pursuit of shared material interests. Each member of the workgroup that has agreed its own definition of a 'fair day's work' can work with a sense that group membership protects them from managerial pressures. The food workers throwing food around the factory are ritually undermining the supervisors' control over their activities. The managers who mock their boss's pretentious language and the managers who refuse to attend their general managers' out-of-hours meetings, are expressing a degree of independence or distance from their senior managers. The strategies of independence that we see in all of these groups are not acts of rebellion or a fight for full autonomy. As part of their implicit contract with their employer, they submit to a certain amount of managerial control but what their collective misbehaviours are in effect saying to those in authority is 'This is who we are. So far and no further'.

Organisational employees who deal directly with customers or clients have an additional need to protect their personal identities and their sense of autonomy. It is not just the manager or supervisor who exerts pressures here on the worker to behave in a certain way. It is also the customer. In many aspects of service and retail work the worker is required to act like a servant. The emotional pressures that this can put on both the worker and the manager alike were looked at in Chapter 5 and the problems of engaging in *emotional labour* were illustrated both by the hospital manager Ken Steary in Cases and Conversations 5.3 and the sex worker Cindy Sutor in Cases and Conversations 5.4. Some important psychic relief from the pressure to act subserviently is thus achieved by the rude labelling of clients in the chip shop and by the motor mechanics always claiming to know better than the motorists what is wrong with their vehicles. The notion of 'getting one's own back' on people who are put into the master or mistress role, *vis à vis* the service worker's role as servant, can take some very unpleasant forms. The ploy of the waiter who, behind the scenes, spits in the diner's food is a classic example of this, but repulsive as such behaviour may seem, it is far from uncommon in the food and drinks industry, at both the customer service end of the business and at the food processing stage. It is rare to find anybody who has worked in a food processing plant who cannot relate tales of people throwing rat droppings into food mixing machines, urinating into beer vats or tipping floor sweepings into hoppers of cereal. Outside the food industry, one hears similar reports of people chalking obscenities on the insides of the items of furniture they are making or leaving hidden parts of metal products insufficiently protected against rust. One hears of unspeakable things being done to dead bodies in hospitals or undertakers' workshops. All of these are human gestures of defiance and demonstrations of personal or group autonomy, however alienated or degraded a form of human expression we may deem them to be.

In the conversation about some of the examples of workplace mischief that they have come across as managers, Hazel Hopeman and Jenny Elgin recognise that there is 'something deeper' going on in what Jenny calls the 'underlife' of organisations.

Activity 10.5

Read the conversation in Cases and Conversations 10.3 between Hazel Hopeman, a manager in an airline, and Jenny Elgin, the manager of a supermarket, and

- note down examples arising in this conversation of the various types of organisational mischief that we identified above (recognising that certain activities may straddle more than one category);

- think about any examples of organisational mischief that you have come across or heard

about that you might have thrown into the conversation if you had joined Jenny and Hazel in their discussion;

- consider the extent to which Hazel and Jenny's attempts to make sense of (or 'theorise' about) these activities, fit with the attempts to understand organisational mischief that have been made in this chapter so far.

Hazel and Jenny probe the underworld

Cases and Conversations 10.3

What really started me thinking about these things was a strange experience I had one day when I was a victim of a practical joke organised by a couple of my departmental managers. I was walking around the shop doing my usual thing of smiling at everyone and having a friendly word with a customer here and a colleague there. One of the customers made a very strange comment. 'You don't look very sore to me', he said. I was puzzled, but carried on. Then one of the checkout operators said, 'You don't look sore to me Jenny'. Again, I said nothing. But when a customer who I'd helped with a query about Sunday opening hours asked me, with a rather enigmatic smile on her face, 'So what are you sore about, Miss Elgin?' I let my puzzlement show. 'Look at your badge, dear,' the customer said. And when I looked at my 'Jenny Elgin, Store manager' badge, I saw that it had been skilfully doctored to say 'Jenny Elgin, Sore Manager'.

I expect that did make you a 'sore manager'.

I was not pleased, I can tell you, Hazel. But I had been rather short tempered with my management team for more than a week. They knew I was having problems with my car and that I was getting tired of having to drive so far to work at this branch. 'Don't take it out on us', the grocery manager had said to me only the day before. He was very understanding. I don't think the others were. They were getting their message over to me another way.

And they were obviously having a good laugh too.

I am sure they were. But what occurred to me was that you always have to look for deeper meanings in these things. There are all sorts of things bubbling away, seething sometimes, beneath the surface – in the underlife of a business, if you like. I'm sure part of the context of 'the laugh' that my managers were having was the fact that I am the only woman manager in the store and that I am the only graduate manager they have ever had close contact with. They know I will be moving on in my career. But I doubt if any of them will. So they 'brought me down a bit'. I said nothing about what happened. But I've never forgotten about it.

I agree that you have to probe beneath the surface, as a manager, when you come across anything like this. One partly hilarious and partly very serious problem I had to deal with was the case of a cabin crew whose male and female members swapped clothes towards the end of a flight. When the passengers were disembarking, there were the cabin crew as usual, thanking passengers for flying with us and very politely wishing them well. But the women were in the men's trousers, and far more peculiarly, the two chaps were in dresses. As you can imagine, we got some complaints.

What was going on, Hazel?

In a way it didn't surprise me. As a management we are well aware of this issue of 'emotional labour' that researchers write about. The man who was behind the jape told me, 'Sometimes you've just got to burst out and be yourself'. 'Cross dressing is being yourself?' I came back – incredulous. 'Well it is for me,' he said, winking at me in a very camp manner. I believed him. 'But what about the others?' I asked. 'Oh, they'd never done it before. But, you ask them, they all say that the laugh did them good.'

So who were they having a go at – the airline, the managers, the passengers?

Oh, I think all of these. And none of them at the same time. I don't think it is as direct or as specific as it was with the case of your managers 'having a go' about your irritability. I think it's all got to do with this 'underlife' that you talk about. All sorts of things are going on behind the scenes in every type of organisation, aren't they?

Yes, but I can't imagine that a lot can go on behind the scenes in an airliner The cabin crew are on display most of the time, aren't they?

Absolutely right – and that's why I was very lenient with them.

And there must be little scope for them to engage in the sort of fiddles that we have to deal with in retailing.

Well, there is just one. The biggest fiddle in the past – one that used to give them a lot of satisfaction as well as being materially rewarding – was the fiddling of time.

Claiming more hours that they actually put in?

Exactly. But that's now gone with computerisation. The only scope they have to line their pockets and 'have one over the airline' at the same time is with regard to complementary alcohol. We can't know how many free drinks passengers have or have not accepted. So a good proportion of those drinks go home with the cabin crew. We are well aware of this. But, as I say, it's the only thing we are aware of. I'm sure it's much more complicated in your business?

It certainly is. We get everything from people hiding stock that they know is going to go down in price the next week to check-out staff keeping vouchers they should give to customers. I've caught staff eating food they have taken off the shelves and which will obviously never go past the till. You get people swapping the tickets on items so that they are scanned at a lower price than they should have been and colleagues giving discounts to friends who are not entitled to them. And a scam was recently discovered in which store managers in one region were getting builders retained by the business to build conservatories on their houses, and charge these to the company.

And do you get people deliberately causing damage?

How do you mean?

I was thinking about what goes on with the men who load and unload planes. They are largely young blokes who are young and very strong. You get the impression that they are very conscious of their masculinity. And I think that their very low status in the airport's pecking order is experienced as some kind of threat to this.

So what do they do?

Well, first, they are always fighting with each other. They have time on their hands when there's no plane to work on and, of course, they have quite a mixture of nationalities and ethnic backgrounds. It can be quite explosive. And when they are not knocking each other to pieces, they are prone to smashing up luggage or bits of freight.

Yes, I've only had a couple of fights to sort out in my career so far. But damage to goods is not uncommon. I had a disgruntled bloke regularly leaving stock out of refrigeration last year and we had a spate recently of staff damaging goods in order to get them reduced in price. There was also the time we caught one of the shelf stackers opening jars of peanut butter and scratching little smiley faces into the surface of the product. What amazed me was that we only received a handful of complaints from customers. Yet he must have contaminated scores of jars, from what we understand. It could have been very damaging for the business. But it didn't even get in the press.

You confined it to the store's 'underlife'?

Thank goodness, yes. The young man who did it apparently felt he was 'having a laugh' at the expense of shoppers who, he said, never bother to speak to him or even smile at him when he is filling shelves.

Oh this is something we are very aware of with our cabin crew. In their training we have to prepare them for ungrateful or rude passengers. They know the score and are generally very good.

Generally?

Well I suppose so. A story is told about one of our crews who got really sick of a man who was regularly rude to them. He was also very demanding. So, one day, they laced his coffee with a strong laxative. That really sorted the bloke out.

Do you think that really happened? I mean it sounds unlikely to me – given that the crew who did it would probably end up cleaning up any mess that got made.

True. But if the story is apocryphal, it is rather interesting, isn't it, that people still take pleasure in passing it on. It always gets a good laugh. It sort of helps keep the customer in their place, psychologically speaking.

Yes, that reminds me of a rather different story – a true one that happened here. But it also has that element of the employee putting a distance between themselves and customers. There was this very attractive young woman who used to shop in here. The male colleagues were always looking out for her coming into the store. Well it turned out that she did some modelling for one of those erotic magazines. When the blokes discovered this, they made sure they obtained plenty of copies of the pictures and passed them round all the staff – men and women alike. It meant that a lot of silly and unpleasant giggling went on whenever she came into the shop. It also led to a game among the lads of 'talent spotting', as they named it. I discovered that they were competing to identify likely models that they might contact a particular magazine about. Fortunately, the first woman who was approached, as far as I know, came straight to me. She was very good about it. But two of those young men no longer work for us!

If only we could get these young men – I'm thinking of our baggage handlers again – to leave their sexuality, and their problems with their masculinity, at home.

And women?

Yes, we ought to be fair here. But I think that the women cabin crew who work for us are all very discreet and sophisticated about how they relate to male passengers. There's no way they could – or, to be honest, we would want them to – leave their sexuality at home. But all sorts of trouble follows if sex does rear its beautiful head at work.

How do you mean?

I was thinking of the time that the airport security caught a couple of our employees having sexual intercourse on the altar of the airport chapel. It was after a party and the place was locked. But they had got a key and thought that no one would disturb them in that part of the building. They were both single and I don't think it even occurred to them that the tabletop they were using was meant to be an altar. But none of this stopped my boss from ordering me to sack both of them. I really had to fight him on this and, in the end, I refused to do it. What amazed me was how hot under the collar he got about the whole business. I mean it really upset him. I argued that there were no serious business or managerial implications whatsoever and that, at the most, it was a minor disciplinary matter. But he had a real problem with it.

I think it's the fear some managers feel about having the lid lifted on this 'underlife', as I call it. Some managers just don't want to acknowledge that people are a lot more than little robots. I think it's the idea that employees are flesh and blood that bothers them. I had a similar difficulty when I discovered that one of the office workers occasionally played this game of leaning out of her office window during her lunch break – the window is immediately above the shop entrance – and passing the time of day with customers. What they didn't know was that, while she was doing this, she was getting served from behind by her boyfriend.

What did you do about that?

Nothing. It was me who caught them. And I decided that their embarrassment at being caught 'at it' was punishment enough. I am utterly confident that they won't do it again. No damage was done. Nobody else knew about it. But when I related this story at a corporate training event, ages after the event, I found that several of the managers there were absolutely appalled. Several people regarded as an utter outrage what I thought was quite an amusing, and even touching, piece of mischief. 'It simply shouldn't have happened' one of them kept muttering. 'The workplace is no place for that sort of thing', another spluttered before walking out of the room.

What was their problem?

What indeed? But I always remember that phrase, 'The workplace is no place for that sort of thing'. If only it were that simple!

This conversation represents a good example of managers taking a step back from their everyday practice and reflecting on the significance of some of the activities that they come across, and indeed have to deal with at work. All of the activities about which they are comparing notes fit more or less with the categories of organisational mischief set out earlier. A series of *practical jokes* or 'wind-ups' make up perhaps the most significant category here. Such a joke is played on Jenny herself and Hazel reports jokes played on airline passengers both as a group (with the cross-dressing farewell) and on one particular passenger who was 'punished' with an unwanted laxative drink. These latter two pieces of mischief to some extent also fit into our category of *putting down customers* – something that would also apply to the 'talent-spotting' *workplace game* Jenny talks about. The same might apply to the office worker communicating to customers from her office window and enjoying the irony of the fact that she was taking certain pleasures they knew nothing of. However, this case, and that of the late night use of the airport chapel for lovemaking was an example of *the use of premises or equipment for private purposes* rather than for organisational ones. *Sabotage* occurs in the loading and unloading of aircraft at the airport and in the interfering with the peanut butter in the shop. We hear of *fiddles* occurring in the airline with regard to alcoholic drinks and both money and goods in the case of the shop.

Jenny and Hazel are doing more in their conversation than simply swapping stories about their respective work organisations. They appear to have a shared interest in making sense of the various examples of organisational mischief that they present to each other. They recognise a straightforward role that these activities play *at a surface level* in organisational members' lives. People enjoy the 'laugh' that follows from the practical joking. Service workers feel better for 'having a go' at or 'keeping in their place' both managers and customers. And employees 'line their pockets', as Hazel puts it, by engaging in fiddles at work. However, both women feel that there is something more significant about these activities, something going on *at a deeper level*. Jenny suggests that there are 'deeper meanings' to these activities and that there are all sorts of things 'bubbling away' or even 'seething' below the surface. Hazel seems to agree with this and takes on Jenny's notion of an organisational 'underlife'. And there is some interesting theoretical reflection that fits with this concept in her interpretation of the behaviour of the cross-dressing cabin crewmembers. She uses a notion of people 'bursting out and being themselves' to make sense of what was occurring here, thus seeing their gesture as a particularly positive form of the 'defence of self' aspect of much organisational mischief. She also connects the fighting and the sabotage that occurs among the young men who load and unload the aircraft with problems that she thinks they have with both their ethnic identities and their masculinity. In thinking about such 'deeper level' factors she is still aware that the behaviour also has a more 'surface level' function of relieving boredom between flights.

Sexuality, humour and the struggle for control

Jenny and Hazel both imply that the area of human sexuality may be one in which clues might be found about the deeper issues that organisational mischief relates to. They both speak of managers who 'had a problem' with the idea of sexual behaviour occurring at work. They were frightened, Jenny suggests, by the prospect of 'having the lid lifted' on the 'underlife' of the organisation. Both sexuality and humour appear to play a major part in the organisational under-life of the organisations that these two managers work in. Can we go more deeply into these matters to explore the full depths of the organisational under-life and what its significance might be in the lives of organisational managers and employees? This is quite a challenging question, and Activity 10.6 is an invitation to take it up.

Activity 10.6

Reread the conversation between Hazel and Jenny and

● Consider why it might be that some of the managers that both Hazel and Jenny have come across seem to be especially troubled about sexual behaviour occurring in the workplace. Why do they consider the workplace to be 'no place for that sort of thing' do you think?

● Look back to the discussion of narratives and stories and how they can be seen as elements of human culture that help people to handle existential problems (pp. 110–18) and reflect on whether the 'laughs' that Hazel and Jenny talk about have a significance which fits with this kind of analysis. Does this workplace humour have a function that goes beyond simply providing 'fun at work' or the pleasure of 'getting one's own back' on certain people?

Jenny Elgin offers one explanation of why managers might be troubled by sexuality in the workplace. To lift the lid from the organisational underlife and contemplate its sexual dimension is to come to terms with 'the idea that employees are flesh and blood'. This means accepting, Jenny thinks, the fact that 'people are a lot more than little robots'. Sexuality, this suggests, stands for the basic humanity – and the fundamental 'animality' we might say – of the people that managers might prefer to treat as cogs in the organisational machine. To be reminded that employees are living creatures with bodies, desires and libidinal drives might make some managers uncomfortable. It reminds them of how limited their capacity to control human beings is. For a manager to be reminded that employees are living animals with emotions and desires is to be reminded that one is being required to control the uncontrol-lable – to 'herd cats' as Mark Merryton so aptly put it in Cases and Conversations 1.1. It is perhaps also discomforting because it reminds the man-ager of their own desires and the sexuality that they too are required to leave behind when they come to work. But sexuality, desire, and indeed the enjoyment of laughter, are not things that can be left behind when the human being goes to work, whether as a manager or as an ordinary employee. And they are behaviours that defy organisational control.

Work organisations are set up to be places where rational and instrumental behaviour occurs and where attention is to be focused on the completion of formal tasks. If there is to be love, it is to be love of work or love of the company. If there is to be passion, it is to be passion for the product or a passion for customer satisfaction. If there is to be desire, it is to be desire for the success of the organisation and a desire for the formal rewards of pay and security that are offered for contributing to that corporate success. For love, passion and desire to be directed to other than corporate ends is to threaten the managerial controls that are intended to achieve those ends. Any display of passion or desire on the part of organisational members for the bodies of other organisational members or for organisational clients is an especially powerful symbolic challenge to that control. We should not be surprised, therefore, that Jenny Elgin speaks of managers arguing emphatically that the workplace is 'no place for that sort of thing'. Indeed, most of us would see the point of their wanting to discourage shop workers spending time identifying which customers might be potential erotic magazine models or wanting to discourage office workers from having sexual intercourse at the window of their offices. However, Jenny and Hazel seem to be implying that a reasonable and sensitive manager would recognise that, while the sexuality of organisational employees may need to kept discreetly under control within the workplace, it is not something that can be completely suppressed. Sexuality may be expressed directly in the workplace through individuals courting each other or engaging in overtly sexual activities. Equally, it may be expressed indirectly through women expressing their femininity and men expressing their masculinity at work through the way they dress or through their style of relating to others. Either way, it is an aspect of the human spirit that will always present a possible challenge to managerial control.

Joking and humour can be seen, like sexuality, as expressions of the 'human spirit'. But humour, again like sex, is associated with pleasure rather than with work. Work organisations are meant to be serious places and not comedy clubs or sites for the pursuit of bodily pleasures. But both sex and humour are serious matters as well, it can be argued. This is partly because they are expressions of human 'spirit' and often express that spirit in the face of managerial attempts to harness human efforts to corporate ends. The office workers having sexual intercourse at the office window were not just finding an opportunity to express their love and desire for each other. They were also making a gesture of independence towards both their employer and the customers of the shop. The cabin crew cross-dressers can be seen as doing something similar with regard to the airline and to the passengers whom they had served. In each of these cases humour and sexuality were both involved in the expression of human autonomy. There was a serious aspect as well as a fun aspect to each of these two pieces of mischief. But the 'seriousness of humour' goes deeper than this.

It might seem strange to talk about humour as a serious matter, but it can be understood as playing a seriously important role in the human construction of identities and the handling of existential anxieties. In Chapter 4 (pp. 115–18) it was argued that narratives, stories, films, news stories, gossip and jokes all play a role in human culture of reassuring people in the face of the life's anxieties. It was pointed out how often these elements of culture lead us to contemplate the horrors of life – horrors ranging from being murdered or having an accident to a sexual partner's infidelity or the loss of one's job. Our engagement with fiction and non-fiction alike, with 'serious' stories as well as with comedy, frequently involves confronting the breakdown of order in our lives as we engage with the story we are reading or watching on a screen – before being reassuringly returned to order and reality as we close the book or leave the cinema. Humour, comedy and joking operate in a similar way. By making work-related jokes or transmitting funny stories about aspects of the work organisation, for instance, we challenge or question the normal order of the work organisation and its control apparatus – an order that is, however, left more or less intact after we have enjoyed 'the laugh' and returned to 'normal service'.

Activity 10.7

Look at the five 'messages from the underground' (one picture and four documents) that have been collected from different work organisations and consider what role you think they might be playing in the lives of the employees of the organisations in which the were circulating.

Messages from the underworld

Cases and Conversations 10.4

Our company was recently in a boat race with two of our competitors. Guess which boat was ours!

If you are unhappy

Once upon a time, there was a non-conforming swallow who decided not to fly south for the winter. However, soon the weather turned so cold that he reluctantly started to fly south. In a short time, ice began to form on his wings and he fell to earth in a barnyard, almost frozen. A cow passed by and crapped on the little swallow. The little bird thought it was the end. But, the manure warmed him and defrosted his wings. Warm and happy, able to breathe, he started to sing. Just then a large cat came by and, hearing the chirping, investigated the sounds. The cat cleared away the manure, found the chirping bird and promptly ate him.

There are three morals to this story. First, everyone who shits on you is not necessarily your enemy, second, everyone who gets you out of the shit is not necessarily your friend and, third, if you're warm and happy in a pile of shit, keep your mouth shut.

Job vacancy: Staffing and administration services sub-assistant

The pay is the market rate less 10% (but with a boredom compensation bonus).

We are a leading financial services company which is creeping into a very long period of unparalleled slow change.

If you are sure, predictable, pedantic and inflexible in your outlook, you could be just what we are looking for. Ideally aged exactly 42.5 years of age, a conservative dresser with at least 22 years experience as the Personnel lady in a building society (or very similar environment) you are a play-it-safe procedure-follower who relishes plodding through long hours.

You will be administering pay and rations to our Head Office staff along with ensuring all paperwork is completed fully on staff movements.

Career prospects are excellent. Keep your nose clean and an increment each year can be yours. In as little as 15 years you could rise to be a Staff and Administration Services Assistant Officer with additional responsibility for sick pay.

Benefits are excellent: pay every month, holidays every year and your own desk and chair.

Interested applicants should apply in writing for a long application form from Major Gen. Horatio Flash-Blindly DSO (ret'd), Staffing and Administration Assistant Sub-General Manager, Newco Financial Services, Staid House, Oldtown. *We think we are an equal opportunities employer and believe this job would especially suit a nice lady.*

In the beginning was the Plan

In the beginning was the Plan.

And then came the assumptions.

And the assumptions were without form.

And the Plan was completely without substance.

And darkness was upon the faces of the workers.

And they spake unto their Supervisors, saying

"It is a crock of crap and it stinketh".

And the Supervisors went unto the Section Heads and sayeth

"It is a pail of dung and none may abide the odour thereof".

And the Section Heads went unto their Managers and sayeth unto them

"It is a container of excrement and none may abide its strength".

And the Managers went unto their Directors and sayeth

"It contains that which aids plant growth and is very strong".

And the Managing Director went unto the Chairman, saying unto him

"It promoteth growth and is very powerful"'

And the Chairman considered the Plan and sayeth unto the Board

"This powerful new Plan will actively promote the growth and efficiency of the Company".

And the Board looked upon the Plan.

And saw that it was good.

And the plan became policy.

Memorandum to all staff
From: the Board of Management
Subject: Retirement policy

As a result of the reduction of money budgeting for departmental areas, we are forced to cut down on the number of our personnel. Under the plan, older employees will be asked to go on early retirement, thus permitting the retention of younger people who represent our future.

Those being required to retire early may appeal to upper management. To make this possible there will be a Survey of Capabilities of Retired Early Workers (SCREW). The appeal process will be known as SHAFT (Scream to Higher Authority Following Termination). Under the terms of the new policy employees may be early retired once, SCREWED twice and SHAFTED as many times as the company deems appropriate.

If the employee follows the above procedures, he or she will be entitled to HERPES (Half Earnings for Retired Personnel's Early Severance). As HERPES is considered a benefit plan, any employee who has received HERPES will no long be SCREWED or SHAFTED by the company.

Management wishes to reassure the younger employees who remain on board, that the company will continue to see that they are well trained through our Special High Intensity Training known as SHIT. The company takes pride in the amount of SHIT our employees receive. We have given our employees more SHIT than any other company in the area. If any employee feels he or she does not receive enough SHIT on the job, see your immediate supervisor. Your supervisor is specially trained to make sure that you receive all the SHIT you can stand.

Each of these documents was widely circulated in the large organisations where they were collected by the researcher. The picture was collected in a hospital, the story of a swallow in a manufacturing company, the mock job advertisement in a building society, the 'In the beginning' text in a pharmaceutical company and the staff memorandum about early retirement in a retailing business. However, it is apparent that these same documents, sometimes in identical form, sometimes with local variations, can be found in one organisation after another. They circulate across societies, it would seem, as well as within organisations.

The documents mock or satirise aspects of the organisation and the way it is managed. They induce mirth by challenging the normal order of these organisations. The picture engages with the notion that the hospital has too many people giving orders (directing the boat), in relation to the numbers of people who are doing the real work (rowing the boat). The story of the swallow satirises those activities we have characterised as 'micropolitical' and implies that the workplace is a dangerous place in which it is difficult to know who is your friend and who is your enemy. The job advertisement apparently mocks the excessively bureaucratic nature of the building society and the poor career opportunities that staff are offered. Its satirical swipe at the employer's claim to be an equal opportunity employer suggests ignorance on the employer's part of the principles of equal opportunities (with the choice of the anachronistic and patronising term 'a nice lady'). It also portrays the management as hypocritical. Senior organisational managers seem to be the main target of 'In the beginning' piece and they are portrayed as plainly stupid, out of touch with common sense and prone to go along with any business nonsense as long as it can be dressed up in the language of planning, efficiency and growth. The workers and the section leaders can see that 'the plan' stinks. The managers, directors and the chairman, however, convince themselves that it is something worthwhile. And, with the retirement policy memorandum, another specific aspect of managerial language and discourse is mocked – the use of acronyms to give weight and importance to relatively routine managerial initiatives. But the document is, more seriously, an attack on what it implies are harsh, unfeeling and exploitative human resourcing policies being pursued by the company.

All of these documents, clearly intended to give employees 'a laugh', deal with serious matters that constitute threats both to employees and to the long- term survival of the organisations themselves (and hence, of course, to the job security of all employees). All comedy, as has been recognised by numerous theorists of humour from Aristotle onwards, deals with incongruity. It focuses upon the unexpected. It plays with the inappropriate. It turns normality on its head. The normal order of each of these organisations is made to look abnormal by being stretched and bent in the distorting mirror of the satirical document. This is exactly what was being done by the airline cabin crew exchanging clothes or by Jenny Elgin's colleagues altering her name badge. These documents and practical jokes distort normality so that we can laugh at and enjoy a temporary suspension of that normality before returning to our normal serious workplace demeanour and getting back to our work.

Workplace humour helps people adjust to aspects of work that they dislike or feel threatened by and it is always possible that some of the satirical intentions of comic interventions may be fulfilled. Mockery of individuals and practices can lead to changes in behaviour and procedures. But workplace humour and joking behaviour

FIGURE 10.3 Glimpsing into the abyss

can be seen as playing a deeper role in people's lives too. It is part of the way we maintain our sanity. We often joke about the things that worry us most. At work for example, it is noticeable that people whose autonomy is most threatened by overbearing customers or managers will tend to make jokes about such customers or managers more often than those who do not experience such pressures. People whose jobs are the least secure tend to joke about 'getting the chop', 'getting the bullet' or receiving the 'little brown envelope' containing a redundancy notice than those who are relatively secure in their jobs. People doing the most dangerous jobs tend to be those who joke most about possible accidents. Those whose work in emergency services, hospitals and mortuaries involves them in matters of life and death, are the most prone to indulge in black humour and 'laugh in the face' of the death and mutilation that their jobs force them to confront. The joking here can be understood as a glimpse into the abyss. A glimpse into the abyss of disorder and madness, we might say, helps us retain our sanity in the light of the dangers that are seething down there and threatening to swallow us up. Much of our engagement with humour and comedy is like the tightrope walker in Figure 10.3 with his quick occasional glimpses down into the abyss over which he is walking.

To get across to the far side of the ravine, the tightrope walker must keep his eyes most of the time on the solid ground that he wants to reach. However, if he too casually or too confidently strides out in this direction, forgetting what horrors are seething beneath his feet, he is likely to slip from his rope. Equally, though, if he looks down too intently into the cauldron below him, he will lose his balance and fall into the pit of horrors. When we move through our everyday lives, intent on our various life, work and family projects, we are like the tightrope walker looking to the solid ground that we wish to reach. But to remind ourselves of the precariousness of our situations, and to come to terms with everything that actually or potentially troubles us about the world, we glimpse into the abyss from time to time. We therefore laugh at the figure slipping over on the banana skin, we laugh at the stupidity of people from a neighbouring society, we laugh at the managers whose pretentiousness or incompetence threatens the security of our employment. Having laughed at what might otherwise frighten us into a loss of control in our lives (madness even), we return to our serious demeanour and travel onwards. When we bring sexuality and humour into the workplace, and when we indulge in the lavatory talk and sexually 'dirty' language of the 'underworld' documents reviewed earlier, we are reminding ourselves and those around us that we are not cogs in the corporate machine. We are demonstrating that we are also both creative human beings (who create jokes, write satires and make each other laugh) and recalcitrant biological animals (who copulate, excrete and refuse to be herded). Sexuality and humour thus play a part in the way each one of us struggles to control our lives and identity. It also plays its part, when it is mischievously brought into the workplace, in the struggle for control that goes on between people with varying degrees of power in the organisational pecking order.

We have concentrated in this chapter on various aspects of the informal and unofficial aspects of organisational life and looked at various challenges that are constantly being made to managerial efforts to shape and control work organisations. In the next chapter we turn to those aspects of the struggle for managerial control that are concerned with obtaining and maintaining 'human resources'.

Summary

In this chapter the following key points have been made:

- Power is most usefully understood as a capacity that is possessed by an individual or group to influence outcomes of situations so that they gain access to whatever resources are scarce and desired in their organisational setting or in society more generally.

- Power operates at various interrelated levels: the level of the relationships between individuals, the level of the structure and culture of work organisations and at the level of the wider society and political economy. One cannot understand the way in which one organisational employee is able to get another to do something they would not otherwise do, for example, without locating that act within the broader organisational of power structure. That power structure, in turn, cannot be understood without looking at the pattern of power and advantage across the society of which the organisation is a part.

- The very way in which work organisations are structured into hierarchies and into sub-units makes it inevitable that organisational members will compete *micropolitically* for access to scarce and desired organisational resources. Especially important is that fact that organisational hierarchies function not only as organisational control devices but are also competitive career ladders for managerial employees. Managers thus tend both to cooperate with each other and to compete with each other for advancement. This competition occurs in the context of considerable ambiguity and uncertainty, all of which creates opportunities for competitive power behaviours.

- There are numerous tactics that can be adopted by parties wanting to improve their organisational power position. However, a perceived ability on the part of a party to deal with strategic uncertainties facing an organisation is especially helpful in advancing that party's interests – as long as they are relatively central to the organisation's operations and are unsubstitutable.

- Micropolitical interests and activities inevitably influence the outcome of any organisational decision-making event. But there are other factors present in the 'garbage can' of the choice situation. There will always be a variety of problems and a variety of solutions 'floating about' in any decision-making situation and the outcome will also be influenced by precisely who is present at the time and how much attention they pay to what is going on.

- A variety of activities go on in every organisation which, like micropolitics, are not officially 'meant to happen' in the organisation. Examples of *organisational mischief* like fiddling, practical joking, sabotage and workplace sexual activity tend to challenge dominant modes of operating in organisations as well as helping people both to further and to defend their interests. They also enable people to protect their personal notions of 'self'. Managers and non-managers alike engage in organisational mischief.

- Sexuality and humour have a particular significance in the 'underlife' of the work organisation as they represent aspects of humanity (including the 'animal' aspects of humanity) that are especially unsusceptible to corporate or managerial control.

- Humour has a very important role in work situations in enabling people both to challenge and adjust to organisational controls and dominant interests. It also helps people control their lives generally and cope with the existential threats to sanity and a sense of order.

Reading

Reading Guides 6, 7 and 24, especially, contain material that supports and takes further much of what is covered in Chapter 10.

CHAPTER 11

Organising, managing and human resourcing

Objectives Having read this chapter and completed its associated activites, readers should be able to:

● See the value of regarding 'human resources' not as people but as the efforts and capabilities that an organisation requires to be able to function in both the short and the long term.

● Recognise that human resourcing and employment issues, while requiring specialist expertise in their management, are nevertheless activities in which all managers are inevitably involved.

● Put into context the alleged 'rise of HRM' as both an academic subject and a managerial practice, noting the considerable ambiguities and conceptual inadequacies associated with the 'HRM' notion.

● Understand the centrality to organisational strategy-making of human resourcing issues and appreciate the inadequacy of treating HR strategy as something that follows from or 'serves' the main corporate or business strategy.

● Relate the day-to-day issues of organisational human resourcing to basic dilemmas and tensions that have to be managed when employing people within industrial capitalist societies and economies.

● See how human resource management plays a particularly strategic role in employing organisations because it necessarily applies to employment issues (a) a corporate rather than a sectional focus and (b) a long-term rather than an immediate or short-term focus.

● Appreciate the distinctive tensions and ambiguities facing HR specialists in their relationships with other departments and managers.

continued

- Recognise that the basic choice between *direct* and *indirect* efforts to achieve managerial control identified in Chapter 8 is central to strategic human resourcing choices and relates to the choice between *low commitment* and *high commitment* HR strategies – a choice which is influenced by how problematic employee constituencies are perceived to be for the organisation's future,

- Come to terms with the fact that employees are not unchanging entities, units of labour or 'human resources' that can be selected, recruited controlled and processed, as some HR thinking tends to assume.

Human resourcing and the employment relationship

Human resourcing and employment issues are much more than a concern of specialist Human Resources (HR) managers. They are utterly central to the existence of work organisations. They not only affect the employment experience of every single member of an organisation, they also pervade every aspect of organisational management. This is not to argue that human resourcing and employment relations work is more important than finance, production or service delivery, say, as a facet of organisational management. Activities in all of these areas are vital to an organisation's performance and long-term survival. The difference with human resourcing matters is that they tend to arise with regard to every other aspect of managerial work. It is probably wise for all managers in an organisation to concern themselves with matters of finance, marketing or service delivery. Yet it is possible for most members of management to leave specialists in these areas to handle the main tasks of marketing, accounting or production. The same is not possible with regard to human resourcing and employment matters however. Most people in managerial positions will have some responsibility for other employees. They thus necessarily get involved in the selection of staff to work in their departments as well as with the training, payment, deployment, appraisal, career development, welfare, grievances, discipline and possible redundancy of these employees. Expert support is likely to be required in all of these areas and managers with corporate HR responsibilities will almost inevitably impose constraints on local managerial discretion. Human resourcing responsibilities, to varying degrees, will form part of the work of most managers in modern organisations, however. Even where a manager does not have direct responsibility for other employees, he or she will still be unable to distance themselves entirely from matters of employment relationships – not least because they are employees themselves with an interest in their own rewards, career development and future deployment.

A frequently heard cliché says that 'people management' is a concern of every manager in an organisation. Is this the argument that is being advanced here? It is not – at least not in these terms. In Chapter 1 it was argued that it is unhelpful to frame managerial work in terms of 'managing people'. This was because such a notion is morally questionable and because the expectation that anyone can actually 'manage people' is utterly unrealistic (something implicitly acknowledged in Mark Merryton's reference to 'herding cats', p. 3).

Human resources	Concept
The efforts, skills or capabilities which people contribute to a work organisation as part of an employment exchange (or a more temporary labour engagement) and which are managerially utilised to enable the organisation to complete tasks carried out in its name, and to continue its existence into the future.	

This recalcitrance or unmanageability of human beings is one of the very factors that make human resourcing issues so central to organisational strategy-making. This point will be developed later in this chapter. But in talking of 'human resourcing' or 'human resource management', are we not adopting a position that is even more morally dubious than what is implied in talk of 'people management'? The answer to this question would most certainly be yes – if we were using the term 'human resources' to mean 'human beings'. To speak of people as human resources, let alone to *relate* to people in such a dehumanising way, is surely to adopt a stance little different from that of slave traders and slave owners. To treat people as means to ends instead of treating them as free and autonomous citizens of a democracy would be to abandon some of the key principles that modern societies are allegedly based upon. Yet people's *services* are acquired by employing organisations in industrial capitalist societies and are exploited to serve ends other than those of the employees themselves. In slavery it was people themselves who were bought and sold. Under capitalism it is people's labour – the work that they can do for an organisation – that is bought and sold. In recognition of this, we need a concept of human resources that avoids treating people as 'resources' while recognising that people bring with them into the employment relationship with a work organisation efforts, skills and capacities which are indeed treated as resources and which managers do try to 'manage'. A key dimension, then, of the overall managerial task in a work organisation is that which concerns itself with obtaining, developing and from time to time dispensing with 'human resources' in this sense and maintaining the basic pattern of employment relationships which make the utilisation of these resources possible. This takes us towards a notion of *human resource management*.

'HRM': an ambiguous and confusing term?

Before we can develop further a useful notion of *human resource management*, we have to come to terms with the rather messy situation that currently exists whereby the term 'human resource management' is used in a confusing variety of ways. This can cause considerable confusion in the study of human resourcing aspects of organisations and the changing ways in which employment issues are being managed.

The term 'HRM' tends to be used in three ways:

- to refer to an academic area of study which brings together what were previously the separate topic areas of personnel management, industrial relations and aspects of 'organisational behaviour' such as motivation, leadership and work design;

- to refer to all those aspects of managerial work that deal with employees (sometimes used interchangeably with 'people management');

- to refer to those activities that were once referred to as *personnel management* ones but which are said to justify a re-labelling as 'HRM' when they take on the features identified in the left-hand column of Table 11.1. In this usage, 'HRM' is a new approach to handling human resourcing and employment issues in organisations.

These alleged differences between something called 'HRM' and something called 'personnel management' are ones that have been put forward by academic writers trying to identify possible trends in how human resourcing and employment management issues are dealt with in work organisations (see Storey, 1995; Legge, 1995, and other references in Reading Guide 21). The labelling of these

TABLE 11.1 A summary of how much academic writing on HRM tends to contrast an aspired to 'HRM' with the 'personnel management' which it rejects

Key features aspired to by 'HRM'	Alleged characteristics of personnel management rejected by 'HRM'
HRM takes on a strategic emphasis and a strong business or 'bottom-line awareness'	Personnel management is said to have an operational emphasis and simply involve itself in 'servicing' the organisation with a supply of suitable and compliant staff
HRM concentrates on building harmonious and reciprocal relationships with employees	Personnel management is said to concentrate on managing conflicts with employees
With HRM, employment and resourcing issues become the concern of all managers	Personnel management was said to keep employment and resourcing issues as its own specialist concern
HRM specialists work as 'business partners' with other managers (insofar as HR specialists are retained, rather than their expertise being outsourced or 'bought in' from consultants)	Personnel managers are said to relate to other managers sometimes by advising them on employee issues and, at other times, by policing them to ensure compliance with corporate personnel policies and procedures
HRM develops a personal and high commitment relationship between the employer and each individual employee	Personnel management is said to find it acceptable to have either a low commitment arms-length relationship with each individual employee or to relate to employees 'collectively' through the intermediary of a trade union
HRM is associated with a high trust organisational culture making significant use of teamworking and other 'indirect control' devices that make close supervision, detailed procedures and strict hierarchies unnecessary	Personnel management is said to be associated with lower trust relationships with employees, more 'direct' management controls and relatively bureaucratic structures and procedures

two approaches as 'HRM' on the one hand and as 'personnel management' on the other has been entirely a choice of academics. In the world of personnel management practice, many practitioners were moving in this alleged 'HRM' direction long before academic observers chose to apply the HRM label to such shifts of emphasis. It is important to recognise, however, that the trend within work organisations to replace the 'Personnel' title with 'HR' is not necessarily connected to the alleged move from personnel practices to 'HRM' practices within organisations. Many personnel departments have indeed been renamed as HR departments but this has largely been a matter of adopting a title that is more fashionable and which is felt to sound more hard-headed or business-like than 'personnel'. It is only marginally connected to the academic distinction between HRM and personnel management. A recognition of this puts into context the irritation expressed by Sue Ridgebridge, an 'HR' practitioner who is also a part-time student of 'HRM', about certain aspects of the academic HRM writing and teaching she has experienced.

Activity 11.1

Read the comments that Sue Ridgebridge makes in Cases and Conversations 11.1 about her trouble with the term 'HRM' and reflect on whether the ways in which you have heard the expression used has created any problems of this kind for you.

Sue Ridgebridge gets cross about HRM   Cases and Conversations 11.1

I sometimes wonder what is going on with this talk of HRM. It seems to mean one thing in the company where I work and several other things to the tutors in the university. At work it's relatively simple. I used to work in a Personnel Department. It was renamed shortly after I joined as 'Human Resources'. Most of the department's work is the same as it was before. Our HR director – who used to be the Personnel Director – has always been a very strategically focused and business-oriented person. She encourages us all to work very hard to support and develop the 'people awareness' of other managers. This is the same as we did when we were 'personnel managers'. And our approach to the trade unions is the same as it was when we were Personnel. We respect what they are trying to do but continue to work, step by step, to get employees to look towards their own manager when they have a problem rather than towards their union representative.

You see no changes accompanying the switch to the HR title then?

Only that we are further down the line with what we were doing when we were 'Personnel'.

So why was the title changed?

Some of us were rather reluctant to do it, in fact. It was mainly in recognition of fashions in management language. Basically 'HR' just sounds more modern. But I suppose we also thought it might help overcome some of the negative associations of 'Personnel'.

Such as?

It was partly the old 'welfare image' that Personnel had once had. And it was also the image of Personnel as a powerful centralised function always telling managers they must do this and they mustn't do that.

So what about your university HRM course?

The university's department of HRM puts on the HRM module I am doing. That department was only formed recently, I understand, and it looks to me as if the university has also gone for a fashionable label. They have no doubt seen a market opportunity to produce courses that sound more appealing than 'personnel management' ones might do.

You sound a bit cynical.

Well, not really. And the courses are quite good actually – they cover all the main sides of the human aspects of management that I am interested in. We get a good mix of work psychology, organisational behaviour as well as the stuff we used to call personnel management.

So, what's the problem?

Two things. First, there is this constant confusion in the course about whether HRM is the *general* business of dealing with staff, employees and all that or whether it is a *particular* approach towards these things. So, one minute for instance, negotiating with unions is treated as part of 'HRM'. But the next minute they are saying that 'HRM' is something that tries to get away from collective bargaining and that developing 'individual contracts' and 'mutuality' is 'the essence of an HRM approach', as one lecturer put it last week. So, in one breath they are saying that HRM is managing employment issues generally and in the next breath they are saying it is a particular approach to employing people. I actually noted down something one lecturer said. He asked the class what they thought the key features were of 'an HRM approach to human resource management'. For goodness sake: confusing or what!

And the other thing?

Oh yes. This is where I get really annoyed. When they are pushing this line that 'HRM' is a particular approach to management, they keep distinguishing it from 'personnel management'. And I find the way they do this utterly insulting to a lot of personnel people and what we were doing for years. The academics create a caricature of what many of us would always have recognised as a bad personnel department and then say that this is how we should characterise all personnel management – as short-termist, fire fighting, reactionary, non-strategic, over-keen on collective bargaining, uninterested in teamworking or empowerment innovations and so on. This is a travesty. It's a rewriting of history. And it's done, I feel, just to put the academic's shiny new 'HRM thing' in a good light.

You are cross!

I think the whole thing is ill informed and definitionally sloppy. They gave us a handout in the lecture: a list of 27 differences between personnel and HR management. I just crossed out the title and wrote in '27 differences between good personnel management and bad personnel management'. I suppose I would have been just as happy with '27 differences between good HR and bad HR'. But to say that the strategic and progressive thing is 'HRM' and the shortsighted reactionary stuff is 'personnel' is – well, words fail me.

But surely you can't expect academics to resort to crude categories like 'good and bad'.

Certainly not. But I think that this is where some of the worst confusions are being created by these academics. Half the time they say they are 'analysing trends' and are not advocating any particular management approach. Next thing, they are slipping over into advocating one particular approach – and using language like 'best practice in HRM'. However objective they pretend to be I think that they are making implicit judgements: 'HRM good, Personnel bad'.

Have you raised this problem?

More than once.

And?

They fall back on this line, 'Oh yes, we must try to sort out the reality from the rhetoric'. Half the bloody articles they ask us to read go on about rhetoric and reality. And it's total hypocrisy, much of the time. I mean, whose bloody rhetoric was it in the first place? These academics create a rhetoric about a shiny new HRM. They then go out and do research on what's happening in practice. And they end up patting themselves on the back for showing an alleged gap between the reality and the rhetoric – a rhetoric that they created themselves.

Sue Ridgebridge notes that the term HRM is used in academic institutions and, she might have added, in book publishing, to refer to a relatively new academic 'subject' that brings together topics that were previously dealt with under different headings. She is aware of the example of the local university at which she is studying and what she has observed there is similar to what has occurred in the business and management faculties of many other universities. The acceptability to the contemporary academic world of the subject of HRM has been signalled not just by the growing numbers of HRM courses being offered or by the growing numbers of departments, texts, courses and 'professors of HRM'. But none of this in itself seems to have particularly confused or annoyed Sue. She seems generally positive about her studies in the department but goes on to demonstrate her credentials as a sharply critical student who can powerfully apply to her study experience the sort of *critical common sense* identified in Chapter 1 (p. 20).

Sue Ridgebridge's critical faculties are first applied to the potentially confusing way academic work jumps back and forth between two uses of the HRM label. Sometimes it uses the term HRM to refer to human resourcing and employment management work generally. At other times it uses the label to refer only to a particular human resourcing and employment management approach – one clearly related, as Table 11.1 indicates, to the *indirect control* structure/culture option examined in Chapters 8 and 9 (and to which we return shortly). Hence we get the nonsense of 'an HRM approach to HRM' suggested by the lecturer of whom Sue is so critical. Second, Sue takes critical aim at the way these human resourcing practices and their associated high commitment or indirect control approach to management is contrasted with 'personnel management'. The personnel/HRM distinction is one which Sue's experience leads her to reject as both spurious and insulting to at least some personnel practitioners. Her more serious accusation, from an academic point of view, is that of a lack of clarity in the work of HRM scholars about whether they are primarily *analysing* ongoing trends in the human resourcing aspects of work organisations or are *advocating* their favoured approach – prescribing certain practices which they either implicitly or explicitly put forward as 'best practice'.

The position taken here is that these criticisms are well-founded and that there is a serious ambiguity in the HRM literature about its analytical and prescriptive elements. There is also a confusing slipping back and forth between referring to all human resourcing and employment management work as 'HRM' and the confining of the term to practices associated with a high commitment/indirect control style of human resourcing. And the popularity of the 'rhetoric versus reality' device in HRM writing suggests an uncritical attachment to Cartesian dualism (Chapter 4, pp. 102–4) which can only be made possible by a worrying lack of awareness of those general developments in philosophy and the social sciences which have established the impossibility of studying social 'reality' in a rhetoric-free manner (Watson, 1995, 1997, Reading Guide 21). To all of this can be added the criticism of much HRM writing as working within the limitations of a broadly systems-control set of assumptions about work organisations (Chapter 2, pp. 43–4). There is a general tone of treating 'human resources' as inputs to organisational systems – systems whose human resourcing sub-systems have to be both 'vertically and horizontally integrated' or 'aligned' with the other organisational sub-systems in order to achieve an effective transformation of inputs into outputs. And these are outputs that accord with the business or other 'goals' of the organisational system.

Not only is there a general and uncritical acceptance of the idea of organisational goals in much of the HRM literature (shown to be highly problematic in Chapter 2, pp. 45–50) but there tends also to be an unquestioning acceptance of the pursuit of 'competitive advantage' as the strategic priority of all organisations (also criticised earlier, pp. 170–1). It seems to be forgotten that a great deal of human resourcing activities in organisations ranging from hospitals and schools to charities and public administrative bodies may be tied to priorities other than competitive ones. There is also a general reluctance in HRM writing to recognise either the significance of the conflicts inherent in industrial capitalist employment relationships or the multiplicity of personal, group and sub-unit interests that clash with each other in the political arenas and career races that inevitably arise in every organisation. The workplace that many HRM writers imply is achievable (by adopting 'HRM' measures of course) is a 'unitary' one in which the adoption of a strong corporate culture, the pursuit of high employee commitment and the encouraging of managers and non-managers to recognise their 'mutual interests' will turn the whole workforce into a cohesive team, all committed to achieving corporate 'high performance', 'world class quality' and, of course, 'sustainable competitive advantage'.

With all of these inadequacies of the current orthodoxies of HRM thinking in mind it is now possible to outline a process-relational approach to human resource management. This is an approach that does not deny the legitimacy of managerial aspirations to achieving a high level of cooperation and mutuality that some of the more prescriptive 'HRM-mongers' imply is realisable, but it is one that gives full recognition to the constraints that limit what is realisable. In doing this, it will more honestly or 'realistically' inform organisational practice than the naïve utopianism of much HRM writing can ever do.

Human resource management: a process-relational view

A central argument of *Organising and Managing Work* has been that it is more helpful to anybody wanting to understand organisational and managerial activities in a way that will inform their practices to 'frame' these activities in process-relational terms rather than to adopt the standard systems-control frame of reference of much management thinking – HRM thinking included. Systems-control assumptions about work organisations usefully draw attention to patterns of cooperation and how different elements of organisations link to each other. They nevertheless tend to avert attention from all the 'conflicts, arguments, debates, ambiguities and sheer guesswork that characterises the *process* and *relationships* that what we might call "real" managerial practice has to cope with all of the time' (p. 58). Systems-control perspectives tend to work with a notion of overall organisational goals, implying through this that organisations are more 'unitary' and have a level of overall consensus about purposes and priorities than has ever been observed in practice. A great deal of HRM writing, as we have already observed, has a strong unitary flavour of this kind. Process-relational perspectives, on the other hand, give full weight to the multiplicity of goals and priorities that exist within every organisation. It recognises that differences of interest and clashes of individual and group priorities have constantly to be coped with – or managed. It also recognises the centrality of *power* and *micropolitical* activities to the way organisational order is negotiated and it acknowledges the significance of various types of *organisational mischief* to organisational functioning. What is required is a notion of *human resource management* that acknowledges the pluralistic, messy, ambiguous and inevitably conflict-ridden nature of work organisations.

A process-relational notion of HRM is one that recognises that managerial work involves attempts to achieve as much productive cooperation and unity of purpose as is realistically possible in any given organisation. It also recognises that this is only ever partially achievable and that HRM work, in every aspect has to handle ambiguities, tensions and conflicts. It will never find panaceas or 'best practices' that will overcome dissent and turn every organisation into a happy family or a unified team. Instead it will engage in a constant struggle to 'manage conflicts', to persuade, put pressure upon and negotiate with employees – making deals and shaping implicit contracts that will enable work tasks to be performed in a way that helps the organisation continue into the future.

Within this process-relational framing of human resourcing work we can put forward a formal definition of HRM.

Human resource management	Concept
That part of managerial work which is concerned with acquiring, developing and dispensing with the efforts, skills and capabilities of an organisation's workforce and maintaining organisational relationships within which these human resources can be utilised to enable the organisation to continue into the future.	

This conception of HRM is essentially strategic in its emphasis on enabling the utilising of employee efforts and capabilities to bring about long-term organisational survival. It incorporates those activities that have always been associated with personnel management, including the recruiting of employees and their training and development. It also acknowledges something that is rarely mentioned in formal definitions of either personnel or human resource management – the fact that a significant element of personnel and HR work has for some decades been the ending of employment relationships with employees, especially through redundancies. The *relational* and *exchange* elements of human resourcing work are acknowledged in the reference to the maintaining of employment relationships. This recognises two important human resourcing tasks: the seeking of compliance, commitment and productive cooperation on the one hand and the handling of conflicts, arguments and employee 'misbehaviours' on the other.

Something that is kept open in the above conception of human resource management is the question of who does this 'HRM work'. The same procedure is being followed here as was followed with regard to 'management' in Chapter 3. Three dimensions of 'management' were identified in Table 3.1: the function of *management* (which has to be carried out regardless of whether a few or many of the organisations employees are directly involved in it); the activity of *managing* (actions taken to achieve the function of managing or shaping the organisation); the formal role of *manager* (which becomes necessary when size or complexity of operations requires a division of labour between managers and others who focus on carrying out direct work tasks). Table 11.2 identifies three equivalent dimensions of HRM.

TABLE 11.2 Three dimensions of human resource management

Human resource management as a *function* is that part of managerial work which is concerned with acquiring, developing and dispensing with the efforts, skills and capabilities of an organisation's workforce and maintaining employment relationships within which these human resources can be utilised to enable the organisation to continue into the future

Human resourcing as an *activity* is the range of actions that fulfil the HRM function:

- monitoring current and likely future staffing requirements to enable some programming of future human resourcing efforts
- collecting and making available for managerial decision-making information on employees, employee capabilities and the deployment of both of these
- selecting and recruiting employees
- hiring labour from agencies and sub-contractors (as an alternative to creating an employment relationship with these providers of labour)
- dispensing with employees whose services are no longer required or who are otherwise deemed incapable of fulfilling tasks required of them
- training, and developing employee capabilities
- consulting, communicating and negotiating with representatives of organised labour (trade unions or professional associations) over whatever conditions or details of employment may have become subject to collective bargaining
- communicating and consulting with employees and employee groupings over employment matters without the intermediaries of trade union representatives
- fixing levels of and administering wages, salaries, fringe benefits and other rewards or 'compensation package' elements
- establishing and ensuring compliance with policies on health and safety, sickness and absenteeism, discipline, fair and equal opportunities – both to maintain the health and goodwill of employees themselves and to ensure compliance with legal requirements

Human resourcing (HR) practitioners occupying a *formal role* are employed in a personnel or HR department to ensure that the human resourcing activities necessary for long-term organisational continuation are carried out, directly through their own efforts and indirectly through their involvement (both enabling and constraining) with other managers

A whole range of processes and activities are carried out in work organisations to fulfil the strategic function of human resource management, as Table 11.2 shows. All of the human resourcing activities identified in the table are meant to ensure that the organisation has both the human skills and capabilities and the degree of social coherence necessary for its continuation into the future. Involved in many of these activities will inevitably be processes of competition, conflict and the wielding of power – all of which can as readily lead to confusion, breakdown and corporate failure as it can help the work organisation 'hold together' and function as a reasonably cooperative enterprise. The challenge faced by those concerned with human resourcing and employment management is enormous, as will be stressed in the consideration of the underlying strategic significance of human resourcing to which we now turn. Once this has been looked at, we will return to the issue of the relationship between human resourcing specialists and other managers with whom they have to work to fulfil the basic HRM function. As Table 11.2 implies – with its reference to there being both an enabling and a constraining role here – this is by no means a straightforward and always harmonious relationship.

The essentially strategic nature of human resourcing

It was argued earlier that human resourcing and employment issues are 'utterly central to the existence of organisations' and that they 'pervade every aspect of organisational management' (p. 368) that was subsequently outlined was said to be 'essentially strategic in its emphasis on enabling the utilising of employee efforts and capabilities to bring about long-term organisational survival'. One inference that could be drawn from this wording is that we are *analytically* privileging the organisation and its survival over the human beings that are involved in it. Perhaps such a position could be defended, on the grounds that it is possible to see an organisation continuing in existence over time in spite of the fact that it has had a complete turnover in the personnel involved in it. However, it is possible to counter this with the recognition that without the human beings that are involved with an organisation at any particular point in time, that organisation would not exist at all. We are back to the centrality of human resourcing and employment issues to the existence of the organisation and to three particular aspects of this centrality:

● the centrality of human resourcing issues to *processes* of organisational strategy-making;

● the role of human resourcing in handling *tensions and contradictions* that underlie the whole employment relationship in industrial capitalist societies;

● the role of the human resourcing function in maintaining *corporate integration* and capabilities to ensure *long-term* organisational viability.

The centrality of human resourcing issues to processes of organisational strategy-making

One frequently hears business leaders and senior managers claim that 'our people are our most important asset'. This wording can readily be criticised as dehumanising employees by treating them as means to ends ('assets' being little different from 'resources'). However, if we generously assume that the word 'people' is simply being used as convenient shorthand for human efforts, skills and capabilities, then perhaps we can acknowledge these words as signalling recognition by those employers that their enterprises are dependent upon the skills and efforts of the people they employ. In fact, we might infer that top managers are coming to recognise that without the people whom they employ – themselves included – the organisation simply would not exist. Yet much of the systems-control thinking that still dominates managerial thinking and a lot of academic writing in this area fails to represent the relationship between general corporate strategies and human resourcing strategies in accordance with this important insight. It treats the human resourcing strategy as something that follows from, supports or serves a main corporate strategy. Malcolm Lossie raises some of the practical issues that can arise from this in Cases and Conversations 11.2.

Activity 11.2

Consider, first, what you think is the most appropriate relationship to exist in an organisation between the shaping of the main corporate or business strategy on the one hand and a human resourcing strategy (in the sense of the general way in which the organisation deals with employment and human resourcing matters) on the other.

Consider whether human resourcing strategies are best understood as subordinate to overall corporate strategies, or as equal in significance to them. Then read the conversation with Malcolm Lossie in Cases and Conversations 11.2 and consider whether you are still happy with your original view in the light of what this HR director has to say.

Malcolm Lossie plays it canny

Cases and Conversations 11.2

It took my predecessor as HR director years and years to get a seat on the main board of this company. He fought like mad to get the right even to listen to what the top men were saying about the direction the business should take. But, just before I took over from him, he told me that he rarely found himself able to speak up about HR matters, even when, in his view, they were key to business decisions that were being made.

And is this different for you now?

After three years in the job, I'd say that I am just beginning to make my voice heard. But it is an uphill struggle. And if I get just one thing wrong, I shall lose every bit of the limited credibility that I have built up.

Yet I thought that you were recruited here precisely because you had credibility – in fact I've heard it said that you were headhunted because they knew that HR issues were vitally important to where the company was going. And they apparently thought that you were one of the few people who was good enough.

Yes, that fits with what I was told. But when it comes to it, there is one attitude that dominates. This is the attitude that engineering issues combined with financial considerations are the most important strategically.

Strategic discussions – board level discussions generally – get little beyond that. The board members would prefer it if they could just follow their engineering instincts about strategic directions – you know, pursue those projects that are the most exciting in engineering terms on the assumption that the world will buy the wonderful things that they produce. That's how it once was, I am told. But they have learned that they must temper this approach with recognition of the financial 'realities' that they must work within. Sometimes I think it would be too much to ask of them, that they should treat human resourcing matters alongside engineering and financial matters. I remember so well one occasion when I got quite forceful and pointed out that a decision that they were moving towards would involve a wave of redundancies. This, coming straight on top of an earlier headcount reduction programme, could have a very destructive effect on morale and recruitment to growing areas of the business, I warned. I was immediately shot down by one of the most powerful non-executive directors. 'You can't let the tail wag the dog, young man', he said, in the most patronising tones I have ever heard. 'If we make the right business decision then it is up to you to make it work in HR terms'. The chairman was much more gentle but suggested that the board thought that they had recruited in me the best HR man available, precisely because some very tricky employment issues were likely to arise from the way they were going to change the business.

So do you accept their definition of the HR role in corporate strategy?

No. I don't.

Sure. But I was looking earlier at your HR mission statement and that is full of stuff about a 'business driven' approach to HR and 'ensuring that the business aims' of the company are 'met through HR policies that are seen as fair, consistent . . .'

Just a minute.

This does sound like the business dog very clearly wagging the HR tail.

Hang on. Get behind the rhetoric. I admit that I am using the language that is preferred along the [directors'] corridor here. I've got to play along with them if I am going to get to where I need to be. It's, you know, 'softly, softly, catchee thief'. I am playing it canny. I know that I have got to talk this language of the 'business coming first' and of the point of HR being to 'help achieve business goals'. But my thinking goes beyond this.

Please go on.

I've got a simple picture in my mind. I see the human resources here as the starting point of our strategic considerations – not as the means of doing whatever suits the shareholders. Now let me make it clear, I am not saying that all the business things we do should be for the sake of the company's employees. But this company is the bundle of brilliant engineering talent that has made it a world leader. The starting point for any strategic discussion has therefore got to be the bundle of core competences that we possess. This is what I am getting my fellow directors to recognise, one by one. As I said to our head of design the other day, 'Where do these brilliant engineering ideas that our future depends on come from in the first place? They come from our human resources'. 'I'd never thought of it like that before', he replied.

Isn't that a bit abstract though?

It's anything but abstract. It is vital that I get my colleagues to think in this way if I am going to make a proper professional contribution to securing the long-term future of this firm. The danger at the moment is that they are looking at separate projects, one at a time. They are inclined to say to me, 'We're starting to work on such and such – so get recruiting a hundred of these and fifty of those. Oh and we are going to run down x and y, so you can lose the people there. Get the accounting chappies to make sure the costs and savings balance out'. No consideration is given to what projects might come along in the future – or indeed where those projects are going to come from – if we try to operate a hire and fire approach in the labour market we are talking about. This is the market for the world's best engineers. So that's what I am working on: getting them to see the human resources as the starting point for strategic thinking and as the source of the efforts that will provide a future for the business. This is all very practical. It is anything but abstract. I recognise that I will continue to recruit in certain areas and lose people in other areas and that, year on year, I will reduce the overall head-count. But I want to do this within a framework of building a secure core of committed engineering and managerial talent that can innovate and take risks and bring home the bacon for another hundred years.

Malcolm Lossie is giving very hard-headed arguments here for refusing to make human resourcing strategies subservient to general corporate strategy concerns. In effect, he claims that by treating the set of human resources that currently make up the organisation as of equal importance to issues of future corporate performance, a better corporate performance is likely to be achieved in the long run. He recognises that a successful corporate strategy and business performance is not just dependent on the human resources that employees supply in the form of willing and cooperative labour but is also dependent on the human resources of creativity and inventiveness. In this sense, he argues, human resources are the starting point for strategic thinking. They are not something that managerial strategic ingenuity (a 'human resource' itself of course) simply looks to an HR director to supply, like so many nuts and bolts, to help fulfil a corporate strategy. This systems-control view of the relationship between corporate and HR strategy-making is a linear one which sees human resource strategy-making as a subsidiary or servant of corporate strategy-making. It is represented on the left-hand side of Figure 11.1 whereas the more processual sort of relationship that Malcolm encourages us to take is represented on the right- hand side. Here there is a continuous interplay between these two aspects of strategy-making and they can be seen as having equal importance.

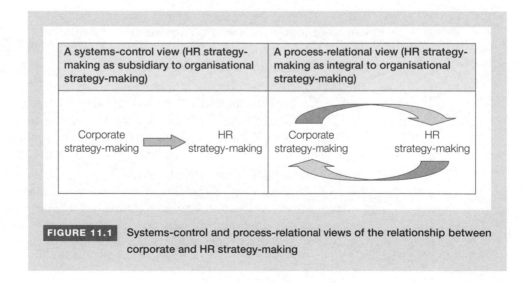

A systems-control view (HR strategy-making as subsidiary to organisational strategy-making)	A process-relational view (HR strategy-making as integral to organisational strategy-making)
Corporate strategy-making → HR strategy-making	Corporate strategy-making ⇄ HR strategy-making

FIGURE 11.1 Systems-control and process-relational views of the relationship between corporate and HR strategy-making

Human resourcing and the handling of tensions and contradictions underlying the employment relationship

A basic challenge facing the management of every employing organisation is that of managers having to *gain some control over, shape* and *exploit* the human resources of labour, skill and capability brought to them by employees. This is necessary for the enterprise to continue in existence. The challenge is a vast one because these 'resources' can only be obtained and utilised through making exchange relationships with human beings – with people who have minds, wills and identities of their own. To gain access to the *human resources* they want, they have to deal with *human beings*. These human beings will inevitably want to make use of the organisation for their own particular purposes (money income, social status, job interest and all the rest) just as much as the organisation wants to make use of them.

There is thus a basic tension that has to be handled. This is a tension, we might say, between the need for organisational managements to have malleable and controllable human resources of effort, skill and capability continually available to them and the basic recalcitrance or sense of independence inherent in the human beings who are the providers of these resources (Chapter 1, p. 6; Chapter 3, pp. 74–5; Chapter 9, p. 286). This profoundly significant tension, which puts pressure on every aspect of managerial work generally and human resourcing work specifically, is not just one that arises at the level of work organisations. It arises in some key principles of the type of economy and society of which all modern work organisations are components. This is the *industrial capitalist* type of political economy that dominates the twenty-first century world, and at the heart of this way of organising economic and social life is the *employment and rational organisation of free labour*. What we have here is a combination of three principles that are essential elements of *modernity* (Chapter 2, pp. 36–8) and which differentiate modern industrial capitalist societies from, say, feudal or tribal societies. They are:

- The principle of *employment* whereby workers sell some of their capacity to work and apply skills and capabilities to an employer (as opposed, say, to the serf working for a lord as a duty inherent in a feudal type of order or a slave working for the person who owns them).

- The principle of the formally rational *bureaucratic work organisation* whereby work activities are located in a technical division of labour, based on rational calculative 'design work' by expert managers, and a hierarchical control structure (as opposed, say, to people carrying out work along lines traditionally associated with the trade or occupation of which they are a part).

- The principle of *free labour* whereby each citizen of society has the legal freedom (or 'democratic right') to choose with whom to make an employment contract and to end that exchange relationship whenever it suits them (as opposed, say, to their being tied into a particular work situation by feudal bonds or by an owner–slave property relationship).

These underlying principles of the modern industrialised society have worked together effectively enough to make this type of social and economic order the dominant one in the contemporary world. In systems terms, it is a system that works. (Although we should never forget that while it has 'worked' to give massive increases in human welfare and democratic freedom it has also made possible some of the most systematic tyrannies and murderous wars of all times.) However, there are contradictory tensions within this way of organising society and economy. In the eyes of the most powerful critic of this system, Karl Marx, these contradictions were such that, in the long run, capitalist societies were bound to collapse. History so far, however, has shown that these contradictions have been *managed* to avoid such a collapse and it is possible to see the human resourcing component of the management of industrial capitalist work organisations as functioning to manage these contradictions. It by no means does this on its own. It performs such a role alongside a whole range of general state provisions and initiatives, in education, health and welfare provisions and employment legislation for example.

The basic contradiction that human resource management helps to 'manage' is that between the principle of *controlling* human activity, which is inherent in the institutions of employment and rational organisation of work, and the principles of *freedom*, *choice* and *autonomy* that are implicit in the institution of free labour. The citizens of industrial capitalist societies are thus given democratic rights, which define them as people who have a right to influence their own destinies and to choose with whom to seek employment. Once in employment though, they find themselves subject to controls imposed both by bureaucratic rules and by 'bosses' who have authority over them in the managerial hierarchy of the organisation in which they have chosen to work. Members of modern societies are encouraged to be free thinking, mobile, assertive individuals vigorously pursuing their own and their families' interests. At the same time, however, they are encouraged to be loyal and obedient citizens and employees. The continuous tension between these two aspects of modern life is one that, we might say, is 'built in' to the sort of societies in which an increasing proportion of people in the modern world live. And at the 'local' level of each employing work organisation, it is a tension with which managers continually have to deal. They strive to achieve a degree of *control* over employees' activities while at the same time having to accept that they must win employees' *willing consent* to work cooperatively in the way required of them.

This analysis has knowingly and deliberately been provided in terms that derive from the tradition of systems thinking about human social arrangements.

← Link   The value and the limitations of using systems thinking to help understand work organisations was a key theme of Chapter 2.

There has been an implicit use of a notion of both the industrial capitalist society and the modern work organisation as *systems* whose various components or organising principles can both function well together, keeping the 'system' going, or come into tension with each other threatening the collapse of that system. Further, it could be argued that 'HRM' has been treated here as a sub-system of organisational and societal systems that performs the function of handling disintegrative tendencies and thus avoiding the collapse of the system. An analogy that suggests itself is one of HRM functioning within work organisations in the same way that the regulator or the safety valve on a steam engine avoids a steam driven machine from blowing up. This analogy, for all its crudity, offers a useful insight.

It is in the spirit of trying to develop insights into the deeper or societal implications of human resource management that the basic systems analogy has been used here. It is not being suggested that societies and organisations *are* systems constructed out of sub-systems that sometimes function to achieve system integration and sometimes fail to function and bring about disintegration or disequilibrium. But it is suggested that the use of such mechanistic analogies can help us temporarily to simplify the immense complexities we confront when we try to generalise about large-scale social and economic arrangements – and thus help generate worthwhile insights. We have therefore looked at social orders and organisations for the moment *as if* they were systems. We have to remember that this is simply a device for making sense of the vast complexities of the human initiatives, conflicts, ambiguities, successes and failures in which we have to struggle to see any kind of pattern. It was accepted in Chapter 2 that *systems-control* ways of thinking have value in drawing our attention to certain 'system-like' characteristics of social life. But the importance was stressed of going beyond systems thinking and looking at the *processes* and ongoing *relationships* that occur within the very limiting 'black box' that systems analysis works with (p. 257). The insight that HRM has a conflict-management or a systems-integrating *function* needs to be combined with consideration of particular activities, processes and relationships like those in which we saw Malcolm Lossie involving himself earlier in Cases and Conversations 11.2. Similarly Inva Gordon's arguments in Cases and Conversations 11.4 for adopting more 'indirect control' or high commitment human resourcing measures in the Viewfield call centre organisation (which we will come to later, p. 399) can be connected to the notion of HRM 'functioning' to manage more effectively certain potentially disintegrative tensions.

The necessarily corporate and long-term focus of HRM

The managerial function of HRM, to which HR specialists and other managers alike contribute, handles basic work and employment tensions and contradictions in a way that gives human resourcing work a centrally strategic significance. Regardless of who carries it out, human resourcing work plays an important *general* role in ensuring that the organisation is able to continue into the future. It does this by trying to balance the managerial need to gain a certain amount of control over employees with recognition that people do not readily submit themselves to such control. There are, however, two more *specific* strategic human resourcing roles, both clearly related to this more general role, which can perhaps only be performed satisfactorily by a corporate HR department. These are:

- *Maintaining corporate integration.* Meeting the need constantly to monitor and influence the comparative treatment of employees across an organisation of any size or complexity to ensure that there is a sufficiently strong general perception of fair treatment and justice across the organisation to prevent a level of conflict, resentment or legal challenge that might damagingly undermine the level of productive cooperation necessary for the organisation's long-term future or might damage its reputation in the labour markets it draws upon.

- *Human resourcing for the future.* Meeting the need to encourage departmental or functional managers with shorter-term and more specific task responsibilities to look beyond the immediate pressures of their day-to-day situation to consider the pattern of skills, capabilities and commitments that the organisation requires for the longer-term.

Activity 11.3

In the light of these two suggested corporate HR roles, consider what particular issues within the range of human resourcing activities (listed in the human resourcing activities section of Figure 11.2) might require the existence of a corporate HR department in an organisation of any size. Then read Jack Avoch's justifications in Cases and Conversations 11.3 for retaining a corporate HR department that he put to Jean-Yves, the new chief executive at Gollachers.

Jack fights his corner

Cases and Conversations 11.3

When Jean-Yves took over as chief executive last year, one of his very first meetings was with me. I had this strange feeling as I went up to his office that, as the recently appointed head of HR, I was either going to be given a key role in the company's future or he was going to say goodbye to me. I was right to be anxious. He told me how much he admired what he had heard about my achievements and how he particularly liked the fact that I had seriously reduced the influence of the company's trade unions as well as having got most of the managers 'turned on to HR issues'. It had occurred to him, however, that the next logical step was for the managers across the organisation to take responsibility for the HR in their own areas and for my HR department to be wound up. He put this in terms of 'really empowering managers' and 'making them accountable for their own actions with regard to how they treat people'. He assured me that his mind wasn't made up on the matter but he also put it to me that 'the logic of this is unassailable, isn't it?' He then asked me whether I believed in 'managers' right to manage?' I was rather thrown by this but felt I had to reply that I did. 'So, if this shouldn't be challenged by trade unions and the like, then surely it shouldn't be challenged any more by a corporate HR department'.

I could see the trap I had walked into. When the union were powerful here, everybody saw a role for a strong personnel or HR department to negotiate with them. They also saw the need to make sure that we didn't get managers making local agreements with their union reps that would lead to comparability claims across the company which would cost the company dear (something that apparently happened several times in the past). What I now needed to do, to fight my corner and defend the people in my HR department, was to persuade Jean-Yves that managers across the organisation simply could not be left to cover every aspect of HR. They would always tend to prioritise local, departmental and immediate issues rather than corporate and long-term ones.

'With the best will in the world', I put it to Jean-Yves, 'You can't expect managers not to give priority to whatever HR issues are most urgent in their own area at any given time. This is the case even if they are very business oriented and strategically aware, as most of our managers are'. I didn't believe what I was saying here, actually, but I knew I would get nowhere if I implied to Jean-Yves that a lot of the managers simply could not be trusted to act in any interest other than that of their own little empire. 'In spite of the unions no longer being the main channel for grievances, this means that it is vital that someone keeps an eye on the whole playing field and ensures that we don't get people in one area being paid more than people in another for similar work.' I told Jean-Yves some stories of recent events that illustrated the problems here. One was the case of a department who organised their own flexi-time arrangements without involving HR. People in three other departments in that building soon decided that they would like to work in this more flexible way, but their managers argued that the work there was different and that they couldn't cope with other than a 9 to 5 arrangement. I pointed out, in the first place, that the manager should not have done that without involving HR. And, in the second place, I observed that if my department had not been there to sort out the rows that blew up, it would have to have been the chief executive who would have needed to 'waste her time' dealing with it.

This last bit seemed to make Jean-Yves think. I also told him about a recent industrial tribunal that had given the company a lot of bad publicity and set back one of our recruitment exercises. I said that this arose because a manager had dismissed an employee without reference to HR and that, again, if we weren't there constantly monitoring this kind of thing, there would be a lot more such tribunals. Just one of these 'every now and again' is damaging for the firm I argued. 'And indeed for the chief executive's own reputation', I dared to add. 'Tell me more', he went on, looking quite worried now. 'Think of it like this', I said. 'These things are bound to happen from time to time even if your managers are really sensitive about good employment practice and all the highly complicated employment legislation. But who would have to go into court to speak for the company, if you didn't have a HR director?', I asked him. And I answered my own question before he had time to. 'It would be down to the chief executive again I am afraid'.

I went on to point out the various corporate initiatives I was currently working on. One of these was an improved graduate recruitment programme. Another was a human resource information system which would be centrally run but which would 'considerably help empower managers by making available to them everything from their staff's training records and holiday entitlements to labour turnover figures and salary details'. 'Who else but an HR department could do these things?' I asked him. And I asked whether he wanted every manager going out and finding his or her own graduates, for example. Jean-Yves started to fight back by arguing that a number of the things that we did could be 'outsourced' or done by consultants. Our annual staff attitude survey was one he pointed to here. 'But what about our very significant work on monitoring current competencies and future skill needs?', I came back at him. 'Left to their own devices, most of our managers are rather unwilling to divert their staff from current tasks in hand to develop the skills they are going to need in the future. But we currently keep them on their toes on this and press them to what we call "investing in the future through HR development"'. You just cannot expect managers, with the departmental and delivery pressures they face every day to look to the long term in this way, without 'being prompted by someone who has this longer-term vision', I insisted.

'Speaking of long-term vision,' Jean-Yves said, standing up and pointing out of his window, 'a lot of restructuring needs to be done across Gollochers'. 'Indeed, I would expect you to be thinking that way,' I commented, feeling my confidence growing by the second. He continued, 'I can see that we are going to be recruiting staff to certain areas at the same time as we are losing people from others – although there might be some scope for redeployment of people if we do this skilfully'. I nodded, and smiled, 'That's not an easy thing to do'.

'Do you think we can do it?', he asked. 'I have done it before', I explained, 'and my staff…'. He cut me off, 'I know what you are going to say. No need. I'll come and see you and your people tomorrow and we'll get the job started'.

Jack appears to have been successful in persuading Jean-Yves to retain a corporate HR department and, indeed, to use Jack and his department to help him restructure Gollochers, though Jack had to work hard to 'fight his corner'. Jean-Yves had clear and well thought out reasons for dispensing with the HR department. It was not a matter of his ignoring the importance of the human resourcing function or, it would appear, having received bad reports about Jack himself. On the contrary, he speaks of the good things he had heard about Jack's achievements. And he could be seen as wanting to strengthen the overall human resourcing *function* (as opposed to *department*), rather than diminishing it. Jean-Yves speaks of making managers more involved in HR issues by getting them to 'take responsibility for how they treat people', and he implies that the existence of a formal HR department tends to constrain managers in this respect. It undermines, he suggests, their 'right to manage'. Jack's response to this is a shrewd one. He carefully avoids being too critical of managers but he suggests that 'with the best will in the world' and with all their 'departmental and delivery pressures' managers could not be expected to pay sufficient attention to broad corporate matters or to the long-term human resourcing needs of the business. He talks of the difficulty they are bound to have in looking at 'the whole playing field' or in considering what human resources will be needed for the longer-term future – unless they are prompted by someone like Jack and his colleagues.

Jack uses a variety of illustrations to support his argument for a corporate HR department – an element of the organisation's overall management that can prompt others to think corporately and long-term about employment matters. The first one is the pay issue and the implication of his few words here is that dangerous perceptions of unfairness could arise if someone was not 'keeping an eye' on what people in different areas were being paid for work of equivalent value. The specific example of one department independently initiating flexible working times is then used to illustrate the sort of problem that can arise. The negative effects of the company having to defend itself in an industrial tribunal are then pointed out. This damages both the organisation's and the chief executive's reputation, might harm recruitment and can take up a lot of management time, Jack suggests. A corporate HR department would presumably avoid this happening too often and would handle such problems if and when they arose. Jack then turns to the implied inefficiencies and inconsistencies that might arise if each department took on the graduate recruitment work currently done by corporate HR and he stresses how departmental managers would benefit from the sort of human resource information system that can only be run corporately. Jack finally wins his case by letting Jean-Yves work out for himself that the very priority that he has set for himself as chief executive – the 'restructuring' of Gollochers – could not really be achieved without HR help at the corporate level. Jack clearly wants Jean-Yves to recognise that with HR devolved to managers across the various operational areas of the company there would be an enormous problem of managing the recruitment of staff for some areas while people were being dismissed from other parts of the company. All of that could be made more acceptable to a workforce, it is implied, if redeployment of people across the areas is made possible. And the inevitable inference that follows from this is that only a corporate HR department could manage this process. Jack and his corporate HR department survive, having established their indispensability to Jean-Yves as a strategically important unit that can play a key role in supporting the HR aspects of his own strategic work.

Running through the story that Jack Avoch tells is the suggestion that relationships between HR specialists and other managers are not simple or straightforward. Jean-Yves seems to be alluding to certain tensions between the two when he brackets HR departments with trade unions as putting limits on managers' 'right to manage'. And implicit in the corporate HR role that Jack argues for is a notion of HR sometimes *supporting* and *enabling* managers (with the HR information system, for example, or on graduate recruitment) but at other times *constraining* them (on how they pay people, settle their working hours, deal with employment law and training matters for example). While Jack Avoch might want to persuade us that there are likely to be unmanageable problems without a corporate HR department, it is clear that the existence of a formal HR presence can, in itself, create problems.

HR specialists and other managers: tensions and ambiguities

When the three main elements of HRM were identified earlier in Table 11.2, it was recognised that human resourcing activities are likely to be carried out by a mixture of human resourcing specialists and other managers. If we look at the role played by those people who are employed in personnel or HR departments we will see that there are four dimensions to their work.

- They carry out specialised administrative tasks relating to human resourcing (from keeping personnel records to placing job advertisements).

- They work with other managers to support them in the fulfilment of human resourcing activities that affect the departments or functions of those managers. This entails, for example, helping managers select, recruit, develop and reward staff that are needed for the department to carry out its tasks and help the department dispense with the services of employees when they are no longer required. This implies a service or *enabling* relationship between HR and other managers.

- They monitor the activities of managers to ensure that they comply with corporate human resourcing policies and procedures necessary to prevent organisational disintegration. This entails, for example, preventing managers from making decisions that have damaging repercussions for other managers (especially on pay and other rewards where perceptions of unfairness across areas can arise), ensuring that managers comply with employment legislation, negotiated agreements with trade unions and with corporate policies on such matters as equal opportunities, disciplinary procedures, communication and consultation. This implies a 'policing' or *constraining* relationship between HR and other managers.

- They monitor the activities of other managers to ensure that they are acquiring and developing human resources that are necessary for the long-term future, as well as for the present. This implies both an *enabling* and a *constraining* relationship between HR and other managers.

This combination of roles creates considerable problems. Somehow, HR departments have *both* to serve or enable managers *and* to control and constrain them. This creates a considerable ambiguity in managers' eyes – often confusing them in practice about whether the personnel or HR department is primarily there to help them in their work or to hinder them. The uncomfortable truth is that both of these tend to be the case, from the point of view of managers concentrating on the priorities of their own department and the immediate pressures faced by their department. The result of this is that in many work organisations there is a tense and ambivalent relationship between HR managers and others. On the one hand, the manager is often dependent upon and appreciative of the help that the HR specialists give. But, on the other hand, they come to resent the limits that are put on their actions and decisions by the HR specialists' insistence that the manager complies with certain corporate or legal requirements. This compliance simply makes the manager's day-to-day life more difficult.

On top of these ambiguities are further ones deriving from the history of personnel management. One half of personnel management's historical roots are in a relatively *tender* or *caring* tradition of employee welfare and industrial social work and the other half of its roots are in a relatively *tough* and *controlling* tradition of labour management and collective bargaining with trade unions. The willingness of personnel specialists in recent years to replace the 'Personnel' title with a 'Human Resources' one can partly be understood as an attempt to play down the welfare and caring dimension of this history (as Sue Ridgebridge implied earlier in Cases and Conversations 11.1). Nevertheless, it is unlikely that employee expectations that Personnel or HR departments can and should show a caring face towards employees will go away. The caring/controlling set of historical ambiguities with regard to the HR department tends to remain alongside the ambiguities created by the dual role of HR as both a service to and a constraint upon the line or departmental manager.

HR specialists are typically presented with the considerable challenge of presenting themselves to the workforce generally as a caring department, concerned with justice and the fair treatment of employees while, at the same time, they must present themselves to corporate management as a department concerned with controlling and exploiting the efforts and capabilities of employees. Simultaneously, they have to present themselves to line or departmental managers as providing a supportive, enabling and empowering service while, to corporate management, they promise to monitor, control and constrain managers so that they do not prioritise their departmental interests with regard to employees over corporate and longer-term strategic concerns.

These ambiguities and tensions are bound to have considerable implications for the way strategic human resourcing is carried out in practice. As we shall now see, there are certain circumstances in which employee groups are more problematic to management than they are in others and the extent to which employee constituencies are perceived as problematic for the organisation's future is likely to be a key influence on the type of human resourcing strategy which emerges. Such a perception tends to put pressure on managers to choose relatively *high commitment* human resourcing strategies. Should the workforce be seen, on the other hand, as less of a problem with regard to the organisation's future, then there is less pressure on managers to choose this more complex and potentially costly approach. A *low commitment* human resourcing strategy, in such circumstances, is more likely to be selected. Such processes of HR strategic choice are not simple or straightforward, however. Ambiguity and differences of value, understanding and interest are always present when strategic choices are made.

Choices and constraints in human resource strategy-making

It was clearly established in earlier chapters that managerial choices about general strategic direction and about the type of structure, culture and job design that are adopted are influenced by a combination of organisational circumstances (or 'contingencies') and managerial interests, values and preferences. No organisational strategy, structure, culture or pattern of work design comes about as a direct consequence, however, of circumstances or contingencies in the way systems-control oriented 'contingency theory' implies. The state of a national or global economy, the market situation of a particular organisation or its size or technological nature does not *determine* what sort of strategy, culture or structure an organisation has. As our earlier analysis recognised, contingencies such as those of organisational environment, size and technology do have important implications for the way in which any organisation is shaped.

Link The relationship between managerial choices and contingent circumstances in the shaping of organisations was closely examined in Chapter 8, pp. 256–66.

The influence of these factors is always mediated by the way managers interpret and *enact* them, and these interpretations of organisational circumstances are taken into managerial decision-making arguments, discussions and debates. It is in this context of interpretation, argument and micropolitical contest that decisions emerge that lead to actions which, when taken together over a period of time, reveal a strategic pattern. This analysis can now be brought forward from its earlier application to how organisations are 'shaped' to our present concern with how human resourcing strategies emerge.

Human resourcing strategy   *Concept*

The general direction followed by an organisation in how it secures, develops, utilises and, from time to time, dispenses with human resources of effort, skill and capability to enable it to continue into the long term.

The way human resourcing strategy is conceptualised here is fully in accord with the concepts of strategy and strategy-making developed in Chapter 6. A human resourcing strategy is not looked at as a plan or as a dimension of a corporate strategic plan. Instead, it is treated as the general pattern that emerges over time as the managers of an organisation seek to supply the organisation with the human resources – in the sense of human efforts, skills and capabilities – that it needs to go forward into a long-term future. To help us see some patterning in the complex mixture of human resourcing activities and procedures that exists in each employing organisation we can utilise a continuum upon which any particular organisation's human resourcing strategy can be placed. The positions at the ends of this continuum are those of a *low commitment* HR strategy at one end and a *high commitment* HR strategy at the other.

- A *low commitment HR strategy* could be characterised as a 'hire and fire' one, in which labour is acquired at the point when it is immediately needed and the employee is allocated to tasks for which they need very little training, with the employment being terminated as soon as those tasks have been completed. The relationship between employer and employee is very much a calculatingly instrumental one and contact between managers and workers very much at 'arms-length'.

- A *high commitment HR strategy* can be identified where the employer seeks a much closer relationship with employees and wants them to become psychologically or emotionally involved with the enterprise. The employer is likely to offer employees opportunities for personal and career development within their employment, which is expected to continue over a longer-term period and potentially to cover a variety of different tasks.

It should immediately become apparent that this continuum of HR strategies has a close relationship with the indirect control/direct control continuum that was used in Chapters 8 and 9 to consider managerial choices about 'organisational shaping'. It is therefore possible to extend the model that was used in Chapter 8 to incorporate those direct/indirect control options into the choice that is made between high and low commitment human resourcing strategies. This recognises that low commitment human resourcing strategies are typically manifested in large part through the use of direct control management practices and procedures, whereas high commitment strategies are expressed in large part through the use of indirect attempts to achieve managerial control. Figure 11.2 is a version of the model introduced in Chapter 8 (p. 258) which has been extended to bring together the notions, on the one hand, of low commitment employment relationships with direct managerial controls and, on the other hand, high commitment employment relationships with indirect management controls.

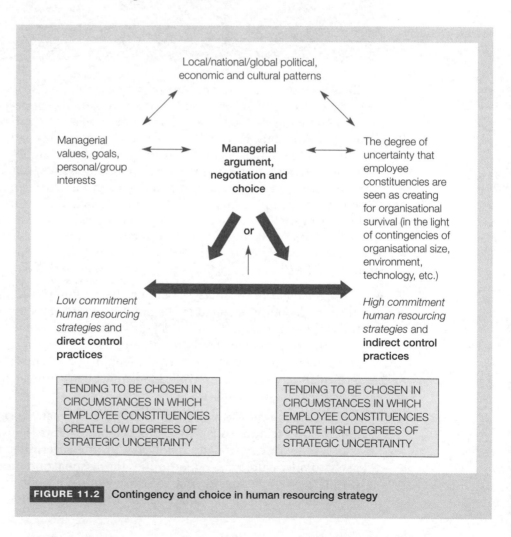

Local/national/global political, economic and cultural patterns

Managerial values, goals, personal/group interests

Managerial argument, negotiation and choice

The degree of uncertainty that employee constituencies are seen as creating for organisational survival (in the light of contingencies of organisational size, environment, technology, etc.)

or

Low commitment human resourcing strategies and **direct control practices**

High commitment human resourcing strategies and **indirect control practices**

TENDING TO BE CHOSEN IN CIRCUMSTANCES IN WHICH EMPLOYEE CONSTITUENCIES CREATE LOW DEGREES OF STRATEGIC UNCERTAINTY

TENDING TO BE CHOSEN IN CIRCUMSTANCES IN WHICH EMPLOYEE CONSTITUENCIES CREATE HIGH DEGREES OF STRATEGIC UNCERTAINTY

FIGURE 11.2 Contingency and choice in human resourcing strategy

The basic claim here is that, all things being equal, a low commitment type of human resourcing strategy is likely to be more appropriate to a situation where employees are not a major source of uncertainty for an employer than one where they create strategic uncertainty. An organisation is not likely to require a highly participative and strong commitment set of arrangements if it has a simple technology and a relatively straightforward business environment that allows it to employ easily obtainable and replaceable employees, for example. However, if an organisation's management sees that its future would be uncertain without meeting the much higher demands that are likely to follow from employing a highly skilled or educated workforce to operate a complex technology or deal with an especially tricky business environment – a workforce that is not easy to obtain or replace – it is much more likely to consider a high commitment set of employment conditions and work arrangements. This is necessary to encourage those people both to stay with the organisation and creatively and flexibly apply themselves to undertaking complex tasks. Note, however, that this proposition was made with the qualification 'all things being equal'. They are not equal, of course.

Managerial values and interests also come into the equation, as do the interpretive processes whereby managers decide how problematic the labour force is, in terms of the organisation's future. It is possible for managers to decide that their social values make them prefer higher commitment employment practices *in principle*. This, however, would tend to create cost problems – making their labour costs higher than competing employers who were more willing to adopt a simpler hire and fire policy. By the same token, a set of HR strategy-makers who disagreed in principle with high commitment practices and indirect management controls, but who employed highly skilled or educated people in a tight labour market would have difficulty retaining staff. In practice, then, there is likely to be interplay between managerial value preferences and perceptions of contingent circumstances making employees more or less strategically problematic (uncertainty-creating). And, given that the individuals within any strategy-making management group are likely to vary in their personal interests, values and priorities, we can expect to see strategic choices emerging out of processes of argument and debate. This was very apparent with regard to some human resourcing issues which arose in the Motoline case in Chapter 8 (and to which we will return below). We will also see this kind of process occurring with the case of the Viewfield call centre company, shortly. First, however, we need to look in more detail at the range of practices and arrangements that tend to be associated with the two ends of the continuum shown in Figure 11.2. Table 11.3 does this by identifying a range of direct–indirect control options that are available with regard to several areas of the organisation and its management that we have considered in earlier chapters – strategy-making practices, culture, structure and work design – together with a number of further areas of organisational management. The table suggests a very inclusive and wide-ranging notion of what human resourcing strategy is about. This is wholly consistent with our conceptualising of human resourcing strategy as the general direction followed

TABLE 11.3 General organisational and managerial options and aspirations related to the basic high commitment/low commiment HRM choice

	General organisational *direct control* options associated with *low commitment HRM*	General organisational *indirect control* options associated with *high commitment HRM*
Strategy-making	• performed by top management, possibly with the aid of strategy experts	• top management provide 'vision' or 'strategic intent' and develop strategy through interaction with other levels
Culture	• rule-based • emphasis on authority • task focus • mistakes punished	• shared values • emphasis on problem-solving • customer focus • learning from mistakes
Structure	• layered hierarchy • top-down influence • centralisation • mechanistically bureaucratic (rigid)	• flat hierarchy • mutual (top-down/bottom-up) influence • decentralisation/devolution • organically bureaucratic (flexible)
Work/job design	• de-skilled, fragmented jobs • doing/thinking split • individual has single skill • direct control of individual by supervisor	• whole, enriched jobs • doing/thinking combined • individual multi-skilled • indirect control within semi-autonomous teams
Performance expectations	• objectives met to minimum level • external controls • external inspection • pass quality acceptable	• objectives 'stretch' and develop people • self controls • self/peer inspection • continuous improvement in quality sought
Rewards	• pay may be varied to give individual incentives • individual pay linked to job evaluation	• pay may be varied to give group performance • individual pay linked to skills, 'mastery'
Communication	• management seek and give information • information used for sectional advantage • business information given on 'need to know' basis	• two-way communication initiated by any party • information shared for general advantage • business information widely shared
Employment relations	• adversarial • collective • win/lose • trade unions tolerated as inconvenient constraints • OR unions used as convenient intermediaries between managers and employees	• mutual • individual • win/win • unions avoided OR unions increasingly by-passed in the hope of their eventual withering away • OR unions involved in *partnership relations* with employers to give a 'voice' to employees in working towards employment security, innovative work practices, fair rewards and investment in training
Employee development	• training for specific purposes • emphasis on courses • appraisal emphasises managerial setting and monitoring of objectives • focus on job	• training to develop employees' skills and competence • continuous learning emphasis • appraisal emphasises negotiated setting and monitoring of objectives • focus on career
HR/Personnel department	• marginal, and restricted to 'welfare' and employment administrative tasks • reactive and *ad hoc* • staffed by personnel specialists	• integrated into management, and working as 'partners' with other managers • pro-active and strategic • staff interchange with the 'line' or other functions

by an organisation in how it secures, develops utilises and dispenses with human resources of effort, skill and capability to enable it to continue into the long term. Such a perspective invites us to see human resourcing strategy as the basic manner or style in which people's work capacities are utilised across every aspect of an organisation. Choices about this manner or style relate to issues ranging from how strategy-making is conducted in the organisation down to the way an HR or personnel department is staffed. At the level of strategy making, for example, a low commitment/indirect control approach only utilises the strategic thinking of a minority of those employed as managers – the very senior managers and their specialist strategic advisers. At the opposite end of the continuum, a high commitment/indirect control approach involves many more people in strategic activities – all managers are seen as having relevant compe-tence in this area. And, with regard to the staffing of an HR department, the former approach tends to treat personnel work as something that can only be done by specialists. The latter style, however, takes a broader view of the capaci-ties of both HR and non-HR managers by suggesting both that their work can to some extent be 'integrated' and that both sets of managers, in certain circum-stances, can work in the other's area of activity.

Many of the options identified at the high commitment/indirect control end of the continuum should perhaps be seen as *aspirations* rather than as 'options' in the strict sense of the term. A number of these options here have been advocated as generally desirable by the *total quality management* move-ment (Wilkinson *et al.*, 1998, and other references in Reading Guide 16), and the virtues of other practices falling at this end of the continuum have been extolled by those wanting to prescribe 'best practice' in areas ranging from work design and pay systems to human resource development. In spite of all this advocacy, however, managers themselves are likely to be aware that these are aspirations that are never likely to be fully realised in practice. They may wish to move towards a culture where more of the values that people within the organisation hold are 'shared' ones. However, it is unlikely that anyone with any familiarity with the world of work is likely to think that it is realistic to achieve an organisational culture in which everyone holds the same values.

The same point applies to the aspiration in the area of employment relations towards 'mutual' relationships rather than adversarial ones and negotiations in which both sides always 'win'. It is by no means unrealistic to seek some move-ment in this direction, as trade unions have tended to acknowledge in calling for employers and trade unions to work together in *partnership relations* to the advantage of corporate and employee interests alike. However, the notion that conflicts between the goals and interests of the multiplicity of parties involved in an organisation can ever be totally overcome is utterly unrealistic. In fact, the very existence of trade unions and the institution of collective bargaining recog-nises differences of interest between employers and employees – interests that these arrangements are intended to manage. And, although trade unions and collective bargaining have become less significant in work organisations in many countries in recent times, they have by no means disappeared. This is recognised in Table 11.3 and the possibility for a continuing trade union role within a high commitment type of HR strategy – one which stresses 'partnership' between employer and employee interests – is included (see Ackers and Payne, 1998; Claydon, 1998, Reading Guide 21).

Activity 11.4

The direction in which Mick Moy and Joy Petty were trying to take Motoline (Chapter 8, pp. 260–4) can be understood as one towards a high commitment type of HR strategy. Reread 'Getting on track at Motoline' and

- use Table 11.3 to note the various ways in which the new management regime was moving towards a high commitment and indirect control approach;

- observe the role that Mick's personal values and background affected his attitude towards trade unions;

- consider how realistic you think Mick is being in considering what might be characterised as a 'partnership' relationship with trade unions in the new Motoline.

Flexibility and dual human resourcing strategies

We have seen that the basic human resourcing style of an organisation can be understood in terms of whether it leans towards an employment style involving *high commitment relationships* between employer and employees and utilises indirect attempts at managerial control of activities or leans towards an employment style involving *low commitment relationships* utilising direct managerial control practices. It is possible, however, that managers in certain organisational situations might want to apply different human resourcing strategies to different parts of their organisation. Why would they do this? To put it at its simplest, it is done in recognition of the fact that the workers who do certain work tasks can be related to in ways that are less costly than others. In economic terms, the *transaction costs* of going to the market for labour in the lower skilled or more peripheral areas of activity are lower than they would be if that labour were employed or incorporated within the bureaucratic hierarchy of the enterprise (see Rowlinson, 1997, Reading Guide 1, on the application of this type of economic thinking to organisations). In circumstances like these, then, organisations might be found to operate a *dual human resourcing strategy*.

Dual human resourcing strategy   *Concept*

A dual human resourcing strategy exists were an organisation applies (a) a high commitment ('relationship') HR strategy involving a long-term employment relationship to core workers and managers and (b) a low commitment ('transactional') HR strategy to more peripheral suppliers of labour (sometimes involving an employment relationship, sometimes involving a market relationship).

The flexible firm

Concept

An organisational pattern in which an organisation seeks some of its human resourcing from a *core workforce* whose members are given employment security, high rewards and skill enhancement opportunities in return for a willingness to adapt and innovate and a *peripheral* workforce whose members are given more specific tasks and less commitment of continuing employment or skill enhancement.

Organisations following a dual HR strategy are adopting features of what has been identified as the *flexible firm* (Atkinson, 1985, Reading Guide 16). The dual HR strategy or 'flexible firm' principle is by no means a new one. It has been used since early industrial times. It even existed during the latter part of the twentieth century when *Fordism* was at is height (Chapter 9, p. 308) and when it appeared that the standard form of work career for most people was becoming one of lifetime employment with a commercial organisation or a public bureaucracy. Its most obvious presence – as today – was in project-oriented industries like building and civil engineering, where organisations had very different requirements for labour at different stages of the projects they undertook. Thus, one source of 'human resourcing' would be labourers, craft workers and technical experts who would be 'bought in' as required. The other source would be the organisation's own employees who were felt to be necessary to integrate activities over time and give continuity to the organisation's development. Also, many organisations through most of the twentieth century had some elements of this dual human resourcing approach *within* its employed workforce, in the form of a differentiation between 'works' and 'staff'. Here the latter employees generally had superior terms and conditions of employment, and, typically, were expected to be 'closer' to management than the former. A higher degree of commitment was sought from these staff members who, however junior they might be, were, in principle at least, on the bureaucratic career ladder – which 'works' employees were not.

With changing social values, the growth of service work and the reduced significance of differences between manual work and office work, employers have tended to abandon the works–staff distinction and have *harmonised* employment terms and conditions across labour categories. The trend is towards the dual human resourcing principles being applied to those who are, on the one hand, a potentially long-term *employed* group and, on the other hand, a short-time *hired* group. The first exception is where, in terms of the model in Figure 11.2, organisations find themselves with relatively stable markets and simple technologies in which a low-commitment direct-control employment strategy is viable (the workforce not being a source of strategic uncertainty for the management). The second exception – where the circumstances will often overlap with those of the first – is in sectors, like certain parts of the hospitality industry, where there are people willing to take on short-term employment. These might be younger people still involved in education or people with family responsibilities who can only manage a partial and perhaps intermittent relationship with employment. Such people are willing to be casually employed because they are only seeking a short-term involvement and this matches the short-term requirement of the employer.

The short-term/long-term distinction is vital to understanding the dual human resourcing approach to achieving flexibility. Managers tend to look for the two different types of flexibility explained in Chapter 9 (p. 313):

- flexibility to meet short-term *adjustment* needs which calls for an ability to bring in and dispense with labour and human expertise as markets fluctuate or as projects begin and end;

- flexibility to meet long-term *adaptability* needs which calls for human commitment and expertise from a core of employees who will willingly and enthusiastically make innovations and actively adapt their practices to ensure that the organisation continues into the long term.

A *transactional* or *market* HR sub-strategy will thus meet the flexibility for short-term adjustment requirement and the *relationship* or *employment* HR sub-strategy will meet the flexibility for long-term adaptability need. And the relative emphasis given to each of the two human resourcing approaches is likely to vary with organisational circumstances. A project-oriented organisation (ship or oil-rig building or civil engineering perhaps) regularly needing to adjust to meet changing demands might give greater emphasis towards a *transactional* (market) approach, for example. An organisation developing and producing high technology consumer products might, on the other hand, use a greater proportion of labour engaged on a *relationship* (employment) basis. In each case, nevertheless, the fact that both types of flexibility are likely to be required in an increasingly competitive economic context means that most organisations will use both means of acquiring human resources of skill, knowledge and labour.

HR strategy-making in practice

The strategic options identified earlier in Table 11.3 are based on thinking and practices covered in literatures on HRM, strategic management, labour market analysis, change management, total quality management and various other attempts at giving managerial advice and selling panaceas for managerial inadequacies. What has been avoided here, however, is any labelling of the two basic styles, the 'high commitment' and the 'low commitment' approaches, as 'old' and 'new' or as 'bad practice' and 'best practice'. This would be to play down the relevance of contingent factors – the extent to which different organisational circumstances may fit better with some types of organisational or managerial practice rather than others. Many readers will nevertheless want to apply value judgements to these alternatives, whether this derives from their own notion of what they believe 'works best' or what they feel about the right and wrong way to 'treat people at work'. This is precisely what happens in the managerial 'arguments, negotiations and choices' processes at the centre of the model in Figure

11.2. One manager in a particular organisation may argue for example that it is morally wrong to use labour as a short-term means to business ends – because it involves people's identities and their livelihoods and denies them the security that any employee in a modern society should have a right to. He might be persuaded, though, by another manager that such a low commitment employment strategy is the one that is most likely to be successful and to justify this he might point to certain organisational circumstances or contingencies. He might observe that the organisation has a very simple technology, faces very seasonal business demands and enjoys a plentiful supply of job applicants who appear to be happy to accept unskilled work with no long-term future. He is pointing out, in other words, that the employee constituencies in his organisation are not particularly problematic: they do not, in strategic exchange terms, create a great deal of uncertainty for those running the organisation, with regard to its overall strategic direction.

Activity 11.5

Read Inva Gordon's account in Cases and Conversations 11.4 of human resource strategy-making at Viewfields and, using Figure 11.2 as an analytical guide, identify the factors that led to a shift in strategic emphasis, noting:

- changing contextual factors at the local or national level;

- the extent to which employees were perceived by the Viewfield management team to be increasingly strategically 'problematic' – in the sense of creating uncertainties for the organisation's continuation and in the light of

changing contingencies (i.e. perceived organisational circumstances);

- the interests, values and goals of members of the management group that influenced how they acted with regard to these contingent and contextual factors ('enacted' them);

- how all these things got mixed together in the managerial arguments or negotiations that occurred – considering in particular any of the factors discussed earlier about the tensions that can arise between HR and other managers.

'Viewfields, how can I help you?'

Cases and Conversations 11.4

It was about a year ago I recognised that I was really going to have to assert myself if I was going to do my HR job properly here at Viewfields. Sandy Viewfield had recruited me as a personnel officer when I was only about a year out of university. I know he was impressed with me but he had it mind that I would be a quiet and compliant recruiter of staff who would very efficiently work the human resourcing machine for him — getting people in when he needed them, making sure that no employment laws were broken and getting rid of people when they were no longer wanted. He seemed happy to appoint a woman to the job, given that he believed that 'people work' was particularly 'suitable for a female' (especially since a lot of the staff were women and Sandy found women 'a bit unpredictable and difficult to understand').

Sandy had left a big telecoms company to set up the call centre business. He had risen from an engineering job up to regional manager level and he brought with him several other people with mainly telephone engineering backgrounds. The accountant, Wesley Nigg, came from a telephone systems manufacturing company. He now calls himself the finance director and he, together with Sandy, Maddy Dornoch – the marketing director – and myself form the senior management group. Sandy uses the word 'strategy' all the time and he likes to think of himself as the great strategist. He talks like this, anyway, always reminding us that he had 'the vision' to set up a business that will stay at the 'cutting edge of call centre technology'. And, yes, by 'technology' he tends to mean the hardware and the computer software that is used. People are just the add-ons that, regretfully, he has to use to work this kit. I am convinced that, in the long run, he thinks that there will be sufficiently intelligent machines available that he won't have to employ operators. For the present, however, he has to have several hundred people working for him on the several dozen accounts that we currently have. As these numbers have grown and as 'personnel problems' have increased in number and frequency he has had to turn to me more and more. It was only after I had proved to him that I was indispensable by rescuing him from what might have been a very damaging court case over a severe harassment affair, did he let me call myself 'HR director' and allow me to play a regular part in senior management meetings. Maddy is in rather a similar position. Sandy is socially unskilled, to put it politely, and he managed to lose several of our best accounts simply by being rude to the people who were bringing him business. That is the main reason he reluctantly decided to get in a marketing expert – or rather let me find someone to take on this role. He didn't like the idea of bringing another woman into the management group. But Maddy was obviously so good that he did the right thing and appointed her. 'Yes, she's clearly the best man for the job', he commented to me after the interviews, demonstrating his less than sophisticated grasp of HR principles!

I am pleased to have a women colleague in the management group. But it worries me at the same time. We end up with women-versus-men sorts of argument all too often. Sandy and Wesley act like stereotypical engineers and accountants and Maddy and I have to play the 'but people matter' line every time. I am sure that Sandy and Wesley resisted a number of the employment innovations that I have made, with Maddy's full support, more than they would have done had either of us been men. I once accused them of being prejudiced against the managerial arguments that Maddy and I were putting forward just because we were women. This was at a meeting that was turning from the intended company policy review into a seriously unpleasant row. Wesley, however, said that he was resisting our ideas purely on cost grounds. And Sandy said that it was much more a matter of his worrying about our 'general naïvety' about human beings as opposed to any specifically 'female naïvety'.

So what were these issues? They were actually rather fundamental ones about the nature of our business as well as about how we treated our employees. Maddy argued that what we primarily sold to our client companies was a 'human service' – a 'warm and helpful interface between their businesses and the people who wanted to deal with those businesses over the telephone'. I argued that we needed to think about our staff as the key to making this possible. It wasn't the quality of the telephone systems we used that would guarantee us a future, any more than it was the software or the quality of the 'scripts' that Maddy's marketing staff were so good at writing and putting in the operators' hands. It was the ability and the willingness of staff to convince the people who called up that they wanted to please and help them. 'Until you can buy robots that sound like warm and intelligent human beings,' I told Sandy that night, 'you are going to have to learn to treat the operators in such a way that they feel committed to the company and are willing to use their initiative to give the callers the quality of service that they – and the client businesses who trust us to represent them – are looking for'.

It was quite fortunate that my mention of robots rather amused Sandy. It might well have angered him if I had spoken less carefully and had seriously implied that he was only capable of relating to machines (which, privately, I sometimes think to be true). In HR work you have got to be subtle and skilled if you are going to get your way. If you start trying to tell managing directors of companies that they are getting it wrong, without being very subtle about it, you are finished – especially if they are men and you are a woman. You've still got to tell them some hard truths, but you tread carefully. You use all the charm and subtlety you can muster to convince them that, unless they listen to you, their business might come unstuck. And we were coming unstuck at Viewfields.

When Viewfields started up it was all very straightforward from Sandy's point of view. He set up the equipment in a rented building on the edge of town and simply advertised in the local paper for staff. There wasn't a lot of competition at that time. Sandy was definitely ahead of the game in the call centre business. He had several big clients and unemployment was high across the region. This meant that he had a plentiful supply of labour, and it was compliant and easily controllable labour too. The technology makes it easy for supervisors to keep a check on the number of calls each operator is handling. It is also easy for them to check that the operators are both following their script and are speaking in a pleasant and helpful manner. Anyone who fell short was simply replaced by the next person in the queue for jobs. The pay was not too bad but there were few rest breaks and there was very limited variety in the work that each person did. Sandy's view was that once a person had 'mastered' a particular script and learned what was expected of them on that client's behalf then time should not be wasted getting them to learn to handle callers on another account. He and Wesley also got very cross if it appeared that operators were going out of their way to be helpful to callers. In fact, it was over their harassing a couple of employees who were accused of this that led to the court case that made Sandy and Wesley recognise that they were not the most skilled at handling people issues.

Times have changed a lot since those early days, as reluctant as Sandy and Wesley were to admit it. The labour market is now much tighter and we have to rely a lot on students who do not take readily to supervisors who bully them or to being instructed in every detail of what they are to say to callers. About a year ago our labour turnover and absence levels were becoming so bad that we were struggling to keep the phones manned. Recruitment costs, Wesley said, were unacceptably high and Maddy warned that several clients were threatening to end their contracts if the number of complaints they were receiving about our staff being brusque and off hand did not reduce significantly. 'They are complaining about staff speaking like robots', Maddy reported – and the irony of this was not lost on Sandy. 'What are we going to do, then?' he asked me. 'What is our HR strategy going to be?'

I explained that we had to take a generally different approach to our staff if the business was going to have a healthy future. Given that we were limited by the standard sort of technology that most call centres use, we could not change things radically – fundamentally upskilling the basic jobs we offer, for example. But we could look for ways of both making people feel less dissatisfied with the work they had to do and also making them feel that the company was one worth staying with and being committed to. The first thing I got accepted was that we would improve some of the basic workplace facilities like the quality of the rest rooms. To my surprise, Wesley said that he could find money to build a small gymnasium for staff to use. Sandy laughed at this, pointing out to us that Wesley had for a long time said that he personally wanted to find a gym to use. But Wesley argued that this kind of thing should be enough to make people prefer to work for Viewfields rather than for any of our rivals, none of which had this kind of facility. I told Wesley that these were just 'hygiene' factors, in motivational terms, and that we had to look for more significant changes relating to the work itself.

When I said that what I had in mind were such things as allowing operators to adapt the basic scripts to suit their personal style, both Sandy and Wesley got very uncomfortable. And when I suggested that we set up development opportunities for staff to learn how to write scripts themselves, by allowing them an hour a week to work with marketing staff, they wanted to end the meeting. Wesley went into a long lecture about unit labour costs, or something of the kind, and Sandy said that it would give us a messy and unmanageable division of labour. 'We can't afford to confuse people about where their place is in the system,' he said, 'and it will put supervisors into an impossible position when they are trying to monitor calls – how will they know whether an

operator is doing the job properly and efficiently if there isn't a defined script and strictly allocated minutes?' 'Oh, I was envisaging getting rid of a separate supervisor's role and allowing operator teams to allocate one of themselves to the monitoring desk each week, with a view to that individual looking for ways of helping colleagues improve their performance, rather than keeping the old system where supervisors basically used the monitoring equipment to police the operators'.

When I went a step beyond this and suggested that we move to a largely internal promotional system and that we recruit all operators as people who can potentially move upwards, eventually having their own client accounts to manage, Wesley lost his temper and told Sandy that he should never have employed a soft-headed and totally unrealistic 'personnel type' like me. He left the meeting and Maddy and I spent the next two hours working on Sandy. He told us that this sounded like revolutionary talk to him. Yet he was willing to give consideration to what was being said because, he claimed, he 'had enough vision to see that this was as much a marketing development as a soppy HR one'. Without Maddy pointing out that it was a 'hard-headed business case' that was being put to him, I don't think we would have got anywhere with my ideas. But Sandy did invite us to develop these ideas further and he promised that he would try to 'bring Wesley round', if we could persuade them that, not only would these ideas overcome some of the 'people problems' that we currently had, but that they would significantly help the business grow.

After several months of argument I got all of this accepted. In fact, the current HR practices go even further than I originally envisaged. The teams not only choose the person to cover the developmental/monitoring role each week, they also organise their own cover for sick colleagues, altering their own shifts to make sure the work is covered. And it would appear that most of the recruitment that we have done recently has been of people introduced by current employees. Each employee, if they want it, can have an hour's 'personal development time' to work with marketing staff or, if they wish, to work on the self-help and distance learning packages that we have on the computers in the 'development room' that was built as an extension to the staff rest area. I've been especially pleased to see that team members are happy to 'trade' development time within the teams. People who are not career-oriented swap their weekly development allowance for time off with people who do want more than an hour a week to develop their career potential.

All of this was hard fought for, I must stress. The company is a much more morally acceptable place to work in, from my personal point of view. But this has only come about because there was a significant business case to put for changing the HR strategy in this way. Having said that, the business case was not one that was immediately obvious to either Sandy or Wesley. Without the hard work put in by Maddy and me to get the men to think differently, little would have changed. Perhaps if the staffing problems had got really out of hand, they might have shifted their ground. But I have no doubt that any changes that Sandy and Wesley would have been capable of making on their own initiatives would have been anything more than minimal – and would not have helped Viewfields survive in the long term. Wesley is still sceptical and constantly complains about the salary costs, in spite of the fact that the rate of our business growth and our growing popularity with both clients and employees gives the company the 'leading edge' position that Sandy is so keen to maintain. As Sandy points out to Wesley, the profits that are being made 'fully justify the higher labour costs'. I suppose the four of us operate quite effectively as a management team but I sometimes wonder how much easier it would all be if business arguments were not always mixed up with the tensions that are always there because Maddy and I are women, are younger than the other two and have not got what Sandy calls a 'proper grounding in telecoms technology' or what Wesley refers to as 'a decent financial education'. This is all nonsense of course – but I long ago realised that, in management, you have to deal with the irrational in people as much as with the rational. Perhaps it all adds to the fun of the job. But I think, as I said to Maddy the other day, that the real reward that I get from seeing our HR strategy in practice is when I hear an operator say to a caller 'how can I help you?' and I get impression that they really mean it.

The final statement that Inva Gordon makes about the sincerity of an operator's offer of help to callers is perhaps rather revealing about her personal values – something also implied by her reference to Viewfields as a more 'morally acceptable place to work'. She brings ethical and caring concerns to her work. Yet we can also imagine Sandy Viewfield, or even Wesley Nigg, taking pleasure in hearing operator's speaking to callers in a seemingly sincere manner, but Sandy and Wesley, we might guess, would be far less concerned than Inva about whether the operators were *actually* sincere in what they said (whether they were engaging in *deep* rather than *surface acting* – see Chapter 5, pp. 145–8). What would matter to them would be that the operators' performances were likely to be 'good for the business'. In spite of the considerable difference of priority and value between the members of Viewfield's strategic management team, a distinctive change had occurred in the HR strategy. This had come about in the light of both varying values and among these four individuals and the changing circumstances, or contingencies faced by the organisation. The 'managerial argument, negotiation and choice' put at the centre of Figure 11.2 was influenced, as the model suggests, by:

- national and local economic and cultural factors – the changing levels of unemployment for example;
- managerial values, goals and interests – these varying from Sandy's ambitions to run a 'leading edge company' and Inva's ethical concerns to Wesley's interest in having a gym available for his own use and the attitudes each of them had towards age and gender;
- the managerially perceived increase in uncertainty being created for the organisation's future by employee constituencies – reflected in absence, labour turnover, recruitment costs and, above all, in the poor level of work performance that was losing Viewfields business. The key contingency behind this was the one of the changing business environment – a higher level of competition in both the main call centre market and in the local labour market.

The managerial choice that emerged from this decision-making *garbage can* (Chapter 10, p. 339) involved shifting along the continuum shown in Figure 11.2 in the direction of a *high commitment human resourcing strategy* accompanied by a related shift in the direction of indirect control practices (team working, emphasis on promotions within an internal labour market etc.). There was no question of a radical shift to a wholly different type of employment practice or a sudden embracing of HR 'best practices'. Instead there was a pragmatic shift in managerial approach resulting from a combination of *choice* and *circumstance*, a combination that took its particular form as a result of processes of argument, challenge and debate and as a result of the specific mix of knowledge, insight, ignorance and prejudice to be found within the group of managers making the shift. The changed contingencies affecting the organisation meant that the main employee constituency was being experienced by managers as more problematic than it was before. The newer human resourcing strategy made a better fit with the organisation's circumstances – a higher commitment and indirect control type of strategy was more appropriate to a situation in which employees were becoming a greater source of strategic uncertainty than they had previously been.

This improved 'fit' between organisational circumstances and human resourcing strategy did not come about automatically – it was chosen by the company's managers. But it was a choice that emerged only after considerable argument, debate and conflict over values. It was also made in an atmosphere of interpersonal tension and in the light of differences of gender, age and occupational background among the group of managers making the strategic choice. Also playing a part in this was a tension between Inva as an HR specialist, on the one side, and Sandy and Wesley on the other. Sandy and Wesley were suspicious of the proposals being developed by Inva, seeing them as naïve and as perhaps too people-oriented or 'caring'. Maddy's support for this was respected but it too was taken less seriously than it might have been, early on, probably because of her gender, work background and relative youth. Inva and Maddy, however, would no doubt have argued that they were the more business and strategically oriented ones, in the long-term sense, because they could see the necessity of adopting a higher HR strategy if the organisation was going to perform well into the long term.

Human resource decision-making does not just occur with regard to the sort of strategic matters that Inva Gordon and her colleagues were tackling. Decisions are made from day to day about which potential employee to recruit, which employees to allocate to which task, which employee to promote, discipline or dismiss. Operational decisions and choices like these are made every day, and they are just as liable to be influenced by ambiguity and differences of interest as are the more strategic types of decision that we have just been looking at.

Selection, choice and discrimination in human resourcing

Human resourcing involves ensuring that work organisations have the necessary human skills, knowledge and capabilities that can be turned into work efforts which will enable the organisation to continue into the future. In practice, this means that decisions regularly have to be made about specific human individuals and about how they are to be treated within a potential or an actual employment relationship. Human resourcing decisions about recruitment and selection, allocation of tasks and rewards, promotions, dismissals and redundancies are routinely made in employing organisations, typically through the combined efforts of human resourcing or personnel specialists and managers who have a more direct authority relationship with the employee. The concern is with getting the 'right person' for a post, a reward, a punishment or a redundancy notice.

Selecting the 'right person' in all of these areas of human resourcing work is, generally speaking, a matter of achieving a decision that is right in two senses. First, the decision needs to be 'right' in the sense that the person selected is the most appropriate one to do a particular job, say, or to go on a particular training course. Second, the decision needs to be 'right' in that it is seen to be broadly fair and acceptable to whatever individuals, groups or authorities that might take an interest in that decision. At the simpler level, this second criterion means that neither the individual employee themselves nor any other employee or manager is likely to be left with a grievance that might lead them to behave in an organisationally disruptive way following the decision. At a more complex level, it means that the decision should neither contribute to a general atmosphere of injustice or low trust within the organisation nor lead to legal actions against the organisation because the employer can be deemed to have unfairly treated or discriminated against an employee in a manner which has been deemed to be illegal in that society – with regard, say, to that employee's gender or race.

For these various reasons, there is considerable pressure on human resourcing decision-makers to make the 'right decision'. A 'wrong decision' can be very costly in a financial sense as well as highly damaging to an organisation's general performance or public reputation. Personnel specialists have therefore been increasingly pressured to find ways of making managers feel confident that they are making the best possible choices when they make selection decisions about employees – when they discriminate between one person and another as a potential employee or a candidate for re-allocation, promotion, reward, punishment or dismissal. Discrimination between one person and another is at the heart of all of these processes. And discrimination means making human judgements that always and inevitably have an ethical dimension to them. To treat one person one way and another person another way inevitably raises questions of justice, fairness, right and wrong. This is something that often makes managers feel uncomfortable – as does the ambiguity and unpredictability inevitably accompanying decisions about human beings and how they are going to behave in the future.

It is perhaps instructive that the term 'discrimination' is widely applied in the employment context only to what might be termed socially unacceptable choices. The notion that there could be a non-discriminatory selection is clearly nonsense (to choose or select is, by definition, to discriminate). Yet it is almost as if managers are trying to convince themselves that they are not discriminating at all and a lot of personnel or human resourcing practice over the years has appeared to support such a possibility. Attempts have thus been made to develop a *rationalistic and bureaucratic personnel management technology* that not only removes ethical uneasiness from personnel decision-making but also plays down the ambiguity and unpredictability that is inevitably associated with judgements made by some human beings about others. Managers have wanted to be equipped with an efficient and neutral set of procedures and technologies which can measure and calculate an employee's, or a potential employee's, appropriateness for treatment of one kind or another (recruitment, promotion, etc.).

It would be foolish to criticise managers, inside and outside HR departments, for trying to devise procedures that enable the best possible person to be chosen for any particular role or treatment or for trying to make that choice in a way that will be deemed to be legal and regarded as generally fair by all concerned. However, there is a considerable danger of managers having too much faith in the ethical neutrality and the predictive powers of human resourcing or personnel techniques and procedures. As we will shortly hear Francesca Carrbridge argue with regard to selection decisions generally, 'At the end of the day a manager must recognise that a choice of one person rather than another involves basic human judgement, intuition and trusting to good fortune. You've got to keep these basic human judgements under control with personnel procedures that try to keep things fair and balanced. But all the selection techniques, personality tests and equal opportunity procedures in the world cannot replace simple human guesswork, a trust in one's "gut feel" and the subjective feeling that you are being as fair as possible when you choose Mrs X rather than Mr Y'.

Activity 11.6

Read what Francesca Carrbridge has to say in Cases and Conversations 11.5 about the difference between her approach to employment decision-making and that of her predecessor, Dag Dunearn, and try to identify the different sets of assumptions, or styles of 'framing' reality, which each of them tends adopt with regard to:

- the nature of work organisations;
- the nature of human beings.

To do this, it should be helpful to draw on the distinction between systems-control and process-relational thinking that has been used throughout previous chapters, having been introduced, with regard to work organisations in Chapter 3, pp. 43–5, and with regard to human beings in Chapter 4, pp. 97–8.

Francesca dismantles the sausage machine
Cases and Conversations 11.5

I noticed, Francesca, that you very much played down the importance of the personality tests that your staff had carried out when it came to the final discussions at the end of today's appointment process.

Yes, I prefer to pay as little attention as possible to personality test results.

Which raises the question of why you use these tests, doesn't it?

Of course it does. When I first came into HR work, I used to argue vehemently against their use. I felt that they were a form of pseudo science that managers might use as a sort of crutch. I feared that test results and 'advice from psychologists' might discourage managers from standing on their own two feet and making basic human judgements that they would have to stand by and cope with once the decision had been made. I didn't want to let managers believe that there is such a thing as the 'right person', let alone someone with the 'right personality' for any particular post. I did a psychology degree myself and was very aware of how poor a predictor of future job performance research shows these things to be. I did my degree dissertation on this at university and what struck me most strongly was not just the poor predictive power of these tests but the point that several writers made about how a person's job performance is much more likely to be influenced by how they are treated once they are in a job than by so-called personality attributes that they bring to the job. That's a pretty powerful thought, isn't it?

Yes, it is. Perhaps we can come back to it.

I just want to stress the importance of managers realising that a selection decision involves a fallible human choice – it is not the outcome of a magic personnel technique. I want them to take responsibility for their decisions. This is really important because it is often how they subsequently deal with the person once they are appointed that makes that appointment a successful or an unsuccessful one.

I see. But you still haven't explained why as HR Director here you spend time and money on occupational testing, something you appear to be against on principle.

I don't oppose all kinds of occupational testing. I'm very happy to use tests which check that people actually have the aptitudes that we are looking for in certain employees. I wouldn't employ an assembly worker who has to manipulate tiny electronic parts who could not pass a standard manual dexterity test any more than I'd take on an office trainee who could not pass a basic literacy test, a sales worker who could not pass a verbal reasoning test or someone to work in our pay office here who failed a numeracy test.

Your problem is with personality tests, then?

It is. Or rather it was. What I recognised after a while was that managers in selection processes did not generally come to rely on test results to anything like the extent that I feared. The tendency that I have observed across many organisations, and years of experience, is that they only take notice of what the testers say when it tends to confirm what their own judgement is telling them. Contrary indications are just ignored.

So why bother with them?

I decided after fighting several battles, especially with a couple of chief executives I worked with, that it wasn't worth it. To put it simply, it appears to make a lot of senior managers feel better if they think that something sort of 'scientific' has gone on somewhere within the selection process. I think it plays a sort of symbolic role for a lot of managers – it is a talisman that makes them feel better about the rather chancy thing they are doing when they are making a decision to appoint, say, someone on £50,000 a year whose later underperformance could cause major difficulties. Recruitment and selection – let alone promotion and deployment decisions – involve a great deal of guesswork. They are very much a gamble, much of the time. And managers are often queasy about this. They feel better if certain procedures have been followed that appear to have something rational or objective about them. I've come to live with this – as long as it does not involve managers denying their responsibility for the decisions they have made, as I just explained. I've therefore become tolerant of the practice of using some personality testing. I'd much prefer to save time and money and drop them though.

Is cost the only problem you have with these tests now?

Oh, I still don't like them. But I admit my predecessor here put me off them. I think I associate testing with his general way of doing HR, or personnel, work.

This is the man you replaced?

Dag Dunearn was a testing maniac. I used to have major battles with him, as his deputy. He used all sorts of tests, some that are relatively uncontroversial as well as some of the more marginal ones, like graphology, to screen out certain applicants for jobs – rejecting them before the managers whose area the job was in had even got to see their applications. Imagine that: you don't even get to have your application put in front of a departmental manager, let alone get an interview, because some charlatan retained by a personnel manager says your handwriting indicates that you are an unreliable person.

But your problems with his approach went further than this?

Indeed. We just didn't see the world in the same way, let alone how you should do personnel work. In the end, the other top managers decided he had to go. He was simply too inflexible, bureaucratic and officious. So I got his job and I think I am well respected. I do put limits on managers' freedom to manoeuvre – over matters like equal opportunities and other areas where employment legislation affects us. And I am fairly bureaucratic in areas where you need to be bureaucratic – over things like accurate employee records and managers following proper procedures in areas like health and safety, discipline, induction, appraisal and all that. But managers generally understand why these things have to be done and realise that I am happy to see all sorts of innovation and experimentation occurring as long as the basic and necessary procedures are followed.

How was it before you took over then?

Dag took what I call a sausage machine approach to HR. He saw the organisation as a big system that ran on sausages. The job of the personnel department, as it was called then, was to act as a sausage machine, producing sausages of the right size and the right type at the right time for each job that had to be done. I don't think he could tell the difference between sausage making and people processing. He would make sure that the organisation contained the right proportion of sausages with black skins and the designated number of disabled sausages, as well as maintaining what he deemed was a correct balance between male and female sausages – if you'll excuse the analogy here. He believed there was a formula for choosing the 'right' person for every job. Every person, just like a sausage, had a fixed set of properties and the job of personnel was to calculate what sort of characteristics were required for every job in the organisation – and then the right sausage would be served up for that post. Do you follow me?

I'm not sure – you are stretching the analogy a bit. Give me an example.

Well, what I had in mind was the way that, whenever there was a vacancy, no action would be taken by the personnel department even to advertise it until the manager concerned had produced a meticulous job description, accompanied by a detailed person specification which would set out in detail exactly what sort of person (I nearly said sausage) that they wanted the personnel department to find for them.

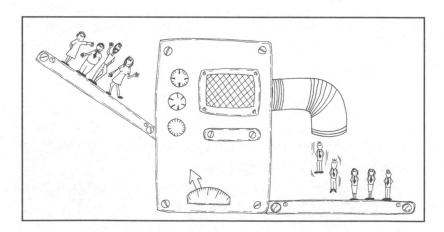

And the problem with this?

Dag saw the organisation's job structure as a much more fixed thing than it is in practice. Managers often said to me that they would be happy to consider a variety of different candidates, with various different strengths, for appointment to an area where there was a vacancy. If they found someone generally useful, then they could adapt the job to fit the person. This went totally against Dag's view of organisations as machines that require human cogs to make them run. He saw his job as getting exactly the right human cog for every little piece of the organisational machine. I remember an argument I had with him over this. He told me that I misunderstood professional personnel management – the basis of which was to make sure that round pegs were found for round holes and square pegs for square holes. It was totally ridiculous, in his view, to go changing the shapes of the 'organisational holes' to make sure that whatever pegs you might chance upon would fit into them. It seems like quite a good idea to me, however.

He was rather mechanistic, you are saying?

Yes, and it was very counterproductive. The business was increasingly requiring flexible and adaptive workers who would themselves influence the jobs they would do once recruited. And Dag was standing in the way of this. His efforts over equal opportunities were equally counterproductive. On several occasions, for example, he held up important selection or promotion interviews for months, until he could get a list of candidates that he deemed to have a reasonable race and gender balance.

The means were getting in the way of the ends for which they were devised, you could say.

Exactly.

And you avoid this happening?

As far as I can. I am passionately concerned about fairness and equal opportunities. But if I were to get obsessed with setting up checks and controls in these areas, like Dag did, it would take us back to a situation where working towards gender and ethnic diversity would simply have a bad name with managers. And they would do everything they could to get round equal opportunity measures wherever they could. My approach is to get managers to believe in the spirit and principle of fairness and equality. It may sound idealistic but I prefer to see the organisation as a sort of moral community – a place in which people can more or less trust each other. That's what I work towards anyway. People are not fixed quantities or objects, like sausages, and I think that if they are encouraged to work together in a good atmosphere they will both develop themselves, as individuals, and change the organisation so that it can cope better with all the changes that are being thrown at it.

So you are much more open and flexible about processes like selection and recruitment?

Indeed, but not only that. Management is not just a technical matter, in my view. When you go through an interviewing process, for example, you are both trying to get to know the candidates, as human beings, and enabling them to get to know you as an employer with a certain culture and set of cultural values. The process is a sort of negotiation between the potential employee and the potential employer. You, as a recruiter, cannot really know what any of these people is really going to be like if you take them on. And they cannot be too sure of just what it is going to be like working for you. So there is a process of weighing each other up. This involves a great deal of ambiguity and awareness that some people are simply more skilled at presenting themselves to a prospective employer than others (from the completing of the application form to what they both mention and avoid mentioning in an interview). And what this all adds up to is that managers have to deploy the basic human skills of eliciting helpful responses from people and judging the likelihood of one person being a better bet for the organisation than another.

That's how you get the right people for the organisation?

No. The 'right person', as you put it, would be the one who you could guarantee would do the job as required. That is just not possible. It is, as I've just said, a matter of who is 'the better bet'. As I was stressing earlier, some of the most important determinants of how well someone does the job (whatever the job turns out to be like, once they start doing it) are ones that arise after the appointment of the individual. How a person is treated once recruited is surely just as important as the recruitment and selection process that brought them into the organisation. On various occasions I have seen what looked like the perfect appointment turning out to be a disaster because the person's abilities were either misused or under used, once appointed. And by the same token, I've seen some potentially high-risk appointments turning out to be great successes because the managers involved worked hard to use the recruits' talents to the best effect. I want managers to recognise all of this and not see HR as a source of administrative and psychological black magic that can find them the 'right person' for every job.

You want managers to make their own judgements and take on their own risks?

Yes, supported by whatever expertise we have to offer in HR. At the end of the day a manager must recognise that a choice of one person rather than another involves basic human judgement, intuition and trusting to good fortune. You've got to keep these basic human judgements under control with personnel procedures that try to keep things fair and balanced. But all the selection techniques, personality tests and equal opportunity procedures in the world cannot replace simple human guesswork, a trust in one's "gut feel" and the subjective feeling that you are being as fair as possible when you choose Mrs X rather than Mr Y.

It is apparent from what Francesca Carrbridge says that she is sensitive to the tensions we identified earlier as typically, if not inevitably, existing between HR and other managers. She manages those tensions by allowing managers flexibility and the chance to innovate, as long as they conform with the basic principles that she lays down to fulfil the HR role of maintaining the organisational workforce as a whole (equal opportunities, compliance with legislation, induction and appraisal procedures, etc.). Her predecessor, Dag Dunearn, on the other hand, exacerbated those tensions by dictating to managers and treating them in an inflexible and officious way. This led to his downfall, it would appear, which Francesca relates to his view of the nature of work organisations. She talks of his view of the organisation as a big machine that requires appropriate employees in the same way that a machine requires cogs. This fits with what we have called a systems-control way of 'framing' organisations (pp. 43–5). It sees the structure of jobs in the organisation as something that is pre-decided in the organisational design – thus making it possible for the personnel department to ask a departmental manager for a precise 'job description' accompanied by a clear 'person specification'. The candidate who fits that specification – with this 'fit' being measured wherever possible by the use of neutral and objective tests – is judged to be the 'right person for the job'. This suggests that Dag sees human beings, and not just organisations, in systems-control terms (pp. 97–8). Each human being 'has' a particular personality or an otherwise similarly fixed set of characteristics – ones that they will carry forward into their subsequent appointment or promotion, regardless of the circumstances in which they find themselves after that appointment.

Francesca scorns this 'sausage machine' approach to HR. Her analogy is a little forced at times but it gives a clear indication of what she has tried to move away from in her regime. She sees the organisation more as a human community, she explains, in which human and fallible judgements are made about employees and prospective employees. The organisation is a much more ambiguous place and every decision has its moral implications, she suggests. The selecting of people is part of a *process*, which continues long after the actual appointment decision is made. It is not part of a sausage-making system. Managers have to take responsibility for their judgements, not just acknowledging the fallibility of their choice-making but accepting responsibility for making the appointment a success after it has been made. All of this suggests a process-relational way of 'framing' both organisations and people. The organisation is seen as a more flexible and negotiable set of arrangements than a systems-control approach would point to. This makes it possible for managers to consider selecting a generally appropriate candidate for an appointment and for the task structure and way of working to be modified once that person becomes involved in it. But Francesca not only avoids regarding the organisation as a fixed entity. She also sees human beings as adaptable – and not as a fixed set of attributes or personality characteristics. How they behave in the organisation is a matter of the processes that they become involved in and the set of relationships in which they play a part.

A process-relational view of the 'people processing' aspect of human resourcing is one that locates choices over such matters as recruitment, promotion, appraisal or deployment within the employment relationship between employees and the employing organisation. The organisation does not itself, in any direct sense, employ people, of course. Managers do this in the organisation's name, and managers are fallible human beings working within bounded rationality and with their judgements shaped by personal beliefs and prejudices as well as by personal and group interests. In effect the HR selection processes in which managers engage are bargaining processes (see Newell and Shackleton, 2001, Reading Guide 21) – albeit bargaining processes in which the parties are rarely equals. They are processes within which an implicit contract is created between employer and employee, an often vague and ambiguous contract that is subject to all sorts of change when the individual finds themselves in the post for which they were selected. Also, their *orientation to work* becomes subject to changes both within and outside the work setting (pp. 126–38). Bargaining is also quite likely to go on between the managers taking part in the selection process themselves. Most HR decisions are made within the sort of 'garbage can' process we examined earlier (pp. 338–46) with a variety of different managerial and personal views and interests coming into play and contributing to the overall *negotiated order* (pp. 74–81) of the organisation. And, just as any selection decision is influenced by how the managerial selectors operate, it will clearly also be influenced by how the employee or respective employee presents themselves. A shrewd candidate for a job, a promotion or a posting will tell credible and appealing stories about themselves and who they are and what they can do, drawing on appropriate *discursive resources* to impress selectors. We saw his very clearly with Mike Kilrock in Cases and Conversations 4.6, and his drawing on discourses of *leadership, entrepreneurship* and *professionalism* to win himself a promotion in his funeral directing organisation.

We do not know how successful Mike Kilrock was in his bid for promotion. Whenever a candidate for selection presents themselves to selectors, they take a risk. They cannot know how their presentation of self and the story they construct about themselves will be received. In the same way, the managers who choose or reject such a candidate cannot know with any certainty that the outcome will be the best one that they could have made. They too are taking a risk. 'At the end of the day', to borrow Francesca Carrbridge's expression from Cases and Conversations 11.5, managerial skills are very much ones of making basic human judgements, shrewd guesses and bargains that will contribute to a greater or a lesser extent to the long-term performance of the organisation that employs them. This analysis applies to human resourcing and other aspects of managerial work alike. Its implications for notions of managerial competence and organisational effectiveness, and the ethical and social implications of both of these, will be taken up in Chapter 12.

Summary

In this chapter the following key points have been made:

- It is both unrealistic and morally dubious to regard human beings themselves as 'human resources'. It is more appropriate to treat *human resources* as the human efforts, skills and capabilities that an organisation requires to be able to operate into the long term.

- Human resourcing issues affect every employee in a work organisation – managers and non-managers alike. And, within management, involvement in human resourcing matters is necessarily a concern of both human resourcing specialists and non-HR managers.

- Human Resource Management (HRM) is a term that is used in a confusing variety of ways. It was largely developed as a concept by academic observers trying to detect significant changes in employment practices. Particular confusion has been caused by academic writers' attempts to differentiate 'HRM' from 'personnel management'. Such a differentiation is only very loosely connected to a trend among practitioners to re-label personnel departments as Human Resources (HR) departments.

- Human resource strategy-making is central to broader practices of strategy-making in employing organisations and the common tendency to see it as following from – or serving – the main business strategy of an organisation can be misleading. It is more helpful to see it as *both* following from and contributing to the main process of corporate strategy-making.

- The human resourcing function of modern work organisations can be understood, in part, as helping to cope with some basic tensions or contradictions inherent in industrial capitalist ways of organising economies and societies. In particular, it has to handle the difficulties caused by the fact that although people are taught to think of themselves as free choice-making citizens in such societies, they are nevertheless subjected to supervisory and managerial control at work. Managerial ways have to be found of both allowing a certain amount of discretion to employees and finding ways of exerting a degree of control over them. The involvement of HR functions in both the 'care' and the 'control' of employees and their concern with both 'welfare' and 'efficiency' reflects this.

- The HR role in organisations is a particularly strategic one because it tends to take on responsibilities for maintaining integration of the workforce at a corporate level and for looking at longer-term employment issues that departmental managers are less likely to be concerned with. This contributes to the tensions and conflicts that often arise between HR specialists and other managers.

- Human resourcing strategies vary from organisation to organisation with some being closer to a *high commitment* pattern of arrangements and practices and others closer to a *low commitment* pattern. The pattern emerging in any particular organisation will be the outcome of various managerial preferences and values on the one hand and certain managerially interpreted contingent or circumstantial factors on the other. All things being equal, a high commitment type of employment strategy will tend to be adopted when managers perceive the employee constituencies to be strategically problematic, in the sense of creating uncertainties for long-term continuation. This might result, for example, from a highly skilled or educated level of workforce being required to operate a relatively complex technology. This would lead employees to place high demands on the employer in terms of both intrinsic and extrinsic rewards. When employee constituencies are much less problematic, on the other hand, and are less able to make strong demands on the employer, for example, there are cost and efficiency pressures on managers to adopt a *low commitment* type of HR strategy.

- The *high* or *low commitment* HR strategic option is closely related to a whole set of other options: ones in areas ranging from job design and pay systems to strategy-making procedures and cultural patterns. In all of these areas an *indirect control* approach will be associated with a *high commitment* HR strategy and direct control approach associated with a *low commitment* HR strategy.

- In certain circumstances, organisations may adopt a dual human resourcing strategy, applying different types of strategy to different parts of the overall work force.

- Human resourcing decisions involving the selection of individuals in areas such as recruitment, promotion, reward, deployment and dismissal are made every day in work organisations. There has been a tendency for a rational and calculative *personnel technology* to be applied to these choices. This involves strongly bureaucratic procedures and the heavy use of such devices as psychological tests. Such a technology is intended to help select individuals in a way that will be deemed efficient, acceptable and fair. However, it tends to become restrictive and counterproductive. Its use can be associated with a systems-control way of thinking about work organisations and people. A more realistic process-relational way of thinking indicates that selection and discrimination processes are highly ambiguous and are dependent on basic human processes of judgement, guesswork, chance taking, debate and negotiation. Selection and HR choice processes in general are better seen as parts of broader and more continuous processes of bargaining and adjustment in which both organisational arrangements and human beings themselves change and adapt within the ongoing negotiated order of the organisation.

Reading

Reading Guide 21, especially, contains material that supports and takes further much of what is covered in Chapter 11.

CHAPTER 12

Managing in a changing world: capability, learning, trust and morality

Objectives

Having read this chapter and completed its associated activites, readers should be able to:

● Bring together many of the themes that have been developed in previous chapters and relate them to questions about what the future of work and work organisations might be, what might make some organisations and managers more effective than others and what part values and ethics play in organisational and managerial work.

● Appreciate that change management is integral to managerial work and that managerial initiatives contribute to as well as react to changes occurring in the world of work.

● Recognise the extent to which the future is more 'open' than is often appreciated, especially with regard to issues of globalisation, technological change, work organisation and what people will expect of work and organisations.

● Understand the role played by trust relations and patterns of reciprocity in the achievement of organisational 'effectiveness'.

● Relate questions of manager effectiveness (or competence) to the capabilities of the general group of managers in an organisation rather than to the characteristics of each individual manager – at the same time recognising that there are individual competencies involving sensitivity to organisational environments, other people, and to knowledge and learning that are relevant to all managers.

● Come to terms with the fact that matters of value, ethics and morality run through every aspect of managerial work and that ethical issues are more usefully understood as one of the ways in which human beings cope with their world rather than as objective absolutes with which people do or do not comply.

continued

415

● Understand that managers themselves have a choice of being either *ethically active* or *ethically assertive* in their everyday work but that, in the end, the ethics and values that will apply to work organisations in the future are matters for broad democratic debate across the world and are something that managers neither can nor ought to be expected to determine.

Continuity, change and managerial choice in the managing of work

Throughout human history, and indeed the prehistory of the human species, people have struggled to make a living. To make something better than a subsistence living, humans have devised various ways of cooperating with each other. These have allowed them to fulfil more complex and productive work tasks than they could have managed working alone. People have also devised exchange relationships that have similarly enabled people, operating in an *organised* way, to trade with each other to their mutual benefit. This too has enabled people, albeit within patterns of inequality and exploitation, to enjoy a better life than would have been possible if each man and woman had tried to struggle on their own to scrape a living from their environment. But whatever type of social and economic order human beings have devised in different places and at different times – be it a hunter-gatherer order, a rural-agricultural order or an urban-centred industrial capitalist order – there have always been common features and continuities. A division of labour – an allocation of different tasks to different people – has been a central feature, as has the need to integrate or coordinate those efforts so that all the separate efforts 'add up' to a level of production above that which might have been achieved by people working separately. What we would nowadays call a *managerial function* has always been a feature of the human organisation of work. This is the case regardless of whether that function, in any given social order, is jointly fulfilled by those doing the work or is allocated to a specialised role holder: chief hunter, head shepherd, slave master, army general, factory superintendent, office supervisor or company director. In each social order that they have devised human beings have found ways of coordinating human work activities and structuring the associated exchange or trading relationships that go with them.

There have been other continuities within the various ways that human beings have found of dividing up work tasks and then integrating and coordinating these into effective forms of productive cooperation. One of the most significant of these has been the need to handle the conflicts and tensions inherent in the work arrangements and the power structures that are associated with them. Conflicts and tensions partly come about as a result of the different levels of reward or benefit that different individuals, groups, castes and classes have always managed to extract from these various working patterns. They have also arisen because of the fundamental 'recalcitrance' – or resistance to control by others – that appears to have characterised human beings in every social order known to us.

Link   The tendency of human beings to act recalcitrantly – to express their autonomy even in the face of seemingly irresistible controls – has been discussed previously in Chapter 1, p. 6, Chapter 3, pp. 74–5, Chapter 9, p. 286 and Chapter 11, p. 382

Conflict between those who have a bigger say and those who have a lesser say in how work is managed has been as much a continuous presence in patterns of work organisation across the ages as has cooperation. There is absolutely no reason to believe that this is going to change in the twenty-first century, as the industrial capitalist form of social order increasingly shapes work enterprises, social institutions and cultures across the globe. How work is managed in the future is therefore going to involve moral and political choices just as much as technical ones.

Working relationships and managerial arrangements cannot be separated from matters of power and social values. The systems-control orthodoxies about organising and managing which we have critically examined in this book imply that effective management and work organisation is a basically technical and politically neutral matter. The process-relational way of understanding organisational and managerial issues sees it very differently: work arrangements, like the lives of the people who make them, are always in process, always undergoing adaptation and change and always subject to the differences of interest, priority and value that characterise human and social relationships. There may well be technical elements in the choices to be made, between, say, one way of using a piece of machinery rather than another or about which pay system or shift pattern to adopt. However, no choice can be made in these or any other areas of work management without taking into account human interests, wants, beliefs, preferences and without considering what it means for people's work orientations and, indeed, their very identities. The value or ethical dimension of all this will be the concern of the later part of this chapter. For the moment, however, the key point to be made is that human interests, wants, preferences and orientations are never fixed and settled. Change is therefore an ever-present aspect of every organisational situation. Process-relational thinking, consequently, would tend to avoid any notion of the 'management of change' as a separate facet of organisational activity or as a specialist activity within managerial work. To manage work is necessarily to manage change. To imagine that one can engage in managerial work and not be significantly involved in coping with change would be very foolish. One of the continuities of work management over time, we might paradoxically say, is that it is always involved in change.

The handling and initiating of change is always an important and integral part of managerial work. Any notion of 'change management' needs to recognise this. Change is integral to managerial work for two main reasons:

- because of the 'emergent' nature of the human beings directly involved in the workplace (p. 106) and the way their wants and expectations change as they move, for example, through different stages of their life cycles; and

- because of the dynamic pressures of competition and innovation that are inherent in capitalist market economies and which involve organisations both in attempting to influence consumer wants and in competing with each other to meet those wants.

Change management   *Concept*

An integral part of all managerial work that (a) copes with the changing patterns of resource input and knowledge available to work organisations and the shifting demands made upon them by the parties with which they deal, and (b) initiates changes that managers perceive to be in their interests or the interests of those who employ them.

To say that managerial work always involves dealing with change is not, however, to deny that the pressures to make changes in the way work is organised will not be greater or lesser at different times. Nor is it to say that, at any particular time, the managers in one organisation may not be under greater pressure to change their practices than the managers in another. Change, we might say, is with us all the time but sometimes it is more an issue for us than it is at other times.

Although they may vary in intensity from time to time and from place to place, there are always pressures on work organisations to change the ways in which they operate. Pressures may come from customers or clients who are no longer satisfied with the goods or services being provided, from investors who are unhappy with the returns they are receiving, from governments who disapprove of their activities or from employees who are no longer willing to perform the tasks required of them. Competition from other organisations is a major and obvious source of pressure for many organisations and this will be heightened by the availability to competitors of new knowledge, new organisational techniques or new technologies. All of this is fairly obvious and seemingly straightforward. What is not so straightforward, in spite of its often being spoken of in managerial circles as if it were straightforward and obvious, is the notion that these can be understood as *drivers* pushing managerial decision-making in a particular direction. Examples of the use of this particular *discursive resource* heard coming from managers' mouths include:

- 'The main drivers in this are the global forces that mean we have no choice but to . . .';
- 'Technological drivers in our business mean that we must . . .';
- 'We will have to do this because market forces are more powerful drivers in the sector than we ever imagined they would become';
- 'Cost drivers have been the most significant ones pushing us in this direction';
- 'Being basically financially driven these days, we have no option but to . . .';
- 'Trends in knowledge management will be the main driver for our business in the future'.

Link   The concept of *discursive resource* was explained in Chapter 4, p. 120 and the significance of particular types of language use among managers was examined in Chapter 5, pp. 160–5.

Statements like these have to be treated carefully and not taken as automatically indicating that the managers who utter them really do see their organisational world in as deterministic a way as their language implies. Managers, especially senior ones, are not unaware that they are as often the authors of these changes as they are their 'victims'. Nevertheless, many managers undoubtedly feel pushed and buffeted by market and technological 'forces' outside of their control. This explains some of their talk of 'drivers'. At other times, however, managers just use the shorthand of 'drivers' to refer to what they are fully aware are much more complex pressures and possibilities than their simplistic terminology might imply. On other occasions, one suspects that they use such language to justify or give legitimacy to actions about which, in practice, they had a great deal more discretion than they wish to reveal. We might, for example, hear managers who find it convenient to relocate the production work of their enterprise saying things like 'Closing these factories is nothing to do with us, the managers – it's all the fault of the markets'. But there are dangers in regularly utilising a discourse of 'drivers' and 'being driven' – with its image of managers being pressured to act in certain ways by mechanical and irresistible forces. The way we *discursively frame* the world around us influences how we act with regard to the world – a point that has been reiterated through this book since it was first made in the early stages of the first chapter. To make constant reference to irresistible drivers is to risk abandoning any notion of strategic managerial choice or creative initiative taking. In theoretical terms, it is to fail to see that organisational strategists do not, in practice, simply react to 'environmental forces'. They actively interpret what is going on and take actions in the light of that sensemaking – they *enact* the organisational environment (Chapter 6, p. 203). There are choices as well as constraints.

Global trends, technological possibilities and organisational options

When it comes to considering the likely future of work organisation and management, the future is far more open – including open to managerial innovation as well as to democratic debate – than is often recognised. At the most general level, what we have called here a process-relational way of looking at the world recognises that human beings both make and are made by the world in which they live and, within that of course, some people have far more influence on the choices that are made than others. Managers tend to have more of a say than non-managers over how work is organised, for example, and senior managers have more influence than do managers working lower down the power hierarchy. However, it is neither circumstances alone nor free managerial choice that will determine the future ways in which work is organised and managed. This is something about which Carlo Relugas, as the chief executive of a Wyvis Computing, has thought deeply.

Activity 12.1

Consider Carlo Relugas's reflections in Cases and Conversations 12.1 on how Wyvis Computing is likely to change in the future and then:

■ note the extent to which his thoughts about managing 'for the future' are integral to his general approach to managerial and strategy-making work, as opposed to being seen as a separate 'change management' aspect of his job;

■ identify factors influencing future patterns that relate (a) to circumstantial constraints upon the organisation and (b) to human choices (managerial and non-managerial) about what is to be.

Carlo contemplates the future

Sometimes, as the chief executive of Wyvis, a large and powerful business in most people's terms, I feel rather foolish. There are going to be major changes in the computing industry in the next twenty years that I intend to be working in it. Nobody would argue with that. And we have got some idea what some of those changes are going to be – continuing minitiaturisation of hardware, radio communication between devices, the widening of the internet and the integration of computing, communications and entertainment – just for starters. There is a sort of relentless technological logic to all of this. Yet just how any of this will work out, I don't really know. This is in spite of the fact that if anybody knew what this future would look like, you would expect it to be me.

I find myself sitting here some evenings wondering just how much we really know about how things will turn out. Technology is said to drive us in certain directions. But I find myself wondering how we are to know what

the buyers of these products will actually want, when it comes to it. I also wonder about how we are to know what our competitors have up their sleeves by way of either influencing or meeting those wants. And I feel equally unsure at times about how we are going to organise ourselves as a business to survive that competition.

I have these thoughts in spite of the fact that I read all sorts of articles saying that the future of computing will be like this and the future of work will be like that. It wouldn't do for me to admit publicly that I am as unsure about the future as I am. But I do tend to say to journalists who ask me about these matters things like, 'Well, it might be like this and it might be like that. We'll have to wait and see'. Yet what I know very well is that it is not just a matter of *waiting* to see. I am very conscious it is decisions which people like me will make that will play a big part in shaping that future. In one's darker moments, this can feel like a frightening responsibility. There are so many unknowns.

There are certain things I feel I can control and certain things that I feel I can't. Let's take this talk of globalisation as an example. Our company could not operate in just one country. No single market is big enough, and we need to source our activities from wherever we can get the best deal across the world. That world feels that it is getting smaller all the time as we communicate across it at great speed, move money backwards and forwards and as we see our products being desired in various countries across the globe, regardless of nationality, political system or religion. But the very words I've uttered give the game away here. I am pointing to all these things that make people say we are living in a globalising world. But at the same time, I mention nationality, politics and religion. These, I feel sure, make things a lot more complicated than some people make out. Just take politics and people's ideas of nationality. If we look at the development of the European Union alone, it is clear that many people in several of the member countries are highly resistant to becoming part of a larger Europe, let alone a larger world. And I see this in Wyvis. We have become a multinational. As I said, this had to happen. But I stress that we are a British multinational. Like several of my colleagues, I am not British myself. But we know that many of those upon whom the future of the company depends wish to have their long-term careers in the country and the culture they grew up in. We are working with some important strategic alliances in China. But our people are only willing to spend a certain amount of time in China. And they resist many of the Chinese ways of doing things. And, let me tell you, there is no way that the Chinese business and authorities that we deal with have any intention of becoming any less Chinese!

There are all sorts of dangers, then, in swallowing simplistic ideas about globalisation. We had a major battle a few months ago in this company about moving production of one of our key products to another country. Certain of our people argued that the cost savings that this would give us on the labour side made such a decision irresistible. We have done this sort of thing several times before. But the product we were arguing about is a more complex one than any of those. This led several of my top management team to argue that we needed to maintain a level of close cooperation and joint production development between our design/development people and our production people for this product that was only achievable if we kept the whole thing here 'in-house', so to speak. That, in fact, is what we have done, in spite of the excellent electronic communications that we could have set up with an overseas operation. I think that this will prove to be a correct decision economically and technically. But, I have to admit, an important factor in the decision was a realisation that a lot of our key technical and managerial people were getting sick and tired of regularly having to fly off abroad to sort things out. We have lost one or two really important people recently to companies that have kept more of their activities in a single country. You cannot deny the significance of this human factor. The way the future unfolds is going to be influenced to a greater extent than is often recognised by what people who work for you will and will not put up with.

The people who work for you are utterly vital to success, especially in a high tech operation like ours. I've illustrated the relevance of people's wants and preferences with my story about overseas executive travel and how this has affected some strategically sensitive decision-making. But it is going to be equally important to the general ways in which we employ people in the future and to the ways in which we organise activities. I am often told that the future is going to give us the 'virtual organisation' and that our company will be in the fore-front of developing this. But I am not so sure. It is true that we have experimented quite a lot in this area. Wyvis has quite a few people operating from home as 'teleworkers' and we have even encouraged people in several areas to stop being employees and become freelance consultants to whom we pay a retainer fee and provide work – as their main client. There have been successes here, but a lot of difficulties too. Our experiences make me very wary of accepting this notion of the organisation of the future as a network of relatively independent contributors which, instead of having employees, draws on the services of a whole lot of people who have 'portfolio careers' – doing a bit of this here and a bit of that here, without a long-term relationship with a single work organisation. We have learned that this suits some people – whether it is just working for us from home via a computer link or whether it is going more fully independent. But there are plenty of people whom it does not suit. I can understand this. I, for example, would go mad working from home – as much as I dislike the drag of commuting into the office every day.

My HR director has looked closely at this. A lot of people have made it clear to us that they want, indeed feel they *need*, a closer long-term relationship with a single employer. And we have got to take heed of that – if we are going to have access to the sorts of high-level skill and commitment that we need to be able to compete in the world. And my mention of commitment is important here. As an organisation, I feel that we need a good propor-tion of our people to be here all the time, working closely together and striving to make innovations to the advantage of a business with which they can identify. I just don't feel that a network of activities would allow suffi-cient control – or focus of the imagination – to make a successful business. In saying this, I am admittedly drawing on my own feelings and my own intuitions as a manager. I could be wrong. This is my whole point – you can't know for sure what will work and what will not. But our experiences here lead me to predict that while we will outsource more of our work to people with whom we will 'network' and while we will have increased numbers working from home, this company will continue to be an employing organisation with a distinctive structure and culture. Of course, Wyvis will be less bureaucratic. It will be more flexible – faster on its feet. But this corporation, or its son or daughter, will still be here when I have retired from the scene.

I acknowledge that I could be wrong about all of this. But where I insist I am right is in keeping an open mind and avoiding all talk of an inevitable future. At the very minimum, we have to avoid making changes for change's sake, or because something is fashionable. More importantly though, we have to proceed thoughtfully but boldly, experimenting with different arrangements and settling on those that suit both our organisational requirements and the requirements of all of those, employees and customers alike, that we depend on to have a future at all.

In reading Carlo's reflections on the future of Wyvis Computing, it is clear that he does not isolate issues of change and of coping with the future from the general way he goes about managing the organisation. He illustrates very effec-tively the point that 'change management' is integral to managerial work generally. He does not speak of the future as something that will 'come along' and confront him at some point. Neither, though, does he view it as something that he and his managerial colleagues will decide upon or choose. While Carlo certainly talks about the predictions that others make about how work will be managed in the future he is anxious to locate his consideration of that future within the normal managerial and strategy-making procedures that he and his fellow managers follow. In fact, to make sense of much of what he says we need to look back to earlier chapters and to our consideration of various parts of the everyday managing of work and the shaping of organisational strategies:

- Carlo is wary of taken-for-granted assumptions that people make about the world and its future. In this and his warnings about the dangers of 'swallowing simplistic ideas about globalisation' he reveals his attachment to a *critical common sense* style of thinking about and analysing organisational situations.

 Link   The value of suspending 'everyday common sense' ways of thinking from time to time and adopting instead a 'critical common sense' style of analysis was explained in Chapter 1, pp. 20–1.

- In pointing out how there are 'so many unknowns', Carlo indicates his recognition of the considerable ambiguity, uncertainty and bounded rationality that surrounds managerial work. He appears to regard this as something that he must live with and deal with through his interaction with other managers, his managerial learning and his intuitive abilities. Ambiguity cannot be overcome, for instance, by turning to firm predictions of the future.

Link   The importance of ambiguity and uncertainty was stressed both in our consideration of the nature of management and in our review of the evidence about how managers go about 'doing management' in practice in Chapter 3, pp. 81–4, and in our examination of strategy-making processes in Chapter 6, p. 171.

- His approach to strategy-making, which involves 'proceeding thoughtfully and boldly' and experimenting with different ways of doing things in order to learn, fits with strategy-making principles of *logical incrementalism*, and *directed evolution* rather than with a long-range *strategic planning* approach.

Link   Close attention is paid to 'logically incrementalist' or 'directed evolution' alternatives to planning-based strategy-making in Chapter 6, especially pp. 189–91.

- He does not treat markets as 'given' aspects of Wyvis's environment to which it must react – he regards them as *enacted* in the sense of their being a matter of how people in organisations interpret and act towards the predispositions of potential customers.

Link   The 'enactment' of aspects of the organisational environment was shown to be central to the managing of resource-dependent relationships and 'strategic exchanges' in Chapter 6, p. 203.

- He is aware of the extent to which managers have options about how they structure the organisations they work in and it would appear that he sees this as more complex than one of simply choosing between a *bureaucratic* and a non-bureaucratic or *networked* set of arrangements. He is clear, however, that the managerial choice of organisational form needs to take into account managerial perceptions of organisational *contingencies* like the type of technology used and the type of people employed. He stresses the dependence of his 'high tech' firm's competitiveness upon people with 'high skill level' for instance. He further recognises that managerial values and preferences come into this process – he says, for example, he is conscious that his analysis draws 'on my own feelings'. He is also explicit about the managerial *debates* that occurred over the strategically important decision about where a complex new product was to be made.

 Link Choices of organisational structure and the cultural features that are associated with them were the concern of Chapters 7 and 8 and the involvement of managerial values, managerial debate as well as the interpretation of 'contingent' factors like organisational size, environment and technology was focused on in both chapters. See, especially, the discussions related to Figures 8.3 (p. 258) and 11.2 (p. 392), for example.

- Carlo places human resourcing matters at the centre of his strategic thinking and his reflections on the future. His taking of the wants and expectations of managers and employees into account when making strategic decisions fits the principle of seeing human resourcing strategy as something integral to overall corporate strategy-making rather than as something 'serving' or following from a main corporate strategy.

 Link The centrality of human resourcing issues to general processes of corporate strategy-making was a key theme of Chapter 11, especially pp. 378–81.

Academic and social debates about the future of work often focus on similar issues to those mentioned by Carlo Relugas. This is not surprising given that the outcomes of all the cultural, political, technological and employment issues that he raises will equally influence the future of 'society' and the future of the business he leads. (Indeed, the strategic decisions made in his company, should it survive, will play their part in shaping the society in which it exists.) The debates that occur, both with reference to matters of work organisation and to the future of societies more generally, all involve questions about the relationship between the 'circumstantial constraints' and the 'human choices' referred to in Activity 12.1. The relationship between these two types of factor is difficult to unravel, however, given that it depends on a distinction that breaks down if pushed too far. One can talk about 'market forces' as a circumstantial constraint on decision-makers for example, but, in the final analysis, markets only exist because consumers choose to buy one product or service rather than another. The same applies to technological trends or to political pressures: in the final analysis these two 'drivers' only become 'realities' because people choose to take up certain technologies (DVD disks rather than videotapes, for instance) or make certain political choices (vote for one set of politicians rather than another, for example). In practice, however, events unfold at a level prior to any 'final analysis' and economic, political and technological trends seem to take on the force of 'drivers' or constraints. If one computer manufacturer suddenly found a way of putting computers on the market at half the price charged by competitors, for instance, the effect of this on those competitor organisations would feel very like an external force 'driving' them to cut costs.

In spite of these reservations about the complexities of choice and constraint in human history, we see in Carlo's reflections on the future a clear recognition that what look like constraints or 'drivers' inevitably involve human choices. And these are choices that he and his managers must take into account when making managerial or business choices and decisions of their own. We can identify three closely related areas of concern on Carlo's part: one with *globalisation*, one with the push towards *virtual or networked organisations* and one with the development of people working within *portfolio careers* instead of seeking long-term employment with particular work organisations. Material on all of these can be found in Reading Guide 18.

Globalisation?

Carlo's concern with globalisation is a good example of how academic and political debates overlap with those in which organisational managers and strategy-makers also engage. Although the term globalisation is used in a variety of different ways, it is generally used to refer to a general shift towards people across the world finding themselves subject to the same cultural, economic, technological and political pressures and living increasingly similar lives, regardless of race, creed or national identity.

Globalisation	*Concept*
A trend in which the economic, cultural and political activities of people across the world come to be increasingly interdependent and similar.	

Carlo, like many commentators on global trends, is aware of emerging patterns that give credibility to a 'globalisation thesis'. Across the world, people are seeking similar commodities, whether these be particular brands of soft drink, training shoe, computer game or musical entertainment. Particularly for products that require a high level of investment, like those supplied by Wyvis

Computing, businesses find it necessary to develop large markets that cross national and regional boundaries that tend to feel less and less significant as a result of fast transport services and electronic communications. These allow people to pass messages back and forth across the world almost instantaneously and they enable money to be transferred from one part of the world to another in a way that challenges the integrity of national economies. In spite of all this, Carlo points out that people across the world still seem concerned to retain what we might call distinctive local, national or religious identities. There is still an interest in defending the integrity of separate nation states – even if those nation states will not be as free as their members might wish and to resist certain global trends.

Carlo supports his argument that people are likely to refuse to abandon 'local' identities by pointing to specific individuals that he knows – managers in his own company in particular. He recognises the growth of 'multinationals' but, he suggests, managers themselves will resist the development of the sort of fully globalised company which would require managers to move about from project to project, regardless of their national or cultural affiliations. British managers, he suggests, wish to stay British and Chinese managers want to remain Chinese. At an even more practical level, he tells us that some employees are actually changing their jobs to avoid too much international travel. Carlo recognises the importance of employers thinking about the type of employment relationship future employees might insist upon. Vital skills could be lost if people are required to be away from home too often by an employer. He also sees managerial issues that question the wisdom of organisations too readily moving production from country to country to gain apparent labour cost benefits. In spite of the sophisticated electronic communications available to coordinate work activities across geographical distances, Carlo and his colleagues recognise that very high levels of productive cooperation and innovation might only be possible if significant parts of their work are kept 'in-house'. Yet again the complexities of human wants and the varied ways in which people provide organisations with the vital human resources of labour, ingenuity and commitment have to be considered. Managerial attention to human choice and preference is more important than reacting to seemingly depersonalised 'drivers' like globalisation.

Virtual organisations?

Similar reservations to those about how far 'globalisation' will go are offered by Carlo with regard the future of work organisations. He has strong doubts about claims that these will largely be virtual or networked organisations – rather than bureaucratically structured employing organisations.

Virtual or networked organisations	*Concept*
Sets of work arrangements in which those undertaking tasks carried out under a corporate name largely relate to each other through electronic communications rather than through face-to-face interaction.	

The experiences of Wyvis Computing show that there are already trends towards people relating to each other through electronic computer-based links rather than coming together in face-to-face working relationships. The company has made use of *teleworking* – having work tasks carried out away from the organisation's own premises using computer links between remote workers and the organisational 'centre'. It has also enabled employees to set up their own businesses and relate to the organisation as commercial suppliers of services rather than as employees. Such trends clearly exist, then. Technological developments make this kind of arrangement increasingly feasible and the organisation is enabled, as Carlo puts it, to be 'more flexible – faster on its feet'. There will undoubtedly be many organisational circumstances in which we can expect to see these trends followed by organisations and, although it is unclear just how significant new internet or 'dot.com' businesses are going to be, there is an increasing use of the internet by established businesses to trade with each other over the internet in a way that not only speeds up supply relationships but also brings an extra competitive pressure into supply chains.

None of these trends are straightforward to understand or to extrapolate from and patterns are often more complex than they look. Teleworking, for example, can take two forms. Sometimes it is done by people who are retained as employees of the organisation. At other times, it is done by people whose services are bought on a project-by-project or task-by-task basis. It would appear that Wyvis Computing has used both types of arrangement. But they clearly see limits to remote working, whether it is done by employees or by contractors. Again, it would appear in part to be a matter of the sort of relationship that people are *willing* to go along with and Carlo has discovered that there are 'plenty of people' whom working from home 'does not suit' and Carlo and his HR director also believe, from an organisational point of view, that certain especially important people will *need* to be retained within the organisation as employees. To achieve very high quality collaborative working relationships and the enthusiastic pursuit of innovation an especially high level of mutual commitment between organisation and worker will be required. This might only be possible within an employment relationship and by people physically working together. Carlo sees such arrangements are important managerially. They are necessary if he and his colleagues are to have the levels of *control* and what he calls 'focus of the imagination' that are necessary for innovation and competitive organisational performance.

Portfolio careers?

Reservations about the viability of virtual organisations are equally relevant to another alleged characteristic of work in the future: the portfolio career. Here the typical worker of the future – be they a highly skilled 'professional' or a supplier of more simple labour – will no longer be an employee of a work organisation. They will be a supplier of services who have a *market* relationship with various organisations rather than an *employment relationship* with just one.

Portfolio or boundaryless career

Concept

A pattern of working in which the individual does not enter an employment relationship with a single work organisation but is engaged by a variety of different organisations on a task-by-task or project-by-project basis.

The obvious reservation that arises with regard to this – in the light of what we have said about the virtual or networked organisation – is that people may simply wish to avoid such a potentially insecure and potentially socially isolated way of earning a living. Carlo's HR colleague says he has found that 'a lot of people . . . want, indeed feel they *need*, a closer long-term relationship with a single employer'. But what Carlo goes on to say about there being *particular* workers that Wyvis would also want to retain in a long-term employment relationship to the corporation is very significant. He talks about 'a good proportion of our people' with whom they wish to retain an employment relationship. The implication of this is that some people in the future are likely to have a choice between an employment relationship with a work organisation and a portfolio career. Others, however, might not have the choice.

It is therefore possible to envisage a working future in which those with high levels of skill, knowledge and generally *marketable competences* can freely choose between a long-term relationship with an employer who is keen to buy their long-term commitment and setting themselves up as a freelance supplier of high level services to organisations who will compete for their services. Those who do not have such an advantageous labour market position, however, may be forced to move from one short-term contract to another, whether they like it or not. This raises the possibility of a future pattern of inequality in which there are very privileged and psychologically secure portfolio workers, on the one hand, and very unprivileged and insecure portfolio workers, on the other. But what about people who stay in employment? Similar inequalities may also arise here. Although Wyvis Computing, given the nature of its technology, may well retain employment slots only for highly skilled workers and managers, there are organisations with different technologies that might be happy to retain employment relationships with a much broader range of workers. Service industries and public organisations that require large numbers of staff to interact face-to-face with clients, patients, passengers, guests and customers may well find that short-term hire-and-fire relationships with 'portfolio' workers will discourage such workers from giving clients and customers the level of care, attention and courtesy that they demand of that organisation.

These matters are all very complex and the pattern that eventually emerges will depend to a considerable extent on what sort of choices people make as consumers, citizens, employees and managers. It may turn out that people will generally be happy to buy as many goods and services over the internet as they can, rather than visit shops and other service organisations. Or it might not. It might turn out that many people want to work from home and not travel into a workplace. Or it might not. It may turn out that people will generally welcome the opportunity to be free of an employer and enjoy a portfolio of different work activities. Or it might not. It might turn out that managers will be happy to abandon jobs running bureaucratically structured work organisations and to seek more direct involvement in producing goods or services. Or it might not.

Activity 12.2

Look back to the staffing and service quality problems that were faced in the hotel by Ken Steary (Chapter 5, pp. 140–1), by Ronnie Brackla in his pub (Chapter 7, pp. 246–8) and by the managers in the Viewfields call centre (Chapter 11, pp. 399–403). Note how all of these problems suggest a managerial solution of developing a fuller, more high-commitment, *employment* relationship rather than the abandonment of an employment link. This inference can most clearly be drawn in the Viewfields case, where such a strategy was followed with apparent success.

Achieving organisational effectiveness

In spite of all the uncertainties that exist about the future, some basic principles will continue to influence how organisational managers go about trying to make their organisations *effective*. These are principles relating to the industrial capitalist social and economic order that, as far as we can tell, will continue to operate into the foreseeable future. Regardless of whether we apply the globalisation label to it or not, an increasingly open set of international markets are developing. This means that competitive pressures on all organisations are likely to increase (these pressures impinging on public and private sector undertakings alike). It further means that managers in all types of work organisation will find themselves under continuous pressure to make their organisations work 'more effectively'. Survival will depend on it. We can therefore expect managers to continue to be under pressure to improve returns on whatever has been invested in their organisations (be this public or private investment). Such pressures will ensure that *change management* will be a continually central component of managers' working lives. They will also ensure that managers will find themselves continuously looking hard at their organisations' employment practices and organisational arrangements to ensure that the organisation is getting the best possible return for what it spends on employing, or otherwise engaging, workers. And to cope with this kind of pressure, a striving for *flexibility* will be central to managerial efforts.

The pursuit of flexibility

Carlo Relugas spoke in Cases and Conversations 12.1 of making Wyvis Computing more flexible and therefore 'faster on its feet'. This would entail making the organisation 'less bureaucratic'. In social science terms this means making the organisation more 'organic' or 'loosely bureaucratised' to cope with the managerially perceived contingency of a less predictable business

A key *contingent* factor influencing managers' choice of a relatively tightly or relatively loosely bureau-cratised organisational structure and culture was shown in Chapter 8 (p. 256) to be the extent to which they perceive their business environment to be either a relatively stable and predictable one or an unstable and unpredictable one. More tightly bureaucratised or *mechanistic* arrangements tend to be chosen to fit with the more predictable type of context while more loosely bureaucratised or *organic* arrangements are developed to cope with unpredictability.

environment. Furthermore, the choice in Wyvis of a more organic type of organisation, in turn, implies the use of an *indirect control* style of managing (pp. 251–5) and the application of a high *commitment human resourcing strategy* – at least to what might be called their *core* highly skilled workforce. In terms of the analysis offered in Chapter 11 (pp. 390–6), managers would be choosing a high commitment HR strategy for their core workers in recognition of the high degree of uncertainty that those employees can create for the organisation's long-term survival. To put this another way, a high quality employment deal would be offered to secure the services of workers upon whom the organisation is highly resource dependent. There might, however, be other workers that the organisation might wish to retain (instead of, as Carlo puts it, 'outsourcing' the tasks that they do) – perhaps to do routine tasks that can more cheaply be done by people on a wage or salary than by buying in their services. In situations like this we can expect to see organisations continuing to follow *dual human resourcing strategies*.

It was recognised in Chapter 11, pp. 396–8, that organisations may find it economically desirable to follow *dual human resourcing strategies* – applying a *high commitment* 'relationship' HR strategy involving a long-term employment relationship to core workers and managers and a *low commitment* 'transactional' HR strategy to more peripheral suppliers of labour (sometimes involving an employment relationship, sometimes involving a market relationship).

This analysis built on the recognition, in Chapter 9, p. 313, that organisations tend to seek two different types of flexibility. Managers will be interested in flexibility to meet short-term *adjustment needs* as well as the sort of flexibility that Carlo Relugas is referring to – flexibility to meet long-term *adaptability* needs. High commitment HR strategies tend to fit with the latter and low commitment strategies with the former.

Reciprocity and high trust relations

The long-term and high commitment relationships that employers can be expected to develop with the core employees upon whom they are particularly dependent will not be relationships of equality. Employers are vastly more powerful than any individual or group of employees except in very rare cases where employees possess unique capacities or resources without which an organisation could not cope. But relationships with employees upon whom the organisation has a high degree of dependence will nevertheless need to be ones of two-way commitment and 'give-and-take'. In more technical language, they will necessarily be relationships of *high reciprocity*.

Link The centrality of reciprocity and exchange to human relationships and to the survival of the human species was emphasised in Chapter 4, p. 111).

In simple terms, core employees are going to have a lot asked of them by way of commitment, creativity, initiative, discretion and a willingness to share ideas and knowledge with others. And in accordance with the basic human *norm of reciprocity*, they are likely to demand quite a lot in return from the employer. In addition to obvious monetary, comfort and security benefits, they are likely to demand freedom from close supervision or short-term monitoring. They will, of course, not be freed from managerial control, but the controls exercised will be the type of *indirect controls* closely examined in earlier chapters (p. 253 and p. 394 especially), and for this to work successfully there is the further requirement of *high trust relations*.

High trust relations

Concept

A situation in which each party to a relationship feels able to take it for granted that broad mutual expectations established between them will be met and continue to be met, without the need closely to specify those expectations or to monitor their fulfilment.

The importance of high trust relations to the general success of a whole economy as well as to group and organisational effectiveness has been widely recognised (Fox, 1974, Reading Guide 16; Fukuyama, 1995, Reading Guide 20, for example). The principle of high trust relations facilitating successful collaborative ventures applies to any kind of cooperative venture, from trading relationships to military alliances and from team sports to work groups or economic enterprises. The principle is that people are likely to be more innovative, creative, accommodating and indeed *giving* in their relationships with others if they feel able to assume that those others will correspondingly act innovatively, creatively, flexibly and in a giving manner towards them. As Fox (1974, Reading Guide 16) significantly pointed out, work relations based on what we have called here *direct managerial controls* are essentially low trust relations. Workers who are blatantly treated as 'means to ends' in themselves will blatantly treat their work as just a 'means to other ends', we might say. They are discouraged from using discretion and tend to find themselves constantly calculating every last penny that they can extract from the employer in return for each unit of work effort they concede to the employer. Such relations lead to a 'spiral of falling trust' in which it becomes impossible to achieve innovative or flexible work performance. On the other hand, if a set of relations can be developed in which employees are confident that they will be well rewarded by the employer and respected for acting innovatively then a 'spiral of rising trust' can be created (Fox, 1974, p. 71). This is likely to lead to higher levels of productive cooperation and hence to high levels of work performance. This is the logic of high trust organisational relations, of indirect management controls and of high commitment human resourcing strategies alike.

Trust relations do not just apply to relations between organisations and their employee constituencies, however. The concept can be applied to all relationships between parties involved with an organisation. We can see this in the way that the high trust principle plays a key part in the concept of *organisational effectiveness* that Bal Blair of Firthside speaks about.

Activity 12.3

Read the discussion in Cases and Conversations 12.2 about 'organisational effectiveness' between the researcher and Bal Blair and Eden Killie. Bal Blair is a main board director of Firthside, a large financial services company, and Eden Killie is the company's organisation development executive. Then

■ try to identity what Bal Blair's notion of an effective organisation is;

■ note how his conception of effectiveness differs from Eden Killie's 'stakeholder' one;

■ consider the extent to which Bal's thinking can be interpreted as bringing together Chapter 6's notion of managing resource dependencies to enable survival into the long-term and the present chapter's concern with high trust relations.

| Faith, trust and the future of Firthside | Cases and Conversations 12.2 |

Although I am interested in what you are doing in Firthside, Bal, I am also interested in how you, as a senior manager, generally go about assessing the 'effectiveness' of different organisations.

BAL: Ok, I'll try. And I'll bring Eden into this. His views are a little different from mine. But let me start. It won't surprise you if I start with the word 'survival', given that we were made to think hard in Firthside three years ago about whether we deserved to survive.

EDEN: That's very true. I remember the new chairman, when he took over, telling us that we had been a 'totally ineffective outfit' for some time and that the only reason we had not faced a survival crisis earlier was because we had fooled people into not noticing our general incompetence.

BAL: OK then. An effective organisation, obviously, is one that is successful. But if you try to isolate and apply any of the standard criteria of success, you find yourselves in difficulties. I have seen financial services firms, for example, that looked successful because they were giving their customers the security of a pension or an insurance policy. But they weren't making a profit. This would lead some to say that they could not be called effective. And I would tend to agree – but not because I see profit as the key indicator of effectiveness. Without a reasonable profit level it is going to be difficult to survive in the long term – and hence be successful in giving customers financial security.

EDEN: What about being a good employer?

BAL: Well, I was going to say that I've seen firms making a good profit but giving a poor service to customers. Again, in the long run that profit will fall as customers turn elsewhere for better terms. And to take up Eden's

point, a firm might look successful because it is known as a good employer. But, again, if you give people a good employment experience but don't maintain your profit level, retain customer satisfaction or avoid getting into trouble with a government watchdog, you won't get the chance to continue to be a good employer for too long. Now this is why Eden is keen on this stakeholder idea. To use your word 'effective', I think he would say that an effective organisation is a good organisation and a good organisation is one that recognises its obligations to all of those who have a stake in it without prioritising any one of them.

I trust Bal isn't putting words into your mouth, Eden?

EDEN: No, he's very fair to me. I've been very taken with the stakeholder idea since it became fashionable in the mid-1990s. I tried to persuade Bal to put a paper to the main Firthside board advocating that we declare ourselves as a stakeholder style of company. I liked the idea of the 'inclusive organisation' that was spoken about and the idea of companies being responsible to all of those in society who had a stake in it. If all your suppliers, customers, employees and the rest – as well as you shareholders – feel that they somehow have a sense of 'ownership' with regard to the company they will serve it better. It can then, in turn, serve all of those interests better. Let's face it, companies – all organisations for that matter – should not be seen as being there primarily for the benefit of those who own them.

But you don't go for this, Bal?

BAL: I applaud the sentiments. And Eden's notion of 'inclusivivity' fits well with the work he does as our organisation development executive. He works largely with our own employees and I see no problem with his encouraging them to see themselves as 'stakeholders' or as having some sense of 'ownership' of their role in the business.

But?

BAL: But – there are lots of buts. This is beyond the simple fact that our current chairman and most of our investors simply would not go along with it – for fairly obvious reasons of self-interest perhaps. As an idea, though, it does have some appeal. The strength of the idea is that it makes us aware that there are lots of different groups that we have got to satisfy to be allowed to continue in business. And I can see how someone who has a pension with us or invests his or her life in a long-term career in us might, in a sense, have a 'stake' in Firthside. But it is to go too far to suggest that all of those who we have to deal with – from suppliers of computing equipment to the journalists on the city pages – have a stake in the business. Take the company who is building our multi-million pound new headquarters building. When they've finished the building and we've paid them off that will be the end of the relationship. In no sense do they now, or will they in the future, be stakeholders.

EDEN: But surely, Bal, it's important not just to have a cold trading relationship with people like those contractors. We want to have a good trusting relationship with them don't we? We want to be able to count on them not to build on shallow foundations or plaster over cracks in walls.

And you'll want to trust them to come back and do any necessary rectifications after the job is meant to be finished, won't you?

BAL: Good. I like that word trust. I want us to establish trusting relationships with everyone we deal with – from the journalists with whom we trade gossip for good write-ups to our shareholders, our customers, our employees and the contractors who provide the food in our company restaurant. To adapt your words, Eden, I'd like to see a warm trading relationship with all these individuals and groups. It's not a matter of having lots of stakeholders, though. It's a matter of making lots of exchanges on the basis of high trust – exchanges that guarantee the organisation a future. And the exchanges we make with our shareholders are no different from any others. I am no keener than you to privilege ownership over other forms of involvement with an organisation.

So an effective organisation is?

BAL: It is simply one in which the management deals with everyone involved with it in such a way that the organisation has a secure and long-term future. And the more you have two-way trust with the people you deal with, the more you are likely to have that future. It is simply so much easier to get your employees to do what you require of them if they trust you and you trust them. It is easier to sell your goods or services if your customers trust you to provide them with what they want and if you can trust them to pay their bills. It is so much easier to get the investment you need if the investors trust you to work for a good return – and so on and so on. In my view effective managers are people who can build trust with whoever they deal with.

EDEN: Building trust with people is not an easy matter though.

BAL: Of course not. It takes a lot of personal and social skills and a lot of time and effort. But once you start to get there, life generally is much easier. It is much easier to captain a ship if everyone on board – officers, passengers and crew – have faith in you, than if they don't.

At the end of this conversation, Bal Blair has moved on from a notion of the effective organisation to a concept of the *effective manager*. We too will turn shortly to the characteristics and orientations that make some managers more able than others to contribute to organisational effectiveness. Staying at the organisational level for the moment, however, it is important to note that Bal's analysis fully accords with the notion of organisational effectiveness that was developed in Chapter 6.

 Link

It was argued in Chapter 6 (pp. 198–202) that because there are so many possible separate and often interdependent criteria of organisational success it is most helpful to see all of these – profitability, growth, service to customers and so on – simply as conditions allowing the meeting of one single criterion of organisational effectiveness: *how well placed it is to continue into the long-term*.

In no way was the notion of long-term survival set up in Chapter 6 as any kind of overarching *goal* or *purpose* of work organisations or of their managers. It was put forward, rather, as a key part of the *logic* within which organisational managements tend to work, in practice. In effect, organisational strategists – with some of them succeeding better than others – orchestrate exchanges aimed at satisfying all of those constituencies upon which the organisation is resource dependent up to a level, and not beyond that level, which will enable the organisation to continue to function into the long term. Bal Blair adds to this the suggestion that such a strategic management function is likely to be easier to fulfil and to be more successful if these exchange relationships can be made in a spirit of mutual high trust. At its simplest, less time and effort will be wasted on negotiating every detail of every single transaction if parties to strategic exchanges can take it for granted that those with whom they are dealing will meet the basic expectations that have been established between them. Everything will be much easier if there does not have to be constant checking up on and 'chasing up' of each party by the other. This does not just apply to employee constituencies. It applies similarly to relationships with shareholders, suppliers and customers. The growing interest of managers in *relationship marketing* fits with this. Relationship marketing involves businesses moving their marketing emphasis away from constantly having to win new customers. Instead they attempt to keep closely in touch with customers after the first transaction has occurred with a view to obtaining 'repeat business'.

Bal Blair puts high trust relations at the centre of managerial efforts to achieve organisational effectiveness for reasons of expedience. An organisation and its management will be seen as effective, he believes, if the organisation is perceived as being well placed to continue into the long term. Bal is well aware that such criteria are very relevant to how organisations are evaluated, indeed 'valued', in modern economies. He is no doubt also aware that higher financial and career rewards tend to go to managers who are seen as particularly effective at achieving secure futures for the organisations that they lead. And Bal has concluded that high trust relations with resource-dependent constituencies will simply make it *easier* to manage all these dependencies in a way that helps to give the organisation a long-term future. The implication is that a potentially disastrous amount of managerial time and attention would be taken up if managers found themselves having to manage a whole series of low trust relations. As Bal points out, 'It is much easier to captain a ship if everyone on board – officers, passengers and crew – have faith in you, than if they don't'. Captains are better able to concentrate on getting ships to their destination if people on board who do not trust their intentions or competence are not constantly challenging them.

Stakeholding or trading?

Eden Killie also argues for the building of high trust relations in the organisational context. He, however, justifies it in terms of an ethical principle, rather than pragmatically. He implies that the various constituencies with which an organisation deals have a *right* to special consideration by the managers of an organisation. They have this right on the grounds of being *stakeholders* in the enterprise. The ethical attraction of this is considerable. It makes it unacceptable for an organisational management to exploit or generally taking advantage of its employees, suppliers, customers or, indeed, any member of the broad community of which stakeholder thinking regards all organisations a part. In effect, organisations are seen as belonging to a community rather than to any one section of that community. They should not therefore favour certain stakeholders over others. Shareholders are just one set of stakeholders among many. They should not be privileged over other stakeholders, all of whom, in effect, have some moral form of ownership of the *inclusive* enterprise (Royal Society of Arts, 1996, Reading Guide 25).

Activity 12.4

Consider, from your own point of view, the   of the role of work organisations in society.
strengths and weaknesses of a *stakeholder* view

The extent to which one favours a stakeholder view of the responsibilities and accountabilities of organisations is very much a matter of one's personal moral position. It is also a matter of the political stance that one takes with regard to the institutions of modern capitalism and a matter of what type of ethical principles one believes should guide economic and corporate behaviour generally. Some people will take the view that those who put the basic financial investment into an enterprise, and hence have ownership rights, have a greater right than others to generally benefit from the activities of that enterprise – with these others gaining specific benefits through a market-based trade with the enterprise. Other people will take the view that financial investment in an enterprise is not essentially different from the investment made in it by those who become its employees or its clients or who, as citizens, allow that enterprise to function in their society. These are matters of one's personal moral and political values.

 Link   The role that managers' personal values play will be considered later in this chapter (pp. 449–62) in the context of the ethical aspects of organisational and managerial work generally.

It is interesting that Bal Blair and Eden Killie come to the same conclusion about the appropriate way for organisations to operate *in practice*. Eden's distinctive stakeholder ethical position leads him to argue for developing high trust relations with all of those with whom Firthside deals. Bal takes a much more expedient route to get to the same destination. Bal seems to have the same basic values as Eden but implies that, in practice, it might make life just too complicated if managers were to commit themselves to treating all of those with whom they deal as if they each had a stake in the enterprise rather than just a trading relationship with it. He therefore prefers to concentrate on making high trust exchanges with all the constituencies that the organisation needs to satisfy to stay in business. And, we might note, he claims to see shareholders as just one of these constituencies. He claims not to privilege ownership rights. How valid such a claim can be in an economic system in which the private ownership of capital plays such a central part is one that we should perhaps not accept uncritically. Nevertheless, Bal chooses to present himself as a manager who is, in some sense, responsible to a wider set of constituencies rather than just the company's shareholders.

Overall, it can be argued that organisations are likely to be more effective, in the sense of being better placed to survive into the long term, if they are *flexible* and *adaptive* and if they are able to establish and maintain *high trust relationships* with those constituencies upon which the organisation is particularly dependent for its long-term survival. None of this is simple to achieve. As our analysis suggests, there are considerable tensions between different aspects of these characteristics. There are tensions which will lead, for example, to some of those who work for organisations being treated in a high commitment and high trust manner (to achieve flexibility for longer-term adaptability) and others in a much shorter-term calculative manner (to achieve flexibility for shorter-term adjustment). Managerial initiative and decisions will thus importantly influence who will be 'winners' and who will be 'losers' in the labour markets of the future. But managers themselves will also find themselves doing more or less well in their own work careers. The challenges that organisations are going to face in the future to be 'effective' will require managers themselves to demonstrate managerial competence of a high level if they are going to be successful in managerial careers.

Achieving manager effectiveness

Given our understanding of what is likely to be required of organisations in the future, it is possible to identify some of the capabilities that managers are likely to require if they are going to contribute to the effectiveness of the organisations that employ them. There has been considerable discussion in recent years of what the *competencies* of a successful manager might be (see Reading Guide 10). A variety of attempts have been made to identify by research how successful managers differ from less successful ones (with success being defined in various ways, ranging from high managerial reputation to the relatively early age of managerial promotion). Valuable insights can be obtained from this work, but there are considerable dangers. The main danger is that of inferring from such studies that there are clearly identifiable traits or skills that an individual possesses, in the same way that they possess a certain physique or hair colour, which mean that the managers will do well once given a managerial appointment. This is unsatisfactory for several reasons. In the first place, such assumptions takes us back to the very limiting and rigid systems-control conception of the human individual that was critically examined in Chapter 4. In the

Link Chapter 4 pointed out the advantages of understanding human beings not as fixed *entities* but as *emergent* characters whose lives are always in process and whose identities are in significant part a reflection of the social and economic context in which they live, the relations they have with others and the way they are continually learning about and adapting to the world in which they find themselves.

second place, crude competency thinking fails to recognise that how well or badly a manager performs in his or her job is very much a matter of how that job has been set up and the extent to which the manager finds himself or herself able to work cooperatively with other managers. It is a lot more than a matter of the 'talents' that he or she brings to the post. Ineffective or 'bad' management of an organisation can result from things other than the employment of 'bad' or incompetent managers.

Activity 12.5

Reread the account of how a confusion arose between 'bad management' and 'bad managers' in the researcher's discussion with Ted Meadows in Chapter 3, pp. 67–8, and

■ note how this influenced the devising of the model shown in Table 3.1 which distinguishes

between 'management', managers' and 'managing';

■ note how this distinction is relevant to the present discussion.

General capability on the part of a manager is something that can only be demonstrated in an organisational situation. It only becomes apparent in the context of a particular management 'team', a specific managerial culture and certain structural arrangements. These are things over which the individual manager may have little direct influence. This is not to say, however, that there are not various personal characteristics, skills, orientations or understandings that *potentially* make some people more effective managers than others. We need to keep separate the question of what managerial *potential* a person might have and how *effective* they might be in practice. To help with this – and working on the assumption made throughout this book, that managers are those people who are formally employed to help direct an organisation as a whole towards its long-term survival – we can offer the paired concepts of *manager competence* and *manager effectiveness*:

Manager competence   *Concept*

The possession of skills, knowledge and aptitudes that a manager can demonstrate in action and which *potentially* enables that manager to bring about the completion of the tasks in their area of responsibility in a way which will make as great a possible contribution to the performance of the organisation and to its long-term survival.

Manager effectiveness   *Concept*

The successful application of the skills, knowledge and aptitudes to the fulfilment of tasks in a manager's area of responsibility so that as great a possible contribution is made to the performance of the organisation and to its long-term survival.

Manager effectiveness is the extent to which a particular manager contributes to the broader and more socially achieved *managerial effectiveness* – managerial effectiveness being effectiveness at the level of a whole management or 'managerial team'. It is the same thing as *organisational effectiveness*: the extent to which the management as a whole is successful at achieving a long-term future for the organisation. And before we make any attempt to identify some of the general characteristics that might make some individuals better able to contribute to overall managerial effectiveness than others, we must note two important things:

- Any particular management team will contain a division of labour within which there will be a variety of managerial jobs, as Stewart's research in particular has demonstrated (1976, 1982, Reading Guide 5). Managers' jobs do not just vary in the amount of seniority that is attached to them or with the functional specialism that they involve (finance, human resourcing, production and the rest). They vary in the amount of discretion that is involved in the position. Jobs also vary from those in which the manager largely relates to people outside the organisation to those in which the manager relates mainly to people within the enterprise. They vary from those in which the manager is in a 'hub' position, relating to people above, below and at the same level in the hierarchy as him- or himself to those in which the manager works alone much of the time. Also, they vary from jobs in which the manager spends most of his or her time supervising the work of subordinates to jobs in which managers work almost exclusively with other managers. All of this means that the mix of managerial competencies required to bring about overall managerial or organisational effectiveness is one that needs to be found at the level of the management team. It is not a mix that has to be found to an equal extent in each individual manager.

- This managerial division of labour means that a 'weakness' in one manager, in general competence terms, might be compensated for by the strengths of another manager within a managerial group. In addition to this, it is possible for a single manager to compensate within his or her own activities for an area of weak personal competence with a particular personal strength – at least for a certain period of his or her career. A good illustration of this is the case of a manager who fell significantly short of the level of capability with budgets that her employer required of her (a 'key competency' in that company's 'management competency handbook'). This manager made a virtue of her difficulties in this area by encouraging her two junior managers to do most of her budgeting work. In the process of developing her deputies in this way she established an especially close and high trust relationship across her departmental management team. This was something she was generally good at doing and it 'paid off' by building a generally high level of effectiveness at the level of the management of that department.

Bearing in mind these reservations about how we make use of it, it is possible to draw up a scheme identifying the characteristics that we can increasingly expect to be required of managers, given the organisational challenges identified earlier of achieving flexibility, adaptability and high trust relations with resource dependent constituencies. The scheme set out in Table 12.1 is closely based on a scheme devised as part of a managerial job undertaken within participant observation ethnographic research in a telecommunications development and manufacturing company (Watson, 2001, Reading Guide 5). The company's directors were anxious to provide managers with information about what it was going to require of them in both their present jobs and jobs into which they might be promoted. They were also looking for a set of background criteria that could be used when making decisions about management appointments, training, promotion and deployment. Table 12.1 does not part significantly from the company's scheme. It simply removes some of the more company-specific criteria used in the original. The scheme has been constructed to be broadly relevant to most organisational situations and the criteria chosen have been derived from a range of sources including the research work done by social scientists on managerial behaviour generally (Chapter 3, pp. 84–8) and on the apparently exceptionally 'successful' managers referred to above. This was supplemented by the author's own research on how managers themselves discriminate between 'good' and 'bad' managers (Watson, 2001, Reading Guide 5). Above all, however, the criteria have been chosen to be consistent with the general thrust of research upon theorising about *how organisations and management actually work in modern societies*. This is the material that has been drawn upon throughout *Organising and Managing Work*.

Activity 12.6

Try to 'test' the Table 12.1 scheme against your own experience and reflect on the relevance of individual managerial competence to broader managerial or organisational effectiveness.

■ Think about:

   (a) the least able manager you have ever come across (choosing, if you wish, someone with managerial responsibilities at a school, college or voluntary association you have experience of),

   (b) the most able manager you have come across.

■ Note down the most significant ways in which each of these did their jobs.

■ Compare your recollections of these two people with the characteristics identified in the two columns in Table 12.1.

■ Consider the extent to which the personal competence or incompetence of these people made an impact on the general managerial effectiveness of the organisation in which they worked. Was the incompetence of your 'worst' manager compensated for by the strengths of other managers, for example, or was the high level of competence of your 'best' manager undermined by other managers or by problems at the level of organisational culture or structure?

TABLE 12.1 Broad characteristics of more able and less able managers		
	The more able or 'competent' manager	**The less able or less 'competent' manager**
Personal orientation		
Achievement and results orientation	Sets high but realistic standards of achievement for self and others, seeks continual improvement in processes and results, and monitors progress against targets	Muddles through without clear objectives, is happy with 'adequate' performance and judges success as the avoidance of trouble
Initiative	Seeks and creates opportunities, initiates actions and wants to be 'ahead of the game'	Reacts to situations and passively follows the initiatives of others
Decisiveness and self-confidence	Believes sufficiently in their own judgement to make decisions and take risks; they accept the possibility of making mistakes from time to time	Is unsure of themselves, they hesitate and procrastinate over decisions; they are risk averse and afraid of making mistakes
Enterprise orientation	Has a strong sense of enterprise and a shrewd grasp of market opportunities; they are cost conscious but strongly aware of the importance of productive investment	Has little awareness of or interest in the financial and market context of business; they either (i) pay little attention to costs – and consequently spend carelessly or (ii) keep down costs regardless of the possibility of later return on present expenditure
Adaptability and capacity to learn	Is flexible in coping with changing circumstances; does not panic in the face of crises or adversity; is constantly learning from their own experiences, from observations and from external sources (contacts, books, papers, media, etc.)	Continues to do things the way they always have, regardless of circumstances; they may panic or retreat when faced with threats or changes; they believe that they know all they need to know
Cognitive style		
Vision and strategic thinking	Can relate current activities to a clear and coherent image of a future state of affairs for the whole organisation and their part of it; they understand the links between everyday activities and the long-term effectiveness of the business – especially with regard to customers; they manage their segment (department, function, etc.) of the organisation as a contribution to the enterprise as a whole. They appreciate the global context in which all organisations increasingly work and are sensitive to differing cultural norms within and across societies	Has a short-term perspective and an inward-looking approach to managing their responsibilities – their departmental or functional objectives are seen as ends in themselves rather than as means to more effective performance of the business as a whole. Minimal attention is paid to customers or clients and there is little awareness of changing global circumstances or of cultural variations that exist within and across societies
Information search	Is constantly collecting and sifting information from a variety of sources and works hard to maintain an information network which will continually feed them with knowledge and intelligence of both a formal and informal nature	Either (i) limits themselves to a few, usually formal, sources of information so that they have little knowledge of or 'feel for' what is going on around them, or (ii) allows themselves to be swamped with information that they receive without discrimination so that they quickly become dazed and out of touch

continued

	The more able or 'competent' manager	The less able or less 'competent' manager
Cognitive style *continued*		
Use of concepts	Is able to sort and make use of information received and gathered through the use of conceptual schemes and theories which might enable them to understand trends and patterns, to see how certain situations have 'come about' and to establish hypotheses which might be 'tested'	Lacks conceptual frameworks for bringing order to what they see going on; they cannot see the 'wood for the trees'; there is little idea of how situations come about and little conceptual basis for trying out new ideas
Creativity	Is imaginative and innovative, devising both new things to do and new ways of doing what was done before	At best, follows established practices and takes the lead given by others and, at worst, is negatively conservative and resistant to new ideas
Judgement and decision-making	Critically and objectively evaluates information and decides upon actions in a logical and rational manner, making use of available evidence but balancing this, where appropriate, with intuition and informed risk-taking	Makes judgements that are subject to bias and prejudice; their actions lack a clear logic and their reasoning may be either (i) coldly based on raw data without the addition of any degree of flair or imaginative interpretation or (ii) based on wild guesses, uninformed hunches, blind self-interest or malice
Interpersonal style		
Sensitivity and listening	Is sensitive to the preferences and emotions of both themselves and of all those they work with (at all levels, inside and outside the organisation); they treat others and their ideas with respect; they listen carefully to the ideas and viewpoints of others, working actively to elicit positive contributions from them	Has little regard for the people they work with; they are insensitive to the feelings of others, concentrating on their own ideas, feelings and objectives regardless of the views or interests of others
Impact and persuasiveness	Has the personal presence and credibility to win support for proposed actions, values and strategies; they use persuasive arguments, symbols and rewards to gain support and they win compliance through selling examples to others	Tends to be taken little notice of and, even when they appear to be given attention, they have little influence either on people's thinking or their behaviour
Planning and organisation	Sets agendas for their teams and works with them to formulate plans, objectives and time targets which are supported with necessary resources	Leaves their teams unclear as to what is expected of them, with vague time horizons and haphazard access to resources
Presentation and communication	Ensures that information and ideas are communicated clearly and unambiguously with the appropriate choice of communication medium to achieve maximum understanding on the part of the audience	Has little appreciation of when to use which means of communication; their writing and their oral communication attempts are muddled, incoherent and ambiguous and they fail to check on how well their audience understands them in the course of their attempts to communicate
Leadership, team building and maintenance	Works with teams they lead to build up a positive climate, an efficient allocation of tasks and they ensure that information is shared and that skills are kept up to date and directed towards effective task achievement and continuous improvement. When they are a member of a team which they are not leading they contribute positively and constructively	Works on their own and tends to maintain power by keeping information from others. The team they are responsible for is left to find its own way of working – often leading to lack of focus, negativity, conflict and under-resourcing. If they are a member of team and not a leader they only play a part when they perceive an opportunity to defend or further a sectional interest

The first thing to notice about the scheme represented in Table 12.1 is that it is consistent with the process-relational conception of the human individual as emergent. It departs from the systems-control way of understanding the human individual as a fixed entity or miniature system with certain given characteristics, personality traits or attitudes. The 'competent manager' is not a particular type of person but someone who acts and thinks in a particular way. Hence the model uses the terms 'orientations' and 'styles' to give an emphasis to this dynamic or processual view of the human individual. The second thing that might be noticed about the scheme is that it is incompatible with a view of management as a specialist occupational activity equivalent to engineering or medicine.

 Link Chapter 2 argued that part of the systems-control orthodoxy about organisations and their managing is that management is a specialised occupation with its own specialist body of knowledge and that doing managerial work involves the application of a neutral technical expertise (p. 44).

The criteria of managerial capability suggested in Table 12.1 fit with Chapter 3's process-relational analysis of the nature of managerial work. This perspective, strongly supported by research into what managers actually do, suggests that managerial work is not most helpfully understood as involving the application of a body of specialist knowledge to the running of an 'organisational machine'. It is much more understood as a matter of deploying social, political and cultural skills to persuading human individuals and groups to think and behave in particular ways. The vital competencies are, therefore, basic human and social ones. The skilled organisational manager is not therefore a technocrat or organisational engineer but a socially, politically and culturally skilled human being. They are skilled at listening to people, talking to people, influencing people, gathering information, analysing information, managing knowledge and looking for different ways of doing things. We can well imagine technical skills in areas like financial or statistical analysis or in computing being used to support all these activities but these are only likely to encourage effectiveness if they are combined with very broad human qualities like determination, creativity, self-confidence and sensitivities to the points of view of other people.

The analysis of manager competence that is emerging here is in danger of sounding very imprecise, trite even. It also risks suggesting that successful managers have to be superhumanly multi-talented and multi-skilled. A picture is painted of an almost impossibly complete and 'fully rounded' person. To be a successful manager, one needs rational and analytical skills yet, at the same time, one has to be able to handle ambiguity and draw on one's intuitive learning. One needs to be a determined, self-confident leader who is willing to direct and monitor other people while, at the same time, being willing to learn from one's mistakes and to play a constructive part in teams when someone else is the leader. In what we might call the 'real world', such paragons of managerial virtue are likely to be rare. Yet all the emerging evidence about what 'works' and 'does not work' in the managing of complex work tasks suggests that these qualities are ones that will be sought by employers of managers. In practice, the strengths and weaknesses of different individuals will be recognised and balanced out across managerial 'teams'. Yet as a manager moves closer to a *general manager* role, the more they are likely to be expected to display competences along the lines of those set out in Table 12.1.

Activity 12.7

Read the account given of Kotter's research (1982, Reading Guide 5) on outstandingly effective general managers (pp. 88–90) and what Peter Brodie (the reputedly very successful general manager of a voluntary organisation) has to say about his working day in Cases and Conversations 3.4. Then consider:

■ to what extent there is a fit between the managerial abilities of these individuals and the scheme set out in Table 12.1;

■ why these competencies appear to be necessary in the work of the general manager.

At first sight, both Peter Brodie and Kotter's effective general managers were not acting in a particularly impressive or systematic way to shape the enterprises for which they were responsible. However, behind the apparent 'madness' of what they were doing was a great deal of 'method', the logic of their behaviour being close to that running through Table 12.1's sketch of the 'more competent' manager. They were endlessly monitoring the activities and expectations of all the various parties or 'constituencies' with which they needed to deal and pulling these people towards compliance with the 'agenda' they had developed for their shaping of their enterprise. And this 'pulling' and 'shaping' occurred through the application of a range of social, interpersonal, political, learning and analytical skills. It did not occur through overt and direct attempts to control behaviours. And why is this? It is because they are highly *dependent* on a large number of other people to achieve their purposes, in spite of the fact that they have a significant degree of formal power or authority, and they have little direct control over the majority of the people upon whom they are dependent. They also have to rely on highly ambiguous information gathered from a wide range of sources to inform all of their persuading, cajoling and 'influencing' activities. A high level of cognitive skills is clearly necessary to make sense of all the information with which the manager is bombarded, as is a capacity to learn continuously from what they see, hear and experience.

The essentially dynamic nature of managerial work makes an ability to learn effectively a fundamentally important competence for managers. The processes of learning about aspects of life that are relevant to managerial work can be seen to start for many people early in their lives. This often happens before the individual enters managerial work itself and it continues through a manager's career as they continually adjust to the circumstances and the pressure that they meet following what managers themselves frequently characterise as the 'sink and swim' process of learning (Watson and Harris, 1999, Reading Guide 5; Watson

2001, Reading Guide 11). The formal process of management development that organisations provide is often haphazard and partial (Storey, Edwards and Sisson, 1997, Reading Guide 11) with managers' attention to texts and 'experts' often happening more with an eye to being familiar with management fads and fashions and the utterances of current 'guru' figures than with a purpose of consciously integrating formal knowledge with personal experience (see Reading Guide 12). It may be, however, that formal management training and education can only ever play a minor part in management learning. Its role may be to act as a support for what is inevitably an intuitive and experiential process that only occurs with significant effects when it is integrated into the more corporate processes associated with the ideas of the *learning organisation* and *knowledge management*.

 Link The significance of the ideas of the learning organisation and knowledge management for organisational strategy making was recognised in Chapter 6, pp. 196–7.

The importance of experiential learning (Kolb, 1984, Reading Guide 11) has repeatedly been stressed and arguments have been put forward for replacing formal academic programmes of management education with *action learning* programmes, where the study of management *ideas* occurs simultaneously with and always in close conjunction with management *practice* (Revans, 1971, 1982, and other references in Reading Guide 11). Management is indeed a 'practice' rather than a 'discipline' or a body of knowledge. It is a practice in which people engage with an ever changing and highly ambiguous world and in which they continually have to negotiate and re-negotiate understandings and relationships with other people. Management education and study can thus play two roles in helping people cope with such challenges. First, it can help sensitise potential managers to these 'realities'. Second, it can provide conceptual and theoretical resources and research-based insights that people involved in managerial tasks, or anticipating such involvement, can incorporate into the personal and practice-based theorising that can only happen when they are doing the job 'for real'. *Organising and Managing Work* is intended to help with both of these roles.

In spite of the importance of the cognitive or intellectual dimension of skilled managerial performance it is vital not to play down the emotional side of managerial work.

 Link The often underestimated significance of the role of feelings and emotions in work organisations generally and in managerial work specifically was stressed in Chapter 5, pp. 138–48.

The basic assumptions of Cartesian dualism in modern thinking (Chapter 3, p. 62) have strongly encouraged the denial or suppression of the emotional side of human life in organisations and have discouraged managers from taking either their own or other people's emotions into account. One sign of a willingness to move away from such a position has been a growing managerial interest in the notion of *emotional intelligence* (Goleman, 1996, 1999, and other references in Reading Guide 10).

Emotional intelligence   *Concept*

An ability to take into account one's own emotions and the emotions of others when deciding how to manage one's own situation and one's relationships with those others.

The notion of emotional intelligence corresponds to the capacity identified in Table 12.1 to be 'sensitive to the preferences and emotions of both themselves and of all those they work with'. The concept is associated with the assumption that it will help people to operate successfully in a social context if they are able to 'manage' both their own emotionality and that of the people to whom they are relating. A parent, for example, would be displaying 'emotional intelligence' and thus acting as a potentially effective parent if, when faced with a first child trying to tip a newly born second child out of its pram, they were able to recognise that child's feeling about the sudden arrival of a sibling and could respond to the child's behaviour with a carefully judged and balanced display of distress and disapproval, on the one hand, and an appreciation of the child's own confusion and distress on the other hand.

An 'emotionally intelligent' manager is one who would act in a similarly sensitive and *balanced* way if, for example, they had to deal with a group of journalists interviewing them about a company's recent and apparently disastrous loss of some major customers. The shrewd manager might display a certain amount of humility and reveal a hint of distress about the vagaries and unpredictability of the market place. But they would balance this with an appearance of confidence that some customers will be won back and new ones found once they and their colleagues have learned from their difficulties and improved their performance. In this way, attention has not just been paid to the desires of the journalists to go away with a 'good story' but thought has been given to how both people within the organisation and those who might buy from it in the future are left *feeling* about what has happened and, more importantly, what is going to happen. The manager has acted in a way that is more likely to assist in the long-term survival of the organisation than if they had acted in a way that was less likely to create relatively positive *feelings* about the organisation's future among all of those who would see or read the journalists' stories.

Using the concept of *emotional intelligence* in this way, we are once again identifying a 'managerial competence' that might be found in any generally socially effective human being, whatever their purpose or social context might be. Its significance is recognised in the thinking of Aristotle, in the parables of Jesus and in the writing of Machiavelli, and it is to be found in the actions of shrewd parents, teachers and lovers everywhere. Yet the tendency has been for management consultants to 'commodify' the concept – to treat it in a very non-processual and non-relational way as a 'thing' that managers might or might not possess. It is also widely treated as something that can be measured in an individual by analysing their responses to a psychologist's specially devised questionnaire. The danger here is that we are taken back to the type of thinking about managerial competence that was rejected earlier: that which saw 'competencies' as inbuilt characteristics or 'traits' of human individuals existing in isolation from their organisational context. It is much more helpful to see competencies, instead, as *emergent* predispositions of people to act in certain ways in the context of relationships, cultural assumptions and ongoing learning and adaptive processes. The concept of emotional intelligence, for example, is likely to be more useful for understanding manager effectiveness if we do not focus on the extent to which managers *are emotionally intelligent* but focus on the extent to which, in particular organisational contexts, managers *act in an emotionally intelligent way*.

The rather 'commodified' way in which the emotional intelligence idea has been taken up managerially raises doubts about just how process-oriented the future recruiters and developers of managers are likely to be in practice. Systems-control thinking still has a powerful grip. It encourages a view of the manager as a small system-like entity with a bundle of 'traits', as well as over-emphasising the potential of structural innovations and organisational 're-engineering' as ways of improving organisational effectiveness. Nevertheless, awareness is increasing of the necessity for management thinking to shift from an emphasis on structures and systems to an emphasis on developing organisational processes that bring out human creativity and enterprise. Such trends fit with the growing interest among strategy-makers in what were earlier characterised as *directed evolution* approaches to the shaping of organisational activities for long-term survival.

Link 'Directed evolution' approaches to strategy-making such as those involving *logical incrementalism* and the principles of the *learning organisation* were examined in Chapter 6, pp. 189–97. The relevance of the types of managerial competence being examined in the present chapter to such a way of managing strategically are illustrated in the story about how 'Ali and Dina come into their own'.

Managing right and wrong

Our consideration of different ways of achieving organisational effectiveness as well as our reflections on how some managers contribute more 'competently' than others to such effectiveness has taken for granted the notion of organisational and managerial effectiveness that has run through *Organising and Managing Work*. Organisational effectiveness has been treated throughout as a matter of achieving the long-term survival of the organisation as a corporate whole. The concept has been repeatedly used from the point at which the basic function of management was first formally conceptualised in such terms (Chapter 3, p. 67). The logic of managerial work is taken to be one of the managers in an organisation working both individually and corporately to fulfil this function. All those specific managerial requirements of satisfying shareholder demands, meeting employee expectations, gaining approval from state agencies, helping clients or securing the business of customers have been treated throughout not as the *ends* of managerial work but as the *means* by which the basic managerial task of taking the organisation 'forward' into the future is achieved.

This emphasis on managing for long-term corporate survival might appear, at first sight, to be a way of avoiding questions of the moral rightness or wrongness of managerial and corporate actions. Indeed, such a view of their role could be used by managers to argue that their work is morally neutral. They could use it to suggest that it is not part of their job to consider the ethical aspects of organisational activities. They might argue that they are employed simply to do what is best for the long-term future of the organisation that pays them. But even if we accept that managers tend not to be employed primarily to 'do good works' in the world, it is a total nonsense to suggest either that their work is morally neutral or that they can do the job without at least taking into account the ways in which their acts and decisions are likely to be judged in moral terms by others. Even if we avoid the morally dubious language of 'managing people' (Chapter 1, pp. 3–6) and are careful not to talk of *people* as 'human resources' (Chapter 11, p. 369), we have to recognise that the treatment of people as means towards ends rather than as ends in themselves is an intrinsic element of managerial work, and questions about the rights and wrongs of *using people* in different ways are at the centre of many ethical debates. Part of Kant's famous *categorical imperative*, an idea that has long been at the centre of the western tradition of philosophical debate, is the injunction to treat people as 'ends in themselves' and not primarily as the means of meeting the needs of others.

No managerial act can be morally neutral because every such act occurs in the context of relationships in which there is, at the very least, a potential for exploitation. By the same token, no manager is likely to succeed in his or her work, at least over any significant period of time, if they fail to take into account how others might morally judge their actions. A manager who gave no attention to whether their actions or decisions were likely to be judged as fair or unfair, just or unjust, honest or dishonest by people both inside and outside their organisation would be a fool. They would be unlikely to survive in their job for long and any manager who assumed that he or she had sufficient authority for no one to question and potentially challenge their actions, would equally be a fool. Glenn Ferness is anything but a fool – but she still talks of the insoluble moral dilemmas that face her in her work.

Activity 12.8

Read what Glenn Ferness, the general manager of a large city branch of Logies department stores, says about the ethical dimension of her work in Cases and Conversations 12.3 and

- note the ways in which moral or ethical criteria come into her managerial work and how these criteria relate to her personal concept of 'self' and her overall life career;

- consider how far you agree with her argument that the only way for a manager to change things they are morally unhappy with in an organisation is to argue 'the business case' rather than the moral case as such.

My company right or wrong?

Cases and Conversations 12.3

Your colleagues tell me that you are a particularly ethically aware manager.

Oh dear.

You don't take that as a compliment?

I suppose I should. But I am rather sensitive to being viewed in that way. Although it is true that I am a very ethically conscious person, I am terribly aware that it can be used by certain people, certain men in the business especially, to suggest that one is less than fully focused on the 'interests of the business'. It doesn't help your career to be seen that way – especially if it can be used by the male dinosaurs who still dominate this company to argue against putting other women into senior positions. I know there has been talk like this about me. And this is in spite of the fact that the only other woman at the very senior level in the organisation has no interest in ethics at all. At work she takes a very simple view of 'my company right or wrong'.

You don't take the view that women make better managers than men precisely because they are more sensitive to the human and ethical nuances of managerial work, and that they therefore make decisions that 'take people along with them' more often that men do?

Oh, I think there may be something in that. But I don't waste time on the argument about whether or not women are different or better than men in management.

Why?

There are several different reasons. In the first place, what sort of evidence have we got? Some of the best managers I know are women (and this doesn't include my senior woman colleague). They are people who would score highly on emotional intelligence tests, I am sure. I suspect that they have no choice but to be sophisticated thinkers. They have to be especially good at what you call 'taking people along' with them if they are to overcome all the barriers against women getting to the top. To put it another way, you will only tend to see exceptionally talented women in senior jobs because, compared to men, they have got to be exceptionally talented to get there at all. You can't take this to suggest that women are inherently better managers than men.

And in the second place?

If you want to fight the cause of getting more women into management, it will get you nowhere to argue to the men who currently rule the roost that women might be better than them. And, thirdly, I don't like the way that people who argue this stuff about women being better managers because of their 'nurturing' qualities and their 'people skills' draw on stereotypes of women. Those stereotypes are just too simplistic – not to say patronising. And, Betty, the other general store manager I was telling you about, is anything but nurturing.

You sound a bit resentful about her?

Oh dear. I had better be careful hadn't I? Betty's appointment, two years before mine, looked like a step forward for women's careers in the company. But it wasn't. When they appointed her, they didn't think out the implications of choosing Betty. The chairman of the time said something like, 'It would look good for the business if we were to be seen putting more women into senior positions'. But they promoted somebody who was not ready for such a job. That was morally wrong. It was wrong because it exploited Betty herself. And it was wrong because it has held back the cause of fair treatment for women managers generally. Because she has been rather bad at the job, she is used as an argument by a number of the men for avoiding appointing other women to such jobs. I am convinced my own promotion was held up on these grounds.

So what looked like a step forward for women's careers was a step back, are you are saying?

That's right. And I have learned from it. I am slowly increasing the proportion of women managers in my own store. But my stated justification for it is that it is 'best for the business' to use all the talents available to us. I argue the same way for the equal opportunities and diversity policies that we apply generally. I have a profound personal moral belief that we should treat everybody with equal regard and that it is desperately wrong to judge people on the basis of their sex, ethnicity, or their age for that matter. But arguing the moral case, in those terms, gets one nowhere. So I argue the case for using all the talents we have got or I argue that it would be 'bad for business' to be known as an employer who unfairly discriminated against various groups.

Bad for business?

Perhaps in terms of recruitment – all sorts of people might avoid joining a company known to be an unfair employer. But we also have to think about the public – our customers especially. We are well aware that a lot of the more 'discriminating' public (in the nicest sense of that word; you know, 'nice people') in this city use our store. A lot of them – quite rightly in my view – would stay away from a shop that did not treat its entire staff with the highest regard. Do you see what I mean?

Yes, are you saying that there are personal 'causes' and moral purposes informing your work but to fight for those causes you have to play down your role as a 'moral crusader' and argue every moral case as a business case.

That's it. I've always thought of myself as something of a crusader, as you've inferred. But I soon realised that being seen in this way would not only ruin my career. It would also make me a rather useless crusader.

But why would a 'crusader' come into retailing at all? What brought you into this business?

I sometimes wonder that myself. For years I expected to go into something like social work, hospital management or even politics. But shopkeeping is also in my blood. My parents ran a small shop for years. So, looking back, it seems as if I tried to resolve these two sides of my character by coming into this top chain store with a view to trying to 'make a difference' to what happens – 'from the inside', so to speak, rather than through going into politics. I think I am having some success with this. But I wouldn't exaggerate it.

So, do you believe that operating ethically as a business is the key to long-term business success?

I used to. But I am afraid it just isn't as simple as that. Let me give you an example. I am currently expanding the food side of our business here. Some old houses were demolished next to us. So we bought up the land and have extended our store. I know it is going to be very profitable to have more space for fresh food. It's more than just the extra sales, though. It's also because it will allow us to cover an even bigger proportion of people's shopping needs in our store. We will simply be a bigger retailing force in the city. That's an important element of our general business strategy. But one of the consequences of this is that we will put out of business several small shops that I know are already struggling in the city.

That troubles you?

With my background you can see why it might. I agonised over the development. It was a real moral dilemma for me. In fact, I talked to my parents about it and, in the end, they helped me reach a position that enabled me to go ahead and put my plan to head office. We concluded that although I had a moral duty to those small shopkeepers I also had a moral duty to my employer. I decided it would be wrong not to tell my employer that there was this opportunity to increase the long-term viability of the company. But I still feel bad about it. There's no 'my company right or wrong' for me.

But what if the company insisted on your doing something that you felt was ethically unacceptable to you personally?

I might have to leave. It might have happened last week for instance. I was taking part in a annual strategy review at head office and one of the issues discussed was our discovery, via the press, that one of the suppliers from whom we were buying a lot of health training equipment was not only using child labour abroad to produce some of their lines but was also, through a subsidiary, selling torture equipment to some very questionable foreign governments. My personal reaction to this was to get straight back to my store and remove every item of that company from our shelves. Although, at the end of the day, I would have felt it necessary to leave my job if the company had not decided to stop buying from that supplier, I was able to join what turned out to be the winning faction of senior managers who argued for ending our contract with the firm. And, guess what? We won the case on the grounds that it would be damaging to our business, in the long term, if we continued to use a supplier that was 'getting a bad press'. We needed to 'protect our reputation for fair dealing in the world' as the chief executive concluded at the end of the debate.

You must have been relieved at this outcome?

I was. But I didn't really expect the decision to go the other way. I actually have a lot of faith in our current chief executive. I know him well and he and I share a lot of personal values. We have only had one significant managerial disagreement since I have been working closely with him.

What was that about?

It was over his proposal to make a link between top managers' bonuses and the business's share price. He saw it as a virtue, as he put it, 'to align manager and shareholder interests'. I saw this as quite wrong. Firstly, it does not feel right to me to align managers' interests with any one stakeholder in the business rather than another. At least with a link between managers' pay and business performance you are rewarding them for contributing to something that might benefit employees and customers as much as shareholders. And, secondly, I pointed out the dangers of pandering to the short-termism of the financial markets. You can imagine managers doing all sorts of things to bump up the share price in the short term.

Such as?

Such as downsizing the workforce in the stores for example. That sort of thing is always popular with certain investment interests.

Go on.

That sort of thing would harm the business in the longer run – long-term share price included, of course. I managed to persuade Chris not to go ahead on that one, I am delighted to say. What pleases me is that, like me, he is acutely aware of the moral dilemmas that we face in management.

Can you give me other examples of managerial moral dilemmas?

One we have talked about several times, very much in private I must stress, is our shared disgust about trends in farming: the way all sorts of risks are taken with the public's health (in the case of the BSE crisis with beef, for example) and even with the very long-term viability of the countryside itself (seen with the effects of the dreadful foot and mouth disease outbreak, for example). As a retailer, Chris and I have reflected on whether Logies should go along with this constant pushing down of food prices with all the evils of industrial farming that follow from it. He experimented with getting a couple of stores just selling organic foods for a period. But our sales went down badly. Both Chris and I would like to see our stores selling mainly locally grown organic fresh foods in the long term. In that we are following our moral impulses. But we will only be able to move in that direction if and when a larger proportion of our customer base comes to share the same values.

You mean being willing to pay more for a more 'ethical' product.

Yes, but it is only 'ethical' at present in the eyes of some of us. For others there's no ethical issue. Life would be so much easier if there was a shared set of values in society, easier for everyone. But, even then, I am not sure how easy being a retailer or manager would be. Say, for instance, we put up the price of food in the interests of a more ethical approach to farming. What would happen to all those poor families that would not be able to afford those prices? How do you solve that one? And, managerially, what do I do about this dilemma: I am generally increasing the discretion that our ordinary shop workers have, you know 'empowering them'. This is to me an obviously morally right thing to do. It gives people a more fulfilling working day – and it seems to be working by making people both happier and more effective as sale persons. Yet it is causing distress to a number of our older supervisors and section managers. They tell me I am letting them down by reducing their authority and their status in the shop – something they earned by years of dedication to Logies. This is, they say, quite simply 'wrong'. And I can see their point of view.

So what you are doing is both morally right and morally wrong – in your own terms?

That's just how messy and ambiguous managing is. There's no way one can be ethically pure in managerial work – any more than I suppose you can in life generally. You have to come to terms with the fact you are going to face a lot of insoluble moral dilemmas. You just have to make the best of things – given the circumstances and given your own moral values.

So what are you doing about the empowerment issue?

What I have had to do is to balance things out in the way I just mentioned – making the best of things without either compromising my own values or my responsibilities to the company that pays me. In this case, like with so many managerial initiatives, there are going to be winners and losers. On this matter I have decided to accept that I have to hurt a section of our workforce (although I will do my best to minimise that hurt) on the grounds that my changes will help the long-term success of my store. But that's not the whole story. There is also a personal moral concern behind my wanting to empower staff. I think it is morally right to give people at work as much control over their situations as is compatible with effective performance. So it pleases me to think that I am improving some people's lives and, at the same time, improving the business that pays me. I've simply got to go away now and think of how I can do my best to help those whose working lives I have spoiled.

Glenn is very anxious to see herself as an ethical person, a generally 'good person' who does the 'right thing' in her life. To help both herself and her interviewer to make sense of how she relates her private moral views to her managerial work she gives us some insight into her own identity, biography, emotions and her broad *orientation to work*.

 Link — Chapters 3 and 4 show the importance of people's biographies, identities and life projects in understanding their work behaviours generally and demonstrate the value of such concepts for understanding how people face the challenges that arise in managerial work particularly.

Glenn's parents and upbringing have clearly been an important influence on her and she still seeks their help when faced with moral dilemmas such as that which caused her to be torn between furthering the interests of the business she worked for and protecting the interests of the small shopkeepers – people with whom she clearly felt empathy. Being 'ethically aware' is important to the sort of person she believes herself to be. Although it is the interviewer who introduces the idea of Glenn as a 'crusader', it is a label that she seems happy to accept. It fits with her earlier career interest in politics and her talk of 'fighting the cause' of getting more women into management.

The sense-making work that Glenn engages in when talking to the researcher can be seen as part of her *managing to manage* – coping with all the pressures of what she calls the 'messy and ambiguous' nature of managerial work. All of this, together with her reference to learning from her experiences, gives us a picture, not of a person with a given bundle of managerial 'competencies', but of an *emergent manager* who is constantly learning and developing herself as she faces the moral and practical dilemmas of changing managerial circumstances (Watson and Harris, 1999, Reading Guide 5). It is also a picture of a *reflective practitioner* who can step back from immediate work pressures and critically examine what they are doing and why (Schön, 1983, Reading Guide 11). Glenn, in her practical management thinking, shows the sort of sensitivity to human values, differences and conflicts of interest that *critical management and organisation study* attempts to highlight in the academic context. She has no doubts, for instance, there often have to be 'losers' as well as 'winners' as a result of managerial decisions and actions.

Link The conception of *critical management and organisation study* established in Chapter 1 stresses the need of everyone interested in managerial work to take fully into account the 'deeply political and value-laden nature of every aspect of organisational and managerial behaviour' (pp. 20–6).

One way we can make sense of Glenn's policy of making a business case, rather than a directly moral or political case, for tackling issues of gender, ethnic and age discrimination or inequality might be that she is aware of the extent to which such matters relate to the broader social and cultural context in which her organisation exists. To try to take on major social change issues from the position of a manager in just one organisation would be highly unrealistic, but a small contribution might be made to such change if the manager seeks opportunities to make business decisions that fit with notions of a fairer society.

Activity 12.9

Look back to the two stories about Rose Markie and The Canalazzo restaurant (Cases and Conversations 1.4 and 1.5) and the story 'Jan and Mohammed come to Mountains' in (Cases and Conversations 7.1) and

■ consider the extent to which in each of these cases there was a combination of discriminatory practice within the work organisation and an influence of wider cultural patterns in the societies of which the organisation owning The Canalazzo and the Mountains organisation were a part;

■ consider what arguments a manager with Glenn Ferness's values, political sensitivity and sense of personal 'cause' might put to other managers in the restaurant company and in Mountains to persuade them to change their practices with regard to employees' race or gender.

Activity 12.10

Reflect on whether, in your experience, there is a difference between the way men and women do managerial jobs (do women show more 'emotional intelligence' than men, for instance?) and, whatever conclusion you come to, decide how far you agree with Glenn that such matters have little practical relevance when it comes to arguing the case within organisations for improving women's managerial opportunities.

It is not too difficult to develop arguments that might be put to managers in either The Canalazzo or Mountains about the business advantages of treating people in a less unfairly discriminatory manner. We cannot, however, judge how effective these arguments might be without some considerable knowledge and insight into the individuals we were dealing with, or an understanding of the norms and values prevailing in those organisations, localities and industries. Glenn has clearly developed this kind of understanding of her own organisation and its social context and she appears to have concluded that she would not get far advancing women's careers in management by taking up arguments based on the view that women are potentially more able managers than men (Rosener, 1990, and other references in Reading Guide 23). She also has ethical reservations about such arguments, recognising the dangers of encouraging stereotypes about men and women that might fuel rather than discourage unfair discriminatory behaviour. Research on men and women managers in practice tends to show that although such managers will *talk about* sex differences in people's management styles, it is nevertheless the case that the women who compete successfully with men for senior positions tend to do so by managing *in practice* in ways little different from those followed by men (Wajcman, 1998, Reading Guide 23, for example).

Glenn Ferness is obviously very sensitive to the politics and ethical dilemmas of managerial work in a way that does not stop with her concern about equal opportunities in the workplace. She tells us about some specific moral positions that she holds and is very explicit about how a whole range of things are either 'right' or 'wrong'. She is nevertheless quite clear that finding complete solutions to ethical dilemmas is impossible. She calls some dilemmas 'insoluble'. Yet she knows that she still has to make decisions and take actions in spite of the dangers of compromising her own values or falling short in her commitment to the company that employs her. Glenn gives us some clear indications of where these personal values and ethical concerns are relevant to her work. She tells us that her company was wrong to 'exploit' Betty by promoting her prematurely. She talks of her 'profound moral belief' that all people should be treated with equal respect and not unfairly discriminated against on grounds of gender, ethnicity or age. She tells us of her belief that 'it is morally right to give people at work as much control' over their circumstances as is compatible with business interests. She does not relate any of this to any explicit set of overarching ethical principles, however. The source of her values is treated as something of a mystery in fact. At one point she says that the proposal to tie managerial rewards to the company share price, for example, did not *feel right* to her, and she talks about herself and Chris following their 'moral impulses' – whatever these might be – with regard to industrial farming practices.

Ethical ambiguity and the inevitability of moral dilemmas

It is difficult to see a pattern in Glenn's personal morality that fits with any of the schemes of *normative ethics* that philosophers or religious thinkers have proposed over the centuries – schemes that give the basic grounds for deciding what one should and should not do in any particular situation. Sometimes she seems to be using what philosophers call *deontological* grounds for deciding what is right and wrong. This is where one simply takes one's duty in the world as a given and makes moral decisions in the light of that duty. This might take the form of following Kant's categorical imperative about treating all human beings as ends in their own right, for example. Her dislike of exploiting employees (like Betty) and her belief in treating all people 'with equal regard' could be related to deontological thinking. At other times, however, she seems to be basing her position on what ethicists often call *consequentialist* (and sometimes 'teleological') grounds. Here, one starts with a notion of what is 'good' in the world (a state of general human happiness, or the pursuit of the virtuous life, say). One then treats as 'right' those acts that help achieve this state of affairs. A 'right action' is one that would bring about the best possible consequences. We see Glenn adopting this type of principle when she suggests that it is 'morally right' to give people at work as much control over their circumstances as is compatible with business interests. Glenn is coming close here to applying *utilitarian* principles. Utilitarianism is perhaps the best known version of consequentionalist thinking and, in its classical form, it involves deciding what is right on the grounds of what will give the greatest amount of happiness to the greatest number of people.

It is perhaps unsurprising that Glenn does not consistently follow any single scheme of normative ethics. It is rare to find someone who does, at least in the world of 'practical affairs'. Also, there are fundamental difficulties with both deontological and consequentionalist approaches to ethical choice-making. In the case of deontology, it is far from clear from where people might take a notion of duty. The human world does not universally respect any single law-giver, god or biblical text. So how can there be a shared notion of duty and hence a shared morality across a variety of different people? There is a serious flaw in consequentialist thinking too. As has often been pointed out, especially with regard to utilitarianism, it could justify executing an innocent person for a crime if, for example, the public is happy that an apparently guilty person had been punished. The utility of such an act, and its contribution to the sum of human happiness, might be even greater if it were seen to deter the commitment of further such crimes. To most of us it would still be far from 'right' to kill that person, however much general human happiness was brought about by such an act. We can imagine Glenn arguing, along lines similar to this classic criticism of consequentionalist ethics, that it would still have been wrong to have promoted Betty into a job in which she was likely to struggle, even if her appointment had led to happy outcomes for people in the company generally.

← Link   The role of the 'foundationalist' aspirations in modernist thinking was identified in Chapter 2, p. 50.

In the end it would appear to be impossible to establish a clear *foundationalist* moral framework that managers, or anyone else in the modern world, can follow. The problem can be solved no more easily by the application of *rational* methods (calculating the relative amounts of human happiness and unhappiness likely to be caused by a certain act, for instance) than it can by taking what philosophers call an *emotivist* line (as Glenn did when she spoke of something *not feeling right* for example). In a modern world where so much emphasis is placed on rational thinking, one might expect however that moral principles might be derived from rational analysis of the human predicament. Max Weber, the key theorist of the rationalisation of the modern world (Chapter 7, pp. 239–42), pointed out why this is impossible (Weber, 1949, Reading Guide 25) and one can see in Glenn Ferness's notion of the insolubility of ethical dilemmas echoes of Weber's important notion of the *ethical irrationality of the world*.

Ethical irrationality of the world	*Concept*
Judgements about what is right and wrong cannot be derived from rational or scientific analysis of the human condition given that no system of values can be established that will make every value consistent with every other or ensure that right actions always lead to right outcomes (or wrong actions necessarily lead to wrong outcomes).	

There are two aspects to the idea of the world as ethically irrational. First there is an *axiological* dimension of this ethical irrationality. This recognises that the world is full of different *and often irreconcilable* human values, goals, purposes and interests. A very obvious illustration of this is the problem that arises for people who believe it is fundamentally wrong to kill another human being while nevertheless being able to envisage a situation in which acts they regard as equally evil are likely be committed, if certain people are not killed. Glenn gives managerial examples of this aspect of ethical irrationality. She recognises, for example, the 'rightness' of charging higher food prices to make possible a more ethically acceptable agricultural system. At the same time she believes in the 'rightness' of providing food that can be afforded by the poorer members of society. But these two things are not compatible. She also points to the impossibility of doing the 'right thing' for the shop workers in Logies without doing the 'wrong thing' with regard to the supervisors and section managers.

The second dimension of Weber's idea of ethical irrationality involves the *paradox of consequences*, something that has enormous implications for all managerial work. Doing what Glenn took to be a 'right thing' for the ordinary shop workers in Logies had the unintended consequence of doing what she felt was a 'bad thing' to the supervisory staff. Such a paradox can also be seen occurring with Logies' appointment of Betty, as the company's first senior manager. Her appointment was intended to lead the way for the appointment of more women to such positions. In practice, it turned out to hinder rather than help the meeting of such a purpose. An act that was, in Glenn's terms, intended to bring about the 'right thing' of increasing women's managerial opportunities had the unintended consequence of holding back the achievement of that 'rightness'. Glenn's awareness of the likely counterproductive consequences of trying to encourage Logies' top managers to work more effectively by relating part of their pay to the business's share price might also be seen as fitting into the paradox of consequences aspect of the 'ethical irrationality'.

Link Numerous examples were given in Chapter 7 (pp. 242–9) of the *paradox of consequences* and how the *means* chosen to achieve certain *ends* often lead to consequences which undermine the ends for which they were originally devised – the various negative aspects of bureaucracy being the most famous examples of this.

Glenn's warning to her chief executive colleague about relating managerial rewards to the share price echoes some powerful warnings that various writers have given about the negative effects on the long-term corporate performance resulting from the general managerial prioritising of the pursuit of shareholder value (Deal and Kennedy, 1999, Reading Guide 19) or of the specific tying of managerial rewards to share values through the issuing of *stock options* to corporate managers (Kennedy, 1999, Reading Guide 25). It is argued by these and other commentators that the long-term future of some previously very successful organisations has been significantly damaged as managers have boosted their own incomes by impressing stock markets through their downsizing, outsourcing, re-structuring and merger activities. Such short-term activities, through their damage to security, commitment and trust within the organisation, can seriously damage long-term corporate performance. The paradox of consequences can clearly operate at the level of a whole political economy as well as at the organisational level.

Morality and managerial practices

In the light of the ethical irrationality of the world and the immense ambiguity that confronts anyone trying to act morally in the world, how can managers and others involved in the managing of work manage to succeed in bringing any moral criteria whatsoever into their actions? Some research suggests that managers have little choice other than to 'bracket' or leave their private moralities 'at home' and to pursue corporate interests ruthlessly and amorally (Jackall, 1988, Reading Guide 25 – see also Chapter 5, p. 158). Other research suggests that managers continuously draw upon, and mix together, criteria of *expedience* (what will 'work') and moral *principle* (what is 'right') in their day-to-day work (Watson, 1996, Reading Guide 25). Thus managers, in explaining their personal 'theories of management' to the researcher, said things like:

- managers *ought* to listen to their workers and, if they do, they will *get better work from them*;
- it is a *good thing* to encourage employees to develop their skills and responsibilities at work and this will mean that people will *do a much better job* if you treat them in this way;
- it is good and *moral* to establish relationships of trust with the people around you and this *pays off* corporately;
- bullying people, being overly secretive and lying is *wrong*, it also tends to be *unhelpful* to managers, in the longer run, in getting them what they want from people.

Arguments like these encourage us to abandon the type of 'either-or thinking' (see Chapter 4, pp. 94–7) that would suggest that people have to be *either* 'pragmatic' *or* 'principled' or have to be *either* 'expedient' *or* 'ethical'. In practice people tend to be 'pragmatically principled' or 'ethically expedient'. This appears to be the case with Glenn Ferness's 'making the best of things' in the light of both her own moral values and the organisational or business circumstances. Such an approach also seems to be behind the position that is taken by all of those arguing for high commitment and high trust work organisations. The implications that it is a 'good thing' for managers to trust and value people within the organisation and that this 'good treatment' is likely to be reciprocated by 'good behaviour' by everyone in the organisation – 'good behaviour' that will make the organisation an effective and successful one, to the benefit of all its members. Such assumptions are implicit in the arguments put forward by Bal Blair and Eden Killie (see above, pp. 432–4), although the former tended to lay the emphasis on the expedient aspect of high trust organisations and the latter the principled aspect.

Eden Killie, in Cases and Conversations 12.2, sought a moral basis for developing a 'high trust' work organisation on the grounds that all of those with whom the organisation deals have the right to be treated well because each of them is a 'stakeholder' in the organisation. Writers influenced by McIntyre's critique of 'bureaucratic managerialism' (1981, Reading Guide 25) have put forward an alternative set of grounds for developing morally responsible managerial practices. Anthony (1986, Reading Guide 25) and Roberts (1984, 1996, Reading Guide 25), for example, take up McIntyre's understanding of the relevance of Aristotle's ideas to management practice. It is argued that managers can find a moral base for their authority and their actions by treating their organisations as *moral communities* in which the interdependence of all members of that community is recognised. Managerial power is morally justified by its dedication to achieving the good life that it makes possible for members of that community. There is a serious catch in this kind of approach, however, if it keeps its focus at the level of the organisation as a moral community. A manager talking about high trust organisations in an ethnographic account of a managerial discussion about management and morality graphically illustrates this catch (Watson, 1998, Reading Guide 25). He says he can envisage an organisation that has high trust relations, caring welfare policies, serious empowerment practices and a strong culture with tight values that all members operate within and benefit from. He then shocks his colleagues by pointing out that such a strongly morally focused organisation could exist, and yet be in the business of contract murder. Would that really be a moral organisation he asks? Of course not, his colleagues inevitably but reluctantly admit.

Morality is something that clearly cannot be localised to the practices within a work organisation. Insofar as managers are going to bring moral criteria into their work, they will have to look to the wider cultural world within which their organisation operates. To do this they can be expected to act in the light of two sets of criteria. First, they will look to the personal values that they bring to the workplace from their own upbringings, cultural roots and sense of 'the sort of person I am'. We saw this very clearly with Glenn Ferness and noted how she recognised that moral circumstances could occur at work that might cause her to leave the company. Second, managers inevitably have to look to the values and moralities of the various constituencies with whom the organisation strategically exchanges to enable it to continue into the future. Glenn gives us the example of the dangers to the survival of Logies that could arise if the sort of people who use their shops were to learn that the company unfairly discriminated against people on grounds of their race, gender or age or if potentially valuable workers were deterred by such a reputation from seeking employment with the business.

> **Link** Managers' own values and preferences have been recognised as important inputs to organisational outcomes at various key points in previous chapters. Especially:
>
> - in Chapter 4 where the values of strategy-makers were recognised as a significant factor in their shaping of strategy. The point is clearly illustrated in the cases of Ali and Dina in *Tigermill* (pp. 180–3 and pp. 192–4) and Donna Dulsie in Strath Guitars (pp. 208–12) and theorised in the analysis of the relationship between organisational and managerial strategic exchange processes (pp. 213–18);
> - in Chapter 8's analysis of the interplay of contingencies and choices in the shaping of organisations (pp.255–66);
> - in Chapter 11's analysis of the interplay of contingencies and choices in the making of human resourcing strategies (pp. 390–6).

Given the ethical irrationality of the world, managers are not going to find a single clear and unified set of ethical principles that all their organisational decisions can be based upon. However, this does not mean there is not a *variety* of ethical schemes or sets of moral principles to which managers will make reference. It is precisely because the world is ethically irrational that human beings have had to *create* cultures and ethical and religious systems, as Weber pointed out.

> **Link** Chapter 4, pp. 110–14 argued that neither human society nor human 'sanity' are possible without cultures and that 'rules and moralities are at the heart of the sets of shared understandings and meanings' that constitute cultures.

There is in the world a complex plurality of cultural and ethical systems and this is a plurality to which managers have to be sensitive. Even if there were a single set of moral rules that were acceptable within and across cultures, it would not avoid people having to face moral dilemmas. Nor would it straightforwardly help them resolve dilemmas. The existence of shared cultures – at an organisational, a societal or even an international level – would simply make the ultimately ambiguous moral aspects of human existence more manageable by providing languages and criteria that human beings can use to debate and contest the rights and wrong of their actions. Glenn Ferness in Cases and

Conversations 12.3, we have shown, made use of more than one type of ethical criterion in developing her personal ethical orientation. She also, when looking at the corporate aspects of decision-making, looked to the plurality of values that impinged on things that the organisation might do: the value that customers would put on the employment reputation of Logies, for example, or the public's current view of the ethics of industrialised agriculture. While most of Logie's customers did not object to current food industry practices, it would not be in the interests of the organisation to move to the more expensive organic and locally-grown foods which Glenn and Chris would prefer, on personal ethical grounds, to sell. Should these values change, Logies could then realistically change its practices to fit better with the personal preferences of these two senior managers.

All of this analysis suggests that managers clearly cannot operate in an ethically neutral way. They are bound to attend to the ethical and cultural expectations of the various parties with which they 'trade'. But does this mean that managers simply *follow* the 'ethical flow' of the world in which their organisations operate? In large part, they do, given the logic of their work as helping the organisation survive into the future through processes of exchange with resource dependent constituencies, all of which bring a vast range of goals, interests and values into the exchange relationship. But to speak of managers 'going with the ethical flow' is to tell only part of the story. There are two basic possibilities for the individual manager.

First there is the possibility of taking an *ethically reactive* stance. This does mean 'going with the flow' of what is sought from their organisation by some of the constituencies with which they deal and which is supported or allowed by other constituencies. Thus if a nation state says it is legal for a company to sell tobacco products within their territory and sufficient customers are willing to pay for those products then the managers in that company may well decide that there is no ethical difficulty in producing and marketing products that are likely to harm the health of many of those who choose to buy them.

Second, there is the possibility of an *ethically assertive* stance. We see this at its simplest in the case of managers choosing not to work for an organisation that, say, makes tobacco products, sells armaments or buys material from what they regard as ethically suspect organisations. We see a stronger version of such a stance with the manager who decides to leave an organisation because of moral qualms about some of its activities (as when Glenn Ferness contemplated leaving Logies if they did not cease to use the supplier of fitness equipment). However, the strongest case of the ethically assertive managerial stance is that which we see exemplified in Glenn's general approach to her managerial work. We are left in no doubt about her strong moral concerns and we are also firmly made aware of her understanding of the role of expedience in managerial work. She brings these two things together with her concept of 'making a business case' for things which, privately, she wishes to bring about for moral reasons. She accepts this compromise, recognising that there is no 'shared set of values to which everyone can be expected to subscribe'. Things that she sees in a moral light might, she recognises, only be seen as 'ethical in the eyes of some of us'. She therefore only presses moral causes for which she believes she can make a 'business case'. 'Arguing the moral case', she has learned, 'gets you nowhere'. For a manager to talk too much in ethical terms is to suggest that he or she is 'less than fully focused on interests of the business'. Hence, Glenn works to further her 'cause' of increasing the proportion of women managers in Logies by arguing that the business is better served by using all the 'talents' available to it. This is much more likely to succeed than directly putting a moral case (in terms such as those of 'women's rights' or of 'equality' presumably). Similar arguments, together with warnings about a poor employer reputation potentially alienating customers, are used to persuade people to go along with other fair treatment policies in the shop.

Glenn Ferness is probably an unusually ethically aware and morally assertive manager and, in the 'competence' terms looked at earlier in this chapter, she appears to be an exceptionally able and, indeed, effective manager. Even in her case though, the scope for making the world a better, fairer or happier place is exceedingly limited. It is inevitably a great deal less for the average manager. Yet managerial decisions and actions, especially as they add up to form larger corporate and intercorporate patterns, make a significant difference to people's lives, as one organisational example after another in *Organising and Managing Work* has shown.

In spite of the very significant role that managerial work plays in modern societies, we cannot look to the managers of modern corporations to determine how people are going to live their lives in the future. Neither can we expect them to be the arbiters of the values and ethics that will guide the people's choices and actions, either as workers or as consumers. Indeed, to re-assert a value position that has been implicit throughout the writing of the present book, we *should not* look to managers to shape our world in this way. To do so would be to condone the type of *managerialism* that was identified as a potential pathology of modern social order in Chapter 2 (p. 53). If we have any belief in the values of democracy and political debate, we are bound to look to political and democratic institutions to balance and channel the considerable power exerted by corporate interests and their managerial servants. To help us most effectively engage in the sort of debates that are necessary both within work organisations and at the level of democratic societies, a critical social scientific study of the organising and managing of work has a modest but significant part to play.

People involved in managerial work are not simply the bigger cogs of an organisational machine whose job is to drive the smaller cogs in order to meet incontestable 'organisational goals'. They may not be free to pursue a moral agenda in the organisations that employ them but everything they do has inevitable political and ethical implications. Each manager has their own way of balancing their personal moral beliefs with the ethical pressures that their organisational situation imposes upon them. It has been suggested in this final chapter that managers are faced in the moral realm with both choices and constraints, as indeed they are in so many of the other aspects of their work that have been reviewed in this book. A choice that each manager can only make for themselves is that of whether they are going to be more or less assertively active in bringing a self-consciously ethical dimension into their work.

The logic of managerial work requires managers to act as agents for the organisations in whose name the activities that they try to shape are undertaken. It requires them to work alongside others to take those organisations forward into the future. Yet, as we have seen throughout the book, such work is full of choices as well as packed with complex challenges, endless ambiguities and inevitable conflicts of interest. *Organising and Managing Work* has not tried to prescribe how choices might be made, to suggest solutions to organisational challenges or to overcome the ambiguities that these choices and challenges entail. Instead, it has sought to offer thoughts, critical insights, concepts, theories and engaging stories that anyone involved in work organisations, in any way whatsoever, can use to inform their choices and practices.

Summary

In this chapter the following key points have been made:

- The management of change is best understood as an integral part of managerial work. This is the case because managing work involves dealing with human beings whose wants and expectations are constantly changing and because it has to handle, at the same time, the ever changing competitive pressures that are part of the dynamics of industrial capitalist economies and the markets within which organisations have to survive.

- Managerial talk that makes use of a notion of global, market, financial or technological 'drivers' can lead to an over-estimation of the extent to which managerial actions are *determined* by external circumstances. There are managerial choices as well as constraints when it comes to shaping work activities and devising patterns of work organisation for the future.

- The future of work is far more open that it is often believed to be. Human choices, among workers and consumers as well as among managers, may well see significant resistance to trends such as those towards the globalisation of human cultures, the development of virtual or networked organisations and the adoption of portfolio or 'boundaryless' careers.

- The development of trust relations, both within work organisations and between organisations and the external constituencies with which they strategically exchange, can be an important means towards making organisations effective and able to survive into the long term. High trust relations, together with high commitment employment relations, can help to make organisations *flexibly adaptive* and thus well placed to cope with pressures for innovation. However, there are also pressures on organisations to be able to make *short-term adjustments*, which can lead them to treat parts of their workforces in a low commitment and low trust way. This suggests that there will be both 'winners' and 'losers' in terms of the quality of work careers and rewards that will be available in the future.

- Individual managers vary in the abilities they bring to their managerial work. Personal orientations, cognitive abilities and the interpersonal styles all make a significant difference to the contribution that any particular manager is able to make, as are those ways of dealing both with one's self and one's relationships that are fashionably labelled as 'emotionally intelligent'. However, the extent to which managerial potential is translated into manager effectiveness, and hence into overall organisational effectiveness, involves more than the sum of the abilities to be found among managers. Those capacities come together in a complex set of managerial relationships and a division of labour in which strengths and weaknesses may or may not be balanced out to the organisation's overall advantage.

- Managerial work can never be carried out in an ethically or politically neutral way – it always and inevitably has value implications and ethical consequences. Managers who do not take the value implications of their actions into account are not only open to moral judgement by commentators on management or by critics of management, they are also unlikely to be successful in their work.

- There is no clear set of uncontested ethical principles to which managers can look to help them in handling the ethical dilemmas that inevitably arise in their work. What is right and wrong in any given situation is not only open to different interpretations by different people operating with different interests and values, it is also complicated by the fact that 'good' acts do not necessarily lead to 'good' outcomes – and vice versa.

- Moral criteria relevant to managerial practice are, in practice, drawn from the cultural (and, often, multi-cultural) contexts in which managers shape their lives and identities and do their jobs. *Ethical* considerations are mixed together in various different ways with considerations of *expedience*.

- The most significant way in which ethical or moral considerations come into managerial work is as a result of managers needing to take into account the values and priorities of all the groups with which their organisation deals. Managers have little option but to take notice of the value preferences and priorities of, for example, customers, clients, employees, potential employees, shareholders and, on the behalf of members of society generally, the nation state. Within all of this, however, some managers will be more ethically assertive than others but, if they do attempt to further a personal ethical agenda, they will generally find it necessary to justify what they propose in terms of the interests of the organisation rather than by giving a direct moral argument for what they wish to bring about.

- People involved in managerial work will continue to play a major role in the shaping of people's lives in the future. In a democratic system, however, it is not their place to determine what will and what will not be valued in the future or influence what is to be regarded as right and wrong.

Reading

Reading Guides 10, 11, 18, 23 and 25 contain material that supports and takes further much of what is covered in Chapter 12.

Concept guide

Alienation The destruction of the integrity of the human self – a splitting of one part of a person's 'being' from another.

Ambiguity (*see also* Uncertainty) Ambiguity exists when the *meaning* of a situation or an event is unclear or confused and is therefore open to a variety of interpretations.

Artefacts Objects that have been created by human hands. They often play a symbolic role within organisational cultures as well as fulfilling a practical function. A manager's desk is an artefact that plays both a practical and a symbolic role, a company flag plays almost exclusively a symbolic role.

Bounded rationality *see* Rationality, bounded.

Bureaucracy The control and coordination of work tasks through a hierarchy of appropriately qualified office holders, whose authority derives from their expertise and who rationally devise a system of rules and procedures that are calculated to provide the most appropriate means of achieving specified ends.

Business process re-engineering (BPR) The restructuring of an organisation to focus on business processes rather than on business functions. Advanced management control information technologies are used together with team working and employee 'empowerment'.

Capitalist labour process *see* Labour process, capitalist.

Career A sequence of social positions filled by a person throughout their life – or through an aspect of their life such as their involvement in work.

Career, subjective The way someone understands or makes sense of their movement through various social positions in the course of their life, or a part of their life.

Change management An integral part of all managerial work that (a) copes with the changing patterns of resource input and knowledge available to work organisations and the shifting demands made upon them by the parties with which they deal, and (b) initiates changes that managers perceive to be in their interests or the interests of those who employ them.

Closure, social The process whereby a group seeks to gain or defend its advantage over other groups by closing its ranks to those it defines as outsiders.

Collective bargaining A method of agreeing work conditions and rewards through a process of formal negotiations between employer representatives and the representatives of employees who are collectively organised, typically in a trade union.

Common sense, critical Analysis based on the basic logic, rationality, hard-headedness to be found in human beings whenever they step back from the immediate situation and critically put their minds to an issue or problem.

Common sense, everyday Analysis based on unthought-out, taken-for-granted, immediately 'obvious', everyday assumptions about the world and human activity within it.

Competence, manager (*see also* Effectiveness, manager) The possession of skills, knowledge and aptitudes that a manager can demonstrate in action and which *potentially* enables that manager to bring about completion of the tasks in their area of responsibility in a way which will make as great a possible contribution to the performance of the organisation and to its long-term survival.

Concepts Concepts are the working definitions that are chosen or devised to make possible a particular piece of scientific analysis. They are the way scientists define their terms for the purpose of a specific investigation. They therefore differ from dictionary definitions which tend to have a much more general applicability.

Conflict Comes about in organisations at two levels. There is (a) *conflict at the level of interests*, where there is difference between employers/managers and employees over desired outcomes (a difference that is not necessarily stated or immediately obvious) and (b) *conflict at the level of behaviour*, where parties seeking different outcomes either *directly* clash over those differences and engage in open dispute or *indirectly* express their differences through such gestures as grudging cooperation, destructive behaviour or generalised belligerence.

Constituencies, strategic All the parties with which an organisation exchanges are strategic in the sense that the exchanges made with them contribute to long-term survival. At any point in time, however, some constituencies are more strategic than others insofar as they create a greater degree of uncertainty with regard to the organisation's long-term future.

Contingencies, organisational *see* Organisational contingencies.

Contract, implicit The tacit agreement between an employing organisation and the employed individual about what the employee will 'put in' to the job and the rewards and benefits for which this will be exchanged.

Contract, manipulating employees' perceived implicit This is at the centre of all motivational, leadership and job design work done by managers. Tasks are shaped and rewards are offered as part of a bargaining process in which managers try to persuade employees to work in the way they want them to work.

Contra-culture *see* Subculture.

Contradiction, organisational The key contradiction is that between the organisation's need to *control* employees and its need to give employees *freedom* to take initiatives and apply discretion in their work. A tension therefore arises between pressures to make people controllable and pressures to allow them discretion.

Control, double control problem The pressure that is put on managers to manage the activities and thinking of others at the same time as they have to manage and shape their own identities, lives and personal projects.

Cooperation, productive The working together of people employed within, or otherwise involved in the organisation, to achieve the tasks that are undertaken in the organisation's name. This has to be achieved in the face of the tendency for people to pursue ends (often cooperatively) which are not consonant with efficient task fulfilment.

Critical common sense *see* Common sense, critical.

Culture The set of meanings shared by members of a human grouping which defines what is good and bad, right and wrong and consequently defines the appropriate ways for members of that group to think and behave.

Culture, organisational The set of meanings and values shared by members of an organisation that defines the appropriate ways for people to think and behave with regard to the organisation.

Deontology The investigation of the nature of duty or obligation. A deontological ethical position is one which says that to do the right thing is to do what is dutiful.

Directed evolution A style of strategic management in which continuous organisational adaptation occurs through processes of trial and error, opportunism, exchange, negotiation, experimentation and learning within a clear sense of general organisational direction and managerial priority.

Discourse A set of connected concepts, expressions and statements that constitutes a way of talking or writing about an aspect of the world, thus framing and influencing the way people understand and act with regard to that aspect of the world.

Discursive framing *see* Framing, discursive.

Division of labour, social or *general* The allocation of work tasks across society, typically into occupations or trades.

Division of labour, technical or *detailed* The breaking down of 'whole' occupational roles into specialised and generally unskilled jobs.

Double control problem *see* Control, double control problem.

Dual human resourcing strategy *see* Human resourcing strategy, dual.

Effectiveness and efficiency An action is judged to be *efficient* if it uses the most appropriate known means to achieve a given end but it is only judged to be *effective* if the action fulfils the intentions behind it.

Effectiveness, manager (*see also* Competence, manager; Effectiveness, organisational/managerial) The successful application of the skills, knowledge and aptitudes to the fulfilment of tasks in a manager's area of responsibility so that as great a possible contribution is made to the performance of the organisation as a whole and to its long-term survival.

Effectiveness, organisational and managerial The ability to satisfy the demands of the range of constituencies inside and outside the organisation so that continued support in terms of resources such as labour, custom, investment, supplies and legal approval is obtained and the organisation enabled to survive into the long term.

Efficiency *see* Effectiveness and efficiency.

Emotional intelligence An ability to take into account one's own emotions and the emotions of others when deciding how to manage one's own situation and one's relationships with those others.

Emotional labour An element of work activity in which the worker is required to display certain emotions in order to complete work tasks in the way required by an employer.

Emotions and feelings *Feelings* are sensations felt bodily which relate to a psychological state. *Emotions* are the way these sensations are made sense of with reference to culture, either privately or socially.

Employment A characteristic institution of both modern industrial capitalist societies and modern work organisations which involves an *exchange* or trade between the employer and the employee whereby certain effort and commitment is offered by the employee to the employer in return for certain monetary and other rewards.

Enacted environment *see* Environment, enacted.

Enactment *see* Environment, enacted.

Environment, enacted The environment of an organisation exists for members of an organisation by virtue of the interpretations they make of what is occurring 'outside' the organisation and the way their own actions influence or shape those occurrences.

Epistemology The investigation of the grounds on which knowledge can be treated as valid or 'true'.

Equity or balance theories of work motivation These theories show how work behaviour is influenced by how people perceive their situation after comparing their work/reward exchange (or 'implicit contract') with the employer to that of other members of the organisation.

Ethical irrationality of the world Judgements about what is right and wrong cannot be derived from rational or scientific analysis of the human condition given that no system of values can be established that will make every value consistent with every other or ensure that right actions always lead to right outcomes (or wrong actions necessarily lead to wrong outcomes).

Ethics The investigation of the moral principles that people apply to their behaviour. *Normative ethics* are sets of moral principles that guide people in their behaviour.

Ethnography A method of social science research in which the subjects are directly observed in their normal pattern of living, with a view to the researcher producing an account of the cultural lives of those research subjects.

Everyday common sense *see* Common sense, everyday.

Exchange *see* Strategic exchange.

Expectancy theories of work motivation These theories show how work behaviour is influenced (a) by the particular wants and expectations which particular employees, in particular circumstances, bring to the organisation and (b) by the extent to which these are met by the employer.

Flexibility Managers of organisations look for two types of flexibility: (a) *flexibility for long-term adaptability*: the ability to make rapid and effective innovations through the use of job designs and employment policies that encourage people to use their discretion and work in new ways for the sake of the organisation – as circumstances require; and (b) *flexibility for short-term predictability*: the ability to make rapid changes through the use of job designs and employment policies that allow staff to be easily recruited and trained or easily laid off – as circumstances require.

Flexible firm, the An organisational pattern in which an organisation seeks some of its human resourcing from a *core workforce* whose members are given employment security, high rewards and skill enhancement opportunities in return for a willingness to adapt and innovate and a *peripheral* workforce whose members are given more specific tasks and less commitment of continuing employment or skill enhancement.

Foundationalism The use of large explanatory systems of ideas to make sense of human history and society – whether these be drawn from religious, scientific or philosophical thought.

Framing, discursive (*see also* Discourse) The process whereby human beings draw on sets of discursive resources (concepts, expressions, statements, etc.) made available in their culture to make sense of a particular aspect of their lives and are thereby influenced in the way they conduct themselves in that part of their life.

Fordism A combining of mass production de-skilled job design in the industrial workplace with employment and state welfare policies that develop workers as both fit workers and willing consumers of the products of industry.

Functionalism A form of social science theorising in which the form and existence of social institutions, or aspects of them, are explained in terms of the functions they fulfil. It should not be confused with *functional analysis*, in which the functions of activities or institutions ('management' for example) are identified without committing the *functionalist error* of explaining the existence of the institution in terms of its function. Just because an institution functions in a certain way, this does not mean that is how or why it came into existence.

Garbage can model of organisational choice Organisational decisions are influenced by the various problems that are around at the time of the decision; the various available solutions which might be attached to these problems; the people who are around at the time; the amount of time these people have available.

Globalisation A trend in which the economic, cultural and political activities of people across the world come to be increasingly interdependent and similar.

Heroes and villains, organisational Characters referred to in organisational stories, jokes, legends, myths and sagas who are used either as inspirational figures ('role models') that current organisational members are encouraged to emulate or as extreme indulgers in behaviours that people in the organisation are meant to avoid.

High trust relations *see* Trust relations, high.

Human resource management That part of managerial work which is concerned with acquiring, developing and dispensing with the efforts, skills and capabilities of an organisation's workforce and maintaining organisational relationships within which these human resources can be utilised to enable the organisation to continue into the future.

Human resources The efforts, skills or capabilities which people contribute to a work organisation as part of an employment exchange (or a more temporary labour engagement) and which are managerially utilised to enable the organisation to complete tasks carried out in its name, and to continue its existence into the future.

Human resourcing strategy The general direction followed by an organisation in how it secures, develops, utilises and, from time to time, dispenses with human resources of effort, skill and capability to enable it to continue into the long term.

Human resourcing strategy, dual A dual human resourcing strategy exists where an organisation applies (a) a high commitment ('relationship') HR strategy involving a long-term employment relationship to core workers and managers and (b) a low commitment ('transactional') HR strategy to more peripheral suppliers of labour (sometimes involving an employment relationship, sometimes involving a market relationship).

Ideal type A model of a phenomenon or a situation which describes what it would look like if it existed in a pure form. It provides, in effect, a benchmark against which actually occurring cases of the phenomenon can be compared. It is often used to characterise 'bureaucracy' but could equally effectively be used in the analysis of 'fascism' or 'serial murder'. 'Ideal' in this context has nothing to do with desirability.

Identity Identity is a notion of who a particular person is – in relation to others. It defines in what ways the individual is like other people and in what ways they differ from other people. It has a *self-identity* component (the individual's own notion of self) and a *social-identity* component (the notion others have of who the person is).

Implicit contract *see* Contract, implicit.

Implicit contract, managerial manipulation of *see* Contract, manipulating employees' perceived implicit.

Indulgency pattern The ignoring by supervisors or managers of selected rule infringements by workers in return for those workers conceding to requests that, strictly speaking, they could refuse.

Instrumental, rationality *see* Rationality, instrumental.

Jargon Language use and terms that are peculiar to a specific cultural setting or group context.

Job design/redesign practices (*see also* Work design) The shaping of particular jobs, especially with regard to how narrow or broad the tasks associated with those jobs are and the extent to which jobholders exercise discretion in carrying out those tasks.

Job enrichment The expansion of the scope of jobs by such means as the re-integration of maintenance or inspection tasks; an extension of the work cycle; an increased degree of delegation of decision-making by job holders.

Jokes Humorous stories or pranks engaged in to cause amusement.

Knowledge management Practices which encourage the acquisition, creation, sharing, manipulation and developing of knowledge (recognised as ways of understanding the world as well as having information about it) within an organisation in order to enhance the effective performance of that organisation and, hence, its strategic success.

Labour process, capitalist In Marxian analysis this is the process whereby managers design, control and monitor work activities in order to extract surplus value from the labour activity of employees on behalf of the capital-owning class who employ them.

Lean production The combining, typically within car assembly, of teamworking with automated technologies. Workers are required both to initiate 'continual improvements' in quality and to ensure that every task is got 'right first time' and completed to a demanding 'just-in-time' schedule.

Learning organisation An organisation in which experimentation, reflection and mutual learning are normal aspects of the work of all organisational members and in which learning provides a key source of satisfaction for individuals as well as enabling the organisation to be innovative and productively adaptive.

Legends, organisational Narratives about events that might or might not have happened in the organisation's past, which have a sense of wonder about them and which point to activities that the listener is encouraged to admire or deplore.

Logical incrementalism An alternative to top-down strategic planning in which strategic development happens in incremental and experimental steps that are taken within a sense of a broad organisational direction or strategic logic.

Management As a *function* management is the overall shaping of relationships, understandings and processes within a work organisation to bring about the completion of the tasks undertaken in the organisation's name in such a way that the organisation continues into the future. As an *activity*, management is the bringing about of this 'shaping' and as a *group of people*, management is the set of organisational employees given official responsibility for fulfilling or carrying out the shaping of relationships, understandings and processes.

Management, the modernist conception of managerial work This sees managers as specialised 'experts' within work organisations who rationally analyse the tasks for which the organisation was set up and the resources required to complete them and, in the light of these analyses, design work systems which achieve sufficient control over work activities to ensure successful task completion.

Manager competence *see* Competence, manager.

Manager effectiveness *see* Effectiveness, manager.

Managerialism A belief that modern societies, and the institutions within them, should be run by qualified managers who can organise society rationally on the basis of their expert knowledge – thus replacing the divisiveness and inefficiency of debate and democracy.

Managism A belief that there is a distinctive managerial expertise based on a body of objective management knowledge which managers should apply to enable them rationally to design, maintain and drive organisational systems in the same way that expert engineers design, maintain and drive machines.

Manipulating employees' perceived implicit contract *see* Contract, manipulating employees' perceived implicit.

Micropolitics/organisational politics Processes occurring within work organisations as individuals, groups and organisational 'sub-units' compete for access to scarce and valued material and symbolic resources.

Mischief, organisational Activities occurring within the workplace that (a) according to the official structure, culture, rules and procedures of the organisation, 'should not happen' and (b) contain an element of challenge to dominant modes of operating or to dominant interests in the organisation.

Modernism The key principle of modernism is the application of rational or scientific analysis to social, political and economic affairs – work organisation included – to achieve greater human control over the world and to bring about general progress in the condition of humankind.

Modernity A period of human social existence dominated by the following of the principles of modernism.

Motivation *see* Equity and Expectancy theories of work motivation.

Myths, organisational Narratives about events that are unlikely ever to have happened but which illustrate some important 'truth' about life in the organisation.

Narratives and stories *Narratives* are accounts of the world which follow a basic form of 'this, then that, then that' and which, when applied to human affairs, typically take on a more developed *story*-like form involving characters with interests, motives, emotions and moralities.

Negotiated order, in organisations The pattern of organisational activities that has arisen or emerged over time as an outcome of the interplay of the variety of interests, understandings, reactions and initiatives of the individuals and groups involved in the organisation.

Norms of behaviour, organisational Regularly recurring pieces of behaviour that become accepted in the organisation as 'the way things are done'.

Official and unofficial aspects of organisations *Official* aspects of organisations are all the rules, activities and values that are part of the formally managerially sanctioned policies and procedures. *Unofficial* aspects are the rules, activities and values that people at all levels in the organisation develop but which do not have formal managerial sanction.

Ontology The investigation of the nature of being. It might consider, for example, in what sense a work organisation can be said to 'exist'.

Open systems thinking *see* Systems thinking, open.

Organisational and managerial effectiveness *see* Effectiveness, organisational and managerial.

Organisational contingencies Organisational circumstances like size, main technology or environment with which organisational structures and cultures need to *fit* or *match* if the organisation is going to function successfully.

Organisational/corporate strategy *see* Strategy, organisational/corporate.

Organisational mischief *see* Mischief, organisational.

Organisations, work Work arrangements involving relationships, understandings and processes in which people are employed, or their services otherwise engaged, to complete tasks undertaken in the organisation's name.

Orientation, work The meaning individuals attach to their work which predisposes them both to think and act in particular ways with regard to that work. There is an *initial orientation* at the point of entry to work and this is liable to change as circumstances and interests change within the continuing employment relationship.

Paradox of consequences, in organisations (*see also* Contradiction, organisational) The tendency of the means chosen to achieve ends in organisations to undermine or defeat the very ends for which they have been adopted.

Portfolio or boundaryless career A pattern of working in which the individual does not enter an employment relationship with a single work organisation but is engaged by a variety of different organisations on a task-by-task or project-by-project basis.

Positivism A view of the social sciences that sees them as equivalent to the natural or physical sciences and therefore able to use the same basic investigative procedures. It regards the social world as a reality external to those who study it and, in its classical form, saw the role of social science as one of helping predict and therefore control social phenomena and events.

Postmodernism A way of looking at the world that rejects attempts to build systematic (or 'foundationalist') explanations of history and society and which, instead, concentrates on the ways in which human beings 'invent' their worlds, especially through the use of language or 'discourse'.

Postmodernity A way of organising human social existence that has rejected the key principles of modernity.

Power The capacity of an individual or group to affect the outcome of any situation so that access is achieved to whatever resources are scarce and desired within a society or a part of that society.

Power, strategic contingency theory of A sub-unit of an organisation will have greater relative power or influence within the organisation the more it (a) is central to the organisation's workflow, (b) cannot be substituted by another unit, (c) reduces uncertainties perceived to be of strategic significance to the organisation.

Pragmatism This, in a general sense, is simply a matter of being sensible, practical or realistic about the world. *Pragmatism*, in a more specific sense, is a philosophical approach that evaluates theories or beliefs in terms of their effects upon practice. We judge one theory to be better than another, for example, if it is more likely to guide us towards success in a project to which both theories have relevance.

Process-relational thinking A way of understanding human beings and their social arrangements which recognises that both of these are *emergent* (always in a process of 'becoming'). It refuses to see human identities and social arrangements (such as work organisations) as fixed entities. It also recognises that human individuality is *relational* (only existing in relation to others) and that social institutions are the creations of ongoing human relationships and interactions.

Productive cooperation *see* Cooperation, productive.

Rationality, bounded The human ability to calculate the most appropriate means of achieving a specified end is limited, or bounded, in two ways: (a) only a small proportion of all the knowledge or information which is potentially relevant to any rational analysis can ever be obtained and (b) the human mind would only cope with a fraction of all the relevant information, were it obtainable.

Rationality, instrumental The calculated choice of appropriate means to achieve specified ends.

Reification/personification The error of treating an abstraction as if it were a concrete 'thing' or a living person. The error is committed, for example, if one talks of an organisation 'making one do something'. Such talk obscures, if not denies, the role of human agency, power or choice in whatever it was that the person was 'made to do'.

Rites, organisational Rituals that are relatively formally (though not necessarily officially) organised and pre-planned.

Rituals, organisational Patterns of behaviour that regularly occur in particular circumstances or at particular times in an organisation.

Sagas, organisational Narratives with a series of events that are said to have unfolded over time and which constitute an important part of the organisation's history.

Scientific management (Taylorism) Work design principles that maximise the amount of discretion over task performance given to managerial experts, who calculate and precisely define how each job is to be carried out.

Self *see* Identity.

Self-actualisation An idealised state of existence in which the human being becomes everything that a human being could possibly be.

Semi-autonomous workgroups *see* Teamworking/semi-autonomous workgroups.

Sense-making A concept increasingly used instead of 'interpretation' – to emphasise the 'active' element of people's efforts to give meaning to phenomena.

Social closure *see* Closure, social.

Social construction The process whereby people, through cultural interaction, give meaning to the world in which they find themselves. It is assumed that the world can only be known by human beings through language-based processes of cultural interpretation and sense-making. Its use should not be taken to imply that there is no world beyond language. The world is only meaningful to us – given a 'reality' – when people make sense of it through language and culture.

Social or *general* division of labour *see* Division of labour, social or *general*.

Socio-technical systems *see* Systems, socio-technical.

Stories *see* Narratives and stories.

Strategic choices Managerial choices about the basic way an organisation is shaped and the relationships it has with the parties with whom it exchanges and which influence the long-term future of the organisation.

Strategic constituences *see* Constituencies, strategic.

Strategic economising (minimised resource outflow within long-term viability) The principle whereby organisations allocate to constituencies upon whom they are *resource dependent* the least costly level of demand compliance that is possible without the constituency withdrawing the level of resource support that is necessary for long-term survival.

Strategic exchange As both individuals and organisations shape themselves and are shaped to continue their existence into the future, the exchange of material and symbolic resources occurs (a) between individuals and others in their social worlds (including employing organisations) and (b) between organisations and their internal and external constituencies upon which they are resource dependent (including employees). An individual taking employment with a work organisation, for example, makes a strategic exchange with that organisation to the extent that their life and circumstances are shaped by that involvement. And the organisation makes a strategic exchange with that individual – in the same way that it does with other constituencies like customers, suppliers and shareholders – to the extent that the organisation's future is going to be shaped by that exchange.

Strategic intent A statement of a clear and specific strategic position that an organisation's management aspires to reach at a specified time in the future and to which employees are persuaded to commit themselves and actively work towards.

Strategic management The element of managerial work that concerns itself with taking the organisation as a whole forward into the long term.

Strategy, organisational/corporate The pattern to be seen emerging over time as actions are taken that enable an organisation to continue into the future.

Stress A sense of distress arising because of pressures experienced in certain social or economic circumstances that render the sufferer emotionally, and sometimes physically, incapable of continuing to behave in the ways expected of them in those circumstances.

Structure, organisational The regular or persisting patterns of action that give shape and a degree of predictability to an organisation.

Subculture/contra-culture A *subculture* may be identified where a section of an organisation follows a cultural pattern that is a variation of the main organisational pattern of meanings and values. When such a pattern includes values that contradict the main organisational ones it is sometimes called a *contra-culture*.

Symbol Any act, word, sound or object acts as a symbol when it stands for 'something else' that is not visible, audible or tangible.

Systems-control thinking A way of understanding human beings and their social arrangements that sees both of these as controllable *entities* which take in various inputs and convert them into outputs. Systems-control views of organisations emphasise the controlling role of managers, who are seen as designing, engineering and maintaining organisations as social entities that have an existence separate from the people and activities that are associated with them. Systems-control views of human beings tend to treat organisational members as relatively fixed individual entities with given *personalities* who are amenable to managerial control through the meeting of their individual system *needs* by managers, who thus *motivate* them to act as the organisational system requires.

Systems thinking, open A way of analysing any complex entity in terms of system inputs, system outputs and an internal conversion process – with communication links or 'control actions' monitoring the outputs to enable any necessary process adjustments to be made.

Systems, socio-technical An approach to work design in which the technical and the social/psychological aspects of the overall workplace are given equal weight and are designed at the same time to *take each other into account*.

Teamworking/semi-autonomous workgroups The grouping of individual jobs to focus work activities on a *whole task*, with team members being fully trained and equipped so that they can be given discretion, as a group, over how the task is completed.

Technical or *detailed* division of labour *see* Division of labour, technical or *detailed*.

Technocracy Rule by experts (*see* Managerialism, which is a version of technocracy).

Technologies Technologies are the applications to task fulfilment of combinations of machines and other material artefacts with associated techniques and knowledge.

Theories Systematic generalisations about the world which are one of the main products of scientific work.

Trust relations, high A situation in which each party to a relationship feels able to take it for granted that broad mutual expectations established between them will be met and continue to be met, without the need closely to specify those expectations or to monitor their fulfilment.

Uncertainty (*see also* Ambiguity) Uncertainty exists when the *understanding* of a future situation or event is unclear or confused and is therefore open to a variety of interpretations.

Virtual or networked organisations Sets of work arrangements in which those undertaking tasks carried out under a corporate name largely relate to each other through electronic communications rather than through face-to-face interaction.

Work design/redesign principles (*see also* Job design and Job enrichment) General principles about how narrow or broad the tasks associated with jobs should be and the extent to which jobholders should use discretion in carrying out those tasks.

Work organisations *see* Organisations, work.

Work Organisation and Management Studies The analysis of the human aspects of work organisation and its management which draws on the social sciences to develop insights, theories and research findings with a view to informing the choices, decisions and actions of people who have a practical involvement with organisations.

Work orientation *see* Orientation, work.

Reading guides

Reading Guide 1 The nature and study of organisations

Aldrich, H.E. (1999) *Organizations Evolving*, London: Sage

Aldrich, H.E. (1979) *Organizations and Environments*, Englewood Cliffs, NJ: Prentice-Hall

Alvesson, M. and Deetz, S. (1996) 'Critical theory and postmodernism approaches to organizational studies' in S.R. Clegg, C. Hardy and W. Nord (eds) *Handbook of Organization Studies*, London: Sage, 191–217

Astley, W.G. (1985) 'Administration science as socially constructed truth', *Administrative Science Quarterly*, 30: 497–513

Astley, W.G. and Van de Ven, A.H. (1983) 'Central perspectives and debates in organization theory, *Administrative Science Quarterly*, 28: 245–270

Baum, J.A.C. (1996) 'Organizational ecology' in S.R. Clegg, C. Hardy and W. Nord (eds) *Handbook of Organization Studies*, London: Sage, 77–114

Bittner, E. (1965) 'The concept of organization', *Social Research*, 32: 239–255

Blau, P.M. and Scott, R.G. (1963) *Formal Organizations*, London: Routledge

Boje, D.M.G., Robert, P. Jr and Thatchenkery, T.J. (eds) (1996) *Postmodern Management and Organization Theory*, London: Sage

Brown, R.K. (1992) *Understanding Industrial Organisations*, London: Routledge

Burrell, G. (1997) *Pandemonium*: *towards a Retro-organization Theory*, London: Sage

Burrell, G. and Morgan, G. (1979) *Sociological Paradigms and Organizational Analysis*, London: Heinemann

Campbell, D. (2000) *The Socially Constructed Organization*, London: Carnac

Carroll, C.R. (1988) *Ecological Models of Organizations*, Cambridge, Mass: Ballinger

Carroll, C.R. (1984) 'Organizational Ecology', *Annual Review of Sociology*, 10: 71–93

Checkland, P.B. (1981) *Systems Thinking, Systems Practice*, Chichester: Wiley

Checkland, P.B. and Scholes, J. (1990) *Soft Systems Methodology in Action*, Chichester: Wiley

Chia, R. (ed.) (1998) *In the Realm of Organization: Essays for Robert Cooper*, London: Routledge

Chia, R. (1995) 'From modern to postmodern thinking styles: implications for organizational analysis', *Organizational Studies*, 10(4): 579–604

Child, J. (1984) *Organization: A Guide to Problems and Practice*, London: Harper & Row

Clegg, S.R. (1990) *Modern Organizations: organization studies in the postmodern world*, London: Sage

Clegg, S.R. and Hardy, C. (1996) 'Organizations, organization and organizing' in S.R. Clegg, C. Hardy and W. Nord (eds) *Handbook of Organization Studies*, London: Sage, 1–27

Clegg, S.R., Hardy, C. and Nord, W. (eds) (1996) *Handbook of Organization Studies*, London: Sage

Cooper, R. (1986) 'Organization/disorganization', *Social Science Information*, 25(2): 299–335

Cooper, R. and Burrell, G. (1988) 'Modernism, postmodernism and organisational analysis: an introduction', *Organisation Studies* 9(1): 91–112

Cooper, R. and Law, J. (1995) 'Organization: distal and proximal views' in S. Bacharach, P. Gagliardi and B. Mundell (eds) *Research in the Sociology of Organizations (Vol. 13): studies of organizations in the European tradition*, Greenwich, CT: JAI Press

Czarniawska-Joerges, B. (1993) *The Three-dimensional Organisation: a constructionist view*, Bromley, Kent: Chartwell-Bratt

Day, R.A. and Day, J. (1997) 'A review of the current state of negotiated order theory: an appreciation and critique', *Sociological Quarterly*, 18: 126–142

Donaldson, L. (1996) *For Positivist Organization Theory*, London: Sage

Emery, F.E. (ed.) (1969) *Systems Thinking*, Harmondsworth: Penguin

Fincham, R. and Rhodes, P.S. (1998) *The Individual, Work and Organization*, third edn, Oxford: Oxford University Press

Fineman, S. and Gabriel, Y. (1996) *Experiencing Organizations*, London: Sage

Gabriel Y. (ed.) (1999) *Organizations in Depth*, London: Sage

Gabriel, Y., Fineman, S. and Sims, D. (2000) *Organizing and Organizations: an introduction*, second edn, London: Sage

Gillespie, R. (1991) *Manufacturing Knowledge: A History of the Hawthorne Experiments*, Cambridge: Cambridge University Press

Grant, D., Keenoy, T. and Oswick, C. (eds) (1998) *Discourse and Organisation*, London: Sage

Hannan, M.T. and Freeman, J.H. (1977) 'The population ecology of organisations', *American Journal of Sociology*, 82: 929–964

Hassard, J. and Parker, M. (eds) (1994) *Towards a New Theory of Organizations*, London: Routledge

Hassard, J. and Parker, M. (eds) (1993) *Postmodernism and Organizations*, London: Sage

Hassard, J. and Pym, D. (eds) (1990) *The Theory and Philosophy of Organizations: critical issues and perspectives*, London: Routledge

Hatch, M.-J. (1997) *Organization Theory: Modern, Symbolic and Postmodern Perspectives*, Oxford: Oxford University Press

Jackson, N. and Carter, P. (2000) *Rethinking Organisational Behaviour*, Harlow: FT Prentice-Hall

Klein, L. and Eason, K. (1991) *Putting Social Science to Work*, Cambridge: Cambridge University Press

March, J.G. and Simon, H.A. (1958) *Organizations*, New York: Wiley

Meyer, J.W. and Rowan, B. (1977) 'Institutionalized organizations: formal structure as myth and ceremony', *American Journal of Sociology*, 83(2): 340–63

Miller, E.J. and Rice, A.K. (1967) *Systems of Organization: the control of task and sentient boundaries*, London: Tavistock

Morgan, G. (1997) *Images of Organization: New Edition*, London: Sage

Morgan, G. (1990) *Organizations in Society*, London: Macmillan

Morgan, G. (1989) *Creative Organization Theory: A Resourcebook*, London: Sage

Mullins, L. (1999) *Management and Organizational Behaviour*, fifth edition, London: FT Pitman

Nicholson, N. (1995) *The Blackwell Encyclopedic Dictionary of Organizational Behaviour*, Oxford: Blackwell

Perrow, C. (1986) *Complex Organizations: a Critical Essay*, third edn, New York: Random House.

Pfeffer, J. (1993) 'Barriers to the advance of organizational science: paradigm development as a dependent variable', *Academy of Management Review*, 18(4): 599–620

Pfeffer, J. and Salancik, G.R. (1976) *The External Control of Organisations: a resource dependence approach*, New York: Harper and Row

Reed, M. (1996) 'Organization theorizing: a historically contested terrain', in S.R. Clegg, C. Hardy and W. Nord (eds) *Handbook of Organization Studies*, London: Sage, 31–56

Reed, M. (1992) *The Sociology of Organisations: themes, perspectives and prospects*, London: Harvester Wheatsheaf

Reed, M. (1990) 'From paradigms to images: the paradigm warrior turns post-modernist guru', *Personnel Review*, 19(3): 25–40

Reed, M. (1985) *New Directions in Organisational Analysis*, London: Tavistock

Reed, M. and Hughes, M. (1992) *Rethinking Organization*, London: Sage

Roethlisberger, F.J. (1968) *Man-in-Organization*, Cambridge, Mass: Belknap Press of Harvard University Press

Roethlisberger, F.J. and Dickson, W.J. (1939) *Management and the Worker*, Cambridge, Mass: Harvard University Press

Rowlinson, M. (1997) *Organisations and Institutions*, Basingstoke: Macmillan

Scott, W.R. (1995) *Institutions and Organizations*, London: Sage

Scott, W.R. and Christensen, S. (eds) (1995) *The Institutional Construction of Organizations: International and Longitudinal Studies*, London: Sage

Scott, W.R. and Meyer, J.W. (1994) *Institutional Environments and Organisations*, Newbury Park, Cal: Sage

Silverman, A. (1970) *The Theory of Organisations*, London: Heinemann

Sorge, A. and Warner, M. (eds) (1997) *The Handbook of Organizational Behaviour*, London: International Thomson Business Press

Strati, A. *Organization Studies: theory and method*, London: Sage

Strauss, A., Schatzman, L., Erlich, D., Bucher, R. and Sabsin, M. (1963) 'The hospital and its negotiated order' in Friedson, E. (ed.) *The Hospital in Modern Society*, New York: Macmillan

Thompson, J.D. (1967) *Organizations in Action*. New York: McGraw-Hill

Thompson, P. (1993) 'Postmodernism: fatal distraction' in J. Hassard and M. Parker, (eds) *Postmodernism and Organizations*, London: Sage

Tolbert, P.S. and Zucker, L.G. (1996) 'The institutionalization of institutional theory' in S.R. Clegg, C. Hardy and W. Nord (eds) *Handbook of Organization Studies*, London: Sage, 190–217

Tsoukas, H. (1994) *New Thinking in Organisational Behaviour*, Oxford: Butterworth-Heinemann

Tsoukas, H. (1992) 'Panoptic reason and the search for totality: a critical assessment of the critical systems perspective', *Human Relations*, 45(7): 637–657

Van Maanen, J. (1995) 'Fear and loathing in organization studies', *Organization Science* 6(6): 687–692

Watson, T.J. (2001a) 'Formal and informal organization' in N.J. Smelser and P.B. Baltes (eds) *International Encyclopedia of the Social and Behaviour Sciences*, Amsterdam: Elsevier

Watson, T.J. (2001b) 'Negotiated orders, in organizations' in N.J. Smelser and P.B. Baltes (eds) *International Encyclopedia of the Social and Behaviour Sciences*, Amsterdam: Elsevier

Wilson, F. (1999) *Organizational Behaviour: A Critical Introduction*, Oxford: Oxford University Press

Willmott, H. (1998) 'Re-cognizing the Other: reflections on a new sensibility in social and organization studies' in R. Chia (ed.) *In the Realm of Organization*, London: Routledge

Reading Guide 2 The nature and study of management

Anthony, P.D. (1986) *The Foundation of Management*, London: Tavistock

Barnard, C.I. (1938) *The Functions of the Executive*, Cambridge, Mass: Harvard University Press

Burnham, J. (1945) *The Managerial Revolution*, Harmondsworth: Penguin

Carroll, S.J. and Gillen, D.J. (1987) 'Are the classical management functions useful in describing work?', *Academy of Management Review*, 12(1): 38–51

Child, J. (1969) *British Management Thought*, London: Allen & Unwin

Earl, M.J. (ed.) (1983) *Perspectives on Management*, Oxford University Press

Eccles, R.G. and Nohria, N. (1992) *Beyond the Hype: rediscovering the essence of management*, Cambridge, Mass: Harvard Business School

Fayol, H. (1949, originally 1916) *General and Industrial Management*, London: Pitman

Fletcher, C. (1973) 'The end of management' in J. Child (ed.) *Man and Organisation*, London: Allen & Unwin, 135–157

Follet, M.P. (1941) *Dynamic Administration*, London: Pitman

Gowler, D. and Legge, K. (1996) 'The meaning of management and the management of meaning: a view from social anthropology' in S. Linstead, R. Grafton Small and P. Jeffcutt (eds) (1996) *Understanding Management*, London: Sage

Grint, K. (1995), *Management: a sociological introduction*, Cambridge: Polity

Gulick, L.H. (1973) 'Notes on the theory of organisation' in L.H. Gulick and L.F. Urwick (eds) *Papers on the Science of Administration*, New York: Columbia University Press

Gulick, L.H. and Urwick, L.F. (eds) (1937) *Papers on the Science of Administration*, New York: Columbia University Press

Hales, C. (1993) *Managing Through Organisations*, London: Routledge

Knights, D. and Willmott, H. (1999) *Management Lives: Power and Identity in Work Organizations*, London: Sage

Lawrence, P. (1996) 'Through a glass darkly: towards a characterization of British management' in I. Glover and M. Hughes (eds) *The Professional Managerial Class*, Aldershot: Avebury

Lennie, I. (1999) *Beyond Management*, London: Sage

Linstead, S., Grafton Small, R. and Jeffcutt, P. (eds) (1996) *Understanding Management*, London: Sage

Mangham, I.L. (1990) 'Managing as a Performing Art', *British Journal of Management*, 1: 105–115

Mant, A. (1979) *The Rise and Fall of the British Manager*, London: Pan

Marglin, S. (1980) 'The origins and function of hierarchy in capitalist production' in T. Nichols (ed.) *Capital and Labour*, Glasgow: Fontana

Mintzberg, H. (1989) *Mintzberg on Management*, New York: Collier-Macmillan

Mintzberg, H. (1977) 'The manager's job: folklore and fact', *Harvard Business Review*, 55(4): 49–61

Palmer, I. and Hardy, C. (1999) *Thinking about Management: Organizational Debates in Practice*, London: Sage

Pascale, R.T. and Athos, A.G. (1982) *The Art of Japanese Management*, Harmondsworth: Penguin

Pfeffer, J. (1981) 'Management as symbolic action' in L.L. Cummings and B.M. Staw (eds) *Research in Organisational Behaviour*, vol. 4, Greenwich, CT: JAI Press

Pugh, D.S. (ed.) (1995) *History of Management Thought*, Aldershot: Dartmouth

Reed, M.I. (1989) *The Sociology of Management*, Brighton: Harvester Wheatsheaf

Reed. M.I. (1984) 'Management as a social practice', *Journal of Management Studies*, 21:3

Selznick, P. (1957) *Leadership and Administration*, Evanston, Ill: Row, Peterson

Smith, V. (1990) *Managing in the Corporate Interest: control and resistance in an American bank*, Berkeley: University of California Press

Stewart, R. (1986) *The Reality of Management*, second edn, London: Heinemann

Teulings, A.W.M. (1986) 'Managerial labour processes in organized capitalism: the power of corporate management and the powerlessness of the manager' in D. Knights and H. Willmott (eds) *Managing the Labour Process*, Aldershot: Gower, 142–165

Thomas, A. (1993) *Controversies in Management*, London: Routledge

Tsoukas, H. (1994) 'What is management? An outline of a metatheory', *British Journal of Management*, 5(4): 289–301

Watson, T.J. (2001), *In Search of Management* (revised edn), London: Thomson Learning (originally 1994)

Watson, T.J (2000) 'Managerial practice and interactive social science', *Science and Public Policy*, 27(3): 31–38

Watson, T.J. (1997) 'Theorising managerial work: a pragmatic pluralist approach to interdisciplinary research', *British Journal of Management*, 8 (special issue): 3–8

Watson, T.J. (1994) 'Managing, crafting and researching: words, skill and imagination in shaping management research', *British Journal of Management*, 5 (special issue): 77–87

Whitley, R. (1989) 'On the nature of managerial tasks and skills', *Journal of Management Studies*, 26(3): 209–24

Whitley, R. (1984) 'The scientific status of management research as a practicality-oriented social science', *Journal of Management Studies*, 21(4): 369–390

Whittington, R. (1992) 'Putting Giddens into action: social systems and managerial agency', *Journal of Management Studies*, 29(6): 693–112

Willmott, H. (1997) 'Management and organization studies as science?', *Organization*, 4(3): 309–344

Willmott, H. (1987) 'Studying managerial work: a critique and a proposal', *Journal of Management Studies*, 24: 249–70

Wren, D.S. (1994) *The Evolution of Management Thought*, New York: Wiley

Reading Guide 3 Human identity, culture and language

Austin, J.L. (1962) *How to do Things with Words*, Oxford: Oxford University Press

Bahktin, M.M. (1981) *The Dialogic Imagination*, Austin: University of Texas Press

Baumeister, R.F. (1986) *Identity: Cultural Change and the Struggle for Self*, New York: Oxford University Press

Berger, P.L. and Luckmann, T. (1971) *The Social Construction of Reality*, Harmondsworth: Penguin

Billig, M. (1987) *Arguing and Thinking: a rhetorical approach to social psychology*, Cambridge: Cambridge University Press

Blau, P. (1964) *Exchange and Power in Social Life*, New York: Wiley

Boden, D. (1994) *The Business of Talk*, Cambridge: Polity

Breakwell, G.M. (1986) *Coping with Threatened Identities*, London: Macmillan

Clark, H., Chandler, J. and Barry, J. (1994) *Organisations and Identities*, London: Chapman and Hall

Dachler, H.P. and Hosking, D.-M. (1995) 'The primacy of relations in socially constructing organisational realities' in D.-M. Hosking, H.P. Dachler and K.J. Gergen (eds) *Management and Organisation: relational alternatives to individualism*, Aldershot: Avebury

Davis, J. (1992) *Exchange*, Milton Keynes: Open University Press

du Gay, P. (1995) *Consumption and Identity at Work*, London: Sage

Edwards, D. and Potter, J. (1992), *Discursive Psychology*, London: Sage

Foucault, M. (1980) *Power/Knowledge: selected interviews and other writings*, Brighton: Harvester

Foucault, M. (1979) *The History of Sexuality Vol. 1*, Harmondsworth: Penguin Books

Geertz, C. (1973) *Interpretations of Culture*, New York: Basic Books

Gergen K.J. (1999) *An Invitation to Social Construction*, London: Sage

Gergen, K. (1994) *Toward Social Transformation in Social Knowledge*, second edn, London: Sage

Giddens, A. (1991) *Modernity and Self-identity: self and society in the modern age*, Cambridge: Polity

Giddens, A. (1984) *The Constitution of Society: outline of the theory of structuration*, Cambridge: Polity

Goffman, E. (1958) *The Presentation of Self in Everyday Life*, Harmondsworth: Penguin

Harré, R. and Gillet, G. (1994) *The Discursive Mind*, London: Sage

Harré, R. and Stearns, P. (eds) (1995) *Discursive Psychology in Practice*, London: Sage

Hassard, J., Holliday, R. and Willmott, H. (eds) (2000) *Body and Organization*, London: Sage

Hoggart, S. (2000a) 'Lego language: how piles of jargon bury English', *The Guardian*, 5 May

Hoggart, S. (2000b) 'Black marks for Byers: but gold star for a Blair babe', *The Guardian*, 12 May

Hosking, D.-M., Dachler, H.P. and Gergen, K.J. (1995) *Management and Organisation: relational alternatives to individualism*, Aldershot: Avebury

Hosking, D.-M. and Morley, I.E. (1991) *A Social Psychology of Organising: people, processes and contexts*, London: Harvester Wheatsheaf

Leach, E. (1982) *Social Anthropology*, Glasgow: Fontana

Manning, P.K. (1995) 'The challenges of postmodernism' in J. Van Maanen (ed.) *Representations in Ethnography*, Thousand Oaks, Cal: Sage

McKinlay A. and Starkey, K. (eds) (1997) *Foucault, Management and Organization Theory: From Panopticon to Technologies of Self*, London: Sage

Mead, G.H. (1962) *Mind, Self and Society*, Chicago: University of Chicago Press

Miller, P. and O'Leary, T. (1987) 'Accounting and the deconstruction of the governable person', *Accounting, Organizations and Society*, 12(3): 235–65

Mumby, D.K. (1988) *Communication and Power in Organizations: Discourse, Ideology and Domination*, Norwood, NJ: Ablex

Murphy, R. (1988) *Social Closure*, Oxford: Oxford University Press

Nicholson, N. (2000) *Managing the Human Animal*, London: Texere

Potter, J. and Wetherall, M. (1987) *Discourse and Social Psychology: beyond attitudes and behaviour*, London: Sage

Sarbin, T.R. and Kitsuse, J.I. (1994) *Constructing the Social*, London: Sage

Shotter, J. (1994) *Cultural Politics of Everyday Life: social constructionism, rhetoric and knowing of the third kind*, Milton Keynes: Open University Press

Shotter, J. (1993) *Conversational Realities*, London: Sage

Strauss, A. (1978) *Negotiations*, New York: Wiley

Taylor, C. (1989) *Sources Of the Self: the making of the modern identity*, Cambridge, Mass: Harvard University Press

Watson, D.H. (1996) 'Individuals and institutions: the case of work and employment' in M. Wetherell (ed.) *Identities, Groups and Social Issues*, London: Sage

Watson, T.J. (2000) 'Discourse and Organisation' (review article), *Human Relations*, 53(4): 559–597

Watson, T.J. (1997) 'Languages Within Languages: a social constructionist perspective on multiple managerial discourses' in F. Bargiela-Chiappini and S. Harris (eds) *The Language of Business*, Edinburgh: Edinburgh University Press

Watson, T.J. (1995) 'Rhetoric, discourse and argument in organisational sensemaking: a reflexive tale', *Organisation Studies*, 16(5): 805–821

Weick, K.E. (1995) *Sensemaking in Organisations*, Thousand Oaks, Cal: Sage

Weick, K.E. (1979) *The Social Psychology of Organising*, Reading, Mass: Addison-Wesley

Whetten, D. and Godfrey, P.C. (eds) (1998) *Identity in Organizations: building theory through conversations*, London: Sage

Wittgenstein, L. (1953) *Philosophical Investigations*, Oxford: Blackwell

Reading Guide 4 Narrative, ethnography and pragmatism

Atkinson, P. (1990) *The Ethnographic Imagination*, London: Routledge

Betelheim, B. (1976) *On the Uses of Enchantment: the meaning and importance of fairy tales*, New York: Knopf

Boje, D.M. (1991) 'The storytelling organisation: a study of storytelling performance in an office-supply firm', *Administrative Science Quarterly*, 38(4): 106–26

Bolman, L.G. and Deal. T.E. (1991) *Reframing Organizations: artistry, choice and leadership*, San Francisco: Jossey-Bass

Bruner, J. (1987) 'Life as Narrative', *Social Research* 5(1): 11–32

Carroll, L. (1962) *Alice's Adventures in Wonderland*, London: The Folio Society

Coffey, A. (1999) *The Ethnographic Self: fieldwork and the representation of identity*, London: Sage

Czarniawska, B. (1999) *Writing Management: organization theory as a literary game*, Oxford: Oxford University Press

Czarniawska, B. (1998) *A Narrative Approach to Organization Studies*, London: Sage

Czarniawska, B. (1997a) *Narrating the Organisation: dramas of institutional identity*, Chicago: University of Chicago Press

Czarniawska, B. (1997b), 'The four times told tale: combining narrative and scientific knowledge in organisation studies', *Organisation*, 4(1): 51–74

Czarniawska-Joerges, B. (1996) 'Autobiographical acts and organizational identities' in S. Linstead, R. Grafton Small and P. Jeffcutt (eds) (1996) *Understanding Management*, London: Sage

Czarniawska-Joerges, B. (1995) 'Narration or Science: collapsing the division in organisation studies', *Organisation*, 2(1): 11–33

Czarniawska-Joerges, B. and Monthoux, P.G. (eds) (1994) *Good Novels, Better Management: reading organizational realities in fiction*, Reading: Harwood

Davidson, D. (1986) 'A coherence theory of truth and knowledge' in E. Lepore (ed.) *Truth and Interpretation*, Oxford: Blackwell

Gabriel, Y. (1998) 'Same old story or changing stories? Folkloric, modern and postmodern mutations' in D. Grant, T. Keenoy and C. Oswick (eds) *Discourse and Organisation*, London: Sage

Gabriel, Y. (1991) 'Turning facts into stories and stories into facts: a hermeneutic exploration of organisational folklore', *Human Relations*, 44(8): 857–875.

Gallie, W.B. (1952) *Pierce and Pragmatism*, Harmondsworth: Penguin

Haack, S. (1996) 'Pragmatism' in N. Bunnin and E.P. Tsui-James (eds) *The Blackwell Companion to Philosophy*, Oxford: Blackwell

Hacking, I. (1999) *The Social Construction of What?*, Cambridge, Mass: Harvard University Press

Hatch, M.J. (1996) 'The role of the researcher: an analysis of narrative position in organisation theory', *Journal of Management Enquiry*, 5(4): 359–374

James, W. (ed. D. Olin) (1992) *Pragmatism in Focus*, London: Routledge

Jeffcutt, P. (1994) 'From interpretation to representation in organizational analysis: postmodernism, ethnography and organizational symbolism', *Organization Studies*, 15(2): 241–274

Law, J. (1994) 'Organization, narrative and strategy' in J. Hassard and M. Parker (eds) *Towards a New Theory of Organizations*, London: Routledge, 248–268

McCloskey, D.N. (1990) *If you're So Smart: the narrative of economic expertise*, Chicago: University of Chicago Press

Mitroff, I.I. and Kilmann, R. (1975) 'Stories managers tell: a new tool for organisational problem solving', *Management Review*, 64(1): 13–28

Mounce, H.O. (1997) *The Two Pragmatisms*, London: Routledge

Nelson, J.S., Megill, A. and McCloskey, D.N. (1987) *The Rhetoric of the Human Sciences: language and argument in scholarship and human affairs*, Madison: University of Wisconsin Press

Parker, I. (ed.) (1998) *Social Constructionism, Discourse and Realism*, London: Sage

Polkinghorne, D.E. (1988) *Narrative Knowing and the Human Sciences*, Albany: State University of New York Press

Potter, J. (1996) *Representing Reality: discourse, rhetoric and social construction*, London: Sage

Putnam, H. (1995) *Pragmatism*, Oxford: Blackwell

Richardson, L. (1995) 'Narrative and Sociology' in J. Van Maanen (ed.) *Representations in Ethnography*, Thousand Oaks, Cal: Sage

Rorty, R. (1989) *Contingency, Irony, and Solidarity*, Cambridge: Cambridge University Press

Rorty, R. (1982) *Consequences of Pragmatism*, Brighton: Harvester

Rorty, R. (1980) *Philosophy and the Mirror of Nature*, Oxford: Blackwell

Rose, D. (1990) *Living the Ethnographic Life*, Newbury Park, Cal: Sage

Rosen, M. (1991) 'Coming to terms with the field: understanding and doing organisational ethnography', *Journal of Management Studies*, 28(1): 1–24

Schwartzman, H.B. (1993) *Ethnography in Organisations*, Newbury Park, Cal: Sage

Terkel, S. (1977) *Working: people talk about what they do all day and how they feel about what they do*, Harmondsworth: Penguin

Thomas, J. (1993) *Doing Critical Ethnography*, Newbury Park, Cal: Sage

Tsoukas, H. (1998a) 'Forms of knowledge and forms of life in organized contexts' in R. Chia (ed.) *In the Realm of Organization*, London: Routledge

Tsoukas, H. (1998b) 'The word and the world: a critique of representationalism in management research', *International Journal of Public Administration*, 21(5): 781–817

Tsoukas, H. (1989) 'The validity of idiographic research explanations', *Academy of Management Review*, 14: 551–561

Urmson, J.O. (1989) 'Truth' in J.O. Urmson and J. Rée (eds) *The Concise Encyclopedia of Western Philosophy and Philosophers*, London: Routledge

Van Maanen, J. (ed.) (1998) *Qualitative Studies of Organizations*, London: Sage

Van Maanen, J. (ed.) (1995) *Representations in Ethnography*, Thousand Oaks, Cal: Sage

Van Maanen, J. (1988) *Tales of the Field*, Chicago: Chicago University Press

Van Maanen, J. (1979) 'The fact of fiction in organizational ethnography' in J. Van Maanen (ed.) *Qualitative Methodology*, Beverly Hills, Cal: Sage, 37–66

Watson, T.J. (2000) 'Ethnographic fiction science: making sense of managerial work and organisational research processes with Caroline and Terry', *Organisation*, 7(3): 513–534

Watson, T.J. (1995) 'Shaping the story: rhetoric, persuasion and creative writing in organisational ethnography', *Studies in Cultures, Organisations and Society*, 1(2): 301–11

Reading Guide 5 Managerial behaviour and practices

Brewer, E. and Tomlinson, J.W.C. (1964) 'The manager's working day', *Journal of Industrial Economics*, 12: 191–197

Burns, T. (1957) 'Management in action', *Operational Research Quarterly*, 8: 45–60

Burns, T. (1954) 'The directions of activity and communication in a departmental executive group', *Human Relations*, 7: 73–97

Carlson, S. (1951) *Executive Behaviour: a study of the workload and the working methods of managing directors*, Stockholm: Strombergs

Child, J. and Ellis, T. (1973) 'Predictors of variation in managerial roles', *Human Relations*, 26(2): 227–250

Currie, G. (1999) 'The influence of middle managers in the business planning process: a case study in the UK NHS', *British Journal of Management*, 10(2): 95–184

Dalton, M. (1959) *Men Who Manage*, New York: Wiley

Dubin, R. and Spray, S.L. (1964) 'Executive behaviour and interaction', *Industrial Relations*, 3(2): 99–108

Golding, D. (1996) 'Management rituals: maintaining simplicity in the chain of command' in S. Linstead, R. Grafton Small and P. Jeffcutt (eds) *Understanding Management*, London: Sage

Golding, D. (1980) 'Establishing blissful clarity in organisational life: managers', *Sociological Review*, 28(4): 763–782

Golding, D. (1979) 'Symbolism, sovereignty and domination in an industrial hierarchical organisation', *Sociological Review*, 27(1): 169–177

Hales, C.P. (1989) 'Management processes, management divisions of labour and managerial work: towards a synthesis', *International Journal of Sociology and Social Policy*, 9: 9–38

Hales, C.P. (1987) 'The manager's work in context: a pilot investigation of the relationship between managerial role demands and role performance', *Personnel Review*, 16(5): 26–33 York.

Hales, C.P. (1986) 'What do managers do? a critical review of the evidence' *Journal of Management Studies*, 23: 88–115

Hales, C.P. and Tamangani, Z. (1996) 'An investigation of the relationship between organizational structure, managerial expectations and managers' work activities', *Journal of Management Studies*, 33(6): 731–756

Hannaway, J. (1989) *Managers Managing: the workings of an administrative system*, Oxford: Oxford University Press

Horne, J.H. and Lupton, T. (1965) 'The work activities of "middle managers" – an exploratory study', *Journal of Management Studies*, 2(1): 14–33

Isabella, L.A. (1990) 'Evolving interpretations as a change unfolds: how managers construe key organisational events', *Academy of Management Journal*, 33 (1): 7–41

Kotter, J.P. (1982) *The General Managers*, New York: Free Press

Kotter, J.P. and Lawrence, P.R. (1984) *Mayors in Action*, New York: Wiley

Lawrence, P. (1984) *Management in Action*, London: Routledge

Livian, Y.-F. and Burgoyne, J.G. (eds) (1997) *Middle Managers in Europe*, London: Routledge

Luthans, F., Hodgetts, R.M. and Rosencrantz, S.A. (1988) *Real Managers*, Cambridge, Mass: Ballinger

Mangham, I.L. and Pye, A. (1991) *The Doing of Management*, Oxford: Blackwell

Mangham, I.L. (1986) *Power and Performance in Organisations*, Oxford: Blackwell

Mintzberg, H. (1994) 'Rounding out the managerial job', *Sloan Management Review*, Fall: 11–26

Mintzberg, H. (1975) 'The manager's job: folklore and fact', *Harvard Business Review*, 53(4): 49–61

Mintzberg, H. (1973) *The Nature of Managerial Work*, New York: Harper & Row

Preece, D., Steven, G. and Steven, V. (1999) *Work, Change and Competition: Managing for Bass*, London: Routledge

Sayles, L.R. (1964) *Managerial Behaviour*, New York: McGraw-Hill

Stewart, R. (1989) 'Studies of managerial jobs and behaviour: the way forward', *Journal of Management Studies,* 26(1): 1–10

Stewart, R. (1983) 'Managerial Behaviour: how research has changed the traditional picture' in M.J. Earl (ed.) *Perspectives on Management*, Oxford University Press

Stewart, R. (1982) 'A model for understanding managerial jobs and behavior', *Academy of Management Review*, 7: 7–14

Stewart, R. (1979) 'The manager's contacts: demand or choice?', *Journal of European Industrial Training*, 3(4): 2–5

Stewart, R. (1976) *Contrasts in Management*, Maidenhead, Berks: McGraw-Hill

Stewart, R. (1967) *Managers and their Jobs*, Maidenhead: McGraw-Hill

Stewart, R., Smith, P., Blake, J. and Wingate, P. (1980) *The District Administrator in the National Health Service*, London: Pitman

Watson, T.J. (2001) *In Search of Management*, London: Thomson Learning (originally 1994)

Watson, T.J. (1998) 'The labour of division: the manager as "self" and "other" in K. Hetherington and R. Munro (eds) *Ideas of Difference*, Oxford: Blackwell

Watson, T.J. and Harris, P. (1999) *The Emergent Manager*, London: Sage

Whiteley, W. (1985) 'Managerial work behaviour: an integration of results from two major approaches', *Academy of Management Journal*, 28(2): 344–362

Willmott, H. (1984) 'Images and ideals of managerial work: A critical examination of conceptual and empirical accounts', *Journal of Management Studies*, 21(3): 349–368

Reading Guide 6 Ambiguity, uncertainty and managerial decision-making

Agor, W. (1989) *Intuition in Organizations*, Newbury Park, Cal: Sage

Agor, W. (1986) 'The logic of intuition: how top executives make important decisions', *Organizational Dynamics*, Winter: 5–15

Behling, O. and Eckel, N. (1991) 'Making sense out of intuition', *Academy of Management Executive*, February: 46–54

Brunsson, N. (1985) *The Irrational Organization: irrationality as a basis for organisational action and change*, Chichester: Wiley

Brunsson, N. (1982) 'The irrationality of action and action rationality: decisions, ideologies and organizational actions', *Journal of Management Studies*, 19(1): 29–44

Chia, R. (1994) 'The concept of decision: a deconstructive analysis', *Journal of Management Studies*, 31(6): 781–806

Cleverley, G. (1971) *Managers and Magic*, London: Longman

Cohen, M.D., March, J.G. and Olsen, J.P. (1972) 'A garbage can model of organizational choice', *Administrative Science Quarterly*, 17(1): 1–25

Cyert, R.M. and March, J.G. (1963) *A Behavioural Theory of the Firm*, Englewood Cliffs, NJ: Prentice-Hall

Feldman, M. (1991) 'The meanings of ambiguity: learning from stories and metaphors' in P. Frost, L. Moore, M. Louis, C. Lundberg and J. Martin (eds) *Reframing Organization Culture*, Newbury Park, Cal: Sage, 145–156

March, J.G. (1998) *The Pursuit of Organizational Intelligence*, Oxford: Blackwell

March, J.G. and Olsen, J.P. (1976) *Ambiguity and Choice in Organisations*, Oslo: Universitetsforlagtt

Miller, S.L., Hickson, D.J. and Wilson, D.C. (1996) 'Decision-Making in organizations' in S.R. Clegg, C. Hardy and W. Nord (eds) *Handbook of Organization Studies*, London: Sage, 293–312

Mumby, D.K. and Putnam, L.L. (1992) 'The politics of emotion: a feminist reading of bounded rationality', *Academy of Management Review*, 17(3): 465–486

Simon, H.A. (1957) 'A behavioural model of rational choice' in *Models of Man*, New York: Wiley

Srivasta, S. and associates (ed.) (1983) *The Executive Mind*, San Francisco: Jossey-Bass

Streeck, W. (1987) 'The uncertainties of management in the management of uncertainty', *Work, Employment and Society*, 1: 281–308

Weick, K.E. (2000) *Making Sense of Organization*, Oxford: Blackwell

Weick, K.E. (1995) *Sensemaking in Organisations*, Thousand Oaks, Cal: Sage

Weick, K.E. (1983) 'Managerial thought in the context of action' in Srivasta, S. and associates (eds) *The Executive Mind*, San Francisco: Jossey-Bass

Weick, K.E. (1979) *The Social Psychology of Organising*, Reading, Mass: Addison-Wesley

Reading Guide 7 Power and politics in organising and managing

Armstrong, P. (1989) 'Management, Labour Process and Agency', *Work, Employment and Society*, 3(3): 307–322

Brown, A.D. (1998) 'Narrative, politics and legitimacy in an IT implementation', *Journal of Management Studies*, 35(1): 35–59

Buchanan, D. and Badham, R. (1999) *Power, Politics, and Organizational Change: winning the turf game*, London: Sage

Burns, T. (1961) 'Micropolitics: mechanisms of institutional change', *Administrative Science Quarterly*, 6: 257–281

Burns, T. (1955) 'The reference of conduct in small groups: cliques and cabals in occupational milieux', *Human Relations*, 8: 467–486

Clegg, S.R. (1989) *Frameworks of Power*, London: Sage

Clegg, S.R. and Palmer, G. (1996) *The Politics of Management Knowledge*, London: Sage

Cohen, M.D., March, J.G. and Olsen, J.P. (1972) 'A garbage can model of organizational choice', *Administrative Science Quarterly*, 17(1): 1–25

Daudi, P. (1986) *Power in the Organisation: the discourse of power in managerial praxis*, Oxford: Blackwell

Fincham, R. (1992) 'Perspectives on power: processual, institutional and "internal" forms of organizational power', *Journal of Management Studies*, 26(9): 741–759

Guth, W.D. and Macmillan, L.C. (1986) 'Strategy implementation versus middle management self interest', *Strategic Management Journal*, 7: 313–327

Hardy, C. (1996) 'Understanding power: bringing about strategic change', *British Journal of Management*, 7 (special issue): 3–16

Hardy, C. (ed.) (1995) *Power and Politics in Organizations*, Aldershot: Dartmouth

Hickson, D.J., Hinings, C.R., Lee, C.A., Schneck, R.E. and Pennings, J.M. (1971) 'A strategic contingencies theory of intra-organizational power', *Administrative Science Quarterly*, 16: 216–229

Huczynski, A.A. (1996) *Influencing Within Organizations: getting in, rising up and moving on*, Hemel Hempstead: Prentice Hall

Jay, A. (1970) *Management and Machiavelli*, Harmondsworth: Penguin Books

Kakabadse, A. (1983) *The Politics of Management*, Aldershot: Gower Publishing

Knights, D. and Murray, F. (1994) *Managers Divided*, Aldershot: Gower

Maccoby, M. (1976) *The Gamesmen*, New York: Simon and Schuster

Mangham, I. (1979) *The Politics of Organizational Change*, Westport, CT: Greenwood Press

McKinlay, A. and Taylor, P. (1998) 'Through the looking glass: Foucault and the politics of production' in A. McKinlay and K. Starkey (eds) *Foucault, Management and Organizational Theory*, London Sage

Mintzberg, H. (1953) *Power In and Around Organizations*, Englewood Cliffs, NJ: Prentice-Hall

Pettigrew, A.M. (1973) *The Politics of Organisational Decision Making*, London: Tavistock.

Pettigrew, A.M. and McNulty, T. (1995) 'Power and influence in and around the boardroom', *Human Relations*, 48(8): 845–873

Pfeffer, J. (1992) *Managing With Power: politics and influence in organizations*, Cambridge, Mass: Harvard Business School Press

Raelin, J.A. (1986) *The Clash of Cultures: managers and professionals*, Cambridge, Mass: Harvard Business School Press

Tannen, D. (1995) 'The power of talk: who gets heard and why', *Harvard Business Review*, September–October: 138–148

Watson, D.H. (1992) 'Power, conflict and control at work' in J. Allen, P. Braham and P. Lewis (ed.) *Political and Economic Forms of Modernity*, Cambridge: Polity

Watson, T.J. (1982) 'Group ideologies and organisational change', *Journal of Management Studies*, 19(3): 259–275

Wildavsky, A. (1979) *The Politics of the Budgeting Process*, Boston: Little Brown

Zugbach, von R. (1995) *The Winning Manager: coming out on top in the organization game*, London: Souvenir Press

Reading Guide 8 Emotion and stress in work and organisations

Albrow, M. (1997) *Do Organisations have Feelings?*, London: Routledge

Cooper, C.L. (2000) *Theories of Organizational Stress*, Oxford: Oxford University Press

Cooper, C.L., Cooper, R.D. and Eaker, L. (1988) *Living With Stress*, Harmondsworth: Penguin

Cooper, C.L. and Smith, M.G.J. (eds) (1985) *Job Stress and Blue Collar Work*, Chichester: Wiley

Cooper, C.L. and Sutherland, V.J. (1992) 'The Stress of the Executive Lifestyle: trends in the 1990s', *Management Decision*, 30(6): 64–68

Damasio, A.R. (2000) *The Feeling of What Happened*, London: Heinemann

Fineman, S. (1999) 'Emotion and organizing' in S.R. Clegg, C. Hardy and W. Nord, (eds) *Handbook of Organization Studies*, London: Sage

Fineman, S. (ed.) (1993a) *Emotion in Organizations*, London: Sage

Fineman, S. (1993b) 'Organizing and emotion', J. Hassard and M. Parker (eds) *Towards a New Theory of Organizations*, London: Routledge

Harré, R. and Finlay Jones, R. (eds) (1986) *The Social Construction of Emotions*, Oxford: Blackwell

Hochschild, A.R. (1985) *The Managed Heart: the commercialization of human feeling*, University of California Press

Hopfl, H. and Linstead, S. (1993) 'Passion and performance: suffering and the carrying of organizational roles', in S. Fineman (ed.) *Emotion in Organizations*, London: Sage

Muchinsky, P.M. (2000) 'Emotions in the workplace: the neglect of organizational behaviour', *Journal of Organizational Behavior*, 21: 801–805

Newton, T., Handy, J. and Fineman, S. (eds) (1995) *Managing Stress: emotion and power at work*, London: Sage

Putnam, L. and Mumby, D.K. (1993) 'Organizations, emotion and the myth of rationality', in S. Fineman (ed.) *Emotion in Organizations*, London: Sage

Sennett, R. (1998) *The Corrosion of Character: the personal consequences of work in the new capitalism*, New York: W.W. Norton

Taylor, S. (1998) 'Emotional labour and the new workplace', in P. Thompson and C. Warhurst (eds) *Workplaces of the Future*, London: Macmillan

Van Maanen, J. (1991) 'The smile factory: work at Disneyland', in E.J. Frost, L.F. Moore, M.R. Louis, C.C. Lundberg and J. Martin (eds) *Reframing Organizational Culture*, Newbury Park, Cal: Sage, 58–76

Van Maanen, J. and Kunda, G. (1989) '"Real feelings": emotional expression and organizational culture', *Research in Organizational Behavior*, 11: 43–103

Wharton, A.S. and Erickson, R.J. (1993) 'Managing emotions on the job and at home: understanding the consequences of multiple emotional roles', *Academy of Management Review*, 18(3): 457–486

Wollheim, R. *On the Emotions*, Yale: Yale University Press

Wouters, C. (1989) 'The sociology of emotions and flight attendants: Hochschild's "managed heart"', *Theory, Culture and Society*, 6(1): 95–123

Reading Guide 9 Manager insecurity and changing careers

Dopson, S. and Neumann, J.E. (1995) 'Uncertainty, contrariness and the double-bind: middle managers' reactions to changing contracts', *British Journal of Management*, 9 (special issue): 53–71

Dopson, S. and Stewart, R. (1993) 'Information technology, organizational restructuring and the future of middle management', *New Technology, Work and Employment* 8(1): 10–20

Dopson, S. and Stewart, R. (1990) 'What is happening to middle management?', *British Journal of Management*, 1(1): 3–16

Hallier, J. and James, P. (1997) 'Middle managers and the employee psychological contract: agency, protection and advancement', *Journal of Management Studies* 34(5): 703–728

Hallier, J. and Lyon, P. (1996) 'Job insecurity and employee commitment: managers' reactions to the threat of outcomes of redundancy selection', *British Journal of Management*, 7: 107–123

Mant, A. (1979) *The Rise and Fall of the British Manager*, London: Pan

McGovern, P., Hope-Hailey, V. and Stiles, P. (1998) 'The managerial career after down-sizing: case studies from the "leading edge"', *Work, Employment and Society*, 12(3): 457–477

Mulholland, K. (1998) '"Survivors" versus "Movers and Shakers": the reconstitution of management and careers in the privatised utilities' in P. Thompson and C. Warhurst (eds) *Workplaces of the Future*, Basingstoke: Macmillan

Newell, H. and Dopson, S. (1996) 'Muddle in the Middle: organizational restructuring and middle management careers', *Personnel Review*, 25(4): 4–20

Redman, T., Wilkinson, A. and Snape, E. (1997) 'Stuck in the middle? Managers in building societies', *Work, Employment and Society*, 11(1): 101–114

Scarborough, H. (1998) 'The unmaking of management? Change and continuity in British management in the 1990s', *Human Relations*, 51(6): 691–716.

Scarbrough, H. and Burrell, G. (1996) 'The Axeman Cometh: the changing roles and knowledges of middle managers' in Clegg, S.R. and Palmer, G. (eds) *The Politics of Management Knowledge*, London: Sage

Scase, R. and Goffee, R. (1989) *Reluctant Managers: their work and lifestyles*, London: Unwin Hyman

Thomas, R. and Dunkerley, D. (1999) 'Careering downwards? Middle managers' experiences in the downsized organization', *British Journal of Management*, 10(2): 95–184

Thornhill, A. and Saunders, M.N.K. (1998) 'The meanings, consequences and implications of downsizing and redundancy: a review', *Personnel Review*, 27(4): 271–295

Westley, F.R. (1990) 'Middle managers and strategy: microdynamics of inclusion', *Strategic Management Journal*, 11: 337–351

Worrall, L. and Cooper, C.L. (1999) *The Quality of Working Life: the 1999 Survey of Managers' experiences*, Institute of Management Research Report, London: Institute of Management

Worrall, L., Cooper, C. and Campbell, F. (2000) 'The new reality for UK managers: perpetual change and employment instability', *Work, Employment and Society*, 14(4): 647–668

Worrall, L., Cooper, C. and Campbell-Jamison, F. (2000) 'The impact of organizational change on the work experiences and perceptions of public sector managers', *Personnel Review*, 29(5): 613–636

Reading Guide 10 Manager competence and leadership

Aktouf, O. (1996) 'Competence, symbolic activity and promotability' in S. Linstead, R. Grafton Small and P. Jeffcutt (eds) (1996) *Understanding Management*, London: Sage

Beatty, C.A. and Lee, G.L. (1992) 'Leadership among middle managers: an exploration in the context of technological change', *Human Relations*, 45(1): 957–980.

Boam, R. and Sparrow, P. (eds) (1992) *Designing and Achieving Competency*, Maidenhead: McGraw-Hill

Boyatzis, R.E. (1982) *The Competent Manager*, New York: Wiley

Brewis, J. (1996) 'The "making" of the competent manager', *Management Learning*, 27(1): 65–86

Bryman, A. (1996) 'Leadership in organizations' in S.R Clegg, C. Hardy and W. Nord, (eds) *Handbook of Organization Studies*, London: Sage, 276–292

Burgoyne, J. (1989) 'Creating the managerial portfolio: building on competency approaches to management development', *Management Education and Development*, 20: 56–61

Burgoyne, J. and Stuart, R. (1976) 'The nature, use and acquisition of managerial skills and other attributes', *Personnel Review*, 15(4): 19–29

Burns, J.M. (1978) *Leadership*, New York: Harper and Row

Conger, J.A.N. and Kanungo, R. (1998) *Charismatic Leadership in Organizations*, London: Sage

du Gay, P. and Rees, B. (1996) 'The conduct of management and the management of conduct: contemporary managerial discourse and the constitution of the "competent" manager', *Journal of Management Studies*, 33(3): 263–282

Dulewicz, V. (2000) 'Emotional intelligence: the key to successful corporate leadership?', *Journal of General Management*, 25(3): 1–14

Goleman, D. (1999) *Working with Emotional Intelligence*, London: Bloomsbury

Goleman, D. (1996) *Emotional Intelligence: why it can matter more than IQ*, London: Bloomsbury

Hosking, D.M. (1991) 'Chief executives, organising processes, and skill', *European Journal of Applied Psychology*, 41: 95–103

Kotter, J.P. (1999) 'What effective general managers really do', *Harvard Business Review*, 77(2): 145–59

Martinko, M.J. and Gardner, W. (1985) 'The observation of high-performing educational managers: methodological issues and managerial implications' in J.G. Hunt, D. Hosking, C.A. Schriesheim and R. Stewart (eds) *Leaders and managers: international perspectives on managerial behaviour and leadership*, New York: Pergamon, 142–162

McClelland, D.C. and Boyatzis, R.E. (1982) 'Leadership motive pattern and long-term success in management', *Journal of Applied Psychology*, 67(6): 737–743

Morse, J.J. and Wagner, E.R. (1978) 'Measuring the process of managerial effectiveness', *Academy of Management Journal*, 21(1): 23–25

Schroder, H.M. (1989a) 'Managerial competence and style', in M.J. Kirton (ed.) *Adaptors and Innovators: Styles of creativity and problem-solving*, London: Routledge

Schroder, H.M. (1989b) *Managerial Competence: the key to excellence*, Iowa: Kendall Hunt

Silver, M. (ed.) (1991) *Competent to Manage*, London: Routledge

Tichy, N. and Devanna, M. (1986) *The Transformational Leader*, New York: John Wiley

Vroom, V.H. and Jago, A.G. (1988) *The New Leadership: Managing Participation in Organizations*, Englewood Cliffs, NJ: Prentice-Hall

Watson, T.J. (1995) 'Entrepreneurship and professional management: a fatal distinction', *International Small Business Journal*, 13(3): 33–45

Weick, K.E. (1999) 'That's moving: theories that matter', *Journal of Management Inquiry*, 8(2): 134–142

Weisinger, H. (1988) *Emotional Intelligence at Work*, San Francisco: Jossey-Bass

Woodruffe, C. (1992) 'What is meant by a competency?' in R. Boam and P. Sparrow, (eds) *Designing and Achieving Competency*, Maidenhead: McGraw-Hill, 16–30

Yukl, G. (1998) *Leadership in Organizations*, Fourth edn, Upper Saddle River, NJ: Prentice-Hall

Zaleznik, A. (1964) 'Managerial behaviour and interpersonal competence', *Behavioural Science*, 9: 156–166

Reading Guide 11 Management learning and development

Argyris, C. and Schön, D.A. (1974) *Theory in Practice: increasing professional effectiveness*, San Francisco: Jossey-Bass

Buchanan, D., Claydon, T. and Doyle, M. (1999) 'Organization development and change: the legacy of the nineties', *Human Resource Management Journal*, 9(2): 20–37

Burgoyne, J.G. (1995) 'The case for an optimistic, constructivist and applied approach to management education: a response to Grey and Mitev', *Management Learning*, 26(1): 91–102

Burgoyne, J.G. (1994) 'Managing by learning', *Journal of Management Learning*, 25(1): 35–55

Burgoyne, J. and Reynolds, M. (1997) *Management Learning: integrating perspectives in theory and practice*, London: Sage

Clutterbuck, D. and Crainer, S. (1988) *Makers of Management*, London: Macmillan

Constable, J. and McCormick, R. (1987) *The Making of British Managers*, London: British Institute of Management

Fox, S. (1997), 'From management education and development to the study of management learning' in J. Burgoyne and M. Reynolds (eds) *Management Learning: integrating perspectives in theory and practice*, London: Sage

French, R. and Grey, C. (eds) (1996) *Rethinking Management Education*, London: Sage

Gold, J. (1997) 'Learning from story telling', *Journal of Workplace Learning* 9(4): 133–41

Golding, D. (1986) 'Inside story – on becoming a manager', *Organization Studies*, 7(2): 193–198

Grey, C. and Mitev, N. (1995) 'Management Education: a polemic', *Management Learning*, 26(1): 73–90

Handy, C. (1987) *The Making of Managers*, London: MSC/NEDC/BIM

Herriot, P., Gibbons, C., Pemberton and Jackson, P.R. (1994) 'An empirical model of managerial careers in organizations', *British Journal of Management*, 5: 113–121

Hill, L.A. (1992) *Becoming a Manager: mastery of a new identity*, Boston, Mass: Harvard Business School Press

Holman, D., Pavlica, K. and Thorpe, R. (1997) 'Rethinking Kolb's theory of experiential learning in management education: the contribution of social constructionism and activity theory', *Management Learning*, 28(2): 135–48

Huczynski, A.A. (2000) *Encyclopedia of Management Development and Organization Change Methods*, Aldershot: Gower

Kolb, D.A. (1984) *Experiential Learning*, Englewood Cliffs, NJ: Prentice-Hall

Lave, J. and Wenger, E. (1991) *Situated Learning: Legitimate Peripheral Participation*, Cambridge: Cambridge University Press

Mabey, C. and Iles, P. (eds) (1994) *Managing Learning*, London: Routledge

McGill, I.A. and Beaty, L. (1995) *Action Learning*, London: Kogan Page

McGoldrick, J. and Stewart, J. (1996) 'The HRM–HRD Nexus' in J. McGoldrick and J. Stewart (eds) *Human Resource Development*, London: Pitman Publishing

Pedler, M. (ed.) (1997) *Action Learning in Practice*, Aldershot: Gower

Revans, R.W. (1982) *The Origins and Growth of Action Learning*, Bromley: Chartwell-Bratt

Revans, R.W. (1971) *Developing Effective Managers*, New York: Praeger

Schön, D.A. (1983) *The Reflective Practitioner: how professionals think in action*, New York: Basic Books

Storey, J. (1992) *Developments in the Management of Human Resources*, Oxford: Basil Blackwell

Storey, J., Edwards, P. and Sisson, K. (1997) *Managers in the Making: development and control in corporate Britain and Japan*, London: Sage

Thomson, A., Storey, J., Mabey, C., Gray, C., Farmer, E. and Thomson, R. (1997) *A Portrait of Management Development*, London: Institute of Management

Watson, T.J. (2001) 'The emergent manager and processes of management pre-learning', *Management Learning*, 32(2): 221–235

Weick, K.E. and Westley, F. (1996) 'Organizational learning: affirming an oxymoron' in Clegg, S.R., Hardy, C. and Nord, W.R. (eds) *Handbook of Organization Studies*, London: Sage

Reading Guide 12 Fads, fashions and gurus in management thinking

Abrahamson, E. (1996) 'Management fashion, academic fashion, and enduring truths', *Academy of Management Review*, 21(3): 616–618

Barley, S. and Kunda, G. (1992) 'Design and devotion: surges of rational and normative ideologies of control in managerial discourse', *Administrative Science Quarterly*, 37: 363–399

Clark, T. and Salaman, G. (1996) 'The managerial guru as organizational witchdoctor', *Organization*, 3(1): 85–107

Collins, D. (2000) *Management Fads and Buzzwords*, London: Routledge

Furestan, S. (1999) *Popular Management Books – how they are made and what they mean for organisations*, London: Routledge

Huczynski, A.A. (1993a) *Management Gurus: what makes them and how to become one*, London: Routledge

Huczynski, A.A. (1993b) 'Explaining the succession of management fads', *The International Journal of Human Resource Management*, 4(2): 443–463

Jackson, B. (1996) 'Re-engineering the sense of self: the manager and the management guru', *Journal of Management Studies*, 33(5): 571–590

Jackson, N. and Carter, P. (1998) 'Management gurus: what are we to make of them?' in J. Hassard and R. Holliday (eds) *Organization–Representations: Work and Organization in Popular Culture*, London: Sage

Kieser, A. (1997) 'Rhetoric and myth in management fashion', *Organization*, 4: 49–74

Ramsey, H. (1996) 'Managing sceptically, a critique of organisational fashion' in Clegg, S.R. and Palmer, G. (eds) (1996) *The Politics of Management Knowledge*, London: Sage

Shapiro, E.C. (1996) *Fad Surfing in the Boardroom*, Oxford: Capstone

Thomas, P. (1999) *Fashions in Management Research: an empirical analysis*, Aldershot: Ashgate

Watson, T.J. (1994) 'Management "flavours of the month": their role in managers' lives', *The International Journal of Human Resource Management*, 5(4): 889–905

Reading Guide 13 Critical management and organisation studies

Alvesson, M. and Deetz, S. (1999) *Doing Critical Management Research*, London: Sage

Alvesson, M. and Willmott, H. (1996) *Making Sense of Management: a critical introduction*, London: Sage

Alvesson, M. and Willmott, H. (eds) (1992) *Critical Management Studies*, London: Sage

Baritz, L. (1960) *Servants of Power*, New York: Wiley

Fournier, V. and Grey, C. (2000) 'At the critical moment: conditions and prospects of critical management studies', *Human Relations*, 53(1): 7–32

Grey, C., Knights, D. and Willmott, H. (1996). 'Is a critical pedagogy of management possible?' in R. French and C. Grey (eds) *Rethinking Management Education*, London: Sage

Nord, W.R. and Jermier, J.M. (1992) 'Critical social science for managers? Promising and perverse possibilities', in M. Alvesson and H. Willmott (eds) *Critical Management Studies*, London: Sage

Perriton, L. (2000) 'Verandah discourses: critical management education in organizations', *British Journal of Management*, 11(3): 227–237

Prasad, P. and Capruni, P. J. (1997) 'Critical theory in the management classroom: engaging power, ideology, and praxis', *Journal of Management Education*, 21(3): 284–291

Reynolds, M. (1999) 'Grasping the nettle: possibilities and pitfalls of a critical management pedagogy', *British Journal of Management*, 10(2): 95–184

Reynolds, M. (1998) 'Reflection and critical reflection in management learning', *Management Learning*, 29(2): 183–200

Reynolds, M. (1997) 'Towards a critical management pedagogy' in J. Burgoyne and M. Reynolds (eds) *Management Learning: integrating perspectives in theory and practice*, London: Sage

Sotorin, P. and Tyrell, S. (1998) 'Wondering about critical management studies', *Management Communication Quarterly*, 12(2): 303–336

Steffy, B.D. and Grimes, A. J. (1986) 'A critical theory organisational science', *Academy of Management Review*, 11(2): 322–336

Thompson, P. and McHugh, D. (1995) *Work Organisations: a critical introduction*, Basingstoke: Macmillan

Watson, T.J. (1994) 'Towards a managerially relevant but non-managerialist organisation theory' in J. Hassard and M. Parker (eds) *Towards a New Theory of Organizations*, London: Routledge

Willmott, H. (1997) 'Critical management learning' in J. Burgoyne and M. Reynolds (eds) *Management Learning: integrating perspectives in theory and practice*, London: Sage

Reading Guide 14 Strategy and strategy-making

Goold, M. and Campbell, A. (1986) *Strategies and Styles: the role of the centre in managing diversified corporations*, Oxford: Blackwell

Grant, R.M. (1998) *Contemporary Strategy Analysis*, Oxford: Blackwell

Hamel, G. and Prahalad, C.K. (1993) 'Strategy as stretch & leverage', *Harvard Business Review*, March–April: 75–84

Hamel, G. and Prahalad, C.K. (1989) 'Strategic intent', *Harvard Business Review*, 89(3): 63–76

Hardy, C. (1994) *Managing Strategic Action: mobilizing change*, London: Sage

Henderson, B.D. (1970) *The Product Portfolio*, Boston: Boston Consulting Group

Hyman, R. (1987) 'Strategy or structure: capital, labour and control', *Work, Employment and Society*, 1(1): 25–55

Johnson, G. (1990) 'Managing strategic change: the role of symbolic action', *British Journal of Management*, 1: 183–200

Johnson, G. (1987) *Strategic Change and the Management Process*, Hemel Hempstead: Prentice-Hall

Kanter, R.M. (1989) *When Giants Learn to Dance: understanding the challenges of strategy, management and careers in the 1990s*, London: Allen & Unwin

Kanter, R.M. (1983) *The Change Masters: corporate entrepreneurs at work*, London: Allen & Unwin

Knights, D. and Morgan, G. (1991) 'Strategic discourse and subjectivity: towards a critical analysis of corporate strategy in organisations', *Organisation Studies*, 12(3): 251–273

Knights, D. and Morgan, G. (1990) 'The concept of strategy in sociology: a note of dissent', *Sociology*, 24: 475–483

Mintzberg, H. (1994) *The Rise and Fall of Strategic Planning*, Hemel Hempstead: Prentice-Hall

Mintzberg, H. (1990) 'The design school: reconsidering the basic premises of strategic management', *Strategic Management Journal*, 11: 171–195

Mintzberg, H. (1988) 'Opening up the definition of strategy' in J.B.Quinn, H. Mintzberg and R.M. James (eds) *The Strategy Process*, Englewood Cliffs, NJ: Prentice-Hall

Mintzberg, H. (1987a) 'Crafting strategy', *Harvard Business Review*, July/August: 66–75

Mintzberg, H. (1987b) 'The strategy concept', *California Management Review*, 30(3): 11–32

Mintzberg, H. (1978) 'Patterns in strategy formation', *Management Science*, 24(9): 934–948

Mintzberg, H. and Waters, J.H. (1985) 'Of strategies deliberate and "emergent"', *Strategic Management Journal*, 6(3): 257–272

Narayanan, V.K. and Fahey, L. (1982) 'The micro-politics of strategy formulation', *Academy of Management Review*, 7(1): 25–34

Ohmae, K. (1989) 'The global logic of strategic alliances', *Harvard Business Review*, March–April: 43–55

Peters, T.J. and Waterman, R.H. Jr (1982) *In Search of Excellence*, New York: Harper & Row

Pettigrew, A.M. (1987) 'Context and action in the transformation of the firm', *Journal of Management Studies'*, 24(6): 649–670

Pettigrew, A.M. (1985) *The Awakening Giant: creativity and change in ICI*, Oxford: Blackwell

Pettigrew, A.M. (1977) 'Strategy formulation as a political process', *International Studies in Management and Organization*, 7(2): 78–87

Pettigrew, A.M., Ferlie, E. and McKee, L. (1992) *Shaping Strategic Change*, London: Sage

Pettigrew, A.M., Thomas, H. and Whittington, R. (2000) *The Handbook of Strategy and Management*, London: Sage

Porter, M. (1985) *Competitive Advantage: creating and sustaining superior performance*, New York: Free Press

Porter, M. (1980) *Competitive Strategy*, New York: Free Press

Prahalad, C.K. and Hamel, G. (1990) 'The core competencies of the organization', *Harvard Business Review*, 68: 79–91

Quinn, J.B. (1980) *Strategies for Change: logical incrementalism*, Homewood, Ill: Irwin

Quinn, J.B. (1978) 'Strategic change, logical incrementalism', *Sloan Management Review*, 20: 7–21

Schilit, W.K. (1987) 'An examination of the influence of middle level managers in formulating and implementing strategic decisions', *Journal of Management Studies*, 24: 271–293

Schoenberger, E. (1995) *The Cultural Crisis of the Firm*, Oxford: Blackwell

Schoenberger, E. (1994) 'Corporate strategy and corporate strategists: power, identity and knowledge within the firm', *Environment and Planning A*, 26: 435–451

Smircich, L. and Stubbart, C. (1985) 'Strategic management in an enacted world', *Academy of Management Review*, 10: 724–736

Stacey, R. (1996) *Strategic Management and Organizational Dynamics*, London: Pitman

Stacey, R. (1995) 'The science of complexity an alternative perspective for strategic change processes', *Strategic Management Journal*, 16: 477–495

Westley, F.R. (1990) 'Middle managers and strategy: microdynamics of inclusion', *Strategic Management Journal* 11: 337–351

Westley, F.R. and Mintzberg, H. (1989) 'Visionary leadership and strategic management', *Strategic Management Journal*, 10: 17–32

Whipp, R. (1996) 'Creative deconstruction: strategy and organizations' in S.R. Clegg, C. Hardy and W. Nord (eds) *Handbook of Organization Studies*, London: Sage, 261–275

Whittington, R. (1996) 'Strategy as practice', *Long Range Planning*, October: 731–735

Whittington, R. (1993) *What is Strategy and Does it Matter?*, London: Routledge

Reading Guide 15 Learning organisations and knowledge management

Argyris, C. (1999) *On Organizational Learning*, second edn, Oxford: Blackwell

Argyris, C. and Schön, D.A. (1978) *Organisational Learning*, New York: Addison Wesley

Blackler, F. (2000) 'Power, mastery and organizational learning', *Journal of Management Studies*, 37(6): 833–851

Blackler, F. (1995) 'Knowledge, knowledge work and organizations – an overview and interpretation', *Organization Studies*, 16(6): 1021–1046

Boisot, M.H. (1999) *Knowledge Assets: securing competitive advantage in the information economy*, Oxford: Oxford University Press

Brown, J.S. and Duguid, P. (1991) 'Organizational learning and communities-of-practice: toward a unified view of working, learning and innovation', *Organization Science*, 2(1): 40–47

Burgoyne, J., Pedler, M. and Boydell, T. (1994) *Towards the Learning Company*, Maidenhead: McGraw-Hill

Coopey, J. (1996) 'Crucial gaps in the "Learning Organization"' in K. Starkey (ed.) *How Organizations Learn*, London: International Thomson Business Press

De Geus, A.P. (1988) 'Planning as learning', *Harvard Business Review*, March–April: 70–74

Easterby-Smith, M., Burgoyne, J. and Araujo, L. (eds) (1999), *Organizational Learning and the Learning Organization: developments in theory and practice*, London: Sage

Garavan, T. (1997) 'The learning organization: a review and an evaluation', *The Learning Organization*, 4(1): 18–29

Gherardi, S. (1997) 'Organizational learning', in A. Sorge and M. Warner (eds) *The Handbook of Organizational Behaviour*, London: International Thomson Business Press

Hodgkinson, M. (2000) 'Managerial perceptions of barriers to becoming a "learning organisation"', *The Learning Organisation*, 7(3/4): 156–166

Jones, A.M. and Hendry, C. (1994) 'The learning organization: adult learning and organizational transformation', *British Journal of Management*, 5(1): 53–62

Kamoche, K. (1997) 'Knowledge creation and learning in international HRM', *International Journal of HRM*, 8(3): 213–225

Keep, E. and Rainbird, H. (2000) 'Towards the Learning Organization?', in S. Bach and K. Sisson (eds) *Personnel Management: a comprehensive guide to theory and practice*, Oxford: Blackwell

Mullin, R. (1996) 'Knowledge management: a cultural evolution', *The Journal of Business Strategy*, 17(5): 56–62

Nahapiet, J. and Ghoshal, S. (1998) 'Social capital, intellectual capital and the organizational advantage', *Academy of Management Review*, 23(2): 242–266

Nonaka, I. (1994) 'A dynamic theory of organisational knowledge creation', *Organization Science*, 5(1): 14–37

Nonaka, I. and Takeuchi, H. (1995) *The Knowledge Creating Company*, Oxford: Oxford University Press

Nonaka. I., Umemoto, K. and Sasaki, K. (1999) 'Three tales of knowledge-creating companies' in G. von Krogh, J. Roos and D. Kleine (eds) *Knowing in Firms: understanding, managing and measuring knowledge*, London: Sage, 146–172

Pedler, M., Burgoyne, J. and Boydell, T. (1997) *The Learning Company: a strategy for sustainable development*, second edn, London: McGraw-Hill

Prusak, L. (1997) *Knowledge in Organizations*, Oxford: Butterworth-Heinemann

Scarbrough, H. (ed.) (1996) *The Management of Expertise*, Basingstoke: Macmillan

Scarbrough, H. and Swan, J. (2001) 'Explaining the diffusion of knowledge management: the role of fashion', *British Journal of Management*, 12(1): 3–12

Scarbrough, H., Swan, J. and Preston, J. (1999) *Knowledge Management and the Learning Organisation*, London: CIPD

Senge, P.M. (1990) *The Fifth Discipline: the art and practice of the learning organisation*, New York: Doubleday

Senge, P., Kleiner, A., Roberts, C., Ross, R., Roth, G. and Smith, B. (1999) *The Dance of Change: the challenges of sustaining momentum in learning organizations*, London: Nicholas Brealey

Starkey, K. (ed.) (1996) *How Organizations Learn*, London: International Thomson Business Press

Teece, D. and Nonaka, I. (2000) *Managing Industrial Knowledge*, London: Sage

Reading Guide 16 Bureaucracy, organisational structures and re-engineering

Atkinson, J. (1985) 'Flexibility: planning for an uncertain future', *Manpower Policy and Practice*, no. 1, Summer

Barnhart, R.K. (1988) 'Structure' and 'culture' in *Chambers Dictionary of Etymology*, Edinburgh: Chambers

Beetham, D. (1996) *Bureaucracy*, Open University Press

Buchanan, D.A. (1997) 'The limitations and opportunities of business process re-engineering in a politicised organizational climate', *Human Relations*, 50(1): 51–72

Burke, R. and Cooper, C.L. (2000) *The Organization in Crisis: downsizing, restructuring and privatisation*, Oxford: Blackwell

Burns, T. and Stalker, G. (1994) *The Management of Innovation*, second edn, Oxford: Oxford University Press (originally 1961)

Champy, J. (1996) *Reengineering Management: The Mandate for New Leadership*, New York: Harper Business

Child, J. (1972) 'Organizational structure, environment and performance: the role of strategic choice', *Sociology*, 6(1): 331–350

Clarke, J. and Newman, J. (1997) *The Managerial State*, London: Sage

Davenport, T. (1993) *Process Innovation: Reengineering work through information technology*, Boston, Mass: Harvard Business School Press

Donaldson, L. (1996) 'The normal science of structural contingency theory', in S.R. Clegg, C. Hardy and W. Nord (eds) *Handbook of Organization Studies*, London: Sage, 57–76

Fox, A. (1985) *Man Mismanagement*, second edn, London: Hutchinson

Fox, A. (1974) *Beyond Contract: work, power and trust relations*, London, Faber

Friedman, A.L. (1990) 'Managerial strategies, activities, techniques and technologies: towards a complex theory of the labour process' in D. Knights and H. Willmott (eds) *Labour Process Theory*, London: Macmillan

Friedman, A.L. (1977) *Industry and Labour*, London: Macmillan

Goleman, D. (2000) 'Leadership that gets results', *Harvard Business Review*, March–April: 78–90

Gouldner, A. (1964) *Patterns of Industrial Bureaucracy*, New York: The Free Press

Grey, C. and Mitev, N. (1995) 'Reengineering organizations: a critical appraisal', *Personnel Review*, 24(1): 6–18

Grint, K. and Willcocks, L. (1995) 'Business process re-engineering in theory and practice: business Paradise regained?', *New Technology, Work and Employment*, 10(2): 99–108

Hammer, M. and Champy, J. (1993) *Reengineering the Corporation*, London: Nicholas Brealey

Hammer, M. and Stanton, S. (1995) *The Reengineering Revolution: A Handbook*, New York: Harper Business Press

Higgs, M. and Dulewicz, V. (1999) *Making Sense of Emotional Intelligence*, London: NFER-Nelson

Jaques, E. (1990) 'In praise of hierarchy', *Harvard Business Review*, 68(1) 127–133

Knights, D. and Willmott, H. (eds) (2000) *The Reengineering Revolution: critical studies of corporate change*, London: Sage

Lawrence, P.R. and Lorsch, J.W. (1967) *Organization and Environment: managing differentiation and integration*, Boston, Mass: Harvard Business School Press

Merton, R.K. (1940) 'Bureaucratic structure and personality', *Social Forces*, 18: 560–568, reprinted in R.K. Merton, *Social Theory and Social Structure*, New York: Free Press

Oliver, N. and Wilkinson, B. (1988) *The Japanization of British Industry*, Oxford: Blackwell

Osborne, D. and Gaebler, T. (1992) *Re-inventing Government*, Reading, Mass: Addison-Wesley

Peters, T. and Waterman, R.H. (1982) *In Search of Excellence*, New York: Harper and Row

Pollitt, C. (1993) *Managerialism and the Public Services*, Oxford: Blackwell

Pugh, D.S. and Hickson, D.J. (1976) *Organisational Structure in it context: The Aston Programme I,* Farnborough, Hants: Saxon House

Pugh, D.S. and Hinings, C.R. (eds) (1976) *Organisation Structure: extensions and replications, The Aston Programme II,* Farnborough, Hants: Gower

Pugh, D.S. and Payne, R.L. (1977) *Organisational Behaviour in its Context: The Aston Programme III,* Farnborough, Hants: Saxon House

Ray, L. and Reed, M. (1994) *Organizing Modernity: Neo-Weberian Perspectives on Work, Organization and Society,* London: Routledge

Redman, T. and Wilkinson, A. (2001) 'Downsizing' in T. Redman and A. Wilkinson (eds) *Contemporary Human Resource Management,* Harlow: FT Prentice-Hall

Ritzer, G. (1998) *The McDonaldization Thesis,* London: Sage

Ritzer, G. (1993) *The McDonaldization of Society,* Thousand Oaks, Cal: Pine Forge

Storey, J. (ed.) (1993) *New Wave Manufacturing Strategies,* London: Chapman

Weber, M. (1978) *Economy and Society,* Berkeley: University of California Press

Wilkinson, A. and Willmott, H. (1995) (eds) *Making Quality Critical: new perspectives on organizational change,* London: Routledge

Wilkinson, A., Redman, T., Snape, E. and Marchington, M. (1998) *Managing with Total Quality Management: theory and practice,* Basingstoke, Macmillan

Willmott, H. (1995) 'The odd couple?: re-engineering business processes; managing human relations', *New Technology; Work and Employment,* 10(2): 89–98

Willmott, H. (1994) 'Business process re-engineering and human resource management', *Personnel Review,* 23(3): 34–46

Woodward, J. (1994) *Industrial Organisation,* second edn, Oxford: Oxford University Press (originally 1965)

Reading Guide 17 Work design, empowerment and teams

Babbage, C. (1832) *On the Economy of Machinery and Manufacture,* London: Charles Knight

Becker, B. and Huselid, M. (1998) 'High performance work systems and firm performance: a synthesis of research and managerial implications', *Research in Personnel and Human Resources,* 16(1): 53–101

Belbin, M. (1993) *Team Roles at Work,* Oxford: Butterworth-Heinemann

Benders, J. and Van Hootegem, G. (1999) 'Teams and their context: moving the team discussion beyond existing dichotomies', *Journal of Management Studies,* 36(5): 609–628

Boje, D.M. and Winsor, R.D. (1993) 'The resurrection of Taylorism: total quality management's hidden agenda', *Journal of Organizational Change Management,* 6(4): 57–70

Braverman, H. (1974) *Labor and Monopoly Capital,* New York: Monthly Review Press

Buchanan, D.A. (2000) 'An eager and enduring embrace: the ongoing rediscovery of teamworking as a management idea', in S. Procter and F. Mueller (eds) *Teamworking,* Basingstoke: Macmillan, 25–42

Buchanan, D.A. (1994) 'Cellular manufacture and the role of teams' in J. Storey (ed.) *New Wave Manufacturing Strategies: organisational and human resource management dimensions,* London: Paul Chapman, 204–225

Buchanan, D.A. (1979) *The Development of Organisational Design Theories and Techniques*, Aldershot: Saxon House

Buchanan, D.A. and McCalman, J. (1989) *High Performance Work Systems: the digital experience*, London: Routledge

Buchanan, D. and Preston, D. (1992) 'Life in the cell: supervision and teamwork in a "manufacturing systems engineering" environment', *Human Resource Management Journal*, 2(4): 55–76

Burawoy, M. (1979) *Manufacturing Consent: changes in the labour process under monopoly capitalism*, Chicago: Chicago University Press

Child, J. (1985) 'Managerial strategies, new technology and the labour process', in D. Knights, H. Willmott and D. Collinson (eds) *Job Redesign*, Aldershot: Gower, 107–141

Dawson, P. (1996) *Technology and Quality: change in the workplace*, London: International Thomson Business Press

De Sitter, L.U., den Hertog, J.F. and Dankbaar, B. (1997) 'From complex organizations with simple jobs to simple organizations with complex jobs', *Human Relations*, 50(5): 497–534

Edwards, R. (1979) *Contested Terrain*, London: Heinemann

Friedman, A.L. (1977) *Industry and Labour*, London: Macmillan

Guzzo, R.A. and Dickson, M.W. (1998) 'Teams in organizations: recent research on performance and effectiveness', *Annual Review of Psychology*, 49: 307–38

Hackman, J.R. and Oldham, G.R. (1980) *Work Redesign*, New York: Addison-Wesley

Hampton, M.M. (1999) 'Work groups', in Y. Gabriel (ed.) *Organizations in Depth*, London: Sage, 112–138

Herzberg, F. (1966) *Work and the Nature of Man*, Chicago, Ill: World Publishing Co.

Hickson, D.J. (1966) 'A convergence in organisation theory', *Administrative Science Quarterly*, 11: 224–237

Jaques, E. (1956) *Measurement of Responsibility*, London: Tavistock

Jones, O. (1997) 'Changing the balance? Taylorism, TQM and the work organization', *New Technology, Work and Employment*, 12(1): 13–23

Marchington, M. (1992) *Managing the Team*, Oxford: Blackwell

Mayo, E. (1933) *The Human Problems of an Industrial Civilisation*, New York: Macmillan

McGregor, D.C. (1960) *The Human Side of Enterprise*, New York: McGraw-Hill

Murakami, T. (1997) 'The autonomy of teams in the car industry: a cross-national comparison', *Work, Employment and Society*, 11(4): 749–758

Murakami, T. (1995) 'Introducing team working: a motor industry case study from Germany', *Industrial Relations Journal*, 26(4): 293–304

Parker, S. and Wall, T. (1998) *Job Work Design: organizing work to promote well-being and effectiveness*, London: Sage

Pollert, A. (ed.) (1991) *Farewell to Flexibility?*, Oxford: Blackwell

Pollert, A. (1988) 'Dismantling flexibility', *Capital and Class*, 34: 42–75

Procter, S. and Ackroyd, S. (2001) 'Flexibility' in T. Redman and A. Wilkinson (eds) *Contemporary Human Resource Management*, Harlow: FT Prentice-Hall

Procter, S. and Mueller, F. (eds) (2000a) *Teamworking*, Basingstoke: Macmillan

Procter, S. and Mueller, F., (2000b) 'Teamworking, strategy, structure, systems and culture' in S. Procter and F. Mueller (eds) *Teamworking*, Basingstoke: Macmillan, 3–24

Rice, A.K. (1958) *Productivity and Social Organisation*, London: Tavistock

Ritzer, G. (1993) *The McDonaldization of Society*, Thousand Oaks, CA: Pine Forge

Royle, T. (2000) *Working for McDonald's in Europe: the unequal struggle?*, London: Routledge

Sewell, G. and Atkinson, B. (1992) 'Empowerment or emasculation? Shopfloor surveillance in a total quality organisation' in P. Blyton and P. Turnbull (eds) *Reassessing Human Resource Management*, London: Sage, 97–115

Sinclair, A. (1992) 'The tyranny of team ideology, *Organization Studies*, 13(4): 611–626

Smith, A. (1974) *The Wealth of Nations*, Harmondsworth: Penguin (originally 1776)

Smith, C. and Thompson, P. (1998) 'Re-evaluating the labour process debate', *Economic and Industrial Democracy*, 19(4): 551–577

Taylor, F.W. (1911) *The Principles of Scientific Management*, New York: Harper

Trist, E.L., Higgin, G.W., Murray, H. and Pollock, A.B. (1963) *Organisational Choice*, London: Tavistock

Watson, T.J. (1986) *Management, Organisation and Employment Strategy*, London: Routledge

Watson, T.J. and Rosborough, J. (2000), 'Teamworking and the management of flexibility: local and social–structural tensions in high performance work design initiatives' in S. Procter and F. Mueller (eds) *Teamworking*, Basingstoke: Macmillan

Wickens, P. (1995) *The Ascendant Organization: combining commitment and control for long term sustainable business success*, Basingstoke: Macmillan

Womack, J.P., Jones, D.J. and Roos, D. (1990) *The Machine that Changed the World*, New York: Rawson

Wood, S. (1989) 'New wave management?', *Work, Employment and Society*, 3(3): 379–402

Wood, S. and Albanese, M. (1995) 'Can we speak of high commitment management on the shop floor?', *Journal of Management Studies*, 32(2): 215–247

Reading Guide 18 Changing organisational, technological, global and 'postmodern' patterns

Ashkenas, R., Ulrich, D., Jick, T. and Kerr, S. (1995) *The Boundaryless Organisation*, San Francisco, Cal: Jossey-Bass

Bartlett, C.A. and Ghoshal, S. (1990) 'Matrix management: not a structure, a frame of mind', *Harvard Business Review*, July–August: 138–145

Beynon, J. and Dunkerley, D. (eds) (1999) *The Globalisation Reader*, London: Athlone

Boddy, D. and Gunson, N. (1997) *Organizations in the Network Age*, London: Routledge

Bridges, W. (1994) 'The end of the job', *Fortune*, 130(6): 62–74

Carr, N. (1999) 'Being virtual: character and the new economy', *Harvard Business Review*, 77(3): 181–90

Casey, C. (1995) *Work, Self and Society: after industrialism*, London: Routledge

Castells, M. (1998) *The information age: economy, society and culture, Vol. III: end of millennium*, Oxford: Blackwell

Castells, M. (1997) *The information age: economy, society and culture, Vol. II: the power of identity*, Oxford: Blackwell

Castells, M. (1996) *The information age: economy, society and culture, Vol. I: the rise of the network society*, Oxford: Blackwell

Chesbrough, H.W. and Teece, D.J. (1996) 'When is virtual virtuous – organizing for innovation', *Harvard Business Review*, Jan–Feb: 65–73

Child, C. and Faulkner, D. (1998), 'Networks and virtuality', in C. Child and D. Faulkner (eds) *Strategies for Co-operation: managing alliances, networks and joint ventures*, Oxford: Oxford University Press, 113–142

Clark, J. (1995) *Managing Innovation and Change: people, technology and strategy*, London: Sage

Clark, J., McLoughlin, I., Rose, H. and King, R. (1988) *The Process of Technological Change: new technology and social choice in the workplace*, Cambridge: Cambridge University Press

Collins, J.C. and Porras, J.I. (1995) *Built to Last: successful habits of visionary companies*, New York: Random House

Cooper, C.L. and Rousseau, D.M. (1999) *The Virtual Organization, Trends in Organizational Behaviour*, Vol. 6, Chichester: Wiley

Cooperrider, D.L. and Dutton, J. (1999) *Organizational Dimensions of Global Change: no limits to cooperation*, London: Sage

Dawson, P. (1994) *Organisational Change: a processual approach*, London: Chapman

Drucker, P.F. (1997) 'Toward the new organization' in F. Hesselbein, M. Goldsmith, and R. Beckhard (eds) *The Organization of the Future*, San Francisco: Jossey-Bass

Elger, T. and Smith, C. (1994) *Global Japanization? The Transformation of the Labour Process*, London: Routledge

Ghoshal, S. and Bartlett, C. (1997) *The Individualised Corporation*, London: Heinemann

Handy, C. (1994) *The Empty Raincoat: making sense of the future*, London: Hutchinson

Harris, M. (1998) 'Re-thinking the virtual organization', in P.J. Jackson and J.M. van der Wielen (eds) *Teleworking: International Perspectives*, London: Routledge, 74–92

Huws, U. (1997) *Teleworking: Guidelines for Good Practice*, Report 329, Brighton: Institute for Employment Studies

Jackson, P.J. and van der Wielen, J.M. (1998) *Teleworking: new international perspectives from telecommuting to the virtual organisation*, London: Routledge

Kumar, K. (1996) *From Post-Industrial to Post-modern Society*, Oxford: Blackwell

Lyotard, J.-F. (1984) *The Postmodern Condition*, Manchester: Manchester University Press

McGrew, A. (1992) 'A global society?' in S. Hall, D. Held and A. McGrew (eds) *Modernity and its Future*, Cambridge: Polity Press

McKinlay, A. and Taylor, P. (2000) *Inside the Factory of the Future*: *work, power and authority in microelectronics*, London: Routledge

McLoughlin, I. and Clark, J. (1988) *Technological Change at Work*, Milton Keynes: Open University Press

McLoughlin, I. (1999) *Creative Technological Change: The Shaping of Technology and Organizations*, London: Routledge

Ohmae, K. (1990) *The Borderless World*, New York: Harper Business

Parker, B. (1996) 'Evolution and revolution: from international business to globalization' in S.R. Clegg, C. Hardy and W. Nord (eds) *Handbook of Organization Studies*, London: Sage, 484–506

Pettigrew, A. and Fenton, E. (eds) (2000) *Process and Practice in New Forms of Organizing*, London: Sage

Prahalad, C.K. and Doz, Y. (1987) *The Multinational Mission*, New York: Free Press

Rifkin, J. (1996) *The End of Work*, New York: Tarcher/Putnam Press

Semler, R. (1994) *Maverick!*, London: Arrow

Thompson, P. and O'Connell Davidson, J. (1995) 'The continuity of discontinuity: managerial rhetoric in turbulent times', *Personnel Review*, 24(4): 17–33

Torrington, D. (1994) *International Human Resource Management: think globally, act locally*, Hemel Hempstead: Prentice-Hall

Venkatraman, N. and Henderson, J.C. (1998) 'Real strategies for virtual organizing', *Sloan Management Review*, 40(1): 33–48

Zuboff, S. (1988) *In the Age of the Smart Machine*, New York: Basic Books

Reading Guide 19 Cultural aspects of organisations

Alvesson, M. (1987) 'Organisations, culture and ideology', *International Studies of Management and Organisation*, 17(3): 4–18

Alvesson, M. and Berg, P.O. (1992) *Corporate Culture and Organizational Symbolism*, Berlin: de Gruyter

Anthony, P.D. (1994) *Managing Culture*, Buckingham: Open University Press

Barney, J. (1986) 'Organizational culture: can it be a source of sustained competitive advantage?', *Academy of Management Review*, 2(3): 656–665

Bartlett, C.A. and Ghoshal, S. (1989) *Managing Across Borders*, London: Hutchinson

Bate, P. (1994) *Strategies for Cultural Change*, Oxford: Butterworth-Heinemann

Berg, P.O. and Kreiner, K. (1990) 'Corporate architecture: turning physical settings into symbolic resources', in P. Gagliardi (ed.) *Symbols and Artifacts: Views of the Corporate Landscape*, New York: Aldine de Gruyter, 41–67

Beyer, J.M. and Trice, H.M. (1988) 'The communication of power relations in organizations through cultural rites', in M.D. Jones, M.D. Moore and R.C. Sayder (eds) *Inside Organisations: understanding the human dimension*, Newbury Park, Cal: Sage, 141–157

Bowles, M.L. (1989) 'Myth, meaning and work organisation', *Organisation Studies*, 10(3): 405–421

Brown, A.D. (1998) *Organisational Culture*, second edn, London: FT Pitman

Brown, A.D. and Starkey, K. (1994) 'The effect of organizational culture on communication and information', *Journal of Management Studies*, 31(6): 807–828

Dandridge, T.C., Mitroff, I. and Joyce, W.E. (1980) 'Organizational symbolism: a topic to expand organizational analysis', *Academy of Management Review*, 5(1): 77–82

Davis, S.M. (1984) *Managing Corporate Culture*, Cambridge, Mass: Ballinger

Deal, T.E. and Kennedy, A.A. (1999) *The New Corporate Cultures: revitalizing the workplace after downsizing, merger and reengineering*, New York: Texere

Deal, T.E. and Kennedy, A.A. (1982) *Corporate Cultures: the rites and rituals of corporate life*, Reading Mass: Addison-Wesley

du Gay, P. (1992) 'Enterprise culture and the ideology of excellence', *New Formations*, 13: 45–62

Feldman, S.P. (1996) 'Management in context: culture and organisational change' in S. Linstead, R. Grafton Small and P. Jeffcutt (eds) *Understanding Management*, London: Sage

Feldman, S.P. (1988) 'How organizational culture can affect innovation', *Organizational Dynamics*, 17(1): 57–68

Fitzgerald, T.H. (1988) 'Can change in organizational culture really be managed?', *Organizational Dynamics*, 17(2): 5–15

Frost, P.J., Moore, L.F., Louis, M.R., Lundberg, C.C. and Martin, J. (eds) (1991) *Reframing Organizational Culture*, London: Sage

Frost, P.J., Moore, L.F., Louis, M.R., Lundberg, C.C. and Martin, J. (eds) (1985) *Organizational Culture*, London: Sage

Gagliardi, P. (1990) *Symbols and Artifacts: views of the corporate landscape*, New York: Aldine de Gruyter

Gagliardi, P. (1986) 'The creation and change of organizational cultures: a conceptual framework', *Organization Studies*, 7(2): 117–134

Graves, D. (1986) *Corporate Culture: diagnosis and change*, New York: St Martin's Press

Green, S. (1988) 'Understanding corporate culture and its relation to strategy', *International Studies of Management and Organization*, 18(2): 6–28

Hampden-Turner, C. (1990) *Corporate Culture: from vicious to virtuous circles*, London: Economist Books

Handy, C.B. (1978) *The Gods of Management*, Harmondsworth: Penguin

Hassard, J. and Sharifi, S. (1989) 'Corporate culture and strategic change', *Journal of General Management*, 15(2): 4–19

Hofstede, G. (1991) *Cultures and Organisations*, London: McGraw-Hill

Hofstede, G., Neuijen, B., Ohayv, D. and Sanders, G. (1990) 'Measuring organizational cultures: a qualitative study across twenty cases', *Administrative Science Quarterly*, 35: 286–316

Jaques, E. (1951) *The Changing Culture of a Factory*, London: Tavistock

Kilmann, R.H., Saxton, M.J., Serpa, R. and associates (eds) *Gaining Control of the Corporate Culture*, San Francisco, Cal: Jossey-Bass

Kotter, J.P. and Heskett, J.L. (1992) *Corporate Culture and Performance*, New York: Free Press

Kunda, G. (1995) *Engineering Culture: Control and Commitment in a High-tech Corporation*, Philadelphia: Temple University Press

Linstead, S. and Grafton-Small, R. (1992) 'On reading organizational culture', *Organization Studies*, 13(3): 331–355

Martin, G. (1992) *Cultures in Organizations: Three Perspectives*, Oxford: Oxford University Press

Martin, J. (1985) 'Can organization culture be managed?' in P.J. Frost, L.F. Moore, M.R. Louis, C.C. Lundberg and J. Martin (eds) *Organization Culture*, London: Sage, 95–98

Martin, J. and Siehl, C. (1983) 'Organizational culture and counterculture: an uneasy symbiosis', *Organizational Dynamics*, Autumn: 52–64

Meek, V.L. (1988) 'Organizational culture: origins and weaknesses', *Organization Studies*, 9(4): 453–473

Ogbonna, E. (1992/3) 'Managing organizational culture: fantasy or reality?', *Human Resource Management Journal*, 3(2): 42–54

Ogbonna, E. and Wilkinson, B. (1990) 'Corporate strategy and corporate culture: the view from the checkout', *Personnel Review*, 19(4): 9–15

Ott, J.S. (1989) *The Organizational Culture Perspective*, Pacific Grove, Cal: Brooks-Cole

Parker, M. (1999) *Organizational Culture and Identity: unity and division at work*, London: Sage

Pascale, R.T. (1985) 'The paradox of corporate culture: reconciling ourselves to socialization', *California Management Review*, 27(2): 26–41

Pettigrew, A.M. (1979) 'On studying organisational cultures', *Administrative Science Quarterly*, December: 570–81

Pondy, L.R., Frost, P., Morgan, G. and Dandridge, T. (eds) (1983) *Organizational Symbolism*, Greenwich, Conn: Jai Press

Ray, C.A. (1986) 'Corporate culture; the last frontier of control?', *Journal of Management Studies*, 23(3): 287–297

Rowlinson, M. and Hassard, J. (1993) 'The invention of corporate culture: a history of the histories of Cadbury', *Human Relations*, 46(3): 299–326

Sathe, V. (1985) *Culture and Related Corporate Realities*, Homewood, Ill: Irwin

Schein, E.H. (1985) *Organisational Culture and Leadership*, San Francisco: Jossey-Bass

Schein, E.H. (1983) 'The role of the founder in creating organizational culture', *Organizational Dynamics*, 12(1): 13–28

Schultz, M. (1995) *Studying Organizational Cultures: Diagnosis and Understanding*, Berlin: De Gruyter

Smircich, L. (1983) 'Concepts of culture and organisational analysis', *Administrative Science Quarterly*, 28(3): 339–358

Strati, A. (1998) 'Organizational symbolism as a social construction: a perspective from the sociology of knowledge', *Human Relations*, 51(11): 1379–1402

Trice, H.M. and Beyer, J.M. (1993) *The Cultures of Work Organizations*, Englewood Cliffs: Prentice-Hall

Trice, H.M. and Beyer, J.M. (1984) 'Studying cultures through rites and organizational ceremonies', *Academy of Management Review*, 9(4): 653–669

Van Maanen, J. and Barley, S.R. (1984) 'Occupational communities: culture and control in organisations' in B. Staw and L. Cummings (eds) *Research in Organizational Behavior 6*, Greenwich, Conn: JAI Press

Weick, K.E. (1987) 'Organizational culture as a source of high reliability', *California Management Review*, 29(2): 112–127

Weick, K.E. (1985) 'The significance of corporate culture', in P.J. Frost, L.F. Moore, M.R. Louis, C.C. Lundberg and J. Martin (eds) *Organizational Culture*, Beverly Hills, Cal: Sage, 381–389

Wilkins, A.L. (1983) 'Organizational stories as symbols which control the organization' in L.R. Pondy, P.J. Frost, G. Morgan and T.C. Dandridge (eds) *Organizational Symbolism*, Greenwich, Conn: JAI Press, 81–92

Wilkins, A.L. and Dyer, W. G. (1988) 'Toward culturally sensitive theories of culture change', *Academy of Management Review*, 13(4): 522–533

Williams, A., Dobson, P. and Walters, M. (1993) *Changing Culture: new organizational approaches*, second edn, London: Institute of Personnel Management

Willmott, H. (1993) 'Strength is ignorance: Slavery is freedom: managing culture in modern organisations', *Journal of Management Studies*, 30(4): 515–552

Wuthnow, R.J., Davison, H., Bergesen, A. and Kurzweil, E. (1984) *Cultural Analysis*, London, Routledge

Reading Guide 20 Cross-cultural and comparative patterns

Barsoux, J.-L. and Lawrence, P. (1990) *Management in France*, London: Cassell

Bjerke, B. (2001) *Business Leadership and Culture*, Cheltenham: Elgar

Calori, R. and Lawrence, P. (1991) *The Business of Europe: managing change*, London: Sage

Child, J. and Kieser, A. (1981) 'Organization and managerial roles in British and West German companies: an examination of the "culture-free" thesis' in D.J. Hickson and C. J. McMillan (eds) *Organization and Nation*, Aldershot: Gower, 51–73

Felstead, A. and Jewson, N. (1999) *Global Trends in Flexible Labour*, Basingstoke: Macmillan

Fukuyama, F. (1995) *Trust: the social virtues and the creation of prosperity*, London: Hamish Henderson

Goffee, R. and Jones, G. (1995) 'Developing managers for Europe: a re-examination of cross-cultural differences', *European Management Journal*, 13(3): 245–250

Hampden-Turner, C.M. and Trompenaars, F. (2000) *Building Cross Cultural Competence: how to create wealth from conflicting values*, Chichester: Wiley

Hickson, D.J. and Pugh, D.S. (1995) *Management Worldwide: the impact of societal culture on organisations around the globe*, Harmondsworth: Penguin

Hofstede, G. (2001) *Culture's Consequences: comparing values, behaviours, institutions and organizations across nation*, second edn, London: Sage

Hofstede, G. (ed.) (1998) *Masculinity and Femininity: the taboo dimension of national cultures*, London: Sage

Hofstede, G. (1993) 'Cultural constraints in management theory', *Academy of Management Executive*, February: 81–94

Hunt, J.G., Hosking, D., Schriesheim, C.A. and Stewart, R. (eds) *Leaders and managers: international perspectives on managerial behaviour and leadership*, New York: Pergamon

Lawrence, P. (1992) 'Management development in Europe: a study of cultural contrast, Britain and France', *Human Resource Management Journal*, 1(1): 1–23

Maruyama, M. (1984) 'Alternative concepts of management: insights from Asia and Africa', *Asia Pacific Journal of Management*, January: 100–111

Redding, G. (1990) *The Spirit of Chinese Capitalism*, New York: de Gruyter

Stewart, R. and Barsoux, J. (1994) *The Diversity of Management*, London: Macmillan

Stewart, R., Barsoux, J.-L., Kieser, A., Ganter H.-D. and Walgenbach P. (1994) *Managing in Britain and Germany*, Basingstoke: Macmillan

Trompenaars, F. (1993) *Riding the Waves of Culture*, London: Economist Books

Watson, T.J. and Bargiela-Chiappini, F. (1998) 'Managerial sensemaking and occupational identities in Britain and Italy', *Journal of Management Studies*, 35(3): 285–301

Whitley, R.D. (ed.) (1992) *European Business Systems: firms and markets in their national contexts*, London: Sage

Reading Guide 21 Human resource management and employment relations

Ackers, P. and Payne, J. (1998) 'British trade unions and social partnership: rhetoric, reality and strategy', *International Journal of Human Resource Management*, 9(3): 529–549

Ackers, P., Smith, P. and Smith, C. (eds) (1996) *The New Workplace Trade Unionism: critical perspectives on work and organisation*, London: Routledge

Ackroyd, S. and Procter, S. (1998) 'British manufacturing organisation and workplace industrial relations', *British Journal of Industrial Relations*, 36(2): 163–183

Anderson, N. and Herriot, P. (eds) (1997) *International Handbook of Selection and Assessment*, Chichester: Wiley

Anderson, N. and Ostroff, C. (1997) 'Selection as socialization' in N. Anderson and P. Herriot (eds) *International Handbook of Selection and Assessment*, Chichester: Wiley

Bach, S. and Sisson, K. (eds) (2000) *Personnel Management: a comprehensive guide to theory and practice*, Oxford: Blackwell

Bacon, N. (2001) 'New patterns of employment relations' in T. Redman and A. Wilkinson (eds) *Contemporary Human Resource Management*, Harlow: FT Prentice-Hall

Bacon, N., Ackers, P., Storey, J. and Coates, D. (1996) 'It's a small world: managing human resources in small businesses', *International Journal of Human Resource Management*, 7(1): 82–100

Beardwell, I. (ed.) (1996) *Contemporary Industrial Relations: a critical analysis*, Oxford: Oxford University Press

Becker, B. and Gerhart, B. (1996) 'The impact of human resource management on organisational performance', *The Academy of Management Journal*, 2(3): 60–79

Beech, N. (1998) 'Literature review: rhetoric and discourse in HRM', *Management Learning*, 29(1): 110–113

Beer, M., Spector, B., Lawrence, P.R., Mill, Q.D. and Walton, R.E. (1984), *Managing Human Assets*, Boston, Mass: Harvard Business School Press

Blyton, P. and Turnbull, P. (eds) (1992) *Reassessing Human Resource Strategies*, London: Sage

Boxall, P. (1996) 'The strategic HRM debate and the resource-based view of the firm', *Human Resource Management Journal*, 6(3): 59–75

Boxall, P.F. (1994) 'Placing HR strategy at the heart of business success', *Personnel Management*, July: 32–35

Boxall, P. (1992) 'Strategic human resource management: beginnings of a new theoretical sophistication?', *Human Resource Management Journal*, 2(3): 60–79

Brewster, C., Hegewisch, A. and Mayne, L. (1994) 'Trends in European HRM' in P. Kirkbride (ed.) *Human Resource Management in Europe*, London: Routledge

Brewster, C., Mayrhofer, W., Morley, M. (eds) (1999) *New Challenges for European Human Resource Management*, Basingstoke: Macmillan

Cappelli, P. and Crocker-Hefter, A. (1996) 'Distinctive human resources are firms' core competencies', *Organizational Dynamics*, 24(3): 7–22

Clark, I. (1999) 'Corporate human resources and "bottom line" financial performance', *Personnel Review*, 28(4): 290–306

Clark, T. (1996) *European Human Resource Management*, Oxford: Blackwell

Claydon, T. (1998) 'Problematising partnership: the prospects for a co-operative bargaining agenda' in P. Sparrow and M. Marchington (eds) *Human Resource Management: the new agenda*, London: FT Pitman

Cooper, D. and Robertson, I.T. (1995) *The Psychology of Personnel Selection*, London: Routledge

Coupar, W. and Stevens, B. (1998) 'Towards a new model of industrial partnership' in P. Sparrow and M. Marchington (eds) *Human Resource Management: the new agenda*, London: FT Pitman

Devanna, M.A., Fombrun, C.J. and Tichy, N.M. (1984) 'A framework for strategic human resource management' in C. Fombrun, N.M. Tichy and M.A. Devanna, (eds) *Strategic Human Resource Management*, Chichester: Wiley

Dipboye, R. (1992) Selection interviews: process perspectives, Cincinnati: South-Western

Edwards, P.K. (2000) 'Discipline: towards trust and self-discipline?' in S. Bach and K. Sisson (eds) *Personnel Management: a comprehensive guide to theory and practice*, Oxford: Blackwell

Edwards, P.K. (ed.) (1995) *Industrial Relations*, Oxford: Blackwell

Edwards, P.K. (1986) *The Theory of Conflict*, Oxford: Blackwell

Ezzamel, M., Lilley, S., Wilkinson, A. and Willmott, H. (1996) 'Practices and practicalities in human resource management', *Human Resource Management Journal*, 5(3): 7–23

Fombrun, C.J. (1983) 'Strategic management: integrating the human resource systems into strategic planning', *Advances in Strategic Management, Vol. 2*, Greenwich, Conn: JAI Press

Fombrun, C., Tichy, N.M. and Devanna, M.A. (eds) (1984) *Strategic Human Resource Management*, New York: Wiley

Gallie, D., White, M., Cheng, Y. and Tomlinson, M. (1998) *Restructuring the Employment Relationship*, Oxford: Oxford University Press

Gennard, J. and Kelly, J. (1994), 'Human resource management: the views of personnel directors', *Human Resource Management Journal*, 5(1): 15–32.

Gospel, H.F. and Palmer, G. (1993) *British Industrial Relations*, second edn, London: Routledge

Grant, D. and Oswick, C. (1998) 'Of believers, atheists and agnostics: practitioner views on HRM', *Industrial Relations Journal*, 29(3): 178–193

Gratton, L., Hope Hailey, V., Stiles, P. and Truss, C. (1999) *Strategic Human Resource Management*, Oxford: Oxford University Press

Guest, D. (1991) 'Personnel management: the end of orthodoxy?', *British Journal of Industrial Relations*, 29(2): 149–175

Guest, D. (1990) 'Human resource management and the American Dream', *Journal of Management Studies*, 27(4): 377–397

Guest, D. (1989a) 'HRM: implications for industrial relations' in J. Storey (ed.) *New Perspectives on Human Resource Management*, London: Routledge

Guest, D. (1989b) 'Personnel and HRM: can you tell the difference?' *Personnel Management*, January: 48–51

Guest, D.E. (1987) 'Human resource management and industrial relations', *Journal of Management Studies*, 24(5): 503–521

Guest, D. and Hoque, K. (1994) 'The good, the bad and the ugly: employment relations in new non-union workplaces', *Human Resource Management Journal*, 5(1): 1–14

Hart, T.J. (1993) 'HRM – time to exorcize the militant tendency', *Employee Relations*, 15(3): 29–36.

Hendry, C. (1994) *Human Resource Management*, Oxford: Butterworth-Heinemann.

Hendry, C. (1993) *Human Resource Strategies for International Growth*, London: Routledge

Hendry, C., Pettigrew, A. and Sparrow, P. (1988) 'Changing patterns of human resource management', *Personnel Management*, November: 31–41

Judge, T.A. and Cable, D.M. (1997) 'Applicant personality, organizational culture and organization attraction', *Personnel Psychology*, 50: 359–394

Kamoche, K. (2001) *Understanding Human Resource Management*, Buckingham: Open University Press

Kamoche, K. (1996) 'Strategic human resource management within resource-capability view of the firm', *Journal of Management Studies*, 33(2): 213–233

Kamoche, K. (1995) 'Rhetoric ritualism and totemism in human resource management', *Human Relations*, 48(4): 367–385

Kamoche, K. (1994) 'A critique and a proposed reformulation of strategic human resource management', *Human Resource Management Journal*, 4(4): 29–47

Keenoy, T. (1990) 'Human resource management: rhetoric, reality and contradiction', *International Journal of Human Resource Management*, 1(3): 363–384

Kelly, J. (1998) *Rethinking Industrial Relations*, London: Routledge

Legge, K. (2000) 'Personnel Management in the Lean Organization', in S. Bach and K. Sisson (eds) *Personnel Management: a comprehensive guide to theory and practice*, Oxford: Blackwell

Legge, K. (1995) *Human Resource Management: rhetorics and realities*, Basingstoke: Macmillan

Legge, K. (1993) 'The role of personnel specialists: centrality or marginalization?' in J. Clark (ed.) *Human Resource Management and Technical Change*, London: Sage, 20–42

Legge, K. (1989) 'Human resource management: a critical analysis' in J. Storey (ed.) *New Perspectives on Human Resource Management*, London: Routledge

Legge, K. (1978) *Power, Innovation and Problem Solving in Personnel Management*, London: McGraw-Hill

Lengnick-Hall, C. and Lengnick-Hall, M. (1988) 'Strategic human resources management: a review of the literature and a proposed typology', *Academy of Management Review*, 13(3): 454–470

Leopold, J., Harris, L. and Watson, T.J. (1999) *Strategic Human Resourcing: Principles, Perspectives and Practices*, London: FT Pitman

Mabey, C., Salaman, G. and Storey, J. (1998) *Strategic Human Resource Management* second edn, Oxford: Blackwell

Mabey, C., Skinner, D. and Clark, T. (eds) (1998) *Experiencing Human Resource Management*, London: Sage

Marchington, M. and Parker, P. (1990) *Changing Patterns of Employee Relations*, London: Harvester Wheatsheaf

McDaniel, M.A., Whetzel, D.L., Schmidt, F.L. and Maurer, S.D. (1994) 'The validity of the employment interviews: a comprehensive review and meta analysis', *Journal of Applied Psychology*, 79: 599–616

Mueller, F. (1996) 'Human resources as strategic assets: an evolutionary resource-based theory', *Journal of Management Studies*, 33(6): 757–785

Newell, S. and Shackleton, V. (2001) 'Selection and assessment as an interactive decision–action process', in T. Redman and A. Wilkinson (eds) *Contemporary Human Resource Management*, Harlow: FT Prentice-Hall

Newell, S. and Shackleton, V. (2000) 'Recruitment and selection', in S. Bach and K. Sisson (eds) *Personnel Management: a comprehensive guide to theory and practice*, Oxford: Blackwell

Newell, S. and Shackleton, V. (1993) 'The use (and abuse) of psychometric tests in British industry and commerce', *Human Resource Management Journal*, 4(1): 14–23

Newton, T. and Findlay, P. (1996) 'Playing God? The performance of appraisal', *Human Resource Management Journal*, 6(3): 42–58

Noon, M. (1992) 'HRM: a map, model or theory?' in P. Blyton and P. Turnbull (eds) *Reassessing Human Resource Management*, London: Sage

Procter, S.J., Rowlinson, M., McArdle, L., Hassard, J. and Forrester, P. (1994) 'Flexibility, politics and strategy: in defence of the model of the flexible firm', *Work, Employment and Society*, 8(2): 221–242

Purcell, J. (1995) 'Corporate strategy and its link with human resource management strategy' in J. Storey (ed.) *Human Resource Management: a critical text*, London: Routledge

Purcell, J. and Ahlstrand, B. (1994) *Human Resource Management in the Multi-Divisional Company*, Oxford: Oxford University Press

Redman, T. and Wilkinson, A. (eds) (2001) *Contemporary Human Resource Management*, Harlow: FT Prentice-Hall

Rosenfeld, P., Giacalone, R.A. and Riordan, C.A. (1995) *Impression Management in Organizations: theory, measurement, practice*, London: Routledge

Schuler, R.S. and Jackson, S.E. (eds) (1999) *Strategic Human Resource Management*, Oxford: Blackwell

Schuler, R.S. and Jackson, S.E. (1996) *Human Resource Management: positioning for the 21st century*, Minneapolis, St Paul: West Publishing

Silverman, D. and Jones, J. (1976) *Organisational Work: the language of grading and the grading of language*, London: Macmillan

Sisson, K. (1995) 'Human resource management and the personnel function' in J. Storey (ed.) *Human Resource Management: a critical text*, London: Routledge

Sisson, K. (1993) 'In search of HRM', *British Journal of Industrial Relations*, 31(2): 201–209

Sparrow, P. and Hiltrop, I.M. (1994) *European Human Resource Management in Transition*, Hemel Hempstead: Prentice-Hall

Starkey, K. and McKinlay, A. (1993) *Strategy and the Human Resource*, Oxford: Blackwell

Storey, J. (ed.) (1995) *Human Resource Management*, London: Routledge

Storey, J. (1994) 'How new-style management is taking hold', *Personnel Management*, January: 32–35

Storey, J. (1992) *Developments in the Management of Human Resources*, Oxford: Blackwell

Storey, J. (ed.) (1989) *New Perspectives on Human Resource Management*, London: Routledge

Storey, J. and Bacon, N. (1993), 'Individualism and collectivism into the 1990s', *International Journal of Human Resource Management*, 4(3): 665–684

Storey, J., Cressey, P., Morris, T. and Wilkinson, A. (1997) 'Changing employment practices in UK banking: case studies', *Personnel Review*, 26(1): 24–42

Tailby, S. and Winchester, D. (2000) 'Management and trade unions: towards social partnership?', in S. Bach and K. Sisson (eds) *Personnel Management: a comprehensive guide to theory and practice*, Oxford: Blackwell

Torrington, D. (1998) 'Crisis and opportunity in HRM: the challenge for the personnel function' in P. Sparrow and M. Marchington (eds) *Human Resource Management: the new agenda*, London: FT Pitman

Torrington, D. and Hall, L. (1998) *Human Resource Management*, London: Prentice-Hall

Torrington, D. and Hall, L. (1996) 'Chasing the Rainbow: how seeking status through strategy misses the point for the personnel function', *Employee Relations*, 18(6): 79–96

Towers, B. (1997) *The Representation Gap*, Oxford: Oxford University Press

Townley, B. (1994) *Reframing Human Resource Management*, London: Sage

Townley, B. (1993) 'Performance appraisal and the emergence of management', *Journal of Management Studies*, 3(2): 221–238

Townley, B. (1989) 'Selection and appraisal: reconstituting social relations?' in J. Storey (ed.) *New Perspectives on HRM*, London: Routledge

Tyson, S. (1995a) *Human Resource Strategy*, London: Pitman

Tyson. S. (ed.) (1995b) *Strategic Prospects for HRM*, London: IPD

Tyson, S. and Fell, A. (1986) *Evaluating the Personnel Function*, London: Hutchinson

Walton, R.E. (1985) 'From control to commitment in the workplace', *Harvard Business Review*, March–April: 76–84

Watson, D.H. (1988) *Managers of Discontent: trade union officers and industrial relations managers*, London: Routledge

Watson, T.J. (2001) 'Speaking professionally – occupational anxiety and discursive ingenuity among human resourcing specialists' in S. Whitehead and M. Dent (eds) *Managing Professional Identities*, London: Routledge

Watson, T.J. (1999), 'Human resourcing strategies: choice, chance and circumstances' in J. Leopold, L. Harris and T.J. Watson (eds) *Strategic Human Resourcing: principles, perspectives and practices*, London: FT Pitman

Watson, T.J. (1997) 'Human resource management, industrial relations and theory – standing back and starting again', *The New Zealand Journal of Industrial Relations*, 22(1): 7–21

Watson, T.J. (1995) 'In search of HRM: beyond the rhetoric and reality distinction or the dog that didn't bark', *Personnel Review*, 24(4): 6–16

Watson, T.J. (1977) *The Personnel Managers*, London: Routledge

Watson, T.J., Leopold, J. and Newsome, K. (1999), 'Conflict and co-operation in employment relations' in J. Leopold, L. Harris and T.J. Watson (eds) *Strategic Human Resourcing: principles, perspectives and practices*, London: FT Pitman

Watson, T.J. and Watson, D.H. (1999) 'Human resourcing in practice: managing employment issues in the university', *Journal of Management Studies*, 36(4): 483–504

Wood, S. (1996) 'High commitment management and payment systems', *Journal of Management Studies*, 33(1): 53–78

Wood, S. (1995) 'The four pillars of HRM: are they connected?', *Human Resource Management Journal*, 5(5): 49–59

Reading Guide 22 Work orientations, careers, contracts and motivations

Adams, J.S. (1965) 'Inequity in social exchange' in L. Berkovitz (ed.) *Advances in Experimental Social Psychology, Vol. 2*, New York: Academic Press

Adams, J.S. (1963) 'Towards an understanding of inequity', *Journal of Abnormal and Social Psychology*, 67: 422–436

Arnold, J. (1997) *Managing Careers into the 21st Century*, London: Sage

Arthur, M.B., Hall, D.T. and Lawrence, B.S. (1989) *Handbook of Career Theory*, Cambridge: Cambridge University Press

Arthur, M., Inkson, K. and Pringle, J. (1999) *The New Careers: individual action and economic change*, London: Sage

Arthur, M.B. and Rousseau, D.M. (eds) (1996) *The Boundaryless Career: new employment principle for a new organisational era*, New York: Oxford University Press

Baldamus, G. (1957) 'The relationship between work and effort', *Journal of Industrial Economics*, 6(3): 192–201

Baldamus, W. (1961) *Efficiency and Effort*, London: Tavistock

Becker, H.S. and Strauss, A. (1966) 'Careers, personality and adult socialization', *American Journal of Sociology*, 62: 404–413

Behrend, H. (1957) 'The effort bargain', *International Labor Relations Review*, 10

Blauner, R. (1964) *Alienation and Freedom: the factory worker and his industry*, Chicago: University of Chicago Press

Carter, P. and Jackson, N. (1993) 'Modernism, postmodernism and motivation, or why expectancy theory failed to come to expectation' in J. Hassard and M. Parker (eds) *Postmodernism and Organisations*, London: Sage

Cohen, L. (2001) 'Careers' in T. Redman and A. Wilkinson (eds) *Contemporary Human Resource Management*, Harlow: FT Prentice-Hall

Collin, A. (1996) 'Organizations and the end of the individual', *Journal of Managerial Psychology*, 11(7): 9–17

Collin, A. (1986) 'Career development: the significance of subjective career', *Personnel Review*, 15(2): 22–8

Collin, A. and Young, R.A. (eds) (2000) *The Future of Career*, Cambridge: Cambridge University Press

Evetts, J. (1992) 'Dimensions of career: avoiding reification in the analysis of change', *Sociology*, 26: 1–21

Goldthorpe, J.H., Lockwood, D., Bechhofer, F. and Platt, J. (1968) *The Affluent Worker: attitudes and behaviour*, Cambridge: Cambridge University Press

Guest, D. (1998) 'Is the psychological contract worth taking seriously?', *Journal of Organizational Behaviour*, 9: 649–664

Hall, D.T. and associates (1996) *The career is dead: Long live the career: A relational approach to careers*, San Francisco: Jossey-Bass

Hall, D.T. and Moss, J.E. (1998) 'The new protean career contract: helping organisations and employees adapt', *Organizational Dynamics*, 26(3): 22–37

Herriot, P. (1992) *The Career Management Challenge*, London: Sage

Herriot, P., Manning, W.E.G. and Kidd, J.M. (1997) 'The content of the psychological contract', *British Journal of Management*, 8(2): 151–162

Herriot, P. and Pemberton, C. (1995) *New Deals: the revolution in managerial careers*, Chichester: Wiley

Hochschild, A.R. (1997a) 'When work becomes home and home becomes work', ,*California Management Review*, 39(4): 79–97

Hochschild, A.R. (1997b) *The Time Bind: when work becomes home and home becomes work*, New York: Holt

Jackall, R. (1988) *Moral Mazes: the world of corporate managers*, New York: Oxford University Press

Kotter, J.P. (1973) 'The psychological contract', *California Management Review*, 15: 91–99

Lawler, E.E. (1971) *Pay and Organizational Effectiveness*, New York: McGraw-Hill

Levinson, H., Price, C., Munden, K. and Solley, C. (1966) *Men, Management and Mental Health*, Cambridge: Harvard University Press

Martin, G., Staines, H. and Pate, J. (1998) 'Linking job security and career development in a new psychological contract', *Human Resource Management Journal*, 8(3): 20–40

Maslow, A. (1968) *Towards a Psychology of Being*, Princeton: Van Nostrand

Maslow, A. (1954) *Motivation and Personality*, New York; Harper & Row

Maslow, A. (1943) 'A theory of human motivation', *Psychological Review*, 50: 37–96

McGregor, D.C. (1960) *The Human Side of Enterprise*, New York: McGraw-Hill

Morrison, D.E. (1994) 'Psychological contracts and change', *Human Resource Management*, 33(3): 353–72

Newell, H. (2000) 'Managing careers', in S. Bach and K. Sisson (eds) *Personnel Management: a comprehensive guide to theory and practice*, Oxford: Blackwell

Nippert-Eng, C.E. (1995) *Home and Work: negotiating boundaries through everyday life*, Chicago and London: University of Chicago Press

Noon, M. and Blyton, P. (1997) *The Realities of Work*, Basingstoke: Macmillan

Rauschenberger, J., Schmitt, N. and Hunter, T.E. (1980) 'A test of the need hierarchy concept', *Administrative Science Quarterly*, 25(4): 654–670

Robinson, S. and Rousseau, D.M. (1994) 'The psychological contract – not the exception but the norm', *Journal of Organisational Behavior*, 15(3): 245–259

Rose, M. (1988) *Industrial Behaviour*, Harmondsworth: Penguin

Rousseau, D.M. (1995) *Psychological Contracts in Organisations: understanding written and unwritten agreements*, Thousand Oaks, Cal: Sage

Schein, E. (1978) *Career Dynamics: matching individual and organizational needs*, Reading, Mass: Addison-Wesley.

Stiles, P., Gratton, L., Truss, C., Hope-Hailey, V. and McGovern, P. (1997) 'Performance management and the psychological contract', *Human Resource Management Journal*, 7(1): 57–66

Stouffer, S.A. and associates (1949) *The American Soldier*, Princeton, NJ: Princeton University Press

Thompson, P. (1989) *The Nature of Work*, second edn, London: Macmillan

Vroom, V.H. (1964) *Work and Motivation*, New York: Wiley

Warhurst, C. and Thompson, P. (1998) 'Hands, hearts and minds: changing work and workers at the end of the century' in P. Thompson and C. Warhurst (eds) *Workplaces of the Future*, Basingstoke: Macmillan

Watson, T.J. (1996) 'Motivation: that's Maslow, isn't it?', *Management Learning*, 27(4): 447–464

Watson, T.J. (1995) *Sociology, Work and Industry*, London: Routledge

Watson, T.J. and Harris, P. (1996) 'Human resources are strategic too: managerial career strategies, planned or realized', *Strategic Change*, 5(6): 1–12

Watson, T.J. and Tansley, C. (2000) 'Strategic exchange in the development of human resource information systems', *New Technology, Work and Employment*, 15(2): 108–122

Wilson, N.A.B. (1973) *On the Quality of Working Life*, London: HMSO

Young, R.A. and Collin, A. (eds) (1992) *Interpreting Career: hermeneutical studies of lives in context*, Westport, Conn: Praeger

Reading Guide 23 Gender in organisations and management

Acker, T. (1990) 'Hierarchies, jobs, bodies: a theory of gendered organizations', *Gender and Society*, 4(2): 139–158

Adler, N. and Izraeli, D. (eds) (1994) *Competitive Frontiers: women managers in a global economy*, Cambridge, Mass: Blackwell

Allen, S. and Truman, C. (eds) (1993) *Women in Business: perspectives on women entrepreneurs*, London: Routledge

Alvesson, M. and Billing, Y. (1997) *Understanding Gender and Organizations*, London: Sage

Alvesson, M. and Billing, Y. (1992) 'Gender and organization: towards a differential understanding', *Organization Studies*, 13(1): 73–103

Arroba, T. and James, K. (1988) 'Are politics palatable to women managers? How women can make wise moves at work', *Women in Management Review,* 3(3): 123–110

Asplund, D. (1988) *Women Managers: changing organisational cultures*, Chichester: Wiley

Bailyn, L. (1993) *Breaking the Mold: women, men and time in the new corporate world*, New York: Free Press

Brewis, J. and Grey, C. (1994) 'Re-eroticizing the workforce: an exegesis and critique', *Gender, Work and Organisation*, 1(2): 67–82

Calas, M.B. and Smircich, L. (1996) 'From "the woman's" point of view: feminist approaches to organization studies' in S.R. Clegg, C. Hardy and W. Nord (eds) *Handbook of Organization Studies*, London: Sage, 218–257

Cavendish, R. (1982) *Women on the Line*, London: Routledge and Kegan Paul

Cheng, C. (ed.) (1996) *Masculinities in Organisations*, Newbury Park, Cal: Sage

Cockburn, C. (1991) *In the Way of Women: men's resistance to sex equality in organisations*, London: Macmillan

Collinson, D. (1992) *Managing the Shopfloor: subjectivity, masculinity and workplace culture*, Berlin: de Gruyter

Collinson, D.L. and Collinson, M. (1989) 'Sexuality in the workplace: the domination of men's sexuality', in J. Hearn, D.L. Sheppard, P. Tancred-Sherrif and G. Burrell (eds) *The Sexuality of Organisation*, London: Sage

Collinson, D.L. and Hearn, J. (eds) (1996) *Men as Managers, Managers as Men: critical perspectives on men, masculinities and managements*, London: Sage

Collinson, D., Knights, D. and Collinson, M. (1990) *Managing to Discriminate*, London: Routledge

Connell, R.W. (1987) *Gender and Power*, Cambridge: Polity Press

Davidson, M.J. and Burke, R.J. (2000) *Women in Management: Current Research Issues, Volume II*, London: Sage

Davidson, M.J. and Cooper, C.L. (1992) *Shattering the Glass Ceiling: the woman manager*, London: Paul Chapman

Ferrario, M. (1994) 'Women as managerial leaders', in M.J. Davidson and R.J. Burke, R.J. (eds) *Women in Management*, London: Paul Chapman

Gherardi, S. (1996) 'Gendered organisational cultures: narratives of women travellers in a male world', *Gender, Work and Organisation*, 3(4): 187–201

Gherardi, S. (1995) *Gender, Symbolism and Organizational Cultures*, London: Sage

Gilligan, C. (1982) *In a Different Voice*, Cambridge, Mass: Harvard University Press

Goffee, R. and Scase, R. (1985) *Women in Charge*, London: Allen & Unwin

Gooch, L. and Ledwith, S. (1996) 'Women in personnel management' in S. Ledwith and F. Colgan (eds) *Women in Organizations*, Basingstoke: Macmillan

Helgesen, S. (1990) *The Female Advantage: women's ways of leadership*, New York: Doubleday

Hochschild, A.R. and MacHung, A. (1997) *The Second Shift*, New York: Avon

Itzin, C. and Newman, J. (eds) (1995) *Gender, Culture and Organizational Change*, London: Routledge

Kanter, R.M. (1977) *Men and Women of the Corporation*, New York: Basic Books

Kerfoot, D. and Knights, D. (2000) *Management, Organization and Masculinity*, London: Sage

Knights, D. and Willmott, H. (eds) (1986) *Gender and the Labour Process*, Aldershot: Gower

Ledwith, S. and Colgan, F. (1996) *Women in Organisations: challenging gender politics*, Basingstoke: Macmillan

Leidner, R. (1991) 'Serving hamburgers and selling insurance: gender, work and identity in interactive service jobs', *Gender and Society*, 5(2): 154–177

Liff, S., Worrall, L. and Cooper, C.L. (1997) 'Attitudes to women in management: an analysis of West Midlands businesses', *Personnel Review*, 26(3): 152–173

Mann, S. (1995) 'Politics and power in organizations: why women lose out', *Leadership and Organization Development Journal*, 16(2): 9–15

Marshall, J. (1995a) *Women Managers Moving on: exploring career and life choice*, London: Routledge

Marshall, J. (1995b) 'Working at senior management and board levels: some of the issues for women', *Women In Management Review*, 10: 21–5

Marshall, J. (1984) *Women Managers: travellers in a male world*, Chichester: Wiley

Mills, A. and Tancred, P. (1992) *Gendering Organization Analysis*, London: Sage

Mills, A.J. (1988) 'Organization, gender and culture', *Organization Studies*, 9(3): 351–369

Powell, G.N. (1999) *Handbook of Gender and Work*, London: Sage

Powell, G.N. (1993) *Women and Men in Management*, Newbury Park: Sage

Pringle, R. (1988) *Secretaries Talk: sexuality, power and work*, London: Verso

Roper, M. (1994) *Masculinity and the British Organisation Man Since 1945*, Oxford: Oxford University Press

Rosener, J.B. (1990) 'Ways women lead', *Harvard Business Review*, Nov–Dec: 119–125

Savage, M. and Witz, A. (eds) (1992) *Gender and Bureaucracy*, Oxford: Blackwell

Simpson, R. (1997) 'Have times changed? Career barriers and the token woman manager', *British Journal of Management*, 8 (special issue): 121–130

Stanko, E. (1988) 'Keeping Women In and Out of Line: sexual harassment and occupational segregation', in S. Walby (ed.) *Gender Segregation at Work*, Buckingham: Open University Press

Tannen, D. (1990) *You Just Don't Understand: women and men in conversation*, New York: William Morrow

Tanton, M. (1994) *Women in Management*, London: Routledge

Wajcman, J. (1998) *Managing Like a Man: women and men in corporate management*, Cambridge: Polity

Wajcman, J. (1996) 'Desperately seeking differences: is managerial style gendered?' *British Journal of Industrial Relations*, 34(3): 333–349

York, P. (1999) 'The gender agenda', *Management Today*, October: 56–63

Reading Guide 24 Mischief, humour and joking in organisations

Ackroyd, S. and Thompson, P. (1999) *Organisational Misbehaviour*, London: Sage

Adams, A. (1992) *Bullying at Work*, London: Virago

Analoui, F. and Kakabadse, A.P. (1991) *Sabotage – how to recognise and manage employee defiance*, London: Mercury

Barsoux, J.-L. (1993) *Funny Business: humour, management and business culture*, New York: Cassell

Boland, R.J. and Hoffman, R. (1983) 'Humour in a machine shop: an interpretation of symbolic action' in L.R. Pondy, P. Frost, G. Morgan and T. Dandridge (eds) *Organizational Symbolism*, Greenwich, Conn: JAI Press

Bradney, P. (1957) 'The joking relationship in industry', *Human Relations*. 10(2): 179–187

Brown, G. (1977) *Sabotage: A Study in Industrial Conflict*, Nottingham: Spokesman Books

Burrell, G. (1992) 'Sex and Organisations' in A.J. Mills and P. Tancred (eds) *Gendering Organisational Analysis*, London: Sage

Collinson, D.L. (1994) 'Strategies of Resistance: power, knowledge and subjectivity in the workplace' in J. Jermier, W. Nord and D. Knights (eds) *Resistance and Power in the Workplace*, London: Routledge

Collinson, D.L. (1992) *Managing the Shopfloor: subjectivity, masculinity and workplace culture*, Berlin: de Gruyter

Collinson, D.L. (1988) 'Engineering humour: masculinity, joking and conflict in shop floor relations', *Organization Studies*, 9(2): 181–199

Dalton, M. (1948) 'The Industrial Rate Buster', *Applied Anthropology*, 7(1): 5–23

Davies, C. (1982) 'Ethnic jokes, moral values and social boundaries', *British Journal of Sociology*, 33(3): 383–403

Di Tomaso, N. (1989) 'Sexuality in the workplace: discrimination and harassment', in J. Hearn, D.L. Sheppard, P. Tancred-Sherrif and G. Burrell (eds) *The Sexuality of Organization*, London: Sage

Ditton, J. (1977a) *Part-time Crime: An Ethnography of Fiddling and Pilferage*, London: Macmillan

Ditton, J. (1977b) 'Perks, pilferage and the fiddle: the historical structure of invisible wages', *Theory and Society*, 4(1): 39–71

Dubois, P. (1977) *Sabotage in Industry*, Harmondsworth: Penguin

Filby, M. (1992) 'The figures, the personality and the bums: service work and sexuality', *Work, Employment and Society*, 6(1): 23–42

Fine, G.A. (1988) 'Letting off steam: redefining a restaurant's work environment' in M.D. Moore and R.C. Snyder (eds) *Inside Organizations: understanding the human dimension*, Newbury Park, CA: Sage, 119–128

Fox, S. (1990) 'The ethnography of humour and the problem of social reality', *Sociology*, 24(3): 431–446

Harlow, E., Hearn, J. and Parkin, W. (1992) 'Sexuality and social work organisations', in P. Carter, T. Jeffs and M. Smith (eds) *Changing Social Work and Welfare*, Buckingham: Open University Press

Henry, S. (1987) *The Hidden Economy: the context and control of borderline crime*, Oxford: Martin Robertson

Jacobson, H. (1997) *Seriously Funny: from the ridiculous to the sublime*, London: Viking

Jermier, J. (1988) 'Sabotage at work: the rational view', *The Sociology of Organisations*, 6: 101–134

Jermier, J., Knights, D. and Nord, W. (1994) *Resistance and Power in Organisations*, London: Routledge

Lee, D. (2000) 'An analysis of workplace bullying in the UK' *Personnel Review*, 29(5): 593–612

Linstead, S. (1985) 'Jokers wild: the importance of humour in the maintenance of organisational culture', *Sociological Review*, 33(4): 741–767

MacKinnon, C.A. (1979) *The Sexual Harassment of Working Women*, New Haven: Yale University Press

Mars, G. (1982) *Cheats at Work: An Anthropology of Workplace Crime*, London: Counterpoint

Mulkay, M. (1988) *On Humour*, Cambridge: Polity Press

Noon, M. and Delbridge, R. (1993) 'News from behind my hand: gossip in organisations', *Organisation Studies*, 14(1): 23–36

Punch, M. (1996) *Dirty Business: Exploring Corporate Misconduct: Analysis and Cases*, London: Sage

Radcliffe-Brown, A.R. (1940) 'On joking relationships', *Africa*, 13: 195–210

Rayner, C. and Hoel, H. (1997) 'A summary review of literature relating to workplace bullying', *Journal of Community and Applied Social Psychology*, 7: 181–191

Roy, D. (1974) 'Sex in the factory: informal heterosexual relations between supervisors and workgroups' in C.D. Bryant (ed.) *Deviant Behaviour*, Chicago: Rand McNally

Roy, D. (1958) 'Banana time: job satisfaction and informal interaction', *Human Organisation*, 18(1): 158–161

Roy, D. (1952) 'Quota restriction and goldbricking in a machine shop', *American Journal of Sociology*, 57(5): 427–442

Stephen, T. (1999) *Bullying and Sexual Harassment*, London: IPD

Stockdale, M.S. (1996) *Sexual Harassment in the Workplace: perspectives, frontiers and response strategies*, London: Sage

Thomas, A.M. and Kitzinger, C. (1994) 'It's just something that happens: the invisibility of sexual harassment in the workplace', *Gender, Work and Organisation*, 1(3): 151–161

Reading Guide 25 Ethics, trust and morality in organising and managing

Ackers, P. (2001) 'Ethics' in T. Redman and A. Wilkinson (eds) *Contemporary Human Resource Management*, Harlow: FT Prentice-Hall

Anthony, P.D. (1986) *The Foundation of Management*, London: Tavistock

Barrett, E. (1999) 'Justice in the workplace: normative ethics and the critique of human resource management', *Personnel Review*, 28(4): 307–318

Cadbury, A. (1987) 'Ethical managers make their own rules', *Harvard Business Review*, Sept–Oct: 69–73

Fox, A. (1974) *Beyond Contract: work, power and trust relations*, London: Faber

Jackall, R. (1988) *Moral Mazes: the world of corporate managers*, New York: Oxford University Press

Kennedy, A.A. (1999) *The End of Shareholder Value*, New York: Texere

Legge, K. (1998) 'The morality of HRM' in C. Mabey, D. Skinner and T. Clark, *Experiencing Human Resource Management*, London: Sage

MacIntyre, A. (1981) *After Virtue: a study in moral theory*, London: Duckworth

Maclagan, P. (1998) *Management and Morality*, London: Sage

Mangham, I. (1995) 'MacIntyre and the manager', *Organization*, 2(2): 181–204

McAuley, J. (1996) 'Ethical issues in the management of change' in K. Smith and P. Johnson (eds) *Business Ethics and Business Behaviour*, London: International Thomson Business Press, 221–242

McMylor, P. (1994) *Alasdair MacIntyre: critic of modernity*, London: Routledge

Mitroff, I.I. (1998) 'On the fundamental importance of ethical management: why management is the most important of all human activities', *Journal of Management Inquiry*, 7(1): 68–79

Parker, M. (ed) (1998) *Ethics and Organization*, London: Sage

Roberts, J. (1984) 'The moral character of management practice', *Journal of Management Studies*, 21(3): 287–302

Roberts, J. (1996) 'Management education and the limits of technical rationality: the conditions and consequences of management practice' in R. French and C. Grey (eds) *Rethinking Management Education*, London: Sage

Royal Society of Arts (1996) *Tomorrow's Company*, Aldershot: Crouler

Smith, K. and Johnson, P. (eds) (1996) *Business Ethics and Business Behaviour*, London: International Thomson Business Press

Sorell, T. and Hendry, J. (1994) *Business Ethics*, Oxford: Butterworth-Heinemann

Statham, A. (1987) 'The gender model revisited: differences in the management styles of men and women', *Sex Roles*, 16(7/8): 409–429

Walton, C.C. (1988) *The Moral Manager*, New York: Harper and Row

Watson, T.J. (1998) 'Ethical codes and moral communities: the Gunlaw temptation, the Simon solution and the David dilemma' in M. Parker (ed.) *The Ethics of Organisation*, London: Sage

Watson, T.J. (1996), 'How do managers think? – morality and pragmatism in theory and practice', *Management Learning*, 27(3): 323–341

Weber, M. (1949) *The Methodology of the Social Sciences*, Glencoe, Ill: Free Press

Winstanley, D. and Woodall, J. (1999) *Ethical Issues in Contemporary Human Resource Management*, Basingstoke: Macmillan

Winstanley, D., Woodall, J. and Heery, E. (1996) 'Business ethics and human resource management', *Personnel Review*, 25(6): 5–12

Woodall, J. (1996) 'Managing culture change: can it ever be ethical?', *Personnel Review*, 25(6): 26–40

Reading guides index

Abrahamson, E. 494
Acker, T. 514
Ackers, P. 507, 508, 518
Ackroyd, S. 500, 507, 516
Adams, A. 516
Adams, J.S. 512
Adler, N. 514
Agor, W. 487
Ahlstrand, B. 511
Aktouf, O. 491
Albanese, M. 502
Albrow, M. 489
Aldrich, H. E. 477
Allen, J. 489
Allen, S. 514
Alvesson, M. 477, 494, 495, 504, 514
Analoui, F. 516
Anderson, N. 507
Anthony, P.D. 480, 504, 518
Araujo, L. 497
Argyris, C. 492, 497
Armstrong, P. 488
Arnold, J. 512
Arroba, T. 515
Arthur, M. 512
Ashkenas, R. 502
Asplund, D. 515
Astley, W.G. 477
Athos, A.G. 481
Atkinson, B. 502
Atkinson, J. 498
Atkinson, P. 483
Austin, J.L. 482

Babbage, C. 500
Bach, S. 508, 510, 511, 513
Bacharach, S. 478
Bacon, N. 508, 511
Badham, R. 488
Bahktin, M.M. 482
Bailyn, L. 515
Baldamus, G. 512
Baltes, P.B. 480
Bargiela-Chiappini, F. 483, 507

Baritz, L. 495
Barley, S.R. 494, 506
Barnard, C.I. 480
Barney, J. 504
Barnhart, R.K. 498
Barrett, E. 518
Barry, J. 482
Barsoux, J.-L. 506, 507, 516
Bartlett, C. A. 502, 504
Bate, P. 504
Baum, J.A.C. 477
Baumeister, R.F. 482
Beardwell, I. 508
Beatty, C.A. 491
Beaty, L. 493
Bechhofer, F. 513
Becker, B. 500, 508
Becker, H.S. 512
Beckhard, R. 503
Beech, N. 508
Beer, M. 508
Beetham, D. 498
Behling, O. 487
Behrend, H. 512
Belbin, M. 500
Benders, J. 500
Berg, P.O. 504
Berger, P.L. 482
Bergesen, A. 506
Berkovitz, L. 512
Betelheim, B. 483
Beyer, J.M. 504, 506
Beynon, J. 502
Billig, M. 482
Billing, Y. 514
Bittner, E. 477
Bjerke, B. 506
Blackler, F. 497
Blake, J. 487
Blau, P.M. 477, 482
Blauner, R. 513
Blyton, P. 502, 508, 510, 514
Boam, R. 491
Boddy, D. 502

Boden, D. 482
Boisot, M.H. 497
Boje, D.M.G. 477, 484, 500
Boland, R.J. 516
Bolman, L.G. 484
Bowles, M.L. 504
Boxall, P.F. 508
Boyatzis, R.E. 491, 492
Boydell, T. 497, 498
Bradney, P. 516
Braham, P. 489
Braverman, H. 500
Breakwell, G.M. 482
Brewer, E. 485
Brewis, J. 491, 515
Brewster, C. 508
Bridges, W. 502
Brown, G. 517
Brown, A.D. 488, 504
Brown, J.S. 497
Brown, R.K. 477
Bruner, J. 484
Brunsson, N. 487
Bryant, C.D. 518
Bryman, A. 491
Buchanan, D.A. 488, 493, 498, 500, 501
Bucher, R. 479
Bunnin, N. 484
Burawoy, M. 501
Burgoyne, J.G. 486, 491, 492, 493, 495, 497, 497, 498
Burke, R. 499, 515
Burnham, J. 480
Burns, J.M. 492
Burns, T. 485, 488, 499
Burrell, G. 477, 478, 491, 515, 517

Cable, D.M. 509
Cadbury, A. 518
Calas, M.B. 515
Calori, R. 506
Campbell, A. 495
Campbell, D. 477
Campbell, F. 491
Campbell-Jamison, F. 491
Cappelli, P. 508
Capruni, P.J. 495
Carlson, S. 486
Carr, N. 502
Carroll, C.R. 477
Carroll, S.J. 480
Carroll, L. 484
Carter, P. 478, 494, 513, 517
Casey, C. 502
Castells, M. 502
Cavendish, R. 515
Champy, J. 499
Chandler, J. 482
Checkland, P.B. 477
Cheng, C. 515
Cheng, Y. 509
Chesbrough, H.W. 502
Chia, R. 477, 480, 485, 487

Child, C. 502
Child, J. 478, 480, 486, 499, 501, 506
Christensen, S. 479
Clark, H. 482
Clark, I. 508
Clark, J. 503
Clark, T. 494, 508, 510
Clarke, J. 499, 510
Claydon, T. 493, 508, 518
Clegg, S.R. 477, 478, 479, 488, 489, 494, 497, 499, 503, 515
Cleverley, G. 487
Clutterbuck, D. 493
Coates, D. 508
Cockburn, C. 515
Coffey, A. 484
Cohen, L. 513
Cohen, M.D. 487, 488
Colgan, F. 515
Collin, A. 513, 514
Collins, D. 494
Collins, J.C. 503
Collinson, D. 515
Collinson, D.L. 500, 515, 517
Collinson, M. 515
Conger, J.A.N. 492
Connell, R.W. 515
Constable, J. 493
Cooper, C.L. 489, 491, 499, 503, 515, 516
Cooper, D. 508
Cooper, R. 478
Cooper, R.D. 489
Cooperrider, D.L. 503
Coopey, J. 497
Coupar, W. 508
Crainer, S. 493
Cressey, P. 511
Crocker-Hefter, A. 508
Cummings, L. 481, 506
Currie, G. 486
Cyert, R.M. 487
Czarniawska, B. 478, 484

Dachler, H.P. 482, 483
Dalton, M. 486, 517
Damasio, A.R. 489
Dandridge, T.C. 504, 505, 506, 516
Dankbaar, B. 501
Daudi, P. 488
Davenport, T. 499
Davidson, D. 484
Davidson, M.J. 515
Davies, C. 517
Davis, J. 482
Davis, S. M. 504
Davison, H. 506
Dawson, P. 501, 503
Day, J. 478
Day, R.A. 478
De Geus, A.P. 497
De Sitter, L.U. 501
Deal, T.E. 484, 504
Deetz, S. 477, 494
Delbridge, R. 518

den Hertog, J.F. 501
Dent, M. 512
Devanna, M.A. 492, 508, 509
Di Tomaso, N. 517
Dickson, M.W. 501
Dickson, W.J. 479
Dipboye, R. 508
Ditton, J. 517
Dobson, P. 506
Donaldson, L. 478, 499
Dopson, S. 490, 491
Doyle, M. 493
Doz, Y. 503
Drucker, P.F. 503
du Gay, P. 482, 492, 504
Dubin, R. 486
Dubois, P. 517
Duguid, P. 497
Dulewicz, V. 492, 499
Dunkerley, D. 491, 502
Dutton, J. 503
Dyer, W.G. 506

Eaker, L. 489
Earl, M.J. 480, 487
Eason, K. 478
Easterby-Smith, M. 497
Eccles, R.G. 480
Eckel, N. 487
Edwards, D. 482
Edwards, P.K. 493, 508, 509
Edwards, R. 501
Elger, T. 503
Ellis, T. 486
Emery, F.E. 478
Erickson, R.J. 490
Erlich, D. 479
Evetts, J. 513
Ezzamel, M. 509

Fahey, L. 496
Farmer, E. 494
Faulkner, D. 502
Fayol, H. 480
Feldman, M. 487
Feldman, S.P. 504
Fell, A. 512
Felstead, A. 507
Fenton, E. 503
Ferlie, E. 496
Ferrario, M. 515
Filby, M. 517
Fincham, R. 478
Findlay, P. 510
Fine, G.A. 517
Fineman, S. 478, 489
Finlay Jones, R. 489
Fitzgerald, T.H. 504
Fletcher, C. 480
Follet, M.P. 480
Fombrun, C.J. 508, 509
Forrester, P. 510
Foucault, M. 482

Fournier, V. 495
Fox, A. 499, 518
Fox, S. 493, 517
Freeman, J.H. 478
French, R. 493, 519
Friedman, A.L. 499, 501
Friedson, E. 479
Frost, P.J. 487, 490, 504, 505, 506, 516
Fukuyama, F. 507
Furestan, S. 494

Gallie, D. 509
Gabriel, Y. 478, 484, 501
Gaebler, T. 499
Gagliardi, P. 478, 504, 505
Gallie, W.B. 484, 509
Ganter, H.-D. 507
Garavan, T. 497
Gardner, W. 492
Geertz, C. 482
Gennard, J. 509
Gergen, K.J. 482, 483
Gerhart, B. 508
Gherardi, S. 497, 515
Ghoshal, S. 498, 502, 503, 504
Giacalone, R.A. 511
Gibbons, C. 493
Giddens, A. 482
Gillen, D.J. 480
Gillespie, R. 478
Gillet, G. 482
Gilligan, C. 515
Glover, I. 481
Godfrey, P.C. 483
Goffee, R. 491, 507, 515
Goffman, E. 482
Gold, J. 493
Golding, D. 486, 493
Goldsmith, M. 503
Goldthorpe, J.H. 513
Goleman, D. 492, 499
Gooch, L. 515
Goold, M. 495
Gospel, H.F. 509
Gouldner, A. 499
Gowler, D. 480
Grafton Small, R. 480, 484, 481, 486, 504, 505
Grant, D. 478, 484, 509
Grant, R.M. 495
Gratton, L. 509, 514
Graves, D. 505
Gray, C. 494
Green, S. 505
Grey, C. 493, 495, 499, 515, 519
Grimes, A.J. 495
Grint, K. 480, 499
Guest, D.E. 509, 513
Gulick, L.H. 480
Gunson, N. 502
Guth, W.D. 488
Guzzo, R.A. 501

Haack, S. 484
Hacking, I. 484
Hackman, J.R. 501
Hales, C.P. 480, 486
Hall, D.T. 512, 513
Hall, L. 511
Hall, S. 503
Hallier, J. 490
Hamel, G. 495, 496
Hammer, M. 499
Hampden-Turner, C.M. 505, 507
Hampton, M.M. 501
Handy, C. 493, 503, 505
Handy, J. 490
Hannan, M.T. 478
Hannaway, J. 486
Hardy, C. 477, 478, 479, 481, 488, 489, 494,
    495, 497, 499, 503, 515
Harlow, E. 517
Harré, R. 482, 489
Harris, L. 510, 512
Harris, M. 503
Harris, P. 487, 514
Harris, S. 483
Hart, T.J. 509
Hassard, J. 478, 479, 482, 484, 489, 495, 505,
    506, 510, 513
Hatch, M.-J. 478, 484
Hearn, J. 515, 517
Heery, E. 519
Held, D. 503
Helgesen, S. 515
Henderson, B.D. 495
Henderson, J.C. 504
Hendry, C. 498, 509
Hendry, J. 519
Henry, S. 517
Herriot, P. 493, 507, 513
Herzberg, F. 501
Heskett, J. L. 505
Hesselbein, F. 503
Hetherington, K. 487
Hickson, D.J. 488, 500, 501, 506, 507
Higgin, G.W. 502
Higgs, M. 499
Hill, L.A. 493
Hiltrop, I.M. 511
Hinings, C.R. 488, 500
Hochschild, A.R. 490, 513, 515
Hodgetts, R.M. 486
Hodgkinson, M. 498
Hoel, H. 518
Hoffman, R. 516
Hofstede G. 505, 507
Hoggart, S. 482, 483
Holliday, R. 482
Holman, D. 493
Hope Hailey, V. 490, 509, 514
Hopfl, H. 490
Hoque, K. 509
Horne, J. H. 486
Hosking, D.-M. 482, 483, 492, 507
Huczynski, A.A. 489, 493, 494

Hughes, M. 479, 481
Hunt, J.G. 492, 507
Hunter, T.E. 514
Huselid, M. 500
Huws, U. 503
Hyman, R. 495

Iles, P. 493
Inkson, K. 512
Isabella, L.A. 486
Itzin, C. 515
Izraeli, D. 514

Jackall, R. 513, 518
Jackson, B. 494
Jackson, N. 478, 494, 513
Jackson, P.J. 503
Jackson, P.R. 493
Jackson, S.E. 511
Jacobson, H. 517
Jago, A.G. 492
James, K. 515
James, P. 490
James, R.M. 496
James, W. 484
Jaques, E. 499, 501, 505
Jay, A. 489
Jeffcutt, P. 480, 481, 484, 486, 504
Jeffs, T. 517
Jermier, J.M. 495, 517
Jewson, N. 507
Jick, T. 502
Johnson, G. 496
Johnson, P. 518, 519
Jones, A.M. 498
Jones, D.J. 502
Jones, G. 507
Jones, J. 511
Jones, M.D. 504
Jones, O. 501
Joyce, W. E. 504
Judge, T.A. 509

Kakabadse, A. 489, 516
Kamoche, K. 498, 509
Kanter, R.M. 496, 515
Kanungo, R. 492
Keenoy, T. 478, 484, 510
Keep, E. 498
Keiser, A. 494
Kelly, J. 509, 510
Kennedy, A.A. 504, 518
Kerfoot, D. 515
Kerr, S. 502
Kidd, J.M. 513
Kieser, A. 506, 507
Kilmann, R.H. 484, 505
King, R. 503
Kirkbridge, P. 508
Kirton, M.J. 492
Kitsuse, J.I. 483
Kitzinger, C. 518
Klein, L. 478

Kleine, D. 498
Kleiner, A. 498
Knights, D. 480, 481, 489, 495, 496, 499, 501, 515, 517
Kolb, D.A. 493
Kotter, J.P. 486, 492, 505, 513
Kreiner, K. 504
Kumar, K. 503
Kunda, G. 490, 494, 505
Kurzweil, E. 506

Lave, J. 493
Law, J. 478, 484
Lawler, E.E. 513
Lawrence, B. S. 512
Lawrence, P. 481, 486, 506, 507
Lawrence, P.R. 486 , 499, 508
Leach, E. 483
Ledwith, S. 515
Lee, C.A. 488
Lee, D. 517
Lee, G.L. 491
Legge, K. 480, 510, 518
Leidner, R. 516
Lengnick-Hall, C. 510
Lengnick-Hall, M. 510
Lennie, I. 481
Leopold, J. 510, 512
Lewis, P. 489
Lepore, E. 484
Levinson, H. 513
Liff, S. 516
Lilley, S. 509
Linstead, S. 480, 481, 484, 486, 504, 505, 517
Livian, Y.-F. 486
Lockwood, D. 513
Lorsch, J.W. 499
Louis, M.R. 487, 490, 504, 505, 506
Luckmann, T. 482
Lundberg, C.C. 487, 490, 504, 505, 506
Lupton, T. 486
Luthans, F. 486
Lyon, P. 490
Lyotard, J.-F. 503

Mabey, C. 493, 494, 510, 518
Maccoby, M. 489
MacHung, A. 515
MacIntyre, A. 518
MacKinnon, C.A. 517
Maclagan, P. 518
Macmillan, L.C. 488
Mangham, I.L. 486, 489, 518
Mann, S. 481, 516
Manning, P.K. 483
Manning, W.E.G. 513
Mant, A. 481, 490
March, J.G. 478, 487, 488
Marchington, M. 500, 501, 508, 511
Marglin, S. 481
Mars, G. 517
Marshall, J. 516
Martin, J. 487, 490, 504, 506

Martin, G. 505, 513
Martin, J. 505
Martinko, M.J. 492
Maruyama, M. 507
Maslow, A. 513
Maurer, S.D. 510
Mayo, E. 501
Mayrhofer, W. 508
McArdle, L. 510
McAuley, J. 518
McCalman. J. 501
McClelland, D.C. 492
McCloskey, D.N. 484
McCormick, R. 493
McDaniel, M.A. 510
McGill, I.A. 493
McGoldrick, J. 493
McGovern, P. 490, 514
McGregor, D.C. 501, 513
McGrew, A. 503
McHugh, D. 495
McKee, L. 496
McKinlay, A. 483, 489, 503, 511
McLoughlin, I. 503
McMillan, C. J. 506
McMylor, P. 518
McNulty, T. 489
Mead, G.H. 483
Meek, V.L. 505
Megill, A. 484
Merton, R.K. 499
Meyer, J.W. 478, 479
Mill, Q.D. 508
Miller, E.J. 479
Miller, P. 483
Miller, S.L. 488
Mills, A. 516
Mills, A.J. 516
Mintzberg, H. 481, 486, 489, 496, 497
Mitev, N. 493, 499
Mitroff, I.I. 484, 504, 518
Monthoux, P.G. 484
Moore, M.D. 504, 506, 517
Moore, L.F. 487, 490, 504, 505
Morgan, Gareth 477, 479, 505, 506, 516
Morgan, Glenn 496, 479
Morley, I.E. 483
Morley, M. 508
Morris, T. 511
Morrison, D.E. 513
Morse, J.J. 492
Moss, J.E. 513
Mounce, H.O. 484
Muchinsky, P.M. 490
Mueller, F. 500, 502, 510
Mulholland, K. 491
Mulkay, M. 517
Mullin, R. 498
Mullins, L. 479
Mumby, D.K 483, 488, 490
Mundell, B. 478
Munden, K. 513
Munro, R. 487
Murakami, T. 501

Murphy, R. 483
Murray, H. 502
Murray. F. 489

Nahapiet, J. 498
Narayanan, V.K. 496
Nelson, J.S. 484
Neuijen, B. 505
Neumann, J.E. 490
Newell, H. 491, 513
Newell, S. 510
Newman, J. 499, 515
Newsome, K. 512
Newton, T. 490, 510
Nichols, T. 481
Nicholson, N. 479, 483
Nippert-Eng, C.E. 514
Nohria, N. 480
Nonaka, I. 498
Noon, M. 510, 514, 518
Nord, W. 477, 478, 479, 488, 489, 494, 495,
    497, 499, 503, 515, 517

O'Connell Davidson, J. 503
O'Leary, T. 483
Ogbonna, E. 505
Ohayv, D. 505
Ohmae, K. 496, 503
Oldham, G.R. 501
Olin, D. 484
Oliver, N. 499
Olsen, J.P. 487, 488
Osborne, D. 499
Ostroff, C. 507
Oswick, C. 478, 484, 509
Ott, J.S. 505

Palmer. G. 488, 494, 509
Palmer I. 481
Parker, B. 503
Parker, I. 485
Parker, M. 478, 479, 484, 489, 495, 505, 513,
    518, 519
Parker, P. 510
Parker, S. 501
Parkin, W. 517
Pascale, R.T. 481, 505
Pate, J. 513
Pavlica, K. 493
Payne, J. 500, 507
Pedler, M. 493, 498, 497
Pemberton, C. 493, 513
Pennings, J.M. 488
Perriton, L. 495
Perrow, C. 479
Peters, T.J. 496, 499
Pettigrew, A.M. 489, 496, 503, 505, 509
Pfeffer, J. 479, 481, 489
Platt, J. 513
Polkinghorne, D.E. 485
Pollert, A. 501
Pollitt, C. 499
Pollock, A.B. 502

Pondy, L.R. 505, 506, 516
Porras, J.I. 503
Porter, M. 496
Potter, J. 482, 483, 485
Powell, G.N. 516
Prahalad, C.K. 495, 496, 503
Prasad, P. 495
Preece, D. 487
Preston, D. 501
Preston, J. 498
Price, C. 513
Pringle, J. 512
Pringle, R. 516
Procter, S. 500, 501, 502, 507, 510
Prusak, L. 498
Pugh, D.S. 481, 500, 507
Punch, M. 518
Purcell, J. 511
Putnam, H. 485
Putnam, L.L. 488, 490
Pye, A. 486
Pym, D. 478

Quinn, J. B. 496

Radcliffe-Brown, A.R. 518
Raelin, J.A. 489
Rainbird, H. 498
Ramsey, H. 494
Rauschenberger, J. 514
Ray, C.A. 505
Ray, L. 500
Rayner, C. 518
Redding, G. 507
Redman, T. 491, 500, 508, 510, 511, 513, 518
Reed, M. 479, 481, 500
Rée, J. 485
Rees, B. 492
Revans, R.W. 493
Reynolds, M. 493, 495
Rhodes, P.S. 478
Rice, A.K. 479, 501
Richardson, L. 485
Rifkin, J. 503
Riordan, C.A. 511
Ritzer, G. 500, 501
Robert, P. Jr 477
Roberts, C. 498
Roberts, J. 519
Robertson, I.T. 508
Robinson, S. 514
Roethlisberger, F.J. 479
Roos, D. 502
Roos, J. 498
Roper, M. 516
Rorty, R. 485
Rosborough, J. 502
Rose, D. 485
Rose, H. 503
Rose, M. 514
Rosen, M. 485
Rosencrantz, S.A. 486
Rosener, J.B. 516

Rosenfeld, P. 511
Ross, R. 498
Roth, G. 498
Rousseau, D.M. 503, 512, 514
Rowan, B. 478
Rowlinson, M. 479, 506, 510
Royal Society of Arts 519
Roy, D. 518
Royle, T. 502

Sabsin, M. 479
Salaman, G. 494, 510
Salancik, G.R. 479
Sanders, G. 505
Sarbin, T.R. 483
Sasaki, K. 498
Sathe, V. 506
Saunders, M.N.K. 491
Savage, M. 516
Saxton, M.J. 505
Sayder, R.C. 504
Sayles, L.R. 487
Scarbrough, H. 491, 498
Scase, R. 491, 515
Schatzman, L. 479
Schein, E.H. 506, 514
Schilit, W.K. 497
Schmidt, F.L. 510
Schmitt, N. 514
Schneck, R.E. 488
Schoenberger, E. 497
Scholes, J. 477
Schön, D.A. 492, 493, 497
Schriesheim, C.A. 492, 507
Schroder, H.M. 492
Schuler, R.S. 511
Schultz, M. 506
Schwartzman, H.B. 485
Scott, W.R. 479
Scott, R.G. 477
Selznick, P. 481
Semler, R. 503
Senge, P.M. 498
Sennett, R. 490
Serpa, R. 505
Sewell, G. 502
Shackleton, V. 510
Shapiro, E.C. 494
Sharifi, S. 505
Sheppard, D.L. 515, 517
Shotter, J. 483
Siehl, C. 505
Silver, M. 492
Silverman, D. 479, 511
Simon, H.A. 478, 488
Simpson, R. 516
Sims, D. 478
Sinclair, A. 502
Sisson, K. 493, 508, 510, 511, 513
Skinner, D. 510, 518
Smelser, N.J. 480
Smircich, L. 497, 506, 515
Smith, A. 502

Smith, B. 498
Smith, C. 502, 503, 507
Smith, K. 518, 519
Smith, M. 517
Smith, M.G.J. 489
Smith, P. 487, 507
Smith, V. 481
Snape, E. 491, 500
Snyder, R.C. 517
Solley, C. 513
Sorell, T. 519
Sorge, A. 479
Sotorin, P. 495
Sparrow, P. 491, 508, 509, 511
Spector, B. 508
Spray, S.L. 486
Srivasta, S. 488
Stacey, R. 497
Staines, H. 513
Stalker, G. 499
Stanko, E. 516
Stanton, S. 499
Starkey, K. 483, 489, 498, 504, 511
Statham, A. 519
Staw, B. 481, 506
Stearns, P. 482
Steffy, B.D. 495
Stephen, T. 518
Steven, G. 487
Steven, V. 487
Stevens, B. 508
Stewart, J. 493
Stewart, R. 481, 487, 490, 492, 507
Stiles, P. 490, 509, 514
Stockdale, M.S. 518
Storey, J. 493, 494, 500, 508, 509, 510, 511
Stouffer, S.A. 514
Strati, D. 479, 506
Strauss, A. 479, 483, 512
Streeck, W. 488
Stuart, R. 492
Stubbart, C. 497
Sutherland, V.J. 489
Swan, J. 498

Tailby, S. 511
Takeuchi, H. 498
Tamangani, Z. 486
Tancred, P. 516
Tancred-Sherrif, P. 515, 517
Tannen, D. 489, 516
Tansley, C. 514
Tanton, M. 516
Taylor, C. 483
Taylor, F.W. 502
Taylor, P. 489, 503
Taylor, S. 490
Teece, D.J. 498, 502
Terkel, S. 485
Teulings, A.W.M. 481
Thatchenkery, T.J. 477
Thomas, A. 481

Thomas, A.M. 518
Thomas, H. 496
Thomas, J. 485
Thomas, P. 494, 503
Thomas, R. 491
Thompson, J.D. 479
Thompson, P. 479, 495, 502, 514, 516
Thomson, A. 494
Thomson, R. 494
Thornhill, A. 491
Thorpe, R. 493
Tichy, N. 492, 508, 509
Tolbert, P.S. 479
Tomlinson, J.W.C. 485
Tomlinson, M. 509
Torrington, D. 503, 511
Towers, B. 511
Townley, B. 511
Trice, H.M. 504, 506
Trist, E.L. 502
Trompenaars, F. 507
Truman, C. 514
Truss, C. 509, 514
Tsoukas, H. 480, 481, 485
Tsui-James, E.P. 484
Turnbull, P. 502, 508, 510
Tyrell, S. 495
Tyson, S. 511, 512

Ulrich, D. 502
Umemoto, K. 498
Urmson, J.O. 485
Urwick, L.F. 480

Van de Ven, A.H. 477
van der Wielen, J.M. 503
Van Hootegem, G. 500
Van Maanen, J. 480, 483, 485, 490, 506
Venkatraman, N. 504
von Krogh, G. 498
Vroom, V.H. 492, 514

Wagner, E.R. 492
Wajcman, J. 516
Walby, S. 516
Walgenbach, P. 507
Wall, T. 501
Walters, M. 506
Walton, C.C. 519
Walton, R.E. 508, 512
Warhurst, C. 514
Warner, M. 479
Waterman, R.H. 499
Waters, J.H. 496
Watson, D.H. 483, 489, 512

Watson, T.J. 480, 481, 483, 485, 487, 489,
    492, 493, 494, 495, 502, 507, 510, 512,
    514, 519
Weber, M. 500, 519
Weick, K.E. 483, 488, 492, 494, 506
Weisinger, H. 492
Wenger, E. 493
Westley, F.R. 491, 494, 497
Wetherall, M. 483
Wharton, A.S. 490
Whetten, D. 483
Whetzel, D.L. 510
Whipp, R. 497
White, M. 509
Whitehead, S. 512
Whitley, R. D. 481, 487, 507
Whittington, R. 481, 496, 497
Wickens, P. 502
Wildavsky, A. 489
Wilkins, A.L. 506
Wilkinson, A. 491, 500, 508, 509, 510, 511,
    513, 518
Wilkinson, B. 499, 505
Willcocks, L. 499
Williams, A. 506
Willmott, H. 480, 481, 482, 487, 494, 495,
    499, 500, 501, 506, 509, 515
Wilson, D.C. 488
Wilson, F. 480
Wilson, N.A.B. 514
Winchester, D. 511
Wingate, P. 487
Winsor, R.D. 500
Winstanley, D. 519
Wittgenstein, L. 483
Witz, A. 516
Wollheim, R. 490
Womack, J.P. 502
Wood, S. 502,
Woodall, J. 519
Woodruffe, C. 492
Woodward, J. 500
Worrall, L. 491, 516
Wouters, C. 490
Wren, D.S. 482
Wuthnow, R.J. 506

York, P. 516
Young, R.A. 513, 514
Yukl, G. 492

Zaleznik, A. 492
Zuboff, S. 504
Zucker L.G. 479
Zugbach, von R. 489

Index

absenteeism 270, 349, 350
alcoholism 136
Albrow, M. 139
Ackers, P. 396
acting, deep and surface 145–8, 403
Adams, J.S. 298
airlines 147, 199–20, 270, 272, 353–6
alienation 148, 293, 311, 465
Alvesson, M. 22
ambiguity 13, 49, 53, 57, 81, 84, 92, 105, 128,
    171, 189, 329, 366, 375–6, 384, 423,
    444, 448, 463, 465
animal aspects of humans 94, 111, 144,
    358–9, 365
Anthony, P. 459
anthropology 17, 19, 273, 291
anxiety 111, 116, 278, 295, 360
    and managerial work 154–60, 168
appraisal, performance 25, 394, 408, 410
Aristotle 446
artefacts 268, 270, 272, 273, 274, 465
Aston studies 257
Atkinson, J. 397
attitudes 98, 104, 105, 260
Austin, J.L. 102, 103, 260

Babbage, C. 307
Baldamus, G. 128
banking 271, 272
Baritz, L. 22
Barnard, C. 75–7, 84
Behrend, H. 128
Billig, M. 103
biography see life strategy
biology 40, 45, 55, 98, 178
black box, systems 58, 91, 257,
boundaryless career see career
Braverman, H. 309
Buchanan, D.A. 314
budgets 244
building management 69
bullying 349, 351
bureaucracy 37, 81, 114, 138, 221, 239–49,
    251, 253, 254–5, 256, 257, 259, 260,
    262–3, 265, 274, 303, 327, 363, 382,
    422, 424, 465
    as structure and culture 239, 349
bureaucratic personality 248
Burnham, J. 52
Burns, T. 253, 254, 256, 265, 327
Bus company management 78–80
business process re-engineering 314–19, 320, 465

call centres 233, 399–403
capitalism, industrial 36, 60, 69, 93, 113, 114,
    124, 128, 207, 238, 293, 306, 369,
    382–3, 416, 417, 418, 463, 470
car assembly 129, 308, 311, 314, 316
career 128, 130, 131, 135, 213, 282, 291, 335,
    368, 394, 465
    see also portfolio careers
Cartesian dualism see dualism, Cartesian
case studies 12
categorical imperative 448
cats, herding 3, 104, 358, 369
    see also resistance, human (to control by
        others)
change management 73, 91, 260–4, 287, 304,
    415, 416–19, 429, 463, 465
charisma 241, 322
charities/voluntary organisations 88–91
cheating, 336, 351
child labour 451
Christianity 38
civil engineering, management 235–7
class and inequality 22, 24, 25, 26, 31, 47, 70,
    114, 128, 226, 246, 293, 323, 416, 428,
    454, 457
Claydon, T. 386
Clegg, S.R. 254
cliques and cabals 336
closure, social 113, 114, 465
Cohen, M.D. 339
collective bargaining 465
    see also trade unions
commitment 252, 253, 303, 368, 370, 374,
    390, 391–5, 404, 413, 427, 428, 430,
    459, 463

common sense 20–1, 28, 29, 32, 99, 104, 293, 300, 301, 373, 423, 466
communication 76, 98, 377, 394, 442
  in bureaucracy 241
community 410, 436
competencies 428
  core 380
  managerial 292, 412, 415, 437, 447, 466
competition and competitors 36, 60, 165, 171, 260–1, 265, 313, 401, 403, 418, 427, 463
competitive advantage 170–1, 218, 375
computer company management 420
concepts 30, 50, 98, 106, 123, 322, 442, 466
conflict 13, 17, 22, 26, 49, 77, 113, 114, 189, 218, 239, 327, 375–6, 384, 416, 417, 463, 466
constituencies, strategic 114, 201, 202–13, 220, 392, 404, 435, 461, 464, 466
consultants 66, 179, 181, 316, 317, 386
contingencies 256–66, 312–13, 318, 320, 392, 404, 424
contraculture 269, 475
contradiction 242, 245, 251–2, 318–19, 378, 382–4, 412, 466
control, managerial xix, 37, 43, 47, 58, 61, 82, 92, 138, 157–8, 171, 221, 222, 234, 250, 252, 265, 272, 305, 318, 383, 427, 466
  direct and indirect 251–5, 274, 302–11, 313–14, 320, 368, 413
  see also systems-control thinking
Cooper, C. 154
cooperative, worker 67, 238
corporate image 64
critical common sense see common sense
critical management and organisation studies 4, 14, 21–6
critical thinking 2, 30–1, 32, 38, 171, 294, 373, 423, 453, 463
culture 17, 60, 93, 105, 107, 110–18, 124, 131, 252, 255, 258, 265, 291, 296, 360
  and structure 223–34, 248, 249–50, 274, 323, 365, 460, 464, 467
  Asian 133
  blame 261, 273
  national xxiv, 225–8, 133, 460
  organisational see organisational culture
customers 12, 31, 114, 127, 195, 203, 204, 207, 247, 248, 261, 265, 270, 273, 290, 314, 316, 342, 350, 357, 422, 433, 450, 461, 462
cyber shops 193

Dachler, H.P. 59
Dalton, M. 77, 84
data 105, 182, 202
database management 243–4
daydreaming 148
de Condorcet Marquis 37
de Geus, A. 197
Deal, T.E. 458
death camps 242
decision-making 17, 18, 339–46, 461
dehumanising customers

democracy 5, 6, 52, 383, 362, 464
deontology 455–6, 467
dependence, manager dependence on others 85, 92, 444
Descartes, R. 37, 96
  see also Dualism, Cartesian
deskilling 306–9, 312, 320, 394
determinism 119, 418–19, 429, 463
Dewey, J. 28
Dickson, W.J. 21, 76, 84, 139, 308, 351
Diderot, D. 37
directors, company 78–81, 316, 324, 380–8
discourse 105, 110, 118–23, 124, 270, 274, 467
discrimination 228, 351, 400, 404–6, 440, 450, 454
discursive resources 119–22, 149, 168, 170, 171, 228, 290, 411, 419
  framing see framing of 'reality'/discursive framing
  ingenuity 121
division of labour 305, 439, 464, 467
documents, illicit organisational 360–3
Donne, J. 97
Dopson, S. 158
double control problem, managerial 160, 168, 466
driver analogy 44, 54, 418–19
dual control problem 160, 466
dualism, Cartesian 62, 63, 96–7, 123, 149, 152, 278, 374, 445
  see also dualities and dualisms
dualities and dualisms 95–6, 98, 107, 134, 149, 459
dysfunctions of bureaucracy 248

economics 17, 30, 51, 198, 199
e-commerce 194, 195
Edwards, P. 445
Edwards, R. 309
effectiveness, 467
  organisational see organisational effectiveness
  managerial see management effectiveness
efficiency 24, 119–20, 467
effort bargain see implicit contract
emancipation, human 22
emergence 2, 88, 105, 106, 108–110, 138, 169,186, 188–9, 196, 206, 213, 222, 229, 302, 417, 453
emotional
  intelligence 446–7, 449, 464, 467
  labour 143, 145–8, 167, 352, 468
  work 145
emotions 99, 100, 105, 107, 123, 138–48, 159, 165, 215, 241, 445, 453, 456–7, 467
  and feelings 143–4, 467
empire building 244, 266
employment 60–1, 114, 282, 300, 382, 468
employment relations 394
empowerment 22, 122, 226, 270, 272, 287, 290, 304, 314, 315, 316, 317, 452
enactment 63, 64, 131, 144, 166, 251, 255–6, 274, 318, 320, 391, 399, 419, 468
engineering 3, 117, 260–4, 379

enlightenment 37, 51, 54
entitiveness 59
enterprise 121
environment, enacted organisational 202–203, 265, 419, 423
environmental issues (ecological) 452
epistemology 27, 468
equal opportunities 227, 363, 377, 409, 450
equity theory of motivation 296, 297, 298–9, 468
essentialism 148
ethical irrationality of the world 457–8, 460, 468
ethically assertive action 461
ethically reactive action 461
ethics and morality xix, 5, 24, 111–12, 201, 267, 268, 399, 436, 447–63, 464, 468
    consequentionalist grounds for 456
    deontological grounds for 455–6
    normative 455–7
    teleological grounds for 456
    utilitarian 456
ethnicity and race 22, 114, 132–4, 228, 351, 357, 408, 450
ethnography 140, 158, 294, 440, 468
ethnographic fiction science xxi–xxii
evolution 40, 112–23, 138, 191
    directed 191–4, 195, 216, 423, 447, 467
exchange 107, 111, 114, 127, 147, 183, 202, 376, 461
    see also strategic exchange
existential challenges 105, 110, 111, 116, 278, 360, 366
expectancy theory 21, 296, 297, 300–1, 468
exploitation 448, 450, 455

family business 180, 192–4
farming 38, 122, 452, 457, 461
fast food 312
Fayol, H. 86
feelings see emotions and feelings
Ferguson, A. 37
fiddles 350, 357
financial management 192
Fineman, S. 144
flexibility 249, 253, 254, 261, 296, 296–99, 313, 422, 427, 437, 463, 468
    for short-term adjustment and long-term adaptability 313–14, 398, 429–30, 437, 463, 468
flexible firm 397, 468
Fordism 308, 397, 469
formal/informal aspects of organisations see informal aspects of organisations
Foucault, M. 119, 122
Foundationalism 50, 52, 456, 468
foundry management 283–5, 287–9
Fox, A. 253, 431
framing of 'reality'/ discursive framing 4–11, 30, 34, 36, 50, 51, 52, 54, 58, 63, 106, 119–22, 124, 135, 217–18, 406, 410, 411, 469
Friedman, A.L. 253–4, 309
Fukuyama, F. 431

functionalism 469
functions of management see management, functions of

games, workplace 351, 357
garbage can theory of decision-making 339–46, 366, 469
gender 22, 114, 227, 230, 261, 271, 272, 273, 359, 400, 404, 408, 450
    see also women in management
Gergen, K. 59
globalisation 36, 122, 318, 421, 425–6, 429, 463, 469
goals see organisational goals
Goffe, R. 158
Goffman, E. 104
Goldthorpe, J. 129
Goleman, D. 446
gossip 27, 85, 87, 159, 360, 434
Gouldner, A. 286
government
    local 78–9, 80, 89
    state 12, 31, 163, 204, 205, 260–1, 265, 271, 273, 315, 324
Greek gods 242
guitar making 208–13
gurus, management 445
Gulick, L.H. 86

Hamel, G. 197
harassment, sexual 349
harmonisation of employment conditions 397
Harris, P. 444, 453
Hawthorne experiments 21, 308, 309, 351
Henderson, B.D. 184
heroes, organisational 153, 271, 469
Hertzberg, F. 295, 305, 309, 310
Hickson, D.J. 253, 257, 330
Hinings, C.R. 257
history xxii, 36, 119, 416
Hobbes, T. 113
Hochschild, A. 145, 154
Hofstede, G. 255
Hoggart, S. 163, 165
home and work 153–4, 217, 358–9
Hosking, D. 59
hospitals 3, 9–10, 77, 205, 218
hotel management 140–3
HR strategies 390–404, 470
    dual 314, 396–9, 430, 467
    and corporate strategies 378–81, 412
    development and training 394, 402
    managers, and other managers 388–90, 413
HRM Ch. 11, esp. 375–7, 469
    and personnel management 370–3
    as an academic subject xx, 13, 14, 15, 367, 370–5, 412
    as essentially strategic 378–88
Human Relations 26, 62
human resource management see HRM
human resources 319, 367, 368–9, 412, 448, 469
Hume, D. 37

humour and joking 89, 116, 270, 312, 345, 348, 351, 357, 359–65, 366
Hunter, T.E. 293

ideal type 241, 303, 470
identity 105, 106, 114, 115–18, 121, 127, 131, 145, 148, 166, 215, 216, 217, 470
implicit contract 125, 126–38, 145, 148, 167, 205, 275, 281–91, 312, 347, 411, 466, 470
inclusive organisations 433
incrementalism *see* logical incrementalism
indulgency pattern 286–7, 320, 470
industrial revolution 37
informal aspects of organisations 19, 76–7, 85
    see also official and unofficial aspects
information systems 244, 386
innovation 44, 258, 305, 313, 410, 418, 427
instincts 111, 114
    of the fox 178
institutional theories of organisation 225–6
intelligence *see* emotional intelligence
iron cage 241

Jackall, R. 158, 458
James, W. 28
Jaques, E. 253
jargon 160, 162, 470
job
    design Ch. 9, esp. 302, 394, 470
    enlargement *see* job redesign
    enrichment *see* job redesign
    evaluation 289, 290
    redesign/work redesign 295, 302–5
jobsworth 246, 248
joking *see* humour
just-in-time management 316

Kafka, F. 242
Kant, I. 37, 448, 456
Kennedy, A.A. 458
kitchen workers 19
knowledge management 197, 445
Kolb, D.A. 445
Kotter, J.P. 87, 444

labour
    markets 6, 19, 381, 404, 428
    process 309, 470
language 1–6, 102–4, 105, 111, 118, 268, 270–1, 272, 273, 307, 460
    managerial 4, 160–5, 168, 363, 380, 419
Lawler, E.E. 300
leadership 11–13, 80, 95, 121, 155, 275, 276, 277, 288, 290, 292, 319, 322, 411
lean production 314, 470
learning 98, 105, 271, 394, 444–5
    action 445
    organisations 196–7, 198, 445, 471
legends, organisational 270, 471
leisure at work 290
leisure centre management 341–4
Levinson, H. 128
linearity 98–102, 144, 219, 223, 278, 297, 381

linguistic repertoires *see* discursive resources
    turn 102, 103
Locke, J. 37
Lockheed corporation 217
logical incrementalism 190–1, 423
logistics 174–6
love 359

Machiavelli, N. 446
Machine/engineering metaphor 40–1, 44, 74, 75, 76, 97–8, 123, 154, 179, 384, 409
management 65–70, 471
    as strategic 68–9, 92, 172
    behaviour (what managers do) 84–91, 92
    classical view of 86, 159
    development 445
    effectiveness xix, 437–47, 464, 467
        see also competences, managerial
    education 11–15, 22, 294, 288, 445
    fashions and 'fads' 159–60, 290, 311
    function 67, 69, 86, 92, 172, 325, 416, 448
    general 87, 444
    knowledge 12, 23, 44, 445
    learning 14, 15
    middle 158
    occupation 37, 443
    of people 3–6, 24, 31, 368–9, 448
    origins 37, 69
    right to manage 5, 388
    social and task dimensions 57, 70–4
managerialism/managerial revolution 33, 52–4, 56, 459, 462, 471
managism 33, 52–4, 56, 155, 157, 168, 471
March, J.G. 339
Marglin, S. 69
market
    awareness 441
    research 3
marketing 3, 11, 161, 203, 263, 316
    relationship 435
markets, 12, 19, 36, 165, 199, 203, 262, 316, 421, 425, 436
    see also labour markets 262–3
Martian, inquisitive 46, 82
Marx, K. 128, 295
masculinity 355, 356, 357
Maslow, A. 292–7, 309, 310, 320
Mayo, E. 308
MBA 3, 154, 156, 157, 162, 180, 187
McGregor, D.C. 252
McHugh, D. 22
McIntyre, A. 459
meaning, human need for 111–12, 267
memory 105
Merton, R.K. 248
metaphors and analogies 172, 190, 223–24
    see also driver analogy, machine/ engineering metaphor, organic analogy
micropolitics/managerial politics 77, 214, 325–38, 363, 365–6, 375, 455, 471
Microsoft 201
military 171–2, 270, 298
Mintzberg, H. 188–9, 190

mischief *see* workplace mischief
mission, corporate 10, 265
modernity, modernism 33, 36–8, 50–2, 53, 54, 55–6, 81, 82, 96, 97, 138, 239, 471, 472
    pragmatic 33, 50–2, 54, 55–6, 83
Montesquieu, C. 37
moral community, the organisation as 410–11, 459
morality *see* ethics and morality
Morley, I.E. 59
motivation 11, 13, 14, 21, 26, 97, 100–1, 105, 275, 276–302, 319
multi–national companies 421, 426
murder 101, 115, 201, 360
myths, organisational 270, 274, 472

narratives and stories xxi, 105, 107, 110, 114, 115–18, 124, 134, 270, 274, 360
negotiated order 74–81, 85, 235, 243, 278, 338, 346, 411, 472
Newell, S. 411
network 333–4, 422, 424
    see also virtual organisation
newspaper management 331–4
Newton, I. 37
norms, of behaviour 271, 272, 273, 274, 350, 472

objectives *see* goals
occupational choice 131
office cleaning 269
official and unofficial aspects of organisations 57, 74–81, 92, 221, 223, 228–30, 234–9, 235, 250, 264–5, 269, 271, 272
Olsen, J.P. 339
ontology 61, 112
operations management 11
organic analogy 38–40, 178, 223–4
organisations, nature of 59–64, 472
organisational
    behaviour (OB) xxi, 3, 11–15, 26, 32, 37, 170, 370
    culture 8, 14, 74, 221, 222–39, 247–8, 467
        and societal culture 225–8, 250
    effectiveness 170, 198–202, 415, 429–37, 447–8, 467
    goals xx, 44, 45–50, 55, 58, 60, 63, 200, 435, 462
    identity 64
    mischief 321, 346–57, 375, 471
    name 63–4
    size 256, 257–8, 266, 312, 318, 392
    structure 8, 10, 11, 17, 19, 95, 221, 222, 223–4, 227, 229, 230–9, 255–65, 394, 440
    structure, mechanistic and organic 253, 254, 256, 265, 394, 429
    structure and culture 223–4, 230–4, 248, 249–50, 274, 323
    structure and societal structure 225–8, 250, 259
organised anarchy 339
orientation to work 125, 126–38, 166, 167, 176, 275, 278, 279–81, 319, 411, 443, 453, 472
    initial 131, 167, 472

owner managers 69
ownership and control of organizations 26, 36, 323, 433

paradox of consequences 243–49, 250, 457, 472
participant observation xxi, 28, 84, 158
partnership approach to employment relations 262, 266, 396
passion 359
patronage 336
pay *see* rewards
Payne, J. 396
Payne, R. 257
people management *see* management of people
perception 98, 105, 281, 298, 299
performance related pay 21
personality 17, 19, 98, 107–8, 137
personality tests 406–7
personification *see* reification
personnel management *see* HRM
perspectives, academic/schools of thought xix, 13–14, 26–7, 35
persuasion 60, 61, 65, 298, 330, 336, 444
Peters, T.J. 184, 195–6, 267
Pierce, J. 28
pin making 306
planning 85, 86, 88–9, 101, 159, 177–85, 186, 188, 189, 192, 197, 361–2, 363, 423
PODSCORB 86
police 18, 25, 31, 90, 122
politics *see* micropolitics
Porter, M. 184
portfolio
    analysis 184
    career 427–9, 463, 472
positivism 51, 472
postmodern organisation 254
postmodernism, 50, 473
power xx, 19, 22, 26, 48, 61, 62, 255, 266, 282, 321, 322–38, 365, 375, 473
pragmatism xxii, 27–30, 32, 69, 173, 256–7, 266, 293–4, 296–7, 305, 459, 473
Prahalad, C.K. 197
Preston, D. 314
printing management 70, 271
prisons, effectiveness of 200
privatisation 78
process-relational thinking xx, 22–3, 29, 34, 35, 54, 57, 58–9, 75, 81, 88, 91, 93, 105, 106, 123, 153, 155, 229, 257, 278, 298, 375, 406, 411, 417, 419, 443, 473
productive cooperation 59, 60, 65, 278, 326, 416, 426, 432, 466–7
profession/professionalisation 10, 121, 326, 411, 428
profit 19, 198–9, 236, 248
protestant ethic *see* work ethic
psychological
    contract *see* implicit contract
    testing 407–9, 447
psychology 17, 19, 30, 51, 62, 106, 107, 123, 137, 141, 291, 407, 447

pub management 246–9
public relations 135–7
publishing 99–100
Pugh, D.S. 257

quality management 8, 72, 261, 304, 395
Quinn, J.B. 190

race *see* ethnicity
rationality 1–7, 51, 81, 82, 83, 105, 165, 171,
    184, 240, 457, 473
    bounded 83, 114, 246, 473
    formal and material 243
Rauschenberger, J. 293
recalcitrance *see* resistance
reciprocity 111, 143, 153, 166, 415, 430–1
recruitment and selection 155, 187, 336, 377,
    386, 389, 405–11
redundancy 25, 108, 364, 368, 380, 405
reification/personification 49, 61, 142, 165,
    223, 473
research xxi, 12, 22, 26, 28, 90, 166, 271, 445
resistance, human (to control by others) 6, 75,
    286, 382, 417, 463
resource dependence 202–13, 222, 461, 474
restaurant management 18–19, 25–6
retail management 41–3, 132–3, 211, 449–53
Revans, J. 445
rewards 20–1, 71, 130, 175, 236
rhetoric 103, 374
Rice, A.K. 310
rites, organisational 17, 271, 274, 473
rituals, organisational 17, 223, 271, 272, 274,
    286, 294–5, 473
Ritzer, G. 312
Roberts, J. 459
Roethlisberger, F.J. 21, 76, 139
role prescription 253
Rorty, R. 28
Rosener, J.B. 455
Rousseau, J.J. 37
Rowlinson, M. 396
Royle, T. 312
rules 8, 10, 61, 74, 85, 76, 95, 111, 223, 229,
    237, 241, 245, 249, 252, 253, 323, 394

sabotage 349, 351, 357
sagas, organisational 271, 474
satire, organisational 363
Scase, R. 158
Schein, E.H. 128, 268
Schmitt, M. 293
Schoenberger, E. 217, 222
Schön, D.A. 453
school management 48, 150–2, 327
science 51, 138, 456
scientific management ('Taylorism') 307–8,
    311–12, 474
Scott, W.R. 225
security management 342–4
selection, employee *see* recruitment
self-actualisation 139, 292, 474

self-identity *see* identity
semi-autonomous workgroup 311
    see also teamwork
sense-making 105, 474
service sector/workers 19, 140–8, 312, 352,
    428–9
sex at work 356, 358–9, 365, 366
sex workers 146–8
Shackleton, V. 411
Sisson, K. 445
Smith, A. 37, 306–7
social
    construction 62–3, 113, 114, 144, 149,
        153, 474
    psychology 17, 19
    sciences xix, 6, 13, 17–21, 23, 26, 32, 37,
        95, 104, 170, 224, 273, 292
socialism 36
sociology 17, 19, 62, 291
socio-technical systems 310–11
stakeholding 432–4, 435–6, 451–2, 459
Stalker, G. 253, 254, 256, 265
state *see* government
Stewart, R. 158, 439
stock options for corporate managers 451–2, 458
Storey, J. 445
story telling 115–18, 264, 341, 446
    see also narrative
Stouffer, S.A. 298
strategic
    alliances 171, 218, 421
    awareness 176, 441
    contingency theory of power 329–38, 473
    economising 207, 474
    exchange 35, 36, 91, 128, 134, 138, 166,
        172, 176, 198, 206, 213–18, 220, 260,
        276, 279, 281, 291, 292, 301, 319, 335,
        337, 399, 423, 460, 474
    focus 182, 193, 195
    intent 197–8, 474
    retreats 336
strategy xx, 12, 14, 15, 57, 68, 91, 114, 260,
        266, 272, 274, 378–87, 394, 424, 475
    and strategic exchange 198–213
    and strategy-makers 213–18, 222
    and the work of all managers 169, 173–7
    and war 171–2, 179, 185–6
    life 91, 106, 107, 110, 126, 138, 186, 215,
        217, 278, 327
    orthodox understandings 177–85, 218
    processual understandings 185–9
    trends in management of 189–97
Strauss, A. 77
stress 139, 148–54, 167, 475
structure *see* structure, organisational
subculture 269, 272, 475
subjectivity 119
supermarket management 353–6
SWOT analysis 178, 183
symbols 17, 223, 268–9, 273, 274, 297
systems 7, 10, 26, 33, 38–43, 60, 62, 64, 76,
    88, 310, 374, 385, 475

see also systems-control thinking
systems-control thinking xx, 22–3, 29, 33,
    34–5, 43–50, 55, 61, 81, 91, 93, 97, 104,
    105, 106, 123, 177, 184–5, 278, 302, 374,
    375, 378, 384, 406, 410, 417, 443, 475

tasks, management of 6, 48, 59, 65, 77, 274,
    Ch. 9
Tavistock Institute 310
Taylor, F.W. 254, 307–8, 311–12
Taylorism *see* scientific management
team leading 8, 226
teamworking 10, 175, 289, 291, 303, 304, 305,
    311, 442, 443, 475
technocracy 53
technology and technical change 36, 51,
    59–60, 256, 257, 258, 263, 265–66, 312,
    316, 318, 392, 399, 400, 401, 406,
    420–2, 424, 425, 475
teleworking 422, 427
theory xx, xxii, 13, 14, 27, 29, 30, 32, 166,
    257, 291, 442, 476
    and practice 16, 23, 28–9, 174, 255–6,
    291, 445
    x and y 252, 254, 255
Thompson, P. 22
Tolbert, P.S. 225
total quality management (TQM) *see* quality
    management
trade unions/organised labour 13, 130–1,
    261–2, 266, 274, 315, 351, 370, 377,
    385, 388, 389, 394, 395–6, 465
Trist, E. 310
trust and trust relations 237, 238, 253, 264,
    303, 317, 370, 415, 430–2, 437, 440,
    459, 463, 476
truth/truth claims for knowledge xxii, 27–9,
    32, 52, 293–4, 296

uncertainty 57, 81–4, 87, 92, 189, 205, 255,
    329–30, 366, 392, 423, 466, 476
underlife, organisational 65, 346

unintended consequences *see* paradox of
    consequences
utopia 196, 250, 326

values 22, 223, 240, 249, 255, 258, 259,
    266–7, 268, 272, 273, 318, 392, 393,
    394, 396, 403, 415, 447–63, 464,
value chain analysis 181
villains, organisational 271, 469
violence 141–3, 159
violin making 306
virtual/networked organisations 422, 426–27,
    428, 463, 476
vision, corporate 155
Voltaire, F.M.A. de 37
Vroom, V. 300

waiters 19
Wajcman, J. 455
Walton, R.E. 254
warehouse management 175–6
Waterman, R.H. 184, 195–6, 276
Watson, T.J. xxi, xxii, 67, 159, 254, 256, 272,
    294, 297, 374, 440, 444, 453, 458, 459
Weber, M. 81, 138–9, 239–42, 243, 252, 303
Weick, K.E. 59
Wilkinson, A. 395
Willmott, H. 22
Wittgenstein, L. 102
women and management 449–50, 454–5
    see also gender
Woodward, J. 256
Work Organisation and Management Studies
    16–19, 476
work orientations *see* orientations to work
work to rule 246
work, design *see* job design
work–life balance 153–4
workplace mischief *see* organisational mischief
Worrall, L. 154

Zucker, L.G. 225